Peaceful Maritime Engagement in East Asia and the Pacific Region

Oceans Law and Policy

Edited by

James Kraska and Myron H. Nordquist

VOLUME 25

The titles published in this series are listed at *brill.com/colp*

Peaceful Maritime Engagement in East Asia and the Pacific Region

Edited by

James Kraska, Ronán Long, and Myron H. Nordquist

TUTA SUB AEGIDE PALLAS · 1683 ·

BRILL
NIJHOFF

LEIDEN | BOSTON

Library of Congress Cataloging-in-Publication Data

Names: Conference on Oceans Law and Policy (44th ; 2021 : Tokyo, Japan). | Kraska, James, editor. | Long, Ronán, editor. | Nordquist, Myron H., editor. | Charles H. Stockton Chair of International Law (Naval War College), sponsoring body. | Nihon Kokusai Mondai Kenkyūjo, host institution.
Title: Peaceful maritime engagement in East Asia and the Pacific Region / edited by James Kraska, Ronan Long and Myron H. Nordquist.
Description: Leiden ; Boston : Brill Nijhoff, [2023] | Series: Center for Oceans Law and Policy, 1872-7158 ; volume 25 | "With this 44th Annual Conference on Oceans Law and Policy (COLP), the event continues under the auspices of the Stockton Center for International Law (SCII) of the US Naval War College. Although the Center for Oceans Law and Policy closed in 2020 ... the 44th COLP was co-hosted in Tokyo (and virtually) by the Japan Institute of International Affairs (JIIA) on 10-12 May 2021"–ECIP preface. | Includes bibliographical references and index.
Identifiers: LCCN 2022038790 (print) | LCCN 2022038791 (ebook) | ISBN 9789004518612 (hardback) | ISBN 9789004518629 (ebook)
Subjects: LCSH: Law of the sea–Pacific area–Congresses. | Security, International–Pacific area–Congresses. | Law of the sea–East Asia–Congresses. | Security, International–East Asia–Congresses. | LCGFT: Conference papers and proceedngs.
Classification: LCC KZA1141 .C66 2021 (print) | LCC KZA1141 (ebook) | DDC 341.4/5–dc23/eng/20220919
LC record available at https://lccn.loc.gov/2022038790
LC ebook record available at https://lccn.loc.gov/2022038791

Typeface for the Latin, Greek, and Cyrillic scripts: "Brill". See and download: brill.com/brill-typeface.

ISSN 1872-7158
ISBN 978-90-04-51861-2 (hardback)
ISBN 978-90-04-51862-9 (e-book)

This book is printed on acid-free paper and produced in a sustainable manner.

This book is dedicated to our dear colleague Satya N. Nandan (July 10, 1936–February 25, 2020) for his many outstanding contributions to the Law of the Sea

Contents

PART 6
Issues Arising Out of Climate Change

Preface

The Annual Conference on Oceans Law & Policy began more than four decades ago at the Center for Oceans Law and Policy at the University of Virginia, when Ambassador John Norton Moore and Professor Myron Nordquist identified the need for a regularly occurring and major international meeting to explore developments in the field. The Conference is an expression of current scholarship by leading figures in the field, a gathering of government officials from throughout the world, and an opportunity for participants from academia, industry, civil society, and international and nongovernmental organizations to learn from each other.

With this 44th Annual Conference on Oceans Law and Policy (COLP), the event continues under the auspices of the Stockton Center for International Law (SCIL) of the US Naval War College. Although the Center for Oceans Law and Policy closed in 2020, the Stockton Center for International Law continues a long-standing commitment to the rule of law in the oceans. When the U.S. Naval War College was established in the late-19th century, the first General Order of the school required that there would be two courses of study at the college – strategy and international law. These two are intertwined to maintain peace and security. In 1895, the international law program at the Naval War College began publication of *International Law Studies*, the oldest journal of international law in the United States. Today the Stockton Center military professors in international maritime law from the U.S. Coast Guard, Navy, U.S. Marine Corps, and hosts numerous visiting scholars and officials to advance our understanding of oceans law and policy, including from the Japan Maritime Self-Defense Force (JMSDF) and the Korea Maritime Institute (KMI). The Stockton Center also is responsible for producing *The Commander's Handbook on the Law of Naval Operations*, a restatement of international maritime law, signed by the U.S. Navy, U.S. Coast Guard, and U.S. Marine Corps.

The 44th COLP was co-hosted in Tokyo (and virtually) by the Japan Institute of International Affairs (JIIA) on 10–12 May 2021, reaching some 1,100 participants. This is the first time COLP was conducted in Japan. The Nippon Foundation and World Maritime University (WMU) – Sasakawa Global Ocean Institute generously co-sponsored the conference, which focused on "Peaceful Maritime Engagement in East Asia and the Pacific Region." This volume is based on presentations made by many experts invited to the Tokyo conference. The sessions featured remarks by distinguished international law scholars and six substantive Parts devoted to identifying and analyzing key issues associated with the conference subject.

Featured Papers begin this volume, the first of which is a tribute to Ambassador Satya N. Nandan to whom this book is dedicated. *Professor Myron H. Nordquist* highlighted just one illustration of Nandan's many contributions to oceans law and policy based on both shared personal experiences and long friendship. The Tokyo Conference was honored with a keynote address by *Judge Shunji Yanai*, the Japanese judge on the International Tribunal for the Law of the Sea (ITLOS). He carefully reviewed the major law of the sea disputes addressed by the International Tribunal for the Law of the Sea (ITLOS) since its founding, noting 27 contentious cases, including three maritime delimitation cases and two advisory opinions. ITLOS has provided interpretations on explicit situations under UNCLOS such as foreign flag vessels operating in another State's EEZ e.g., bunkering. At the same time, new challenges not even implicitly covered in the Convention require new legislation e.g., Marine Biodiversity of Areas Beyond National Jurisdiction (BBNJ).

The third featured speaker was *Michael W. Lodge*, the Secretary-General of the International Seabed Authority. He discussed the legal regime of the deep seabed as a paradigm for global governance of natural resources. A former President of ITLOS, *Judge Rüdiger Wolfrum*, then makes a comprehensive survey of the international law-making field. He is uniquely qualified to comment on the multifaceted actors in the international normative order and his pointed insights are truly valuable. The comprehensive contribution by *Professor Ronán Long* and *Mariamalia Rodriguez Chaves* dealing with the difficulties that must be overcome to attain the conservation and sustainable use of biodiversity beyond national jurisdiction in the Southeast Pacific merit a featured status in this book. Their paper evaluates state practice in the region and concludes that substantial reform is needed in the littoral States' current legal mandates. The draft BBNJ Agreement is postulated as having the potential to herald in a new era of marine biodiversity conservation in areas beyond national jurisdiction for the entire Pacific Basin, thereby providing a remedy for the Southeast region. *Professor Atsuko Kanehara* concluded with thoughts on our "manifold but common maritime order" as demonstrated at the Tokyo conference. She emphasized the global reach of the common nature of the law of the sea.

Part 1 of the conference, on baselines and archipelagic States, began with *Professor Clive Schofield* of WMU and *David Freestone*, professor at George Washington University, and focused on climate change-driven impacts on the ocean. They point to global sea level rise and the major threats to archipelagic atoll coasts and provide scientific projections for damage implications. *Henry S. Bensurto. Jr.* with extensive personal research experience next wrote a detailed opposition brief on China's attempt to designate the Spratly Islands with archipelagic legal status. He is very critical of China's "expansionist" activities in the South China Sea. Next is a paper by *Professor James Kraska* who heads the Stockton Center of International Law at the US Naval War College. His detailed and well-documented analysis updates the literature about the US legal position on China's proclaimed baselines. The subsequent paper in this part is written by U.K. *Professor Richard Barnes* on the legal status of dependent archipelagic waters. He cites many arguments in favor of conferring such status.

Part 2 deals with navigation rights and law enforcement. *Dr. David S. Goddard* of the U.K. Foreign Office introduces the topic of the applicability of human rights treaties in maritime law enforcement. He points out that extraterritorial jurisdiction is much more complicated at sea than on land. *Professor David Letts* then provides a practical guide to navigation and law enforcement from an Australian perspective. He rightly points out that UNCLOS sets out an overarching legal framework but does not answer all the questions that arise with respect to law enforcement at sea. *Professor Kyo Arai* from Doshisha University in Kyoto next analyzes maritime interception operations (MIO) on the high seas against suspected ships sailing under foreign flags as part of the War on Terror. He argues that an expansive interpretation of self-defense is inadvisable to maintain a free and open maritime order. *Professor Masahiro Kurosaki* of the National Defense Academy of Japan then cautions against escalations into the use of force and armed conflict particularly where the coastal State forcibly evicts foreign flag State vessels from its territory. His presentation also offers an optimal framework for de-escalating a coastal State's actions.

Part 3 is addressed to Arctic shipping. *Professor Aldo Chircop* in his usually competent fashion postulates governance considerations for low impact corridors in Canadian Arctic waters. His analysis explores principal governance issues of such corridors against the legal and regulatory backdrop of Canada. An examination of the Northern Sea Route (NSR) in Russia is next given by *Professor Kentaro Wani*. He concludes that Russian requirements for shipping along the NSR do not comport with UNCLOS but that a tailored interpretation of Article 234 of UNCLOS might be a possible remedy. The role of East Asian port States in addressing ship-source pollution from Arctic shipping is the subject of a paper by *Zhen Sun* from WMU. She advocates the use of port State extraterritorial jurisdiction enforcement to implement applicable international rules and standards.

Part 4 deals with the complicated subject of East China Sea maritime boundaries. *Professor Hironobu Sakai* explains the natural prolongation theory for China and for Japan advances the equidistance approach for continental shelf delimitation. He urges both States to "rediscover" an Agreement they signed in 2008 as a starting point for negotiating a broader solution. The submission by *Professor Stuart Kaye* is among the best of any papers we have ever had over many years of editing this COLP series. He confronts the technical issues with clarity and succinctly maps out sensible approaches needed for both China and Japan to move toward on resolving this very volatile dispute. *Professor Robert Beckman* and *Vu Hai Dang* from Singapore's Centre for International Law next provide a useful clarification about the role that ASEAN plays in the resolution of maritime disputes in the South China Sea. They emphasize that ASEAN wants to maintain its central role in dealing with regional issues but remain neutral in competition between major powers.

Part 5 takes up preservation of the marine environment with a special focus on the hazard of plastic debris. *Professor Tomofumi Kitamura* of the University of Tokyo introduces the problem of millions of tons of plastic that leak into the oceans each year. His paper also considers how the basic structure of an instrument tackling marine plastic pollution might be designed. *Aleke Stöfen-O'Brien* then considers the role of common but differentiated responsibilities as a guiding principle toward a potential international treaty on plastic and marine litter. She sees many options available on the application and operationalization of this principle in such a treaty. *Joanna Mossop* from the Law Faculty at Victoria University of Wellington cites regional arrangements and the implications of a new treaty for marine biodiversity in the Asia Pacific area. She outlines the position of States in the area and projects their likely reaction.

Part 6 covers issues arising from climate change. *Professor Karen Scott* from the University of Canterbury in New Zealand reviews the BBNJ negotiations. She examines whether current draft arrangements provide an opportunity to connect the law of the sea and climate change. The goal would be to integrate climate concerns into high seas decision-making affecting biodiversity and ecosystems. *Professor Naoki Iwatsuki* from Rikkyo University in Japan looks at the relation between UNCLOS and climate change law. He notes the compulsory judicial procedures under UNLOS and suggests that these procedures could work effectively "if collaboration and coordination" are pursued through standard-setting by both systems.

We are pleased to offer this volume as a worthy successor to the process initiated by John Norton Moore and Myron H. Nordquist decades ago. COLP and this volume continues to serve as a record of emerging scholarship and thought oceans law and policy. The 45th Annual Conference carries on this tradition in 2022 under the co-sponsorship of the Maritime Institute of Malaysia (MIMA) in Kuala Lumpur.

Myron H. Nordquist
Distinguished Fellow, Stockton Center for International Law
James Kraska
Charles H. Stockton Professor of International Maritime Law and Chair, Stockton Center for International Law

Acknowledgements

This volume is a tribute to Japan's role in developing oceans law and policy.

Open access to this volume was made possible by the Japan Institute of International Affairs (JIIA).

Illustrations

Figures

Tables

Maps

Notes on Contributors

Kyo Arai

has been Professor of International Law, the Faculty of Law, Doshisha University, Kyoto, since 2007. He received an LL.M from the Graduate School of Law, Doshisha University, in 1995. Areas of his academic interests are: International Humanitarian Law, Law of Naval Warfare, and International Criminal Law. He has contributed to many books and journals, including the *Japanese Yearbook of International Law*, and the *Journal of International Law and Diplomacy* (published by the Japanese Society of International Law).

Richard Barnes

is Professor of International Law at the University of Lincoln. He is also Adjunct Professor of Law at the Norwegian Centre for the Law of the Sea. He has published widely on international law of the sea, including *Property Rights and Natural Resources* (Hart, 2009) and co-edited *The United Nations Convention on the Law of the Sea: A Living Instrument* (BIICL, 2016), *Research Handbook on Climate Change, Oceans and Coasts* (Edward Elgar, 2020) and *Frontiers in International Environmental Law: Oceans and Climate Challenges* (Brill 2021). Richard is Current Legal Developments Editor of the *International Journal of Marine and Coastal Law*. He has advised a range of public and private bodies, including the WWF, the European Parliament, and the UK Department for Environment, Food and Rural Affairs, and appeared on numerous occasions before Parliamentary committees to provide expert evidence on fisheries and law of the sea issues.

Robert Beckman

is an Emeritus Professor at the Faculty of Law of the National University of Singapore (NUS). He has specialized in Ocean Law and Policy and in the International Regulation of Shipping, and he currently teaches a course on International Regulation of the Global Commons. Prof. Beckman was the founding Director of the Centre for International Law (CIL), a university-level research institute at NUS, and he is currently the head of CIL's Ocean Law & Policy Programme. He is also a Senior Advisor to the Maritime Security Programme of the Institute for Defence & Strategic Studies (IDSS) at Nanyang Technological University (NTU). Prof. Beckman is a member of the Governing Board of the Rhodes Academy of Oceans Law and Policy.

Henry S. Bensurto Jr.
is a career diplomat and the Philippine Foreign Affairs Lead Counsel in the *South China Sea Arbitration*. He authored the Zone of Peace, Freedom, Friendship and Cooperation in the South China Sea (ZOPFFC) as the Philippine's foreign policy approach in the SCS; and later, as part of the core legal framework of the suit against China. He is a recipient of various Presidential awards for his foreign policy contributions including the Order of Lakandula with the Rank of Grand Officer Commander (2015), and the Gawad Mabini with the Rank of Dakilang Kasugo (2009). Mr. Bensurto is an alumnus of the University of the Philippines (Political Science), San Beda College of Law (LLB), and Oxford University (Distinction in Public International Law). He has a Diploma on the Law of the Sea, Rhodes Academy of Oceans Law and Policy, and a Certificate on National Security, Center for National Security Law, University of Virginia School of Law.

Mariamalia Rodríguez Chaves
has more than fifteen years of experience working with environmental non-governmental organizations and as an independent consultant on diverse environmental topics. She has a law degree, and a master's degree in Environmental Law, from the University of Costa Rica; and a PhD in Law from the School of Law of the National University of Ireland, Galway (NUIG). She successfully completed the United Nations-Nippon Foundation of Japan Fellowship and is the Global representative of its Alumni network of over 200 fellows worldwide. Currently, Mariamalia is a Post-Doctoral Fellow researcher in the Empowering Women for the United Nations Decade of Ocean Science for Sustainable Development programme at the WMU-Sasakawa Global Ocean Institute; a consultant for the High Seas Alliance, where she is responsible for coordinating the approach of Latin American countries in negotiating new treaty on biodiversity beyond national negotiations at the United Nations; and the programme coordinator of the DOALOS/Norway programmes of assistance to meet the strategic capacity needs of developing states in the field of ocean governance and the law of the sea.

Aldo Chircop
is professor of law and Canada Research Chair at the Marine & Environmental Law Institute, Schulich School of Law, Dalhousie University, Canada. His fields of research are in the law of the sea and international maritime law.

Vu Hai Dang
is an Ocean Law and Policy Senior Research Fellow at the Centre for International Law – National University of Singapore. His expertise includes international

law, law of the sea, international environmental law, protection of the marine environment with a geographical focus on Southeast Asia and the South China Sea. He has a broad experience, having worked in the various fields of the legal service, diplomacy, the civil service, and academia.

David Freestone

is Professorial Lecturer and Visiting Scholar at the George Washington University Law School, Washington DC. He has been the Co-Rapporteur of the ILA Committee on International Law and Sea Level Rise since 2012. He is also the Executive Secretary of the Sargasso Sea Commission. From 1996–2008 he worked in the Legal Office of the World Bank – initially as Chief of the Environment and International Law practice group, retiring as Deputy General Counsel/Senior Adviser. He is the Editor in Chief of the *International Journal of Marine and Coastal Law*. His recent books include *Legal Dimensions of Sea Level Rise: Pacific Perspectives*, The World Bank and GFDRR, 2021 (with Duygu Çiçek); *Conserving Biodiversity in Areas beyond National Jurisdiction*, Brill Nijhoff, 2019; *Sustainable Development and International Environmental Law* (Edward Elgar, 2018).

David S. Goddard

is a barrister and Assistant Legal Adviser at the UK Foreign, Commonwealth and Development Office. During a previous career in the Royal Navy, he served as a legal adviser on various maritime and joint operations, and as a military professor at the Stockton Center for the Study of International Law at the US Naval War College. His research has focused on the law of the sea, international human rights law and the intersection of international law and military operations.

Naoki Iwatsuki

is professor of international law at Rikkyo University (Japan) since 2012. He earned an LL.M from the University of Tokyo in 1998 and DEA from the University of Paris 1, Pantheon-Sorbonne, in 2000. He was visiting fellow at the European University Institute (2010–2011), at the Lauterpacht Centre for International Law, the University of Cambridge (2011), and at the University of Rome *La Sapienza* (2011–2012). His principal field of research is the peaceful settlement of international disputes, especially focusing on the legal regulation of non-military coercive measures during the process of amicable settlement of disputes, or countermeasures. On this subject, he has published many journal articles and chapters, including 'Legal Nature of Non-forcible Unilateral Measures by Third States in Case of Grave Violation of Human Rights: Critical Analysis on the Doctrine of "Third-party Countermeasures,"' in: Y. Iwasawa,

K. Morikawa, T. Mori, and Y. Nishimura (eds.), *Dynamics of International Law: In Memory of Professor Akira KOTERA* (Tokyo, Yuhikaku, 2019), pp. 131–164 [in Japanese] and 'Chapter 81 Procedural Conditions of Countermeasures', in: J. Crawford, A. Pellet, S. Olleson and K. Parlet (eds.), *The Law of International Responsibility* (New York, Oxford University Press, 2010), pp. 1149–1156 (in collaboration with Yuji Iwasawa).

Atsuko Kanehara
is Professor of Public International Law at Sophia University, President of the Japanese Society of International Law. She was an advocate for the Government of Japan in "Southern Bluefin Tuna" Cases, and a counsel for the Government of Japan in "Whaling in the Antarctic" Case. She is also serving as Councilor of the Sasakawa Peace Foundation. She is a member of the Governing Board of IMO International Maritime Law Institute, and Visiting Lecturer at the Institute (2007–2011, 2018-present). She delivered a course of lectures at the Hague Academy of International Law, and her article based upon them was published in the *Recueil des cours*, Volume 399 (2019).

Stuart Kaye
is Director and Distinguished Professor of Law within the Australian National Centre for Ocean Resources and Security (ANCORS) at the University of Wollongong. He is a former Dean and Winthrop Professor of Law at the University of Western Australia and held a Chair in Law at the University of Melbourne from 2006 to 2010. He was Dean and Professor of Law at the University of Wollongong between 2002 and 2006. He holds degrees in arts and law from the University of Sydney, winning the Law Graduates' Association Medal, and a doctorate in law from Dalhousie University. He is admitted as a barrister of the Supreme Courts of New South Wales, Tasmania and Queensland.

Tomofumi Kitamura
is an associate professor of international law at the University of Tokyo (Japan). Before taking up the current position in April 2016, he was an associate professor at the Tokyo Metropolitan University (Japan) (2011–2016). He received his bachelor's, master's, and doctoral degrees from the University of Tokyo. His areas of research include international trade law, law of treaties, state responsibility, and international dispute settlement.

James Kraska
is Charles H. Stockton Professor of International Maritime Law and Chair of the Stockton Center for International Law at the U.S. Naval War College and Visiting Professor of Law and John Harvey Gregory Lecturer on World Organization at

Harvard Law School. He has served as Visiting Professor of Law at the College of Law, University of the Philippines, and Visiting Professor of Law at Gujarat National Law University. He previously was Mary Derrickson McCurdy Visiting Scholar at Duke University Marine Laboratory and Chief of Naval Research Fellow at Woods Hole Oceanographic Institution. He has published numerous books and scholarly articles and is General Editor of *International Law Studies* and Editor-in-Chief of the treatise, *Benedict on Admiralty: International Maritime Law*. He is also a Visiting Professor at University of Reading School of Law and a Permanent Member of the Council on Foreign Relations. Professor Kraska served as a U.S. Navy officer and lawyer, with multiple tours of duty in Japan and the Pentagon.

Masahiro Kurosaki
is an Associate Professor of International Law and the Director of the Study of Law, Security and Military Operations at the National Defense Academy of Japan. He has published a range of articles and book chapters on the law of international security, the law of armed conflict, international criminal law, and Japanese security laws, which include: "Towards the Special Computer Law of Targeting: 'Fully Autonomous' Weapons Systems and the Proportionality Test," in Claus Kreß and Robert Lawless (eds.), *Necessity and Proportionality in International Peace and Security Law* (Oxford University Press, 2021); *Strengthening the U.S.-Japan Alliance: Pathways for Bridging Law and Policy* (Columbia Law School, 2020)(co-edited with Nobuhisa Ishizuka and Matthew C. Waxman); "The Fight against Impunity for Core International Crimes: Reflections on the Contribution of Networked Experts to a Regime of Aggravated State Responsibility," in Holly Cullen, Joanna Harrington, and Catherine Renshaw (eds.), *Experts, Networks and International Law* (Cambridge University Press, 2017).

David Letts
holds academic appointments at the Australian National University, Canberra and the Australian National Centre for Ocean Resources and Security, University of Wollongong. Prior to pursuing his academic career, David enjoyed more than thirty years of full-time service in the Royal Australian Navy. He regularly teaches and writes on the law of the sea and maritime security topics, as well as assisting a number of United Nations and non-governmental agencies with law of the sea dissemination activities.

Michael W. Lodge
has been the Secretary-General of the International Seabed Authority since 2017. He is a British national. He received his law degree from the University of

East Anglia, UK, and has an MSc in marine policy from the London School of Economics and Political Science. He is a barrister of Gray's Inn, London. With more than 30 years of experience, Michael Lodge has a strong background in the field of law of the sea as well as ten years' judicial experience in the UK and South Pacific. He spent many years living and working in the South Pacific and was one of the lead negotiators for the South Pacific Island States of the 1995 UN Fish Stocks Agreement. Mr Lodge has published and lectured extensively on the international law of the sea, with over 35 published books and articles on law of the sea, oceans policy and related issues.

Ronán Long
is the Director of the WMU-Sasakawa Global Ocean Institute at the World Maritime University (WMU) in Malmö, Sweden, and the Nippon Foundation Professorial Chair in Ocean Governance and the Law of the Sea. He is the author/co-editor of 12 books and over 300 scholarly contributions on oceans law and policy. He read for his PhD at the School of Law Trinity College Dublin, he has been a Senior Visiting Scholar-in-Residence at the University of California, Berkeley, and a Visiting Scholar at the 'Centre for Oceans Law and Policy' at the University of Virginia. Additionally, Professor Long teaches on the Law of the Sea programme at Harvard Law School. Prior to his academic career, he was a permanent staff member at the European Commission and undertook over 40 missions on behalf of the European Institutions to the Member States of the European Union, the United States of America, Canada, Central America as well as to African countries. His research interests are focused on regulatory and governance arrangements pertaining to new technologies, marine biodiversity, the law of climate change, as well as human rights. He writes and advocates on the interests and needs of the Global-South in ocean affairs and with view to supporting a rules-based international order.

Joanna Mossop
is an Associate Professor in the Law Faculty at Victoria University of Wellington, New Zealand. Her research interests lie in the law of the sea, and she has published on a number of topics including: maritime security, marine biodiversity beyond national jurisdiction, dispute settlement and the continental shelf beyond 200 nautical miles. She has provided advice and training to the New Zealand government and is an observer on the New Zealand delegation to the international negotiations for the BBNJ Treaty. In 2016 the New Zealand government nominated her to the list of arbitrators and conciliators under Annexes V and VII of UNCLOS. She is on the board of several journals including Marine

Policy; she is a member of the IUCN Commission on Environmental Law and a co-chair of the Oceans and International Environmental Law Interest Group of the Australia New Zealand Society of International Law.

Myron H. Nordquist
is currently the Distinguished Fellow at the Stockton Center for International Law at the U.S. Naval War College. He is the former Associate Director of the Center for Oceans Law and Policy at the University of Virginia School of Law. Professor Nordquist has edited more than 60 books, mostly on law of the sea topics. He is Editor-in-Chief of the eight-volume set titled UN Convention on the Law of the Sea 1982: A Commentary sponsored by the Virginia Center. He has authored and delivered uncounted academic presentations as well as numerous scholarly articles on oceans law, national security law and international law.

Hironobu Sakai
is Professor of International Law at Graduate School of Law, Kyoto University, and Dean of Kyoto University Law School. He holds LL.M. in 1989 from Kyoto University. His recent publications in English include: "*La bonne administration de la justice* in the Incidental Proceedings of the International Court of Justice," *Japanese Yearbook of International Law*, Vol.55 (2012), pp. 110–133, "New Relationship between the United Nations and Regional Organizations in Peace and Security: A Case of the African Union," in S. Hamamoto, H. Sakai & A. Shibata (eds.), *"L'être situé," Effectiveness and Purposes of International Law, Essays in Honour of Professor Ryuichi Ida* (Brill, 2015), pp. 165–189, "After the *Whaling in the Antarctic Judgment*: Its Lessons and Prospects from a Japanese Perspective," in M. Fitzmaurice & D. Tamada (eds.), *Whaling in the Antarctic: Significance and Implications of the ICJ Judgment* (Brill, 2016), pp. 308–345.

Clive Schofield
is Professor and Head of Research, WMU-Sasakawa Global Ocean Institute, World Maritime University (WMU), Malmö, Sweden and Professor, Australian Centre for Ocean Resources and Security (ANCORS), University of Wollongong, Australia. He holds a PhD in Geography (Durham) and an LLM in International Law (UBC). His research relates to international maritime boundaries, boundary dispute resolution, ocean governance and technical aspects of the law of the sea, resulting in over 200 publications. Clive is an Observer on the Advisory Board on the Law of the Sea (ABLOS) and a Member of the ILA Committee on International Law and Sea Level Rise.

Karen N. Scott

is a Professor of Law at the University of Canterbury in New Zealand, President of the *Australian and New Zealand Society of International Law* (ANZSIL) and Editor-in-Chief of *Ocean Development and International Law* (ODIL). Karen is on the board of seven journals including the *Brill Research Perspectives on the Law of the Sea* and the *Australian Yearbook of International* Law. She researches and teaches in the areas of public international law, law of the sea and international environmental law. Karen has published over 70 edited books, journal articles and book chapters in these areas.

Aleke Stöfen-O'Brien

is Associate Research Officer at the WMU-Sasakawa Global Ocean Institute, World Maritime University in Malmö, Sweden. Prior to joining WMU, Aleke worked at the Federal Environment Agency of the Federal Republic of Germany, the Secretariat of the Convention on Biological Diversity (CBD), Montréal, Canada, the European Commission, the United Nations Institute for Training and Research (UNITAR) as well as the WHO/Europe representation to the EU working on aspects such as marine environmental protection, marine litter, aquaculture, sub-seabed CO2 capture and storage, capacity-building and broader aspects of international and European law. Aleke co-convened Chapter 12 on Marine Litter of the Second World Ocean Assessment which was published in summer 2021 and she was nominated by the Nippon Foundation to contribute to the development of The Economist Plastics Management Index which was published in October 2021.

Zhen Sun

is a Research Officer at the WMU-Sasakawa Global Ocean Institute, World Maritime University in Malmö, Sweden. She is the Co-Principal Investigator on multiple research and capacity building programmes. Her main research interests include the law of the sea, regulation of international shipping, gender equality, ocean governance and the protection of the marine environment. Prior to joining WMU, Zhen was a Research Fellow at the Centre for International Law, National University of Singapore. Zhen received her law degrees from Hainan University, China University of Political Science and Law, the University of Edinburgh and the University of Cambridge.

Dai Tamada

is Professor of International Law at Graduate School of Law, Kyoto University. He holds M.A. (Kyoto University 2000) and Ph.D. (Kyoto University 2014). His research areas cover international dispute settlement, international investment law, the law of treaties, and the law of the sea. He has been committee member in several Government organs, including Ministry of Foreign Affairs (MOFA), Ministry of Economy, Trade and Industry (METI), and Ministry of Justice (MOJ) of Japan. His recent publications include Malgosia Fitzmaurice and Dai Tamada (eds.), *Whaling in the Antarctic: Significance and Implications of the ICJ Judgment* (Brill/Nijhoff, 2016), and Dai Tamada and Keyuan Zou (eds.), *Implementation of the United Nations Convention on the Law of the Sea: State Practice of China and Japan* (Springer, April 2021).

Kentaro Wani
LLB (Sophia University, 1999), MA (the University of Tokyo, 2001), PhD (the University of Tokyo, 2007), is Associate Professor of Public International Law at Osaka University, Japan (since October 2010). From 2007 to 2010 he was Assistant Professor of Public International Law at the University of Tokyo. He maintains a special interest in the law of armed conflict; the use of force in international law; the law of the sea; and the history of international law. His principal publications include *Neutrality in International Law: From the Sixteenth Century to 1945* (Routledge, 2017); "Development of the Law of the Sea and the Legal Status of International Straits in Time of International Armed Conflict," *Japanese Yearbook of International Law*, Vol. 61 (2019); and "The Status of Rebels in Non-International Armed Conflict: Do They Have the Right to Life?," in Karen N. Scott, Kathleen Claussen, Charles-Emmanuel Côté, and Atsuko Kanehara, eds., *Changing Actors in International Law* (Brill, 2020). He has won the 43rd Adachi Mineichiro Memorial Award (Adachi Mineichiro Memorial Foundation) in 2010 for his work on the law of neutrality.

Rüdiger Wolfrum
is a Professor for National Public Law and International Public Law at the Law Faculties of the Universities of Mainz (1982), Kiel (1982–1993) and Heidelberg (1993–2012); Director at the Max Planck Institute for Comparative Public Law and International Law, Heidelberg (1993–2012); 2013- 2020 Managing Director of the Max Planck Foundation for International Peace and the Rule of Law. Membre de l'Institut de Droit International (since 2007); Manley O. Hudson Medal, American Society of International Law, 2020. Judge at the International Tribunal for the Law of the Sea (1996- 2017); President (2005–2008); member or chair at several arbitral tribunals and conciliator at a conciliation commission. He has numerous publications on general international law, United Nations law, human rights, the law of the sea, international trade law, environmental law and on international dispute settlement. He also has publications on national and comparative public law, in particular constitutional law.

Shunji Yanai
is a Judge of the International Tribunal for the Law of the Sea (President 2011–2014); and Board Director, Japan Investment Advisor Co., Ltd. After having studied law at the University of Tokyo, he joined the Japanese Foreign Service in 1961 and held various positions including Consul General in San Francisco, Legal Advisor to the Foreign Minister, Executive Secretary of the Prime Minister's PKO Office, Director-General of the Foreign Policy Bureau, Deputy-Foreign Minister, Vice-Foreign Minister and Ambassador to the United States. Following retirement from the Foreign Service, Professor of Law until 2007 at Waseda University and Chuo University in Tokyo; Board Director, Mitsubishi Electric Corporation until 2012; and the Chairman of the Advisory Panel on Reconstruction of the Legal Basis for Security until 2014.

Featured Papers

CHAPTER 1

Tribute to Ambassador Satya N. Nandan

Myron H. Nordquist

Satya Nandan was a close friend of me and my family for over four decades. He and I worked together for many years which included productive months at the Third United Nation's Convention on the Law of the Sea (UNCLOS) negotiations. Satya was a skilled diplomat who made many substantive contributions to the peaceful order of the oceans.[1] His contributions were comparable to just a few others such as Tommy Koh of Singapore, who was the President of the Law of the Sea Conference.

My remarks here refer to just one brief period of Satya's long life. The rationale for this approach is to offer one concrete example of many available to illustrate the seminal role he played in the Law of the Sea. The period selected hopefully provides a manageable focus suitable for an introduction and tribute to Satya. The events occurred during his activities in 1975 when Satya was Rapporteur of the Second Committee at the Third Conference in Geneva. And I personally was regularly involved with him in this period of the negotiations.

Satya was an extraordinary public servant for his native Fiji, the United Nations, the International Seabed Authority and UNCLOS viewed as a whole. His contributions need to be honored and preserved for humankind, not the least of which are for serious LOS scholars. My relationship with Satya started at the UN General Assembly in the early 1970s (shortly after the "Principles Resolution" was adopted) when Satya was a young diplomat from Fiji posted to its UN Mission in New York.

When the Conference officially started in 1973, Satya was elected as a representative of the Asian Regional Group to serve as Rapporteur of the Second Committee under a chairman selected by the Latin American Group. The Second Committee following the List of Subjects and Issues adopted for the Conference was assigned the most important substantive issues at UNCLOS. These included the territorial sea, innocent passage, international straits transit, archipelagic regime, exclusive economic zone (EEZ), fisheries, continental shelf, high seas, and regime of islands.

1 See M.W. Lodge and M.H. Nordquist (eds.), *Peaceful Order in the World's Oceans: Essays in Honor of Satya N. Nandan*, (Leiden/Boston: Brill Nijhoff), 2014.

 | DOI:10.1163/9789004518629_002

The focus of the limited scope of my remarks here is on the single article in the 1982 Convention pertaining to islands: Article 121. The substantive session of UNCLOS opened in Caracas in 1974 with well over 100 countries giving for the first time ever an outline of their general positions on the law of the sea. This opening stage was followed by States submitting literally hundreds of detailed proposals based on the list of subjects and issues assigned to the three Main Conference committees.

The Second Committee dealing with the traditional law of the sea had, of course, to deal with these hundreds of official proposals. Delegates faced a dauting task to reach a single text for a draft Convention that was considered necessary for presentation to the next Conference session planned for Geneva in 1976.

The only realistic way delegates found out of a political deadlock (and conference failure) in 1975 given the overwhelming number of competing State proposals was to adopt unique procedural rules for the UNCLOS negotiations. The delegations knew that they had to provide a "fair reading and review" procedure for each of the proposals submitted from many sovereign States. Moreover, the conference had to proceed on a "consensus" basis in its task of reaching an agreed draft text. Delegations resolved the problem of trying to produce a single negotiating text by bestowing an unprecedented procedural power on the "Chairmen" of the three main conference committees. Each chairman was personally mandated by the UNCLOS delegates to prepare the actual language for a draft convention text. The prepared text was then to be submitted to his full committee allowing all delegates to review it. Satya's role in 1975 thereby immediately evolved into drafting the textual proposals for the Second Committee's Chairman. This extraordinary step was accepted as the only practical way to obtain a single text for a convention at this stage of the negotiations. That is, a single draft text was seen in 1975 as critical for the success or failure of the Third Conference.

Here it is noteworthy that the draft submissions from the Second Committee to the Plenary Committee of the Conference were written in English, not Spanish, which was the native language of the Chairman. The reason is that Rapporteur Nandan and the few UN staff (most notably Gudmunder Eiriksson of Iceland) who did the actual drafting or research selection read and wrote in the English language. Further noteworthy for the limited focus of these remarks is that both Satya and Gudmunder were from island States. By their backgrounds they understood more than most delegates about the complexity posed by islands throughout the world and their controversial status, particularly with respect to disputed ownership of associated ocean entitlements. As noted, no records were kept of their drafting research or writing but hints of influence emerged from informal working group meetings that were sometimes held on certain articles. These informal meetings in 1975 were open to all delegations but no definitive conclusions can be drawn from what was said there.

As a matter of traceable Conference history, the drafts submitted to the Chairman of the Second Committee by Satya Nandan were accepted, adopted by the Chairman, and forwarded to the Second Committee Plenary just as Satya had written them. Even more amazing is the fact that the Single Negotiating Text (SNT) from 1975 which became Article 121 in the Convention remained substantively unchanged from what Satya had drafted and handed to his Chairman in 1975. To make the point completely clear, Satya's language for Article 121 remained subsequently unchanged despite several detailed reviews of the exact language in full committee meetings from 1976 to 1982. His draft as submitted in 1975 is now the binding text in Article 121 of the 1982 Convention.

The Vienna Convention on the Law of Treaties provides customary international law rules for the interpretation of treaty text. The general rule there is found in article 31 which provides that the ordinary meaning is to be given to the terms of the treaty in their context. The sources of international law are listed in Article 38 of the Statute of the International Court of Justice (which is part of the UN Charter). Article 38(a)(1) expressly provides first for the application for international conventions for settling disputes. Judicial decisions and opinions of academic experts are expressly given a "subsidiary" role.

The point is that text accepted by sovereign State consent controls what is international law. In the case of the regime of islands, paragraph 1 of Article 121 reads: "An island is a naturally formed area of land, surrounded by water, which is above water at high tide."

This language selected for the SNT in 1975 originated in Article 10 of the 1958 Convention on the Territorial Sea and Contiguous Zone which in turn was taken from slightly modified language drafted by the ILC in 1956 for the First Conference. Unlike the First Conference, the International Law Commission was not tasked to prepare draft treaty provisions for the Third Conference. The Third Conference negotiations could have saved a great deal of time, energy and angst had it started in 1974 with what was equivalent to an SNT for most articles. But we have what we have.

In any event the words "naturally formed" in Article 121 were not only familiar to most delegations but also part of the legal lexicon for many countries at the Third Conference. Satya wisely selected these exact words for his text and Second Chairman Galindo Pohl of El Salvador readily endorsed this in the text for the SNT draft of Article 121(1) in 1975.

The second paragraph of Article 121 just repeated the 1958 Convention's general concept that treated islands as having the same ocean space entitlements as "other land territory". The problem now, however, was that the new 200-mile EEZ and expanded continental margin claims at the Third Conference vastly increased the reach and expansion of island ocean entitlements. Most of this expansion was in the international area beyond national jurisdiction which had now been deemed the Common Heritage of Mankind. The landlocked/geographical group led in large part by Tommy Koh was a major political force in the negotiations by 1975. Satya obviously decided it was necessary to reduce the entitlement of islands to make the island regime more acceptable. Thus, the third paragraph came into being.

A new paragraph 3 exception for "rocks" was seen by Satya as necessary to reduce the impact of island entitlement. Rocks that could not "sustain human habitation or an economic life of their own" were to have no EEZ or continental shelf. Presumably, rocks under international law still would rate a territorial sea and contiguous zone.

The third paragraph of Article 121 thus contains a new rule of international law. Satya and his small group of fellow draftsmen in 1975 deftly employed the well-established drafting technique of "deliberate ambiguity" to encapsulate this new rule. By doing so, the draftsmen hoped that contending spokesmen on contested island regime issues would compromise sufficiently to accept the new rule in the UNCLOS in the context of the tide of political pressures to achieve a convention.

The 121(1) reference to a "naturally formed" area of land for an island definition unfortunately remained unclear. The main reason is that it is not obvious "when" the required natural formation must take place. Possibilities from the text could include when the 'big bang' created the universe, when the earth split apart (Siberia used to be connected to Alaska), when the continental masses drifted apart, when Captain Cook marked his charts, when a volcano erupted or even when a dispute settlement case required a determination.

All interested parties want to know what was intended in drafting the text of articles in a Convention. This is where the value of Satya's reflections come to the fore. He selected or drafted key text in the 1982 Convention on the Law of the Sea. For that reason, it was very fortunate that he was able to finalize his book *Reflections on the Making of the Modern Law of the Sea* before his untimely passing in 2020.[2] We therefore have a record of his remarkable

2 S.N. Nandan with K.E. Dalaker, *Reflections on the Making of the Modern Law of the Sea* (Singapore: NUS Press), 2021.

personal contribution to world order in the oceans which cover over 70% of the earth's surface. Finally, we might remember that he made a special historical impact for the newly independent state of Fiji when he deposited in 1982 the first ratification of the United Nations Convention on the Law of the Sea. He was first in line even at the end.

My bet is that he is still smiling with satisfaction about that.

CHAPTER 2

Reflections on Peaceful Maritime Engagement in East Asia and the Pacific Region

Shunji Yanai

Professor Nordquist, Professor Kraska, Ambassador Sasae, distinguished panelists, and participants, ladies and gentlemen, it is a distinct honor and pleasure for me to give opening remarks at the Conference on Oceans Law and Policy 2021. When the conference was postponed last year due to the COVID-19, I was hoping that it could be held this year as an in-person event. Unfortunately, the pandemic has continued to linger. In the meantime, however, all of us have been accustomed to attend conferences via the Zoom webinar format. And I know that many are participating remotely in this year's conference from all over the world.

Almost four decades have elapsed since the adoption of the United Nations Convention on the Law of the Sea (the Convention). The Convention put an end to legal disorder reigning in respect of the seas and oceans under the 1958 Geneva Conventions. At the third United Nations Conference on the Law of the Sea (UNCLOS III), States finally agreed on the breadth of the territorial sea and established new regimes such as the 200-nautical miles Exclusive Economic Zone (EEZ), straits used for international navigation, and archipelagic waters. They also redefined the continental shelf within and beyond 200 nautical miles.

Further, the Convention created an entirely new international maritime regime, that of the deep seabed, defining that the seabed and ocean floor and subsoil thereof, beyond the limits of national jurisdiction (the Area), and its resources are the common heritage of mankind. For these decades, the Convention, which is often referred to as the "Constitution of the Sea," has been the mainstay in the efforts to maintain peace and the rule of law on the seas and oceans, and to encourage the sustainable development of marine resources for future generations.

As the Convention comprises complex provisions such as laws concerning the continental shelf, which are difficult to implement or may give rise to disputes between State Parties to the Convention, it sets up an institutional framework for interpreting and implementing its provisions. In addition to such existing institutions as the United Nations, the specialized agencies,

 | DOI:10.1163/9789004518629_003

and the International Court of Justice (ICJ), the Convention established the Commission on the Limits of the Continental Shelf (CLCS), the International Seabed Authority (ISA), and the International Tribunal for the Law of the Sea (ITLOS). This is to ensure the proper interpretation or the smooth implementation of these complex provisions. Cooperation among State Parties and the support of these institutions are indispensable for preventing disputes over law-of-the-sea matters, peacefully settling any disputes that nevertheless arise, and establishing the rule of law over the seas and oceans.

The drafters and negotiators of the Convention were wise to devise this institutional framework which facilitates the Convention to address various issues, including new challenges. This is in addition to setting out laws in the Convention to govern a wide range of law-of-the-sea matters. All three institutions created by the Convention have worked hard to implement or interpret its complex provisions that are not always clear, as the Convention is a product of compromise among many States with different interests and backgrounds. ISA has adopted regulations on the exploration for and exploitation of mineral resources in the Area and has drawn up many formal plans of work. CLCS has examined many submissions from coastal States, concerning the continental shelf beyond 200 nautical miles and made recommendations on matters related to the establishment of the outer limits of their continental shelf. ITLOS, for its part, has dealt with twenty-seven contentious cases, including three maritime delimitation cases and two advisory opinions in the twenty-five years since it started its operation.

In connection with maritime delimitation disputes, the important contribution by the ICJ should be underlined. As is well known, the Convention only provides that the delimitation of the EEZ and the continental shelf respectively shall be effected by agreement on the basis of international law in order to achieve an equitable solution. However, the Convention does not offer any criteria for the delimitation nor does it specify the method to be applied for achieving an equitable solution. The ICJ devised a three-stage method of delimitation, which has come to be known as the "equidistance/relevant circumstances method." ITLOS has applied this method in the past delimitation cases on the merits.

Although long and thorough negotiations were conducted on a wide range of maritime issues at UNCLOS III, new challenges have arisen through the law of the sea after the adoption of the Convention. These include some issues that States were not aware of or were not fully discussed. For example, States did not discuss at UNCLOS III, the question of the right of a flag State with respect to a container ship having multinational composition of its crew and multiplicity of interests that may be involved in the cargo on board a single ship. Also, in shipping, bunkering by foreign tankers to foreign fishing vessels in the EEZ of a coastal State is a shipping business that developed after the adoption of the Convention. Regarding the right of a flag State with respect to a container ship, ITLOS ruled in the M/V "SAIGA" (No.2) Case that the flag State has the right to protect the vessel flying its flag irrespective of the nationalities of the persons involved in the shipping operations concerned. ITLOS stated in its judgment that the ship, everything on it, and every person involved or interested in its operations are treated as an entity linked to the flag State. This has come to be known as a "ship-as-a-unit principle." With respect to bunkering in the EEZ, there is no explicit provision in the Convention as this is a business practice that developed only after the adoption of the Convention. However, in the M/V "Virginia G" Case, ITLOS ruled that the regulation by a coastal State of bunkering of foreign vessels fishing in its EEZ is among those measures which the coastal State may take in its EEZ to conserve and manage its living resources under the Convention.

The Convention codified the customary rules of international law regarding piracy on the high seas. However, different types of piracy and armed robbery occurred frequently in the EEZ and the territorial sea of certain countries in Asia and Africa after the adoption of the Convention. This is another challenge to the law of the Sea.

Further, the Convention covers only mineral resources in the area, and living resources on the deep seabed beyond national jurisdiction were not a subject of the negotiations at UNCLOS III. As we all know, active negotiations are being conducted in the United Nations with a view to adopting a new legal instrument on the biological diversity beyond national jurisdiction under the Convention. In addition, the impact of climate change on the law of the sea is another new challenge that was not aware of at UNCLOS III.

As mentioned above, the right of a flag State to protect the vessel flying its flag and bunkering in the EEZ are the issues that fall within the scope of the interpretation or application of the Convention even though it has no explicit provisions on these matters. On the other hand, other kinds of challenges have arisen and may arise in the future, which cannot be resolved only through the interpretation or application of the provisions of the Convention as they now stand. The Marine Biodiversity of Areas Beyond National Jurisdiction (BBNJ) is a typical case of this kind of challenges which is not covered by the Convention even implicitly, and therefore requires new international legislation.

It is gratifying to note that together with traditional issues, new challenges to the law of the sea are included in the agenda of the 2021 Conference on Oceans Law and Policy, such as the impact of climate change, including sea level rise and Arctic shipping, combat against maritime crimes, and the preservation of the marine environment, including the hazard of plastic debris. I earnestly hope that panelists and participants will have fruitful discussion at this conference and come up with useful proposals.

I cannot close my remarks without expressing my serious concern about attempts in East Asia to change the maritime legal order in violation of international law, including, in particular, the law of the sea.

CHAPTER 3

The Legal Regime of the Deep Seabed as a Paradigm for Global Governance of Natural Resources

Michael W. Lodge

I wish to congratulate Professor James Kraska and the Stockton Center for International Law for taking over the responsibility for organization of these annual conferences from the University of Virginia.[1] The Virginia conference series started some 40 years ago, and the collected proceedings form an impressive record of the progressive development of the international law of the sea. I wish James and his team all the very best as they work to continue this legacy. I am very happy to see that Professor Myron Nordquist, as well as Judy Ellis, will continue their association with the conference programme.

I also wish to congratulate our host institution, the Japan Institute of International Affairs, for its support for this conference. I understand that it has been extremely challenging to organize it in the current circumstances and that we all would have wished to have been together in Tokyo for this event. The personal connections that are made in conferences such as this are invaluable and cannot be replicated over video. Nevertheless, I commend the institute for moving forward with the conference despite the formidable challenges.

Before I turn to the subject matter of my intervention, I wish to make one comment. Since 2019, in my capacity as Secretary-General of the Authority, I have been honoured to have been recognized as an International Gender Champion by the International Gender Champions Network, which is a network of global leaders committed to advancing gender equality. As part of my own commitment to that objective, I had signed the IGC Panel Parity Pledge to champion gender balance at events such as this.

I cannot help but reflect that none of today's keynote speakers are women, none of the moderators are women, and out of 24 speakers for the conference, only four are women. Indeed, three out of the seven panels are exclusively male panels. This is not a good reflection of the diversity of the global community

1 The views expressed in this essay are those of the author and do not necessarily reflect the views of the International Seabed Authority or of its members.

DOI:10.1163/9789004518629_004

of law of the sea scholars and practitioners. I do hope that the organizers can take this comment on board for future conferences. The Virginia conference is possibly the most prestigious law of the sea gathering in the world and it is important that it reflects who we are as a community.

The theme of the conference is peaceful maritime engagement in East Asia and the Pacific region. I would like to use the opportunity of this keynote address to take a broader outlook and to reflect on the way in which Part XI of the Convention[2] and the 1994 Agreement[3] have ensured peace and order in the ocean beyond national jurisdiction, not just in East Asia and the Pacific, but around the world.

The history of the international law of the sea is one of a tension between exclusive jurisdiction of coastal States in areas close to the coastline and open access to natural resources in the parts of the ocean beyond national jurisdiction.[4] In areas beyond national jurisdiction, each State had the right to use the sea and to exercise jurisdiction over ships flying its flag, and the duty to ensure that its freedoms were exercised with reasonable regard for the exercise of high seas freedoms by other States.

The evolution of the law, even up to the present day, is fundamentally associated with advances in the technological ability of States to control the sea at ever greater distances from the shore and to utilize the natural resources it contains.[5] In this sense, one of the great achievements of the Convention was to replace a plethora of conflicting and competing claims by coastal States with universally agreed limits on the territorial sea, the contiguous zone, and the exclusive economic zone, as well as clarity on the rights and duties of coastal States within those zones.[6]

The Convention, and customary international law, also reflects a strong preference for carving up the natural resources of the sea into different regulatory domains controlled by coastal States and against international regulation of these resources by international agencies. We see this exemplified not only

---

2 United Nations Convention on the Law of the Sea (done 10 December 1982, entered into force 16 November 1994) 1833 UNTS 397.

3 Agreement relating to the implementation of Part XI of the United Nations Convention on the Law of the Sea of 10 December 1982 (done 28 July 1994, entered into force 28 July 1996) 1836 UNTS 41.

4 Alan O. Sykes & Eric Posner, *Economic Foundations of the Law of the Sea* (John M. Olin Program in Law and Economics Working Paper No. 504, 2009).

5 Ibid.

6 Michael W. Lodge, 'Enclosure of the Oceans versus the Common Heritage of Mankind', 97 Int'l L. Stud. 803 (2021).

in the maxim that the 'land dominates the sea',[7] but also in the way in which the Convention relegates the interests of the international community in the delineation of the continental shelf to a procedural afterthought.[8]

The fact that common pool resources could be subject to over-exploitation and that international rules may be necessary to ensure proper conservation and management as well as equity over access to such resources was not lost on the participants in UNCLOS III. Both President Nixon's 1970 proposal for a UN Convention on the International Seabed Area[9] and the draft Ocean Space Treaty proposed by Malta in 1971,[10] recognized the need for international regulation of access to resources beyond national jurisdiction as well as distribution of the proceeds for the economic advancement of developing countries.

In the end, of course, these early proposals were substantially watered down. Partition of the ocean and its resources according to the national interests of States became the dominant approach. It was decided to limit the jurisdiction of the International Seabed Authority to the mineral resources located in the seabed beyond national jurisdiction and to give the Authority no role at all in the delineation of the spatial limits of its jurisdiction. Whilst there was some recognition of the legitimate interests of developing States in equitable redistribution of wealth, there were fundamental disagreements over the appropriate economic measures to be used to respond to these concerns.[11]

It was only with the adoption of the Implementation Agreement of 1994 that it became possible to resolve these disagreements. That agreement marked a major step forward, not only in the way it addressed the substantive concerns of States while reiterating the core principles contained in the Convention, but also in the way in which it was so tightly woven together with the fabric of the Convention.

Any instrument of ratification or accession to the Convention following the adoption of the Agreement would also represent consent to be bound by the Agreement.[12] Furthermore, no State was allowed to ratify the Agreement

---

7 North Sea Continental Shelf Cases (Federal Republic of Germany v Denmark) (Merits) [1969] ICJ Rep 3.

8 Lodge, n. 6 *supra*.

9 H. Gary Knight, 'The Draft United Nations Convention on the Law of the Sea, Background, Description and Some Preliminary Thoughts', *San Diego Law Review*, Vol. 8, No. 3 (May 1971).

10 Draft Ocean Space Treaty: Working Paper Submitted by Malta, U.N. Doc. A/AC.138/153 (1971), reprinted in Report of the Committee on the Peaceful Uses of the Sea-Bed and the Ocean Floor Beyond the Limits of National Jurisdiction, 26 GAOR., at 105–93, Supp. No. 21, UN Doc. A/8421 (1971).

11 Sykes & Posner, n. 4, *supra*.

12 1994 Agreement, Article 4(1).

unless it had previously or at the same time acceded to the Convention.[13] All States that were already party to the Convention prior to the adoption of the Agreement were considered to have established their consent to be bound by the Agreement unless they 'opted-out' within a period of 12 months.[14]

These measures ensured prompt entry into force of the Agreement, but more importantly ensured that there would be a single regime formed by the Convention and the 1994 Agreement together. Accordingly, any possibility of overlapping or conflicting regimes was denied while preventing the development of a new regime that could potentially undermine the existing regime. Most importantly, these measures substantially reinforced the overall objective of peace and order in the ocean beyond national jurisdiction which is the centrepiece of the Convention.

In this aspect, there are perhaps some important lessons to be considered in relation to future implementation agreements. So how do we measure the success of the regime created by the Convention and the 1994 Agreement?

First, the mere fact that the Convention establishes a legal regime for the Area that limits access to resources and prevents unrestrained exploitation is itself a benefit to humanity and an important contribution to peaceful maritime engagement. Through the development and implementation of a set of rules and standards governing deep sea mining and related activities, including marine scientific research in the Area, it becomes possible to balance the need for resource extraction with the preservation of the marine environment.

Second, the regime has succeeded in its objective of preventing unilateral claims to deep seabed resources. Initially this was achieved by the pioneer investor regime under resolution II,[15] which was subsequently grandfathered into the current regime by the 1994 Agreement. Since 1982, all claims to potential mine sites have been dealt with strictly in accordance with the provisions of resolution II, the 1994 Agreement and the regulations adopted by ISA.[16]

---

13 1994 Agreement, Article 4(2).

14 1994 Agreement, Article 5(1). See also Shabtai Rosenne, 'The United Nations Convention on the Law of the Sea, 1982', 29 *Israel Law Review* 491 (1995).

15 Resolution II Governing Preparatory Investment in Pioneer Activities Relating to Polymetallic Nodules, annexed to the Final Act of the Third United Nations Conference on the Law of the Sea, Montego Bay, 10 December 1982.

16 Regulations on Prospecting and Exploration for Polymetallic Nodules in the Area, ISBA/6/A/18, Annex, (adopted in 2000, revised in 2013 as ISBA/19/C/17); Regulations on Prospecting and Exploration for Polymetallic Sulphides in the Area, ISBA16/A/12/Rev.1 (2010); Regulations on Prospecting and Exploration for Cobalt-Rich Ferromanganese Crusts in the Area, ISBA/18/A/11 (2012).

There have been no unilateral claims, even though some key States remain outside the regime created by the Convention and the 1994 Agreement.

It is clear that, whatever the political positions expressed in some countries, industry is not prepared to take the risk to operate outside the framework of the Convention. One of the decisive factors in this regard is the security of tenure that is guaranteed under the contract with ISA, which resolves one of the key problems for all open access regimes of a lack of enforceable property rights.[17]

Third, is the fact that the regime forces States to act by consensus. One criticism of all international regimes is that they can only operate with the consent of all or most States, which makes them slow and inefficient.[18] It is true that it takes a long time to build consensus, especially where there are many conflicting interests. This is certainly the case with respect to the rules for exploitation of seabed minerals, which have been under negotiation since 2015.[19] On the other hand, the fact that States are forced to make all efforts to reach consensus makes the ultimate regime stronger and more broadly representative of the interests of all. It also promotes regulatory stability and predictability, which are important incentives for investment.

Of course, States will submit to an international regime only if they expect the gains from cooperation to be greater than the potential returns from unilateral action.[20] This is why the Convention and the 1994 Agreement establish one of the most complex power-sharing arrangements in international law.[21] The composition and decision-making rules in the Council ensure that decisions are made in a way that reflects a balance between the major interests in seabed mining.

Fourth, the fact that there is a single global regime covering more than 50 per cent of the global seafloor brings profound benefits on two important levels. It ensures a level playing field for industry, whether funded by international capital, States or in the form of the Enterprise, but even more importantly, it ensures effective and comprehensive protection of the marine environment.

---

17 Sykes & Posner, n. 4, *supra*.

18 Sykes & Posner, n. 4, *supra*.

19 All draft texts and details of the negotiating process can be found at www.isa.org.jm. A summary of the negotiation process up to and including 2021 appears in ISA document ISBA/26/C/44.

20 Sykes & Posner, n. 4, *supra*.

21 Michael W. Lodge, 'The Deep Seabed', in DR Rothwell, AG Oude Elferink, KN Scott and T Stephens (eds) *The Oxford Handbook of the Law of the Sea* (OUP Oxford 2015) 226–53.

Under this single global regime, the default position is that the seabed is off limits to mining except where expressly permitted by ISA following a lengthy process of approval. Even at the exploration phase, the most stringent environmental regulations apply to ensure that the precautionary approach is applied, and that environmental data are collected and shared with the regulator. ISA is currently in the process of establishing the most comprehensive system for environmental impact assessment and subsequent regulation for any activity taking place beyond national jurisdiction.[22] All environmental decisions are based on the best available science and a precautionary approach.

Fifth, the existence of a shared space for decision-making has proved to act as a catalyst for innovative action on many of the underlying concerns relating to equity that were at the core of the Maltese proposal in 1971.

In this regard, whilst the objectives of the original text of the Convention were hampered by the imposition of clumsy and divisive economic measures such as mandatory transfer of technology and subsidization of the Enterprise, there has always been a broad consensus around the application of general utilitarian ethics to the problem of equitable distribution of benefits. There is no disagreement with the general principle that poorer countries should receive transfers from richer countries, although there may be very strong disagreements as to the form those transfers should take.

One of the core objectives of the Part XI regime was to ensure equality of access to seabed mineral resources by both developed and developing States. The regime has been remarkably successful in meeting this objective. Today, out of 31 exploration contracts issued by ISA, eight are held by developing countries, including six small island developing States.[23] I must mention here the important contribution that was made in this regard by the Seabed Disputes Chamber of ITLOS in its advisory opinion of 2011.[24] By clarifying the law on the responsibilities and obligations of sponsoring States, the Chamber reinforced the provisions of the Convention and opened the door to full participation by the developing countries.

Many of the non-monetary benefits of the Part XI regime are specified in Article 150 of the Convention, including increased availability of minerals, rational management of the resources and expansion of opportunities for participation.[25] However, there is no limit to the category of non-monetary

---

22 See the draft Regulations on Exploitation of Mineral Resources in the Area, ISBA/25/C/WP.1, available at www.isa.org.jm.

23 These are Cook Islands, Kiribati, Nauru, Singapore and Tonga.

24 *Responsibilities and Obligations of States with Respect to Activities in the Area (Advisory Opinion)* (1 February 2011) [2011] ITLOS Rep 10.

25 United Nations Convention on the Law of the Sea, 1982, Article 150.

benefits, and it is not possible to quantify all these benefits as they may change over time. They certainly include the protection of the marine environment, capacity-building, increased scientific knowledge of the marine environment and increased availability of marine technology.

The Part XI regime and the International Seabed Authority has always been a unique experiment in international relations. As the pressure to use ocean resources in a sustainable manner that benefits all of humanity increases, we can expect to see increased focus on the role and functions of ISA.

It is worth recalling the words of the current Secretary-General of the United Nations to the effect that the governance of critical global public goods, including peace and the natural environment, needs to be reinforced and reimagined. The starting point for this is respect for and compliance with international law.[26]

I am convinced that the Part XI regime offers a convincing template for international governance of shared resources that will become increasingly important to the maintenance of peace and good order in the ocean. The regime has demonstrated that it is resilient, whilst also adaptable to changing political and economic circumstances. It has benefited from the support of the vast majority of the international community, and it deserves continued support as it seeks to fulfil its mandate of a fair and equitable distribution of the resources of the seabed beyond national jurisdiction for the benefit of all humanity.

26 Statement by Antonio Guterres, Secretary-General of the United Nations, to the Seventy-Fifth Session of the United Nations General Assembly (September 2020).

CHAPTER 4

International Law Making

Rüdiger Wolfrum

1 Introduction

Since the seventies of the last century, the system of international law making has changed dramatically. Until then the development of new international rules rested on bilateral international agreements or multilateral ones prepared by legal experts, predominantly the International Law Commission, as was the case with the Vienna Convention on the Law of Treaties. Multilateral treaties developed spontaneously at a multilateral conference were few in number but had a lasting effect on international relations. Prime examples were the Hague Conferences of 1899 and 1907, which codified the first comprehensive regime on the rules in international armed conflicts. Meanwhile multilateral agreements are gaining ground and in relevance concentrating on issues which are in the interest of the international community. Or to describe the situation differently – the agreements elaborated rather than developing international law merely codify it. What do I mean by the reference to community interest-oriented agreements? These are multilateral treaties, which serve the interests of the international community. One may differentiate between three different types of issues which may be qualified as such:

- Treaties on international spaces – which means spaces which are not under the jurisdiction of a State such as the high seas or outer space;
- Issues which cannot be managed without the participation of at least most States such as treaties concerning the protection of the world climate; and
- Issues which constitute the ethical basis for international law such as the international human rights regime.

The content of such new international regimes, which occupy a growing space in the international normative system have resulted in new forms – or you may say procedures of law making or, in other words, in new institutionalized forms of the international normative order resulting in the acknowledgement of further actors besides States and international organizations. The new actors are NGOs, interest groups and other representatives of civil society.

DOI:10.1163/9789004518629_005

This development took place hand in hand with a particular procedure for the establishment of new regimes and new fora for deliberations such as multilateral conferences inaugurated and prepared by an international organization, conferences of parties, and treaty bodies. All constitute institutionalized forms of cooperation among States. These new forms of institutionalized cooperation between States are considered more flexible as far as the implementation of the mandate of each forum is concerned.

However, the relevance of other sources of international law underwent significant changes. This is true for General Principles of Law, customary international law, decisions of international organizations and unilateral acts of States (such as unilateral declarations).

2 The Institutional Aspect

2.1 *Multilateral Conferences*

Multilateral conferences constitute the main fora to develop or prepare the development of new international norms, mostly international treaties. They have undergone a significant development since one of the first of such conferences in Europe, namely the Vienna Conference of 1815.[1]

As already indicated, multilateral conferences may be differentiated as to whether they work on the basis of a draft agreement prepared by an expert body or which operate on the basis of political guidelines such as the Third UN Conference on the Law of the Sea (Codification Conferences v. Law Making Conferences). The differences in mandate have an influence on the working methods. The Rio Conference on Environment and Development, 1992 and the subsequent conferences thereto may serve as an example. In these conferences, not only States participated but also international organizations, intergovernmental institutions and non-governmental organizations[2] as observers. The widening in participation is one of the hallmarks of modern multilateral conferences with the mandate to develop regimes, which serve international community interests.

1 The Westphalian Peace Conferences, ending the Thirty Years' War in Germany, often referred to as multilateral conferences, were different in structure and format from subsequent multilateral conferences, in particular the peace conferences in The Hague 1899 and 1907.

2 See Rule 64 Draft Rules of Procedure of the Conference on Sustainable Development, decided at the 2012 Rio Conference on Sustainable Development and formalized by A/RES/67/290of 9 July 2013.

2.2 *Conferences/Meetings of Parties*

All multilateral agreements concerning the protection of human rights, the protection of the environment, on international trade as well as other issues serving the interests of the international community have established conferences/meetings of parties.[3] They constitute a form of institutionalized cooperation of parties different from international organizations and multilateral conferences. Since all State Parties to the international agreement concerned are automatically the members of such conferences/meetings, these are often explicitly referred to as the supreme body of the international agreement concerned. These conferences/meetings of parties are the necessary institutional feature if a regime is to be qualified as serving community interests. They guarantee the permanent influence of the international community on the development of the regimes in question. Their decisions may be considered as subsequent practice and as such contribute to the interpretation of the norm in question. The Meeting of States Parties referred to in Article 319 UNCLOS does not fit into the traditional pattern of responsibilities of other Meetings of States Parties.

2.3 *Treaty Bodies (Human Rights)*

Treaty bodies consist of experts selected by the States Parties for a defined period of time. They are obliged to act independently and impartially, and the treaties concerned provide that all geographical regions are adequately represented.

The mandate of all human rights treaty bodies can be generally described as monitoring the implementation of the international human rights agreement concerned. However, the functions of human rights treaty bodies have developed beyond what is being provided for in the human rights treaties concerned. By general comments or general recommendations they contribute to the interpretation of the relevant regime.

---

3 The terminology varies. The term "Conference of parties" is mostly reserved to the "mother-agreement" often a framework Convention such as the UN Framework Convention on Climate Change, 1992, (ILM vol.31 (1992) p. 849), whereas in respect of the Kyoto Protocol the equivalent plenary body is referred as meeting of parties. In spite of the fact that the membership in the mother-agreement and the Protocol to such an agreement may differ frequently the Conference of parties serves as the Meeting of Parties. In such a case States parties to the mother-agreement but not to the Protocol serve as observers.

2.4 *Other Actors (Individuals, NGOs, Multinational Enterprises)*

There are several other actors in international relations such as individuals or groups thereof, NGOs and multinational enterprises. An increasing literature argues that individuals have become subjects of international law.[4] I do not share this view although it cannot be denied that individuals are directly addressed by international law.

The situation is different in respect to groups of individuals. For example, the representations of the various groups of indigenous peoples exercise some influence in international relations, although the scope of their activities is limited to issues directly affecting the rights of indigenous peoples. An example to that extent is their participation in the Arctic Council.

NGOs,[5] although frequently considered as new subjects or actors, have been active in international relations for a long time. Several such organisations were founded in the 19th century pursuing idealistic or scientific objectives. The term "non-governmental organisations" has been defined by ECOSOC Resolution 1996/31 as "any such organization that is not established by a governmental entity or international agreement."

NGOs concentrate on human rights, international humanitarian law, disarmament and environmental law (national as well as international). Due to the amalgamation of environmental and developmental policies,[6] the focus of NGOs has broadened. NGOs perform functions on the international norm-making level as well as on the implementation of international law. NGOs play a significant and by now established role at multilateral conferences and summits. However, they also initiate new policies either by approaching UN organs or regional organizations or political organs at the national level. Their influence is particularly significant as far as implementation of international norms

4 Anne Peters, *Beyond Human Rights: The Legal Status of the Individual in International Law*, CUP, Cambridge, 2016, speaks of a "paradigm shift" in international law (at 1) in which "human beings are becoming the primary international legal person"; Walter, 'Subjects of International Law' in *Max Planck Encyclopedia of Public International Law*, (hereinafter MPEPIL) OUP, Oxford, 2007 <www.mpepil.com>.

5 The literature on NGOs is numerous; see for example Markus Wagner, 'Non-State Actors', in MPEPIL (note 4) <www.mpepil.com> (21 August 2020); Andrea Bianchi (ed.), *Non-State Actors and International Law*, Ashgate Farnham, 2009; Pierre-Marie Dupuy and Luisa Vierucci (eds.), *NGOs in International Law: Efficiency in Flexibility*, Elgar, Cheltenham, 2008; Anne Peters, Lucy Koechlin, Till Forster and Gretta Fenner Zinkernagel (eds.), *Non-State-Actors as Standard Setters*, CUP Cambridge, 2009.

6 Wagner, 'Non-State Actors', (above, note 5), 2013.

is concerned. Finally, some international courts and tribunals accept amicus curiae briefs from NGOs.[7]

It is frequently argued that NGOs reflect the views of the international society.[8] In such generality this statement is hard to sustain. NGOs focus on particular aspects without necessarily taking into account other equally valid concerns. Frequently it is unclear why a particular policy is being pursued and to what extent funders may have a direct or indirect influence on the policy pursued. However they were, the persistent promotors of the Convention on the Prohibition of the Use, Stockpiling, Production and Transfer of Anti-Personnel Mines and Their Distraction, 1997,[9] the Biodiversity Convention and the Rome Statute, just to name some examples.

As far as multinational enterprises (or Transnational Corporations) are concerned, it is of relevance to ask whether they may be directly obliged under international law. This is relevant in respect of environmental law as well as under international human rights regimes or in respect of minimal social and labour standards. In particular the core international labour standards come into play. International law has developed or is in the process of developing under the notion of "global governance"[10] mechanisms, which fence in activities of multinational enterprises with the consequence of direct responsibility in case of non-compliance. The mechanisms used to that extent are the establishment of standards and practices being of a non-legal nature. Nevertheless, they are enforceable and are enforced.

3 The Normative Influence of the Main Actors

3.1 *The Role of States in Respect of Forming the International Normative Order*

As far as the normative contribution of individual States is concerned, one has to distinguish between the different levels on which international norms

7 Hobe, 'Article 71', in Simma et al., *Charter of the United Nations*, MN 22 -25; Treves, *The Expansion of International Law*, RdC vol 398, 112–126.

8 Agata Kleczkowska, 'Armed Non-State Actors and Customary International Law', in: Summers and Gough (eds.), *Non-State Actors and International Obligations* (Leiden, Boston: Brill Nijhoff, 2018), at 60–85 seems to argue that the participation of NGOs would strengthen the legitimacy of the regime concerned. This is not the position taken here.

9 2056 UNTS, 211.

10 The term has been coined in political science: James N. Rosenau, 'Governance, Order, and Change in World Politics', in: *Governance without Government* (J. N. Rosenau and E.-O. Czempiel, eds.), 1992, 1.

are being initiated, developed and adopted. It is in practice rare that a single State imitates the deliberations of an international norm (treaty or soft law instrument). Mostly, this is the undertaking of a group, which may involve other actors besides States. However, there are exceptions to that. For example, the development of the regime on deep seabed mining was initiated by the permanent representative of Malta to the United Nations, Ambassador Arvid Pardo, by addressing the General Assembly. However, the general practice is that such initiatives are carried formally by a group of States such as in the case of marine biological resources beyond national jurisdiction (BBNJ).

3.2 *The Normative Contributions of International Organizations*

Only a few international organizations have direct legislative functions such as the Security Council of the United Nations or the International Seabed Authority or the Meeting of Parties of the Montreal Protocol. Others have a more indirect influence on the normativity of the international order.

3.3 *The Normative Contributions of Multilateral Conferences*

Multilateral conferences, even so-called law-making ones, have, strictly speaking, no law-making functions. International treaties developed in this context have to be ratified by States to enter into force. Therefore, such multilateral conferences just constitute an intermediary stage in the development of an international normative order. However, the legal impact such draft treaties may have should not be underestimated. The results reached at such conferences may be of relevance for State practice even before the draft treaty in question enters into force.

Most relevant is the development of general principles, agendas and work programs by multilateral conferences. The Rio Conference of 1992 and the subsequent conferences thereto are telling examples about how multilateral conferences may shape the international normative order.

3.4 *The Normative Influence of Conferences and Meetings of Parties*

The functions of conferences/meetings of parties differ significantly if the regime concerned is administered by an international organization. Two examples may illustrate this point. According to article 319(2)(e) UNCLOS the Secretary General shall "...convene necessary meetings of State Parties in accordance with this Convention." The functions of these meetings of States Parties are of an administrative nature. The mandate of "freestanding" conferences/meetings of Parties is substantially different. For example, the powers and functions of the UN Framework Convention on Climate Change[11] are as follows:

> The Conference of the Parties, as the supreme body of this Convention, shall keep under regular review the implementation of the Convention and any related legal instruments that the Conference of the Parties may adopt, and shall make, within its mandate, the decisions necessary to promote the effective implementation of the Convention.

The mandate for conferences/meetings of other multilateral environmental agreements is similar.

In spite of all differences mentioned so far, all conferences/meetings of Parties enjoy legislative competences in varying degrees. This mandate oscillates between interpretation and law making.

The second type of decisions of conferences/meetings of parties are the ones which are binding without the consent of the States concerned. They are issued by the conferences/meetings of parties based on an authorization by the "mother agreement". The Montreal Protocol may serve as an example. Its article 14(4)(b) and (c) provides that the Meeting of Parties decides on any adjustments or reductions referred to in paragraph 9 of article 2(c) and on any addition to, insertion in or removal from any annex of substances and on related control measures in accordance with article 2(10). These decisions broaden the scope of the applicability of the Montreal Protocol and the Meeting of Parties has made ample use of this mandate. They are adopted by a two thirds majority and are binding upon all States Parties. The basis for such law-making is a delegation of legislative competences by a decision of the States Parties.

The Paris Agreement developed a sophisticated system of delegating legislative competences to the Meeting of Parties. It provides two avenues for the Meeting of Parties to issue legally binding obligations, first by adopting them in mandatory language based on a treaty provision that provides for a legal obligation for each Party, for example under articles 4(2), 8, 9, 11 et seq. of the Paris Agreement. These nationally determined contributions are to be qualified as unilateral acts of States reflecting a binding commitment.

The second avenue is a treaty provision that authorizes to adopt binding decisions as provided for under article 4(8) and 4(13) of the Paris Agreement.[12]

---

11 Article 7(2) UNFCCC.

12 See Daniel Bodansky, 'The Paris Climate Change Agreement: A new hope?' AJIL 110 (2016), 288–319; Petra Minnerop, 'The Legal Effect of the "Paris Rulebook" under the Doctrine of Treaty Interpretation' in Cameron, Mu, and Roeben (eds), *Global Energy Transition,*

In both cases, the guidelines or the decisions of the Meeting of Parties are based upon a mandate of the Paris Agreement and accordingly covered by the consent of the States Parties. The Paris Rulebook to the Paris Agreement[13] elaborates on this point further.

The third type of rules developed by conferences/meetings of Parties are those which are not explicitly mandated in the mother-agreement. Even in this situation a conference/meeting of parties may function as a legislator, albeit the mandate is limited in substance. As has been stated by the ILC: "[I]t cannot simply be said that because the treaty does not accord the Conference of States Parties a competence to take legally binding decisions, their decisions are necessarily legally irrelevant and constitute only political commitments".[14]

3.5 *Normative Contribution of Treaty Bodies (Human Rights)?*

As already mentioned, the human rights treaty bodies have transformed the mechanism of General Comments/General Recommendations into a veritable tool of progressively developing the human rights treaties concerned. The policy and practice of the treaty bodies differ considerably though; the most active treaty body is the Committee of the International Covenant on Economic, Social and Cultural Rights (ICESCR).

The General Comment No. 8 of the Treaty Body (17th session) dealt in detail factually and legally with the relationship between economic sanctions and the respect for economic, social and cultural rights. In particular in Iraq, the treaty body came to the conclusion that economic sanctions were in violation with the Covenant. This statement influenced the sanctions system of the United Nations.

General Comment No. 15: The right to water[15] establishes a new economic right, namely the right to water, invoking articles 11 (right to food) and 12 (highest attainable standard of health) of the Covenant. Through this the scope of the ICESCR has been expanded. This right to water has become a mechanism

---

Hart Publishing, 2021, 6; Lavanya Rajamani, 'The 2015 Paris Agreement: Interplay between Hard, Soft and Non-Obligations', JEL 28 (2016), 337; in general on the normative influence of conferences and meetings of Parties see Rüdiger Wolfrum, *Solidarity and Community Interests: Driving Forces for the Interpretation and Development of International Law*, RdC vol. 416 (2021), 90 at 282 et seq.

13 Decision of the Conference of Parties acting as Meeting of Parties to the Paris Agreement, 1/CP.21 FCCC/CP/2015/10/Add.1.

14 ILC Report covering the work the seventieth session to the General Assembly, UN Doc. A/73/10, ILC Yearbook, 2018, vol. II, Part Two. Commentary to draft conclusion 11, para. 26.

15 Twenty-ninth session (2002), UN Doc. HRI/GEN/1/Rev.9 (Vol. I), 97.

on the implementation of international environmental law concerning surface and ground water.

The same mechanism is being used by the conferences/meetings of parties referred to above. There is, however, a significant difference between the two institutions.

3.6 *The Contribution of Internationally Accepted Standards as Mechanisms for the Development of the International Normative Order*

Internationally accepted standards are often developed in soft law instruments. This format is chosen to avoid the rigidity of international treaties. They are frequently referred to as guidelines, codes of conduct or recommendations. They may be developed by a group of enterprises, with or without governmental involvement or by international organizations. The involvement of experts, interest groups and representatives from civil society groups is standard.

As to their content some variety exists; they may be dealing with a specific subject only or be of a general nature. By way of generalisation, one may distinguish between those instruments which supplement international legally binding norms and those which stand for themselves instead of an international treaty. This distinction is fluid.

An example where the development of international standards has been transferred to expert bodies by an act of delegation of legislative powers are the standards concerning sanitary and phytosanitary measures by the Agreement on the Application of Sanitary and Phytosanitary Measures (SPS Agreement)[16] to certain other functional institutions. According to article 3(1) of the SPS Agreement, States Parties are called upon to "harmonize sanitary and phytosanitary measures on as wide a basis as possible" based on "international standards, guidelines or recommendations, where they exist". The SPS Agreement itself does not contain any international standards, nor does it provide for such standards by the WTO; it rather refers to standards developed by the *Codex Alimentarius* Commission, the standards developed by the International Office of Epizootics (for animal health) and the standards developed under the auspices of the Secretariat of the International Plant Protection (for plants).[17] These standards are not binding but they are made binding upon the assumption of the article 3(2) SPS Agreement that provides

16 Text in https://www.wto.org/english/tratop_e/sps_e/spsagr_e.htm.

17 Oliver Landwehr, Article 3 SPS, in: *WTO: Technical Barriers and SPS Measures*, Max Planck Commentaries on World Trade Law (R. Wolfrum, P.-T. Stoll and A. Seibert-Fohr, eds.), Martinus Nijhoff Publishers, Leiden, Boston, 2007, article 3, MN 1, 7.

national measures based upon these standards are considered compatible with WTO law. One of these standards is the *Codex Alimentarius* developed by a committee established by FAO and WHO which involves experts, representatives of interest groups and of the civil society.

International standards are also developed by the IMO. According to its Statute, it has the mandate "to encourage and facilitate the general adoption of the highest possible standards in matters concerning the maritime safety, efficiency of navigation in prevention and control of marine pollution from ships."[18] The IMO adopts a great number of codes of conduct, guidelines, standards and recommendations to prevent and control pollution from ships. These instruments are technically non-binding; nevertheless, they are accepted in practice and implemented by States. They are even enforced against vessels under a foreign State by coastal States and port States.[19]

The OECD has been engaged in standard setting intensively; they are commonly issued as recommendations. It is the particularity of these standards that they constitute norms in themselves and are not interwoven with hard law like the standards developed by IMO and ICAO. Standards issued by OECD are non-binding and form part of the extensive body of the soft law produced by the organisation. Within the OECD recommendations entail a strong political commitment by members which are expected to take measures for the implementation of the recommendation concerned. Often, these recommendations include reporting obligations concerning implementation. Such reporting obligations exercise a pressure to implement. This approach is comparable in object and purpose to the reporting system common concerning the implementation of international human rights as well as in respect of more recent multilateral environmental treaties such as the Paris Agreement. Apart from the internal effects of OECD recommendations, it is to be noted that some of them worked as a blueprint beyond the realm of OECD. In particular, OECD developed the first comprehensive code for corporate social responsibility,[20] which had a significant impact in international law in general. It is the particularity of these guidelines that they provide for a dispute settlement procedure. It should be noted that the Council of the OECD in 2019 issued Recommendations on Artificial Intelligence[21] which refers and establishes relevant Guidelines in the Sustainable Development Goal set out in the 2030

18 Article 1.

19 See article 218(1); 219(1); and 220(1) UNCLOS.

20 OECD Guidelines for Multinational Enterprises: http://mneguidelines.oecd.org/guidelines.

21 OECD Recommendations of the Council on Artificial Intelligence, OECD/LEGAL/0449.

Agenda for Sustainable Development. One recent example shall complete this point. The OECD issued a guideline concerning the origin of certain minerals.[22] This soft law instrument was included into an EU Regulation 2017/812, which will become effective on 1 January 2021.

Finally, the FAO Code of Conduct on Responsible Fisheries has been developed as an alternative for a treaty-based regime covering the same regulations. This Code of Conduct is freestanding as are the OECD guidelines, that is to say it is implemented without any recourse to any international legally binding norm. It is implemented via a system of reporting obligations. This Code is not unique.

4 Concluding Remarks

The foregoing has demonstrated that the contributions of various actors to the international normative order are multifaceted. In general – and this constitutes a simplification – one may identify several different levels of norm making: The initiation of new norms is undertaken by all actors and further developed by politically oriented fora; the new norms may be negotiated on the basis of the outcome from the politically oriented fora in multilateral conferences. However, the process does not end here. The international norms established are not static. They are progressively developed by means of interpretation by conferences/meetings of parties and treaty bodies. Finally, one should add a new and growing category of norms, namely international standards, mostly not developed by actors in international relations but by institutions governed or influenced by professional societies and representatives from the civil society. These standards are integrated into international norms through blanket rules – these are rules, which have to be filled and concretized before they can be implemented. This development briefly outlined here has significantly altered international normativity.

22 OECD Due Diligence Guidelines for Responsible Supply Chains of Minerals from Conflict-Affected and High-Risk Areas www.oecd.org/corporate/mne/mining.htm.

CHAPTER 5

Governance of Marine Biodiversity beyond National Jurisdiction: Searching for Sustainable Solutions in the Southeast Pacific

Ronán Long and Mariamalia Rodríguez Chaves

1 Introduction*

Strung in a receding line between Central America and Cape Horn, the four States of Colombia, Ecuador, Peru and Chile are all defined by their striking coastal geography, as well as their relationship with the ocean and its bountiful resources in the Southeast Pacific. They also constitute the four members of the Permanent Commission for the South Pacific, commonly known by its Spanish acronym CPPS, which stands for the 'Comisión Permanente del Pacífico Sur'.[1] The latter is a venerable intergovernmental organisation that traces its roots back to the genesis of modern international law of the sea and to the unilateral practice of Latin American States in extending their maritime jurisdiction and sovereignty over living and non-living natural resources in sea areas adjacent to their coasts pursuant to the Santiago Declaration of 1952.[2] Since its establishment, CPPS embodies a distinctive regional alliance for the coordination

* This study will be expanded and updated in our forthcoming book: M. Rodríguez Chaves and R. Long, Biodiversity of Areas Beyond National Jurisdiction: The Costa Rica Thermal Dome and Other International Case Studies (Leiden/Boston: Brill/Nijhoff, 2023). The chapter was researched and written by R. Long based on an early draft prepared by M. Rodríguez Chaves. The authors wish to thank Ambassador Méntor Villagómez for reading and commenting on the text in a personal capacity, as well as Ms. Judy Ellis for her professional editorial skills.

1 CPPS is a legal entity under international law in accordance with the provisions of the Convention of Paracas, Peru, 14 January 1966. On the role of CPPS and BBNJ, see *inter alia*: C. Durussel, Challenges in the Conservation of High Seas Biodiversity in the Southeast Pacific (Doctor of Philosophy Thesis, University of Wollongong, 2015); C. Durussel, E.Soto Oyarzún, S. Urrutia, "Strengthening the Legal and Institutional Frame-work of the Southeast Pacific: Focus on the BBNJ Package Elements", (2017) 32(4) *International Journal of Marine and Coastal Law*, 635–671; UNEP-WCMC, Governance of Areas beyond National Jurisdiction for Biodiversity Conservation and Sustainable Use: Institutional Arrangements and Cross-Sectoral Cooperation in the Western Indian Ocean and the Southeast Pacific, UN Environment World Conservation Monitoring Centre, Cambridge (UK), 2017.

2 Declaration on the Maritime Zone, 18 August 1952. 1006 UNTS 323.

 | DOI:10.1163/9789004518629_006

of the national maritime policies of its members, all of which are developing States, especially in relation to the sustainable use of offshore resources and the protection of the marine environment of the Southeast Pacific.

In view of its unique role, this Chapter explores a number of themes through the lens of CPPS, including: the shared regional vision of sustainable economic development of offshore resources for the benefit of impoverished coastal communities; the willingness of Governments to undertake high-stakes international diplomacy and to coordinate regional state practice in pursuing their national interests by means of the progressive development of the law of the sea; as well as the practical aspects and difficulties encountered in coordinating regional policies in maritime affairs over the past seven decades and more. In this discussion, particular emphasis is placed on regional efforts to protect biodiversity on the basis of the ecosystem approach. As addressed elsewhere in the specialist literature, the latter is an essential normative tool that can be applied in managing human activities that impinge upon the conservation status of marine living resources.[3] As such, its practical application as an environmental concept remains poorly understood, principally in relation to how it impacts upon the navigational entitlements and maritime security interests of third States in sea areas within and beyond national jurisdiction.[4]

With the foregoing in mind, the Chapter opens by describing the abundance of deep-ocean biodiversity in the Southeast Pacific and the anthropogenic pressures it faces today. We then outline the birth and progressive evolution of modern law of the sea from a Latin American perspective.[5] This is followed by a review of the legal mandate of CPPS and the practical aspects of its working relationships with other intergovernmental bodies including those concerned with the management of fisheries and seabed mining, two of the gravest environmental challenges faced by humanity worldwide. Thereafter we turn to the development of the BBNJ Agreement from the perspective of the CPPS member States. The Chapter concludes by outlining some lessons that may be

3 D. Langlet, R. Rayfuse (ed.), *The Ecosystem Approach in Ocean Planning and Governance: Perspectives from Europe and Beyond* (Leiden/Boston: Brill/Nijhoff, 2019).

4 C. Engler, 'Beyond rhetoric: navigating the conceptual tangle towards effective implementation of the ecosystem approach to oceans management', 23(3) (2015) *Environmental Reviews* 288–320.

5 See *inter alia*: F. García-Amador, 'The Latin American Contribution to the Development of the Law of the Sea'. *American Journal of International Law*, 68(1), 33–50. doi:10.2307/2198801; Verner, Joel G. 'Changes in the Law of the Sea: Latin American Contributions and Rationales', *Social and Economic Studies* 30, no. 2 (1981): 18–44. http://www.jstor.org/stable/27861936; A. Mawdsley, (1992). 'The Latin American Contribution to the Modern Law of the Sea'. *Netherlands International Law Review*, 39(1), 63–88.

derived from State practice and the regional approach to the conservation of biodiversity in areas within and beyond national jurisdiction and how these can be applied to shape the design of new high seas governance arrangements for the Costa Rica Dome (CRD) in the Central Tropical Pacific.

Before delving into the analysis, it ought to be recalled that Panama and Costa Rica are the two closest Central American States to the Southeast Pacific. Moreover, the four States of Panama, Ecuador, Colombia and Costa Rica have established the Eastern Tropical Pacific Marine Corridor (CMAR) initiative to connect a series of MPAs in their respective maritime zones with each other.[6] By virtue of geography, their shared history in law of the sea matters, along with their common interests in safeguarding the marine environment, Costa Rica and Panama are thus inalienably linked to their sister States to the south in the search for viable solutions to the conservation and sustainable use of high seas biodiversity. In order to further understand these issues and to explore the intricate geopolitical and legal relationships that have shaped the distinctive regional approach to ocean matters for well over half a century, we first provide a brief glimpse of the offshore geography, the extraordinary marine biodiversity of the Southeast Pacific, as well as some of the unsustainable activities that are impacting on its conservation.

2 Remarkable Biodiversity and Unsustainable Activities

The Pacific Ocean occupies an entire hemisphere. Moreover, the Eastern Pacific Ocean has been described as 'one of the last bastions of what ocean biodiversity would look like in a pristine world', constituting a 'living laboratory for scientific research' on life in the ocean.[7] From a law of the sea perspective, there is no universally accepted geographical definition of the Southeast Pacific. For the purpose of this Chapter, the region is therefore understood to extend from Central America to Cape Horn on the southern tip of Chile, taking in the maritime zones of Colombia, Ecuador, Peru and Chile, and includes the

6 Eastern Tropical Pacific Marine Corridor (CMAR). Available at: http://www.cmarpacifico.org. See also: Eastern Tropical Pacific Marine Corridor (CMAR). Action Plan of the Eastern Tropical Pacific Marine Corridor (CMAR). 2019–2024. Available at: http://www.cmarpacifico.org/sites/default/files/content/files/Plan%20de%20Accion%20CMAR%2030-7-2019.pdf; S. Ryan Enright, R. Meneses-Orellan, I. Keith, 'The Eastern Tropical Pacific Marine Corridor (CMAR): The Emergence of a Voluntary Regional Cooperation Mechanism for the Conservation and Sustainable Use of Marine Biodiversity Within a Fragmented Regional Ocean Governance Landscape', *Front. Mar. Sci.*, 02 June 2021.

7 See, A. Hearn, *The Guardian*, 2 November 2021.

high seas westwards of those countries.[8] Among its biogeographic features, it counts the oceanic archipelagos of the Galápagos Islands belonging to Ecuador with their world renowned ecosystems, as well as Juan Fernández and Easter Islands under Chile's sovereignty and jurisdiction. The maritime boundaries of coastal States in the Southeast Pacific are demarcated by parallels of latitude, some of which have been the subject of dispute resolution proceedings in international courts and tribunals, including most notably a longstanding dispute between Peru and Chile concerning their EEZ limits.[9] The seabed geomorphology consists of a relatively narrow band of continental shelf running the length of South America dropping steeply to the Atacama Trench, which forms a natural barrier along with the Humboldt Current dividing marine ecosystems in the deep ocean from their coastal equivalents. There are several fracture zones due to seabed spreading, as well as a chain of distinctive and complex underwater geological elevations, which extend laterally out into the Pacific and include seamounts, plateaux, caps, rises, banks, spurs and ridges. Rising from the depths of the ocean floor, the biodiversity and marine ecosystems associated with Gómez and Nazca ridges warrant special protection measures in their own right under the law of the sea.[10]

In designing appropriate biodiversity conservation schemes for the region, further regulatory complexity arises from the environmental processes at play in the Eastern Pacific Ocean, with El Niño and La Niña events in particular influencing the winds, thermoclines and the temperatures of the warm water Peruvian and cold-water Humboldt currents. The prevailing conditions have a major bearing on the ecological functioning and ambulatory nature of marine ecosystems. There are high levels of species endemism at specific seafloor features including hydrothermal vents sites.[11] In addition, the region

8 On the political geography of the Eastern Pacific, see V. Prescott, C. Schofield, *The Maritime Political Boundaries of the World* (Leiden/Boston: 2ed., Martinus Nijhoff, 2005) 397–459.

9 Maritime Dispute, *Peru* v *Chile*, Judgment, ICJ GL No 137, [2014] ICJ Rep 4, ICGJ 473 (ICJ 2014), 27th January 2014, International Court of Justice [ICJ].

10 Daniel Wagner, Liesbeth van der Meer, Matthias Gorny, Javier Sellanes, Carlos F. Gaymer, Eulogio H. Soto, Erin E. Easton, Alan M. Friedlander, Dhugal J. Lindsay, Tina N. Molodtsova, Ben Boteler, Carole Durussel, Kristina M. Gjerde, Duncan Currie, Matthew Gianni, Cassandra M. Brooks, Marianne J. Shiple, T. 'Aulani Wilhelm, Marco Quesada, Tamara Thomas, Piers K. Dunstan, Nichola A. Clark, Luis A. Villanueva, Richard L. Pyle, Malcolm R. Clark, Samuel E. Georgian, Lance E. Morgan, 'The Salas y Gómez and Nazca ridges: A review of the importance, opportunities and challenges for protecting a global diversity hotspot on the high seas', *Marine Policy*, Volume 126, 2021.

11 D. Wagner *et al.*, Also see: A.M. Friedlander, et al., 'Marine Biodiversity in Juan Fernández and Desventuradas Islands, Chile: global endemism hotspots', 11 (2016) PLoS One, e0145059.

is characterised by important migration routes and feeding grounds for cetaceans, pinnipeds, marine reptiles, tunas, sharks and rays, and seabirds.[12] Five of the seven sea turtle species are found in the Southeast Pacific with some estimates suggesting that many migratory species remain in the region between 45% and 75% of the year.[13] That said, major scientific knowledge gaps exist on the extent and distribution of marine species in the tropical, subtropical and temperate marine ecosystems, partly because the South Pacific is less studied and sampled by marine scientists than other ocean regions.[14] As a result, many species and marine ecological interactions remain unknown to science. Accordingly, one can anticipate that the regulatory priorities for conservation measures may well change in the fullness of time, especially as new scientific information comes to hand about the impacts of anthropogenic activities on the loss of marine species and habitats.[15]

A case in point relates to the impacts of fisheries on biodiversity. In this regard, the South Pacific is the third most productive region in the world for commercial sea fisheries and aquaculture according to the FAO.[16] Indeed, the importance of fisheries and the abundance of marine life was highlighted during the course of the aforementioned maritime boundary dispute settlement proceedings between Peru and Chile, with the International Court of Justice noting that 18 to 20 per cent of the world's fish catch comes from the Large Marine Ecosystem associated with the Humboldt Current.[17] In the northern part of the region, tuna and shrimp fisheries are particularly important for Colombia and Ecuador. There are significant anchovy fisheries in Peru's EEZ, as well as in northern and central marine areas under the jurisdiction of Chile, with artisanal demersal fisheries to the fore farther to the south. Due to the widespread and catastrophic impacts on biodiversity, fisheries in general need to be managed very carefully to ensure the conservation of marine living

12 D. C. Dunn, et al., 'The importance of migratory connectivity for global ocean policy', (2019) *Proceedings of the Royal Society B*, 286(1911), 20191472.

13 A.L. Harrison, 'Estudio sobre la importancia socioeconómica de las áreas fuera de la jurisdicción nacional (ABNJ) en la región del Pacífico Sudeste'. Proyecto STRONG High Seas, 2021, 37.

14 M. Bebianno et al., cited in United Nations, *The Second World Ocean Assessment*, Volume I, at 144. Available at: https://www.un.org/regularprocess/sites/www.un.org.regularprocess/files/2011859-e-woa-ii-vol-i.pdf.

15 A. Chatwin (2007) *Priorities for coastal and marine conservation in South America*. United States of America: The Nature Conservancy, 1, 38.

16 FAO. 2020. *The State of World Fisheries and Aquaculture 2020. Contributing to food security and nutrition for all*. Rome.

17 Maritime Dispute, Peru v Chile, above n. 9.

resources and to safeguard marine ecosystems. In particular, the activities of IUU vessels pose a calamitous threat to critically endangered species such as hammerhead sharks, who breed in the vicinity of Darwin Island.[18] These iconic species are protected under the Convention on International Trade on Endangered Species (CITES) and the Convention on Migratory Species (CMS) but continue to be targeted illegally for their valuable fins.[19] Rigorous enforcement of these instruments is thus required to safeguard their conservation status.[20]

The productive nature of the marine living resources is also borne out by the trade data on the export of fishery products comprising primarily shrimp, tuna, salmon and fishmeal from Ecuador, Chile and Peru.[21] Fishery productivity is linked to the strong biological interconnectivity between coastal State waters and ABNJ of the Southeast Pacific, especially for highly migratory species including skipjack (*Katsuwonus pelamis*), bigeye (*Thunnus obesus*), and yellowfin tuna (*Thunnus albacares*).[22] Subject to seasonal variation, intensive fishing activities tend to concentrate in areas associated with the upwelling systems of the Pacific and in the vicinity of the extensive range of seamounts, the most important of which are the Nazca ridge and the Sala y Gómez seamounts, seaward of the Exclusive Economic Zones of Ecuador, Peru and Chile.[23] Together, both ranges are estimated to makeup over half the number of seamounts of the Southeast Pacific.[24] The absence of appropriate regulation and rigorous oversight schemes poses a major risk to the fragile ecology of the latter features and their dependent ecosystems. This risk extends to the activities of the long-distance fleets of China, Japan, South Korea and Taiwan.[25] Farther to the north towards the Central Tropical Pacific, a similar conservation threat arises from the activities of large industrial vessels from Southeast Asia fishing in high seas areas to the east of the Galápagos Islands and outside of the jurisdiction of Costa Rica, Panama, Colombia, Ecuador and Peru.

---

18 See discussion infra on challenges and pressures: fisheries and seabed mining.

19 On the relevant law applicable to CITES and CMS protected species, see E. Techera, N, Klein, *International Law of Sharks* (Boston/Leiden: Brill/Nijhoff, 2017) 35, 45 and 99.

20 Ibid.

21 FAO above n. 16, 80.

22 See: M. Olivares-Arenas, et al., 'Estudio sobre la importancia socioeconómica de las áreas fuera de la jurisdicción nacional (ABNJ) en la región del Pacífico Sudeste'. Proyecto STRONG High Seas, 2021, 17.

23 Ibid. Proyecto STRONG High Seas, 2021, 17, 41.

24 Ibid.

25 Ibid. Also see: Chatwin, above n. 15, 3.

The risks posed by the various fishing fleets are compounded by the absence of data on the wider environmental impacts of fishing on biodiversity.[26] What is more, the risks and impacts are further exacerbated by the myriad sources of marine pollution in the region including by the terrestrial mining industries, aquaculture, coastal development, urbanisation, invasive species, debris accumulating at or near the South Pacific Ocean Gyre,[27] as well the catastrophic consequences of the climate emergency.[28] The evidence of the latter is nothing short of unsettling, primarily because the South Pacific is warming above the global average and the circulation systems are also experiencing changes, which will impact on the abundance and distribution of fish stocks across the region.[29] This also jeopardises the delicate balance of marine ecosystems and is already contributing to the existential crisis faced by many coastal communities in Latin America, where there are few alternatives to employment other than in the fisheries and aquaculture sectors. Furthermore, changes in the Humboldt Current System are influencing different countries in different ways, especially in relation to the upwelling off Chile and the decrease of a similar phenomenon off the coast of Peru.[30] Ominously, marine heatwaves are forecast to become 'more frequent and pronounced in the future'.[31] This will bring its own set of environmental and management challenges concerning the survivability and the future functioning of marine ecosystems in the Southeast Pacific.

On the positive side, it is heartening to note that major scientific efforts are underway in the region to understand the consequence of these phenomena and to study the health and resilience of the ocean. Apart from satellite remote sensing and ocean observation tools, the results of ship-based technical field

26 Ibid. Proyecto STRONG High Seas, 2021, at 24.

27 See *inter alia*: G. Luna-Jorquera, el al., 'Marine protected areas invaded by floating anthropogenic litter: an example from the South Pacific', *Aquat. Conserv. Mar. Freshw. Ecosyst.* 29 (S2) (2019) 245–259; M. Thiel, et al., 'Impacts of marine plastic pollution from continental coasts to subtropical gyres-fish, seabirds, and other vertebrates in the SE Pacific', *Front. Mar. Sci.* 5 (2018) 238.

28 CPPS (2012) Plan de Acción Estratégico para la CPPS del siglo XXI. Available at: http://cpps.dyndns.info/cpps-docs-web/publicaciones/PAE-CPPS-XXI.pdf, at 17. Also see Stanford University study, notes 22 and 23 Durussel.

29 IPCC, H.-O. Pörtner, et al., 2019 IPCC Special Report on the Ocean and Cryosphere in a Changing Climate.

30 United Nations, World Ocean Assessment II above n. 14, citing Bertrand, Arnaud, and others (2019). Climate change impacts, vulnerabilities and adaptations: Southwest Atlantic and Southeast Pacific marine fisheries. Impacts of Climate Change on Fisheries and Aquaculture, 325.

31 Ibid, 486.

work are helping to shine a rare chink of light on the extraordinary abundance of marine biodiversity and the dynamic nature of regional ecosystems. Notable examples include the research cruises undertaken in the Nazca-Desventuradas Marine Park by Ecuador in 2015 and by Chile in 2016.[32] These surveys revealed high levels of marine endemism in the biodiversity associated with the Sala y Gómez and Nazca Ridges.[33] The latter features constitute an ecologically or biologically significant marine area (EBSA) under the Convention on Biodiversity. Their scientific importance and vulnerability to anthropogenic impacts is further highlighted by the Global Ocean Biodiversity Initiative, the Global Census of Marine Life on Seamounts, as well as their designation by Mission Blue as a Hope Spot. Despite these impressive endorsements of scientific merit and ecological fragility, spatial specific protection measures are yet to be adopted for areas beyond national jurisdiction, a major shortcoming that is most critical in relation to the EBSA of the Salas y Gómez and Nazca ridges.[34] This regulatory failure may be contrasted with the considerable progress that has been made by coastal States to protect areas within national jurisdiction. Notably in this regard, Chile has undertaken extensive MPA designations including the establishment of no take zones in areas within national jurisdiction in the vicinity of Rapa Nui, Salas y Gómez, the Desventuradas Islands, as well as the Juan Fernández Archipelago.[35] In addition, all seamounts located within the Chilean waters are protected to some degree from bottom trawling.[36] Furthermore, Peru has also demonstrated strong leadership on marine conservation issues by prohibiting extractive activities below the 600 metre isobath in the areas designated as the Nazca Ridge National Reserve.[37]

Taken together, these measures amount to a modest start to marine ecosystems conservation but much remains to be done.[38] The scale of the latter challenge should not be underestimated as Latin American States face many

---

32 Ibid, 443.

33 D. Wagner *et al.*, The Salas y Gómez and Nazca ridges, above n. 10.

34 Ibid.

35 See discussion infra on challenges and pressures: fisheries and seabed mining, as well as on the CMAR initiative.

36 Ibid.

37 Peru created Nazca Ridge National Reserve, its first fully marine protected area. Available at: https://andina.pe/ingles/noticia-peru-creates-nazca-ridge-national-reserve-its-first-fully-marine-protected-area-847733.aspx. See also: Supreme Decree that establishes the Nasca Dorsal National Reserve N° 008-2021-MINAM. Available at: https://busquedas.elperuano.pe/normaslegales/decreto-supremo-que-establece-la-reserva-nacional-dorsal-de-decreto-supremo-n-008-2021-minam-1960402-2/.

38 United Nations, *The Second World Ocean Assessment*, above n. 14, 55 and 278.

other pronounced difficulties in the economic and social spheres, including the severe impacts of the COVID-19 pandemic, with a 2021 UN Report recording that Latin America and the Caribbean had close to one third of total deaths globally with less than 8 per cent of the world's population.[39] The human scale of this tragedy thus provides a stark backdrop to regional efforts to improve ocean governance and to safeguard marine biodiversity within and beyond national jurisdiction.[40] In charting a way forward on these issues, one has to take into consideration the vanguard and in many ways the catalytic contributions made by Latin American States to the development of modern law of the sea over the past seventy years and more, a matter to which we now turn.

3 Regional Approaches to Marine Biodiversity: Legal Genesis and Geopolitical Context

At many levels, the legal genesis and geopolitical context for conserving marine biodiversity in areas beyond national jurisdiction can be traced back to the interests and practices of States bordering the Southeast Pacific since the late 1940s.[41] From that time forward, they are very much associated with a positivist approach to international law, as evidenced by State practice and its influence on customary and treaty law, principally in relation to the rolling out of maritime limits, the articulation and implementation of new concepts such as the EEZ, the vexed question of how best to regulate high seas fisheries under international law, as well as the development of the legal regime that applies to the International Seabed Area.[42]

Right up to the 1940s, it may be recalled that apart from the narrow band of coastal waters constituting the territorial sea, the ocean in its entirety was high seas and therefore subject to freedom of fishing and other unrestricted uses

39 Economic Commission for Latin America and the Caribbean (ECLAC), Disasters and inequality in a protracted crisis: towards universal, comprehensive, resilient and sustainable social protection systems in Latin America and the Caribbean (LC/CDS.4/3), Santiago, 2021, 9.

40 See discussion infra on CPPS member states and the BBNJ Agreement.

41 See inter alia: F. García-Amador, 'The Latin American Contribution to the Development of the Law of the Sea', *American Journal of International Law*, 68(1), 33–50. doi:10.2307/2198801; J. Verner, 'Changes in the Law of the Sea: Latin American Contributions and Rationales'. *Social and Economic Studies* 30, no. 2 (1981): 18–44. http://www.jstor.org/stable/27861936 A. Mawdsley, (1992). 'The Latin American Contribution to the Modern Law of the Sea', *Netherlands International Law Review*, 39(1), 63–88.

42 Y. Tanaka, *International Law of the Sea* 3ed., (Cambridge: CUP, 2019).

conducted in conformity with international law as it then was. After World War Two, however, State practice in the Southeast Pacific was influenced greatly by the Truman Proclamation on the Continental Shelf of the United States, as well as the maritime claims of Mexico and Argentina.[43] Specifically, Argentina claimed an extensive area of sea lying above the continental shelf, the so-called epicontinental sea, as territorial sea in 1946. The following year, Peru and Chile laid claim to 200-mile zones, with El Salvador following suit in 1950. Similar claims were made by Costa Rica without disregard to the lawful rights of other States, based on reciprocity, in the Central East Pacific and the Caribbean Sea.

The most significant milestone on this journey and its emphasis on what States do in practice was the signature of the Declaration of Santiago on the Maritime Zone by Chile, Ecuador and Peru in 1952.[44] The extension of exclusive sovereignty and jurisdiction over marine resources out to 200 miles was for 'the purposes of the conservation, development and exploitation of these resources, to which the coastal countries are entitled'.[45] Although it was clearly the outcome of an intergovernmental political process, the Santiago Declaration had the elevated legal status of an international treaty and was negotiated and agreed at the Conference on the Exploitation and Conservation of the Marine Resources of the South Pacific and the Regulation of Maritime Hunting Operations in the Waters of the South Pacific, held in Santiago in August 1952.[46] The same conference also adopted the Joint Declaration concerning Fishing Problems in the South Pacific, as well as the constituent instrument of a new regional body, namely: the Agreement relating to the Organization of the Permanent Commission of the Conference on the Exploitation and Conservation of the Marine Resources of the South Pacific. Following on from this, six other instruments were adopted in Lima in December 1954 and in Quito in May 1967. Interestingly, the Government of Costa Rica subscribed to the Protocol of Adherence to the Santiago Declaration in 1955 but the President of the country subsequently vetoed a domestic bill to ratify the instrument in 1966.[47]

---

43 J. Vargas, *Mexico and the Law of the Sea: Contributions and Compromises*, (Leiden/Boston, Nijhoff, 2011).

44 See above n. 2.

45 Santiago Declaration. Para 3(1).

46 The four 1952 instruments (including the Santiago Declaration) were registered on 12 May 1976 (United Nations Treaty Series (UNTS), Vol. 1006, pp. 301, 315, 323 and 331, Registration Nos. I-14756 to I-14759). The United Nations Treaty Series specifies that the four 1952 treaties came into force on 18 August 1952 upon signature.

47 F. García-Amador, above n. 41, footnote 18.

All of these initiatives placed considerable emphasis on the biological unity and ecological resilience of the ocean. At that particular time, there were major geopolitical and marine resource considerations at play within the region, especially in relation to the exploitation by foreign vessels of the rich tuna, anchovy and cetacean resources in the Southeast and Central Pacific. At a geopolitical level, the three signatory States to the 1952 Santiago Declaration were also pursuing a vision of peace, solidarity and cooperation on matters of common interest in their respective maritime zones. An overriding political imperative was the need to address the deplorable poverty of the region, as well as the special needs of coastal communities. In tackling these issues through the rolling out of their extensive maritime claims, Chile, Peru and Ecuador sought first and foremost to bring the living resources of the Large Marine Ecosystems of the Peruvian and Humboldt Currents within national control. Furthermore, although they lacked the technical, scientific and industrial capability to exploit offshore resources at national and regional levels, they were steadfast in their joint commitment to counteract the hegemony and resource exploitation by foreign vessels from distant industrialised nations including those from the United States and Japan, as well as the activities of the Onassis whaling fleet in the coastal waters of Peru.[48]

Significantly, from the perspective of this discussion, it is germane to note that the signatory States to the Santiago Declaration were acutely aware and concerned about the fragile ecological balance of marine ecosystems, as evidenced by the various *démarche* tabled by their diplomatic representatives at the United Nations and other intergovernmental bodies. In 1956, for instance, a senior Chilean diplomat informed the Sixth (Legal) Committee of the United Nations General Assembly that the joint action of the parties to the Santiago Declaration in extending their maritime zones was triggered by the need to protect all 'the marine flora and fauna living in the Humboldt Current, as all the various species depended on one another for their existence and have constituted a biological unit which had to be preserved'.[49] This ecological nexus was also reflected in the Santiago Declaration itself, which explicitly acknowledged the 'geological and biological factors, which determine the existence, conservation and development of marine fauna and flora in the waters along the coasts' of the signatory States.[50] Crucially, parties to the Santiago Declaration agreed to coordinate further on the regulation of fishing and the

48 See Tanaka above n. 42, 149–151.

49 Cited by the International Court of Justice in Maritime Dispute, Peru v Chile, Judgment, ICJ GL No 137, [2014] ICJ Rep 4, ICGJ 473 (ICJ 2014), 27th January 2014, para. 106.

50 Santiago Declaration. Article 3(1).

exploitation of natural resources of common interest within their respective maritime zones.[51]

When viewed with the benefit of hindsight, it is evident that there were many compelling geographical, economic, environmental, social, cultural and indeed philosophical arguments underpinning the Santiago Declaration. Although these arguments have stood the test of time and remain tenable today, the legal basis for extending maritime limits out to a distance of 200 miles from the coast at the time was inherently weak in the absence of *lex lata* and can thus be characterised as *de lege ferenda*.[52] Importantly in that regard, the 1952 Santiago Declaration contributed to the subsequent development of the concept of EEZ under UNCLOS, along with its rapid acceptance as part of customary international law.[53] Furthermore, the conservation of living resources of ABNJ and the biological unity of the ocean continued to inform the positions of Latin American States at the three law of the sea codification conferences in 1958 (UNCLOS I), 1960 (UNCLOS II) and again at UNCLOS III between 1973 and 1982.[54]

One can make several further observations about state practice in the Southeast Pacific and its contribution to the development of the law of the sea including its influence on the practice of Latin American states right up to the present day in the broader context of the BBNJ Agreement.

The first point relates to an *avant-garde* commitment to a regional treaty and the advancement of community interests in high stakes international diplomacy and state practice. More pedantically, from the viewpoint of the New Haven School of jurisprudence and public policy, it is also evident that the Santiago Declaration advanced a regional coordinated approach to bringing about changes to the public order of the ocean around the values of equity, development, conservation, and human dignity.[55] At that particular time, Latin American States were effectively disenfranchised by the *status quo* in the international legal order as it applied to the ocean. Their extravagant claims to extended maritime jurisdiction were based upon the importance of the ocean as a source of food and the need of the coastal States to feed their dependent

51 Santiago Declaration. Article 3(VI).

52 See discussion. Vargas above n. 43, especially 140.

53 Continental Shelf (Libya v Malta), Judgment, ICJ 1985, p. 33, para 34.

54 UNEP-WCMC (2017) *Governance of areas beyond national jurisdiction for biodiversity conservation and sustainable use: Institutional arrangements and cross-sectoral cooperation in the Western Indian Ocean and the Southeast Pacific*. Cambridge (UK): UN Environment World Conservation Monitoring Centre, 7.

55 R. Derrig, *International Law and the Democratic Character: An Intellectual History of the New Haven School*, (Oxford: OUP, forthcoming 2023).

and growing populations. The underlying precept of community interests was thus tied to regional state practice. According to this analysis, the Santiago Declaration can be characterised as one of the first regional initiatives to shape the international law of the sea by developing States in the Global South more generally. The commitment to regionalism was perhaps best typified by the establishment of the CPPS, tasked with an express mandate to coordinate regional interests in maritime matters. The signatory States reached out to sister States farther to the north including Costa Rica and Panama to work with CPPS. Indeed, the Declaration of Santo Domingo sought to muster 28 countries in Latin America and the Caribbean to adopt a common approach to marine resource exploitation, pollution and marine scientific research.[56] Colombia acceded to the CPPS in 1979, thereby increasing and strengthening the scope of the regional alliance.[57]

The second aspect was the manner in which regionalism influenced multilateralism and the negotiation of the so-called Constitution of the Oceans at the UN in the 1970s and early 1980s. In this context, although the Montevideo Conference on the Law of the Sea 1970 was largely unsuccessful in mobilising regional interests, it paved the way for the successful Lima Conference in the same year, and the subsequent coordinated approach adopted by 16 Latin American States participating and shaping the outcomes of the Third Law of the Sea Conference (UNCLOS III). At that particular time, there was a flurry of regional diplomatic initiatives in Latin and Central America concerning the development of the law of the sea including: the Montevideo Declaration on the Law of the Sea in 1970; the Lima Declaration of Latin American States on the Law of the Sea of 1970; the Declaration of Santo Domingo of 1972; and the Resolution of the Inter-American Juridical Committee of 1973. The President of the final sessions of UNCLOS III, H.E. Tommy Koh, writing with H.E. Jayakumar, has since noted that 'the Latin American Group was the most united and effective in coming to homogenous positions on law of the issues' at UNCLOS III.[58] Of course, this was greatly facilitated by their joint regional interests in expanding coastal State jurisdiction over the high seas and the conservation of the resources and marine ecosystems therein.

The third striking characteristic of State practice is the manner in which economic and ecological values continued to inform the regional approach

56 Declaration of Santo Domingo, 892.

57 CPPS Statute. Article 1.

58 T. Koh, S. Jayakumar 'The Negotiation Process of the Third United Nations Conference on the Law of the Sea, in M. H. Nordquist, (Ed.) *United Nations Convention on the Law of the Sea 1982: A Commentary*, Vol. 1, (Leiden: Nijhoff, 1985), 83.

to the management of high seas fisheries resources and their associated biodiversity right up to the present day. These values are of course linked with the construct of patrimony and the special interests of Latin American States in modern law of the sea,[59] as well as the advancement of the aggregate of their claimed offshore entitlements to meet future needs. In a maritime legal context, the concept and term *Mar Presencial* was devised in 1970 to describe an ocean area that falls under the influence of coastal States in the Southeast Pacific. Subsequently, the concept was enshrined in the Santo Domingo Declaration of 1972 and informed the diplomatic positions adopted by Latin American States participating in the Seabed Committee negotiations at the United Nations in 1973.[60] To a large degree, the economic resources and related environmental interests of coastal States were subsumed and reflected in the Exclusive Economic Zone and the continental shelf provisions of UNCLOS.

In the early 1990s, however, the concept of *Mar Presencial* resurfaced yet again in national legislation and regional diplomatic positions adopted by Latin American States prior to the Fish Stocks Conference in 1995. Most notably, Chile sought its application to the management of straddling and highly migratory fish stocks on the high seas in the Southeast Pacific.[61] Marine ecosystem considerations were once more put forward to justify and prioritise the special economic interests of coastal States over high seas living resources in areas adjacent to their EEZs, the right to control marine scientific research, as well as the right to take unilateral measures to advance their national interests in the absence of effective international management mechanisms.[62] Remarkably, as can be seen in Figure 5.1, Chile claimed that *Mar Presencial* applied over the high seas of the Southeast Pacific from its EEZ limits out to a median at the edge of continental shelf of Easter Island, and from the Arica Parallel to the South Pole. The socio-biological unity of the ocean, the need

59 H. Caminos, et al., 'The Latin American Contribution to International Law', Proceedings of the Annual Meeting (American Society of International Law), vol. 80, *American Society of International Law*, 1986, pp. 157–72.

60 Vargas, above n. 43, 165.

61 See inter alia: J. Dalton, 'The Chilean Mar Presencial: a harmless concept or a dangerous precedent?' 8 IJMCL 397–418 (1993); E. Molenaar, 'New Maritime Zones and the law of the sea' in H. Ringbom (ed) *Jurisdiction over Ships -Post UNCLOS Developments in the Law of the Sea* (Leiden: Nijhoff, 2015) 249–277. On the geographical scope of *Mar Presencial*, see Article 2, No. 24 of Chile's General Law on Fisheries and Aquaculture, as amended, to take into account the maritime boundary between Peru and Chile pursuant to ICJ ruling of January 27, 2014.

62 Kibel, Paul Stanton. "Alone At Sea: Chile's Presencial Ocean Policy." *Journal of Environmental Law*, vol. 12, no. 1, Oxford University Press, 2000, pp. 43–63.

to manage environmental connectivity and offshore resources on the basis of the ecosystem approach, and the sharing of high seas resources on an equitable basis with developing countries, were all considerations that pervaded the writings of Vicuña and other Latin American scholars.[63] They sought to influence the outcomes of the 1995 Fish Stock Conference and to advance the concept as a precept to resolve many of the intractable issues concerning the international regulation of high seas fisheries. There was, however, considerable international resistance to the unilateral claims of Chile in light of its fundamental incompatibility with both the letter and spirit of UNCLOS. At all levels, *Mar Presencial* marked a radical departure from customary and treaty law as it applied to the ocean. Subsequently, its practical application never came to fruition and was rendered nugatory by the 1995 Straddling Fish Stocks Agreement, as well as the orderly functioning of the regional fisheries management bodies in the South and East Pacific.

That said, the legal arguments pertaining to the principle of interdependence and the unity that coexists between offshore living resources and the needs of coastal populations have not gone away entirely and resurfaces periodically in regional statements and practices on law of the sea matters.[64] For instance, at a meeting celebrating the Sixtieth Anniversary of the Santiago Declaration in 2012, in the "Commitment of Galápagos for the XXI Century" CPPS member States affirmed the need to take into account the ecosystem approach and the precautionary principle in the protection of sea areas under their national sovereignty and jurisdiction, as well as a guide to their actions beyond those areas, including the Pacific Basin.[65] As will be seen below, the ecosystem approach and the needs of coastal populations were raised vociferously by Latin American States and other negotiating blocks representing the Global South at the BBNJ intergovernmental conference 2018–2022.[66]

This brings the discussion to the penultimate point, which relates to State practice and the ongoing search for sustainability solutions to conserve biodiversity in the Southeast Pacific both within and beyond national jurisdiction. Today, only two CPPS member States are party to UNCLOS and its two

63 F. O. Vicuna (1995) "Trends and issues in the law of the sea as applied in Latin America", 26(2) *Ocean Development & International Law*, 93–103, DOI: 10.1080/00908329509546051.

64 Ibid, 149.

65 The VIII Meeting of Ministers of Foreign Affairs of the Permanent Commission for the South Pacific (CPPS), Commitment of Galápagos for the XXI century. Para 1. Available at: http://cpps.dyndns.info/asambleas/x_asamblea/Commitment%20of%20Gal.

66 K. Hassanali, "CARICOM and the blue economy – Multiple understandings and their implications for global engagement", *Marine Policy*, Volume 120, October 2020.

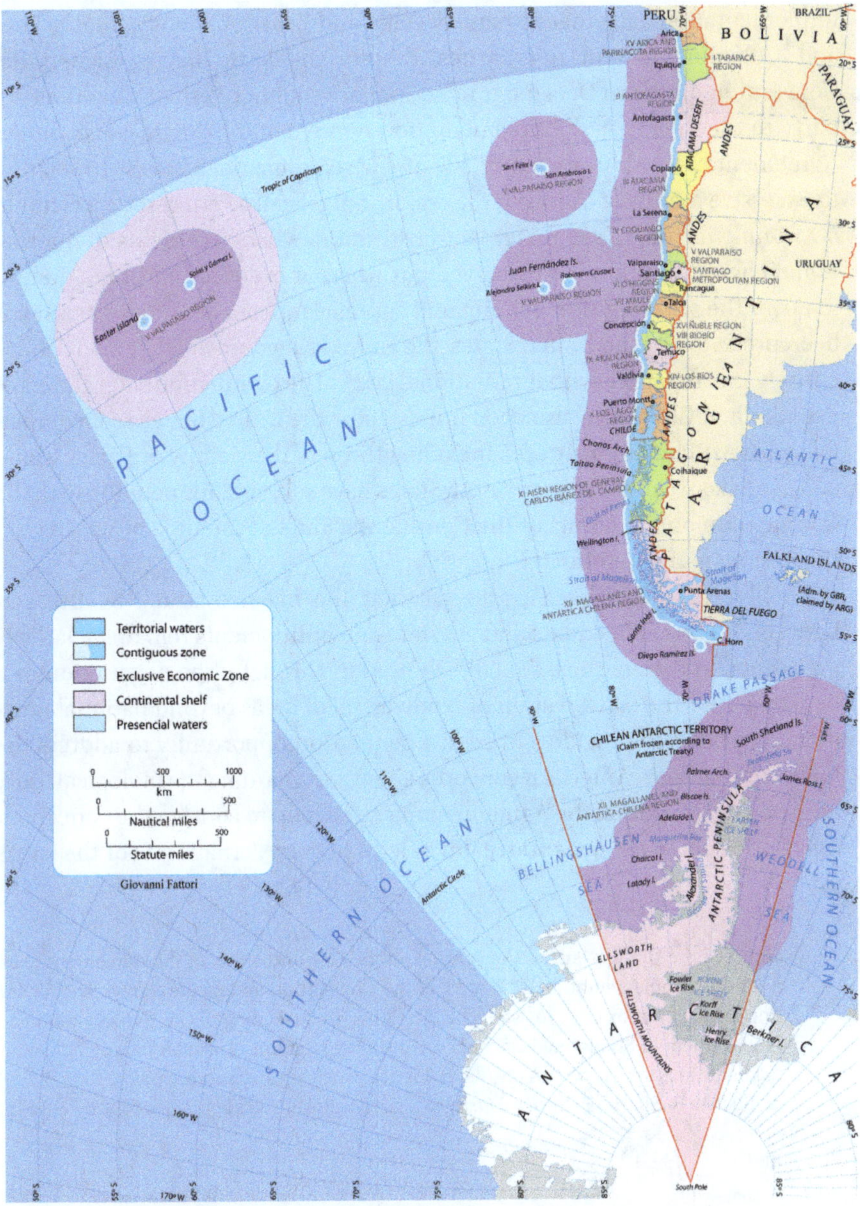

FIGURE 5.1 Chile mar patrimonial (*Mar Presencial*)
SOURCE: LIGA MARITIME DE CHILE, 2014

implementation agreements, namely Chile and Ecuador. Inauspiciously, Peru and Colombia remain non-parties, despite the latter having signed the Convention on the 10 December 1982. Similarly, neither Peru or Colombia are party to the 1994 Part XI Implementation Agreement or the 1995 Fish Stocks Agreement.[67] In addition, major law of the sea difficulties persist in relation to excessive maritime claims in the region. Specifically, Peru asserts a claim to a 200-mile territorial sea under its Constitution, where free rights of international communication are preserved but where it exercises maritime dominion over the seabed, water column and suprajacent airspace.[68] This claim has been protested by the United States, the United Kingdom and Germany and is entirely incompatible with international law.[69] The continental shelf claims of Ecuador and Chile have also been protested by the United States as incompatible with Article 76 of UNCLOS, including those in the vicinity of Easter Island and the Salas y Gómez ridges.[70] Both States have submissions pending with the Commission on the Limits of the Continental Shelf at the time of writing but these remain undetermined.[71]

Finally, it is relatively easy to see that the balance struck by UNCLOS between high seas freedoms and coastal State entitlements remains relatively precarious in the Southeast Pacific. Viewed in this light, the negotiation of a new treaty for the conservation of biodiversity of areas beyond national jurisdiction appears to provide a once in a generation opportunity to address the longstanding Latin American concerns about safeguarding the biological unity of the ocean. If it does, the Agreement may well help to consign the concept of *Mar Presencial* to the pedantic realm of legal history. Perhaps one of the levers

67 Status of the United Nations Convention on the Law of the Sea, of the Agreement relating to the Implementation of Part XI of the Convention and of the Agreement for the Implementation of the Provisions of the Convention relating to the Conservation and Management of Straddling Fish Stocks and Highly Migratory Fish Stocks at 27 June 2019. Available at: https://www.un.org/depts/los/reference_files/status2019.pdf.

68 A. Roach, B. Smith, *Excessive Maritime Claims*, (Boston/Leiden: Nijhoff, 3ed., 2012) at 146–148.

69 Ibid.

70 Ibid. 194–197.

71 See Partial Submission of Chile to the Commission on the limits of the continental shelf. Eastern Continental Shelf of Easter Island Province. Available at: https://www.un.org/depts/los/clcs_new/submissions_files/chl87_20/chle.pdf. See also: Joint partial submission of data and information on the outer limits of the continental shelf of the republic of Costa Rica and the republic of Ecuador in the Panama basin pursuant to part vi of and Annex II to the United Nations Convention on the law of the sea. Available at: https://www.un.org/depts/los/clcs_new/submissions_files/criecu_86_2020/PART-I%20(secured).pdf.

to doing so and to moving forward on some of the most pressing issues concerning the conservation of high seas biodiversity relates to the institutional mechanism for the coordination of maritime policies within and beyond the region, which we will explore next.

4 Venerable Maritime Regional Organization

The Permanent Commission for the South Pacific was established within the broader framework of the Santiago Declaration on the 18 August 1952 and tasked with coordinating the maritime polices of its three founding members including their efforts to halt illegal fishing and whaling in the region.[72] More recently, Chile, Ecuador and Peru affirmed its legal identity as an intergovernmental body under international law by ratifying the 1978 Convention on the international legal personality of the Permanent Commission of the South Pacific.[73] Vitally, the latter provided a legal basis for the appointment of a Secretary-General, who is the legal representative of the body and is responsible for discharging its day-to-day functions. As mentioned previously, membership grew when Colombia joined in 1979. In addition, there have been longstanding overtures to Panama to become a full member in view of its longstanding affiliation with the work of CPPS and as a party to the Southeast Pacific Action Plan.

In recent years, the role of CPPS has become considerably more arduous and now entails coordinating regional maritime policies pertaining to marine resource exploitation, conservation measures, environmental protection, and facilitating various aspects of marine scientific research.[74] For geopolitical reasons, its functions have always been limited to the softer dimensions of coordination and the provision of advisory services, thereby forming an important nexus between its four permanent members, who categorise it as a Maritime Regional Organization in its legal relations with themselves and other international and intergovernmental bodies.[75] By international standards, the institutional

72 UNEP-WCMC above n. 54, 71.

73 Convention on the International Legal Personality of the Permanent Commission of the South Pacific. UNTS 1098. Entered into force on 29 July 1978.

74 C. Durussel, at al., 'Strengthening the legal and institutional framework of the Southeast Pacific: focus on the BBNJ package elements', 32 (2017) *Int. J. Mar. Coast. Law*, 635–671.

75 CPPS (2012). Compromiso de Galápagos para el Siglo XXI. VIII reunión de ministros de relaciones exteriores de la Comisión Permanente del Pacifico Sur. Puerto Ayora, Galápagos, Ecuador. 17 de agosto de 2012, para. 6.

structure to discharge this mandate is relatively slim and consists of an Assembly, an Executive Committee, the national sections, as well an array of working groups. Decisions are taken on the basis of consensus and the work of the organisation is supported by a Secretariat with a headquarters in Guayaquil (Ecuador).[76] The annual budget of the organisation is very modest and in the order of USD 688.000.[77] Almost tiny to run an international organisation with serious intergovernmental responsibilities.

Since its foundation, CPPS and its member States have sought to advance the conservation and sustainable use of marine living resources, an objective that went to the very heart of multiple regional declarations including the Cali Declaration,[78] the Declaration of Viña del Mar,[79] the Declaration of Quito,[80] the Declaration of Lima,[81] the Declaration of Bogota,[82] and the Declaration of Santiago.[83] For much of its institutional life, the bulk of the work undertaken by CPPS has been focused on coordinating issues concerning areas within member state sovereignty and jurisdiction, including their islands in the Pacific. However, the discussion below pays special attention to various initiatives under its auspices pertaining to the conservation of biodiversity of areas beyond national jurisdiction. In large measure, this role stems from the broadening of its functions in 1981 when it became the Executive Secretariat of the Southeast Pacific Regional Seas Programme under the Convention on the Protection of the Marine and Coastal Areas of the Southeast Pacific (Lima Convention). Thereafter, it assumed specific responsibilities in relation to its associated Plan of Action for the Protection of the Marine Environment and Coastal Areas of the Southeast Pacific.[84] Although the Regional Seas Programme

76 Ibid. Article 6.

77 Comisión Permanente del Pacífico Sur. XV Asamblea Extraordinaria. SG/CPPS/AE/XV/05. 15 Diciembre del 2020. Asamblea, available at: http://cpps.dyndns.info/cpps-docs-web/circulares/2021/003.Circular%20003-2021_Acta%20Final%20XV%20Asamblea%20Extraordinaria%20CPPS.pdf.

78 Cali Declaration, 24 January 1981, on considering the Area and its mineral resources as common heritage of mankind.

79 Viña del Mar Declaration, 10 February 1984, on the conservation and optimal use of marine resources beyond 200 nautical miles.

80 Declaration of Quito, 10 December 1987, on considering CPPS as the relevant regional organisation to coordinate the common interest in preserving marine resources in ABNJ.

81 Declaration of Lima, 4 March 1993.

82 Declaration of Bogota, 4 August 1997.

83 Declaration of Santiago, 14 August 2000.

84 UNEP. *Southeast Pacific Regional Seas Programme.* Available at: http://www.unep.org/regionalseas/south-east-pacific. See also: Convention for the Protection of the Marine Environment and Coastal Areas of the Southeast Pacific (Lima Convention). 1102 UNTS 2. Entered into force on 19 May 1986. See: CPPS. *Action Plan for the protection of the marine*

applies to the EEZs of Chile, Peru, Ecuador, Colombia and Panama, the ambit of the Lima Convention is nonetheless considerably more expansive in that it aims to prevent, reduce and control pollution of the marine environment; enhance cooperation in emergency situations; promote joint programmes for monitoring pollution in the Southeast Pacific area, within and beyond national jurisdiction; and strives to advance scientific and technological cooperation between its members.[85] The geographical scope of the Lima Convention thus covers the maritime zones of contracting parties, as well as ABNJ up to a distance within which pollution of the high seas may affect that area.[86] Moreover, as a consequence of Panama's membership of the Southeast Pacific Action Plan, the geographical footprint of CPPS extends northwards as far as Central America.[87] Although Costa Rica is not party to the Lima Convention, it nonetheless has a longstanding history of working with CPPS member states on matters of common concern. In implementing the Action Plan, CPSS also works very closely with UNEP and over twenty other agencies, programmes and the Secretariats of international treaties.

Several environmental protection and pollution related protocols supplement the Lima Convention and provide the framework for the adoption of conservation measures.[88] One of the most important is the 1989 Protocol for the Conservation and Administration of the Marine and Coastal Protected Areas of the Southeast Pacific.[89] This instrument aims to protect and preserve ecosystems that are fragile, vulnerable or have unique natural value, as well as where the flora and fauna are threatened by depletion and extinction.[90] The protocol applies to the EEZs of contracting parties, as well as the entire continental shelf where it extends beyond the 200 nautical mile limits. Importantly, it provides a legal basis for the establishment of protected areas in the form

---

environment and coastal areas of the Southeast Pacific. Available at: http://cpps.dyndns.info/cpps-docs-web/planaccion/docs2014/publicaciones/documentos-tecnicos/TextosBasicos-4Edicion-CPPS.pdf, 147.

85 Lima Convention. Articles 4, 6, 7, 10.

86 Ibid. Article 1.

87 UNEP-WCMC, above n 54, 72.

88 They include inter alia: the 1983 Protocol for the protection of the Southeast Pacific against pollution from land-based sources; the 1989 Complementary Protocol to the Agreement on Regional Cooperation to Combat Pollution of the Southeast Pacific by Hydrocarbons and other Harmful Substances. Protocol for the protection of the Southeast Pacific against radioactive contamination.

89 Protocol for the Conservation and Management of Marine and Coastal Protected Areas of the Southeast Pacific, 21 September 1989, in force 24 January 1995.

90 Protocol for the conservation and management of protected marine and coastal areas of the Southeast Pacific. Recital 3.

of parks, reserves, flora and fauna sanctuaries. In relation to such areas, the focus is on providing a framework for sustainable development. To this end, it sets down requirements concerning the adoption of integrated management plans, environmental impact assessment, the prohibition of any activity liable to have adverse effects on the ecosystem or the fauna and flora of such areas, as well as the establishment of buffer zones around MPAs for management and enforcement purposes.[91]

With a view to fostering enhanced regional cooperation on maritime matters, CPPS member States have adopted a Strategic Action Plan for the organisation of its work around specific action lines, namely: strengthening competitiveness for sustainable development; implementing the ecosystem approach; strengthening of knowledge of the ocean and atmosphere interactions; and consolidating regional strengths and knowledge.[92] Furthermore, the work of CPPS and its member states on the protection of marine biodiversity and living resources in the Southeast Pacific is based upon the precautionary principle and ecosystem-based management of the offshore environment.[93] In light of its modest resources, the CPPS work programme is nothing short of ambitious and touches upon many aspects of ocean governance including: the progressive development of the law of the sea through participation in international and regional processes; coordinating joint approaches to regional regulations; scientific and environmental assessments of natural resources and fisheries; and coordinating action to prevent, reduce and control pollution of the marine environment.[94] Since 2013, prominent accomplishments include the adoption and implementation of regional action plans on marine and coastal protected areas, marine mammals, turtles, and mangroves, as well as projects on marine litter, micro-plastics and municipal litter. Indeed, CPPS member States were among the first regional groups worldwide to address marine debris and to undertake specific initiatives on the production, recycling and responsible consumption of plastic materials that pollute the marine environment.[95] An

---

91 Ibid. Article 1. See also: R. Warner, *Protecting the Oceans Beyond National Jurisdiction. Strengthening the International Law Framework* (Leiden, Boston: Martinus Nijhoff, (2009), 191.

92 Protocol for the conservation and management of protected marine and coastal areas of the Southeast Pacific. Article 5.

93 CPPS Statutes. Article 3(a).

94 Ibid. Article 3(c), (I), (J).

95 CPPS. 2007. Marine litter in the Southeast Pacific Region: a review of the problem. Permanent Commission for the South Pacific. Guayaquil, Ecuador. 29 p. See also: CPPS. 2014 Implementation of the CPPS/UNEP Project: "Development and implementation of Local Action Plans to promote the management of the marine debris in coastal

important dimension of the work programme extends to sharing environmental and climatic data with IATTC and SPRFMO for fisheries management and biodiversity conservation purposes.[96] The MOU between CPPS and IATTC expired in 2020 and the working relationship between the two bodies is sometimes reported as fractious.[97] Less problematically, CPPS fosters regional partnerships to monitor and forecast oceanographic and climatic variability.[98] At the multilateral level, it remains fully engaged with law of the sea processes at the UN and makes substantial scientific contributions to the UN World Ocean Assessment Reports, and participates as an observer at the BBNJ negotiations at the UN.

The 2012 Galápagos Commitment highlights the importance of economic valuation of ecosystem services as a tool for the planning and management of the marine environment. The same instrument promoted the role of CPPS in advancing regional cooperation among its members on conservation matters, as well as broader engagement and coordination with other intergovernmental bodies within and beyond the region including coastal and island States in the West Pacific.[99] This dimension of its work is continuously expanding and extends to the conclusion of an agreement with the Secretariat of the Pacific Environment Programme to cooperate in the protection of a more extensive area of the Pacific. The latter objective is particularly appropriate in view of the long-term regional opposition to nuclear tests in the Pacific, its support for processes and targets set under the Convention for Biological Diversity including those on sustainability of fishery resources, marine ecosystems, and marine protected areas, as well as the effective implementation of the Sustainable Development Goals under the 2030 Agenda. Furthermore, because of the disparate nature of ocean governance arrangements in the Southeast Pacific,[100] CPPS is obliged to interact with at least a dozen other intergovernmental and international organisations including those concerned with living and non-living resources of areas beyond national jurisdiction, intractable topics that merit further consideration here.

communities in the Southeast Pacific". 2014. Available at: http://cpps-int.org/index.php/actividades-pda-m/2014/67-pda-basura-2014.

96 UNEP-WCMC, above n 54, 80.

97 Cremers, K., Wright, G., and Rochette, J. (2020). Options for Strengthening Monitoring, Control and Surveillance of Human Activities in the Southeast Pacific Region. STRONG High Seas Project. Potsdam: Institute for Advanced Sustainability Studies (IASS).

98 WOA II, Vol. I, above n. 14, 54.

99 UNEP-WCMC, above n 54, 80.

100 R. Mahon, L. Fanning, 'Regional ocean governance: Polycentric arrangements and their role in global ocean governance', 107 (2019) *Marine Policy* Table 2.

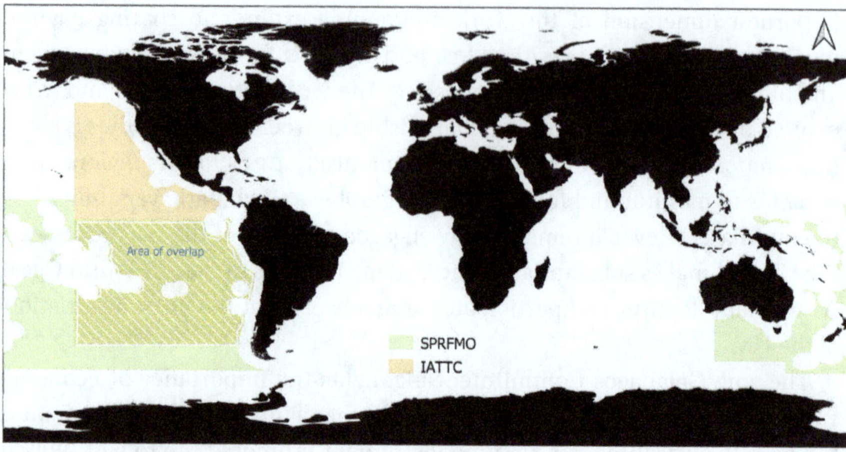

FIGURE 5.2 Regional fisheries organizations: geographical area of overlap SPRFMO and IATTC
SOURCE: WMU-GOI

5 Challenges and Pressures: Fishing and Seabed Mining

The discussion in this Chapter shows that many pivotal legal questions concerning high seas biodiversity are linked inextricably with the progressive development of international law. The search for successful environmental solutions is therefore more often than not contingent upon the adoption of appropriate regulatory measures, as well as the application of cutting-edge normative principles and approaches by competent international and intergovernmental bodies. With this in mind, our treatment of the subject below concentrates on high seas fisheries and seabed mining of the International Seabed Area (the Area), two of the most formidable regulatory challenges that must be overcome to ensure the conservation and sustainable use of biodiversity in the Southeast Pacific.

5.1 *Fisheries in the Southeast Pacific*

The management of high seas fisheries raises many contentious elements concerning the mandates and work of the two regional fisheries management organisations, namely: the Inter-American Tropical Tuna Commission (IATTC) and the South Pacific Regional Fisheries Management Organisation (SPRFMO). The geographical scope of these bodies overlap, as can been seen from Figure 5.2. Furthermore, they have very different approaches to the conservation of biodiversity and the application of the ecosystem approach to lessen the impacts of fisheries on marine ecosystems.

We shall start with the SPRFMO, first established in 2013 pursuant to the Convention on the Conservation and Management of High Seas Fishery Resources in the South Pacific Ocean.[101] The SPRFMO is responsible for managing non-highly migratory fisheries and the protection of biodiversity in the marine environment in high seas areas of the South Pacific Ocean.[102] Suffice to note here that the SPRFMO is well placed to adopt appropriate conservation measures and to mitigate the impacts of fisheries on marine ecosystems. This is particularly true in view of its broad membership of 15 contracting parties including China and three CPPS member states (Chile, Peru and Ecuador), as well as four cooperating parties that include Colombia.[103] According to the Preamble of the SPRFMO Convention, the organisation aims to 'avoid adverse impacts on the marine environment, preserve biodiversity, maintain the integrity of marine ecosystems and minimise the risk of long-term or irreversible effects of fishing'.[104] In practice, progress by SPRFMO in discharging its treaty mandate to protect biodiversity has been very much like the proverbial Curate's egg, that is to say, good and bad in places. For instance, it has prohibited the use of large-scale pelagic nets and deep-water gill nets, adopted management measures to reduce the impact of fishing on seabirds and gone some of the way to addressing VMEs through restrictions on bottom fishing, as well as setting down a legal requirement to undertake a research assessment of potential environmental impacts prior to opening new bottom-fishing areas.[105] Laudably, SRFMO and its member States have heeded scientific advice on conservation measures and this contributed in large measure to the recovery of the stock of Jack Mackerel, which was facing collapse due to over-exploitation and poor management decisions. In contrast to many other RFMOs, the success of SRFMO has been facilitated by a decision-making procedure that allows for majority voting procedures if the members fail to reach agreement on management measures based on consensus.[106] Crucially as well,

101 Convention on the Conservation and Management of High Seas Fishery Resources in the South Pacific Ocean (SPRFMO Convention). Entered into force on 24 August 2012.

102 Ibid. Article 5.

103 Australia, Chile, China, Cook Islands, Cuba, Ecuador, European Union, Denmark [in respect of the Faroe Islands], Republic of Korea, New Zealand, Peru, Russia, Chinese Taipei, USA, and Vanuatu. The cooperating parties are Colombia, Curaçao, Liberia, and Panama.

104 SPRFMO Convention. Preamble.

105 See, P. Ridings, et al., Report of the South Pacific Regional Fisheries Management Organisation Performance Review Panel (1 December 2018), 35–37.

106 See: Schiffman, H.S. "The South Pacific Regional Fisheries Management Organization (SPRFMO): An improved model of decision- making for fisheries conservation?" *J. Environ. Stud. Sci.* 2013, 3, 209–216.

in view of the oceanic scale of its Convention area, SRFMO applies a sophisticated array of MSC tools to monitor and enforce its conservation measures.

All of the foregoing represent progress but at the same time much remains to be done to ensure the long-term sustainability of fisheries and the safeguarding of biodiversity in high sea areas adjacent to the maritime zones under the sovereignty and jurisdiction of CPPS member States. Indeed, according to the performance review published in 2018, the SRFMO needs to enhance its capacity to undertake ecosystem-based management by taking into consideration deep-water chondrichthyans, seabird mitigation measures for all fisheries, habitat mapping, and examination of climate change impacts.[107] Furthermore, the review concluded that area-based management tools ought to be applied to link conservation measures with the identification of EBSAs and VMEs.[108] By any account, there is an urgent need to adopt spatial management measures for the high seas pocket between the UNESCO designated Galápagos Marine Reserve and the EEZ of Ecuador. According to Global Fishing Watch, this area is subject to intensive fishing activity by a large fleet of 200 vessels flying the flag of China and targeting protected species of shark as well as the squid fisheries.[109] We will return to the latter topic below in our discussion of the Eastern Tropical Pacific Marine Corridor.

The second RFMO mentioned above is the IATTC, the oldest of the tuna fisheries intergovernmental bodies. Despite its longevity, this organisation is still beset by many practical problems in discharging its mandate in the management and conservation of the tuna fishery resources and related species under the Antigua Convention. The geographic scope of the latter covers an extensive area of the Southeast Pacific. Chile, however, remains a cooperating non-party, a significant membership shortcoming. The catch of the IATTC-regulated fleet of tuna vessels is taken primarily from ABNJ including in the yellowfin, albacore, skipjack, bigeye, and Pacific bluefin tuna fisheries. The IATTC applies a comprehensive array of fisheries management measures including spatial closures, catch limits, and technical conservation measures to limit bycatch, which are underpinned by compliance and enforcement rules. Despite the sophisticated nature of many of these measures and its expertise in using risk assessment models to inform fishery decision-making and stock assessment, the performance of IATTC in the protection of biodiversity and trophic interactions in ABNJ falls well short of international standards. As a

107 See, P. Ridings above n. 105, 35–37.

108 Ibid.

109 BBC 'Ecuador on alert over huge Chinese fishing fleet off Galápagos Islands' 29 July 2020. Available at: https://www.bbc.com/news/world-latin-america-53562439.

result, tuna fisheries conducted under the auspices of IATTC continue to have significant impacts on marine ecosystems and high seas biodiversity, including billfishes, marine mammals, sea turtles, sharks and rays, as well as other fauna, as is evident from an assessment published in 2018.[110] One can conclude from the latter report that the commitment of IATTC to implement the ecosystem approach in line with its obligations under the Antigua Convention and the 1995 FAO Code of Conduct for Responsible Fisheries leaves much to be desired. This is disappointing in view of its considerable science capacity to conduct stock assessments and to undertake technical field work on the impacts of fisheries on marine ecosystems.[111] Remarkably, although the IATTC has a strong legal mandate and considerable success in reducing dolphin mortality in the EPO under the Agreement on the International Dolphin Conservation Program (AIDCP), it has been slow to develop or implement appropriate scientific tools for ecosystem management such as the adoption of biological and ecological indicators of species and ecosystem integrity impacted by its fisheries.[112] At the time of writing, IATTC has major difficulties in adopting appropriate management measures governing fish aggregating devices (FADs) in the EPO, and this is also impacting biodiversity adversely.

As seen elsewhere in this volume, the activities of IUU vessels impacts considerably on living resources worldwide including on biodiversity. This is also true in relation to the Southeast Pacific. Indeed, one of the major regulatory challenge for the region is to how to improve the enforcement and compliance of fisheries laws both within and beyond national jurisdiction including by the parties and the cooperating non-parties to the regional agreements. In this regard, the two aforementioned regional fisheries organisations have significant roles to play and are working in concert with CPPS member states on matters of common concern including VMS, observer schemes and port state measures. Crucially, apart from Colombia, all CPPS member are party to the 2009 Port State Measures Agreement. However, it is reported that some CPPS members have traditionally been reticent about sharing fisheries information including on the activities of IUU vessels in their respective maritime zones.[113] With an eye to mitigating this shortcoming and to reinforcing regional cooperation in fisheries law enforcement, Peru, Chile, Ecuador, Panama and Costa Rica concluded an agreement with Global Fishing Watch to share information

110 See: L. Duffy, S Griffiths, Ecosystem Considerations, ICCAT Doc. SAC-09-11.

111 See: IATTC Performance Review 2016, available at: tuna-org.org/Documents/IATTC-AIDCP-Performance-Review-Final-ReportENG.pdf.

112 See L. Duffy above n. 110.

113 UNEP-WCMC, above n 54, 81.

on IUU vessels in the region[114] Moreover, CPPS has been active in forging regional approaches to IUU fishing by hosting workshops on strengthening regional coordination to combat IUU fishing in waters under national jurisdiction of the CPPS member States, hosting meetings of judicial authorities and the maritime authorities of its member states, as well as conducting training sessions on regional monitoring control and surveillance schemes to implement port state measures. However, many challenges remain, including in relation to extending the observer programme coverage adopting more effective compliance mechanisms, as well as greater engagement by NGOs in compliance procedures.[115]

5.2 *Seabed Mining in the Southeast Pacific*

Several studies indicate that many species and benthic communities will be lost forever should seabed mining activities commence at commercial industrial levels.[116] Fortunately, at the time of writing there are no exploration contracts in place for the Area of the Southeast Pacific. As alluded to previously however, this may change as there are significant mineral resources associated with the seamounts and the hydrothermal vents systems including polymetallic nodules and cobalt rich crusts in the region. Thus, it is entirely understandable that important decisions have already been taken at national levels on the basis of the precautionary principle to safeguard marine ecosystems within and beyond national jurisdiction. Specifically, Chile has prohibited seabed mining in seabed areas within national jurisdiction in the vicinity of Easter Island.[117] There is also a moratorium on seabed mining in designated protected areas within national jurisdiction in the vicinity of the Nazca Ridge. That said, a broader prohibition on seabed mining is not mentioned specifically in the 2012 Galápagos Commitment, which calls for coordinated action

114 Global Fishing Watch. Transparency Programme in Latin America. Available at: https://globalfishingwatch.org/transparency-program-latin-america/. CPPS Secretariat has co-ordinated Declarations to combat IUU fishing. See: CPPS. Circular CPPS/SG/157/2020. Available at: http://cpps.dyndns.info/cpps-docs-web/circulares/2020/157.Circular%20157-2020_Propuesta%20de%20Declaracion%20sobre%20Pesca%20INDNR.pdf. Also: Ministry of Foreign Affairs of Peru. Available at: https://www.gob.pe/institucion/rree/noticias/312274-declaracion-conjunta.

115 K. Cremers, above n. 97, 32–36.

116 See, for example, D. Miljutin, et al., "Deep-Sea Nematode Assemblage Has Not Recovered 26 Years after Experimental Mining of Polymetallic Nodules (Clarion-Clipperton Fracture Zone, Tropical Eastern Pacific)". *Deep Sea Res., Part I* 2011, *58* (8), 885– 897, DOI: 10.1016/j.dsr.2011.06.003.

117 Wagner, et al., above n. 10, 5.

by member states in relation to the living and non-living resources of ABNJ, as well as recording a commitment to search for 'alliances to tackle common challenges with coastal States of the West Pacific'.[118]

In considering the potential but real risks should mineral extraction activities commence in the Southeast Pacific at some future point in time, one has to keep in mind that there are significant geopolitical issues at play in the regional approach to this contentious topic under the law of the sea. First and foremost, three CPPS member states, Chile, Peru, and Ecuador, have significant terrestrial mining interests and considerable technical expertise in extracting minerals from land-based sources. For well-honed and perhaps logical domestic political reasons, they are keen to insulate their national industries from further international competition arising from the development of mining activities of the Area. That said, all CPPS member states are long-standing proponents of the principle of the common heritage of mankind in relation to mineral resources of the Area. The CPPS enjoys observer status at the ISA and keeps a watching brief on regulatory developments and other matters of concern to its members.[119] The development of the mining code by the ISA is also followed closely by Latin American States more broadly, several of whom play an active part in the work of the various subsidiary bodies of the Authority. Surprisingly in many respects in view the concentrations of seabed minerals and high levels of biodiversity, there are currently no areas closed to seabed mining or designated as an Area of Particular Environment Interest in the Southeast Pacific under the regulatory regime applicable to the Area. In the absence of exploration contracts and commercial interest in the region, the ISA has yet to develop a regional marine environment plan for the Southeast Pacific.[120]

The absence of commercial interest in the Southeast Pacific may well change in the fullness of time. Indeed, one anticipates that many of the conservation issues will come to a head as soon as the BBNJ Agreement is adopted and comes into force. One also has to bear in mind that the approach of Latin American States to the ongoing work on the development of the regulatory framework for seabed mining by the ISA is shaped by their membership of the Group of

118 CPPS (2012). Compromiso de Galápagos para el Siglo XXI. VIII reunión de ministros de relaciones exteriores de la Comisión Permanente del Pacific Sur. Puerto Ayora, Galápagos, Ecuador. 17 de agosto de 2012, para. 20.

119 F. Armas Pfirter (2013) *State of the legislation relating to seabed mining: Its application to the Southeast Pacific, including proposals to promote the adoption of regional measures on oceanic mining*. Ecuador: CPPS, 53.

120 K.A. Miller, K.F. Thompson, P. Johnston, D. Santillo, "An overview of seabed mining including the current state of development, environmental impacts, and knowledge gaps", *Front. Mar. Sci.*, 4 (2018), p. 418.

Latin America and Caribbean Countries (GRULAC). The latter is one of the five Regional Groups at the UN and that counts 33 member States, or 17 per cent of total UN membership, which is a sizeable block in any decision-making or law-making context at the ISA. Notably in this regard, Costa Rica, Panama and Chile, as well as seven other member States of GRULAC, have actively sought the completion of the regulatory code by the ISA on matters such as the environmental code, the Regional Environmental Management Plans, the rules on inspection and enforcement, the benefit sharing mechanism, as well as the various environmental standards and guidelines, before any plan of work for mining of the Area is considered by the Council.[121]

6 Seeking Greater Regulatory Coherence: The Eastern Tropical Pacific Marine Corridor

At many practical levels, one of the most difficult regulatory challenges encountered in the Eastern Pacific Ocean stems from the ambulatory nature of marine ecosystems and the migratory range of marine species within and across the Eastern Tropical Pacific and the Southeast Pacific. One can therefore ask: is it possible to mitigate the transboundary impacts of human activities on marine ecosystems and species that straddle and migrate between areas within and beyond national jurisdiction through the application of spatial management tools under the law of the sea?

An example in point relates to the tropical and sub-tropical ecosystems that extend southwards from the Gulf of California to the north of Peru, covering sea areas under the jurisdiction and sovereignty of close to a dozen coastal States, as well as a considerable portion of the high seas.[122] Although Costa Rica has been a longstanding promoter of regional approaches to marine environmental stewardship, it faces many intergovernmental difficulties as evidenced by the marked reluctance of States to ratify the 2002 Antigua Convention for the North East Pacific.[123] Although the latter was signed by Mexico, El Salvador,

---

121 Letter to the ISA Secretary-General, from Argentina, Bahamas, Chile, Costa Rica, Cuba, Dominican Republic, Guyana, Jamaica, Panama and Trinidad and Tobago, 7.10.2021 (copy shared with the authors).

122 M. Spalding, et al. (2007). "Marine ecoregions of the world: a bioregionalization of coastal and shelf areas". *BioScience* 57, 573–583.

123 Convention for Cooperation in the Protection and Sustainable Development of the Marine and Coastal Areas of the Northeast Pacific. Signed in Antigua, Guatemala, on 18 February 2002.

Honduras, Nicaragua, Guatemala, Panama, Costa Rica and Colombia, it has attracted only two ratifications to date, Guatemala and Panama, which is two countries short of the number to bring the instrument into force.

Notwithstanding this absence of committment, there appears to be greater political appetite in recent years to develop a more coherent regional approach to transboundary marine environmental issues that link the Central Tropical Pacific with the Southeast Pacific. Notably, a rejuvenated chapter in intergovernmental relations appears to have commenced in 2021 with the signature of the Declaration for the Conservation of the Marine Corridor of the Eastern Tropical Pacific (referred to CMAR) by the Presidents of Ecuador, Colombia, Panama and Costa Rica on the margins of the Climate Change COP 26 in Glasgow. This political initiative formalises regional arrangements that connect several MPAs within the national jurisdiction of the four signatory States with each other by means of marine corridors (migravías). The corridor is shown by the shaded in Figure 5.3 below.[124] Disappointingly, the precise geographical limits of the corridor remains undefined but to all intents and purposes appears to exclude areas beyond national jurisdiction, including the high seas pocket between Galápagos and Gorgona, where there is intense fishing activity, as highlighted previously. Even though this is a serious geographical flaw that will undermine its long-term effectiveness, the Declaration signals an important development in regional marine environmental policy, particularly as its implementation will entail a moratorium on fishing activity in the corridor to protect the migratory routes of species such as sea turtles, blue whales, hammerhead sharks and rays, as well as coral reefs and mangroves in coastal waters.[125]

Today this regional initiative is more urgent than ever due to the relentless loss of biodiversity and destruction of marine habitats in the Eastern Pacific. Perhaps less well known is that CMAR is not entirely new in so far as its stems from the 2004 San Jose Declaration, a non-binding political agreement by the same countries to establish a corridor connecting MPAs in the five groups of islands and offshore archipelagos consisting of the following: Malpelo and Gorgona belonging to Colombia; the Coiba MPA in the EEZ of Panama; the Galápagos Marine Reserve under the sovereignty and jurisdiction of Ecuador;

124 See: http://www.cmarpacifico.org.

125 Michelle Soto. 'Costa Rica, Panama, Colombia and Ecuador are heading to create a Marine Biosphere Reserve between islands of the Eastern Tropical Pacific'. Ojo al clima. Available at: https://ojoalclima.com/costa-rica-panama-colombia-y-ecuador-se-encaminan-a-crear-una-reserva-de-la-biosfera-marina-entre-islas-del-pacifico-oriental-tropical/.

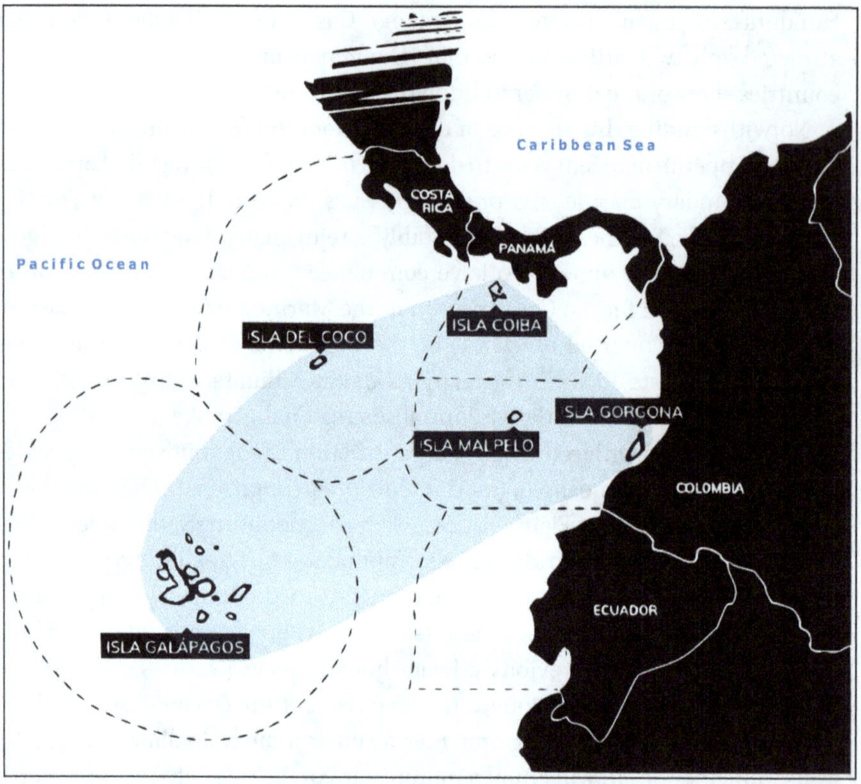

FIGURE 5.3 Eastern Tropical Pacific Marine Corridor
SOURCE: WMU-GOI

and the Cocos National Marine Park established and managed by Costa Rica.[126] Apart from Gorgona, all of the MPAs are recognised as UNESCO World Heritage Sites, thus underscoring their global status and the need for specific conservation measures and management plans. In addition, Coco and Galápagos enjoy further protection under the Ramsar Convention, with the latter and Malpelo designated as Particularly Sensitive Sea Areas by the IMO. As discussed above, many of the protected areas such as the Galápagos Marine Reserve enjoy high levels of marine endemism and several species are protected under CITES

126 CMAR, (2004). Corredor marino de conservación y desarrollo sostenible del pacifico este tropical entre las islas Coco – Galápagos – Malpelo – Coiba – Gorgona. Antecedentes y consideraciones técnicas para su definición. Documento Técnico, San José, Costa Rica. Marzo.

and CMS.[127] Due to its environmental significance and the need for further conservation measures, the CMAR is part of an Ecologically and Biologically Significant Area under the Convention on Biological Diversity.

Although the 2004 San Jose Declaration was first agreed close to ten years ago, the corridor in the intervening years was characterised by inherently weak governance structures and inaction on the part of the signatory States, especially in relation to monitoring and compliance mechanisms, as well as failures to adopt appropriate laws and policies to ensure the conservation of biodiversity in areas within national jurisdiction.[128] In order to tackle these shortcomings, the 2021 CMAR initiative entails the implementation of a Regional Action Plan 2019–2024 along with a range of conservation and management activities of the signatory States to combat illegal fishing and to preserve the biodiversity of the corridor, which will constitute a UNESCO biosphere reserve. The overall aim of the initiative is to improve the conservation and sustainable use of the region's marine and coastal resources through ecosystem-based management and the development of regional intergovernmental strategies with the support of NGOs and international bodies. There are several other innovative aspects of the 2021 CMAR initiative, which bode well for the establishment of a more robust protection scheme. For instance, the 2021 Declaration is financed by the Development Bank of Latin America and entails a debt swap for the conservation of the marine environment. As such, it also reflects a regional approach that is underpinned by a shared institutional structure along with common values including: the precautionary principle, stakeholder engagement, transparency in decision-making, adaptive management of the offshore environment, as well as the pooling of regional expertise and resources. All management decisions are adopted by consensus, but the real powers remain at national levels, in so far as the principal mechanisms for the delivery of specific actions are the National Commissions in each of the signatory States.

From the perspective of this analysis, it is significant to note that there are several regulatory and policy linkages between the corridor initiative and other conservation schemes in the Southeast Pacific. Thus, for example, the MPAs associated with the Galápagos, Malpelo, Gorgona, and Coiba are also part of the regional MPA network of the Southeast Pacific pursuant to the Biodiversity Protocol of the Lima Convention. Within this framework, there appears to be considerable scope for the CMAR signatory States to work further with CPPS

127 A Hearn, et al. (2021). A Proposal for Marine Spatial Planning of Ecuador's Exclusive Economic Zone around the Galápagos Marine Reserve. Technical Document.

128 See Enright *et al.* Also, Mahon, R., and Fanning, L. (2019a). "Regional ocean governance: integrating and coordinating mechanisms for polycentric systems". *Mar. Policy*, 5.

and its member States on matters of common conservation concern. The scheme of protection afforded by the corridor could, for instance, be extended to cover areas beyond national jurisdiction, most especially to address the illegal activities of vessels operating in the high seas pocket between the Galápagos and continental Ecuador.[129] In principle, and provided that Central American States can muster sufficient political support from Costa Rica, Panama and Nicaragua, it is also conceivable that the corridor could be rolled out farther north to cover the CRD, a proposal that we will return to below. Suffice it to say here that any such development will mark the attainment of a major regional milestone in the protection of marine biodiversity of the Eastern Pacific, bearing in mind that both the CMAR and the CRD are component parts of the same Large Marine Ecosystem that straddle areas beyond national jurisdiction along with the maritime zones of Mexico, Guatemala, El Salvador, Honduras, Nicaragua, Costa Rica, Panama, Colombia, and Ecuador. Realistically, for this to happen the CRD will have to be designated as a high seas MPA under the processes set down by the BBNJ Agreement. As will be seen next, Latin American States have shaped the substantive content and cross-cutting provisions of the latter instrument.

7 CPPS Member States and the BBNJ Agreement

The conservation of marine ecosystems remains of paramount importance for countries bordering the Southeast Pacific since the 1940s. After the coming into force of the 1995 Fish Stocks Agreement however, individual and joint efforts to protect biodiversity in areas beyond national jurisdiction encountered strong headwinds at various regional processes concerned with the protection of marine ecosystems in the region. Indeed, neither the 2000 Galápagos Agreement nor its 2003 Protocol took legal effect due to the absence of political support at national levels among the signatory States.[130] As a result, the CPPS was denied formal treaty powers to take binding legal measures on behalf of its members in relation to high seas biodiversity. Despite regional inaction on

129 See: El País. *"Un acuerdo internacional para proteger las islas Galápagos" Available at:* https://elpais.com/sociedad/2020-09-25/un-acuerdo-internacional-para-proteger-las-islas-Gal

130 Framework Agreement for the Conservation of Living Marine Resources on the High Seas of the South Pacific, Santiago de Chile, 14 August 2000, (not in force); Modificatory Protocol to the Framework Agreement for the Conservation of Living Marine Resources on the High Seas of the South Pacific, Lima, 27 November 2003, (not in force).

such matters, CPPS member States nonetheless remained highly engaged in various multilateral processes concerned with protecting the marine environment, including most notably the BBNJ intergovernmental conference, which convened at the UN between 2017 and 2022. This was greatly facilitated by their membership, and at times leadership of an important negotiation and advocacy group in the international law-making process, commonly known by the acronym CLAM, denoting the Core of Latin American Countries. Apart from Ecuador withdrawing from CLAM for a brief period in 2019 and 2020, this alliance includes all CPPS member States, as well as Argentina, Brazil, Costa Rica, El Salvador, Guatemala, Honduras, Mexico, Panama, Paraguay, Dominican Republic and Uruguay. From a law of the sea perspective, the CLAM group brings a disparate mix of States together, including those with large coastlines, as well as the land-lock country of Paraguay, States with important fisheries interests, States with islands, and States that are party and non-party to UNCLOS. In view of its diversity of maritime interests, CLAM was well placed to contribute to the search for middle ground solutions in the negotiations of a new multilateral treaty on high seas biodiversity.[131] Interestingly, although not a member of CLAM *per se*, the land-locked State of Bolivia actively led the negotiations at the IGC during the course of its presidency of G77/China in 2018 and used its position to advocate for the rights of nature approach to high seas biodiversity.

The unified approach of CPPS member states to the BBNJ negotiations is unsurprising when one considers that the 2012 Galápagos Commitment affirmed their shared goal to enhance the conservation and sustainable use of biodiversity in the entire Pacific Basin.[132] By virtue of the same instrument, they committed themselves to a range of regional actions that have major law of the sea implications including: the establishment of alliances to develop joint projects and exchange of experiences on maritime issues; collaboration on scientific research programmes pertaining to the marine environment within and beyond national jurisdiction; tackling pollution of the marine environment; promoting the conservation and non-lethal use of whales in international fora; creating new MPAs and consolidating a regional network of marine and coastal protected areas in the Southeast Pacific; along with the adoption and support of the Plan of Action for the Protection of the Marine Environment and Coastal Areas of the Southeast Pacific.[133] Furthermore,

131 Statement by Uruguay, Joint Intervention – Core Latin American Group (Clam) General Exchange of Views at the Third Session of the BBNJ IGC, 19 August 2019.

132 Galápagos Declaration. Paras. 1, 7, 20.

133 Ibid. Para. 2, 19, 21, 22, 23, 24, 26, 29.

CPPS was tasked with coordinating regional responses to these issues on foot of its advisory competences.[134] To take the BBNJ agenda forward, the CPPS Assembly established technical working groups to examine various topics that were central to the negotiations including: the conservation and sustainable use of biodiversity and marine genetic resources; the sustainable management of fisheries and the conservation of biodiversity of deep waters and ecosystems; and the development of an Integrated Regional Ocean Policy to serve their common interests.[135] In parallel, the CPPS raised its international profile at various law of the sea processes more broadly and articulated its views on some of the key issues by contributing to the United Nations Regular Process for global reporting and assessment of the state of the marine environment, including socioeconomic aspects.[136] This engagement extended to participation in research initiatives including the STRONG High Seas project on high seas governance arrangements for biodiversity in the Southeast Pacific and the Southeast Atlantic.[137]

On the various cross-cutting elements of the BBNJ package, CPPS member States have a common history and strong geopolitical reasons to support the codification of normative principles and approaches for environment management including the ecosystem approach.[138] As seen above, this is entirely understandable because the ecosystem approach is linked with the *raison d'être* of CPPS, as well as many practical aspects of its work programme.[139] The BBNJ Agreement may thus redress the longstanding concerns of CPPS member states about the application of this normative paradigm in areas beyond national jurisdiction, especially if they can apply it in a way that reflects the principles of interdependence and social justice, thereby contributing to the wellbeing of coastal communities and States of the Southeast Pacific. Indeed, according to the CPPS statutes, the ecosystem approach will be 'successfully

134 UNEP-WCMC, above n 54, 80, 90.

135 CPPS. *Working Groups*. Available at: http://www.cpps-int.org/cpps-docs/gt/GT-B-RGM/TDR-GT-CPPS-B-RGM.pdf. See also: CPPS. Resolution CPPS/AO/XII/N03/2015, 25 November 2015.

136 United Nations Division for Ocean Affairs and the Law of the Sea. *A Regular Process for global reporting and assessment of the State of the marine environment, including socioeconomic aspects.* Available at: http://www.un.org/depts/los/global_reporting/global_reporting.htm.

137 PROG (2017) *Strong high seas – IKI project launched at UN Ocean Conference.* Available at: http://www.prog-ocean.org/strong-high-seas-iki-project-launched-at-un-ocean-conference/#more-275 See also: CPPS. Biodiversidad Fuera de la Jurisdicción Nacional en la Región del Pacífico Sudeste. Available at: https://abnj-pacifico.org/mas-informacion/.

138 CPPS Statutes. Article 2.

139 Ibid, article 5.

achieved if it maintains or increases the capacity of an ecosystem to produce the desired benefits, and increases the capacity of society to equitably distribute the associated benefits and costs'.[140] To this end, one of the tasks of the CPPS is to propose long-term strategic guidelines, taking into consideration the ecosystem-based approach, and to protect ecosystem services for the benefit of states parties, their peoples and the marine environment.[141] As seen previously, important work is underway under the auspices of CPPS in relation to economic and social evaluations of the benefits derived from marine biodiversity and their associated ecosystems within the region.

Another significant aspect of the BBNJ Agreement is that the entire instrument pivots around the provisions promoting international cooperation between States and among relevant legal instruments and frameworks, as well as between global, regional, subregional and sectoral bodies.[142] Similar to many other law of the sea treaties, the principle of cooperation permeates all aspects of the Agreement and will ultimately provide an important avenue for improving ocean governance worldwide including in the Southeast Pacific. In this context, the BBNJ Agreement may provide an incentive for the member states to further empower CPPS, so that it has a more extensive range of powers to engage in multilateral and regional processes on their behalf.[143] Currently, the principal mechanisms for collaboration are cooperation agreements, including the arrangements that have been concluded with the Economic Commission for Latin America and the Caribbean on marine resources and regional development;[144] the FAO on fisheries planning and research on living marine resources;[145] and the State Oceanic Administration from China on oceanic activities undertaken in the Pacific basin.[146] Additionally, CPPS has signed a Memorandum of Understanding with CBD,[147] and with the Inter-American Tropical Tuna Commission.[148] Overall, however, cross-sectoral collaboration

140 Ibid.

141 Ibid. 2.

142 Draft BBNJ Agreement. Articles 1, 6.

143 UNEP-WCMC, above n 54, 78.

144 Cooperation Agreement between CPPS and ECLAC/UNDP. Available at: http://cpps.dyndns.info/consulta/documentos/legal/cooperacion/2.AC.CPPS-CEPAL-PNUD-1983.pdf.

145 Cooperation Agreement between CPPS and FAO. Available at: http://cpps.dyndns.info/consulta/documentos/legal/cooperacion/3.AC.CPPS-FAO-1985.pdf.

146 UNEP-WCMC, above n 21, 79.

147 MoU between CPPS and CBD Secretariat. Available at https://www.cbd.int/doc/agreements/agmt-cpps-1998-06-03-moc-en.pdf.

148 MoU between CPPS and IATTC. Available at: http://www.iattc.org/PDFFiles2/CPPS-IATTC-MOU-Jun-2015.pdf.

between various intergovernmental bodies remains fundamentally weak and has not been developed to any degree in the Southeast Pacific, according to the CPPS Secretariat.[149]

In line with their collective interests, the CPPS member States have followed a regional approach to the negotiation of the four substantive strands of the Agreement. This includes on the many contentious provisions pertaining to marine genetic resources, where they have aligned their positions with CLAM and G77/China more generally. Remarkably, there are no regional specific instruments on the use, access to and benefit sharing of marine genetic resources that apply in ABNJ of the Southeast Pacific, even though they constitute marine living resources and thus fall within the scope of the 2012 Galápagos Commitment. By any measure, the high seas freedoms to collect and use MGRs appear to constitute a major lacuna in regional ocean governance arrangements, especially when one considers the number of hydrothermal vent sites and other areas of great scientific interest that merit special protection in their own right. The CPPS has long strived to plug this legislative gap by hosting a number of regional workshops on the scientific and legal aspects of developing a *sui generis* regulatory framework governing the exploration and collection of MGRs in areas beyond national jurisdiction of the Southeast Pacific.[150]

In contrast to the absence of regulatory measures on marine genetic resources, CPPS member States have considerable expertise and a number of regional obligations pertaining to the environmental impact assessment of offshore activities, which is the second substantive strand of the BBNJ package. More specifically, within the framework of the Lima Convention, CPPS Parties have adopted technical guidelines on EIA to assist member states and other actors on the planning of projects and to minimize their harmful impacts on the marine environment of the Convention Area. The latter, it may be recalled, encompasses ABNJ to the extent that is necessary to control pollution of the marine environment.[151] Moreover, the Protocol for the conservation and management of protected marine and coastal areas of the Southeast Pacific stipulates that Parties must undertake the following: assess the environmental impact of any activity liable to produce adverse effects on protected areas; establish an integrated analysis procedure; and exchange of information on

149 UNEP-WCMC, above n 54, 80.

150 See: STRONG high seas capacity development series – introduction to marine genetic resources. 18 November 2021. Available at: https://www.prog-ocean.org/events/strong-high-seas-capacity-development-series-introduction-to-marine-genetic-resources/.

151 Lima Convention. Article 1, 8. Para 1.

alternative activities or measures for preventing such effects.[152] In practice, however, the picture is less rosy in so far as the aforementioned assessment requirements are not applied in relation to projects conducted exclusively in ABNJ of the Southeast Pacific.[153] In view of the transboundary impacts of many anthropogenic activities, this may be considered a major weakness in the regional approach to the protection of marine biodiversity both within and beyond national jurisdiction. One anticipates that this governance gap will ultimately be closed by the EIA provisions in the BBNJ Agreement, as soon as they come into force.

On the third strand of the BBNJ package on area-based management tools and the establishment of MPAs in areas beyond national jurisdiction, much remains to be done despite the considerable progress that has been made in coastal waters. Impressively, close to half of Chile's EEZ is designated as protected areas and management measures extend to a number of "no take" zones for fisheries. At a scientific level, the latter prohibitions are crucially important in light of the ecological connectivity between the biodiversity associated with the oceanic archipelagos under Chile's sovereignty and maritime jurisdiction and the health of the broader marine environment of the Pacific.[154] As seen above, despite its longstanding affinity with the concept of *Mar Presencial* in the Southeast Pacific, Chile has not sought to impose obligations in relation to the activities of third parties in high seas areas adjacent to MPAs in waters under national jurisdiction. Furthermore, it is difficult to discern a broader regional commitment to establish MPAs on the high seas. This reluctance is all the more notable when one considers that a protocol to the Lima Convention addresses specifically the conservation and management of protected marine and coastal areas of the Southeast Pacific.[155] The latter instrument recognises the need to adopt appropriate measures for the protection and preservation of fragile, vulnerable and unique ecosystems, as well as threatened species, and calls for the establishment of protected areas.[156] Significantly the geographical

152 Paipa Protocol. Article 8.

153 Durussel above n. 1. See also: Gjerde, K.M., Wright, G., and Durussel, C., Strengthening high seas governance through enhanced environmental assessment processes: A case study of mesopelagic fisheries and options for a future BBNJ treaty, STRONG High Seas Project, 2021.

154 A.M. Friedlander, C.F. Gaymer "Progress, opportunities and challenges for marine conservation in the Pacific Islands" (2021) 31(2) *Aquat. Conserv. Mar. Freshw. Ecosyst.*, at 221–231.

155 CPPS. Protocol for the conservation and management of protected marine and coastal areas of the South-East Pacific (Paipa Protocol, hereafter). Adopted on 21 September 1989. Available at: http://www2.ecolex.org/server2neu.php/libcat/docs/TRE/Full/En/TRE-001085.txt.

156 Ibid. Recital 1, 3.

scope of the Protocol encompasses the EEZs of the Contracting Parties, as well as the entire continental margin extending beyond 200 nautical miles.[157] The Protocol therefore provides a legal basis for the establishment of protected areas on the extended continental shelf beyond the 200 miles EEZ limits and in areas where the super-adjacent water column is high seas.[158] In marked contrast to the practice of States on the Atlantic coast of Europe such as Portugal, at the time of writing, no Latin American State has established an MPA on its outer continental margin beyond 200 nautical miles. That said, Costa Rica and Ecuador have made a joint submission in relation to the Panama Basin to the Commission on the Limits of the Continental Shelf under Article 76 of UNCLOS.[159] Chile has made a submission in respect of the Eastern Continental Shelf of Easter Island Province.[160] If these claims are determined favourably in whole or in part by the Commission in due course, then these countries will be in a position to establish MPAs on their respective continental margins. If they do, the Protocol addresses the relevant criteria that apply to establishing MPAs; the regulation of activities within MPAs including the very significant prohibition on seabed mining and any other activity liable to have adverse effects on species, ecosystems or biological processes; measures to prevent, reduce and control pollution; as well as provisions on regional cooperation and capacity building.[161]

The hesitancy of CPPS member states in establishing high seas MPAs is compounded by the marked reluctance of multilateral bodies in applying sector specific spatial tools.[162] By any standard, there is a strong scientific case supporting the application of area-based management tools in particular to safeguard biodiversity, especially when one considers that there are 21 EBSAs in the Eastern Tropical and Temperate Pacific. This total takes into account

---

157 Ibid. Article 1.

158 See Warner above n. 91, 191.

159 UNCLOS. Article 76(4)-(6). See joint submission by Costa Rica and Panama on 16 December 2020. Available at: https://www.un.org/depts/los/clcs_new/commission_submissions.htm. See also: See Preliminary information indicative of the outer limits of the continental shelf beyond 200 nautical miles submitted by Costa Rica. Available at: http://www.un.org/depts/los/clcs_new/submissions_files/preliminary/cri2009informacion_preliminar.pdf and the reservation note made by Nicaragua in relation to the preliminary information by Costa Rica. Available at: http://www.un.org/depts/los/clcs_new/submissions_files/preliminary/nic_re_cri_2010_en.pdf.

160 See submission made by Chile on 21 December 2020. Available at: https://www.un.org/depts/los/clcs_new/commission_submissions.htm.

161 CPPS. Protocol for the conservation and management of protected marine and coastal areas of the South-East Pacific. Articles 4, 5, 7, 10.

162 UNEP-WCMC, above n 54, 92.

15 in the CPPS geographical area,[163] including six that are located in ABNJ, namely: Salas y Gómez and Nazca Ridges;[164] Equatorial Front and Carnegie Ridge;[165] Equatorial High-Productivity Zone;[166] an area of the Eastern Tropical Pacific Marine Corridor;[167] an area of the Galápagos Archipelago and Western Prolongation;[168] and the Grey Petrel Feeding Area in the South-East Pacific Rise.[169] Several of the EBSAs constitute high productivity areas of upwelling systems, similar to the oceanographic features that take place in the CRD.[170] One therefore anticipates that the aforementioned EBSAs will constitute priority areas for protection and designation under the BBNJ Agreement.[171]

The fourth strand of the latter instrument concerns capacity-building and technology transfer, which are of fundamental importance for CPPS member States in view of their status as developing States. These topics are addressed by both the 1981 Lima Convention and the 1989 MPA Protocol.[172] As highlighted above, there is a pressing need for more scientific research in the Southeast Pacific and the sharing of international resources to do so. Moreover, in contrast to the majority of coastal States in the Global South, Chile and Peru have significant scientific infrastructure including deep ocean research vessels, which are well capable of undertaking the technical fieldwork to support the implementation of the BBNJ Agreement.[173] A regional approach on

163 CBD (2017) *EBSAs Regions Eastern Tropical and Temperate Pacific*. Available at: https://www.cbd.int/ebsa/ebsas.

164 CBD (2017) *Salas y Gómez and Nazca ridges*. Available at: https://chm.cbd.int/database/record?documentID=204100.

165 CBD (2017) *Equatorial front and Carnegie ridge*. Available at: https://chm.cbd.int/database/record?documentID=204048.

166 CBD (2017) *Equatorial high-productivity zone*. Available at: https://chm.cbd.int/database/record?documentID=204046.

167 CBD (2017) *Eastern Tropical Pacific Marine Corridor*. Available at: https://chm.cbd.int/database/record?documentID=204045.

168 Marine Conservation Institute (2017) *MPAtlas*. Seattle, WA. Available at: http://mpatlas.org/map/high-seas-protections/.

169 CDB (2017) *Grey petrel feeding area in the South-East Pacific Rise*. Available at: https://chm.cbd.int/database/record?documentID=204074.

170 See, M. Rodriguez Chaves and R. Long, *Biodiversity of Areas Beyond National Jurisdiction: The Costa Rica Thermal Dome and other International Case Studies* (Leiden/Boston: Nijhoff, 2022).

171 An initiative for the establishment of a high seas MPA to protect the Nazca ridge has been endorsed by the Chilean Government. See: https://sdgs.un.org/news/president-pinera-announces-chile-will-advance-proposal-fully-protect-area-high-seas. Also: Wagner et. al, above n. 10.

172 1981 Lima Convention. Article 10; 1989 MPA Protocol, Articles IX, X.

173 IOC-UNESCO. 2020. Global Ocean Science Report 2020–Charting Capacity for Ocean Sustainability. K. Isensee (ed.), Paris, UNESCO, at 26–29.

capacity-building will also accord with the mandate of CPPS, which extends to strengthening scientific cooperation and capability in the region, particularly as it relates to tasks associated with environmental and fisheries management, combatting climate change and efforts to mitigate the risks associated with natural phenomenon.[174] As seen previously, notable examples in this regard include: the coordination of the El Niño Regional Research Programme (ERFEN);[175] national and regional initiatives to protect the marine environment;[176] as well as collaboration with the SPRFMO and other partners in the implementation of a major GEF project on sustainable fisheries management. Indeed, one of the objectives of the CPPS working group on fisheries management and biodiversity conservation of deep-sea living marine resources and ecosystems in ABNJ is to build capacity to assess the status of deep-sea fisheries and the conservation status of VMEs in areas beyond national jurisdiction.[177] To this end, collaboration agreements have been concluded by CPPS with the Economic Commission for Latin America and the Caribbean;[178] FAO;[179] the State Oceanic Administration from China;[180] CBD;[181] and the IATTC.[182] Furthermore, the BBNJ Agreement may improve the scope for cross-sectoral collaboration on capacity building and technology transfer between multilateral, regional and national bodies concerned with the conservation and sustainable use of biodiversity in the Southeast Pacific.[183] If it does so, this will be a major accomplishment that is long overdue under Parts XIII and XIV of UNCLOS. As such, it will have an immediate and discernible effect on ensuring

174 CPPS Statutes. Article 3(l).

175 UNEP-WCMC, above n 54, 75.

176 Ibid.

177 CPPS. First meeting of the Working Group on Sustainable Fisheries and Conservation of Biodiversity of the CPPS. Available at: http://www.cpps-int.org/cpps-docs/gt/GT-PSCB/2013/ago/informe-i-videoconf.pdf. See also: FAO (2017) *Sustainable fisheries management and biodiversity conservation of deep-sea living marine resources and ecosystems in the ABNJ.* Available at: http://www.fao.org/in-action/commonoceans/projects/deep-seas-biodiversity/en/.

178 Cooperation Agreement between CPPS and ECLAC/UNDP. Available at: http://cpps.dyndns.info/consulta/documentos/legal/cooperacion/2.AC.CPPS-CEPAL-PNUD-1983.pdf.

179 Cooperation Agreement between CPPS and FAO. Available at: http://cpps.dyndns.info/consulta/documentos/legal/cooperacion/3.AC.CPPS-FAO-1985.pdf.

180 UNEP-WCMC, above n. 54, 79.

181 MoU between CPPS and CBD Secretariat. Available at: https://www.cbd.int/doc/agreements/agmt-cpps-1998-06-03-moc-en.pdf.

182 MoU between CPPS and IATTC. Available at: http://www.iattc.org/PDFFiles2/CPPS-IATTCMOU-Jun-2015.pdf.

183 UNEP-WCMC, above n 54, 80.

that Latin American States can give full effect to, and derive benefits, from the implementation of the BBNJ Agreement.

8 Lessons for the CRD

High seas governance in the Southeast Pacific is a complex and compelling field of international law. Complexity arises out of the unique blend of geopolitical, legal, scientific and social considerations at play in shaping the precise contours of the regional approach to regulating the conservation of marine biodiversity both within and beyond national jurisdiction. At this point in the discussion, it is therefore appropriate to review if and how the practice of CPPS member states in law of the sea matters can influence the establishment of new governance arrangements for the CRD in the Central Tropical Pacific.

In both the Southeast Pacific and the Central Tropical Pacific, we can start by pointing out that all of the primary actors are developing States in the push to improve sustainability practices under international law and the development of new norms and instruments for doing so. There is also a collective understanding that the socio-biological unity of the ocean has underpinned regional coordinated action on important law of the sea matters since the adoption of the Santiago Declaration in 1952. Today, regional recognition of the unity of marine ecosystems lies at the very heart of the mission of CPPS and its member States, which are all committed to the implementation of the three pillars of sustainable development.[184] There are, of course, inherent tensions in the region on matters such as maritime boundaries and access to fishery resources, but the CPPS member states are nonetheless willing to work hand-in-hand with other members of CLAM to attain successful outcomes from the BBNJ negotiations at the intergovernmental conference under the auspices of the UN. They are also keen to provide leadership on conservation issues, albeit within national jurisdiction and to partner with their sister States to the north for this purpose.[185] Their global marine environment stewardship credentials are greatly enhanced by the establishment of the Eastern Tropical Pacific Marine Corridor (CMAR) to protect migratory species by linking MPAs in sea areas within national jurisdiction. However, one should not forget that a similar initiative pursuant to the 2004 San Jose Declaration failed to deliver the anticipated conservation benefits due to inherently weak governance

184 CPPS (2012) Plan de Acción Estratégico para la CPPS del siglo XXI. Available at: http://cpps.dyndns.info/cpps-docs-web/publicaciones/PAE-CPPS-XXI.pdf, 3.

185 Ibid. 14.

structures and enforcement mechanisms.[186] Vitally, the 2019–2024 Action Plan recommends expanding the CMAR initiative to include other MPAs and countries in the region, which potentially opens the door for its application to the CRD,[187] without including it specifically by name. A possibility that we will return to below.

The second lesson relates to the coordinating role that CPPS plays through its work programme, which is primarily expert led and structured around science-based decision-making in policy and regulatory processes. A case in point is the working-group on IUU fishing that focuses among other matters on regional implementation of Port State measures.[188] There is also a strong emphasis on reducing the bycatch of fisheries, as seen in the work undertaken by the Technical Coordination Committee for Sharks, which advises CPPS on the implementation of a Regional Action Plan for the conservation and management of sharks, rays and chimaeras in the Southeast Pacific Region (PAR-Tiburon).[189] As highlighted previously, the establishment of working groups to examine ABNJ related topics by the CPPS Assembly contributed enormously to the adoption of a unified approach to the international regulation of high seas biodiversity and shaped the negotiation positions adopted by CLAM in the treaty deliberations at the UN. In addition, it should be borne in mind that CPPS is committed to delivering science to inform environmental impact assessment, as well as area-based management tools, even though it does not have a legal mandate to implement area-based planning *stricto sensu* in ABNJ.[190] In addition, it promotes marine scientific research and capacity building,[191] including global and regional programmes for the conservation of biodiversity and the protection of the environment, as well as to ensure that appropriate scientific and climatic data is readily for this purpose.[192] This extends to supporting a regional oceanographic cruise programme and the dissemination of the results of marine scientific research to inform policies and actions on

186 WildAid (2010). *An Analysis of the Law Enforcement Chain in the Eastern Tropical Pacific Seascape*. Available online at: https://www.issuelab.org/resources/26036/ 26036.pdf; See also: Cremers above n. 97.

187 Corredor Marino del Pacífico Este (CMAR) (2019a). Plan de acción 2019–2024. San José, Costa Rica, 46.

188 CPPS. *IUU fishing*. Available at: http://www.cpps-int.org/index.php/pesca-indnr.

189 CPPS. *Technical coordination committee for sharks*. Available at: http://www.cpps-int.org/index.php/ctc-par.

190 Galápagos Declaration. Para. 1.

191 CPPS Statutes. Article 3(l).

192 UNEP-WCMC, above n 54, 81.

matters of global and regional environmental concern.[193] A commendable example is the study of the El Niño phenomenon in the Southeast Pacific undertaken by CPPS in partnership with two dozen scientific institutions.[194] CPPS also contributes to the Global Ocean Observing System (GOOS) regional alliance for the Southeast Pacific.[195]

Perhaps the most important lesson that can be derived from the Southeast Pacific is that coastal States in the Central Tropical Pacific, such as Costa Rica, will have to take on responsibility for protecting the CRD and build strong regional arrangements for doing so. In particular, they will have to muster considerable support from a broad range of countries within and beyond region, as well as from a willing and strong cohort of intergovernmental bodies, especially those that have conservation interests and regulatory mandates in the Eastern Pacific. The nature of this challenge should not be underestimated and some of the initial portends are less than favourable, particularly so when one considers that there was little or no engagement from regional bodies such as IATTC and the SPRFMO in the BBNJ negotiation processes at the UN to develop a new implementation agreement under UNCLOS. Moreover, as seen above, multilateral organizations such as the ISA and the IMO are slow to adopt regulatory measures tailored to address the conservation requirements of the Southeast Pacific. The need for such measures is particularly acute in relation to the Nazca Ridge, which borders a major international shipping route and has high concentrations of seabed minerals. The harsh reality is that much of the burden to champion the protection of high seas biodiversity rests with the modestly resourced CPPS, which has an inherently weak legal mandate to advance the conservation agenda.

9 Safeguarding Marine Ecosystems in the Southeast Pacific

Although CPPS member states were *avant-garde* on many maritime matters for well over half a century and provided strong international leadership on

193 CPPS. *Regional oceanographic cruise programme*. Available at: http://cpps-int.org/index.php/crucero-inicio. This Programme has developed a Protocol for the use of seabird CTD and data processing in the South Pacific to standardise the procedures for the operation of the equipment and processing of the collected data. CPPS (2015) *Protocol for the use of sea-bird CTD and data processing in the South Pacific*. Ecuador: CPPS, 2.

194 CPPS. *Regional Scientific Committee for the regional study of the El Niño phenomenon in the Southeast Pacific*. Available at: http://www.cpps-int.org/index.php/sobre-erfen.

195 CPPS. *GOOS regional alliance for the Southeast Pacific*. Available at: http://www.cpps-int.org/index.php/grasp-contactos.

ecosystem-based management of the marine environment, one has to conclude this chapter on a relatively cautious note. Undoubtedly, States bordering the Southeast Pacific share many similarities with their neighbors in Central America in so far as they are all developing or low middle-income countries, which are struggling to climb the rankings in the Human Development Index. Apart from their membership of CLAM, they have common economic, social and geo-political interests in establishing a stable and effective international treaty regime governing high seas biodiversity. In recent years, however, state practice has focused almost exclusively on protecting the marine environment under coastal States jurisdiction. Constructively in this regard, CPPS promotes large marine ecosystem-based management considerations in national policies and programmes, working in concert with international organisations such as the FAO.[196]

Governance arrangements in the Southeast Pacific are multifaceted and face many challenges including the scourge of IUU fishing.[197] Somewhat ironically, in light of their longstanding commitment to legal concepts that are premised on the ecological unity of the ocean, Latin American States bordering the Pacific have not taken any substantive measures to protect marine biodiversity in areas beyond national jurisdiction over and beyond giving effect to the measures adopted by the regional fisheries bodies. Aside from the latter, they have not sought to press high seas ecosystems-based obligations on vessels flying their national flags, or indeed the flags of third states. More remarkably, they have not elevated the regional seas programme to a fully-fledged regional seas treaty, similar to the approach taken in other ocean regions. These regulatory shortcomings are particularly lamentable in relation to the biodiversity associated with the Salas y Gómez and Nazca ridges, which is predominantly in areas beyond national jurisdiction and has extraordinary levels of marine endemism.[198] Paradoxically, Chile supported the adoption of the 2021 Madrid Declaration by CCAMLR parties to advance the designation of new marine protected areas in Antarctica and is a strong proponent, along with Argentina, of international efforts to safeguard the marine environment more generally in the Southern Ocean.

---

196 R. Mahon, L. Fanning, 'Regional ocean governance: Integrating and coordinating mechanisms for polycentric systems', 107 (2019) *Marine Policy* Table 3.

197 See CPPS above n 113. Available at: http://cpps.dyndns.info/consulta/documentos/xiii_asamblea_extra_declaracion.pdf.

198 D. Wagner *et al.*, The Salas y Gómez and Nazca ridges: A review of the importance, opportunities and challenges for protecting a global diversity hotspot on the high seas, above n 10.

In contrast to the constructive endeavors of CPPS member states in multilateral and regional processes under UNCLOS and other international instruments, it nonetheless appears that ecological concerns play a paltry second fiddle to the powerful fishing interests in Latin America. Perhaps this failing is most egregious in relation to high seas biodiversity in the region. In this context, one should not forget that the primary State actors are all from the region, with respective percentages of total fishing effort in the Southeast Pacific being accounted for by Peru (60%), Chile (26%), and Ecuador (7%).[199] According to this narrative, one is left with the overriding impression that States within the region have to a certain degree coalesced in keeping CPPS relatively weak as the regional maritime coordination body. In particular, they have deprived it of the resources to ensure effective and ambitious conservation leadership within the dozen or so national, regional and multilateral bodies concerned with ocean governance and the protection of the marine environment in the Southeast Pacific. By any analysis, a major lacuna stems from the absence of substantive CPPS powers to adopt legally binding conservation measures that apply beyond national jurisdiction, other than within the narrow confines of the 1991 Lima Convention and Article 4 of its Statute.

All in all, without substantial reform, it is difficult to see at this point in time how CPPS can grow its membership or extend its geographical scope to include the CRD, particularly in view of its limited mandate pertaining to the conservation of biodiversity in areas beyond national jurisdiction.[200] Nonetheless, history teaches us that the interconnectivity of ocean ecosystems and the need for coherent regulatory systems will continue to influence the practice of all Latin American States in the Eastern Pacific. Looking to the future, if they are to remain true to the spirit and letter of the Santiago Declaration, it will greatly serve their interests to ratify and support the expeditious implementation of the BBNJ Agreement by all states concerned with conservation issues in the entire Pacific Basin. Overall, the picture that emerges from the discussion in this chapter is that much remains to be done in the Southeast Pacific before it can be used as a template for the establishment of new ocean governance arrangements for the CRD. The BBNJ Agreement thus has the potential to herald in a new era of marine biodiversity conservation and should therefore be ratified and implemented by all Latin American States.

---

199 Durussel above n. 1, 44. See also: C. Durussel, E. Soto Oyarzún, S. Urrutia, above n 1, 640.

200 CPPS (2012) Plan de Acción Estratégico para la CPPS del siglo XXI. Available at: http://cpps.dyndns.info/cpps-docs-web/publicaciones/PAE-CPPS-XXI.pdf, 14.

CHAPTER 6

Our Manifold but Common Maritime Order

Atsuko Kanehara

It is not an easy task for me to conclude this Conference, but I would like to focus particularly on the "manifold" nature of the law of the sea. This is because this Conference has eloquently demonstrated that manifold nature. Furthermore, the manifold nature is even multilayered. I would like to propose three layers that form the manifold nature of the law of the sea. I will conclude the Conference by applying the three perspectives that demonstrate these multiple layers, one by one. Each perspective forms a set of terms that are in contrast to each other. They are: first, "holistic but specific"; second, "static but dynamic"; and third, "theoretical but practical." These three sets of terms reflect the multiple layers constructing the manifold nature of the law of the sea. I really hope these sets of terms will work as perspectives for concluding this wonderful Conference.

1 Holistic but Specific

The first perspective is that the law of the sea is "holistic but specific." How is it that, in this Conference, we find two factors that are in contrast to each other?

It goes without saying that UNCLOS, the so-called "Constitution of the Oceans," covers almost all the fields of public international law in its seventeen Parts and three hundred and twenty Articles.

Regarding the content of this Conference, looking at the Programme, the titles of the seven panels may seem, at a glance, specific. This is because the title of the Conference is spotlighting East Asia and the Pacific Region. But, in many ways, this Conference has significantly demonstrated its wide coverage. I will explain this through the following four points.

First, under the title of each panel, speakers richly enlarged and widened the discussion. For instance, Panel 1 on Baselines and Archipelagic States touched upon not only these legal concepts but also unilateral and confrontational ambition in the widening jurisdictional sea areas based upon a problematic use of archipelagic baselines. The panel also addressed the issue of sea level rise. Panel 4 on East China Sea Maritime Boundaries analyzed the issue of maritime delimitation with deep consideration of dispute settlement, too.

Second, this Conference dealt with issues that UNCLOS treats in a relatively succinct manner, namely issues of maritime security and the Arctic. Panel 2 and Panel 3 of the Conference took up these issues. Maritime security is becoming an acute issue for the law of the sea, and particularly to the East China Sea and the South China Sea. In this regard, Professor James Kraska and the Naval War College took the initiative in the discussions at this Conference. Panel 2 examined the issues of navigation rights and law enforcement, each of which is doubtlessly a very important issue of the law of the sea. "Law enforcement" does not have a clear definition under UNCLOS. In this regard, Panel 2 dealt with "law enforcement" in relation to navigation rights. Such a viewpoint is really indispensable to the law of the sea, and therefore, very useful.

Third, the panels of the Conference did not take up – at least directly – some of the main parts of UNCLOS, specifically issues of natural resources development and dispute settlement. These issues seemed not to have been part of the themes of any of the six panels of the Conference. Nonetheless, we had the honor to have, as keynote speakers and a moderator, Judges of ITLOS, Judge Shunji Yanai, former ITLOS President and Judge Rüdiger Wolfrum, and Judge Jin-Hyun Paik, as well as Secretary-General of the International Seabed Authority, Mr. Michael Lodge. Their keynote speeches and their chairing of the panels certainly added to this Conference the viewpoint of dispute settlement and natural resources development.

Fourth, the Conference paid attention to the new issues that UNCLOS did not sufficiently know at its adoption in 1982. They are, for instance, BBNJ, plastic litter, and global warming. In dealing with these issues, panelists enlarged their examination, not confining themselves to UNCLOS but considering the relationships among multiple legal regimes. The relationships were namely between the law of the sea or UNCLOS, on the one hand, and the treaties on environmental protection and the WTO, on the other hand. Really, by the efficient interplay among the relevant international legal regimes, the law of the sea could contribute to achieving the goals of the conservation and sustainable use of BBNJ, combatting global warming, and the protection of the marine environment from the harmful effects caused by plastic litter.

This fourth point brings us to the second set of factors providing the perspective for concluding this Conference. That is "static but dynamic."

2 Static but Dynamic

The law of the sea is one of the oldest fields in international law. Over at least several centuries, humankind established and further refined the fundamental principles and concepts of the law of the sea. They still hold solid significance under UNCLOS, which succeeded the four 1958 Geneva Conventions on the law of the sea. To understand this, it is enough for us to think about the legal regimes of high seas, and territorial seas, and the concepts forming the essential elements of these legal regimes. These are, for instance, the freedom of high seas, navigation rights, innocent passage, and territorial sovereignty. UNCLOS, in the latter half of the 20th century, introduced its complicated system of the distribution of jurisdiction to coastal States, flag States, and port States under the refined zone system of sea areas, such as territorial sea, contiguous zone, exclusive economic zone, archipelagic waters, continental shelf, and deep seabed.

In the long history of its development, the law of the sea has fostered and maintained its fundamental principles and concepts. This means the static aspect of the law of the sea and UNCLOS. We find some of the fundamental concepts of the law of the sea in the titles of the panels of this Conference, such as baselines, archipelago, archipelagic baselines, navigational rights, law enforcement, and maritime boundaries. The unchanging significance of these concepts for the law of the sea eloquently proves the static nature of it. To respect the historical existence of the law of the sea, this Conference had, as the moderator for Panel 1, Professor Masaharu Yanagihara, an expert of the history of international law.

In contrast, the law of the sea is facing very radical and rapid changes due to the development of technologies for various marine uses and the growing harmful impacts on oceans of such uses. The relatively new issues of the law of the sea are, for instance, marine environmental protection, BBNJ, combatting global warming in the context of the law of the sea, particularly sea level rise, and coping with plastic litter. These could be included as issues of marine environmental protection under Part XII of UNCLOS. UNCLOS could cover these issues through the interpretation and application of the relevant provisions mainly under Part XII. However, far beyond that, these issues may strongly require some amendments of UNCLOS, and even the creation of new rules of the law of the sea in order to most effectively tackle these newly emerging issues.

Please allow me to add the issue of combatting the pandemic to the list of the new issues with which UNCLOS is facing serious challenges. Due to the COVID-19 pandemic, all the participants and attendants of this Conference had difficulty getting together for the Conference which was initially scheduled for 2020. Unfortunately, the harmful effects of the pandemic are still impacting our globe. For this reason, even this year, in 2021, we could not convene the Conference in person. So, everybody here would surely not deny the necessity of international law to effectively counter such a devastating natural disaster. Certainly, this is the case with the law of the sea. As reported worldwide, the Diamond Princess was anchored at Yokohama Port, Japan with persons infected with COVID-19 onboard. In taking the necessary measures to prevent the further spread of the infection, Japan seriously considered the relationship between flag State jurisdiction and port State jurisdiction in relation to foreign vessels present in ports in internal waters. The experience of COVID-19 has raised further difficult issues to be examined for the purpose of necessary amendments of the law of the sea and even the possible creation of new rules for it.

These newly emerging issues could require changes of the key concepts and even the fundamental ideas of the law of the sea, for instance, the distribution of jurisdiction to port States, coastal States, and flag States, and even the solid zone system of sea areas. By flexibly responding to such changes, the law of the sea would really acquire a dynamic nature.

Thus far, I have explained the second set of factors that gives me one perspective for concluding the Conference, namely, "static but dynamic." Then, how can the law of the sea keep its longevity by coping with the newly emerging issues? It is by holding practical attitudes that should necessarily accompany theoretical approaches.

Here, we have come to the third set of factors that are in contrast to each other, "theoretical but practical."

3 Theoretical but Practical

Regarding the content of this Conference, it aimed to deal with both law and policy, and it focused upon peaceful maritime engagement in East Asia and the Pacific Region. Therefore, the law of the sea was discussed with a particular regional concern for East Asia and the Pacific Region. It undoubtedly gave us an indispensable practical attitude that should accompany the theoretical discussions on the issues of the law of the sea.

Let me explain the achievements of this Conference in this regard with some examples. East Asian countries have serious concern with China's unilateral and even aggressive ambition and conduct. Such concern is, certainly, shared commonly by South Asian countries. Panel 1, regarding archipelagic baselines, gave thorough theoretical consideration of the interpretation of UNCLOS and the possible existence of customary international law. Furthermore, it conducted a very practical examination that was keenly motivated not only by South Asian States, but also by East Asian States as well. Panel 3 touched upon the issue of the Arctic. In this panel, not only the voices of the coastal States of the Arctic, but also the viewpoints of the non-coastal States were heard for the purpose of building the Arctic regime. The voices of the non-coastal States significantly added, to the theoretical analysis of the possible Arctic regime, a reflection of their practical desires. As non-coastal countries of the Arctic, East Asian countries are trying to become essential stakeholders, in some sense, in a competitive manner. Panel 5 and Panel 6 did not stop at theoretical evaluation of the relevant legal regimes for the themes of the panels. They also dealt with the impact of BBNJ on the Pacific Region, plastics, and the issue of global warming, particularly by emphasizing sea level rise. In this sense, practical viewpoints were never missing from these panels, either. Thus, these ways of examining the issues under the panels undeniably proved to be fine combinations of the theoretical and practical viewpoints of this Conference.

In addition, I would like to highlight the valuable participation, in this Conference, by both academic and diplomatic societies. These speakers really embodied the theoretical and practical viewpoints in dealing with the themes of this Conference.

Thus far, I have explained the manifold nature of the law of the sea. To do so, I applied three perspectives, namely, three sets of factors that are in contrast to each other. These are, "holistic but specific," "static but dynamic," and "theoretical but practical." These multiple layers really form the manifold nature of the law of the sea. The content and contributors of this Conference impeccably represent this manifold nature of the law of the sea.

4 Conclusion

I would like to emphasize the "common" nature of the law of the sea.

From a time-oriented viewpoint, it is remarkable that this Conference is the forty fourth Conference on Oceans Law and Policy. We had the honor of receiving a superb introduction given by Professor Myron Nordquist. He has continuously taken a leading role in ensuring the success of these conferences. The law of the sea needs to survive newly emerging challenges. For that goal, all of us, gathering here, have a heavy but very honorable duty to uphold the traditional law of the sea, and to collaborate to maintain our maritime order. Beyond that, from now on, we need to work together to pass the maritime order in our hands on to future generations.

From a space-oriented viewpoint, we should not forget that every maritime issue and its handling have both regional and global implications. We certainly know that the oceans cover our globe entirely. Many uses of oceans are taking place at the same time all over the globe. The handling of a maritime issue in one region doubtlessly has impacts on other regions of the world.

Taking seriously into consideration these points, both from a time perspective and from a space perspective, we will never leave any States, nor anyone else, as bystanders to the maritime order.

This is because all of us share a common maritime order, meaning our common but manifold maritime order.

PART 1

Baselines and Archipelagic States

CHAPTER 7

Archipelagic Atoll States and Sea Level Rise

Clive Schofield and David Freestone

1 Introduction

This chapter outlines scientific projections for sea level rise and highlights the potential implications of this especially for low-elevation atoll and reef island features. It builds on the earlier work of the authors on the legal implications of the impacts of sea level rise on coasts and islands, in particular a recent preliminary risk assessment of the threats that sea level rise poses to all archipelagic States.[1] This chapter narrows the focus of the previous work to concentrate on the threats that sea level rise poses to low-elevation States and territories wholly or predominantly comprised of coral atolls. This group of States includes the Maldives in the Indian Ocean and Kiribati, the Marshall Islands, Tokelau and Tuvalu in the Pacific Ocean. Additionally, a number of other archipelagic States possess low-elevation atoll and reef island features as do a number of dependent island territories.

Following discussion of recent sea level rise estimates, a brief summary of the legal regime relating to archipelagos is provided. The connection and relationship between atolls and sea level rise is then discussed and competing scientific theories on this critical issue explored. What becomes clear is that sea level rise not only has the potential to threaten coastal areas of these States and territories, their infrastructure and their associated populations, but also the very validity of their archipelagic baselines and potentially even their ability to maintain their archipelagic status. This could lead to major reductions in the scope of their maritime jurisdiction defined adjacent to their threatened territories. The chapter closes with some considerations on the response options open to archipelagic island States in light of the foregoing discussion and some concluding thoughts.

---

1 D. Freestone and C.H. Schofield, 'Sea Level Rise and Archipelagic States: A Preliminary Risk Assessment', *Ocean Yearbook*, 35, 2021, 340–387. See also David Freestone and Duygu Çiçek, *Legal Dimensions of Sea Level Rise: Pacific Perspectives*, The World Bank and Global Facility for Disaster Reduction and Recovery (GFDRR), 2021, VIII + 71 pp.

 | DOI:10.1163/9789004518629_008

2 Sea Level Rise Projections

There is broad consensus in the scientific community that global climate change has already had and is continuing to have multiple impacts on the oceans. Substantial impacts on marine environments are predicted to result from increasing water temperatures,[2] changes to the chemistry of seawater including ocean acidification[3] and expected increases in the geographical range, frequency and intensity of extreme weather events.[4] It is also clear that, as a direct result of anthropogenic emissions of greenhouse gases, (GHG) global sea levels are rising at unprecedented rates and that they seem likely to continue to rise for the next millennia. The ultimate scale and rates of sea level rise is, however, dependent on the degree to which the international community is able to constrain GHG emissions.[5]

The factors contributing to sea level rise are multifaceted and complex, but the climate change-related ocean warming and the melting of grounded ice such as from glaciers and ice sheets are considered to be key drivers. For example, in its 2013 Fifth Assessment Report (AR5) the Intergovernmental Panel on Climate Change (IPCC) estimated mean sea level will rise between 0.52 m and 0.92 m by 2100. Subsequently, in its 2019 *Special Report on Oceans and the Cryosphere* it raised the upper end of the estimates to 1.1 m, whilst observing that this projection was conservative.[6] IPCC AR5 also concluded, with high

2 The IPCC's Fifth Assessment Report (AR5) of 2013 concluded unequivocally that the Earth's system as a whole is warming and that the global ocean will continue to warm in the 21st century. See, *Inter-governmental Panel on Climate Change* (*IPCC*), *Climate Change 2013: The Physical Science Basis, Contribution of Working Group I to the Fifth Assessment Report of the Intergovernmental Panel on Climate Change* (Cambridge, United Kingdom and New York, NY, USA: Cambridge University Press, 2013), 4; and IPCC, *Climate Change 2014, Synthesis Report, Contribution of Working Groups I, II and III to the Fifth Assessment Report of the Intergovernmental Panel on Climate Change* (IPCC, 2015), pp. 11 and 60.

3 Ocean waters interact with the atmosphere so that increasing levels of atmospheric carbon dioxide result in solution in sea water and consequently increase acidification of the oceans. See, *Climate Change 2014, Synthesis Report*, 41.

4 The IPCC suggests that it is likely that extreme sea levels such as those experienced during storm surges have increased since 1970 mainly as a result of rising mean sea level. *Ibid.*, 8 and 53.

5 IPCC, *Climate Change 2021: The Physical Science Basis*, Working Group I contribution to the Sixth Assessment Report of the Intergovernmental Panel on Climate Change, (Cambridge, Cambridge University Press, 2021) available at https://www.ipcc.ch/report/ar6/wg1/. See also, IPCC, *Climate Change 2022: Impacts, Adaption and Vulnerability*, Working Group II contribution to the Sixth Assessment Report of the Intergovernmental Panel on Climate Change, (Cambridge, Cambridge University Press, 2022).

6 IPCC, *Special Report on the Ocean and Cryosphere in a Changing Climate* [IPCC Special Report], approved at its 51st Session, 20–23 September 2019.

confidence, that there are strong indications that the rate of sea level rise has accelerated, with the rate of sea level rise since the mid-19th century being larger than the mean rate during the previous two millennia.[7] Moreover, in its 2019 Special Report, the IPCC indicated that that global mean sea level rise in the period 2006–2015 has been two and a half times the rate for the period 1901–1990.[8]

Additionally, the IPCC report concerning the physical science basis for its Sixth Assessment Report (AR6), issued in August 2021, strongly reinforces this message.[9] AR6 found that the average rate of sea level rise had increased almost three-fold from 1.3 mm per year in the period 1901–1971 to 3.7 mm per year in 2006–2018 with human influence considered 'very likely' to be the main driver for these changes.[10] This report also indicated that not only is it 'virtually certain' that, with high confidence, global mean sea level will continue to rise over the 21st century, but that 'sea level is committed to rise for centuries to millennia … and that it will remain elevated for thousands of years'.[11] Further, the IPCC warned that under continued high GHG emission scenarios, significantly higher sea level rise, approaching 2 metres by 2100 and 5 metres by 2150 "cannot be ruled out, due to deep uncertainty in ice sheet processes."[12] These projections have led to serious concerns that low-elevation coasts and islands, including those of archipelagic atoll island States will be inundated and/or could be rendered uninhabitable.

In the present context it is also important to note that in the Pacific Ocean region, where the majority of archipelagic atoll States are located, the rate of sea level rise is highest in the tropics and the maximum predictions already suggest they could exceed 2 meters by 2100.[13] In 2018, the Pacific Marine Climate Change Report Card suggested that the Pacific Islands experienced sea level rise of 3–6 mm per year in the period 1993–2017 but with "some notable differences" across the region with sea level rise experienced by islands in the

7 See, *Climate Change 2014, Synthesis Report*, 42.

8 See, Ocean and Cryosphere in a Changing Climate.

9 IPCC, 2021.

10 *Ibid.*, at TS-44.

11 *Ibid.*

12 *Ibid.*, at SPM-28. The emissions scenarios related to this projection are Shared Socio-economic Pathways (SSPs) 5 to 8.5, corresponding to very high emission scenarios. This projection was made with low confidence due to the deep uncertainties involved.

13 J.A. Hall *et al.*, *Regional Sea Level Scenarios for Coastal Risk Management: Managing the Uncertainty of Future Sea Level Change and Extreme Water Levels for Department of Defense Coastal Sites Worldwide* (U.S. Department of Defense, Strategic Environmental Research and Development Program, 2016).

Western Pacific[14] being markedly higher than in the Eastern Pacific.[15] Further, studies taking into account observed sea level change between 1950 and 2009 in the West Pacific region coupled with assessment of variations in vertical uplift/subsidence have suggested that sea level rise in this region is of the order of three times the global average.[16]

3 The Legal Regime of Archipelagos

As the authors have discussed in detail elsewhere,[17] the codification of the concept of archipelagic status is essentially a creature of the Third UN Conference on the Law of the Sea, 1973–1982 (UNCLOS III). There had been a long history of discussion of the issue – stretching back even before the famous 1930 Hague Codification Conference,[18] to a proposal in 1924 by Professor Alvarez to the International Law Association,[19] although no agreement on the issue was possible in 1930, principally because the breadth of the territorial sea was still in dispute.[20] At the Second Conference on the Law of the Sea in 1960 (UNCLOS II), the two leading proponents of the archipelagic concept made the case for the special position of mid-ocean archipelagos, but the issue was deferred for further study.[21] Concerns over archipelagic status for mid-ocean archipelagos

---

14 For example, the Solomon Islands, Papua New Guinea and Marshall Islands.

15 For example, Samoa and Kiribati. See, Commonwealth Marine Economies Programme (CMEP), *Pacific Marine Climate Change Report Card 2018*, Townhill, B. *et al.* (eds), (CMEP, 2018).

16 Becker, M., Meyssignac, B., Letetral, C., Llovel, W., Cazenave., & Delcroix. T., 'Sea level variations at tropical Pacific Islands since 1950', *Global and Planetary Change*, 2012, 80–81, 85–98.

17 Freestone and Schofield, 'Sea Level Rise and Archipelagic States: A Preliminary Risk Assessment' 2021, 340, 354–367.

18 D.P. O'Connell, *The International Law of the Sea*. Ed., I.A. Shearer (Oxford, 1982) at pp. 237–8. See also generally O'Connell's seminal paper: 'Mid Ocean Archipelagos in International Law', *British Yearbook of International Law*, 45, 1971, 1–78.

19 Cited in A/CONF. 13/18 (1957), Part 1, section 1, UNCLOS I, I Off. Rec 289, 291 and in *UN Convention on the Law of the Sea: A Commentary.* S. Nandan and S. Rosenne, eds. (Martinus Nijhoff, 1993) Vol II, p. 423 (hereinafter *Virginia Commentary*). See also O'Connell, (1971), p. 5, citing *Report of 33rd Conference of ILA* (Stockholm, 1924) pp. 259 et seq. Alvarez was chair of the Committee on Neutrality.

20 Although there was some support at that point by Japan and Germany, *Ibid.* p. 239.

21 Namely Philippines and Indonesia. The delay was in large part because the Philippines based its case on an argument of historic waters – an issue that the UN General Assembly had already decided to study. UNCLOS II *Official Records* 51, cited O'Connell, n. 3 above, p. 246.

were addressed at UNCLOS III leading to the drafting of Article 46 of LOSC which provides that:

> For the purposes of this Convention:
> (a) "archipelagic State" means a State constituted wholly by one or more archipelagos and may include other islands; and
> (b) "archipelago" means a group of islands, including parts of islands, interconnecting waters and other natural features which are so closely interrelated that such islands, waters and other natural features form an intrinsic geographical, economic and political entity, or which historically have been regarded as such.

The most important aspect of this negotiated compromise definition is that these special rules may only be applied to States composed entirely of islands or parts of islands and the interconnecting water between them.[22] The requirements for the drawing of archipelagic baselines are laid out in Article 47 that can be summarised as follows:

1. that archipelagic States "may draw straight archipelagic baselines joining the outermost points of the outermost islands and drying reefs of the archipelago" provided that the "main islands" of the archipelagic State are included within the archipelagic baseline system;[23]
2. that the ratio of water to land within the baselines must be between 1:1 and 9:1;[24]
3. that the length of any single baseline segment must not exceed 125 M;[25]
4. that no more than three per cent of the total number of baseline segments enclosing an archipelago may exceed 100 M;[26] and,

22 It has been noted that the term 'other natural features' in art. 46(b) is somewhat obscure. However, this terminology can be taken to be a reference to drying reefs as mentioned in art. 47(1). See, J.R.V. Prescott and C.H. Schofield, *The Maritime Political Boundaries of the World*, (Leiden/Boston: Martinus Nijhoff Publishers, 2005), pp. 167–168.

23 Art. 47(1) LOSC. This represents the critical test of the validity of a system of archipelagic baselines. The intent of this provision appears to be to exclude both coastal States dominated by a few large islands and those whose islands are particularly dispersed, such as the United Kingdom and the Federated States of Micronesia (FSM) respectively.

24 Art. 47(1) LOSC.

25 Art. 47(2) LOSC.

26 *Ibid.* The requirement that no more than three per cent of baseline segments may exceed 100 M in length appears restrictive. However, this is misleading. *Handbook on*

5. that such baselines "shall not depart to any appreciable extent from the general configuration of the archipelago."

Of particular note for present purposes is the stipulation in Article 47(1) that, in defining the State's system of archipelagic baselines, these baselines should link "the outermost points of the outermost islands and drying reefs of the archipelago." Fundamentally, a system of archipelagic baselines comprises a series of base points located on or above the normal baseline along the coast of a number of insular features. Consequently, archipelagic baselines are reliant on potentially ambulatory low-water lines along the coast to ensure that the baseline system is "closed".[27]

The insular features involved may include low-tide elevations both falling within the breadth of the territorial sea measured from an above high-tide coast and low-tide elevations lying beyond that distance so long as such features have a lighthouse or similar installation located on them.[28] While this may mean that the maximum amount of area may be enclosed, the incentive to increase the area enclosed also arguably encourages the use of features that are inherently peripheral and also possibly insubstantial and therefore potentially especially vulnerable to sea level rise.

The loss of features that constitute key basepoints or turning points in the archipelagic baselines system may mean that the remaining basepoints are further apart than the Convention permits or it may mean that the resulting water to land ratio proportions no longer meet the necessary ratio requirements.[29] Leaving aside for the present the impact such changes might have on the State's maritime zone claims, such changes might actually compromise the State's ability to maintain valid archipelagic baselines. Although the group of islands would still remain an archipelago geographically and politically, it would lose all the special advantages of archipelagic status that the LOSC confers.

---

the Delimitation of Maritime Boundaries, (New York: United Nations, 2000), p. 8; and, Freestone and Schofield, 'Sea Level Rise and Archipelagic States: A Preliminary Risk Assessment' (2021) 361.

27 See, United Nations, *Baselines: An Examination of the Relevant Provisions of the United Nations Convention on the Law of the Sea* (UN Office for Ocean Affairs and the Law of the Sea, New York, 1989), p. 23.

28 *Ibid.*, p. 36. The United Nations Group of Technical Experts on Baselines indicated that this rule combines the provisions of arts. 13(1) and 7(4) of the LOSC and "so differs from the rules for applying the method of straight baselines."

29 Art. 47(1) and (2).

4 Archipelagic Atoll States

A number of island States are entirely or predominantly composed of low-elevation coral atolls and related reef islands which gives rise to particular concerns in the context of sea level rise related threats. These include the Maldives, Marshall Islands, Tokelau and Tuvalu.[30]

The Maldives comprises 1,190 islands, of which around 200 are inhabited, spread across 26 distinct atolls stretching 822 km from 7° N. to just south of the Equator.[31] The largest atoll is Bodu Thiladhunmathi while Huvadhu atoll has the greatest number of islands. The Marshall Islands consists of 29 atolls and five isolated reef island features as well as the feature termed Enenkio by the Marshall Islands but known as Wake Island to the United States, which also claims sovereignty over the feature and administers it in practice.[32] Tokelau, which is non-self-governing territory of New Zealand, comprises three low-lying atoll island features,[33] whilst the independent State of Tuvalu consists of nine low-lying atolls and 101 reef island features.[34]

Additionally, the State of Kiribati consists of 32 atolls and reef island features together with one raised island feature, Banaba (Ocean) Island, of higher elevation. There are also a number of other States and territories, which possess some higher elevation islands, but are also partially composed of low-lying reef features. While these jurisdictions are not in danger of complete inundation, they can still be considered to be subject to high levels of vulnerability to sea level rise impacts. These include the Cook Islands and the Federated States of Micronesia (FSM). The Cook Islands are a self-governing State in

30 L. Bernard, S. Kaye, M. Petterson and C.H. Schofield, C.H., 'Securing the Limits of Large Ocean States in the Pacific: Defining Baselines amidst Changing Coastlines and Sea Level Rise', 11 (2021) *Geosciences*, no.9, 394–404, at pp. 406–408.

31 See, Embassy of the Maldives, 'Maldives: Geography and location', available at https://www.maldivesembassy.be/en/about-maldives/geography-location.

32 D. Freestone and C.H. Schofield, 'Current Legal Developments: The Marshall Islands', 31 *International Journal of Marine and Coastal Law*, 2016: 720–746; and, United Kingdom Hydrographic Office (UKHO), *Pacific Islands Pilot*, Volume I, NP60 (11th edition, Taunton, 2007).

33 Tokelau does, however, have its own political institutions whereby, for example, the Head of Government rotates between the leaders of the three atolls. Tokelau also has its own judiciary, public services and full control over its budget. See. New Zealand, Foreign Affairs and Trade, "About Tokelau", available at, https://www.mfat.govt.nz/mi/aid-and-development/our-aid-partnerships-in-the-pacific/tokelau/about-tokelau/.

34 P.S. Kench, M.R. Ford and S.D. Owen, 'Patterns of island change and persistence offer alternative adaption pathways for atoll nations', *Nature Communications*, 9, 605 (2018), https://doi.org/10.1038/s41467-018-02954-1.

Free Association with New Zealand. They consist of 15 islands, nine are low-lying atoll or reef island features with the remaining six being higher elevation features.[35] Of particular note in the present context is that around two-thirds of the Cook Islands extensive EEZ claims are dependent on low-lying atoll island features, namely, Penrhyn Atoll, Manihiki Atoll, Pukapuka Atoll, Suwarrow Atoll and Palmerston Atoll, all located in the northern part of the Cook Islands.[36] Although FSM includes high elevation features among each of the four major island groups making up the federation, Kosrae, Pohnpei, Chuuk and Yap, multiple outlying and intervening low-elevation atolls and reef islands are likely to be vulnerable to sea level rise. These include, from west to east, Ulithi Atoll, Eauripik Atoll, Pulusuk Atoll, Sapwuahfik Atoll, Minto Reef and Kapingamarangi Atoll.[37]

Further, there are a number of outlying atolls and reef island features associated with the States of Fiji, Palau, Papua New Guinea (PNG), and the Solomon Islands. The maritime claims associated with the Pacific territories of extra-regional States, including French Polynesia, New Caledonia, the United Kingdom's overseas territory of the Pitcairn Islands as well as the Northwestern Hawaiian Islands and a number of U.S. remote Pacific island territories including Howland and Baker Islands, Jarvis Atoll, Johnston Atoll, Kingman Reef, Palmyra Island, and the aforementioned Enenkio/Wake Island can also be viewed as being particularly vulnerable to sea level rise impacts.[38]

Higher elevation island groups, often of volcanic origin, such as Nauru, Niue, Samoa, Tonga and Vanuatu can be considered to be subject to more limited risks from sea level rise. That said, such higher elevation islands are by no means immune to sea level rise impacts, as the majority of the population and the infrastructure on such islands is concentrated on the low-lying coastal fringes rather than the higher elevation core. Moreover, it can be anticipated

35 UKHO (United Kingdom Hydrographic Office), *Pacific Islands Pilot*, Volume I, NP60 (11th edition, 2007).

36 N. Biribo and C.D, Woodroffe, 'Historical area and shoreline change of reef islands around Tarawa Atoll, Kiribati', 8 *Sustainability Science*, 2013:345. https://doi.org/10.1007/s11625-013-0210-z. See also, Bernard, et. al., 'Securing the Limits of Large Ocean States in the Pacific', at p. 407.

37 C.H. Schofield and R, Van de Poll, 'Treaty between the Federated States of Micronesia and the Independent State of Papua New Guinea concerning maritime boundaries between the Federated States of Micronesia and the Independent State of Papua New Guinea and co-operation on related matters', in *The International Maritime Boundaries of the World*, Vol. IX, (Leiden/Boston: American Society of International Law (ASIL)/Martinus Nijhoff, 2021). Bernard, et. al., 'Securing the Limits of Large Ocean States in the Pacific', at p. 407.

38 Bernard, et. al., 'Securing the Limits of Large Ocean States in the Pacific', at pp. 407–408.

that ecosystem services associated with coastal ecosystems will be negatively impacted under such a scenario.[39]

5 Persistent or in Peril?

The first model for the formation of atolls is attributed to Charles Darwin who suggested that atolls form as ocean seamounts subside. Darwin's theory suggested that as ocean volcanoes become extinct, they cool and subside and a ring of coral reefs forms on top of the extinct volcano and that over time corals and eroded coral sands become the dominant deposits overlaying volcanic rock.[40] Consequently, atolls tend to comprise coralline rock and rubble, cemented to a volcanic rock foundation and often feature low-lying (1–4 m elevation) islands surrounding a shallow lagoon. A fresh-water lens often forms under such features which is linked to the habitability of these islands. How saline this lens of fresh water is depends on levels of rainfall and the degree of saltwater intrusion.[41]

The IPCC Report of 2021 suggests that it is "very likely" that sea level rise will occur around small islands and that this, coupled with storm surges and waves that are likely to "exacerbate coastal inundation with potential to increase saltwater intrusion into aquifers in small islands."[42] This report further projects, with high confidence, shoreline retreat "along sandy coasts of most small islands."[43] These findings appear to align with the concerns of States wholly or partially composed of atolls and reef islands. There is, however, some uncertainty concerning the capacity of coral features to respond to changing sea levels, especially in the context of a warming and more acidic ocean, with

39 Coastal ecosystems provide diverse services of environmental, economic, socio-cultural value to humans including, for example, in relation to fisheries, tourism, recreation and coastal protection.

40 See, C.R. Darwin, *Journal of researches into the natural history and geology of the countries visited during the voyage of H.M.S. Beagle round the world, under the command of Captain Fitz Roy, R.N.*, (2d edition, London, John Murray, 1860); and, Darwin, C.R., *The Structure and Distribution of Coral Reefs*, (2d edition, London: Smith Elder and Co, 1874). Other atoll islands formation theories relate to sea level changes across different geological epochs with the formation of atoll islands resulting from sediment deposition controlled by tidal, wave, wind and current factors as well as sea level.

41 Bernard, et. al., 'Securing the Limits of Large Ocean States in the Pacific', at pp. 401–402.

42 IPCC, *Climate Change 2021*, TS-97.

43 *Ibid.*

implications both for the habitability of such features and their persistence above sea level.

Much of the commentary on sea level rise and low-elevation coral islands, including atoll island features, characterizes these features as fragile and threatened environments, which will increasingly and inevitably become less and less habitable and will progressively be inundated. There are, however, competing views on the persistence of atolls in the context of climate change impacts. The critical consideration in this context relates to sediment supply and whether this will enable the island-building processes to continue to occur, on reefs. There is support in the scientific literature for the view that they will not be able to stay above water, for instance on the basis of the analysis of wave and storm dynamics.[44] These findings suggest that even if sea level rises only relatively moderately, the reefs surrounding and protecting island features will increasingly be overwhelmed leading to the islands themselves bearing the brunt of wave and storm action leading to enhanced erosion, inundation and salt water intrusion into freshwater aquifers, thereby reducing the capacity of reef islands to support human habitation.[45]

The counterpoint to these perspectives are the scientific studies that demonstrate that coral reefs and islands can be remarkably robust and enduring features, capable of natural adaptation to sea level rise over time.[46] For example, Webb and Kench have provided a particularly instructive paper in which they reviewed and analyzed 27 atoll islands in the central Pacific, comparing historical aerial photography with modern satellite imagery in order to assess whether these features had in fact, been subject to erosion – as might have been anticipated were conventional wisdom regarding the influence of sea level rise on coral islands correct. Despite the fact that the period covered by the survey coincided with sea level records for the central Pacific

44 See, C.D. Storlazzi, E.P.L. Elias and P. Berkowitz, 'Many atolls will become uninhabitable within decades due to climate change', *Scientific Reports* 2015, 5:14546, doi: 10.1038/srep14546; and, C.D. Storlazzi, S.B. Gingerich and A. van Dongeren, 'Most atolls will be uninhabitable by mid-21st century because of sea level rise exacerbating wave-driven flooding', *Scientific Advances*, 2018, 4, 1–9. See also, Bernard, et. al., 'Securing the Limits of Large Ocean States in the Pacific', at pp. 413–414.

45 *Ibid.*

46 P.S. Kench, 'Understanding Small Island Dynamics: A Basis to Underpin Island Management', pp. 24–28 in 38 in H. Terashima (ed.), *Proceedings of The International Symposium of Islands and Oceans*, (Tokyo: Ocean Policy Research Foundation, 2009). See also, A.P. Webb, 'Coastal Vulnerability and Monitoring in the Central Pacific Atolls', pp. 33–38 in Terashima, *ibid.*; and, Bernard, et. al., 'Securing the Limits of Large Ocean States in the Pacific', at pp. 415–416.

establishing sea level change of the order of 2.0mm yr^{-1}, fully 86 per cent of the islands analyzed were as large as (43 per cent) or larger than (43 per cent) they had been previously.[47] Indeed, multiple studies by Kench and colleagues suggest that atoll islands are capable of dynamic evolution in the face of sea level rise, whereby coastlines may change so that individual features may well change shape but the islands themselves are persistent over time.[48] Further, as Webb has observed, there exist examples of net-island growth which run counter to "established thought, non-scientific reports in the popular media and modelling" and are suggestive of the complexity of shoreline responses to sea level rise.[49]

This line of scientific thinking runs contrary to traditional concerns that coral reef and atoll islands are likely to be imperiled in the face of significantly accelerated sea level rise, especially against the backdrop of warming and acidifying oceans which may seriously impair the ability of natural systems such as coral reefs to autonomously adapt to changing sea levels. The work of Kench and others suggests that sea level rise will actually enhance the likelihood that such islands remain above sea level. This hypothesis is based on research suggesting that sediment transport between islands will be enhanced as sea levels rise, with positive implications for the persistence of reef features.[50] A further dimension to this thinking is that increased frequency and intensity in extreme weather events, whilst resulting in the erosion of parts of islands, simultaneously results in major supplements to sediment supply, essentially building islands up.[51]

It must be noted, however, that the observations of island changes differ between urbanized atoll islands and those features which are more natural and undisturbed. Urban atolls such as South Tarawa in Kiribati, are home to

---

47 A.P. Webb and P.S. Kench, 'The Dynamic Response of Reef Islands to Sea-level Rise: Evidence from Multi-decadal Analysis of Island Change in the Central Pacific', *Global and Planetary Change*, 72 (2010) (3): 234–246.

48 See, for example, P.S. Kench, R.F. McLean and S.L. Nichol, 'New model of reef-island evolution: Maldives, Indian Ocean', *Geology*, 33(2), 2005, 145–148; P.S. Kench, R.F. McClean, R.W. Brander, S.L. Nichol, S.G. Smithers, M.R. Ford and M. Aslam, M., 'The Maldives before and after the Sumatran tsunami;' *Geology*, 34, 2006, No.3; P.S. Kench, M.R. Ford and S.O. Owen, 'Patterns of island change and persistence offer alternate adaptation pathways for atoll nations', *Nature Communications*,9, 2018, 1–7.; and, R. McLean and P.S. Kench, 'Destruction or persistence of coral atoll islands in the face of 20th and 21st century sea-level rise?', 6, *Wiley Interdisciplinary In 2018 Reviews-Climate Change,* 2015, no.5), 445–463.

49 Webb, 'Coastal Vulnerability and Monitoring in the Central Pacific Atolls', at p. 37.

50 Kench et.al., 'Patterns of island change and persistence'. See also, Bernard, et. al., 'Securing the Limits of Large Ocean States in the Pacific', at p. 405.

51 Bernard, et. al., 'Securing the Limits of Large Ocean States in the Pacific', at p. 405.

substantial populations and feature numerous man-made interventions on the coast such as sea defenses and land reclamation projects. Such interventions on the coast tend to disrupt sediment supply and transport, impairing the dynamic island-building system and causing 'knock-on' impacts elsewhere along the coast or on the coasts of other islands.

Although the scientific debate regarding the persistence of atoll island features remains unsettled, it is reasonable to conclude that numerous low-elevation atoll islands are at risk from sea level rise impacts, including substantial changes to features and associated ecosystem services, if not inundation and disappearance. This is especially the case for heavily urbanized features and with respect to the degree of sea level envisaged by the IPCC under high GHG emissions scenarios. For archipelagic atoll island States this necessarily has the potential to impact the validity of archipelagic baseline system and even the ability of such States to maintain archipelagic status.

6 Response Options Open to Archipelagic Atoll Island States

As noted above, especially in the context of urbanized atolls, man-made interventions aimed at stabilizing atoll and reef islands or, alternatively, land-reclamation and island-building activities aimed at enhancing the spatial scope of islands or creating new artificial islands have become commonplace. Such interventions are not without considerable economic and environmental costs. Singapore, for example has substantially extended its land territory over time – by approximately 25 percent over the past two centuries with most of this expansion occurring since independence in 1964.[52] While this expansion came at great expense, it has taken place to meet the needs of a growing city where land values are high.[53] In a small developing State context, this approach has also been taken in the Maldives, that has built a large artificial island, Hulhumalé, close to the capital, Malé, on which a new city is being

52 See, Tanya Ong, "S'pore's land area expanded by 25% in past 200 years", *Mothership*, 27 September 2018 available at, https://mothership.sg/2018/09/singapore-land-reclamation-increase-size/. See also, "Total Land Area of Singapore", available at, https://data.gov.sg/dataset/total-land-area-of-singapore.

53 See, Singapore Urban Redevelopment Authority, "Creating Spaces for Our Growing Needs", available at, https://www.ura.gov.sg/Corporate/Planning/Master-Plan/Themes/A-Sustainable-and-Resilient-City-of-the-Future/Creating-Spaces. See also, Samanth Subramanian, "How Singapore is Creating More Land for Itself", *New York Times*, 20 April 2017, available at, https://www.nytimes.com/2017/04/20/magazine/how-singapore-is-creating-more-land-for-itself.html.

constructed.[54] It is reported to cover four hundred hectares, rising to a height of three metres above current sea level, to house a hospital, schools, government buildings and housing for 40,000 people, with a projected future population of 240,000 people and to have cost "hundreds of millions of dollars."[55] The objective of this development is to provide more land area for safe human habitation. These initiatives are, of course, understandable when set against what is often perceived to be an existential threat to these vulnerable States, but not likely to be affordable for many small threatened States.

An additional or alternative option relates to the fixing and declaring of the location of baselines along the coast, delineated outer limits to maritime claims and delimited maritime boundaries. As the authors have explored elsewhere,[56] there is substantial emerging State practice on this issue as well as significant moves to address these issues at the international legal level.

The International Law Association (ILA) Committee on International Law and Sea Level Rise has been looking at the legal implications of sea level rise since 2014 and issued its first full report in Sydney in 2018.[57] It is due to report again in June 2022 at the ILA Conference in Lisbon. In 2018 in response to the

54 See Nenad J. Dauenhauer, "On the front line of climate change as Maldives fights rising seas", *New Scientist*, 20 March 2017.

55 See Emma Allen, "Climate Change and Disappearing Island States: Pursuing Remedial Territory" Brill Open Law (2018), pp. 1–23, at 5. In 2012, the Maldives were reported to have commissioned a Dutch engineer to design floating islands as "life-boats" for the population in the case of extreme events. See, D. Black, "Floating islands to the rescue in the Maldives", *The Star*, 23 August 2012, available at, https://www.thestar.com/news/world/2012/08/23/floating_islands_to_the_rescue_in_the_maldives.html; and, Housing Development Corporation "Hulhumalé", available at, https://hdc.com.mv/hulhumale/. See further Freestone and Çiçek (2021).

56 D. Freestone and C.H. Schofield, 'Republic of the Marshall Islands: 2016 Maritime Zones Declaration Act: Drawing lines in the sea' (2016) 31 *International Journal of Marine and Coastal Law* (*IJMCL*) 720–746; 'Securing ocean spaces for the future? The initiative of the Pacific SIDS to develop regional practice concerning baselines and maritime zone limits' (2019) 33 *Ocean Yearbook* 58–89; 'Islands awash amidst rising seas: Sea level rise and insular status under the law of the sea' in Proceedings of the 2018 Singapore Conference on Climate Change (2019) 34 *IJMCL* 391–414; 'Sea level rise and archipelagic States: A preliminary risk assessment' (2021) 35 *Ocean Yearbook* 340–387.

57 See Davor Vidas, David Freestone and Jane McAdam, "International Law and Sea Level Rise: The New ILA Committee" (2015) 21 (2) *International Law Students' Association* (*ILSA*) *Journal of International and Comparative Law* pp. 397–408. After an interim report to the ILA Johannesburg meeting in 2016, the 2018 Report is published as Davor Vidas, David Freestone and Jane McAdam, *International Law and Sea Level Rise*. Brill Research Perspectives in the Law of the Sea (Davor Vidas and Donald R Rothwell, eds.) Brill Nijhoff, 2019, ix +87 pp.

Committee's proposal the International Law Association 78th Conference in Sydney passed a Resolution endorsing the Committee's proposal that:

> … on the grounds of legal certainty and stability, provided that the baselines and the outer limits of maritime zones of a coastal or an archipelagic State have been properly determined in accordance with the 1982 Law of the Sea Convention, these baselines and limits should not be required to be recalculated should sea level change affect the geographical reality of the coastline.[58]

Since then, in 2019 International Law Commission (ILC) established a Study Group on "Sea-level rise in relation to international law."[59] The debates in the UN Sixth Committee on the two reports issued to date by the ILC Study group indicated widespread support among UN Members for the position taken by the ILA.[60]

There is now considerable evidence of emerging State practice among the South Pacific Island States, and indeed elsewhere,[61] in support for the view that once maritime baselines and limits have been notified to the UN Secretary General in accordance with the requirements of LOSC that they are not required to be recalculated even if there are coastline changes as a result of sea level rise. This State practice reached its clearest articulation on 6 August 2021, when the leaders of the eighteen Members of the South Pacific Forum at their virtual 51st Annual Meeting issued the *Declaration on Preserving Maritime Zones in the Face of Climate Change related Sea-Level Rise*.[62] This Declaration is the culmination of a long process but also arguably marks a significant change. In particular, rather than indicating that the States concerned seek to change

58 ILA, 'Resolution 5/2018: Committee on International Law and Sea Level Rise', 2018, available at, http://www.ila-hq.org/images/ILA/Resolutions/ILAResolution_5_2018_SeaLevelRise.pdf.

59 Freestone and Schofield, 'Sea Level Rise and Archipelagic States: A Preliminary Risk Assessment' (2021) 350–351.

60 Ibid.

61 See n 58 below.

62 Communiqué, attached as Annex 1 to Freestone and Schofield (2021), pp. 693-695. Available at https://www.forumsec.org/2021/08/11/declaration-on-preserving-maritime-zones-in-the-face-of-climate-change-related-sea-level-rise.The eighteen Member States are: Australia, the Cook Islands, the Federated States of Micronesia, Fiji, French Polynesia, Kiribati, Nauru, New Caledonia, New Zealand, Niue, Palau, Papua New Guinea, the Republic of the Marshall Islands, Samoa, Solomon Islands, Tonga, Tuvalu and Vanuatu.

international law in the future, they clearly articulate their understanding of the obligations imposed by the Convention in this regard and firmly declare the way in which they—as a group—intend to interpret them in the future.[63]

Very shortly after the Pacific Island countries issued their August 2021 Declaration, the Heads of State and Government of the Alliance of Small Island States (AOSIS)[64] issued a complementary Leaders' Declaration.[65] AOSIS is a global alliance established in 1990 in the run-up to the 1992 Rio Conference on Environment and Development and now has 39 members – composed of island States and also low-lying States – like Suriname. Their Declaration therefore represents the agreed position of States from all over the globe. It is clear that the AOSIS Declaration is the result of close co-ordination with the Pacific Island Forum Members. In relation to the issue of maritime zones the September Declaration states that the Heads of State and Government of AOSIS:

> *Affirm* that there is no obligation under the United Nations Convention on the Law of the Sea to keep baselines and outer limits of maritime zones under review nor to update charts or lists of geographical coordinates once deposited with the Secretary-General of the United Nations,

and that,

> such maritime zones and the rights and entitlements that flow from them shall continue to apply without reduction, notwithstanding any physical changes connected to climate change-related sea-level rise.[66]

These declarations, coupled with growing State practice regarding the fixing of baselines, limits and boundaries presage a substantial evolution in the interpretation of the international law of the sea on these matters.

---

63 D. Freestone and C.H. Schofield, 'Pacific Islands Countries Declare Permanent Maritime Baselines, Limits and Boundaries', Current Legal Developments: The South Pacific, *International Journal of Marine and Coastal Law* (2021).

64 The Declaration highlights SIDS challenges and issues guidance on Climate Change, Sustainable Development, and Ocean issues. It is dated 21 September 2021. The authors are grateful to Professor Davor Vidas (chair of the ILA Committee) for bringing this Declaration to their attention.

65 The Declaration is published at AOSIS webpage, at https://www.aosis.org/launch-of-the-alliance-of-small-island-states-leaders-declaration/.

66 Ibid.

7 Conclusions

It is abundantly clear from the scientific literature that global mean sea levels are rising and the rate of sea level rise has escalated. Further, IPCC projected *likely* sea level rise projections do not to date factor in the potential disintegration of marine ice sheets and ice cliffs around Antarctica and the faster than currently projected dynamic ice loss from the Greenland ice sheet due to the deep uncertainties relating to these processes.[67] This means that even more substantial increases in the scale and speed of sea level rise cannot be ruled out. Moreover, even if the scientific debate regarding the long-term persistence of atoll island features is, as yet, unsettled, there is little doubt that the impacts of climate change including sea level rise are likely to be most keenly felt by low-elevation atoll island archipelagic States for whom these are perceived as existential threats.

The level of threat was highlighted vividly during the COP26 negotiations in Glasgow in November 2021 when the Foreign Minister of Tuvalu, Simon Kofe, delivered an address whilst standing knee deep in the ocean of an area that had previously been land and is now submerged. During his address he commented that "We are actually looking at legal avenues where we can retain our ownership of our maritime zones [and] retain our recognition as a state under international law."[68] This statement is consistent with the clear and consistent practice the Pacific Island States as well as other threatened island States. It is clear from this practice as well as high-level diplomatic statements such as the Pacific Islands Leaders Declaration, that island States, including atoll island archipelagic States, are intent on retaining their maritime entitlements.

This is an area where the progressive development of the international law of the sea is very much a 'work-in-progress'. There is now therefore a substantial body of declared practice regarding the interpretation of the obligations contained in the LOSC regarding maritime zones. in large part driven by the practice of small island developing States that are most vulnerable to the impacts of sea level rise This includes low-lying atoll island archipelagic States whose archipelagic status, maritime entitlement and, indeed, statehood are in peril. But the reactions of the general international community to these developments will be crucial.

While the majority of other States appear sympathetic to the plight of low-lying small island developing States in particular, there remains some diversity

67 IPCC, 2021, at TS-45.

68 "Tuvalu seeks to retain statehood if it sinks completely as sea levels rise", *The Guardian*, 11 November 2021.

in views.[69] Further, there is growing realization that there are very few coastal States whose coastline and coastal infrastructure will not be adversely affected over the next few decades by the impacts of the levels of sea level rise that the IPCC is now predicting. It remains to be seen whether these perspectives will shift as the climate crisis becomes ever more apparent, yielding broad acceptance of the interpretation advocated by the Pacific Island States and others, and thus securing the archipelagic status and entitlements of atoll island States.

69 See 2020 UN Sixth Committee Debates referenced above at n 53.

CHAPTER 8

"Archipelagic Spratlys": China's Desperate Attempt to Preserve Expansionist Policy?

Henry S. Bensurto Jr.

Following[1] the 2016 South China Sea Arbitration, Professor Alexander L. Vuving wrote: "*By clarifying the legal status of most of the South China Sea, the ruling goes a long way in shedding light as to which actions were lawful and unlawful.*"[2] He concluded,

> In one stroke, a tribunal verdict has shifted the strategic landscape in the South China Sea. The ruling puts an *end to the age of ambiguity* that has characterized the game nations have been playing in the South China Sea for decades. It also creates the conditions for a more binary configuration of how states line up on the issue. Although the tribunal has no army to enforce its verdict, its decision has legitimacy. And those who directly benefit from the ruling will try their best to make it enforceable.[3]

On 12 July 2016, The Hague-based *ad hoc* Arbitral Tribunal that was constituted 3 years earlier in 2013 under Part XV and Annex VII of the United Nations Convention on the Law of the Sea (UNCLOS) issued its ruling on the merits of the case *The South China Sea Arbitration* (*The Republic of the Philippines vs. The People's Republic of China*).[4]

The Tribunal invalidated China's claim for historic waters in its 9-dash line map.[5] It likewise clarified the character of the relevant features in the Spratlys

1 The opinions expressed herein are the author's personal views and do not in any way represent the views of his Institution.

2 Alexander L. Vuving, Professor at the Daniel K. Inouye Asia-Pacific Center for Security Studies https://thediplomat.com/2016/07/why-the-south-china-sea-ruling-is-a-game-changer/.

3 Ibid.

4 The members of the Arbitral Tribunal were Judge Thomas A. Mensah (President), Judge Jean Pierre-Cot, Judge Stanislaw Pawlak, Prof. Alfred Soons, and Judge Rüdiger Wolfrum. Details and materials on the case may be accessed at www.pca-cpa.org/en/cases/7/.

5 Award, PCA Case No 2013–19, In the Matter of the South China Sea Arbitration Before an Arbitral Tribunal Constituted Under Annex II to the 1982 United Nations Convention on the Law of the Sea Between the Republic of the Philippines and the People's Republic of China, 12 July 2016, p. 111–116.

© HENRY S. BENSURTO JR., 2023 | DOI:10.1163/9789004518629_009

and Panatag Shoal (Scarborough Shoal). None of the relevant features in the Spratlys including Itu Aba[6] and Scarborough Shoal[7] qualifies as an island under Article 121 of UNCLOS.[8] The Philippines' exclusive sovereign rights over the EEZ and Continental Shelf including Recto Bank (Reed Bank) under UNCLOS were unequivocally affirmed.[9]

As a result, the area in the South China Sea that China claimed has been significantly reduced. In other words, the vast sea space including some reefs and shoals that may otherwise be considered disputed because of China's claim absent an arbitration is now unquestionably beyond dispute as China could not claim them under international law, specifically UNCLOS.[10]

The Spratlys alone comprise no more than 5 km^2 of land feature, and more than 410,000 km^2 of maritime space. This entire area used to be disputed because of the 9-dash line claim of China and the lack of clarity on the extent of maritime entitlements that each of the relevant features in the Spratlys are entitled to. Ambiguities both in the claim of China and the character of the relevant features cloaked China's aggressive assertion over the entire area with some semblance of legitimacy. As a result of the 2016 Ruling, China's supposed "*right*" to dispute is now significantly reduced to the 5 km^2 of land feature plus the 12 NM Territorial Sea that may be individually appropriate on the relevant features. In effect, only about 13,000 km^2 out of the more than 410,000 km^2 sea space in the Spratlys which would otherwise be wholly disputed without arbitration, now remains disputed.[11]

Likewise, on the maritime side of the Philippines, about 500,000 km^2 out of the 550,000 km^2 of its EEZ was impacted by the 9-dash line claim of China together with the ambiguous character of the features in the Spratlys. With arbitration, about 540,000 km^2 of the Philippines' EEZ is now unambiguously out of any dispute from China including Recto Bank. Only about 13,000 km^2 remains arguably disputed because of the relevant land features in the Spratlys.[12]

---

6 Ibid., pp. 253–254.

7 Ibid., pp. 143–144.

8 Ibid., pp. 143–174.

9 Ibid., pp. 261–286.

10 "With these key judgments, a vast swath of the South China Sea is legally no longer disputed. The ruling has in fact reduced the disputed area from more than 80 percent of the South China Sea to less than 20 percent of it. What remains under dispute is now only pockets of 12-nm radius circles from the disputed features, plus the overlapping areas of the EEZs from the mainland of the coastal states.", Vuving, *Op. Cit.*

11 Figures are approximations using the Geographic Information System (GIS).

12 Ibid.

And although the South China Sea Arbitration is legally binding only on the Philippines and China as parties to the arbitration, nonetheless its implications go beyond the two countries. The ruling likewise has implications on the other littoral States impacted by the expansive claim of China as well as the other user-States which traverse the South China Sea under the freedom of navigation. If China's 9-dash line claim has no legitimacy *vis-à-vis* the Philippines because it is inherently invalid, then it must arguably have no legitimacy as well *vis-à-vis* the EEZ and Continental Shelves of the other littoral States. In the same manner, it will also have no legitimacy on the High Seas in the 'doughnut hole' of the South China Sea. Accordingly, these maritime areas could now be considered as being beyond what China could claim under international law. If such is the case, then the total sea space cleared from the expansive claim of China would be much more than the 500,000 km^2 EEZ of the Philippines.

More significantly, the 2016 Arbitral Ruling stripped China of any legal justification for its expansionist claim and creeping assertion in the South China Sea and the West Philippine Sea. Absent such legal cover, China's creeping assertion simply amounts to nothing but pure and simple aggression. Should China persist on pursuing the same course of action despite the 2016 Ruling, such action would constitute a violation of the *jus cogens* principle of international law against the use of force or threat of use of force.

Suddenly China is faced with a difficult policy dilemma. *How would China behave towards the Arbitral Ruling? What would be its attitude in the South China Sea in light of the 2016 Arbitral Ruling? Will it eventually comply with the 2016 Arbitral Ruling and behave responsibly?* It appears that China would have three possible policy responses: ONE, to recognize and comply with the Arbitral Ruling as a responsible member of the international community (*Rule Of Law Approach*); TWO, to continue with its belligerent attitude and not recognize the 2016 Arbitral Ruling in utter disregard of the rule of law, and continue with its creeping assertion without legal justification (*Power Politics or 'Who Cares' Approach*); or THREE, to not recognize the arbitration, continue with its creeping assertion but justifying the same under another 'international law' principle (*Hybrid Power Politics and Rule of Law Approach*).

Instead of honorably and humbly accepting the outcome of the Arbitration as India did in its dispute with Myanmar, China's policy response was to not recognize the ruling, undermine its enforcement, continue with its creeping assertion, cloak its expansive claim within a new legal framework of Archipelagic Concept and straight baselines, and try to preserve them within the context of bilateral mechanism and the proposed regional Code of Conduct.

This paper will try to examine China's policy response to the *South China Sea Arbitration* and the 2016 Arbitral Ruling. To do this, it will *first*, attempt to discuss the 2016 Ruling of the Tribunal and then examine its implications for China's policy agenda in the South China Sea; *second*, it will attempt to discuss China's policy response to arbitration including its effort to treat the Spratlys as a single entity capable of archipelagic baselines under Article 46 and 47 as well as the use of straight baselines under Article 7 of UNCLOS, in order to keep as much sea space within its claim which had otherwise been ruled as part of the Exclusive Economic Zone and Continental Shelf of the Philippines. In this respect, the Paper takes the view that the letter and spirit of Articles 46 and 47 as well as Article 7 preclude China from availing itself of those provisions. The Paper will also attempt to examine how China is trying to preserve its expansionist agenda and creeping assertion within the context of the ongoing discussions on the proposed ASEAN-China Code of Conduct. But before an analysis of China's policy response could be made reasonably, a prior understanding of China's expansionist policy and creeping assertion – main drivers to China's policy response – would be necessary. In this regard, this paper takes the view that the 9-dash line map was never the reason for China's creeping assertion. China's expansionist policy and creeping assertion preceded the 2009 interpretation of China's 1947 9-dash line map. Lacking any other viable legal justification to protest the Unilateral and Joint Submission for Extended Continental Shelf of Malaysia and Vietnam in 2009, China interpreted in haste the 1947 map to protest the said submission and to rationalize its expansionist policy and provide legal cover to its creeping assertion in the South China Sea. This paper takes the perspective that the real driver behind China's creeping assertion in the South China Sea is its expansionist policy. Thus, China did not participate in the arbitration to allow itself the flexibility of being able to question the outcome later, which it actually did especially when the arbitral result was not in its favor. Initially premised on making the South China Sea a sphere of influence and security buffer, that hegemonic policy has quickly taken a drastic paradigm shift from breaking US containment of China within the first-island chain and towards attaining strategic parity with the United States by using the South China Sea as a springboard for its nuclear-powered submarines capable of launching intermediate nuclear missiles into the continental United States. By doing so, China could achieve real deterrence against First Strike possibilities from the United States. Corollarily, a prior understanding of the international community's response to China's expansionist policy and creeping assertion prior to arbitration is likewise important especially as the region and the world assess their options *vis-à-vis* China's attempt to preserve its hegemonic policy behind the archipelagic concept. In this respect, the Paper takes the view that appeasement contributed to the escalation of the China's expansionist and aggressive mindset. That said, this paper would then be in a better position to make a reasonable analysis leading hopefully to some policy prescriptions in its conclusion.

1 China's Expansionist Policy & Creeping Assertion

The Philippines filed the suit in 2013 against China in light of the latter's claim of "*indisputable sovereignty*" and jurisdiction over almost the entire South China Sea as expressed in its 9-dash line map. On the basis of that claim, China interfered with the Philippines' right to exclusively explore and exploit its resources in its 200 NM Exclusive Economic Zone (EEZ) and Continental Shelf.

The freedom of the Philippines, and for that matter all the other littoral States in the semi-enclosed sea, to peacefully explore and exploit their own resources is seriously threatened by China's expansionist policy and creeping assertion in the West Philippine Sea and South China Sea.

Although there exists a territorial dispute between the Philippines and China (together with other States such as Vietnam, Malaysia, and Brunei) on some or all the relevant features[13] in the Spratlys, and a maritime dispute on their overlapping EEZ and Continental Shelf north of Luzon, the real serious threat to peace and even to the existential interest of the Philippines is the expansionist policy of China of preposterously expanding these limited disputes beyond where they may reasonably be[14] to areas where they legally ought not to be.[15]

In 2009, China for the first time officially declared to the world its claim to a vast area of the South China Sea in order to protest the unilateral and Joint Submissions of Vietnam and Malaysia for extended continental shelf in the semi-enclosed sea. It did so by attaching a 1947 Chinese map to its protest Note showing an arbitrary drawing of 9 dashes or dotted lines on the South China Sea map. The map *per se* indicates nothing. However, the covering Diplomatic Note implies that China exercises "*indisputable sovereignty and jurisdiction*" over all the areas enclosed by the 9-dotted line. In other words,

13 Rocks.

14 The overlap in their 200 NM EEZ north of Luzon and South of mainland China; Rock features in the Spratlys. The 9-dash line claim extended these disputes up to the limits of the 9-dotted lines.

15 Second Thomas Shoal, Mischief Reef and other low-tide elevations which form part of the Continental Shelf of the Philippines, Recto Bank, Areas 3 & 4, water surfaces that forms part of the Philippine EEZ.

the 9-dotted lines represent the extent of China's national jurisdiction in the South China Sea.

Unfortunately, the 9-dotted line goes beyond China's 200 NM EEZ and extends very deeply South into the 200 NM EEZ of the other littoral countries surrounding the semi-enclosed South China Sea including the Philippines, Malaysia, Brunei, Indonesia and Vietnam. This means that China shares ownership and jurisdiction with all the aforementioned coastal States in the overlapped areas. In effect, all of the affected States will have to share their resources with China. Put in another way, none of the affected States would have the unilateral right to explore and exploit resources found in the overlapped area, without China's approval or concurrence.

Accordingly, Vietnam and Malaysia cannot submit unilaterally or jointly a claim for an Extended Continental Shelf in the South China Sea since these are situated within the "*indisputable sovereignty or jurisdiction*" of China.

In the case of the Philippines, it cannot fish in its 200 NM EEZ or drill oil in its 200 NM Continental Shelf including Recto Bank without the consent of China. About 80 to 85 percent of the waters and continental shelves of the Philippines are impacted by this sweeping claim of China.

All the affected countries obviously do not agree with China's claim. From their perspectives, China's claim is not just expansive. It is also preposterous and devoid of any legal basis. Amid the protestations of all the affected States, China has been asserting its absurd claim in a creeping manner. Strangely, China's assertion very much preceded the official announcement of its claim, which was represented by its self-serving and legally-irrelevant 1947 map.[16]

As early as the 1970s, China forcibly took control of the Paracels from Vietnam.[17] In the 1980s, China went down South in the Spratlys and took control of the Fiery Cross Reef after a naval battle with Vietnam, which resulted in the death of 72 Vietnamese.[18] Then in the 1990s, China began occupying Mischief Reef, which is about 126 M from the coast of the Philippine island of Palawan.

16 This is the reason why the 1947 9-dotted line map is not the problem *per se*, but the expansionist ambition of the Communist Leadership of China. The map is being used as a convenient excuse by the leadership for its real expansionist agenda. "Grab now, Explain Later" creeping policy.

17 Marwyn Samuels, *Contest for the South China Sea* (New York and London: Methuen, 1982), at 100–101.

18 Mark J. Valencia, Jon M. Van Dyke, and Noel A. Ludwig, *Sharing the Resources of the South China Sea* (Honolulu: University of Hawaii Press, 1997), at 21–22.

A seeming pause in China's assertion ensued with the conclusion of the ASEAN-China "*Declaration of Conduct of Parties in the South China Sea*" (DOC) in 2002. China used the DOC to legitimize its new *status quo*, consolidate gains, and cloth its otherwise invalid claim with some semblance of basis and implied recognition (at least of the existence of a dispute which would otherwise not be so as the claim is empty *ab initio*) by ASEAN. On this ground, China really never stopped with its creeping assertion.

The assertion continued in a quiet manner with the aggrieved country being forced to suffer in silence the impact of such assertion within the confines of its bilateral dialogue with China. China was obviously using bilateral dialogue as a trap to suppress the noise of its oppressive assertion from spilling into the international arena. During this time, China was telling the Philippines that it cannot exploit Recto Bank without violating the DOC. China's approval was also asserted as necessary before the Philippines could proceed with any development of the area. It proposed joint development of the Philippines' Recto Bank as the way forward.

With the official announcement of its 9-dash line map in 2009, China stepped up its creeping assertion. This time, China's assertion became more intense, aggressive, and wider in coverage: harassment of vessels in the Recto Bank (Reed Bank) continental shelf (2010);[19] laying of claim on Philippine oil blocks 3 and 4 (2011); forcible occupation of Philippines' Scarborough Shoal (Bajo de Masinloc) (2012); imposition of fishing bans on Vietnam and Philippines' EEZs (2012);[20] frequent sovereignty patrols along the area covered by its 9-dash line claim;[21] use of water cannons and other harassment tactics to forcefully drive away Filipino fishermen from Bajo de Masinloc;[22] public bidding of 9 oil blocks within the EEZ of Vietnam (2012); show of force in the James Shoal in the coast of Malaysia and Brunei (2013);[23] naval blockade on the Philippines' Second Thomas Shoal (Ayungin Shoal);[24] deployment of an oil

19 Simone Orendain, "Philippines Says China Harassed Oil Exploration Vessel," 4 March 2011, at http://www.voanews.com/content/philippines-says-china-harrassed-oil-exploration-vessel-117457638/136022.html.

20 "China starts annual South China Sea fishing ban," *English.xinhua.cn*, 16 May 2013, at http://news.xinhuanet.com/english/china/2013-05/16/c_132386383.htm.

21 Paterno Esmaquel III, "Philippines slams China over 'sovereignty patrols", *Rappler.com*, 18 August 2014, at http://www.rappler.com/nation/66582-philippines-china-sovereignty-patrols-recto-bank.

22 http://www.bbc.com/news/world-asia-26320383.

23 "Chinese navy flexes muscles in South China Sea," March 27, 2013, at http://archive.news10.net/news/national/238097/5/Chinese-navy-flexes-muscle-in-South-China-Sea.

24 Jaime Sinapit and Pots de Leon, "Chinese vessels harass, but fail to stop, resupply mission for PH Navy ship at Ayungin Shoal, " *InterAksyon.com*, 29 March 2014, at

rig off Vietnam's EEZ (2014);[25] ramming of other littoral States' vessels in the South China Sea;[26] and, massive conversion of reefs into artificial islands in the Spratlys, including Gavin Reef, Fiery Cross Reef, Johnson Reef, Calderon Reef, Subi Reef and Mischief Reef (2014–2015).

1.1 *International Dilemma: Appeasement vs. Rule of Law*

Amid China's aggression, two main divergent international views have emerged. One view is more accommodating to China's expansive claim and overlooks the dangers of its aggressive assertion. It sees no urgency in the resolution of territorial or maritime disputes, and seems to consider that the interests of the weaker littoral countries are not so vital as to elicit a firmer international response. This perspective regards international law as important but is likely to overlook its application for politically expedient reasons. Because of its resemblance to the original Appeasement policy of former British Prime Minister Neville Chamberlain in the 1940s, it may be referred to as Neo-Appeasement or the New Appeasement.

Another is a perspective that puts emphasis on the full and decisive application of international law in the resolution of disputes in the South China Sea. While this approach recognizes and encourages the peaceful rise of China and the opportunities brought about by its development, it does not accept the thinking that China's rapid development can be used as an excuse to disregard international law in asserting what it thinks is its rightful claim. Every country, big or small, must abide by the rule of law.[27] Because of its adherence on the

---

http://www.interaksyon.com/article/83734/chinese-vessel-harasses-but-fails-to-stop-resupply-mission-for-brp-sierra-madre-at-ayungin.

25 Chris Brummit, "Vietnam tries to stop China oil rig deployment," May 7, 2014, at http://www.usatoday.com/story/news/world/2014/05/07/vietnam-china-oil-rig/8797007/.

26 Vu Trong Khanh and Nguyen Anh Thu, "Vietnam, China Trade Accusations of Vessel-Ramming Near Oil Rig," June 24, 2014, at http://www.wsj.com/articles/vietnam-china-trade-accusations-of-vessel-ramming-near-oil-rig-in-south-china-sea-1403608970; Sharon Tiezzi, "Philippines accuses China of ramming boats in South China sea," *The Diplomat,* February 5, 2015, at http://thediplomat.com/2015/02/philippines-accuses-china-of-ramming-boats-in-south-china-sea.

27 As President Barack Obama has stated, "Obviously, with a huge population, a growing economy, we want to continue to encourage the peaceful rise of China. I think there's enormous opportunities for trade, development, working on common issues like climate change with China. But what we've also emphasized – and I will continue to emphasize throughout this trip – is that all of us have responsibilities to help maintain basic rules of the road and an international order so that large countries, small countries, all have to abide by what is considered just and fair, and that we are resolving disputes in peaceful fashion." President Barack Obama, Delivered at a Joint Press Conference with President Obama and Prime Minister Abe of Japan, Tokyo, Japan, April 24, 2015.

rules-based management and resolution of disputes, it may be called as the Rule of Law Approach.

1.2 *The Lure of Appeasement: False Sense of Peace*

Appeasement, the policy of making concessions to an opposing power to avoid conflict, is most often identified with the foreign policy of Prime Minister Neville Chamberlain as he dealt with Hitler's Germany from 1937–1939.[28]

The attitude of appeasement in the current context could perhaps be observed from the statement of former US Secretary of State Henry Kissinger[29] that *"The U.S. and China should look to the example of Deng Xiaoping when it comes to defusing China's territorial spats in the South China Sea."*[30] According to Kissinger, *"China and the U.S. should remove the urgency of the debate."* He added that *"Deng Xiaoping dealt with some of his problems by saying not every problem needs to be solved in the existing generation."* He said, *"Let's perhaps wait for another generation but let's not make it worse."*[31]

Unfortunately, this approach of appeasement and accommodation – though perhaps well-intentioned – became the genesis for China's continuing pattern of expansion and creeping assertion in the South China Sea. It all began with the much-celebrated US-China Rapprochement in 1972.

Against the backdrop of an escalating conflict in Vietnam in the late 60s to the 70s, the United States under President Richard Nixon explored ways of improving relations with the People's Republic of China. The thinking at the time was that improvements in the US-China relations would lessen the conflict between the United States and China; weaken the bond between the communist Parties from China, Vietnam, North Korea and the Union of Soviet Socialist Republic (USSR), and in the process isolate the government of North Vietnam. US Secretary of State Henry Kissinger shuttled between Beijing and

---

28 Frank McDonough, *Hitler, Chamberlain and Appeasement* (Cambridge Perspectives in History), (Cambridge University Press, 2002); Alice Mary Smyth (ed), *The Oxford Book of Quotations* (Oxford University Press, 1941). "Peace for our time" was a phrase spoken by Prime Minister Chamberlain on 30 September 1938 in his speech concerning the Munich Agreement after ceding Sudetenland to Nazi Germany. The lines read, "My good friends, for the second time in our history, a British Prime Minister has returned from Germany bringing peace with honour. I believe it is peace for our time."

29 Henry Kissinger was the Secretary of State during Richard Nixon's presidency. He was the architect of Nixon's historic 1972 trip to China that led to the opening of diplomatic ties between the two countries.

30 Sharon Chen and Andrea Tan, "Kissinger Urges Return to Deng's Way on South China Sea Spat," March 29, 2015, at http://www.bloomberg.com/news/articles/2015-03-29/u-s-should-use-deng-approach-in-south-china-sea-kissinger-says.

31 Ibid.

Washington DC to negotiate the terms of normalization of relations between the two countries.[32]

To pave the way for the full normalization of relations with China, the US supported China's entry and assumption of a seat in the UN Security Council. It also agreed on the one-China policy that recognizes Taiwan as part of China. With these major concessions, PROC's Mao Zedong received US President Nixon in Beijing during the latter's historic trip to China February 21–28, 1972. During that trip, the two governments signed the Shanghai Communique which articulated the aforementioned fundamental principles on the Taiwan issue.[33]

Indeed, US-China Rapprochement is a milestone in US-China relations. But it may also be a double-edge sword. On one hand, one may argue its positive impact in the de-escalation of tension between the US and China and the re-shaping of the Cold War, perhaps even of its demise. But on another, it may also have the unintended consequence of encouraging Chinese adventurism in the South China Sea with disastrous implications four decades afterwards.

On January 16, 1974, two years after the Nixon visit to China and the signing of the Shanghai Communique, China took advantage of the normalization in US-China relations and the downscaling of US presence in the South China Sea by launching an invasion of the Crescent Group in the Paracel Islands.[34] This area was previously held by Republic of Vietnam or South Vietnam. The Chinese takeover by force was a surprise. Prior to this, China had never taken any unilateral action that subverted the *status quo* in the Paracel Islands.[35] Despite being an ally to South Vietnam, the United States and practically the World cast a blind eye on China's actions.

Emboldened by its successful occupation of Paracels without international opposition, China continued with its creeping assertion in the South China Sea, methodically altering the status quo *via* a pattern of *"grab, pause & stay." First,* China grabs or occupies a limited piece of its neighbor's territory or maritime space. The grab is done either surreptitiously or by force. *Second,* China would then pause to observe international reaction. *Third,* when tension arises,

32 "Rapprochement with China, 1972", Office of the Historian, Foreign Service Institute, United States Department of State, https://history.state.gov/milestones/1969-1976/rapprochement-china.

33 Ibid.

34 Ngo Minh Tri and Koh Swee Lean Collin, "Lessons from the Battle of the Paracels Islands", *The Diplomat,* January 23, 2014, https://the diplomat.com/2014/01/lessons-from-the-battle-of-the-paracel-islands/.

35 "...the status quo ... the Amphitrite Group in the eastern Paracels and the Crescent Group were respectively under Chinese and Vietnamese control.", ibid.

China employs diplomacy not really for the purpose of resolving the source of tension but in order to deflect international attention and quiet down international uproar. Bilateral dialogue is used as the main diplomatic tool for this purpose. Accordingly, everything is forgotten in the spirit of *"friendship and good bilateral relations."* Tension goes down and everything seems to be back to normal. But China remains in possession of the territory or maritime space they just grabbed. *Fourth*, when everything appears to have quieted down, China then again proceeds to grab the next target territory and maritime space.

This pattern is repeated over and again. Each time, the existing *status quo* is altered and a new one is created. After a period of time, China would negotiate an agreement or a *modus vivendi* that legitimizes the new status quo. Ironically, the ASEAN-China DOC served this purpose in 2005. The future ASEAN-China Code of Conduct (COC) will also most likely legitimize the gains of China in the second phase of its creeping assertion after 2005 – the conversion of almost the entire South China Sea into a *"disputed area,"* takeover of Scarborough Shoal, and the construction and development of reefs into artificial islands in the Spratlys.

Thus, after more than four decades, the status quo in the South China Sea has been unilaterally altered by China – from the forced expulsion of the Vietnamese from the Paracels in the 70s, through the forced occupation of Fiery Cross Reef in the 80s, Mischief Reef in the 90s, Scarborough Shoal in 2012, and the massive conversion of reefs into artificial islands in the West Philippine Sea and the Spratlys.

Years from now, China will consolidate all these gains by using the international modality of acquiring territories which is *'Effectivite'* or Effective Jurisdiction. Luckily, the 2016 Arbitral ruling may have strategically pre-empted this China ambition.

In the final analysis, China's series of creeping assertion in the South China Sea and the West Philippines Sea became possible because of international apathy, accommodation and appeasement. The evil that appeasement sought to avoid is instead materializing and gaining significant momentum.

1.3 *Philippine Experience: The Paradox of Appeasement*

The Philippines also experimented with appeasement in its engagement with China. The experimentations may have arguably gained the Philippines some short-term tactical benefits but definitely caused it disastrous long-term strategic loss and disadvantages.

The Philippines first toyed with the idea in the late 1990s after China occupied Mischief Reef. Mischief Reef is a low-tide elevation about 126 nm off the Philippine Island of Palawan. Between 1994 to 1997, China surreptitiously surveyed, probed, and built structures in the Reef. When discovered, the Philippines initially took a robust stand against China and embarked on internationalizing the incident.

China applied soft diplomacy and convinced the Philippines to stop internationalizing. China urged the Philippines to engage instead in bilateral discussions. Having gained no ground and support from the international community including its ally, the United States, the Philippines relented and abandoned its initial policy of internationalizing China's occupation of Mischief Reef. Over a karaoke sing-along of "*Love me Tender*" by Elvis Presley and "*Let Me Call You Sweetheart*" aboard the Presidential yacht, BRP Ang Pangulo, between President Ramos and Premier Jiang Zemin, the matter of China's occupation of Mischief Reef was swept under the rug.[36] The issue quieted down and China remained in Mischief Reef. Today, the Reef is converted into an artificial island with military installations complete with an airstrip and concrete piers.

Appeasement was again adopted for the second time by the Philippines during the first half of President Gloria Macapagal Arroyo's Administration. Lured by the seeming calmness and friendly relations with China, the Philippine National Oil Company (PNOC) was allowed to enter into a Joint Marine Seismic Undertaking (JMSU) in 2005 with China's Chinese National Offshore Oil Corporation (CNOOC) and Vietnam's PetroVietnam for the joint survey of the Kalayaan Island Group (KIG). The Philippines took the false belief that with the warming of bilateral relations with China, the latter's expansionist ambition in the South China Sea and the West Philippines Sea had finally come to a stop. Somehow, the DOC with its provision on paragraph 5 also reinforced this false belief. Paragraph 5 of the DOC provides:

> The Parties undertake to exercise self-restraint in the conduct of activities that would complicate or escalate disputes and affect peace and stability including, among others refraining from action of inhabiting on the presently uninhabited islands, reefs, shoals, cays and other features and to handle their differences in a constructive manner.[37]

Unfortunately, this was not going to be the case. Soon after the JMSU took effect, China was invoking its provisions to tell the Philippines it cannot issue a license to a private company, British Forum, to drill oil or natural gas at Recto

36 Farolan, Ramon, "Mischief Reef – Where It All Started", *Philippine Daily Inquirer*, https://opinion.inquirer.net/140311/mischief-reef-where-it-all-started.

37 https://humanrightsinasean.info/wp-content/uploads/files/documents/Declaration_on_the_Conduct_of_Parties_in_the_South_China_Sea_0.pdf.

Bank. Doing so would also violate the spirit of the DOC, according to China. When the Philippines refused to renew the JMSU after it lapsed in 2008, China shifted to another reasoning in telling the Philippines it could not unilaterally develop Recto Bank. This time, China said that Recto Bank is a disputed area. When asked why it is disputed, China's reply was that because the latter has a claim on it. When asked about the basis for such claim, it did not give any more explanation except to say that its claim is historic in nature without giving any further details.

By that time, it was becoming clear that China is now unilaterally broadening the area of dispute by arbitrarily expanding its claim. China's claim is no longer confined to the rock features (above water at all times) in the Spratlys and as well as the low-tide elevations (visible during low tide, but disappears during high tide) in the western continental shelf of the Philippines such as Mischief Reef. China was also now claiming completely submerged areas outside of the Spratlys and within the Philippines' 200 NM Continental Shelf.

Suddenly, Recto Bank is a "*disputed*" area, only because China says so. As a "*disputed*" area, the Philippines could not develop it unilaterally. The Philippines therefore must negotiate with China for the future of Recto Bank. In order to avoid conflict while at the same time appearing as a magnanimous neighbor, China would use Deng Xiaoping's formula of setting aside disputes and engage in cooperation. Specifically, China is proposing joint development of Recto Bank by the Philippines and China to manage the alleged "*dispute*" on the Reef. By laying claim on Recto Bank and creating an appearance of a dispute, China is now able to leverage for itself free access to resources in an area that would otherwise be only for the exclusive benefit of the Philippines.

Later, China would also lay claim and dispute Philippine oil blocks 3 & 4, which are 36 and 34 NM away respectively from Palawan.

The third time the Philippines played appeasement with China was during the administration of President Rodrigo Duterte. Immediately after taking office in June 2016, the Duterte Government warmed relations with China. Later, the Government would project mixed signals regarding the rulings of the Arbitral Tribunal after its publication on July 12, 2016, affirming it on one point then downplaying it on another; resume bilateral dialogue with China; distance itself from the Philippines' traditional ally, the United States; and abandon internationalization of China's aggression in the South China Sea within and outside of ASEAN. The Administration would later call this new foreign policy approach "*Independent Foreign Policy*."

Yet, despite the government's "*Independent Foreign Policy*" and the warming of relations with China, the latter's expansion and aggression in the South China Sea never stopped. On the contrary, China became more aggressive, open, and intense. Towards the latter part of the Duterte Administration, the Government specifically its Foreign Affairs Secretary Teodoro Locsin and Secretary of Defense Delfin Lorenzana took a much firmer stance on the matter.

Based on the Philippine experience, one could observe that appeasement may allow a temporary de-escalation or lull in tension, but its long-term consequence may be much worse, for it allows a tyrannical mindset to develop unscathed and turn into a dangerous habit of unfettered bullying and aggression.

1.4 *Appeasement: Lessons from the Past*

Clearly, appeasement has not worked. Appeasement did not work in the past.[38] It is still not working now. It will also not work in the future.

China is still going full speed with its creeping assertion. Even more intensely and with impunity and with no end in sight. In a manner of speaking, it was no longer subtle (e.g., when it occupied Mischief Reef in the 1990s), but more blatant in its creeping assertion (e.g., open grab of Scarborough, massive island building, sovereign patrols, etc.). The Philippines and the other littoral States

---

38 Driven by Adolf Hitler's ambitious expansionist agenda, Germany rebuilt its military despite the prohibitions of the Treaty of Versailles. From 1936 to 1938, Germany remilitarized the Rhineland and 'united' with Austria. In September 1938, Hitler demanded that Sudetenland, a region in Czechoslovakia with a large ethnic German population, be handed over to Germany. Great Britain took the cudgels of negotiating with Germany. British Prime Minister Neville Chamberlain met with Hitler at Berchtesgaden on 15 September 1938 to resolve the Sudetenland problem. Without discussing with the Czech, Chamberlain pledged to give Germany all areas of Sudetenland with a German population of more than 50 per cent. Hitler agreed, but later on increased his demands and asked for all of Sudetenland. The Munich Agreement signed on 29 September 1938 stated that Germany would receive Sudetenland but would leave the rest of the Czech Republic alone. The Munich agreement became the symbol of the policy of appeasement. The mood at the time is often imputed for the choice of policy. Lingering memories of the First World War had left Europe war weary. Chamberlain's policy of appeasement was born of a desire to avoid armed conflict. He spoke of this in his famous statement broadcast on radio on 27 September 1938: "I am myself a man of peace to the depths of my soul; armed conflict between nations is a nightmare to me … War is a fearful thing." Moreover, neither Britain nor France was ready for war military-wise. The economic hardship from the Great Depression, combined with a generally pacifist public sentiment, did not create a favorable environment for rearmament. By 13 March 1939, Germany violated the Munich Agreement by invading the rest of Czechoslovakia. On 01 September 1939, Germany attacked Poland. Honoring their promise to come to Poland's aid in case of Nazi aggression, Great Britain and France declared war on Germany on 03 September 1939. Chamberlain's so-called "peace for our time" turned out to be short-lived and eventually led to the most devastating war in human history.

in the South China Sea have lost significant grounds and are struggling furiously to try to recover what was lost and preserve what is left of their seas and reefs. Freedom of navigation and overflights in the South China Sea are more at risk now than during World War II. The US is doing more and deploying more assets in and around the South China Sea to keep these sea-lanes of communication open to navigation and unhampered flow of goods. As a result, the peoples of the region now live in a more tense environment. Many thanks to appeasement.

There are several theories as to why appeasement failed that we could ponder upon in the present context. Hans Morgenthau (1967), renowned scholar of political realism, regards appeasement as *"a corrupted policy of compromise, made erroneous by mistaking a policy of imperialism for a policy of the status quo."*[39] By offering Czechoslovakia, Britain and France expected to satisfy Hitler enough to settle for the *status quo*. In reality, Hitler would not settle for less than the world. Moreover, they believed Germany would act in good faith and keep its promises. It is apparent now that Germany had no interest in the *status quo* other than to break it.

For a nation with an expansionist agenda, small 'sacrifices' – even offerings of small countries – are never enough. In Morgenthau's (1967) words, *"Successive demands are but links of a chain at the end of which stands the overthrow of the status quo."*[40]

While nations continue to appease China on the belief that it would change its ambitions, China has been building artificial structures and fortifying its military presence in "disputed waters." Inarguably, these acts are deliberate attempts to change the *status quo* right under the world's nose.

It is worth contemplating whether or not the appeasing side even has the capability to satiate the opposing party's demands in the first place. JL Richardson (1988) opines that *"the fundamental reason for the failure of appeasement was that Hitler's goals lay far beyond the limits of reasonable accommodation that the appeasers were prepared to contemplate."*[41] This was a problem with Hitler, whose demands are essentially too large to fulfill.

China's claim is not exactly world domination, but the territory and natural resources within its vaunted nine-dash-line comes close. It overlaps many interests, not only of the claimants themselves but also those of major powers

39 Hans Morgenthau, *Politics among Nations: The Struggle for Power and Peace*, 4th ed, (New York: Knopf, 1967).

40 *Ibid.*

41 J.L. Richardson, "'New Perspectives on Appeasement: Some Implications for International Relations," *World Politics*, Vol. 40, No. 3, (Cambridge University Press, 1988), pp. 289–316.

with respect to their security and economic interests in the region. Moreover, the South China Sea is a major shipping lane where more than half of the world's annual merchant fleet tonnage (roughly USD 5.3 trillion in commodities) passes through.[42] It is not something easily offered in a box with a bow.

Another problem with appeasement is that it causes belligerent nations to grow more brazen. China is obviously not the Germany of the past. However, China's creeping assertion in the South China Sea and the West Philippine Sea is eerily reminiscent of Germany and Italy in the pre-WWII years. Hitler and Mussolini realized that its neighbors were determined to avoid confrontation, and thus continued to test their limits with initially tentative and then increasingly flagrant violations of international norms. In October 1935, Mussolini invaded Abyssinia with little more than token sanctions from the League of Nations. In March 1936, Hitler blatantly violated the Treaty of Versailles by remilitarizing the Rhineland, again without facing the expected reprisal from the British and the French. During the Spanish Civil War, Germany and Italy sent military troops and assets to rebels despite a standing Non-Intervention Agreement.[43] Impotent responses from the international community showed Nazi Germany that they had a very wide berth when it comes to employing normally unacceptable behavior. Steve Chan (1984) believes that "their concession – made at the expense of their ally Czechoslovakia – appears only to have whetted Hitler's appetite for additional territory. According to the appeasement theory of war, World War II might have been averted if the democracies had been more resolute in their opposition to Hitler's earlier aggressions. The moral of the lesson of Munich is that appeasement discredits the defenders' willingness to fight, and encourages the aggressor to escalate his demands."[44]

Over the past decades, countries continue to accommodate China. ASEAN has also done so to a significant degree. The United States is notable in that despite its collective security agreement with the Philippines under the 1947 Mutual Defense Treaty, it kept a blind eye on China's expansionism multiple times, i.e., China's occupation of Fiery Cross Reef, Mischief Reef and Scarborough Shoal. After the Scarborough Shoal fiasco, the US began to

42 United Nations Conference on Trade and Development (UNCTAD), *Review of Maritime Transport 2011*, as cited in U.S. Energy Information Administration, 'Analysis Brief, The South China Sea,' February 7, 2013, <http://www.eia.gov/countries/regions-topics.cfm?fips=scs>.

43 Frank McDonough, *Hitler, Chamberlain and Appeasement (Cambridge Perspectives in History)* (Cambridge University Press, 2002).

44 Steve Chan, *International Relations in Perspective: The Pursuit of Security, Welfare and Justice*, (New York: Macmillan, 1984), at 88–89. Britain and Czechoslovakia were not allies.

undergo a paradigm shift in its policy approach *vis-à-vis* China's expansionist policy and creeping assertion which by this time had spilled over into the East China Sea over the Senkaku Island with Japan.

It is worth noting that decades of this approach have not resulted in less aggressive behavior in the South China Sea or the East China Sea. In fact, it seems to have bolstered China's assertiveness and encouraged threatening language towards the region. Continuing to appease China is unlikely to change, much less improve its behavior, especially when escalating belligerence is consistently met with mild reproaches from the international community.

Perhaps it is easy for certain nations to opt for appeasement towards China because of distance and detachment. During Chamberlain's time, Hitler's designs on Czechoslovakia was a major concern yet remains the problem of 'the other.' This distinct uncoupling is reflected in Chamberlain's words when he called the crisis *"a quarrel in a faraway country, between people of whom we know nothing."*[45] No country expects another state to be its keeper. However, we live in an interconnected world where promoting and maintaining a stable and rules-based environment – one where states abide by certain normative behavior and do not just claim whatever territory they desire – is in *everyone's* interest. The eventual war in Europe despite the Czech matter being simply a quarrel in a "faraway country" is a fine example of why nations should care for another's troubles. This is even more evident in our time, where geographic stability reaps economic dividends not only for individual countries but for entire regions. Even more apropos is this scenario where many of the nations involved are connected *via* a formal "ASEAN Community" as full members and dialogue partners. *Where is the sense of community, and how should such stakeholders behave when the region is on the precipice of regressing into an environment driven by brute might rather than rule of law?*

The region and the rest of the world would benefit from a peaceful, rules-based environment. Similarly, no one gains from having an empowered and increasingly belligerent power. There are no dividends to be had in allowing a blossoming region to transform into one that allows blatant disregard of internationally accepted norms. Belligerent behaviour should not be fostered with appeasement, because this will only encourage an even more aggressive behaviour. When the region finally does reach its 'breaking point,' it may be too late.

---

45 Broadcast (27 September 1938), quoted in "Prime Minister on the Issues", *The Times* (28 September 1938), at 10.

1.5 *Rule of Law: Peace Not Appeasement*

Therefore, for a small country like the Philippines, the choice is clear. True peace in the South China Sea must be anchored on the rule of law. Rule of law is the supremacy of international law in the conduct of inter-state relations; it is the maxim that constrains states in their behavior *vis-a-vis* each other.[46]

From the Philippine perspective, rule of law in the South China Sea context is the respect for relevant applicable international law, particularly the universally-recognized "Constitution for the Oceans" – the UN Convention on the Law of the Sea (UNCLOS). UNCLOS provides a comprehensive regime in the use and management of the seas and oceans. It sets out the legal framework which serves as the basis of the legitimate maritime entitlements and maritime rights of coastal States. A country cannot claim maritime rights that go beyond the rights accorded by the UNCLOS. Therefore, China's 9-dash line claim which encroaches on the legitimate maritime entitlements of other littoral States in the South China Sea contravenes UNCLOS.

Rule of law also refers to the observance and respect of international norms, particularly the norms of conduct and principles that are designed to manage disputes such as the peaceful resolution of disputes, non-use or threat of use of force, and sovereign equality. Rule of law likewise means respect for the institutions and mechanisms that have been established to implement and promote international law such as the dispute settlement mechanism under UNCLOS including arbitration.

Ironically, China uses international law as pretext for its expansive claims and aggression on the territorial and maritime spaces of others. China's leadership has invoked the international legal concept of historic rights allegedly evinced by its 1947 map. All the littoral States in the semi-enclosed sea impacted by that claim obviously disagree with China also on the basis of international law including UNCLOS. Therefore, a clarification of these conflicting rights by the same measure of international law that China uses to justify its actions may perhaps help de-escalate the tension and allow the Philippines to enjoy its own maritime space and resources. As Johann Wolfgang von Goethe once observed, *"And the law can only bring us freedom."*[47]

The hope is that an arbitral clarification may bring back sense to China to behave within the limits of international law. This hope, however, is based on

---

46 Renata Gianini in the Issue brief "The Rule of Law: State Sovereignty vs. International Obligations," GA Sixth Committee (Legal) 2010, at http://al.odu.edu/mun/docs/Issue%20brief%202010,%20The%20rule%20of%20law.pdf.

47 Bartlett, John, *Familiar Quotations*, 14th Edition, published by Little, Brown and Co., 1968, p. 479.

the assumptions that China sincerely believes in the lawfulness of its current actions, and that its actions are impelled by international law, meaning that the Chinese believe that the reason why they are in the waters of others is because they have a better right to be in those seas.

But what if this belief is not sincere? What if international law is not really the reason why China is doing what it is doing? What if China merely uses international law or its interpretation as mere instrument to cover its real intention? What if the real reason is really to expand and control the South China Sea and gain free access to the resources of its littoral neighbors? Does this make Arbitration a futile exercise? Does it mean that the Philippines should not have taken the pain of filing and going through Arbitration?

The author believes otherwise. It is with more reason that Arbitration should be pursued. The Philippines was right in pursuing this course of action. If indeed expansionism and power politics are the real compulsion for China's actions, then Arbitration was a correct path to take. As Abraham Lincoln once said, "*Let us have faith that right makes might, and in that faith let us to the end dare to do our duty as we understand it.*"[48]

But the mere filing of arbitration and the subsequent issuance of its ruling are not enough. We must also all work with a strong sense of urgency and resolve for its enforcement. This is not just for the Philippines, but the international community. As former US President Franklin Delano Roosevelt once observed:

> The epidemic of world lawlessness is spreading. When an epidemic of physical disease starts to spread, the community approves and joins in a quarantine of the patients in order to protect the health of the community against the spread of the disease .... The will for peace on the part of the peace-loving nations must express itself to the end that nations that may be tempted to violate their agreements and the rights of others will desist from such a course. There must be positive endeavors to preserve peace.[49]

To do nothing would be negatively consequential. We and the rest of the world will pay a high price if we neglect this responsibility. As John Locke articulated more than 300 years ago in his *Second Treatise of Government* in 1690: "*Wherever*

48 Abraham Lincoln, Farewell Address, Springfield, Illinois [February 11, 1861], Bartlett, John, *Familiar Quotations*, 14th Edition, published by Little, Brown and Co., 1968, p. 636.

49 President Franklin Delano Roosevelt, the *"Quarantine the aggressor"* speech, Chicago [October 5, 1937], Bartlett, John, *Familiar Quotations*, 14th Edition, published by Little, Brown and Co., 1968, p. 971–972.

Law ends, Tyranny begins."[50] This would be repeated by William Pitt, Earl of Chatham in 1770: "*Unlimited power is apt to corrupt the minds of those who possess it; and this I know, my lords, that where laws end, tyranny begins*."[51]

Tyranny is a mindset. It is a contagion. It is also addicting, especially when it meets no opposition. Unopposed, China's aggression in the South China Sea will not stop there. Potentially, such mindset will carry over in its conduct of foreign relations elsewhere.

A case in point was China's aggressive assertion in the Senkaku Islands following its successful takeover by force of the Philippines' Scarborough Shoal, 124 NM off Luzon. In April 2012, China wrested control of Scarborough Shoal from the Philippines by initially provoking the latter with Chinese fishing vessels poaching in the Shoal, followed by a Chinese white vessel coming to their aid, allegedly in response to their harassment by the Philippine Navy. Not too far away from the area was a grey PLA big ship. Eventually, multiple fishing vessels manned by PLA personnel squeezed the lone Philippine Coast Guard vessel and the Philippine civilian research vessel into moving out of the area. This became known as the "Cabbage Strategy."[52] This same strategy was employed by China immediately thereafter on the Senkaku Islands, which are occupied and administered by Japan but disputed by China. Japan, however, stood firm and employed forces to repel Chinese attempts. The United States also stood by Japan. China relented. The Senkaku islands thus remained in the hands of Japan.

It is thus important for China not to fall into this mindset as such a mindset is dangerous. It creates an opportunity for war and suffering. Just the thought of it is dreadful. A strong international voice and solidarity are imperative if we have to help China turn away from this destructive mindset. We all have a responsibility to stand for international law.

> History proves that dictatorships do not grow out of strong and successful governments, but out of weak and helpless ones. If by democratic methods people get a government strong enough to protect them from fear and starvation, their democracy succeeds; but if they do not, they grow impatient. Therefore, the only sure bulwark of continuing liberty is

---

50 John Locke, *Second Treatise of Government* [1690], sec. 202, Bartlett, John, *Familiar Quotations*, 14th Edition, published by Little, Brown and Co., 1968, p. 372.

51 William Pitt, Earl of Chatham, Case of Wilkes, Speech, Bartlett, John, *Familiar Quotations*, 14th Edition, published by Little, Brown and Co., 1968, p. 426.

52 Harry Krazianis, "China's Expanding Cabbage Strategy", at https://thediplomat.com/2013/10/chinas-expanding-cabbage-strategy/.

> a government strong enough to protect the interests of the people, and a people strong enough and well enough informed to maintain its sovereign control over its government.[53]

In the absence of a supreme government in international relations, it is important to have a strong rule of law in lieu of it. When rule of law is absent or weakened, international relations will be dominated instead by power politics and "*power politics is the diplomatic name for the law of the jungle.*" The law of the jungle is described in the poem "Law of the Yukon" by Robert Willian Service, to wit -

> This is the Law of Yukon, that only
>   The strong shall thrive;
> That surely the weak shall perish, and
>   only the fit survives.
> Dissolute, damned and despairful, crippled
>   and palsied and slain,
> This is the will of the Yukon – Lo,
>   how she makes it plain![54]

True peace in the South China Sea could only come if there is a strong rule of law.

2 Arbitration to Restore Rule of Law

On 22 January 2013, the Philippines initiated arbitral proceedings against China under Article 287 and Annex VII of the United Nations Convention on the Law of the Sea (UNCLOS). After it was constituted and organized pursuant to Annex VII of UNCLOS, the Tribunal conducted hearings on Jurisdiction and Admissibility on 7–13 July 2015. The Tribunal published its Award on Jurisdiction and Admissibility on 29 October 2015. After which, the Tribunal proceeded with the hearings on the Merits from 24–30 November 2015. On 12 July 2016, the Tribunal issued its Ruling on the Merits.[55]

---

53 *Op Cit,* Franklin D. Roosevelt ... Fireside Chat [April 14, 1938], Bartlett, John, *Familiar Quotations,* 14th Edition, published by Little, Brown and Co., 1968, p. 972.

54 Robert William Service, *The Law of the Yukon,* Bartlett, John, *Familiar Quotations,* 14th Edition, published by Little, Brown and Co., 1968, p. 932.

55 Award., *Op. Cit.*

The Tribunal ruled decisively on the 15 Submissions proffered by the Philippines. The 15 Submissions may be summed up into four main issues: *first*, is on the validity of China's historic right claim over a vast area of sea beyond its 200 NM Exclusive Economic Zone (EEZ) and extending up to the limits of its 9-dash line drawing on a map;[56] *second*, is on the legal character of Scarborough Shoal and the relevant features in the Spratlys, whether or not any or all of the relevant features are to be considered as islands, rocks, or low-tide elevations (LTEs) under Article 121[57] of UNCLOS;[58] *third*, is on whether or not China had violated the Philippines' sovereign rights over living and non-living resources in its EEZ;[59] and *fourth*, is on whether or not China caused the destruction of the marine environment in Scarborough Shoal and in the area of the Spratlys.[60]

The Tribunal ruled:

- That China's claim of historic rights over all the waters enclosed in its 9-dash line map (Figure #1) is without basis under public international law especially UNCLOS.[61] Accordingly, the rights of the Philippines under UNCLOS over its territorial sea, contiguous zone, 200 nm Exclusive Economic Zone, and continental shelf prevail over China's unsubstantiated claim of historic rights over the same;
- That none of the relevant geological features including Scarborough Shoal constitute an island under Article 121 of UNCLOS. These features are either "rocks" or "low-tide elevations" (LTEs) in accordance with the Convention;[62]
- That China had violated the Philippines' sovereign rights in its exclusive economic zone through (a) interference with Philippine fishing and petroleum exploration,[63] (b) construction of artificial islands,[64]

56 The Philippine Submissions No. 1 and 2.

57 Part VIII, Regime of Islands, Article 121:\ 1. An island is a naturally formed area of land, surrounded by water, which is above water at high tide.

2. Except as provided for in paragraph 3, the territorial sea, the contiguous zone, the exclusive economic zone and the continental shelf of an island are determined in accordance with the provisions of this Convention applicable to other land territory.

3. Rocks which cannot sustain human habitation or economic life of their own shall have no exclusive economic zone or continental shelf.

58 The Philippine Submissions No. 3 to 7.

59 The Philippine Submissions No. 8 to 10.

60 The Philippine Submissions No. 11 to 14.

61 *See* paragraphs 277–278 of *The South China Sea Arbitration Award*, pp. 116–117.

62 *See* paragraphs 643 to 647 of *The South China Sea Arbitration Award*, pp. 259–260.

63 *See* paragraph 716 of *The South China Sea Arbitration Award*, p. 286.

64 *See* paragraph 1043 of *The South China Sea Arbitration Award*, p. 415.

and (c) failure to prevent Chinese fishermen from fishing in the area;[65] and
- That China committed destruction of the marine environment in and around the relevant geographical features of the Spratlys and Scarborough Shoal.[66]

The Tribunal likewise ruled that Itu Aba is not an island under Article 121 of UNCLOS. Rather, that is a rock. As such, it is only entitled to a 12 NM Territorial Sea and not the maximum 200 NM EEZ. Taiwan, in lieu of the PROC, had submitted a Position Paper arguing that Itu Aba is an island under Article 121 of UNCLOS.[67] This allowed the Tribunal to dwell extensively on the question of Itu Aba.

A year earlier in 2015, the Tribunal issued a separate preliminary ruling affirming its jurisdiction over the case and the issues raised by the Philippines consistent with Article XV and ANNEX VII of UNCLOS, thus paving the way for the aforementioned Tribunal to finally rule on the merits of the case.[68]

3 China's Policy Response to Arbitration

When the Tribunal in the South China Sea Arbitration invalidated China's claim for historic waters under its 9-dash line map and clarified the rock or low-tide character of the relevant features in the Spratlys including Itu Aba, a large part of the South China Sea ceased *ipse jure* to be disputed.

The 2016 Ruling laid bare China's creeping assertion in the South China Sea and the West Philippine Sea as nothing but pure and simple aggression. Now devoid of any legal cover, China has to explore for an alternative legal justification to sustain its unfinished expansion while consolidating the gains from its creeping assertion and convert the same into a new *status quo* in the South China Sea. China needs to protect the supposedly new *status quo* it had generated from its previous assertive actions. It also needs for that "new *status quo*" to have some international recognition and acceptance including the norms, practices, and protocols that China would slowly impose over a period

65 *See* paragraph 757 of *The South China Sea Arbitration Award,* p. 297.

66 *See* paragraphs 992–993 of *The South China Sea Arbitration Award,* p. 397.

67 *Amicus Curiae Submission by the Chinese (Taiwan) Society of International Law* (23 March 2016), at http://www.assidmer.net/doc/SCSTF-Amicus-Curiae-Brief-final.pdf.

68 *Award on Jurisdiction and Admissibility,* 29 October 2015. Accessed at https://pcacases.com/web/sendAttach/2579.

of time *i.e.,* fishing ban, maritime governance, Air Identification Zone (ADIZ), Maritime Traffic Safety Law, *etc.* From the geo-strategic and security perspective, China still needs to complete the unfinished business of completing its envelopment of the South China Sea into a sphere of influence. China wants to avoid containment by the United States and its allies, with the semi-enclosed sea being considered as a security buffer zone and at the same time a springboard for Chinese submarines to launch into the Pacific Ocean where they can provide more accurate and lethal deterrence to the US mainland.

A possible route which China could perhaps take to accomplish all of the above objectives with some semblance of normality and legality would be to: *first,* impugn and undermine the *South China Sea Arbitration*; *second,* adopt a new legal framework as an alternative or in addition to its claim for historic waters that would accord China's creeping assertion some semblance of legitimacy. It would not matter even if such legal framework is invalid in the context of the South China Sea situation. All that is important is that it must have some iota or semblance of validity and connection with international law, specifically UNCLOS, to create doubt (on the 2016 Arbitral Ruling). China's policy mix of soft and hard power is expected to fill any remaining legal gap, and; *third,* preserve such claim under the cloak of another multilateral understanding with the other littoral States in the South China Sea including the Philippines that in effect would countervail the legal implications of the South China Sea Arbitration. A good candidate for this purpose would be the proposed ASEAN-China Code of Conduct.

A cursory observation of evolving developments in the South China Sea seems to indicate such a trend.

3.1 *On China's Attempt to Cloud 2016 South China Sea Arbitration*

Perhaps due to lack of confidence as to the validity of its claim or out of sheer arrogance as a big and powerful country, China refused to participate in the third-party adjudication of its claims and assertions in the South China Sea. At the very outset, China had tried to block, stop and subvert the arbitration process.

In its 19 February 2013 Reply-Note to the Philippines, China expressed its opposition to the former's filing of a complaint against the latter and expressed the view that on the South China Sea, its position "*has been consistent and clear.*" It added that "[*a*]*t the core of the disputes between China and the Philippines in the South China Sea are the territorial disputes over some islands and reefs of the Nansha Islands.*" It pointed out that [t]he two countries also have overlapping jurisdictional claims over parts of the maritime area in the South China Sea, "*which both sides agreed to settle through "bilateral negotiations*" and "*friendly consultations*."[69]

Instead of participating officially in the Arbitration, China submitted its legal position to the Tribunal in several indirect ways. For example, at the initial stage of the proceedings, China deposited with the Permanent Court of Arbitration (PCA) as Register of the Tribunal a copy of its "*Position Paper of the People's Republic of China on the Matter of Jurisdiction in the South China Sea Arbitration Initiated by the Republic of the Philippines,*" which it published on 7 December 2014. In its note verbale to the Tribunal transmitting said Position Paper, the Chinese Embassy in the Netherlands reiterated its non-acceptance of the Arbitration proceedings initiated by the Philippines and a caveat that the Paper should not be construed as acceptance by China of the Arbitration process.[70]

Later, when the Tribunal issued its ruling on the matter of jurisdiction, China issued on 30 October 2015, a "*Statement ... on the Award on Jurisdiction and Admissibility of the South China Sea Arbitration by the Arbitral Tribunal Established at the Request of the Republic of the Philippines.*" In said Statement, the Chinese Foreign Ministry expressed the following points:

> The award rendered on 29 October 2015 by the Arbitral Tribunal established at the request of the Republic of the Philippines ... on jurisdiction and admissibility of the South China Sea arbitration is null and void, and has no binding effect on China.
>
> I. China has indisputable sovereignty over the South China Sea Islands and the adjacent waters. China's sovereignty and relevant rights in the South China Sea formed in the long historic course, are upheld by successive Chinese governments, reaffirmed by China's domestic laws on many occasions, and protected under international law including the United Nations Convention on the Law of the Sea (UNCLOS). With regard to the issues of territorial sovereignty and maritime rights and interests, China will not accept any solution imposed on it or any unilateral resort to a third-party dispute settlement.
>
> II. The Philippines unilateral initiation and obstinate pushing forward of the South China Sea arbitration by abusing the compulsory procedures for dispute settlement under the UNCLOS is a political provocation under the cloak of law. It is in essence not an effort to settle disputes but an attempt to negate China's territorial sovereignty and maritime rights and interests in the South China Sea. In the

69 Award, *Op. Cit.*, p. 12.

70 Award, *Op. Cit.*, p. 14.

Position Paper of the Government of the People's Republic of China on the Matter of Jurisdiction in the South China Sea Arbitration Initiated by the Republic of the Philippines, which was released by the Chinese Ministry of Foreign Affairs on 7 December 2014, upon authorization, the Chinese government pointed out that the Arbitral Tribunal has no jurisdiction over the arbitration initiated by the Philippines, and elaborated on the legal grounds for China's non-acceptance of and non-participation in the arbitration. The position is clear and explicit, and will not change.

III. As a sovereign State and a State Party to the UNCLOS, China is entitled to choose the means and procedures of dispute settlement of its own will. China has all along been committed to resolving disputes with its neighbors over territory and maritime jurisdiction through negotiation and consultations. Since the 1990s, China and the Philippines have repeatedly reaffirmed in bilateral documents that they shall resolve relevant disputes through negotiations and consultations. The Declaration of Conduct of Parties on the South China Sea (DOC) explicitly states that the sovereign states directly concerned undertake to resolve their territorial and jurisdictional disputes by peaceful means through friendly consultations and negotiations. All these documents demonstrate that China and the Philippines have chosen, long time ago, to settle their disputes in the South China Sea through negotiations and consultations. The breach of this consensus by the Philippines damages the basis of mutual trust between states.

IV. Disregarding that the essence of this arbitration case is territorial sovereignty and maritime delimitation and related matters, maliciously evading the Declaration on optional exceptions made by China in 2006 under Article 298 of the UNCLOS, and negating the consensus between China and the Philippines on resolving relevant disputes through negotiations and consultations, the Philippines and the Arbitral Tribunal have abused relevant procedures and obstinately forced ahead with the arbitration, and as a result, have severely violated the legitimate rights that China enjoys as a State Party to the UNCLOS, completely deviated from the purposes and objectives of the UNCLOS, and eroded the integrity and authority of the UNCLOS. As a State Party to the UNCLOS, China firmly opposes the acts of abusing the compulsory procedures for dispute settlement under the UNCLOS, and calls upon all parties concerned to work together to safeguard the integrity and authority of the UNCLOS.

v. The Philippines' attempt to negate China's territorial sovereignty and maritime rights and interests in the South China Sea through arbitral proceedings will lead to nothing. China urges the Philippines to honor its own commitments, respect China's rights under international law, change its course and return to the right track of resolving relevant disputes in the South China Sea through negotiations and consultations.[71]

When the Tribunal proceeded with the hearing on the merits of the case, the Chinese Foreign Ministry Spokesman issued the following comments on 21 December 2015:

> The Chinese side will neither accept nor participate in the South China Sea arbitration unilaterally initiated by the Philippines. The long-standing position is fully supported by international law and subject to no change.
>
> In the hearing, the Philippine side attempted to negate China's sovereignty over the Nansha Islands and deny the validity of the Cairo Declaration and the Potsdam Proclamation in disregard of historical facts, international law and international justice. It testifies to the fact that the South China Sea dispute between China and the Philippines is in essence a territorial dispute over which the arbitral tribunal has no jurisdiction. It also shows that the so-called arbitration is a political provocation under the cloak of law aiming at negating China's sovereignty and maritime rights and interests in the South China Sea instead of resolving the disputes.
>
> It is the Chinese people rather than any other individuals or institutions that master China's territorial sovereignty. When it comes to issues concerning territorial sovereignty and maritime delimitation, China will not accept any dispute settlement approach that resorts to a third party. The Chinese side urges the Philippine side to cast aside illusions, change its course, and come back to the right track of resolving disputes through negotiations and consultations.[72]

Roughly two months before the promulgation of the Tribunal's Ruling on 12 July 2016, perhaps anticipating its outcome, China issued several statements again impugning the Tribunal and reiterating its position not to recognize the arbitration. One such statement was made by the Director General of the

71 Award, *Op. Cit.*, pp. 20–21.

72 Award, *Op. Cit.*, p. 28.

Chinese Department of Treaty and Law of the Chinese Foreign Ministry, Xu Hong, who expressed the following legal position of China:

> China has made it clear on multiple occasions that because the Arbitral Tribunal clearly has no jurisdiction over the present Arbitration, the decision to be made by such an institution that lacks the jurisdiction to do so has obviously no legal effect, and consequently there is no such thing as the recognition or implementation of the Award. Some people wonder whether China's position above is consistent with international law. Today, I would like to elaborate on China's position from the international perspective ....
>
> The first question is what is the scope of the jurisdiction of the Tribunal?
>
> ... to settle international disputes by peaceful means is one of the fundamental principles of international law. However, it should be noted that there are a variety of means to settle disputes peacefully, and compulsory arbitration is merely a new type of procedure established under the UNCLOS. Compulsory arbitration is subsidiary and complimentary to negotiation and consultation, and its application is subject to several preconditions ...
>
> First, compulsory arbitration can only be applied to settle disputes concerning the interpretation and application of the UNCLOS. If the subject matters are beyond the scope of the UNCLOS, the disputes shall not be settled by compulsory arbitration. The issue of territorial sovereignty is one such case. Consequently, States shall not initiate compulsory arbitration on disputes concerning it; and even if they do, the arbitral tribunal has no jurisdiction over them.
>
> Second, a State Party to the UNCLOS may declare in writing that it does not accept compulsory arbitration with respect to disputes concerning maritime delimitation, historic bays or titles, military and law enforcement activities, etc. Such exclusions are effective to other State Parties. With respect to disputes excluded by one party, other parties to the dispute shall not initiate compulsory arbitration; and even if it does, the arbitral tribunal has no jurisdiction over them.
>
> Third, if parties to a dispute have agreed on other means of settlement of their own choice, no party shall unilaterally initiate compulsory arbitration; and even if it does, the arbitral tribunal has no jurisdiction over the dispute.

Fourth, at the procedural level, parties to a dispute are obliged to first exchange views on the means of dispute settlement. Failing to fulfill this obligation, they shall not initiate compulsory arbitration; and even if they do, the arbitral tribunal has no jurisdiction over the dispute.

The above four preconditions act as the "four bars" for States Parties to initiate compulsory arbitration, and for the arbitral tribunal to establish its jurisdiction. They form a part of the package system of dispute settlement, which shall be interpreted and applied comprehensively and in its entirety.

... if we apply the four preconditions to the arbitration initiated unilaterally by the Philippines, it is not difficult to see that the Philippines, by initiating the arbitration, has violated international law in at least four aspects.

First, the essence of the subject-matter of the arbitration is territorial sovereignty over several maritime features in the South China Sea, which is beyond the scope of the UNCLOS. Second, even assuming some of the claims were concerned with the interpretation or application of the UNCLOS, they would still be an integral part of maritime delimitation, which has been excluded by China through its 2006 Declaration and consequently is not subject to compulsory arbitration. Third, given that China and the Philippines have agreed to settle their disputes in the South China Sea through negotiation, the Philippines is precluded from initiating arbitration unilaterally. Fourth, the Philippines failed to fulfill the obligation of exchanging views with China on the means of dispute settlement.

In summary, the Philippines' initiation of the arbitration is a typical abuse of the compulsory arbitral procedures stipulated in the UNCLOS ... in 2014 the Chinese Government issued a Position Paper to elaborate, from an international law perspective, on the question why the Tribunal lacks jurisdiction over the Arbitration ...

However, the Tribunal is not objective or just. On several occasions, it distorts the provisions of the UNCLOS to embrace the claims of the Philippines. In violation of the fundamental principle that the jurisdiction shall be established based on facts and law, the Arbitral Tribunal concluded that it had jurisdiction over the Philippines' claims, which is neither convincing nor valid in international law. For such an award, China certainly has good reasons not to recognize it. The opinions made by the Tribunal,

> as an institution that manifestly lacks jurisdiction and should not exist in the first place, are personal views of the arbitrators at best and are not legally binding, not to mention its recognition or implementation.[73]

Five years after the promulgation of the ruling on the South China Arbitration, China still maintains its position rejecting the said ruling as being null and void. China's Foreign Ministry Spokesperson Zhao Lijan issued on 12 July 2021, during the fifth year anniversary of the Tribunal's ruling, the following remark, *"The award of the arbitration is illegal, null and void. It is nothing more than a piece of wastepaper."*

China has been thought to have hosted or supported international fora and conferences of international law academics and practitioners that produced papers critical of the Arbitration and its ruling. Other countries have also been reportedly approached to support China's position.

Amid China's efforts, the provision of UNCLOS in Article 296 on Finality and binding force of decisions, is clear and unequivocal, to wit:

> 1. Any decision rendered by a court or tribunal having jurisdiction under this section shall be final and shall be complied with by all the parties to the dispute.

China's effort to undermine the *South China Arbitration* never gained traction. In contrast, many countries have expressed support for the South China Sea Arbitration and its 2016 Arbitral Ruling including the United States, Australia, Japan, Vietnam, Indonesia, India, and European States, among others.

In April 2021, US State Department Spokesperson Ned Price indicated that "We [meaning US] have reiterated our strong support for the Philippines and we have called on the PRC to abide by the 2016 arbitral tribunal award under the Law of the Sea Convention, which is final and legally binding on all parties." The statement was issued at the height of the Whitsun incident when Chinese vessels were reportedly swarming the said reef similar to what they did at Bajo de Masinloc (Scarborough Shoal).[74] Most recently, during the fifth year anniversary of the Arbitral Ruling, US Secretary of State Antony Blinken called on Beijing to *"abide by its obligations under international law, cease its provocative*

73 Award., *Op. Cit.*, pp. 32–34.

74 "US calls on China to abide by arbitral tribunal's ruling", Joyce Ann L. Rocamora, April 8, 2021. https://www.pna.gov.ph/articles/1136137.

behavior, and take steps to reassure the international community that it is committed to the rules-based maritime order that respects the rights of all countries, big and small." Blinken likewise reiterated the United States' 13 July 2020 policy[75] and US security commitments to the Philippines noting that any armed attack on Philippine forces, vessels, or aircraft in the West Philippine Sea would

75 The United States champions a free and open Indo-Pacific. Today we are strengthening U.S. policy in a vital, contentious part of that region – the South China Sea. We are making clear: Beijing's claims to offshore resources across most of the South China Sea are completely unlawful, as is its campaign of bullying to control them. In the South China Sea, we seek to preserve peace and stability, uphold freedom of the seas in a manner consistent with international law, maintain the unimpeded flow of commerce, and oppose any attempt to use coercion or force to settle disputes. We share these deep and abiding interests with our many allies and partners who have long endorsed a rules-based international order. These shared interests have come under unprecedented threat from the People's Republic of China (PRC). Beijing uses intimidation to undermine the sovereign rights of Southeast Asian coastal states in the South China Sea, bully them out of offshore resources, assert unilateral dominion, and replace international law with "might makes right." Beijing's approach has been clear for years. In 2010, then-PRC Foreign Minister Yang Jiechi told his ASEAN counterparts that "China is a big country and other countries are small countries and that is just a fact."

The PRC's predatory world view has no place in the 21st century. The PRC has no legal grounds to unilaterally impose its will on the region. Beijing has offered no coherent legal basis for its "Nine-Dashed Line" claim in the South China Sea since formally announcing it in 2009. In a unanimous decision on July 12, 2016, an Arbitral Tribunal constituted under the 1982 Law of the Sea Convention – to which the PRC is a state party – rejected the PRC's maritime claims as having no basis in international law. The Tribunal sided squarely with the Philippines, which brought the arbitration case, on almost all claims. As the United States has previously stated, and as specifically provided in the Convention, the Arbitral Tribunal's decision is final and legally binding on both parties. Today, we are aligning the U.S. position on the PRC's maritime claims in the SCS with the Tribunal's decision. Specifically:

- The PRC cannot lawfully assert a maritime claim – including any Exclusive Economic Zone (EEZ) claims derived from Scarborough Reef and the Spratly Islands – vis-a-vis the Philippines in areas that the Tribunal found to be in the Philippines' EEZ or on its continental shelf. Beijing's harassment of Philippine fisheries and offshore energy development within those areas is unlawful, as are any unilateral PRC actions to exploit those resources. In line with the Tribunal's legally binding decision, the PRC has no lawful territorial or maritime claim to Mischief Reef or Second Thomas Shoal, both of which fall fully under the Philippines' sovereign rights and jurisdiction, nor does Beijing have any territorial or maritime claims generated from these features.
- As Beijing has failed to put forth a lawful, coherent maritime claim in the South China Sea, the United States rejects any PRC claim to waters beyond a 12-nautical mile territorial sea derived from islands it claims in the Spratly Islands (without prejudice to other states' sovereignty claims over such islands). As such, the United States rejects any PRC maritime claim in the waters surrounding Vanguard Bank

invoke the mutual defense commitments of the U.S. and the Philippines under the 1951 U.S.-Philippines Mutual Defense Treaty.[76]

(off Vietnam), Luconia Shoals (off Malaysia), waters in Brunei's EEZ, and Natuna Besar (off Indonesia). Any PRC action to harass other states' fishing or hydrocarbon development in these waters – or to carry out such activities unilaterally – is unlawful.

– The PRC has no lawful territorial or maritime claim to (or derived from) James Shoal, an entirely submerged feature only 50 nautical miles from Malaysia and some 1,000 nautical miles from China's coast. James Shoal is often cited in PRC propaganda as the "southernmost territory of China." International law is clear: An underwater feature like James Shoal cannot be claimed by any state and is incapable of generating maritime zones. James Shoal (roughly 20 meters below the surface) is not and never was PRC territory, nor can Beijing assert any lawful maritime rights from it. The world will not allow Beijing to treat the South China Sea as its maritime empire. America stands with our Southeast Asian allies and partners in protecting their sovereign rights to offshore resources, consistent with their rights and obligations under international law. We stand with the international community in defense of freedom of the seas and respect for sovereignty and reject any push to impose "might makes right" in the South China Sea or the wider region. US Position on Maritime Claims, *Press Statement*, Michael R. Pompeo, US secretary of State, 13 July 2020. https://2017-2021.state.gov/u-s-position-on-maritime-claims-in-the-south-china-sea/index.html.

76 Freedom of the seas is an enduring interest of all nations and is vital to global peace and prosperity. The international community has long benefited from the rules-based maritime order, where international law, as reflected in the UN Law of the Sea Convention, sets out the legal framework for all activities in the oceans and seas. This body of international law forms the basis for national, regional, and global action and cooperation in the maritime sector and is vital to ensuring the free flow of global commerce. Nowhere is the rules-based maritime order under greater threat than in the South China Sea. The People's Republic of China (PRC) continues to coerce and intimidate Southeast Asian coastal states, threatening freedom of navigation in this critical global throughway. Five years ago, an Arbitral Tribunal constituted under the 1982 Law of the Sea Convention delivered a unanimous and enduring decision firmly rejecting the PRC's expansive South China Sea maritime claims as having no basis in international law. The Tribunal stated that the PRC has no lawful claim to the area determined by the Arbitral Tribunal to be part of the Philippines' exclusive economic zone and continental shelf. The PRC and the Philippines, pursuant to their treaty obligations under the Law of the Sea Convention, are legally bound to comply with this decision. The United States reaffirms its *July 13, 2020 policy* regarding maritime claims in the South China Sea. We also reaffirm that an armed attack on Philippine armed forces, public vessels, or aircraft in the South China Sea would invoke U.S. mutual defense commitments under Article IV of the 1951 U.S.-Philippines Mutual Defense Treaty. We call on the PRC to abide by its obligations under international law, cease its provocative behavior, and take steps to reassure the international community that it is committed to the rules-based maritime order that respects the

3.2 *On China's Attempt to Preserve Expansionist Policy through Archipelagic and Straight Baseline Concept*

China appears to be resorting to the use of the archipelagic concept and the use of archipelagic baselines under Article 46 and 47 of UNCLOS, or straight baselines under Article 7 of UNCLOS, to try to preserve its assertion and claim on a large body of water and continental shelf in the South China Sea that it had lost because of the 2016 Arbitral Ruling.

On 12 December 2019, Malaysia submitted to the United Nations Commission on the Limits of the Continental Shelf (CLCS) its claim for Extended Continental Shelf (ECS) in the South China Sea.[77] The recent submission for ECS claim is a partial submission for the "remaining portion of the continental shelf of Malaysia beyond 200 nautical miles in the northern part of the South China Sea."[78] Malaysia, together with Vietnam, previously submitted an ECS claim in the South China Sea, which was deferred for consideration of the CLCS in view of the protests made by China and the Philippines.

On the same day, China filed its protest against the ECS submission of Malaysia. In its Note Verbale CML/14/2019 dated 12 December 2019 addressed to the Secretary-General of the United Nations, China urged the United Nations Commission on the Limits of the Continental Shelf (CLCS) not to consider the submission stating that:

> China has sovereignty over Nanhai Zhudao, consisting of Dongsha Qundao, Xisha Qundao, Zhongsah Qundao and Nansha Qundao; China has internal waters, territorial sea and contiguous zone, based on Nanhai Zhudao; China has exclusive economic zone and continental shelf, based on Nanhai Zhudao; China has historic rights in the South China Sea. The above positions of China comply with relevant international law and practice. They are clear and consistent, and are known to the international community including the Government of Malaysia.[79]

---

rights of all countries, big and small. Fifth Anniversary of the Arbitral Ruling on the South China Sea, *Press Statement*, Antony J. Blinken, 11 July 2021. https://www.state.gov/fifth-anniversary-of-the-arbitral-tribunal-ruling-on-the-south-china-sea/.

77 *See* https://www.un.org/Depts/los/clcs_new/submissions_files/mys85_2019/2019_12_19%20CLCS%20notification.85.2019.LOS_e.pdf.

78 *See* Note No. HA 59/19 of 12 December 2019 from the Permanent Mission of Malaysia to the Secretary-General of the United Nations, https://www.un.org/depts/los/clcs_new/submissions_files/mys85_2019/2019_12_12_MYS_NV_UN_001.pdf.

79 See Note No. CML/14/2019 dated 12 December 2019 from the Permanent Mission of the People's Republic of China to the Secretary-General of the United Nations https://www.un.org/depts/los/clcs_new/submissions_files/mys85_2019/CML_14_2019_E.pdf.

It may be worth noting that the above statement differs from the previous protest notes from China on the joint ECS submission by Malaysia and Vietnam (CML/17/2009) and on Vietnam's unilateral ECS submission (CML/18/2009). In said notes, China stated that:

> China has indisputable sovereignty over the islands in the South China Sea and the adjacent waters, and enjoys sovereign rights and jurisdiction over the relevant waters as well as seabed and subsoil thereof (see attached map). The above position is consistently held by the Chinese Government, and is widely known by the international community.

While the formulation differs, China's meaning and intent remain the same: that it has sovereignty claims over the islands and a large swathe of maritime area in the South China Sea.

However, from a straightforward 9-dash line claim, they are now laying sovereignty claims on the alleged four island groups: (1) Dongsha Qundao (Pratas Islands); (2) Xisha Qundao (Paracel Islands); (3) Zhongsah Qundao (Macclesfield Bank; and (4) Nansha Qundao (Spratly Islands). This makes it appear that their claim for 200 nautical miles (M) Exclusive Economic Zone (EEZ) and 200 M Continental Shelf is UNCLOS-based.

In particular, China's statement appears to claim that the island groups, specifically the Spratly Islands, can be treated as archipelagoes and can be enclosed within a system of archipelagic baselines or straight baselines, and consequently accorded with concomitant maritime entitlements. This Paper argues that China cannot use archipelagic baselines or straight baselines in the island groups in the South China Sea. This is because the use of such baselines is allowed only under certain conditions as provided for under the UN Convention on the Law of the Sea (UNCLOS), and China's application of archipelagic baselines or straight baselines in the island groups in the South China Sea, particularly the Spratly Islands, would be contrary to UNCLOS.

3.2.1 UNCLOS Provisions on the Baselines

Baselines are the reckoning point from which the maritime limits and boundaries of a coastal States are measured. It serves as a fence that separates the internal waters and archipelagic waters from the territorial sea and other maritime zones. Taking into account the varying geographic configuration of countries, UNCLOS provides various types of baselines that could be applied by states as follows: (1) normal baselines; (2) straight baselines; and (3) archipelagic baselines.

Normal baselines refer to the low-water line along the coast as marked on the official large-scale charts of the coastal State.[80] However, in the case of islands situated on atolls or of islands having fringing reefs, the baseline for measuring the breadth of the territorial sea is the seaward low-water line of the reef, as shown by the appropriate symbol on charts officially recognized by the coastal State.[81]

Straight baselines are used in localities where the coastline is deeply indented and cut into, or if there is a fringe of islands along the coast in its immediate vicinity, the method of straight baselines joining appropriate points may be employed in drawing the baseline from which the breadth of the territorial sea is measured. Specifically, Article 7 of UNCLOS provides:

> 1. In localities where the coastline is deeply indented and cut into, or if there is a fringe of islands along the coast in its immediate vicinity, the method of straight baselines joining appropriate points may be employed in drawing the baseline from which the breadth of the territorial sea is measured.

A third kind of baselines is archipelagic straight baselines. This type of baseline is applicable in the case of archipelagic States. Article 46 of UNCLOS provides:

> Article 46 Use of terms.
> For the purposes of this Convention:
> (a) "archipelagic State" means a State constituted wholly by one or more archipelagos and may include other islands;
> (b) "archipelago" means a group of islands, including parts of islands, interconnecting waters and other natural features which are so closely interrelated that such islands, waters and other natural features form an intrinsic geographical, economic and political entity, or which historically have been regarded as such.

Instead of drawing normal baselines in and around each island of an archipelago, an archipelagic State, which is considered as one geographic, political

80 Article 5 of the United Nations Convention on the Law of the Sea, Montego Bay, Jamaica, 10 December 1982, in force 16 November 1994, http://www.un.org/Depts/los/convention_agreements/texts/unclos/unclos_e.pdf. (hereafter referred to as UNCLOS).

81 UNCLOS Article 6.

and economic entity, has the option to enclose said group of islands into a single entity by designating basepoints on the outermost points of the outermost islands and connecting them through a series of straight baselines. Article 47 of UNCLOS provides:

> 1 An archipelagic State may draw straight baselines joining the outermost points of the outermost islands and drying reefs of the archipelago provided that within such baselines are included the main island and an area in which the ratio of the area of the water to the area of the land, including atolls, is between 1 to 1 and 9 to 1.
>
> ...

By using either the straight baselines under Article 7 or Article 47 of UNCLOS, China would supposedly be able to continue making claim on a sea space that it otherwise would have none in light of the ruling in the South China Arbitration.

An examination of Article 7 and Article 47 of UNCLOS *vis-à-vis* the features in the South China Sea including the Spratlys indicates that China cannot use either the straight baselines under Article 7 to enclose the group of features as a single entity or Article 47 as an archipelagic state.

3.2.2 On Article 7, Straight Baselines

As stated, the use of straight baselines under Article 7 is applicable in a situation "where the coastline is deeply indented and cut into, or if there is a fringe of islands along the coast in its immediate vicinity." This concept originated from the Anglo-Norwegian Fisheries case decided in the 1950s where the validity under international law of the methods used to delimit Norway's territorial sea/ fisheries zone was questioned by the United Kingdom. Specifically, the United Kingdom requested the court to decide if Norway had used a legally acceptable method in drawing the baseline from which it measured its territorial sea.[82] Because of the special circumstances of its coast which is deeply indented, Norway applied straight baselines to connect the outermost points of its coast including the outlying features. Norway considered the *skjaergaard* as constituting a whole with the Norwegian mainland, with the waters between the baselines of the belt of territorial waters and the mainland considered

82 Anglo-Norwegian Fisheries, U.K. v. Norway, Order, 1951 I.C.J. 117 (Jan. 18), http://www.worldcourts.com/icj/eng/decisions/1951.12.18_fisheries.htm.

internal waters.[83] The Court in the case ruled that the method employed for the delimitation of the fisheries zone by the Royal Norwegian Decree of July 12th, 1935, is not contrary to international law; and that the baselines fixed in the said Royal Decree in application of this method are not contrary to international law.[84] This principle on straight baseline was later incorporated in Article 7 of UNCLOS.

A closer examination of the Spratlys clearly indicates that its coasts are not deeply indented as that of the *skjaergaard* of Norway. It is not configured as to constitute a fringe of islands grouped around or in the immediate vicinity of one or more larger islands. The extensive sea areas surrounding these very tiny features also do not meet the requirement of being "sufficiently closely linked to the land domain to be the subject to a regime of internal waters."

3.2.3 On Article 47, Archipelagic Baselines

The use of archipelagic baselines in the Spratlys under Article 47 of UNCLOS would also be inappropriate. It cannot be given an archipelagic status entitled to archipelagic baselines since neither the Spratlys itself nor China which is claiming it is an archipelagic State is an archipelagic State. Under Article 47 in relation to Article 46 of UNCLOS provides that only an archipelagic State is entitled to use archipelagic baselines.

Further, the water to land ratio in the Spratlys does not satisfy the ratio requirement under Article 47, which "is between 1 to 1 and 9 to 1." The Spratlys comprise no more than 5 km^2 of land territory, and more than 410,000 km^2 of maritime space. Therefore, the water to land ratio would be approximately 82,000:1.[85]

The matter of whether or not the concept of archipelagic concept or single entity can be applied in the Spratlys was also addressed by the Tribunal at a supplemental stage of the proceedings.

The Tribunal in that case specifically ruled:

> The use of archipelagic baselines (a baseline surrounding an archipelago as a whole) is strictly controlled by the Convention, where Article 47(1) limits their use to "archipelagic states" …
>
> China, however, is constituted principally by territory on the mainland of Asia and cannot meet the definition of an archipelagic State …

83 *Ibid.*

84 *Ibid.*

85 Supplemental Written Submission of the Philippines to the South China Sea Arbitration.

> ... Article 47 of the Convention limits the use of archipelagic baselines to circumstances where "within such baselines are included the main islands and an area in which the ratio of the area of the water to the area of the land, including atolls, is between 1 to 1 and 9 to 1." The ratio of water to land in the Spratly Islands would greatly exceed 9:1 under any conceivable system of baselines....[86]

The Tribunal further added:

> ... the Tribunal is aware of the practice of some States in employing straight baselines with respect to offshore archipelagos to approximate the effect of archipelagic baselines. In the Tribunal's view, any application of straight baselines to the Spratly Islands in this fashion would be contrary to the Convention. Article 7 provides for the application of straight baselines only "[i]n localities where the coastline is deeply indented and cut into, or if there is a fringe of islands along the coast in its immediate vicinity." These conditions do not include the situation of an offshore archipelago. Although the Convention does not expressly preclude the use of straight baselines in other circumstances, the Tribunal considers that the grant of permission in Article 7 concerning straight baselines generally, together with the conditional permission in Articles 46 and 47 for certain States to draw archipelagic baselines, excludes the possibility of employing straight baselines in other circumstances, in particular with respect to offshore archipelagos not meeting the criteria for archipelagic baselines. Any other interpretation would effectively render the conditions in Articles 7 and 47 meaningless.[87]

3.3 *On the Code of Conduct Preserving China's Expansionist Policy*

Although the ruling in the South China Sea Arbitration is final and legally binding on the China and the Philippines,[88] nonetheless, there is nothing in the said ruling or international law that prevents the parties to the said dispute from entering into a subsequent agreement that differs from the said ruling. Such agreement may be in the form of a bilateral agreement or may also be contained in a multilateral agreement such as the proposed ASEAN-China Code of Conduct. China seems to be taking this path in order to protect its

86 Award, *Op. Cit.*.

87 Award, *Op. Cit.*

88 *Article 296, Finality and binding force of decisions,* UNCLOS "1. Any decision rendered by a court or tribunal having jurisdiction under this section shall be final and shall be

expansionist policy, preserve its creeping assertion, and regain what it had otherwise lost in the arbitration.

No wonder, China's attitude vis-à-vis the conclusion of the Code of Conduct (COC) has taken a sharp turn-around. Since the 1990s, the Philippines had been pushing hard for the conclusion of a Code of Conduct with China initially through bilateral diplomacy, and later multilaterally via the ASEAN platform. China, on the other hand, was never keen on its conclusion and dragged its feet despite public articulations to the contrary. Worse, it used COC discussions as cover to mask its continuing assertion on the ground, deflect international attention, and contain international protests and fallout after every aggressive action it intermittently initiates. At most, it only agreed to a watered-down Declaration of Conduct of Parties in the South China Sea in 2005, which it disregarded later.

This is how it was until the Philippines filed the arbitration against China in 2013. Suddenly, China appeared to be interested in a Code of Conduct with the Philippines and the other nine members of ASEAN. China initially dangled the possibility of agreeing to a negotiation on the Code of Conduct, so as to entice the Philippines, and for ASEAN to persuade the latter from proceeding with the arbitration. When this failed and the Arbitration nonetheless proceeded and ended up with its 12 July 2016 Ruling, China shifted gear and suddenly agreed to expedite negotiation and conclusion of the Code of Conduct. For this purpose, China agreed with ASEAN on a single negotiating draft. ASEAN and China have recently agreed on the Preambular provisions of the Code of Conduct. China also expressed optimism that China and ASEAN would be able to complete the COC in 2022.

However, a closer examination of the single negotiating draft and the possible use of the COC to subvert the 2016 Arbitral Ruling, it seems that the South China Sea is better off without the ASEAN-China Code of Conduct. A Code of Conduct that is shaped and formed based on the current negotiating text would be more detrimental rather than beneficial to the peace and security of the South China Sea region.

Of course, it is just a negotiating text, a draft. So far, ASEAN and China have only agreed on the preambular paragraphs. The main body or the operative paragraphs are yet to be argued and agreed upon. These may still change, or, they may not. Either way, there is a strong indication that the "strategic ambiguities" that have been deliberately embedded into the draft to accommodate

complied with by all the parties to the dispute. "2. Any such decision shall have no binding force except between the parties and in respect of that particular dispute."

the competing and even opposing interests of the Claimant-States, is likely to be preserved in the future agreement.

China and the other Claimant countries went into the COC negotiations with differing objectives. On one hand, China is using the COC to preserve its expansive claim over almost the entire South China Sea (initially, as "historic water" covered by the 9-dash line map, and later through the concept of archipelago under UNCLOS). On the other, Vietnam and the Philippines are trying to protect the 2016 ruling on the South China Sea Arbitration in the COC.

In its current state, the COC[89] looks more like a *chop suey* – a mix of varying and often contradictory interests. It lacks focus and direction. A cumulation of various competing interests fitted together within the negotiating framework of "agreeing to disagree" especially on the matter of territorial and maritime claims. Deliberate ambiguity in the COC would allow all the Parties to go along with the conclusion of the COC. From the public relations standpoint, it will be good for ASEAN. It will also be good for China. But in reality, it would be a huge strategic blunder with far-reaching consequences and fundamental implications on the peace, stability and security in the South China Sea region. The deliberate ambiguity in the Code of Conduct would augur well for China and will be exploited by it in the same way it exploited the 2002 Declaration of Conduct (DOC) of State Parties in the South China Sea. The 2002 DOC is being hailed as a milestone document for ASEAN and China in the attainment of durable peace and security in the South China Sea. It may be so. But perhaps it may not.

If one has to use the standard of frequency and magnitude of aggression, tension and conflict, one can empirically come to the conclusion that the South China Sea is a more dangerous place after the conclusion of the DOC in 2002 than before it. Of course, it would not be fair to attribute the rise in tension in the South China Sea solely to the DOC. Nonetheless, there is no doubt that the DOC was exploited by China as an important tool for its expansionist policy in the South China Sea.

In particular, China abused the DOC to tell the Philippines in 2005 to refrain from unilaterally exploring and exploiting Reed Bank lest it violates the letter and spirit of paragraph 5 of the Declaration. Paragraph 5 of the DOC provides,

89 Single Draft Code of Conduct in the South China Sea (COC) Negotiating Text, as of 26/7/2018.

> The Parties undertake to exercise self-restraint in the conduct of activities that would complicate or escalate disputes and affect peace and stability including, among others, refraining from action of inhabiting on the presently uninhabited islands, reefs, shoals, cays, and other features and to handle their differences in a constructive manner.

China was able to abuse the provision of paragraph 5 because of the ambiguity in the definition of disputed areas in the South China Sea. The DOC does not contain any provision defining the areas of dispute in the South China Sea. China exploited this ambiguity by claiming almost the entire South China Sea through its assertion of historic waters allegedly evinced by its 9-dash line map (impliedly in 2005 and expressly in 2009). By doing so, China forced a dispute (though illegally) on the entire high seas (so-called donut hole), approximately 80–90 percent of the Exclusive Economic Zones and continental shelves of the Philippines, Vietnam, Malaysia, and Brunei and to lesser degree that of Indonesia (around the Natuna Island). By doing so, China is able to argue for the applicability of the DOC, particularly paragraph 5 even on the Exclusive Economic Zones and continental shelves of the littoral States.

Further, China began its third wave of creeping assertion in the South China Sea highlighted by its seasonal fishing ban on the South China Sea, forced occupation of Scarborough Shoal, building of artificial islands, and increased sovereignty patrols on the land and sea-space covered by its 9-dash line claim.

Because China's claim is both ambiguous and lacking in international legitimacy, it thrives in unclear and ambiguous concepts and agreements to hide and preserve the same. This, in fact, is the reason why it disdains the clarity and transparency in the ruling of the international Arbitral Tribunal in the South China Sea Arbitration.

China is again repeating the mistakes of the DOC by pushing ASEAN (ASEAN Claimant Members) to the point of deliberate ambiguity in the COC. By doing so, it can allow the survival and preservation of its expansive claims in the South China by using the COC as a legal platform to modify the effects of the 2016 Arbitral Ruling. The sum effect of such legal ingenuity on the part of China is the eventual archiving of the Arbitral Ruling as a mere historical record.

Under such circumstances, the South China Sea will again be pushed back to its helpless period before the 2016 Arbitral Award, although with significant differences: China would have achieved its strategic objective and would have consolidated the same with some semblance of legitimacy provided by the

COC. More dangerously, it will pave the way for a much stronger China with a robust mindset that is more aggressive and feeling invincible to a more adventurous policy and assertion.

South China Sea's peace and security will then become volatile and precarious. In such a post-Code of Conduct scenario, the South China Sea will be less stable, less safe and less secured. Instead of creating a condition for durable peace and security in the South China Sea, it can breed the emergence of a fourth wave of China's creeping assertion to now spill over into the Pacific Ocean, the Indian Ocean and the East China Sea.

This is the reason why it is imperative not to de-link the COC from the 2016 Arbitral Tribunal. The COC cannot afford not to integrate the ruling in its substance. The ruling is the best security for the COC in terms of its clarity as antidote to the ambiguity that China is deliberately trying to force on the COC. That ambiguity will create the vacuum that is so abhorred by security. Thus, ASEAN should not allow a dichotomy between the 2016 Arbitral Ruling and the Code of Conduct. This is the only way by which the Code of Conduct becomes relevant. Either come up with a Code of Conduct that is linked with the 2016 Arbitral Ruling, or; or leave the South China Sea without a Code of Conduct. In case of the latter, the 2016 Arbitral Ruling provides a good safety net even in the absence of a Code of Conduct.

4 Conclusion

The 2016 ruling in the South China Sea Arbitration is a major contribution for the rule of law in the region. The Ruling clarified the maritime entitlements of the Philippines. It also clarified what China can and cannot claim under international law, specifically UNCLOS. It is fair for the Philippines. But it is also fair for China. Despite China's protestations, the Ruling did not strip it of any entitlements that it is otherwise entitled to under UNCLOS. The Tribunal likewise clarified the objective character of the relevant features without regard to who has title over them. In effect, the Tribunal's clarification only stripped China of what it could not claim under a Convention that it negotiated and agreed with together with the rest of the other 168 countries that also signed and ratified the same. More than that, the Ruling also clarified indirectly the maritime entitlements of other littoral States by implication despite the fact that the ruling is only legally binding to the parties to the arbitration. In the context of a semi-enclosed sea that is critical in the exchange of goods via its sea lanes of communications, the Ruling is also huge in its contribution of adding clarity to freedom of navigation in the South China Sea.

Despite the fairness and reasonableness of the Tribunal's Ruling, China has opted not to recognize the ruling and instead engaged in undermining the same, most recently by implying the use of archipelagic baselines and straight baselines. This is for China not only to recover as much sea space that has otherwise been lost in arbitration, but more importantly, to have a semblance of legal justification for its expansionist policy. Fortunately, this particular matter has already been resolved by the same Tribunal in the South China Sea Arbitration. China's behavior in the aftermath of the Ruling only confirms the thinking that the problem in the South China Sea is not the existence of overlapping territorial and maritime claims. Rather, at the root of the disputes in the South China Sea and West Philippine Sea is the expansionist policy of China. This hegemonic ambition is the main driver behind China's creeping assertion in the South China Sea.

Appeasement has reinforced this mindset. It took some time for many countries to realize this. By the time they realized this, China has already extensively altered the *status quo* in the South China Sea with its quick and massive assertions. Fortunately, there was the South China Sea Arbitration. Its clarification of the disputes in the South China Sea has allowed other stakeholders to weigh in correctly on the matter. It also drew the line for China. Now it is up to the international community to work together for the enforcement of the Ruling. The Ruling is not only a just cause for the Philippines. It is as well for the rest of the international community. If the world has to avoid a conflagration in the future, it must take the necessary policy approach now with clear resolve and commitment.

In this context, the Paper notes the overly excessive discussions in some circles as to the enforceability of the Ruling. Unfortunately, in the aftermath of the ruling, the discussions on Arbitration have centered quite extensively (unreasonably from the author's perspective) on the issue of whether or not it is enforceable, rather than on how to enforce it. From this paper's perspective, this overemphasis on the supposed unenforceability of the Tribunal's ruling detracts from the real and more important issue of how to enforce the same. It also shows a lack of understanding of public international law and its progressive nature.

Many critics of international law have criticized it as not being true law. Their criticisms center on the lack of a supreme authority or government as in a domestic setting. Another is the lack of an international military force to enforce it, like that of a local police force in a domestic setting. The argument against the enforceability of the Tribunal's ruling is anchored very much on the same argument against public international as true law. But international law is true law as a body of laws and norms that regulates inter-State relations. Every State recognizes this.

In like manner, the enforceability of international law is different from the enforceability of municipal laws in a domestic setting. Owing to the unique nature of international law, the enforceability of the ruling is not solely determined by the existence or absence of an international police force, but rather through some other means of international pressure, such as international isolation, international trade or some forms of sanctions, among others. One only needs to have the will and creativity to do it.

Food that is served us on our table will not fill and nourish us unless we physically lift our hands and use our faculties to feed ourselves that food. In the same manner, the Tribunal's ruling will not benefit us unless we ourselves work for its enforcement.

Though the path to its enforcement may be narrow and difficult; yet the road to peace that the Tribunal has laid out for us is rather clear and decisive. It should not be wasted.

Sources

Anglo-Norwegian Fisheries, U.K. v. Norway, Order, 1951 I.C.J. 117 (Jan. 18), http://www.worldcourts.com/icj/eng/decisions/1951.12.18_fisheries.htm.

Amicus Curiae Submission by the Chinese (Taiwan) Society of International Law (23 March 2016), at http://www.assidmer.net/doc/SCSTF-Amicus-Curiae-Brief-final.pdf.

Award on Jurisdiction and Admissibility, 29 October 2015. Accessed at https://pcacases.com/web/sendAttach/2579.

Award, PCA Case No 2013–19, In the Matter of the South China Sea Arbitration Before an Arbitral Tribunal Constituted Under Annex II to the 1982 United Nations Convention on the Law of the Sea Between the Republic of the Philippines and the People's Republic of China, 12 July 2016.

John Bartlett, *Familiar Quotations*, 14th Edition, published by Little, Brown and Co., 1968.

Chris Brummit, "Vietnam tries to stop China oil rig deployment," May 7, 2014, at http://www.usatoday.com/story/news/world/2014/05/07/vietnam-china-oil-rig/8797007/.

Steve Chan, *International Relations in Perspective: The Pursuit of Security, Welfare and Justice*, (New York: Macmillan, 1984).

Sharon Chen and Andrea Tan, "Kissinger Urges Return to Deng's Way on South China Sea Spat," March 29, 2015, at http://www.bloomberg.com/news/articles/2015-03-29/u-s-should-use-deng-approach-in-south-china-sea-kissinger-says.

"China starts annual South China Sea fishing ban," *English.xinhua.cn*, 16 May 2013, at http://news.xinhuanet.com/english/china/2013-05/16/c_132386383.htm.

"Chinese navy flexes muscles in South China Sea," March 27, 2013, at http://archive.news10.net/news/national/238097/5/Chinese-navy-flexes-muscle-in-South-China-Sea.

Ramon Farolan, "Mischief Reef – Where It All Started," *Philippine Daily Inquirer*, https://opinion.inquirer.net/140311/mischief-reef-where-it-all-startedhttps://humanrightsinasean.info/wp-content/uploads/files/documents/Declaration_on_the_Conduct_of_Parties_in_the_South_China_Sea_0.pdf.

Fifth Anniversary of the Arbitral Ruling on the South China Sea, Press Statement, Antony J. Blinken, 11 July 2021. https://www.state.gov/fifth-anniversary-of-the-arbitral-tribunal-ruling-on-the-south-china-sea/.

Vu Trong Khanh and Nguyen Anh Thu, "Vietnam, China Trade Accusations of Vessel-Ramming Near Oil Rig," June 24, 2014, at http://www.wsj.com/articles/vietnam-china-trade-accusations-of-vessel-ramming-near-oil-rig-in-south-china-sea-1403608970.

Frank McDonough, *Hitler, Chamberlain and Appeasement* (Cambridge Perspectives in History), (Cambridge University Press, 2002).

Ngo Minh Tri and Koh Swee Lean Collin, "Lessons from the Battle of the Paracels Islands," *The Diplomat*, January 23, 2014, https://the diplomat.com/2014/01/lessons-from-the-battle-of-the-paracel-islands.

Hans Morgenthau, *Politics Among Nations: The Struggle for Power and Peace*, 4th ed, (New York: Knopf, 1967).

Note No. HA 59/19 of 12 December 2019 from the Permanent Mission of Malaysia to the Secretary-General of the United Nations https://www.un.org/depts/los/clcs_new/submissions_files/mys85_2019/2019_12_12_MYS_NV_UN_001.pdf.

Simone Orendain, "Philippines Says China Harassed Oil Exploration Vessel," 4 March 2011, at http://www.voanews.com/content/philippines-says-china-harrassed-oil-exploration-vessel-117457638/136022.html.

Paterno Esmaquel III, "Philippines slams China over 'sovereignty patrols,'" *Rappler.com*, 18 August 2014, at http://www.rappler.com/nation/66582-philippines-china-sovereignty-patrols-recto-bank. http://www.bbc.com/news/world-asia-26320383.

"Rapprochement with China, 1972," Office of the Historian, Foreign Service Institute, United States Department of State, https://history.state.gov/milestones/1969-1976/rapprochement-china.

Renata Gianini in the Issue brief "The Rule of Law: State Sovereignty vs. International Obligations," GA Sixth Committee (Legal) 2010, at http://al.odu.edu/mun/docs/Issue%20brief%202010,%20The%20rule%20of%20law.pdf.

J.L. Richardson, "'New Perspectives on Appeasement: Some Implications for International Relations," *World Politics*, Vol. 40, No. 3, (Cambridge University Press, 1988).

Joyce Ann L. Rocamora, "US calls on China to abide by arbitral tribunal's ruling," Philippine News Agency, April 8, 2021. https://www.pna.gov.ph/articles/1136137.

Marwyn Samuels, *Contest for the South China Sea* (New York and London: Methuen, 1982).

Jaime Sinapit and Pots de Leon, "Chinese vessels harass, but fail to stop, resupply mission for PH Navy ship at Ayungin Shoal," *InterAksyon.com*, 29 March 2014, at http://www.interaksyon.com/article/83734/chinese-vessel-harasses-but-fails-to-stop-resupply-mission-for-brp-sierra-madre-at-ayungin.

Single Draft Code of Conduct in the South China Sea (COC) Negotiating Text, as of 26/7/2018.

Alice Mary Smyth (ed), *The Oxford Book of Quotations* (Oxford University Press, 1941).

Supplemental Written Submission of the Philippines to the South China Sea Arbitration.

Sharon Tiezzi, "Philippines accuses China of ramming boats in South China sea," *The Diplomat*, February 5, 2015, at http://thediplomat.com/2015/02/philippines-accuses-china-of-ramming-boats-in-south-china-sea.

United Nations Convention on the Law of the Sea, Montego Bay, Jamaica, 10 December 1982, in force 16 November 1994, http://www.UN.org/Depts/los/convention_agreements/texts/unclos/unclos_e.pdf. (hereafter referred to as UNCLOS.).

United Nations Conference on Trade and Development (UNCTAD), *Review of Maritime Transport 2011*, as cited in U.S. Energy Information Administration, 'Analysis Brief, The South China Sea,' February 7, 2013, <http://www.eia.gov/countries/regions-topics.cfm?fips=scs>.

US Position on Maritime Claims, Press Statement, Michael R. Pompeo, US secretary of State, 13 July 2020. https://2017-2021.state.gov/u-s-position-on-maritime-claims-in-the-south-china-sea/index.html.

Mark J. Valencia, Jon M. Van Dyke, and Noel A. Ludwig, *Sharing the Resources of the South China Sea* (Honolulu: University of Hawaii Press, 1997).
Alexander L. Vuving, https://thediplomat.com/2016/07/why-the-south-china-sea-ruling-is-a-game-changer.

CHAPTER 9

China's Excessive Straight Baseline Claims

James Kraska

1 Introduction

China's maritime laws reflect the country's sense of weakness as a geographically disadvantaged state in Northeast Asia. While China is a large continental power, it lacks strategic depth along its maritime approaches and is unable to reach the high seas without going through the exclusive economic zone (EEZ) of its neighbors, from Russia to Japan to the Philippines. To address this sense of exposure or vulnerability, China has sought to develop a sense of greater security through excessive or unlawful maritime claims or assertions of entitlement to its maritime approaches or near seas. China has advanced a series of excessive or unlawful maritime claims that seek to place more water under its sovereignty, sovereign rights, and jurisdiction at the expense of its neighbors and even distant coastal States.

These departures from standard state practice and black letter legal doctrine, coupled with China's bold (sometimes galling) disregard for the lawful maritime boundaries of virtually all of its neighbors, reflects the country's increasing economic and military power and the confidence they have engendered. This dynamic has also caused clashes with Japan, the United States, and other maritime powers. Japan is affected by Chinese offshore claims because moving Chinese baselines farther east purports to move the equidistant line from which maritime boundary negotiations use as a point of departure. Any effect on Japan has ramifications for American security, which is linked to Japanese stability, prosperity, and security in East Asia. China's claims also attempt to reduce the operating space of foreign naval forces, such as the U.S. Navy. Likewise, because Japanese security is linked to the United States, any diminution of U.S. and allied operational flexibility or maritime operating space resulting from Chinese excessive claims in the oceans undermines Tokyo's security, sovereignty, and independence.

DOI:10.1163/9789004518629_010

2 China's Baseline Claims

2.1 *Baselines*

A state's maritime zones are measured from baselines. The rules for drawing baselines are contained in articles 5 to 11 and 13 and 14 of UNCLOS. The Law of the Sea Convention distinguishes between normal baselines, which follow the low-water marks along the coast, and straight baselines, subject to specific geographical circumstances. Improperly drawn baselines may significantly extend coastal State jurisdiction seaward in a way that prejudices freedom of navigation and overflight and other internationally lawful uses of the sea. An objective application of the baseline rules contained in UNCLOS restrains extravagant coastal State claims over the global commons and protects the rights and freedoms of all nations.

Normal baselines run along the low-water mark of the coast.[1] The United States recognizes normal baselines as the principal method for drawing baselines. In the case of islands situated on atolls or of islands having fringing reefs, the normal baseline is the seaward low-water line on the drying reef chartered as being above the level of chart datum.[2] While UNCLOS does not address reef closing lines, any such line may not diminish freedom of navigation and overflight and other internationally lawful uses of the sea.

Straight baselines may be appropriate to enclose waters which, because of their close interrelationship with the land, have the character of internal waters. By using straight baselines, a state may also eliminate complex patterns of geometry or smooth out contiguities in the coastline, such as enclaves, in its territorial sea, that otherwise would result from the use of normal baselines. Straight baselines can eliminate these irregularities or enclaves in the territorial sea that would otherwise result from the use of normal baselines.[3] Properly drawn straight baselines do not result in a significant extension of the limits of the territorial sea seaward from those that would result from the application of normal baselines. Furthermore, with the introduction of the EEZ, the rationale for the use of straight baselines has all but disappeared since they were proposed originally to internalize coastal State fisheries near the coast. By using lawful low water basepoints along the coast to measure the territorial sea and EEZ, states may address irregularities that appear on the coast without

1 United Nations Convention on the Law of the Sea art. 5, Dec. 10, 1982, 1833 U.N.T.S. 397 [hereinafter UNCLOS].

2 UNCLOS, art. 6.

3 United Nations, *Baselines: An Examination of the Relevant Provisions of the United Nations Convention on the Law of the Sea* 17 (1989).

exceeding entitlements for the outer reaches of the territorial sea, and especially the EEZ. The effect of an irregular coast on maritime claims diminishes the farther out in the water that you go. Straight baselines are based on the principles set forth in the 1951 Anglo-Norwegian Fisheries Case decided by the International Court of Justice.[4] The decision held by a vote of eight to four that Norway's methodology for drawing modest straight baselines to smooth out coastal irregularities by using *skjærgaard* along its jagged coastline were not contrary to international law. These offshore formations, including low-tide elevations, hug the coastline, which is deeply indented and cut into.

The use of straight baselines today in a way that prejudices international navigation, overflight, and communications interests of other states is counter to the vision of UNCLOS as a constitution for the world's oceans and protection of community interests. Consequently, the United States asserts that straight baselines should be used sparingly, and where they are used, they should be drawn conservatively to reflect the one rationale for their use that is consistent with the UNCLOS, namely the simplification and rationalization of the measurement of the territorial sea and other maritime zones off highly irregular coastlines.

Straight baselines in accordance with these rules may be used only in geographic situations where the coastline is deeply indented and cut into or if there is a fringe of islands along the coast in the immediate vicinity of the coast.[5] In such cases, states may continue to use normal baselines running along the low-water mark along the coast. The U.S. view is that "deeply indented and cut into" refers to a very distinctive coastal configuration in which a locality is deeply indented and cut into dash there exist at least three indentations that are deep and in close proximity to one another.[6] The depth of penetration of each deep indentation from the proposed straight baseline is, as a rule, greater than half the length of that baseline segment. The "fringe of islands along the coast in the immediate vicinity of the coast" refers to several islands.[7] The United States asserts that the most landward point of each island should lie no more than 24 miles from the mainland coastline. Each island to which a straight baseline is to be drawn is not more than 24 miles apart from the island from which the

4 Anglo-Norwegian Fisheries Case (U.K. v. Nor.), Judgment, 1951 I.C.J. Rep. 116, 128, 142–43 (Dec. 18).

5 UNCLOS, art. 7.

6 United Nations Convention on the Law of the Sea, Message from the President of the United States Transmitting, Sen. Treaty Doc. 103–39, p. 9 (Sen. Treaty Doc. 103–39).

7 UNCLOS, art. 121.

straight baseline is drawn. The islands should mask at least 50 percent of the mainland coastline in any given locality.

Straight baselines must not depart to any appreciable extent from the general direction of the coast and the sea areas lying within the lines must be sufficiently closely linked to the land domain to be subject to the regime of internal waters.[8] The United states has taken the position that to be consistent with this provision, straight baseline segments must not depart to any appreciable extent from the general direction of the coastline, by reference to general direction lines which in each locality shall not exceed 60 miles in length; not exceed 24 miles in length individually; and result in sea areas situated landward of the straight baseline segments that are sufficiently closely linked to the land domain to be subject to the regime of internal waters.[9] Minor deviations from these rules do not necessarily mean the straight baselines are inconsistent with the law of the sea.

Straight baselines shall not be drawn to and from low tide elevations, unless lighthouses or "similar installations" which are permanently above sea level have been built on them or except in instances where the drawing of baselines to in from such elevations has received general international recognition.[10] "Similar installations" are those that are permanent, substantial, and used for safety of navigation. "General international recognition" includes recognition by the major maritime users over a long period of time. Basepoints for all straight baselines must be located on land territory and situated on or landward of the low water line. No straight baseline segment may be drawn to a base point located on the land territory of another state.[11]

The United States adheres to the regime of baselines as set forth in UNCLOS. While the United States is not party to UNCLOS, it relies on the Presidential Proclamation of March 10, 1983, which states that the treaty reflects customary international law in respect to the principles that underlie the proper and legal establishment of baselines.[12] The normal baseline for measuring the breadth of the territorial sea is the low-water line along the coast.[13] Straight baselines are limited to two specific geographic situations: (1) "localities where the coastline is deeply indented and cut into, and (2) "if there is a fringe of islands along the coast in its immediate vicinity."[14] Furthermore, "the sea areas lying within

8 UNCLOS, art. 7(3).
9 Sen. Treaty Doc. 103–39, p. 9.
10 UNCLOS, art. 7(4).
11 Sen. Treaty Doc. 103–39, p. 10.
12 UNCLOS, arts. 5–11 and 13–14.
13 UNCLOS, art. 5.
14 UNCLOS, art. 7.

the lines must be sufficiently closely linked to the land domain to be subject to the regime of internal waters."[15]

2.2 *China's Baseline Law*

China has widespread use of straight baselines and does not apply them conservatively. In 1958, China claimed for all territories a 12 nm territorial sea measured from straight baselines, including along the mainland and territories of Taiwan and its islands, the Pescadores (Penghu) Islands (an archipelago of 90 islands and islets in the Taiwan Strait), Pratas (Dongsha or Tungsha) Islands (administered by Taiwan), the Paracel (Xisha or Hsisha) Islands, Macclesfield Bank (Chungsha or Qiongzhou), Spratly (Nansha) Islands and "all other islands belonging to China."[16] The claims did not include specific geographic points.

Numerous islands inside the baselines were claimed as "islands of the Chinese inland waters."[17] These include Dongyin (Tungyin) Island, Gaodeng Island (Kaoteng Island), some 36 Matsu Islands, the Paichuan Islands, Wuchiu Island, the Greater and Lesser Quemoy Islands, Tatan Island, Erhtan Island and Tungting Island.[18] China also claims the waters in Bohai Bay (Gulf of Pohai) and Chiungchow (Hainan) Strait enclosed in baselines as "inland waters."[19]

China has few indentations along the mainland coast, and these are relatively modest and may qualify as historic bays, but not justify the complete straight baseline system along the entire length of the coast of mainland China. In the Fisheries Jurisdiction Case, for example, the Court held that Norway's coastline typifies an area amenable to straight baselines because the contiguity is "[v]ery broken along its whole length, it constantly opens out into indentations often penetrating for great distances inland: the Porsangerfjord, for instance, penetrates 75 sea miles inland."[20] While parts of China's coastline are deeply indented and cut into, the indentations are quite modest, while China has pushed straight baselines miles out into the ocean.

On February 25, 1992, The Law of the People's Republic of China on the Territorial Sea reiterated territorial title claims over mainland of China and

15 UNCLOS, art. 7(3).

16 Declaration on the Territorial Sea (September 4, 1958), ¶ 4, reprinted in Department of State, Limits in the Seas No. 43, Straight Baselines: People's Republic of China 2–6 (July 1, 1972, July 31, 1978).

17 Id., ¶ 2.

18 Id., ¶ 2.

19 Declaration on the Territorial Sea (September 4, 1958), ¶ 3.

20 Id., 133.

its offshore islands and waters contiguous to them.[21] Areas claimed include Taiwan and the various affiliated islands including the Senkaku (Diaoyu) Islands, Pescadores (Penghu) Islands, Pratas (Dongsha) Islands (administered by Taiwan), Paracel (Xisha) Islands, Nansha (Spratly) Islands and "other islands ..."[22] China uses straight baselines as its general method for drawing baselines, rather than normal baselines running along the low-water marks along the coast. Neither the 1958 nor the 1992 legislation refers to normal baselines or the baseline running along the low water line along the coast, which is a departure from state practice.

On May 15, 1996, China declared straight baselines along most of its coastline, from which it measures the breadth of its territorial sea, contiguous zone, and its other claimed maritime zones.[23] That same day, China claimed an EEZ and ratified UNCLOS. China announced the baselines of part of its territorial sea adjacent to the mainland and those of the territorial sea adjacent to the Paracel (Xisha) Islands. The baseline system is comprised of 49 base points along the coast running from Shandong Peninsula to the west coast of Hainan Island. The 48 segments that connect the 49 base points total 1,734.1 miles.[24] The segments range in length from 0.1 miles (segment 45–46 on Hainan Island) to 121.7 miles (segment 8–9 off the northeast coast of China).[25] China notified the United Nations of these geographical coordinates on July 5, 1996. The 1996 Declaration did not address China's baseline from its land boundary terminus with North Korea, including the Pohai (Bo-Hai) area, or along its coast in the Gulf of Tonkin, or around other islands it claims in the South China Sea. Unlike Vietnam, however, China has not claimed Tonkin Gulf as historic internal waters, despite the straight baseline connecting Hainan Island to the mainland.[26]

Over half of the baseline segments (25 of the 48 segments) are more than 24 miles in length, with three (6 percent) of the segments exceeding 100 miles.[27]

21 *Law on the Territorial Sea and the Contiguous Zone* of 25 February 1992, reprinted in Annex 2, Department of State, *Limits in the Seas* No. 117, *Straight Baseline Claims: China* (July 9, 1996).

22 Law on the Territorial Sea and the Contiguous Zone of 25 February 1992, art. 2.

23 Declaration of the Government of the People's Republic of China on the baselines of the territorial sea, 15 May 1996.

24 Department of State, *Limits in the Sea* No. 117, at 4.

25 *Limits in the Sea* No. 117, at 4.

26 Department of State, *Limits in the Seas No. 99, Straight Baselines: Vietnam* 9–10 (1983). In 2000, China and Vietnam entered into a maritime boundary agreement in the Gulf of Tonkin that entered into force June 30, 2004. Report No. 5–25, at 3745–3758 (2005).

27 *Limits in the Sea* No. 117, at 4.

Most of this coastline is smooth, and not deeply indented or cut into or featuring a fringe of islands.

China also uses low-tide elevations to connect its straight baseline system in violation of UNCLOS. Low-tide features may be used in accordance so long as they are within 12 nm of the mainland or an island.[28] China purports to use at least one low-tide elevation beyond this limit, however.[29]

The length and location into the sea of many of China's baseline points indicate that the straight baseline system along the mainland coast is incompatible with UNCLOS, and that China should be using a normal baseline system along its coast. The United States has stated that baseline segments should not exceed 24 miles in length.[30] The 24-mile maximum segment length is implied from a close reading of the relevant articles UNCLOS.[31]

Baselines shall be in the "immediate vicinity" of the coast.[32] Furthermore, "the sea areas lying within the line must be sufficiently closely linked to the land domain to be subject to the regime of internal waters."[33] The U.S. views this text as a strong implication that the waters to be internalized would otherwise be part of the territorial sea.[34] From this perspective it is "difficult to envision a situation where international waters (beyond 12 miles from the appropriate low-water line) could be "sufficiently closely linked" as to be converted to internal waters.[35] A 1989 U.N. study concluded that determination of whether conditions apply that would permit the use of straight baselines requires application of the "spirit as well as the letter of the first paragraph of article 7."[36]

Furthermore, even if the baselines were valid, the right of non-suspendable innocent passage still "shall apply" to such areas that previously were open to navigation and later enclosed within straight baselines.[37] The continuance of transit rights through the regime of innocent passage preserves pre-existing

---

28 UNCLOS, art. 13.

29 *Limits in the Sea* No. 117, at 6 (DMA chart 94260, point 10).

30 U.S. Department of State Dispatch Supplement, *Law of the Sea Convention, Letters of Transmittal and Submittal and Commentary*, Vol. 6, February 1995, p. 8. See also, Victor Prescott, *The Maritime Political Boundaries of the World* 69 (1985).

31 *Limits in the Sea* No. 117, at 5.

32 UNCLOS, art. 7(1).

33 UNCLOS, art. 7(3).

34 *Limits in the Sea* No. 117, at 5.

35 Id.

36 United Nations, *Baselines: An Examination of the Relevant Provisions of the United Nations Convention on the Law of the Sea*, 1989, p. 17.

37 UNCLOS, art. 8(2).

access to the waters that were territorial in nature before the application of straight baselines and makes it untenable to assert a straight baseline segment exceeding 24 miles.[38] In any event the United States suggests that a maximum "reasonable limit" on the distance between baseline points is a straight baseline no greater than 48 miles, or quadruple the breadth of the territorial sea.[39]

China also skirts the rules on fringing islands.[40] Although there is a fringe of islands farther south along the Taiwan Strait, most of the basepoints are disconnected from them and they lie at a distance greater than 12 miles from the coast, and at one point some 50 miles.[41] China's basepoints purport to enclose waters that are not "closely linked to the land domain."

The straight baseline systems along the mainland coast of China also cuts off the eastern approaches to Hainan (Qiongzhou) Strait, a strait used for international navigation. The right of transit passage applies in the strait.[42] China might suggest that this straight baseline is lawful because it predates adoption of rules in UNCLOS, but this position is not convincing for the same reason all of China's historic claims fail – the entire point of the treaty was to ensure states conform to the new metrics.

China also may claim that for ships of all flags except Vietnam or China or Tonkin Gulf destination shipping, Qiongzhou Strait qualifies for the "Messina exception" to transit passage, thereby limiting international shipping to non-suspendable innocent passage because a route of similar convenience already exists to the east and south of Hainan Island.[43] For example, a container ship underway from the port of Yokohama bound for Busan via the Strait of Malacca certainly has a route of similar convenience outside of Hainan Strait. This appears to be a reasonable argument for most international shipping that is transiting the South China Sea and not entering Tonkin Gulf. Regardless of whether the navigational regime of non-suspendable innocent passage in the "Messina exception" might apply for most international shipping through Qiongzhou Strait, this exception to transit passage is not dependent on the validity of straight baselines.[44]

---

38 *Limits in the Sea* No. 117, at 5.

39 Department of State, *Limits in the Sea* No. 106, *Developing Standard Guidelines for Evaluating Straight Baselines* 14 (August 31, 1987).

40 UNCLOS, art. 7(1).

41 *Limits in the Sea* No. 117, at 7.

42 UNCLOS, art. 37.

43 UNCLOS, art. 38(1).

44 James Kraska, "China and Canada are Unlikely to Collaborate on Unlawful Straight Baselines," 19 *Chinese Journal of International Law* 803, 804 (2020).

Even Chinese scholars admit the country's approach to maritime baselines is problematic: "The straight baselines set forth in the [Chinese] Law on the Territorial Sea constitute the basis for demarcating the outer limits of the EEZ and the continental shelf. China applies the method of straight baselines to all its coasts no matter whether they are deeply indented or not, which is controversial in international law, so it may be queried whether China's practice conforms to the relevant provisions of [UNCLOS]."[45]

2.2.1 Paracel Islands Straight Baseline Claims

A second system of straight baselines is declared around the Paracel Islands, surrounded by 28 basepoints completely enclosing the islands.[46] the law of the sea convention, however, restricts the application of archipelagic straight baselines 2 archipelagic States there are "constituted wholly by one or more archipelagos and may include other islands."[47] An "archipelago" "means a group of islands, including parts of islands, interconnecting waters and other natural features which are so closely inter related that such islands, waters and other natural features form an intrinsic geographic, economic and political entity, or which historically have been regarded as such."[48]

The United States, the Philippines, and Vietnam protested the Chinese claims. On June 26, 1998, for example, Vietnam stated in a note verbal that China's establishment of straight baselines of the Hoang Sa (Paracel) archipelago, part of Vietnamese territorial sovereignty, run counter to international law and is absolutely null and void."[49] This mid-ocean archipelagic baseline system is unlawful. The Philippine-China arbitration tribunal. The tribunal wrote:

> The convention also provides, in Article 7, for states to make use of straight baselines under certain circumstances, and the tribunal is aware of the practice of some states in employing straight baselines with respect to offshore archipelagos to approximate the effect of archipelagic baselines. In the tribunal's view any application of straight baselines to the Spratly islands in this fashion would be contrary to the convention.

45 Zou Keyuan, *China's Marine Legal System and the Law of the Sea* 92–94 (2005).
46 *Limits in the Seas* 117 at 8 (citing China's 1992 and 1996 laws).
47 UNCLOS, art. 46.
48 Id.
49 Vietnam, Dispute Regarding the law on the exclusive economic zone in the continental shelf of the People's Republic of China, which was passed on 26 June 1998, communicated by the Permanent Mission of the Socialist Republic of Viet Nam to the United Nations in a note verbale dated 6 August, 1998, reprinted in 38 Law of the Sea Bulletin 54–55 (1998).

> Article 7 provides for the application of straight baselines only "in localities where the coastline is deeply indented and cut into or if there is a fringe of islands along the coast in its immediate vicinity." These conditions do not include the situation of an offshore archipelago. Although the convention does not expressly preclude the use of straight baselines in other circumstances, the tribunal considers that the grant of permission in Article 7 concerning straight baselines generally, together with the conditional permission in Articles 46 and 47 for certain states to draw archipelagic baselines, excludes the possibility of employing straight baselines in other circumstances, in particular with respect to offshore archipelagos not meeting the criteria for archipelagic baselines. Any other interpretation would effectively render the conditions in articles 7 and 47 meaningless. Notwithstanding the practice of some states to the contrary, the tribunal sees no evidence that any deviations from this rule have amounted to the formation of a new rule of customary international law that would permit a departure from the express provisions of the convention.[50]

On December 28, 2016, the United States delivered a note verbale to China's July 12–13 repudiation of the Tribunal's award, which stated:

> [T]to the extent China's claim to "internal waters" contemplates waters within straight baselines around any South China Sea Island, the United States objects … Consistent with international law as reflected in the Law of the Sea Convention, including Articles 5, 7, 46, and 47, China cannot claim straight or archipelagic baselines in the Paracel Islands, Pratas Island, Maccelesfield Bank, Scarborough Reef, or the Spratly Islands. Similarly, China's claims related to what it calls "Nanhai Zhudao (the South China Sea Islands)," and to "Dongsha Qundao (the Dongsha Islands), Xisha Qundao (the Xisha Islands), Zhongsha Qundao (the Zhongsha Islands) and Nansha Qundao (the Nansha Islands)" would be unlawful to the extent they are intended to include any maritime claim based on grouping multiple islands together as a single unit for purposes

50 South China Sea Arbitration (Phil. v. China), Case No. 2013-19, Award, ¶ 575–576 (Perm. Ct. Arb. 2016).

of establishing internal waters, territorial sea, contiguous zone, exclusive economic zone and continental shelf or any other maritime claim.[51]

2.2.2 Senkaku Islands Straight Baseline Claims

The 1996 declaration published geographical coordinates for straight baselines for most of the Chinese coastline, and the Paracel (Xisha) Islands. China claimed straight baselines around the Senkaku Islands in a statement on September 10, 2012.[52] Aside from the overlapping claims of sovereignty by Japan and China, the United States objected based on excessive straight baseline claims. The U.S. does not recognize these claims and protested them in 1996 and 2013 and conducted operational assertions in fiscal years 1997, 2011, 2013 through 2016.[53]

On March 7, 2013, the United States sent a diplomatic note to the Ministry of Foreign Affairs of the People's Republic of China regarding a "Statement of the Government of the People's Republic of China on the Baselines of the Territorial Sea of Diaoyu Dao and Its Affiliated Islands," dated September 10, 2012 ("Statement"). The U.S. diplomatic note protests the establishment by China of straight baselines around the Senkaku Islands, contrary to customary international law as reflected in the UN Convention on the Law of the Sea.[54] The baseline rules in international law distinguish between "normal baselines" (following the low-water mark along the coast at low tide) and "straight baselines," which may only be employed in certain limited geographic situations. The United States has lodged diplomatic protests regarding excessive straight baseline claims of many countries, including a previous protest to China regarding its assertion of straight baselines around mainland China (including Hainan Island) and the Paracel Islands. Excerpts follow from the March 7, 2013, U.S. diplomatic note to China state:

---

51 United States Note Verbale to People's Republic of China, December 28, 2106, available at https://usun.usmission.gov/wp-content/uploads/sites/296/200602_KDC_ChinasUnlawful.pdf.

52 China, "Statement of the Government of the People's Republic of China on the Baselines of the Territorial Sea of Diaoyu Dao and Its Affiliated Islands," 10 September 2012, reprinted in 80 *Law of the Sea Bulletin* 30–31 (2012).

53 Department of Defense Representative for Ocean Policy Affairs (REPOPA), *Maritime Claims Reference Manual* (MCRM) (January 2017). (Issued pursuant to DoD Instruction S-2005.01, Freedom of Navigation (FON) Program (U), October 20, 2014).

54 *Digest of United States Practice in International Law* 369–370 (CarrieLyn D. Guymon, ed. 2013).

The Government of the United States notes that the Statement lists 17 base points that connect to create two straight baseline systems around two groups of islands known collectively in the United States as the Senkaku Islands (China refers to the islands as the Daioyu Islands). The first system of straight baselines consists of 12 segments enclosing Uotsuri Shima (Diaoyu Dao), Kuba Shima (Huangwei Yu), Minami Kojima (Nanxiao Dao), and certain other features. The second system of straight baselines consists of 5 segments surrounding one island, Taisho To (Chiwei Yu) and its surrounding features.

The United States recalls that, as recognized in customary international law and as reflected in Part II of the [UNCLOS], except where otherwise provided in the Convention, the normal baseline for measuring the breadth of the territorial sea is the low-water line along the coast, as marked on large-scale charts officially recognized by the coastal State. As provided for in Article 7 of the Convention, only in localities where the coastline is deeply indented and cut into, or if there is a fringe of islands along the coast in its immediate vicinity, may the coastal State elect to use the method of straight baselines joining appropriate points in drawing the baseline from which the breadth of the territorial sea is measured.

The Senkaku Islands comprise several small features spread over an area of approximately 46 square nautical miles. The United States takes no position on the ultimate sovereignty of the Senkaku Islands. Irrespective of sovereignty claims, international law does not permit the drawing of straight baselines around these features. The Senkaku Islands do not meet the specific geographic requirements for the drawing of straight baselines because their coastline is not deeply indented and cut into, and they do not constitute a fringe of islands along the coast in its immediate vicinity.

To the extent that the Statement might be intended to suggest that archipelagic baselines may be drawn around the Senkaku Islands, this also would be inconsistent with international law. Under customary international law, as reflected in Part IV of the Law of the Sea Convention, only "archipelagic States" may draw archipelagic baselines joining the outermost points of an archipelago. Coastal States, such as China and the United States, do not meet the definition of an "archipelagic State" reflected in Part IV of the Convention. China, therefore, may not draw

> archipelagic baselines enclosing offshore islands and waters, and the proper baseline for such features is the low-water line of the islands.
>
> … These baselines, as asserted, impinge on the rights, freedoms, and uses of the sea by all nations by expanding the seaward limit of maritime zones and enclosing as internal waters areas that were previously territorial sea.
>
> The United States requests that the Government of China review its current practice on baselines, explain its justification under international law when defining its maritime claims, and make appropriate modifications to bring these claims into accordance with international law as reflected in [UNCLOS]….[55]

2.2.3 China's Historic Internal Waters Claims

Internal waters are those landward of the baseline.[56] Article 2 makes clear the generally recognized rule that coastal State sovereignty extends to internal waters. In articles 218 and 220, the Convention adds to general notions of sovereignty and jurisdiction over internal water by expressly authorizing port state enforcement action within internal waters for pollution violations that have occurred elsewhere. This authorization does not imply any limitation on other enforcement actions that coastal States may choose to exercise in their ports or other internal waters.

Subject to ancient customs regarding the entry of ships in danger or distress (force measure) and the exception noted below, the convention does not limit the right of the coastal State to restrict entry into or transit through its internal waters, port entry, imports, or immigration. The exception to the right of the coastal State to deny entry into or transit through its internal waters is found in Article 8(2), which provides:

> When the establishment of a straight baseline … has the effect of enclosing as internal waters areas which had not previously been considered as such, a right of innocent passage as provided in this convention shall exist in those waters.

If a foreign flag vessel is found in a coastal State's internal waters without its permission, the full range of reasonable enforcement procedures is available

---

55 China's claimed baselines of the territorial sea of the Senkaku Islands, *Digest of United States Practice in International Law* Ch. 12, 369–370 (2009–2013).

56 UNCLOS, art. 8(1).

against a foreign commercial vessel. With respect to foreign warships and other government ships on non-commercial service, which are immune from the enforcement jurisdiction of all states except the flag State, it may be inferred that a coastal State may require such a vessel to leave its internal waters immediately.[57] Furthermore, a port State has the right to refuse to permit foreign ships from entering or remaining within its internal waters.

China's dashed line claim in the South China Sea is an attempt at a claim of historic internal waters. Yet, there is no coherent legal basis for its "Nine-Dashed Line" claim in the South China Sea, which was formally announced in a note verbale in 2009. As Secretary of State Michael Pompeo stated, "China uses intimidation to undermine the sovereign rights of Southeast Asian coastal States in the South China Sea, bully them out of offshore resources, assert unilateral dominion, and replace international law with "might makes right."[58] Beijing's approach has been clear for years. In 2010, then-PRC Foreign Minister Yang Jiechi told his ASEAN counterparts that "China is a big country and other countries are small countries and that is just a fact."

An Annex VII Arbitral Tribunal constituted under UNCLOS held unanimously on July 12, 2016, that China's maritime claims have no basis in international law and do not perfect valid historic internal waters claims. On July 13, 2020, the United States aligned itself with the Tribunal's decision.

Claims to historic waters should comport with the three-part test in international law as restated by the United Nations in 1962: (1) exercise of authority over the waters; (2) continuity of the exercise of authority; and (3) acquiescence or acceptance by neighboring states.[59] China's "nine-dash line" claim does not pass this three-part test. Furthermore, sovereignty over land features may be claimed under international law only in five circumstances: (1) accretion, that is a build-up through natural geologic processes, such as a volcanic eruption, (2) cession, or voluntary transfer via treaty, (3) conquest, but only before adoption of the UN Charter in 1945, (4) occupation of *terra nullius*, that is not mere inchoate discovery, but actual occupation, and (5) prescriptive exercise of authority that is public, peaceful and extending over a long period of time. The burden of proof is on the claimant state to present facts and law in support of the claim.

---

57 Id., arts. 25 and 30.

58 Michael R. Pompeo, U.S. Secretary of State, U.S. Position on Maritime Claims in the South China Sea, July 13, 2020.

59 UN Doc. A/CN.4/143, "Juridical Regime of Historic Waters Including Historic Bays – Study prepared by the Secretariat," 2 *Yearbook of the International Law Commission* 1–27 (1962).

China's attempts to construct a geostrategic advantage through its promiscuous use of straight baselines is part of it psychological, or legal "warfare" (lawfare) to position itself as the dominant power in the Pacific region. The emergence of coastal States employing these "psycho-legal" boundaries were foretold decades ago.[60] No state has leveraged this tool more effectively than China. China's baselines claims have strategic consequences for Japan's independence, since they assert the exercise of sovereignty over Japanese territory in the Senkaku Islands and limit the viability of U.S. and allied maritime presence and operations in areas surrounding Japan, making defense of Japanese sovereignty more difficult. Limitations on American or Australian naval operations in East Asia undermine the ability of U.S. forces to respond effectively and with overwhelming force to a regional contingency. This strategic dimension is the most important impact of China's unlawful claims and mean that Japan's interests are intertwined with its partner nations in the region and with the United States from outside the region.

60 Ken Booth, *Law, Force, and Diplomacy at Sea* 164 (1985).

CHAPTER 10

Revisiting the Legal Status of Dependent Archipelagic Waters from First Principles

Richard Barnes

1 Introduction

An archipelago is a 'group of islands, including parts of islands, interconnecting waters and other natural features which are so closely interrelated that such islands, waters and other natural features form an intrinsic geographical, economic and political entity, or which historically have been regarded as such'.[1] For the most part the law on archipelagic States is well-settled. Part IV of the United Nations Convention on the Law of the Sea 1982 (LOSC) defines an archipelagic State and the status of archipelagic waters. It establishes rules for drawing baselines around the archipelago, and it delimits specific navigational and other rights within archipelagic waters. Churchill and Lowe observe that the law has worked well since the entry into force of the LOSC and that the regime appears to balance well the interests of archipelagic and maritime States.[2] Similarly, Davenport notes that the LOSC settled years of debate over the status of groups of islands and established an effective regime.[3] However, such remarks concern the regime of archipelagic States or mid-ocean archipelagos. This refers to groups of islands that are States in their own right, such as Indonesia, Philippines, Fiji, and Nicobar and Andaman. The law of the sea draws a distinction between archipelagic States and other archipelagos, namely coastal archipelagos and dependent or outlying archipelagos. Coastal archipelagos constitute fringes of islands and other features close to the coastline, such as the skjargard along Norway's coast, and similar features along the coasts of Sweden, Finland and parts of Canada. Dependent archipelagos are groups of islands that form part of a State that is comprised mainly

1 Article 46(b), United Nations Convention on the Law of the Sea 1982, 1833 UNTS 3.

2 RR Churchill and AV Lowe, *The Law of the Sea* (3rd edn, Manchester University Press, 1999), 130.

3 T Davenport, 'The archipelagic regime', in D.R. Rothwell, A. G. Oude Elferink, K.N. Scott and T. Stephens (eds), *The Oxford Handbook of the Law of the Sea* (Oxford: Oxford University Press, 2015) 134–158, 158.

DOI:10.1163/9789004518629_011

by a continental landmass. Examples include the Azores (Portugal), Faroes (Denmark), Galapagos (Ecuador) and the Falkland Islands (UK). As a matter of treaty law, the LOSC regime on archipelagos applies only to archipelagic States. And only archipelagic States may enjoy the benefits of the special regime established under Part IV of the LOSC. Of course, coastal archipelagos are covered by the rules on straight baselines.[4] And so they may benefit in part from the inclusion of some littoral waters within the baseline as internal waters, as well as the seawards extension of their maritime zones.

In contrast to archipelagic States, the legal position of dependent archipelagos remains uncertain or as Davenport describes it: 'mired in uncertainty'.[5] Whilst it is clear that the LOSC only addresses archipelagic States, some writers take the view that under customary international law, dependent archipelagos are also entitled to make use of straight baselines to enclose waters with the island group.[6] Others, such as Roach, reject this, arguing that State practice is simply too inconsistent to satisfy the requirements for the formation of a customary rule.[7] Much of the recent debate has focused specifically on China's claims in the South China Sea Arbitration, which generated a slew of scholarship advocating China's rights to assert archipelagic status over various features in the South China Seas.[8] It is possible that the contentious nature of this particular set of claims may colour how the position of dependent archipelagos more generally should be considered. Indeed, a quick survey of the legal basis of such claims indicates that the question is not as clear cut as first appears.

The legal basis for archipelagic baselines can be traced to the *Fisheries case* (1951), where the ICJ acknowledged the use of straight baselines in certain

4 DR Rothwell and T Stephens, *The International Law of the Sea* (Hart, 2010) 183.

5 Ibid, p. 156. See further, S Kopela, *Dependent Archipelagos in the Law of the Sea* (Martinus Nijhoff, 2013).

6 See for example, Chinese Society of International Law, 'The South China Sea Arbitration Awards: A Critical Study' (2018) 17(2) *Chinese Journal of International Law* 207–748, at paras 558, 588.

7 JA Roach, 'Offshore Archipelagos Enclosed by Straight Baselines: An Excessive Claim?' (2018) 49 *Ocean Development and International Law* 176–202.

8 See J Li and Z Jie, 'A Preliminary Analysis of the Application of Archipelagic Regime and the Delimitation of the South China Sea' (2010) *China Oceans Law Review* 167–185; J Nan, 'On the Outlying Archipelagos of Continental States' (2012) *China Oceans Law Review* 41–57; H Nong, L Jianwei, and C Pingping, 'The Concept of Archipelagic State and the South China Sea: UNCLOS, State Practice and Implication' (2013) *China Oceans Law Review* 209–239; K-C Fu, 'Freedom of Navigation and the Chinese Straight Baselines in the South China Sea' in MH Nordquist, JN Moore, R Beckman and R Long (eds.), *Freedom of Navigation and Globalization* (Brill, 2015) 190–196.

exceptional circumstances.[9] Where a coastline is deeply indented, the baseline becomes independent of the low water mark and becomes determined by geometrical construction.[10] The *Fisheries case* is the general authority for the idea that exceptional geographic and other circumstances justify a departure from the ordinary rule that baselines must be drawn along the low water mark. Indeed, the Court observed that where the reasons for the exception become so many, then the normal rule would disappear under the exceptions.[11] The permissibility of drawing straight baselines is reflected in Article 7(1) of the LOSC: 'In localities where the coastline is deeply indented and cut into, or if there is a fringe, of islands, along, the coast in its immediate vicinity, the method of straight baselines joining appropriate points may be employed in the drawing of baselines from which the width of the territorial sea is measured'. Although this rule originally concerned coastal baselines, the acceptance of the principles underlying the exceptions opened the door to its application in other circumstances, specifically the case for a special regime of archipelagic waters.

During the negotiation of the LOSC, archipelagic States argued that their exceptional geographic and political situation merited the development of special rules that allowed them to assert a higher degree of control over the waters of the archipelago.[12] In general, the negotiations involved three connected elements. The first element focused on the special status of archipelagos, i.e., identifying which special circumstances justified special rules for archipelagos. The second element focused on how such claims were to be balanced against the interests of other States and in particular any reduction in navigational freedoms that would result from potential enclosure of large ocean areas within exclusive coastal State control. The third element focused upon how baselines should be drawn to ensure that they reflected such a balance of interests. These three elements of the negotiations ultimately resulted in a special regime for archipelagic States, as found in Part IV of the LOSC. All three elements are connected, but it is worth emphasising that whilst baselines are of upmost practical importance and will define the extent of the archipelago, the drawing of such lines is an entitlement that flows from a special status attaching to the State.

In recent years, it would appear that the debate about archipelagic claims has moved away from questions about the status of the archipelago to challenges

---

9 *Fisheries Case* (*United Kingdom v Norway*) (1951) ICJ Reports 116, 128–132.

10 Ibid, 128.

11 Ibid, 129.

12 See generally Kopela (n 5).

to the validity of baselines drawn by archipelagic States, and whether they are drawn in a way that is consistent with the LOSC. Arguably this shift has gone so far as to marginalize consideration of the basic requirements justifying archipelagic status. Thus, the enjoyment of specific rights focuses mostly upon the drawing of baselines rather than special features of the archipelago.[13] Or, in other words, it has shifted to the practice of States making claims rather than any considered assessment of the justification or legal basis for making such claims. The legal justification of the claims is either skipped over or given superficial consideration. However, logic dictates that any legal rights in archipelagic waters are enjoyed because of the special status attaching to the archipelago. As Su correctly notes, the drawing of baselines is merely a technical step in determining the extent of such rights.[14] However, if this is the case, and the debate on dependent archipelagic claims is collapsed into an assessment of baselines, then it is not clear the extent to which the features of an archipelago, i.e., the geographic, economic and political unity of the archipelago, can or should continue to play a role in the critical first stage of the process – determining the permissibility of archipelagic claims per se.

This paper seeks to revisit this aspect of claims to archipelagic waters to consider the extent to which the geographic, economic, and political unity of the archipelago can and should influence dependent archipelagic claims. These conditions are important for two reasons. First, the requirements for geographic, economic, political, and historical unity serve to ensure there is a material connection between legal claims or maritime jurisdiction and the underlying social, economic and geopolitical reality. This is critical because, as I argue elsewhere, law must be sensitive to the material conditions at play in our oceans.[15] At an ontological level, law of the sea must relate to the physical world and be part of a constructive process. This means that the law should respond to the fluid and dynamic nature of ocean systems, as well as reflect the contingent relationship between humans and resource systems. In an

13 See for example the papers cited at footnotes 7 to 8.

14 See J Su, 'The Unity of Status of Continental States' Outlying Archipelagos' (2020) 35 *IJMCL* 801–835, 819. However, Su then appears to analyse the simple assertion of baselines as evidence of a unity, or at least taking this as an implication that a unity exists (pp. 819–23).

15 See further R Barnes, 'Environmental Rights in Marine Spaces' in S Bogojevic and R Rayfuse (eds), *Environmental Rights in Europe and Beyond* (Hart, 2018) 49–85; R Barnes, 'The Construction of Ocean Space in Areas beyond National Jurisdiction. A fisheries perspective' in V De Lucia, L Nguyen and AG Oude Elferink (eds) *International Law and Marine Areas beyond National Jurisdiction: Reflections on Justice, Space, Knowledge and Power* (Brill, 2022) 275–315.

archipelagic context this is importance because it is reflected in the idea of a fundamental relationship between the islands and ocean spaces, and with the peoples who live in those spaces. Second, since there is no discreet legal basis for dependent archipelagos under Part IV of the LOSC, I argue that any special status they enjoy must arise under customary international law. Furthermore, I argue that customary international law permits claims to dependent archipelagos. However, such claims should demonstrate the geographic, economic and political unity of mid-ocean archipelagos. This is because such claims must be consistent with the existing legal framework that frames such entitlements. These arguments are advanced in the second part of the paper. In the third part of the paper, the geographic, economic, political, and historical requirements for an archipelago are unpacked. The purpose here is to consider how such factors play a role in mediating claims to offshore archipelagos.

2 Claims to Archipelagic Waters for Dependent Archipelagos

If Part IV of the LOSC is not exhaustive of archipelagic claims, then there are two possibilities for the use of straight baselines around dependent archipelagos. The first is for the general provisions on straight baselines in Article 7 to be applied to dependent archipelagos. The second is to identify a rule on dependent archipelagos under customary international law. In this latter case, then the requirements for the existence of a rules of customary international law must be satisfied.

Either approach appears to be ruled out by the tribunal in the *South China Sea* arbitration. Here the tribunal noted the existence of practice by some States using straight baselines around offshore archipelagos to approximate the effect of archipelagic baselines but rejected this as applicable to the Spratly Islands.[16] The tribunal explicitly rejected the application of Article 7 to offshore archipelagos, observing that Article 7 applies only to islands that fringe the main coastline. The tribunal accepted that there were other situations where straight baselines could be used but observed that this does not include offshore archipelagos. The tribunal reasoned that to extend Article 7 further would effectively render the provisions of Articles 7 and 47 meaningless. The reasoning on this point was unclear, but presumably it was meant that that this would render straight baselines generally applicable rather than exceptional.

16 *In the Matter of the South China Sea Arbitration* (The Republic of the Philippines v The People's Republic of China), Award, 12 July 2016, [575].

The tribunal summarily dismissed the notion that deviations from the rules in the Convention amounted to a new customary rule permitting departure from the express provisions of the Convention.[17] However, the reasoning behind this finding was unclear. Underlying the tribunal's decision appears to be the assumption that the Convention dealt exhaustively with baselines. Or perhaps that the Convention intended to freeze developments on this issue outside of the Convention. However, given the paucity of reasoning of the tribunal on these points, these assumptions should be challenged.

First, there is nothing in the language of Article 7 that limits its application to continental coastlines. The logic of Article 7 is to account for complex geography and economic factors in the drawing of baselines; it is intended to simplify the drawing of baselines along deeply indented coastlines. This provision is derived from the *Fisheries case*, where the Court considered the specific situation of a mainland coastline. However, there is nothing in the judgment to suggest that the Court's reasoning was limited only to continental coastlines. Indeed, as the Court concluded, 'The real question raised in the choice of base-lines is in effect whether certain sea areas lying within these lines are sufficiently closely linked to the land domain to be subject to the regime of internal waters. This idea, which is at the basis of the determination of the rules relating to bays, should be liberally applied in the case of a coast, the geographical configuration of which is as unusual as that of Norway'.[18] Norway was an exemplar of a more general recognition that exceptional geographic conditions required exceptional treatment in law.

Secondly, as observed in the wider literature on the law of the sea, the LOSC is a living instrument, one that is intended to adapt to changed circumstances.[19] This adaptability is particularly important in respect of matters not directly addressed by the Convention. According to this understanding of LOSC, we should accommodate legal developments that go with the grain of the LOSC.[20] Arguably, this includes the position of dependent archipelagos. The LOSC favours exceptions to the ordinary rules on baselines and indeed the delimitation of maritime entitlements when geographic or exceptional conditions justify this. These is some State practice in support of this as regards dependent archipelagos. Furthermore, a review of the *travaux preparatoires*

17 Ibid., 576.

18 *Fisheries* case (n 9), 133.

19 See the contributions in J Barrett and R Barnes (eds) *Law of the Sea. UNCLOS as a Living Treaty* (BIICL, 2016).

20 M Wood, 'Reflections on the United Nations Convention on the Law of the Sea: A Living Instrument', in Barrett and Barnes, ibid., LXXVII–LXXXII.

makes it clear that States' opinions were divided on how to deal with offshore archipelagos. All that can be concluded was that the exclusion of rules on dependent archipelagos was a consequence of a lack of agreement on how to regulate such archipelagic claims and not a deliberate decision to preclude the application of alternative rules. Even if one cannot read the text of the LOSC to accommodate dependent archipelagos, this cannot and should not rule out the development of customary rules on dependent archipelagos.

If we look at the development of customary rules, then I would argue that as long as the practice accords with the general tenor of the LOSC then this is an acceptable development in the law of the sea. However, what is critical here is that the developments are in line with the same general constraints that apply to coastal and archipelagic States. These constraints should extend to offshore archipelagos. This means at a minimum ensuring consistency with existing principles so that 'the sea areas lying within the lines must be sufficiently closely linked to the land domain to be subject to the regime of internal waters'.[21] It also means that the preconditions of Article 46 are respected, i.e. that dependent archipelagos manifest some geographic, economic, political and historical connection, and, finally, that baselines respect the rules in Article 47.

If one looks at the literature on archipelagic claims, then it appears that the assessment of customary entitlements to dependent archipelagic waters is something of a numbers game. Below is Table 10.1, indicating the range of current claims to dependent archipelagos, alongside the claimant State, those States in the nearest geographic vicinity, protesting States, and a final column indicating whether there is some geographical, political, economic or historical connection between the archipelago and the metropolitan territory.

Of 15 claims to dependent archipelagos, eight seem to have been protested. In seven of these cases, the protest was by the US alone. The US was joined on two occasions by other States. In light of this, Roach argues that State practice fails to support a rule in favour of dependent archipelagic waters.[22] Whomersley interprets this practice differently, arguing that since the sole objector in most cases was the US, and that most other States have not objected to the claims, this suggests that State practice favours the recognition of offshore archipelagic claims.[23] It is always going to be a challenge to conclusively determine the meaning of State practice. Accordingly, a more nuanced conclusion from the

21 LOSC, Art. 7(3).

22 Roach, above (n 7).

23 C Whomersley, 'Offshore Archipelagos Enclosed by Straight Baselines: A Reply to J. Ashley Roach' (2018) 49 *Ocean Development & International Law* 203–207.

TABLE 10.1 Dependent archipelagic claims (based on data from Roach 2018)[a]

	Feature	Claimant State	Neighbouring States/entities	Protests	Unity features
1	Faroes	Denmark	UK, Iceland, Norway, Denmark	US	Arguable
2	Diayou/ Senkaku	China/ Japan	Japan, Taiwan, South Korea, Philippines	US	Sovereignty dispute
3	Azores	Portugal	Morocco, Western Sahara, Spain	US	Arguable
4	Falklands	UK	Argentina, Chile	US	Arguable
5	Hainan	China	Vietnam, Philippines	US	Arguable
6	Xisha/ Paracel	China	Vietnam, Philippines	US, Philippines, Vietnam	Sovereignty dispute
7	Galapagos	Ecuador	Colombia, Peru, Panama, Costa Rica, Nicaragua, Honduras, Guatemala, and Mexico.	US, UK, Germany, Belgium, Spain, Sweden	Arguable
8	Coco and Preparis	Myanmar	Bangladesh, India, Thailand, Malaysia, Indonesia	Bangladesh	Arguable
9	Svalbard	Norway	Russia, Greenland, Iceland	No objections	Arguable
10	Canary Islands	Spain	Morocco, Western Sahara, Portugal, Mauritania	No objection. IMO PSSA	Arguable
11	Kerguelen Islands	France		No objections	Arguable
12	Malvinas	Argentina	Chile	No objection?	Sovereignty dispute

TABLE 10.1 Dependent archipelagic claims (based on data from Roach 2018) (*cont.*)

	Feature	Claimant State	Neighbouring States/entities	Protests	Unity features
13	Turks and Caicos	UK	Cuba, Dominican Republic, Haiti, United States	No objections	Arguable
14	Guadeloupe	France	Dominica, St Lucia, British Virgin Islands, Puerto Rico, Barbados, Grenada	No objection	Arguable
15	Loyalty Islands	France	Vanuatu, Fiji	No objection	Arguable
16	Hawaii	US		Not claimed	Arguable
17	Andaman and Nicobar	India	Thailand, Myanmar, Indonesia, Bangladesh	Not claimed	Arguable
18	Balearic Islands	Spain	France, Italy, Tunisia	Not claimed	Arguable

a The final column, unity features refer to the existence of some or all of the three elements for archipelagic status: geographic, economic or political. In some cases this is difficult to discern due to an ongoing sovereignty dispute over the islands. This at least cast doubt on the connectivity of the islands with one or more of the disputing States.

data is that practice remains inconclusive, but it certainly does not rule out the permissibility of offshore archipelagic claims.

Furthermore, if, as it seems to be the case, the existence of a customary rule on dependent archipelagos is a numbers game, then I would suggest that this game, like in a casino, is stacked in favour of the house. And the house is the State asserting a claim to an offshore archipelago. First, in terms of mere self-interest, it seems reasonable to assume that States with a geographical configuration favourable to a claim are likely to make their own claims and recognise similar claims by other States. Furthermore, such claimant States will seek to maximise their advantage by pushing the boundaries of what is legally permissible. It may also be noted that States are not compelled to claim archipelagic status and so a failure to extend a claim cannot automatically be taken as negative position on such an entitlement.

Second, the dynamics of practice, including that of specially interested States, is likely to favour support for a rule of custom allowing dependent archipelagic claims. The formation of customary international law requires a generality of practice, and this might suggest that relatively small amounts of practice, as noted above, are inconclusive. However, any evaluation of practice would likely give more weight to the practice of the most interested States, i.e., those possessing dependent archipelagos. Even if the rules on the formation of custom do not quite give specially interested States a greater say in the formation of a rule, they do require that the assessment of State practice must include that of specially interested States.[24] At the end of the day, States with the most to gain or lose will be most active in the framing of any claim to expanded maritime jurisdiction. Thus, States with dependent archipelagos will push hard for recognition of such claims, and States unaffected or not in the vicinity of such claim areas are likely to have little interest in protesting such claims. Indeed, most States are silent on archipelagic claims, and this can easily be construed as acceptance or acquiescence. Treating silence as acquiescence is supported by the *Fisheries case*, where the Court took the view that a toleration of a certain practice may indeed serve as evidence of acceptance of something as law if it represents concurrence in that practice.[25]

Of course, this assumption about acquiescence needs to be qualified. The ILC has stated that two requirements must be satisfied to ensure that tolerance is connected to the practice in question.[26] First, a reaction should generally be called for in the sense that the practice is one that directly or indirectly affects another State and so should cause a response. Second, the acquiescent State should be able to react, meaning it must have had knowledge of the practice and sufficient time and ability to act. It could be argued that maritime delimitation always has an international aspect, and so this demands a more general reaction from States.[27] However, to assume that specific delimitation

24 *North Sea Continental Shelf cases, Judgment,* (1969) ICJ Reports 3, at p. 43, para. 74.

25 *Fisheries* case (n 9), 139.

26 Conclusion 2. ILC, *Draft conclusions on identification of customary international law, with commentaries* (2018), UN Doc A/73/10. Reproduced in *Yearbook of the International Law Commission,* 2018, vol. II, Part Two. Available at https://legal.un.org/ilc/texts/instruments/english/commentaries/1_13_2018.pdf.

27 *Fisheries* case: 'The delimitation of sea areas has always an international aspect; it cannot be dependent merely upon the will of the coastal State as expressed in its municipal law

settlements require more widespread level of support does not reflect what happens in practice. With the notable exception of the United States, most States have a limited capacity or interest in responding to distant maritime claims. A single State making a marginally excessive or exceptional claim to maritime entitlements, such as to a dependent archipelago, is unlikely to provoke responses from distant States, especially if this has no direct impact on their fishing, navigation, or resource interests. Of course, this begs a question as to which States would be affected by such a claim. This would seem to include States with navigation interests, neighbouring States, and States with similar claims. Obviously, the latter group of States is likely to support claims to dependent archipelagic waters since this provides a precedent for making their own such claims. If the waters subject to archipelagic status are not in significant navigation routes, then there is likely to be little cause for concern by other States, even those with general navigational interests. This leaves neighbouring States as being the most interested States and having the most to lose by a potential claim. However, these States are likely to be few in number. In many instances, offshore archipelagos are at a distance from other territories and so baselines may have little impact upon other States' maritime claims. As such, other States may have no interest in protesting a claim to draw baselines around a dependent archipelago. In summary, these factors tend to help stack the odds in favour of the claimant State having its claim recognised, or at least not protested.

So far, the focus has been on practice. Little has been said about *opinio juris*. *Opinio juris* is important in this context since, as I argue below, not only is it required to identify a rule of custom, but it also helps to shape how such a rule is framed. In the literature on dependent archipelagos, practice and custom are treated closely. Kopela considers *opinio juris* by way of inference from State practice, or in the context of protest or acquiescence by other States to particular claims.[28] Similarly, Roach considers this mainly in the context of protests.[29] Whomersley does not mention it at all.[30] In practice, explicit statements about the legal basis for a claim to dependent archipelagic waters are uncommon, so this light touch approach to assessing *opinio juris* is understandable. It is consistent with common understandings of how custom operates, and it seems

---

… the validity of the delimitation with regard to other States depends upon international law'. Above (n 9), 132.

28 Kopela, (n 5) 166–181.

29 Roach, (n 7), 189–90.

30 Whomersley (n 23).

to favour a traditional approach to identification of *opinio juris* by focusing on some evidence of a subjective belief as manifest through statements made by a State.[31] Here what matters is not so much the genuine nature of the belief, but that it is asserted as a belief, explicit or otherwise.

Here I take a different approach and argue for a more robust assessment of *opinio juris*. I take the view that emergent claims to customary international law should also be formulated in a systemic fashion, that is to say, it must be formed with reference to existing rules of law about what is legally permissible. *Opinio juris* entails a sense of legal entitlement or duty, and this can only be meaningful if one refers to the existing legal context within which the alleged customary rule is situated. As the ILC Draft conclusions state: *opinio juris* 'must be accompanied by a conviction that it is permitted, required or prohibited by customary international law'.[32] In the *North Sea Continental Shelf* cases, the court referred to *opinio juris* as conforming to what amounts to a legal obligation: 'Not only must the acts concerned amount to a settled practice, but they must also be such, or be carried out in such a way, as to be evidence of a belief that this practice is rendered obligatory by the existence of a rule of law requiring it'.[33] This speaks again to the idea of coherence with existing standards of conduct. The ILC Draft Conclusions do not explicitly refer to coherence with existing rules in the context of *opinio juris*, but this must be implicit in the nature of *opinio juris*. Otherwise, the idea of a sense of obligation would collapse into pure, unmitigated subjectivity. Accordingly, *opinio juris* cannot be pure belief – it must connect to and be reasoned in accordance with some sense of legal entitlement based upon an existing legal framework. Although States do not have to explain their reasons or motives, the fact that the rules on the formation of customary international law exclude other non-legal motives such as comity, political expedience or convenience means that the basis of a State's belief or reasoning is fundamentally relevant to its claims.[34] This approach, which focuses on the systemic coherence of *opinio juris*, makes it possible to assess novel claims. It is consistent with the reason-based nature

---

31 See for example, M Akehurst, 'Custom as a Source of International Law' (1974–75) 47 *BYIL* 1, 36.

32 ILC, above (n 26) Commentary on Conclusion 9, p. 138.

33 Above (n 24) para 77.

34 ICJ in the North Sea Continental Shelf cases: 'The frequency, or even habitual character of the acts is not in itself enough. There are many international acts, e.g., in the field of ceremonial and protocol, which are performed almost invariably, but which are motivated only by considerations of courtesy, convenience or tradition, and not by any sense of legal duty'. Ibid.

of law and the idea of intelligible argument in law.[35] It is consistent with the view that law should be a coherent system of rules (i.e. lack of rule conflicts).[36] Notably, the ILC Draft conclusions do acknowledge the importance of coherence elsewhere – observing that this justifies the application of a two-element approach across all areas of international law, noting that international law 'is a single system'.[37]

It follows that a claim to dependent archipelagic waters must manifest some degree of coherence with the existing legal basis for claims to mid-ocean archipelagic waters and the rationales applicable to the use of straight baselines since these are the most relevant contexts for assessing such claims. There is some precedent for this. Thus, Danish claims to draw baselines around the Faroe Islands were rationalised on the basis of the 'compact nature of the group of islands, as well as the economic interests (in fishing) peculiar to the region, and as evidence by long usage.[38] This connects to the so-called unity requirements set forth in Article 46 of the LOSC. These requirements are examined next.

3 What Claims to Archipelagic Status Are Permissible?

Under the LOSC, an archipelago is defined as 'a group of islands, including parts of islands, interconnecting waters and other natural features which are so closely interrelated that such islands, waters and other natural features form an intrinsic geographical, economic and political entity, or which historically have been regarded as such'.[39] This sets out the concept of an archipelago which is distinct from an archipelagic State, which is further defined as a 'State constituted wholly by one or more archipelagos and may include other islands' Part IV only applies to what are termed mid-ocean archipelagos, thereby excluding coastal archipelagos and dependent archipelagos from its provisions on baselines, status of waters and rights therein. From Article 46 of the LOSC, we

35 See H Marcos, 'A Reason-Based Approach to Coherence in Customary International Law (September 1, 2021). Interpretation of Customary International Law: Methods, Interpretative Choices and the Role of Coherence. 2nd TRICI-Law Conference, 2nd and 3rd of December 2021, The Hague, Available at SSRN: https://ssrn.com/abstract=3930018.

36 See further M Adenas et al, (eds), *General Principles and the Coherence of International Law* (Brill Nijhoff 2019).

37 ILC, above (n 26), Commentary on Conclusion 2, p. 126.

38 American Embassy Copenhagen telegram 07435, 24 October 1991, discussed in Kopela (n 5) 168.

39 LOSC, Art 46(b).

can derive three key elements of an archipelago: of geographic, economic, and political factors. These three elements must meet two qualitative thresholds of being closely interrelated and intrinsic. Cumulatively, these conditions reflect the underlying reasons for the special status granted to archipelagic States. The elements are by no means discreet since the ideas of integration and forming 'an intrinsic ... entity' point to the sum (or unity) of these elements as being important, rather than them being alternative, individual conditions. A separate and additional criterion is that of historic recognition.

Whilst the status of an archipelago should be distinct from the question of how baselines are drawn, in practice this distinction is not easy to maintain. Although the ICJ stated in the *Qatar/Bahrain* case that archipelagic status must be *claimed* before a State is able to enjoy the rights of an archipelagic State,[40] it is not clear how the Court arrived at this conclusion since there is strictly speaking no requirement within the LOSC for a State to claim archipelagic status. Furthermore, the benefits of archipelagic status are somewhat contingent upon the drawing of baselines in order to delimit archipelagic waters under Article 47. However, this seems to be more of practical requirement than a formal legal precondition as to status. Rothwell and Stephens observe that even if a State meets the criteria of Article 46, a failure to comply with the rules on drawing baselines will compromise its ability to proclaim archipelagic status. However, this has not stopped some States from maintaining archipelagic waters contrary to the requirements of Article 47.

Let us consider these elements in turn.

3.1 *The Geographic Requirement*

The principal geographic feature of an archipelago is that it is a group of islands, but beyond this, things become less certain. The development of archipelagic waters was based heavily on arguments of geography.[41] In the *Fisheries case*, the ICJ was strongly influenced by the geographic realties of Norway's coast. Here the ICJ focused on the 'more or less close relationship existing between certain sea areas and the land formations which divide or surround them',[42] and it held that baselines around coastal archipelagos 'must not depart to any appreciable extent from the general direction of the coast'.[43] Thus we are concerned

40 *Maritime Delimitation and Territorial Questions between Qatar and Bahrain, Merits, Judgment*, (2001) ICJ Reports p. 40, paras. 180–183 and 214.

41 See T Markus 'Article 46' in A Proelss (ed.), *United Nations Convention on the Law of the Sea. A Commentary*, p. 351, para 40.

42 *Fisheries Case* (n 9), 133.

43 *Fisheries Case* (n 9), 133.

with the physical idea of a space and a relationship within that space. Space is a social construct, and so it is not a given that it must be perceived in a particular way.[44] However, it is important to note that the way space is conceived in archipelagos speaks to a close relationship between land, water and the people in those spaces. Indeed, archipelagos have been described as a body of waters studded with islands, rather than islands surrounded by waters,[45] thus emphasising the fundamental importance of the waters to the identity of the State.

At a minimum, there must be two or more islands. Presumably some of the island group must fit with the definition of islands per Article 121 of the LOSC. However, this does not preclude other maritime features being regarded as part of an archipelago because Article 46 refers to 'other natural features', such as low tide elevations or rocks, in the definition of the archipelago.

The islands must be located in a way that makes them a geographic entity. Yet, quite what a 'geographic entity' means is anyone's guess. Indeed, it is the significant diversity of geographic conditions that seems to have presented most challenges for the development of a complete legal regime for archipelagos. Here variables appear to include the number, size and shape of islands, or their relative proximity. The islands may also share a common submarine platform.[46] Beyond referring to some physical situation, no more specific geophysical or geological criterion have been articulated in law. This openness of definition favours treating each case on its own merits, but there should be some limits to keep the notion of archipelago meaningful. Amerasinghe suggests the conditions need to be exceptional – in the sense that they distinguish archipelagos from other features.[47] But without knowing what the measure of a geographic relationship is, this is unhelpful. Instead, Markus suggests that geographic factors refer to propinquity or adjacency.[48] However, he soon concedes that the criterion of geography is too vague. This reflects the earlier views of O'Connell who understood the limits of geography, remarking that: 'It is, however, doubtful whether geography is as important as the lawyers have, on occasions, suggested, particularly in the matter of the vexed question of archipelagos'.[49]

---

44 See Barnes (n 15).

45 JR Coquia, 'The Problem of the Territorial Waters of Archipelagos' (1959) 7 *Far Eastern Law Review* 435.

46 D Andrew, 'Archipelagos and the Law of the Sea: Island straits states or island-studded sea space?' (1978) 2 *Marine Policy* 46–64, 47–8.

47 CF Amerasinghe, 'The Problem of Archipelagos in International Law' (1974) 23 *ICLQ* 539–575, 564.

48 Markus, above (n 41) para 40.

49 DP O'Connell, 'Mid-Ocean Archipelagos in International Law' (1971) 45 *BYIL* 1–77, 1.

Even though we accept the relevance of geography, we should note that it is a necessary but insufficient condition for archipelagic status. According to Miron, unlike the continental shelf, archipelagic waters do not exist ipso facto; it is a status that must be claimed.[50] This is reinforced by the decision of the ICJ in the *Qatar/Bahrain* case.[51] This indicates that simple physical facts cannot be determinative of legal status. Despite this, the literature keeps returning to geographic elements.[52] It also reflects the views of some States.[53] This seems to collapse the test of geography into a test of proximity. Perhaps this explains the emphasis on Article 47 of the LOSC in the literature to assess the validity of archipelagic claims because geography bleeds so easily into Article 47's focus on the ratio of land to waters and the maximum length of baselines.

In summary, what appears to be common across accounts of geographic criteria is a need for some special degree of closeness or interrelationship between land and sea.[54] This favours assessing claims according to some notion of proximity between the islands, and on seeking a link between the islands and surrounding sea space. In the case of dependent archipelagos, most can satisfy these criteria since the islands form identifiable and proximate geographic groups.

3.2 *The Economic Requirement*

Some archipelagic States have claimed that the seas between their islands are an important source of food and other resources for their inhabitants.[55] This economic dependence has only increased as populations have grown. Economic dependence has focused on three main resources. First, there are fisheries, principally as a means to provide livelihoods for local populations.[56] A particular concern was that local fishermen would find it difficult to compete with better developed distant water industrial fleets. Archipelagic waters

50 A Miron, 'The Archipelagic Status Reconsidered in Light of the *South China Sea* and *Düzgit Integrity* Awards' (2018) 15(3) *Indonesian Journal of International Law* 306–340, 312.

51 Above note (40).

52 See for example, G Fitzmaurice, 'Some Results of the Geneva Conference on the Law of the Sea. Part I. The Territorial Sea and Contiguous Zone and Related Topics' (1959) 8 *ICLQ* 73–121, 88; Kopela above (n 5) 110.

53 Statement of the Philippines, United Nations Conference on the Law of the Sea 1958, Official Records, vol 3, p. 239.

54 Amerasinghe above (n 47) at 564; H P Rajan, 'The Legal Regime of Archipelagos' (1986) 29 *German Yearbook of International Law* 137, 145.

55 Coquia (n 45) 435.

56 See arguments by JR Coquia, 'The Territorial Waters of Archipelagos' (1962) 1(1) *Philippine International Law Journal* 139, 155ff; JW Dellapenna, 'The Philippines Territorial Water Claim in International Law' (1970) 5 *Journal of Law and Economic Development* 45, 57.

secure a degree of exclusive access to waters for local fishing communities. Second, there are mineral resources. At an early stage, both Indonesia and the Philippines asserted exclusive control over mineral resources of the seabed and sub-soil as a benefit of the archipelagic principle.[57] The third economic benefit is communication, as indicated by the ICJ in the *Fisheries case*.[58] Thus, waters serve as arteries of economic life, or inter-islands transport and communication. This is particularly important for local communities. Indeed, Lucchin and Voeckel link this to the Faroe Islands, Galapagos and the Kergeuelan Islands,[59] and Kopela identifies this as important in the cases of Loyalty Islands, Turks and Caicos, and Svalbard.[60]

Amerasinghe suggests there must be more than a superficial economic relationship.[61] Further, he argues there are three factors of importance.[62] First, there must be a strong dependence of the inhabitants of the islands on the economic resources of the oceans surrounding them. Second, such dependence must be established for all the islands in respect of all the oceans. It is not sufficient for individual islands to be dependent on individual surrounding oceans. Third, such economic interests should be proven to have been enjoyed for a period of time (unspecified). Rajan follows Amerasinghe's approach.[63] O'Connell reflecting on the *Fisheries case*, highlighted the specific relevance of economic considerations when assessing archipelagic claims.[64] These were key criteria in respect of coastal archipelagos, and he argued that they would be no less relevant to mid-ocean archipelagos. He suggested that to draw any distinction between them as regards the importance each State attaches to marine resources would be artificial.[65] This distinction can helpfully be used to distinguish populated islands that are subject to substantial economic activities from highly dispersed islands where little economic activity exists, and so mediate more expansive claims to archipelagic waters. In any event, there seems to be no reason why arguments based upon economic dependency should not extend to dependent archipelagos. To treat such economic interests differently would be discriminatory and artificially selective.

57 See O'Connell above (n 50) 37, 42.

58 *Fisheries case*, above (n 9) 127–8.

59 L Lucchini and M Voelckel, *Droit de la mer: La mer et son droit; Les espaces maritimes* (Paris: Pedone, 1990) 381–2.

60 Kopela (n 5) 185.

61 Amerasinghe above (n 47) at 564.

62 Rajan above (n 54) at 146.

63 Rajan, ibid. 146.

64 O'Connell, above (n 49) 15.

65 Ibid., 15–6.

3.3 *The Political Requirement*

The third requirement is for there to be political connection between the islands. At a basic level this requires the archipelago to be part of a single State and this clearly excludes island groups that form more than one sovereignty from being treated as an archipelago – as is the case of the Caribbean. The literature offers little guidance on what further meaning might be given to the political dimension of unity, other than to connect it to security concerns. Thus, Rajan indicates that the political requirement is linked to security noting that the islands under the sovereignty of a single State mean 'that security considerations, apart from the consideration of unity among the inhabitants of the island, become cogent'.[66] Amerasinghe observes that exclusive control of waters would enable protection of the archipelagic State's interests, for example to control smuggling or illegal entry.[67] O'Connell also noted that for Indonesia and Philippines, economic considerations were used to reinforce security-based arguments, whereas for other archipelagos, where there was no security concern, economic motives were more important.[68] This suggests that political concerns may not be critical, other than the single sovereignty requirement. Even if more nuanced security concerns have to be demonstrated, it would not be a difficult case for any State claiming dependent archipelagic waters to show such concerns existed.

In most cases dependent archipelagos are not disputed territories, so this minimal level of political connection seems unlikely to be determinative of entitlement to claim archipelagic waters. Although some dependent archipelagos may enjoy a degree of autonomy from the metropolitan territory (e.g., Faroe Islands), this does not significantly interrupt the political connections between parts of the State.

3.4 *The 'Unity' Requirement*

Article 46 requires a close and intrinsic unity of the foregoing three features in order to constitute a legal archipelago. Thus, the features should be 'so closely related' as to 'form an intrinsic geographical, economic and political entity …'. Underpinning the above requirements is the idea that the integrity or unity of the archipelago should be protected. As Senator Tolentino, a strong advocate of the Philippines' archipelagic claims argued: 'it is unthinkable and impossible for us to lend our support to any proposal which may be interpreted, even more remotely, as impairing any of our historic rights, and which

66 Rajan, above (n 54) 146.

67 Amerasinghe, above (n 47) 557.

68 O'Connell, above (n 49) 53.

may be used as an excuse by foreign vessels and fishermen to penetrate with impunity into the very heart of our archipelago'.[69] A similarly strong reason for integration is reflected in Indonesian practice. Thus, the Indonesian delegate to the Conference stated that 'Indonesian language equivalent for the word "fatherland" ... is "tanah air" meaning "land-water", thereby indicating how inseparable the relationship is between water and land to the Indonesian people. The seas, to our mind, do not separate but connect islands. More than that, these waters unify our nation'.[70] This idea of unity is something that is deeply rooted in cultural practices and serves to distinguish archipelagic claims from other claims to extended maritime jurisdiction. It also suggests that it is not merely one or other of the elements that should exist, but some degree of all three. This is reflected more generally in the requirement that there should be a close connection between the waters within a baseline and the land domain.[71]

In geographic terms, this implies some degree of proximity. However, Munawar also suggests that 'ecological and environmental factors may also serve as indicators of the close relationship between the islands and other natural features and the interconnecting waters of the island group'.[72] Economic coherence is generally recognised as relevant, but as discussed, it lacks a precise objective content since any archipelagic entity may point to some economic reasons for unity. As such, economic unity becomes a relative and subjective criterion. Accordingly, higher degrees of economic activity within and across the archipelago will strengthen any claims to archipelagic status. Alongside the political dimension, it points towards the survival of the State. Political coherence goes little beyond requiring the features of the archipelago to belong to the same State. This means that disputed features such as the Spratly Islands cannot be considered as meeting this requirement.

3.5 *Historical Requirement*

The historical criterion is framed as an alternative, rather than complementary criterion for archipelagic status. This means that even where the entity does not meet the intrinsic geographic, economic and political criteria, it may still be considered as an archipelago if it has historically been considered as an

69 Official Records of the Second United Nations Conference on the Law of the Sea, (Committee of the Whole – Verbatim Records of the General Debate), p. 77.

70 Mochtar Kusumaatmadja, UNCLOS III, Official Records, vol. I, 187.

71 See the comment by ICJ in the *Fisheries case* cited above (n 18).

72 M Munawar, *Ocean States, Archipelagic Regimes in the Law of the Sea*, (Martinus Nijhoff Publishers 1995) 113.

archipelago. This requirement is important because it brings into play questions of recognition or acquiescence. In practice most archipelagos meet the other pre-requisites, but historical recognition may be important in respect of aspects of archipelagic claims that are not consistent with the core definition, such the inclusion of distant outlying islands or the drawing of baselines around the archipelago that are not consistent with Article 47.[73] There is no reason in principle why historic title cannot apply also to dependent archipelagos. Title on this basis is recognised in a range of exceptional claims, at least in combination with other factors.[74] However, for present purposes, the historic basis of the claim is unlikely to add much value to an assessment of claims to archipelagic waters based on a sense of legal entitlement as a matter of *opinio juris* since historic claims must be evidenced by constant and long usage and so becomes inseparable from acts of State practice.

3.6 *Other Requirements*

Not unrelated to security is the argument that non-exclusive control of the waters within the archipelago could result in the environmental degradation of such waters. Historically, environmental factors played a major role in helping to justify claims to archipelagic waters *per se*.[75] Thus, several States have advanced a desire to control the movements of tankers in coastal waters during the negotiation of the LOSC.[76] More generally, Fiji asserted that it was vital to control the development of its marine environment to ensure it was in its best interests and would prevent any form of depredation or pollution of the marine environment.[77] There is scientific evidence to support the claim that archipelagic waters are more vulnerable to pollution.[78] This could be used to justify wider authority to protect such waters and to extend such protections around the vulnerable ecosystems. For example, Ecuador has used

---

73 See for example the inclusion of the Darwin and Wolf islands as part of the Galapagos. See US State Department, *Limits in the Seas No 42 Straight Baselines: Ecuador* (1972) 10.

74 See for example, the Norwegian arguments in the *Fisheries case*: 'The Norwegian Government does not rely upon history to justify exceptional rights, to claim areas of sea which the general law would deny; it invokes history together with other factors, to justify the way in which it applied the general law'. Above (n 9) 133.

75 See Kopela, above (n 5) 237ff; O'Connell (n 49) 54.

76 Kopela, above (n 5) 29.

77 Ibid.

78 AR Farhan and S Lim, 'Vulnerability assessment of ecological conditions in Seribu Islands, Indonesia' (2012) 65 *Ocean & Coastal Management* 1–14; D Ferrol-Schulte et al 'Coastal livelihood vulnerability to marine resource degradation: A review of the Indonesian national coastal and marine policy framework' (2015) 52 *Marine Policy* 163–171.

this argument to justify its claims to archipelagic status for the Galapagos: 'It reaffirms that the said lines in the Galapagos Archipelago are determined by the common geological origin of those islands, their historical unity and the fact that they belong to Ecuador, *as well as the need to protect and preserve their unique ecosystems*'.[79] However, neither the legal basis nor the extent of archipelagic waters is connected to any quality of the marine ecosystem or its vulnerability.

It is possible to link environmental concerns to geographic conditions. Here we should recall the perceptiveness of O'Connell who remarked upon the special nature of coral islands, which are of particular relevance to archipelagos: 'The areas of intersection of land and sea are subject to incessant biological and chemical interaction, whereby the land is preserved from ultimate destruction. Pollution of these areas can destroy the organisms that are essential for the coastal mud to retain its vitality and support the flora, notably mangroves, which in many instances constitute an essential rampart against the sea'.[80] This points to a more nuanced physical relationship between the land and sea. There is in principle, no reason why such arguments should not extend to dependent archipelagos where such waters are particularly vulnerable to harm.

That said, environmental conditions alone are not something advanced within the specific provisions on archipelagos in the LOSC, neither is it a concern that is exclusive to archipelagos. All States have an interest in and duty to protect the marine environment.[81] Notably, the LOSC does not differentiate archipelagic waters for special treatment in this respect either in Part IV or Part XII. Whilst some degree of natural connectivity between coastal and oceanic systems may be particular to an island group, it would be difficult to extrapolate from this a generalisable basis for claiming dependent archipelagic waters. At best, it provides an additional political reason for claiming archipelagic waters that taps into more widely recognised concerns about the need for improved environmental protection. It is suggested that environmental considerations ought primarily to be focused on ensuring that any specific vulnerability of archipelagos be addressed through stronger regulation on activities in coastal waters. There is a range of tools available to support this including designation of marine protected areas or particularly sensitive sea areas.

---

79 Para VI of Declaration made when Ecuador Acceded to the Convention (24 September 2012). Emphasis added.

80 Connell above (n 49) 54.

81 See LOSC, Part XII.

3.7 *Evaluating the Requirements*

Following her review of State practice, Kopela argues that geographic considerations should be determinative of the regime of archipelagos since this is the most common feature referred to in practice.[82] This is perhaps a compelling conclusion given the principal focus on drawing of baselines around geographic features. However, it is possible to counter this conclusion, especially since there are so few explicit references to geography being the actual basis of claims. Kopela's conclusion is drawn from an implicit assessment of the general geography of the claimed features.[83] If one reviews the legislation claiming archipelagic waters, then one sees that geography is seldom cited as the basis of the claim. Denmark's legislation on the Faroe Islands baselines makes passing reference only to exclusive fisheries within the baseline.[84] China's legislation for the Diaoyu Islands,[85] and the Hainan and Xisha Islands[86] make no reference to any characteristic of the islands – other than to describe the features. The same applies to Portugal's legislation on the Azores,[87] UK legislation for the Falkland Islands[88] and Turks and Caicos Islands,[89] Ecuador for the Galapagos Islands,[90] Myanmar for the Coco and Preparis Islands,[91] Norway for Svalbard,[92] and Spain for the Canary Islands.[93] Most States simply delimit waters around such island groups using straight baselines or a combination of straight baselines and low water marks. Indeed, few States make explicit reference to the criteria for archipelagos in the LOSC, with Indonesia somewhat exceptionally referring to the reciprocal relationship between land and waters, and singular geographical, economic, security and defence and political unity

---

82 Kopela, above (n 5), p. 147.

83 Kopela, ibid., chapter 3.

84 See Prime Minister's Department Decree No. 156 of April 24, 1963. Available at https://2009-2017.state.gov/documents/organization/62005.pdf.

85 Statement of the Government of The Peoples' Republic of China on the Territorial Sea Baselines for Diaoyu Dao and Its Affiliated Islands 10 September 2012. Available at http://www.chinese-embassy.org.za/eng/zt/topic1/t971217.htm.

86 Declaration Of the Government of the People's Republic of China on the Baseline of the Territorial Sea of the People's Republic of China 15 May 1996.

87 Decree-Law No. 495/85 of 29 November 1985.

88 The Falkland Islands (Territorial Sea) Order 1989.

89 The Turks and Caicos Islands (Territorial Sea) Order 1989.

90 Supreme Decree No. 959-A on June 28, 1971 (Official Register No. 265 of July 13, 1971).

91 The Law amending the Territorial Sea and Maritime Zones Law (The State Peace and Development Council Law No.8/2008), 5 December 2008.

92 Regulations relating to the limits of the Norwegian territorial sea around Svalbard (Royal Decree of 1 June 2001).

93 Royal Decree No. 2510/1977 of 5 August 1977.

of intrinsic nature of the archipelago.[94] However, as discussed above, there does not appear to be any reason why the elements of geographic, economic and political connection between island and water space to justify mid-ocean archipelagos cannot be extended to dependent archipelagos. The main distinction in this case is that the idea of unity becomes somewhat detached in cases where the dependent archipelago is located at an extended distance from the metropolitan State. For some dependent archipelagos this is not an issue (e.g., Svalbard, Hainan, Xisha/Paracel, and Coco and Preparis). For others the islands are at least the closest to the metropolitan State (e.g., Azores). In others, the territories tend to be distant dependencies. However, applying the unity requirement robustly depends on one taking the view that unity must extend to the whole of the State. This would appear to suggest that international law demands that the territories of States must have some degree of proximity. This is clearly not the case in all situations.

There are at least two arguments that could be used to counter my argument that the preconditions for archipelagic status (i.e., the unity requirement) should play a role in evaluating dependent archipelagic claims, and more specifically as helping to frame the sense of legal entitlement to such a claim as a matter of customary international law. The first is that archipelagic status must be claimed and proclaimed. As Miron notes, archipelagic status does not exist ipso facto in the same way that a continental shelf exists.[95] As such it is contingent upon some further act, and this may weaken the relevance of the unity requirement. It places emphasis on the claim, rather than the basis of the claim. Second, the review of the literature above suggests that there is no mathematical method capable of determining the content of the unity requirement. Rather, each requirement is a merely a broad basis upon which claims for archipelagic status may be advanced. This allows flexibility, but at the price of uncertainty, and this is manifest in the variety of claims advanced to archipelagic status. As Jayewardene suggests, the diverse motives advanced by some States to support their claims for special status have had the result of making it more difficult to evaluate those claims.[96] If there are no determinable measures of geography, politics or economics that can be used to set a threshold for archipelagic status then this renders application so variable as not to be a meaningful determinant of any claim. Ultimately, legal rules

---

94 Article 1(3) of the Act on Indonesian Waters 1996.

95 A Miron, 'The Archipelagic Status Reconsidered in Light of the *South China Sea* and *Düzgit Integrity* Awards' (2018) 15(3) *Indonesian Journal of International Law* 306–340.

96 HW Jayewardene, *The Regime of Islands in International Law* (Martinus Nijhoff, 1990) 110.

require a degree of precision if they are to function effectively. Of course, just because something is difficult does not mean it is impossible and that it should not be attempted.

Article 46 is a provision that operates qualitatively. It provides a wider range of contextual factors that can be used by States to assess archipelagic claims. Unlike mathematically precise rules, these allow space for nuance and compromise. For example, in the face of challenges to the drawing of baselines around some maritime features, some States have revised their baselines. Fifty years ago, when assessing the criteria for coastal archipelagos advanced by the ICJ in the *Fisheries case*, O'Connell concluded that to exclude economic factors would be to wrongly constrain the scope for legal evaluation of claims.[97] The Court's judgement 'cannot but be regarded as emancipating the archipelagic question from the confines of precise limits, specific shape and abstract definition in which all previous discussion has sought to enmesh it ….'[98] In short, these criteria remain important in framing the assessment of claims. Returning to my initial observation about the importance of ensuring a connection between legal regimes and the underlying material reality, this recognition of the importance of a wider legal assessment of claims remains critical in ensuring that legal claims are not divorced from physical, political, and economic realities, and that such claims are consistent with existing laws.

4 Concluding Thoughts

The drawing of baselines is an important step it in determining the extent of maritime entitlements. However, in the case of archipelagos this can only be done after it has been established that there is a justifiable basis in law for treating an island group as an archipelago. This means establishing that there are islands which comprise a geographic, economic, and political unity, or have been historically regarded as such. The LOSC applies these conditions to archipelagic States. Assuming that dependent archipelagos are permissible under custom, it is inconceivable that dependent archipelagos could be claimed under customary international law without meeting the same requirements for archipelagic status under the LOSC. Otherwise, they would potentially be treated more favourably than mid-ocean archipelagos. As argued above, the requirement of geographic, economic, and political unity satisfies both the

97 O'Connell, above (n 49) 15–6.
98 Ibid., 16.

need for a strong material connection between the islands and surrounding waters and further justifies their exceptional status in the law of the sea.

When we consider the process and requirements of custom formation, and apply this to the claims to dependent archipelagic waters, it is difficult to resist the argument that States have an entitlement to draw straight baselines around dependent archipelagos. Practice as well as the structural bias towards claimant States tend to favour this. Additionally, when we consider the systemic fit of such claims within the relevant body of rules on the law of the sea, either pertaining to the use of straight baselines or archipelagic status, then it also is difficult to argue that claims to dependent archipelagos should be treated differently than mid-ocean archipelagos. In most such cases there exist the same geographic, economic or political connection between the islands. Kopela concludes her study by noting that the considerable variations in the geography mean that it is difficult to develop a highly uniform regime.[99] She also notes that as far as possible, law should treat like cases alike. It is difficult to disagree with these findings. Of course, this means trying to achieve a balance between flexibility and coherence. By focusing on the core elements that justify the special treatment of archipelagos, we at least ensure that the development of a regime for dependent archipelagos is based upon similar limiting factors. This may not provide categorical answers to questions of entitlement, but it does at least ensure some degree of coherence in the dialogue about the legitimacy of maritime claims.

99 Kopela (n 5) 260.

CHAPTER 11

Straight or Archipelagic Baseline with Respect to Offshore Archipelago?

Dai Tamada

1 Introduction

It is generally thought that China has already established a straight baseline on the Spratly Islands—which is the southern part of the South China Sea—and as we shall see below, it is very controversial whether China has already established or not the offshore archipelago or mid-ocean or outlying archipelago (we can use these terms interchangeably in this paper). This paper aims to examine the issues whether China is entitled to employ the straight baseline or archipelagic baseline in the Spratly Islands under the Law of the Sea Convention (LOSC). If the LOSC is not applicable, next question is whether there is a customary international law rule established for admitting straight baseline on the offshore archipelago. There are two different discussions in this context.

2 LOSC Provisions

Let's move on to LOSC provisions. There are four articles relevant to the baselines. The first is normal baselines. I would like to skip this one. The second is straight baselines. There are some paragraphs, but the most important part is paragraph one. In localities where the coastline is deeply indented and cut into—this is the first requirement—or if there is a fringe of islands along the coast in its immediate vicinity—this is the second requirement in question. So, the question is whether China can satisfy these requirements in the case of the Spratly Islands. The method of straight baseline may be employed in drawing the baseline. This is applicable for all criteria and applicable provisions of LOSC firstly. I will skip the remaining paragraphs and let's move on to Article 46.

In Part IV, entitled archipelagic states on paragraph (a) "archipelagic State" means a State constituted wholly by one or more archipelagos and may include other islands, very simply defined. The next paragraph, (b) "archipelago" means

© DAI TAMADA, 2023 | DOI:10.1163/9789004518629_012

a group of islands and so on. We are going back to this definition under Article 46, and the very controversial article is Article 47 about archipelagic baselines. An archipelagic State, defined here in Article 46, may draw straight archipelagic baselines under some requirements, especially as already pointed out by the previous presenter Professor Schofield, an area in which the ratio of the area of the water to the area of the land, including atolls, is between 1 to 1 and 9 to 1 and shall not exceed 100 nautical miles. These are applicable requirements which China has to satisfy if it intends to apply the archipelagic baselines.

3 China's Position

I would like to skip the other paragraphs and jump to the China's position on the straight or archipelagic baselines. Going back to the beginning of the statement by China expressed in 1955, China adopted a straight baseline in some parts including the South China Sea. However, the straight baselines surrounding each island in the South China Sea are not established or published. The problem is whether China already implemented and applied straight baselines or not, then published or not. Afterwards, in 1992, according to the Law on the Territorial Sea and Contiguous Zone, Article 3, the method of straight baselines composed of all the straight lines joining the adjacent base points shall be employed.

But there's no precise information about where the straight baselines were adopted by Article 3 in this 1992 law. Afterwards, the 1996 Declaration on the straight baseline in the Paracel Islands—also in the South China Sea—but western part which is very close to the Vietnam. Next one is 2012 when China established straight baseline surrounding the Diaoyu/Senkaku Island. It's a quite controversial issue between China and Japan, but unfortunately, I cannot touch upon these two maritime features; Paracel Islands and Senkaku Islands in this presentation.

Here is a summary of China's position before 2012. According to Professor Zhang, he contributed to the publication of my book. Hua Zhang, Chinese scholar, said that it cannot be excluded the possibility that China would apply the straight baselines to three other groups of islands in the South China Sea especially the Nansha/Spratly Islands in the foreseeable future. A little bit more aggressive evaluation was expressed by Mr. Tsuruta, Japanese scholar. He also contributed to the publication of my book. According to him, China may have already applied the straight baselines (also in the Spratly Islands) without making them disclosed or published. This is much more nuanced evaluation.

Probably, China has already established straight baselines in the Spratly Islands but not yet disclosed it. Later, we're going to check this fact.

4 Award in the SCS Case (2016)

Let's see the reaction from the tribunal in the South China Sea case. In the South China Sea case, the statement of China on the legal status of the Spratly Islands was interpreted by the tribunal in two ways. I am going to deal with the second way, that is the second interpretation of the tribunal according to which the employment of archipelagic baseline or the straight baseline applied to the offshore archipelago was adopted by China. The tribunal denied this possibility as follows. It's a little bit long inside quotation.

Firstly, with regard to Articles 46 and 47, the Spratly Islands should be enclosed within a system of archipelagic or straight baselines, this is assertion of China, but the Tribunal cannot agree—it has very clearly denied it—and strictly controlled by LOSC. Article 47 (1) limits their use to archipelagic States which is defined in Article 46 and China is constituted principally by territory on the mainland of Asia and cannot meet the definition of the archipelagic State. As it is not an archipelagic State, it cannot establish archipelagic baseline, quite clearly. Then, if China can satisfy the requirements of being an archipelagic State, it cannot satisfy another requirement of ratio of water, as it is expressed by the Tribunal.

Next, in paragraph 575, the Tribunal examines the applicability of Article 7. As I said, it's about straight baselines and the practice of some States in employing straight baselines with respect to offshore archipelagos to approximate. The tribunal admits that there are some practices like China's practice—and any application of straight baselines to the Spratly Islands in this fashion would be contrary to LOSC. This is the conclusion of the Tribunal. Then, the reason is expressed here. These conditions do not include the situation of offshore archipelago. We cannot apply the Article 7 to the offshore archipelago because there's a requirement of immediate vicinity. China's argument cannot satisfy this requirement according to the tribunal.

Then, last part, the grant of permission, Article 7, and the conditional permission in Articles 46 and 47 finally excludes the possibility of employing straight baselines in other circumstances. So, there is no exception outside these articles. In particular, with respect to offshore archipelago not meeting the criteria for archipelagic baselines—this is the conclusion. This is also the conclusion part; notwithstanding the practice of some States to the contrary—this is a quite controversial part to be subjected to later discussion among scholars—the Tribunal sees no evidence that any deviation from this rule have amounted to the formulation of new rule of customary international law. There is no customary law established with regard to the position of China. This is the conclusion of the Tribunal.

As a summary, I divided the finding of the tribunal into three parts. As far as Article 47 archipelagic baseline is concerned, China is not archipelagic State. Even if it is so, it doesn't satisfy other requirements. This is the first part and with regard to straight baseline with regard to offshore archipelagos is not applicable to the Spratly Islands because Article 7 is not applicable to offshore or mid-ocean archipelago. The second one is that the general permission and the conditional permissions exclude the possibility of straight baselines in other circumstances. As I said, there's no exception. So, under three articles of LOSC, China is not entitled to establish archipelagic or straight baseline in the Spratly Islands. There is no customary international law rule apart from LOSC even though there are some contrary State practices as admitted by the tribunal as exception.

5 China's Critique (2018)

China criticized the Tribunal's award. I would like to skip this part. So, what is the legal basis argued by China? The first one is that the negotiation history shows that the LOSC does not regulate the issue of continental States' outlying archipelagos as such, and continental States have effectively preserved the regime of outlying archipelago as a unit. It's not touched upon by the LOSC. It has been established in customary international law including internal waters, and then it is also repeated by China that it is customary international law regime of outlining archipelagos that should be applied and without inquiring into customary international law; this is a problem in the arbitral award. So, China's suggestion is very important because in this critical study published by China, it is stated that China has promulgated that straight baselines method shall be employed to determine the baselines of the territorial sea of Nansha Qundao, the Spratly Islands, but has not published detailed basepoints or baselines with finality.

So, as I said, probably China already established the straight baselines in the Spratly Islands but not yet published this fact or not disclosed the detailed basepoints or baselines with finality. Probably, it's still very provisional decision by the Chinese government. I'd like to skip here, and a summary of China's position. Offshore archipelago baseline can be established, and this is justified not by the LOSC, this is beyond the scope of the Law of the Sea Convention but by customary international law rule existing outside the Convention which has been established by enough amount of State practices. So, the discussion moves on to the customary international law rather than the LOSC.

6 Remaining Issues to Be Discussed

Remaining issues to be discussed in Section 5. Just briefly, the question is, is there any customary international law rule admitting the employment of a straight baseline with respect to the offshore archipelago? From the Chinese scholar's viewpoint, there is still controversial and confusion in the calculation of State practices in each study but 18 State practices of this kind have been described and used for justification of State practices, since the early 20th century.

The first point is that many State practices are pre-LOSC practices. This means that there were such kind of State practices before the entry into force of the LOSC, and there are a variety of situations in each case, and some practices were criticized very heavily by other states, especially by the United States of America. United States has consistently objected to such kind of State practices.

From here, I'm going to check and introduce the discussion between two parts. One is the pro-China and the second one is the anti-China position. First, Roach, legal advisor of the US Department of State, 2013. Six of the 15 claims to enclose offshore archipelagos have been protested by nine states and the United States protests against employments of straight baselines at offshore archipelagos in the case of Canada, Denmark, Ecuador, Portugal, Sudan, UK, etc.

This is in chronological order from 2013. Afterwards, it's important to check the position of China expressed in the critical study in paragraph 586. The practice of continental States in drawing baselines around their outlying archipelagos as units has only encountered sporadic, isolated and selective protests. This means that the US protests were sporadic, isolated and selective. So, the United States is the only one persistent objector according to the position of China. So, the protests against Ecuador, Denmark, Portugal, China but not all. There are many other exceptions. These protests are selective and inconsistent. They are largely aimed at ensuring the access of US military vessels and aircraft to the major oceans and the seas in the world. This is policy-oriented protests by the United States against all the states. It's very sporadic, isolated and selective.

This is the positions of China and, very interestingly, some authors, not Chinese, but in this case, it's UK, former UK Foreign and Commonwealth Office official supported the position of China. So, according to him, according to the preamble of the LOSC, it is said, affirming that matters not regulated by this Convention to be governed by general international law which means customary international law according to this author, and there exist widespread and consistent State practices. The US is persistent objector but cannot prevent the establishment of customary international law rule. This is probably same as China's position of persistent objector, but there is the establishment of customary international law.

The second argument is based on Article 7, which is broad enough to admit the straight baseline at the offshore archipelago, but he keeps the application of the requirements namely that if an offshore archipelago satisfies the condition of where the coastline is deeply indented and cut into, Article 7 (1) is applicable. As far as Article 7 (1) is satisfied, there can be justification in the case of China as well. I would like to skip the kind of repetition of arguments by Roach, no customary international law, and he attempted to elaborate the State practice analysis; 15 State practices exist and nine states protested against nine practices. Some states do not employ—there are other State practices, not to employ the straight baselines in offshore archipelago like US, India and Spain. So, there's no customary international law rule nor the subsequent agreement in the context of interpretation under the Vienna Convention on the Law of Treaties concerning Article 7 of the LOSC.

7 Conclusions

To conclude, at the level of fact, it is required to pay attention to the official position of China, expressed in a variety of ways, towards the straight baseline of the offshore archipelago, especially in the Spratly Islands. We need to clarify the legal status of the straight baseline prior to offshore archipelago before the China's future official decision to apply it to the Spratly Islands. In my understanding, China already established a straight baseline in the Spratly Islands, but it's not disclosed. It doesn't disclose this fact clearly yet. The next point as in point 2, at the level of interpretation of the LOSC. The South China Sea arbitral award clearly denied the argument of China to employ the straight baseline in question within the LOSC. The second issue is the comprehensiveness of the LOSC must be the most powerful argument against straight baseline of the offshore archipelago. We have to discuss this one much more deeply.

The third issue is the most controversial one. At the level of customary international law, there remains a strong criticism by China against the finding of the tribunal supported by some scholars including non-Chinese scholars as we already saw in the foregoing. Its argument is based on the existence of a customary international law rule. It seems difficult, at least for the moment, to admit the establishment of a customary international law rule because (I) it is contrary to the provision of the LOSC itself, and (II) it is based on the State practice before the entry into force of the Convention, and (III) State practices are criticized by other States for the moment. This is my evaluation. Even if customary international rules have been existing before the entry into force of the Law of the Sea Convention, it should be understood as being superseded by the LOSC. Probably, there can be some connection between comprehensiveness and supersede, the term used by the Tribunal in the South China Sea case by the Tribunal.

This is the conclusion of my presentation, and the last one is advertisement of publication. I referred to some articles in my presentation, which are actually Hua Zhang's article, 'The Application of Straight Baselines to Mid-Ocean Archipelagos Belonging to Continental States: A Chinese Lawyer's Perspective'.[1] Finally, he justifies the China's position. Against this, Yurika Ishii, Japanese scholar, criticized that position very critically.[2] If you're interested, please see the two articles in my book. Professor Keyuan Zou and I edited this book and very recently published by Springer.

1 Hua Zhang, "The Application of Straight Baselines to Mid-Ocean Archipelagos Belonging to Continental States: A Chinese Lawyer's Perspective," in Dai Tamada and Keyuan Zou (eds.), *Implementation of the United Nations Convention on the Law of the Sea: State Practice of China and Japan* (Springer, 2021), pp. 115–131.

2 Yurika Ishii, "A Critique Against the Concept of Mid-Ocean Archipelago," ibid., pp. 133–147.

PART 2

Navigation Rights/Law Enforcement

CHAPTER 12

The Applicability of Human Rights Treaties in Maritime Law Enforcement

David S. Goddard

1 Introduction

The applicability of human rights treaties in maritime law enforcement (MLE) is important for two main reasons.[1] First, it can provide additional mechanisms by which a State may be held accountable for its actions, including, for some States, the possibility of complaints brought by individuals. Second, the application of human rights law may entail additional substantive obligations, over and above those that arise under other bodies of law, including, most notably, the law of the sea.

Consider the example of force used to compel a vessel to stop and yield to enforcement action. From a law of the sea perspective, it is well established that the use of force is to be avoided, and, where it cannot be avoided, its use must go no further than what is reasonable and necessary in the circumstances.[2] In practice, this normally requires the giving of warnings and a process of escalation through increasingly forceful measures.[3] However, whatever the substance of these obligations, the options for bringing States to account for breaching them may be very limited. Even where compulsory dispute resolution is available – which will not always be the case[4] – it will not be available to individuals.

1 The views expressed in this article are the author's own and do not necessarily reflect the views of the United Kingdom government.

2 See, in particular, *M/V 'Saiga' (No 2)* (*Saint Vincent and the Grenadines v Guinea*) (Merits, Judgment of 1 July 1999) ITLOS Reports [155], where the International Tribunal for the Law of the Sea held that '*…the use of force must be avoided as far as possible and, where force is unavoidable, it must not go beyond what is reasonable and necessary in the circumstances. Considerations of humanity must apply in the law of the sea, as they do in other areas of international law*'.

3 Ibid. [156].

4 Considering, for example, the options available under the United Nations Convention on the Law of the Sea (adopted 10 December 1982, entered into force 16 November 1994) 1833 UNTS 397 (UNCLOS), aside from the issue that some States are not parties, UNCLOS

 | DOI:10.1163/9789004518629_013

On the other hand, not only does human rights law require force to be necessary and proportionate, but it also carries other substantive obligations. The right to life under human rights law has been interpreted as requiring, for example, that operations involving the use of force be planned and controlled so as to reduce the risk that lethal force will be required,[5] as well as requiring that individuals using force have been properly trained to do so.[6] It also carries obligations to investigate deaths brought about through the use of force, and to hold individuals to account where their use of force is found to have been unlawful.[7] Moreover, human rights treaties may allow for *individual* rights of complaint,[8] or at least further avenues for accountability under a range of other mechanisms.[9]

The potential significance of human rights law is not limited to the use of force. For example, the right to liberty and security of the person not only limits the circumstances in which individuals may be lawfully detained, but also entails a range of procedural obligations when they are.[10] The right to life may require States to make provision for rescue services, including air-sea rescue,[11]

---

permits States to opt out of its compulsory dispute resolution provisions for some purposes, including disputes concerning military activities. Ibid. art 298(1)(b).

5 See, for example, *McCann and Others v the United Kingdom Series A no 324 (ECtHR)*, in which the UK was held by the European Court of Human Rights not to have properly controlled an operation, so as to avoid a situation where special forces soldiers were required to use lethal force. Ibid [202]–[214]. See also *Nadege Dorzema et al v Dominican Republic* (Merits, Reparations and Costs) Inter-American Court of Human Rights Series C No 251 (24 October 2012) [84].

6 See, for example, *Nadege Dorzema* (n 5) [81]; 'Basic Principles on the Use of Force and Firearms by Law Enforcement Officials' (Adopted by the Eighth United Nations Congress on the Prevention of Crime and the Treatment of Offenders, Havana, Cuba, 27 August–7 September 1990) UN Doc A/CONF.144/28/Rev.1, 112 paras 18–20.

7 See, for example, Walter Kälin and Jörg Künzli, *The Law of International Human Rights Protection* (OUP 2009) 188–89. The European Court of Human Rights has held the procedural obligations under the right to life to continue 'to apply in difficult security conditions'. *Al-Skeini and Others v the United Kingdom* ECHR 2011 [164].

8 As is the case for the ECHR, in respect of which individuals may bring cases against States at the European Court of Human Rights. However, such a right does not exist in every human rights system.

9 Such mechanisms include inter-State complaints, as well as periodic review of State implementation by individual treaty bodies, or under the UN Human Rights Council's system of Universal Period Review.

10 For a detailed consideration of this subject, see Anna Petrig, *Human Rights and Law Enforcement at Sea: Arrest, Detention and Transfer of Piracy Suspects* (Brill Nijhoff 2014).

11 See, for example, *Milan Furdik v Slovakia* (Admissibility) App no 42994/05 (ECtHR, 2 December 2008). The Court held that '…*the State's duty to safeguard the right to life must also be considered to extend to the provision of emergency services where it has been brought to the notice of the authorities that the life or health of an individual is at risk on account of*

and potentially to provide assistance to particular individuals in distress at sea.[12] The prohibition of non-refoulement may prevent the return of individuals to a State in which there is a real risk that they fundamental rights will be violated.[13] Even where enforcement action would be otherwise lawful, it may have to be balanced against competing freedoms of expression and assembly,[14] such as in the case of protest at sea.[15]

These rights may provide demanding standards against which States' conduct in MLE is to be measured. However, their relevance as a matter of law depends, to a large extent, on the applicability of the human rights treaties under which they are protected. Notwithstanding the possibility that certain rights might apply to a specific situation as a matter of custom,[16] it is the applicability of a particular human rights *treaty* that will bring into play the possibility for accountability and redress under its provisions. Establishing whether or not this is the case can be especially difficult in the context of MLE, which will often take place beyond a State's territory, and which will therefore engage the vexed subject of the *extraterritorial* application of human rights treaties.[17]

This crucial threshold of applicability is the subject of this essay. It does not purport to provide a comprehensive answer to the questions involved, but

---

injuries sustained as a result of an accident. Depending on the circumstances, this duty may go beyond the provision of essential emergency services such as fire-brigades and ambulances and, of relevance to the instant case, include the provision of air-mountain or air-sea rescue facilities to assist those in distress'. Ibid.

12 For a recent example, including some interesting conclusions on applicability, see UN Human Rights Committee, 'Views adopted by the Committee under article 5 (4) of the Optional Protocol, concerning Communication No. 3042/2017' (Communication submitted by A.S., D.I., O.I. and G.D. (represented by counsel, Mr. Andrea Saccucci)) (Views adopted 4 November 2020) UN Doc No CCPR/C/130/D/3042/2017.

13 For an instance of the principle of non-refoulement being applied in the maritime domain, see *Hirsi Jamaa and Others v Italy* ECHR 2012.

14 Such freedoms are protected under several instruments. In the case of the ECHR, the freedoms of expression and assembly are protected by articles 10 and 11 respectively. For an example of the freedom of expression in the maritime domain, see *Women on Waves and Others v Portugal* App No 31276/05 (ECtHR, 3 February 2009), which concerned the provision of family planning services from a vessel located in Portugal's territorial sea.

15 See, for example, *The Arctic Sunrise Arbitration* (*The Kingdom of the Netherlands v The Russian Federation*) (Merits) PCA Case No 2014-02 (14 August 2015).

16 The extent to which this may be the case is beyond the scope of this essay.

17 The question of the extraterritorial applicability of human rights treaties has generated copious literature. See, for example, Marko Milanovic, *Extraterritorial Application of Human Rights Treaties: Law, Principles, and Policy* (OUP 2011); Karen da Costa, *The Extraterritorial Application of Selected Human Rights Treaties* (Martinus Nijhoff 2013). Nevertheless, many issues remain unresolved.

rather to explain their contours and identify the key points of doubt and controversy. It does so by considering, first and foremost, the applicability of the European Convention on Human Rights (ECHR);[18] however, reference will also be made to other relevant instruments, including the International Covenant on Civil and Political Rights (ICCPR)[19] and American Convention on Human Rights (ACHR).[20]

This essay first gives a brief summary of the applicability of human rights treaties in general, before considering how those principles apply in the context of MLE, particularly those that take place outside a State's territory. To assist the analysis, it describes a generic maritime enforcement operation and asks when, during this narrative, the threshold of extraterritorial applicability will be crossed. At certain stages of the operation, it is relatively uncontroversial that the necessary jurisdictional link will be established, whereas at others the situation is less clear. The analysis does not aim to resolve these issues, but rather to sketch out the key areas of doubt and controversy.

2 The Applicability of Human Rights Treaties

The ECHR, like the ICCPR and ACHR, contains an express applicability provision, applying the ECHR to 'everyone within [a State party's] jurisdiction'.[21] The equivalent provisions in the ICCPR[22] and ACHR[23] are drafted in slightly different term; nevertheless, the applicability of both turns, as it does for the ECHR, on whether an individual is within a State's jurisdiction.[24] However,

18 Convention for the Protection of Human Rights and Fundamental Freedoms (European Convention on Human Rights, as amended) (ECHR).

19 International Covenant on Civil and Political Rights (adopted 16 December 1966, entered into force 23 March 1976) 999 UNTS 171 (ICCPR).

20 American Convention on Human Rights: 'Pact of San José, Costa Rica' (signed 22 November 1969, entered into force 18 July 1978) 1144 UNTS 144 (ACHR).

21 ECHR (n 18) art 1.

22 'Each State Party to the present Covenant undertakes to respect and to ensure to all individuals within its territory and subject to its jurisdiction the rights recognized in the present Covenant ...'. ICCPR (n 19) art 2(1).

23 'The States Parties to this Convention undertake to respect the rights and freedoms recognized herein and to ensure to all persons subject to their jurisdiction the free and full exercise of those rights and freedoms ...'. ACHR (n 20) art 1(1).

24 There remains a minority view, shared by the United States, that article 2(1) ICCPR should be read as requiring an individual *both* to be within a State's territory *and* subject to its jurisdiction. For a critical account of this issue, see, for example, Milanovic (n 17) 222–27;

'jurisdiction' should not be read as coincident with its meaning in other contexts. Instead, it has developed as a standalone concept, albeit incorporating elements from wider international law, as this essay will explain.

Jurisdiction can be either territorial or extraterritorial. However, while the necessary jurisdictional link will usually be established in the former case simply on the basis of an individual being within a State's territory, the exercise of extraterritorial jurisdiction is exceptional, requiring 'special justification in the particular circumstances of each case'.[25] Quite how easily such jurisdiction can be established has been a major point of contention as the law has developed. While the jurisprudence has evolved over time, and differences have arisen in the approaches taken by different courts and treaty bodies, the essential point remains that extraterritorial jurisdiction must be established on the facts of the case at hand.

Of particular importance in the context of MLE, the necessary jurisdictional link has been recognised as arising between a State and the vessels that fly its flag, at least for the purposes of some treaties.[26] However, more generally, it can arise on either a spatial or personal basis: through the effective control that a State exercises over an *area*; or through the authority and control that a State's agents exercise over an *individual*.[27] Importantly, at least so far as the ECHR is concerned, while the former entails the applicability of the whole treaty, where jurisdiction is established on a personal basis, rights may be 'divided and tailored'.[28] This means that only those rights pertinent to a particular situation need apply – and, crucially, it is no bar to applicability that a State may not be able to give effect to the full range of rights, as would be the case where jurisdiction is established through effective control over an area.

Although these bases for jurisdiction are now well-established in principle, their precise contours are less certain. In the case of personal jurisdiction, a particular issue is exactly which forms of authority and control will be sufficient. While it is now uncontroversial that the jurisdictional link will be

---

Beth Van Schaack, 'The United States' Position on the Extraterritorial Application of Human Rights Obligations: Now is the Time for Change' (2014) 90 Intl L Studies 20.

25 *Banković and Others v Belgium and Others* ECHR 2001–XII 333 [59]–[61].

26 In the context of the ECHR, this was expressly recognised in ibid [73]. The principle was applied in *Hirsi Jamaa and Others v Italy* ECHR 2012, in which the Grand Chamber of the European Court of Human Rights found that irregular migrants were within Italy's jurisdiction when they were brought on board 'military ships flying the Italian flag', while those ships were on the high seas. ibid [76]–[78].

27 *Al-Skeini* (n 7) [130]–[142]. This is sometimes referred to as the 'personal model'.

28 Ibid. [137].

established in respect of an individual who has been detained,[29] it is less clear whether – or at least when – it might be established through the use of physical force alone.

3 Applicability of Human Rights Treaties to Maritime Law Enforcement

MLE activities may be conducted in every maritime zone, and thus either within or beyond areas that form part of a State's territory. A State's sovereignty extends throughout its internal waters and territorial sea, as well as throughout any archipelagic waters it may have.[30] As such areas therefore form part of the State's territory,[31] it follows that jurisdiction for the purpose of human rights treaties is established within them on a territorial basis, just as it is within a State's land territory.[32]

However, a State may also conduct MLE activities beyond its territorial sea, in any contiguous zone it may claim,[33] or to protect the sovereign rights it enjoys in an exclusive economic zone or on the continental shelf.[34] It may also take extraterritorial enforcement action against vessels it has pursued under the rules of hot pursuit,[35] against vessels engaged in piracy,[36] or in a range of other circumstances.[37] In all of these situations it will be necessary to consider

29 See, for example, *Al-Saadoon and Mufdhi v the United Kingdom* ECHR 2010. The case concerned the applicability of the ECHR to Iraqi nationals detained by UK forces in Iraq, and held in a UK-controlled detention facility.

30 UNCLOS (n 4) art 2(1).

31 See, for example, James Crawford, *Brownlie's Principles of Public International Law* (8th edn, OUP 2012) 203; Malcolm N Shaw, *International Law* (7th edn, CUP 2014) 352. See also International Law Commission, 'Draft Articles on the Law of Treaties with Commentaries' [1966] 2 United Nations YB of the Intl L Commission 187 (Draft Articles on the Law of Treaties with Commentaries), 213. Admittedly, this point of view is not universally held. See Douglas Guilfoyle, *Shipping Interdiction and the Law of the Sea* (CUP 2009) 226.

32 This is a common conclusion, though not always explained in detail. See, for example, John E Noyes, 'The Territorial Sea and Contiguous Zone' in Donald R Rothwell and others (eds), *The Oxford Handbook of the Law of the Sea* (OUP 2015) 104.

33 UNCLOS (n 4) art 33.

34 Ibid., arts 56, 77.

35 Ibid., art 111.

36 Ibid., arts 105, 110(1)(a).

37 For example, under UNCLOS, States enjoy a right of visit in respect of foreign vessels suspected of involvement in the slave trade or unauthorised broadcasting, as well as in respect of vessels without nationality. Ibid., art 110. Enforcement action against foreign vessels can also be permitted under bilateral or multilateral treaties, agreed on a case-by-case basis, or authorised by the UN Security Council.

whether the threshold of *extraterritorial* applicability is crossed on the basis of the facts at hand.

In considering this question, it is helpful to sketch out what how a typical MLE operation might typically be conducted.[38] First, State authorities will become aware of a target vessel in respect of which it wishes to conduct law enforcement activity. Perhaps following a period of surveillance, a decision will be taken to interdict the vessel. The interdicting ship will usually make contact with the vessel, instructing it to stop and submit to investigation. If it doesn't comply, there may be an escalation through increasingly forceful measures – including warning shots, as well as non-disabling and disabling fire – to bring it under the interdicting ship's control.[39] At some point, the interdicting ship may send a boarding party, which might use force to take control of the vessel and maybe detain those on board. The vessel itself might then be escorted or even towed to port, while individuals may be detained and brought onboard the interdicting ship, perhaps with a view to prosecution.

Working backwards through this narrative, at the point that detained individuals are brought on board the interdicting ship, the threshold of applicability will almost certainly have been crossed. As noted above, one of the specific situations in which the necessary jurisdictional link has been recognised, at least so far as the jurisprudence of the ECtHR (European Court of Human Rights) is concerned, is in respect of the jurisdiction enjoyed by a State over vessels flying its flag. More generally, detention is the archetype of state agent authority and control over individuals, and well established as a circumstance giving rise to extraterritorial applicability.

But what of individuals on the target vessel? If they are detained, in the sense of being confined to a particular location on board, then there is no reason to doubt that the threshold of authority will have been crossed, just as it would on land. However, what if they are able to move around the vessel, or a large part of it, but the vessel *as a whole* is under the control of the interdicting ship? In essence, the question is whether authority and control over individuals through the control being exercised over the vessel as a whole, is – or can be – sufficient.

The jurisprudence of the ECtHR would suggest an answer in the affirmative. In *Medvedyev and Others v France*[40] the Grand Chamber of the ECtHR

38 For an example of a publicly available account of relevant practice, see Royal Netherlands Navy, 'Fundamentals of Maritime Operations: Netherlands Maritime Military Doctrine' (2014) 349–54.

39 Ibid., 351–52.

40 *Medvedyev and Others v France* ECHR 2010.

considered an interdiction of a Cambodian vessel by French forces, in which the vessel was ultimately placed in tow, with the crew remaining on board. Although the applicants had claimed to have been confined to their cabins, this was disputed, and does not appear to have been determinative.[41] Considering the question of extraterritorial applicability, the Grand Chamber held that it had been established as a consequence of the 'full and exclusive control over the [interdicted vessel] and its crew, at least *de facto*, from the time of its interception, in a continuous and uninterrupted manner until they were tried in France'.[42] Indeed, in considering the related question of whether the crew had been deprived of its liberty, the Grand Chamber found this to have been the case because 'the ship's course was imposed' by the interdicting authorities.[43]

As a matter of principle, this isn't an especially surprising result. For applicability to rest on the degree of freedom individuals enjoy *within* a vessel, while the vessel itself is under another's control, would seem somewhat arbitrary. Arguably, it would also be arbitrary for applicability to rest on the specific modality of the control exercised over the vessel – whether, for example, the vessel is placed under tow, as in *Medvedyev*, or yields to instruction. Nevertheless, while *Medvedyev* is an important point of reference, particularly in the context of the ECHR, it remains a relatively unusual instance of these issues being considered in detail,[44] and it would perhaps be a mistake to extrapolate too far from its particular facts, or to assume that another court would necessarily follow its reasoning.

Moving one step back, what about actions that an interdicting ship might take to compel the target vessel to yield? As noted above, this will generally involve an escalation through a series of forceful measures, which undoubtedly have the potential to affect the right to life. The crucial question, however, is whether the use of such measures is sufficient to give rise to the *applicability* of the right to life in the first place. Put another way, can the use of force against an individual amount – absent anything else – to an exercise of authority and

41 The facts are set out at ibid., [9]–[19].

42 Ibid., [67].

43 Ibid., [74].

44 Consistent with this, see *JHA v Spain*, in which the Committee Against Torture considered, in the context of the Convention Against Torture, a vessel to be within the jurisdiction of a State providing assistance from the point the vessel had been 'rescued', at which point it was placed under tow. UN Committee Against Torture, 'Decision of the Committee Against Torture under Article 22 of the Convention Against Torture and Other Cruel, Inhuman or Degrading Treatment of Punishment Concerning Communication No 323/2007' (Communication submitted by JHA on behalf of PK et al, concerning Spain) (21 November 2008) UN Doc CAT/C/41/D/323/2007 (JHA v Spain) para 8.2.

control, such as to establish extraterritorial applicability according to the personal model?[45]

This is a key area of controversy, and an issue on which different courts and treaty bodies appear to have taken different positions. The Human Rights Committee (HRC), for example, has adopted an entirely functional approach. For example, in its General Comment 36, dealing primarily with the right to life under Article 6 of the ICCPR, the HRC considers that States' obligations are engaged extraterritorially in respect of 'persons located outside any territory effectively controlled by the State whose right to life is nonetheless affected by its military or other activities in a direct and reasonably foreseeable manner'.[46] According to this position, there seems little doubt that the HRC would consider the right to life to be engaged when a State uses force to effect an interdiction.

The Inter-American Commission on Human Rights has adopted a similarly functional approach. For example, in *Armando Alejandre Jr, Carlos Costa, Mario de la Peña and Pablo Morales v Republic of Cuba*,[47] the Commission found Cuba's human rights obligations to have been engaged when Cuban military aircraft allegedly shot down two civilian aircraft in international airspace.[48] It has similarly held Ecuador's obligations potentially to be engaged when members of its army shot Colombian citizens in Colombian territory,[49] and Colombia's obligations to have potentially been engaged when bombs dropped by its armed forces in Ecuadorian territory were alleged to have harmed Ecuadorian citizens.[50]

---

45 For a discussion of the issue in the context of a case in which the UK High Court decided that physical force could be sufficient to bring about the extraterritorial applicability of the ECHR, see David S Goddard, 'Applying the ECHR to the Use of Physical Force in Al-Saadoon' (2015) 91 Intl L Studies 402. Notably, this aspect of the decision was reversed on appeal. See *Al-Saadoon and others (Appellants) v The Secretary of State for Defence (Respondent), Rahmattullah and another (Appellant) v The Secretary of State for Defence and another (Respondents)* [2016] EWCA Civ 811.

46 UN Human Rights Committee, 'General comment No. 36 (2018) on article 6 of the International Covenant on Civil and Political Rights, on the right to life' (30 October 2018) UN Doc CCPR/C/GC/36 para 63.

47 *Armando Alejandre Jr, Carlos Costa, Mario de la Pena y Pablo Morales v Cuba*, Case 11.589, Report No 86/99, Inter-American Commission on Human Rights, OEA/Ser.L/V/II.106 Doc 3 rev at 586 (1999).

48 Ibid. [1].

49 *Danny Honorio Bastidas Meneses and others v Ecuador*, Admissibility, Petition 189–03, Report 153/11 (IACHR, 2 November 2011).

50 *Franklin Guillermo Aisalla Molina v Ecuador*, Case IP-02, Report No 112/10, Inter-American Commission on Human Rights, OEA/Ser.L/V/II.140 Doc 10 (2010).

It has been argued that such an outcome is the inevitable conclusion of the reasoning that underpins the personal model of jurisdiction, and that to deny its application in the case of physical force would be to make an arbitrary distinction from other forms of authority and control, such as detention.[51] Nevertheless, at least so far as the ECtHR is concerned, physical force *is* treated differently from other forms of authority and control. Looming especially large in the Court's jurisprudence is the case of *Banković and Others v Belgium and Others*,[52] in which the Court held the ECHR not to apply in the case of individuals harmed by NATO's bombing of a radio station in Belgrade during the conflict in Kosovo.[53] In so doing, the Court set out a very limited conception of extraterritorial jurisdiction, which was largely limited to effective control over territory, albeit recognizing certain other specific situations, such as in the case of vessels flying under a State's flag.[54]

Admittedly, the ECtHR has subsequently expanded its conception of extraterritorial applicability. As noted above, in *Al-Skeini and others v United Kingdom*, it provided a restatement of its position,[55] recognizing the potential for extraterritorial applicability to arise according to *both* personal and spatial models. However, it stopped short of unambiguously rejecting its earlier approach in *Banković*. While the Court held that individuals were subject to the authority and control of the respondent State's forces when the latter used armed force against them, this was apparently the case only in the context of the respondent State's forces exercising 'public powers'.[56] This arguably allowed the Court to reconcile its findings on the facts in *Al-Skeini* with the decision in *Banković*, although the continuing authority of the earlier decision has been questioned.[57] The ECtHR appears recently to have reaffirmed that *Banković* remains good law,[58] at least as an exception to the applicability of the

51 See, for example, Milanovic (n 17) 207–9.
52 *Banković* (n 25).
53 Ibid. [6]–[11].
54 Ibid. [71]–[73].
55 *Al-Skeini* (n 7) [130]–[142].
56 Ibid. [149].
57 Including by the UK High Court, as discussed at Goddard (n 45) 418, though noting that this aspect of the High Court's decision was ultimately reversed on appeal.
58 *Georgia v Russia (II)* ECHR 2021 [127]–[144]. For discussion, including of this aspect, see Marko Milanovic, 'Georgia v. Russia No. 2: The European Court's Resurrection of Bankovic in the Contexts of Chaos' (*EJIL Talk!*, 25 January 2021) <https://www.ejiltalk.org/georgia-v-russia-no-2-the-european-courts-resurrection-of-bankovic-in-the-contexts-of-chaos/> accessed 28 September 2021.

ECHR in the case of armed force used during the active phase of hostilities in international armed conflict.

To some extent, therefore, whether or not physical force used in interdiction will alone give rise to extraterritorial applicability remains in doubt. While it seems clear that some bodies, such as the HRC, will have no difficulty in finding the required jurisdictional link to have been established, for others – the ECtHR in particular – it is less certain. While it is plausible that the ECtHR might consider the use of force in the course of an interdiction to be analogous to that used in *Al-Skeini*, i.e., in the context of something akin to the exercise of public powers, it cannot be excluded that it will instead follow reasoning closer to that in *Banković*. As things stand, the jurisprudence is not clear enough to draw a firm conclusion.

However, stepping even further back, is it possible that a vessel could be subject to a State's jurisdiction, such as to give rise to extraterritorial applicability, before an interdiction even begins, i.e., right from the start of the narrative set out above? This would be the case if extraterritorial applicability were established on a spatial, rather than personal, basis – if the target vessel is within an area over which the State in question exercises effective control.

As a matter of principle, there seems no fundamental reason why this could not be possible at sea, just as it is on land. However, if the same standards are applied,[59] the key question is whether a State will ever exercise *sufficient* control over an area of sea. The standard has been taken to be the ability to give effect to the full range of rights protected under a treaty,[60] and it is difficult to conceive of many situations where control over an area of sea will meet that standard. Nevertheless, it has been suggested that the standard could be met, for example, in the region where a multinational force conducts a counter-piracy operation.[61] However, this would require a wholly different standard to be applied. In the case of the operation cited, no more than a handful of warships conducted counter-piracy operations – and no other mode of control – over a vast area of ocean. It has also been suggested that there might be a radius around State ships within which they exercise effective control, wherever they may be.[62] However, this conflates the *potential* for a ship to exercise

59 For a statement of the relevant standard in the context of the ECHR, see *Al-Skeini* (n 7) [138]–[139].

60 See, for example, the views of the UK High Court in *Al-Saadoon and Others v Secretary of State for Defence* [2015] EWHC 715 (Admin) [67] ('…it follows that the test of effective control over the area will not be satisfied unless the state has the practical ability to secure the full package of Convention rights'.).

61 Robin Geiß and Anna Petrig, *Piracy and Armed Robbery at Sea* (OUP 2011) 108.

62 Ibid.

control with the question whether it actually does so; and, if a ship *does* do something to exercise control over another vessel, then arguably this is really just an incidence of State agent authority and control under the personal, rather than spatial, model.

Notwithstanding these objections, the possibility of a State exercising sufficient control over an area of sea cannot be ruled out. This is perhaps most plausible in relatively small areas, such as safety zones established around installations.[63] Even then, the control exercised by the State in question will be limited to a relatively narrow range of security-related matters – and still rather different from the level and type of control that would allow a State to give effect to the full range of rights. Consequently, extraterritorial jurisdiction on this basis remains decidedly speculative.

4 Conclusion

This short essay has sought to sketch out some of the issues surrounding the applicability of human rights treaties to MLE operations, particularly those that are conducted beyond a State's territory. This threshold question is important not only for the substantive rights that may be engaged, but also for the possibility that States might be brought to account through additional mechanisms that may become available, including the possibility of individual complaints.

Considering a generic MLE operation, it is relatively uncontroversial that the threshold will be crossed at least at the point that individuals are detained, especially so if they are brought onboard the interdicting ship. There is also good reason to think that the threshold can be met where authority and control is exercised over individuals via control over their vessel as a whole. However, it remains much less clear whether the necessary jurisdictional link will be established prior to control over the vessel being established, including at the point that forceful measures might be employed. On this question, there are considerable differences in the approaches taken by different courts and bodies, and a coherent account remains elusive. Even more speculative is the possibility that extraterritorial applicability could arise from effective control over an area of sea; although not inconceivable, it seems unlikely that the standard established on land could be met at sea in all but the narrowest of circumstances, if at all.

63 UNCLOS (n 4) art 60.

CHAPTER 13

Navigation Rights and Law Enforcement: An Australian Perspective

David Letts

As the law of the sea slowly formed over many centuries, the right to use the world's ocean spaces with relative freedom, predominantly for the purposes of facilitating trade and commerce between communities, was one of the earliest components of the law that was developed. Accompanying this development was the realisation that maritime traffic could also provide a threat to towns and cities along coastlines in a variety of different ways, and that some form of regulation of this traffic was necessary. However, the precise nature, and the permissible extent, of maritime regulation has been the source of ongoing dispute between coastal States and the users of maritime spaces.

One area in which disputes have regularly arisen is the regulation of maritime traffic when people are trying to seek asylum through arrival in a state by boat. Australia has had a long history of dealing with boat arrivals containing people seeking asylum, and over the course of many years Australia's approach towards these boats has altered markedly. There has been a resultant impact on the international community's approach to this topic as well, with a range of measures being adopted including amendments to applicable conventions and the use of similar operational tactics to those used by Australia.

The first part of this chapter will outline what is meant by freedom of navigation and identify some of the friction points that exist between states when navigation, especially close to the coastline, occurs. The next part of the paper will examine how force can be used during law enforcement activities at sea and draw some principles from the key cases and incidents that have informed state practice in these types of operations. Following that, a seminal maritime incident arising during Australia's border protection operations, 'the *Tampa* incident', will be examined. The paper will conclude with an assessment of whether or not Australia's law enforcement operations at sea have been undertaken in a manner that is consistent with the law of the sea.

DOI:10.1163/9789004518629_014

1 Freedom of Navigation

It is widely recognised that modern concepts of freedom of navigation can be traced to the writings of Hugo Grotius in the early seventeenth century with the publication of his dissertation *Mare Liberum*[1] and the subsequent responses that were evoked to its publication.[2] Although *Mare Liberum* was originally published anonymously, the publication had the clear purpose of defending the right of the Dutch East India Company to trade and travel in waters which at that stage the Portuguese claimed as solely their own. It was not until the 1860s that the author of *Mare Liberum* was unambiguously established, and Grotius' work is now regarded as instrumental in establishing the fundamental principle that governs the law of the sea – the freedom of navigation.

Freedom of navigation has manifested itself as part of customary international law as the concept is considered to be one of the fundamental rights available to vessels of all nations, particularly in so far as this right relates to the high seas.[3] In essence, the high seas have been viewed as part of a vast global common upon which vessels of all states have freedom of navigation, fishing and other lawful uses of the seas, although the genesis of this view clearly lies in the '... notion of freedom [being] used as an ideological tool' in furtherance of national objectives.[4]

Freedom of navigation was also a central theme running through the attempts at codifying the law of the sea that occurred during the twentieth

1 Two English language versions of the publication, originally written in Latin, provide slightly different wording for the title: 'The Freedom of the Seas or the Right which belongs to the Dutch to take part in the East Indian trade' is the title of the translation by Ralph Van Deman Magoffin (New York, Oxford University Press American Branch, 1916) available at https://oll.libertyfund.org/title/scott-the-freedom-of-the-seas-latin-and-english-version-magoffin-trans while 'The Free Sea or A Disputation Concerning the Right Which the Hollanders Ought to Have to the Indian Merchandise for Trading' is the title of the translation by Richard Hakluyt in *The Free Sea, trans. Richard Hakluyt, with William Welwod's Critique and Grotius's Reply*, ed. David Armitage (Indianapolis, Liberty Fund, 2004) available at https://oll.libertyfund.org/title/hakluyt-the-free-sea-hakluyt-trans.

2 For further discussion, see D.P. O'Connell, (I.A. Shearer ed.) *The International Law of the Sea Volume 1* (Oxford, Oxford University Press, 1984) pp. 9–18. Also C.J. Colombos, *International Law of the Sea* (6th rev. ed, London, Longmans, 1972), pp. 62–64; R.R. Churchill and A.V. Lowe, *The Law of the Sea* (2nd ed, Manchester, Manchester University Press, 1988), pp. 3–4; and E.D. Brown, *The International Law of the Sea Volume I* (Aldershot, Dartmouth,1994), pp. 6–7.

3 The interplay between coastal State rights and the navigation rights of foreign vessels has been a subject of interest for many decades. See, for example, the discussion on this topic in K.C. Frazer, 'The I'm Alone Case and the Doctrine of Hot Pursuit', 7 *North Carolina Law Review*, 1929, 413.

4 E.D. Brown, *supra* n 2, p. 278.

century, and is now embodied in various parts of the 1982 UN Convention.[5] In this regard, the concept of 'innocent passage in the territorial sea' emerged as being not only a customary right, but also appeared as one of the cornerstones of the 1958 Convention.[6] During the long negotiations that ultimately resulted in the LOSC being opened for signature at Montego Bay, Jamaica, on 10 December 1982, freedom of navigation in the territorial sea remained a crucial issue.[7] The LOSC provided further advances in freedom of navigation by the inclusion of the transit passage regime through straits used for international navigation,[8] as well as the new right of archipelagic sea lanes passage in Part IV of the Convention.[9] The LOSC expressly provides there 'shall be no suspension' of either transit passage or archipelagic sea lanes passage.[10] While it could be considered that the inclusion of the 'transit passage' regime was little more than acknowledgement of the customary nature of the decision of the International Court of Justice in the *Corfu Channel Case*,[11] the President of UNCLOS III[12] has stated that 'transit passage' was in reality a new concept.[13]

The entry into force of the 1982 LOSC in November 1994 had a profound impact on navigation rights that should not be underestimated. The establishment of twelve nautical miles as the maximum breadth of the territorial sea,[14] the introduction of the exclusive economic zone,[15] and the recognition of the unique circumstances pertaining to archipelagic States[16] under the LOSC have all contributed to a fundamentally altered maritime operating environment

5 *United Nations Convention on the Law of the Sea*, 1833 UNTS 397 (hereafter LOSC). Also reprinted and indexed in UN Publication (Sales No. E.97.V.10), *Official Text of the United Nations Convention on the Law of the Sea of 10 December 1982* (New York, United Nations, 1997).

6 *Convention on the Territorial Sea and the Contiguous Zone of 29 April 1958*, 515 UNTS 205, Article 14.

7 LOSC, *supra* n 5, article 18.

8 Ibid., articles 37–44.

9 Ibid., article 53.

10 Ibid., articles 44 and 54.

11 16 *ILR* (1949) 155.

12 In conforming with accepted practice, the 1958, 1960 and 1982 UN Conferences on the Law of the Sea are referred to as UNCLOS I, UNCLOS II and UNCLOS III respectively.

13 Tommy T.B. Koh, 'A Constitution for the Oceans', *United Nations Law of the Sea Text* (1983) at xxxiv.

14 LOSC, *supra* n 5, article 3.

15 Ibid., articles 55–75.

16 Ibid., articles 46–54.

from that which existed prior to the LOSC being concluded.[17] Additionally, while the major impact has certainly been on those States that are party to the LOSC, there has also been a clear impact among those states that have not become party to the Convention, as so much of the operative parts of the LOSC are now accepted as being part of customary international law.[18]

The modern concept of freedom of navigation is firmly based on the LOSC and encompasses various navigational rights and freedoms that apply differently in each of the maritime zones recognised in the Convention.[19] The most expansive navigational rights and freedoms exist in the high seas, which are those sea areas that are beyond the jurisdiction of any state,[20] while in those maritime zones that are closer to the coastline there is greater capacity for a coastal State to regulate elements of passage. Nevertheless, a *right* of passage exists in all maritime zones recognised under the law of the sea with the exception of internal waters.

Challenges to freedom of navigation can take many different forms, and measures to address these challenges can be equally diverse. Adopting an expansive view, the impact of issues ranging from a lack of common understanding of the LOSC's provisions, through to protection and health of the marine environment, are all capable of being potential challenges to freedom of navigation in one way or another.[21]

17 For an early appreciation of the LOSC's impact on Australia, see M. Tsamenyi, S. Bateman and J. Delaney (eds.) *The United Nations Convention on the Law of the Sea: What It Means to Australia and Australia's Marine Industries* (Wollongong, Centre for Maritime Policy, 1996). In particular, note the contribution by I. A. Shearer 'Should Australia have Ratified the Convention?' at pp. 55–65 for a 'devil's advocate' approach to the question of Australia's ratification of the Convention.

18 It is clear that the LOSC did not simply represent a codification of existing customary law, as it introduced too many new concepts for such a proposition to be legally or factually sustainable. Nevertheless, parts of the LOSC do now represent customary law. For example, in relation to the exclusive economic zone (EEZ) Brown, *supra* n 2, p. 224 is clear that "there is no doubt that the general concept of the EEZ has been accepted into the body of customary law". See also *Oceans: The Source of Life – United Nations Convention on the Law of the Sea 20th Anniversary (1982-2002)* at page 15 where the status of the LOSC on its 20th anniversary was assessed by the UN Division for Ocean Affairs and the Law of the Sea, http://www.un.org/Depts/los/convention_agreements/convention_20years/oceanssourceoflife.pdf (accessed 19 Sep 21).

19 S. Bateman, *Freedoms of navigation in the Asia-Pacific region* (Oxford, Routledge, 2020), p. 13.

20 LOSC articles 86 and 87.

21 Bateman, *supra* n 19, p. 13.

2 Law Enforcement at Sea

Law enforcement at sea is conducted in a way that is distinctly different from the way in which law enforcement occurs on land. By its very nature, the maritime environment brings challenges to law enforcement activities such as the need to cope with the movement of vessels as they bounce around in unpredictable ways on the ocean. This, in turn, leads to careful consideration of the level of force that can legitimately be used during law enforcement operations at sea.

The use of force at sea is not a new concept. Battles between naval vessels have occurred regularly throughout history, and vessels have also been used for security and law enforcement activities for many centuries. This paper is not going to deal with activities that occur at sea during periods when the laws of armed conflict apply and where the law of naval warfare is the relevant *lex specialis*. Rather, the focus of this paper is upon those situations that arise when security or law enforcement activities are undertaken and where the relevant legal authority might be, for example, a UN Security Council Resolution or coastal State domestic law that is firmly based on a state's international legal rights and obligations.

Looking at security and law enforcement activities at sea, an appropriate starting point is to begin with some issues that relate to how the use of force should be framed, including examining who, or what, force might be used. In the maritime context there seems to be a number of factors at play, including the use of force against the vessel itself (i.e., trying to stop the vessel from proceeding in a certain direction or carrying out a certain activity) and this activity is somewhat remote from consideration of the status of any persons onboard the vessel.

The LOSC reflects this division in Article 110 (Right of Visit) and Article 111 (Hot Pursuit) as action in both cases is directed against 'a ship'. This type of force could be exerted without actually boarding a vessel, and would also be typified by an escalation of measures that are designed to compel those navigating the vessel to comply with the direction of those intercepting the vessel. Measures could include, in a graduated scale, request by voice/radio, signaling an intention to get the vessel to act in a certain way, maneuvering the intercepting vessel in a manner designed to initiate compliance, sending a boarding party to a vessel to deliver instructions or apprehend the vessel, use of a device to interfere with the vessel's propeller or steering, the firing of warning shots near a vessel or actually firing at the vessel to compel compliance.

The use of force at sea during law enforcement operations was analysed in detail by the International Tribunal for the Law of the Sea in the M/V Saiga case.[22] After assessing the relevant factual circumstances in the case, the Tribunal noted that the LOSC does not actually contain any express provisions that deal with the use of force when a vessel is being arrested.[23] The Tribunal also noted, however, that international law is to be applied by a court or tribunal that is exercising jurisdiction under LOSC Part XV[24] and on that basis ITLOS proceeded to examine the principles that have emerged from law enforcement operations at sea over many years.

Key among these principles is the requirement for force to be '... avoided as far as possible and, where force is unavoidable, it must not go beyond what is reasonable and necessary in the circumstances'.[25] The Tribunal then outlined the normal practice used at sea to stop a ship, including the range of escalatory actions that might follow should those onboard a ship not comply with the direction for the ship to stop. In providing this assessment, ITLOS referred to two earlier law enforcement cases with approval: the *I'm Alone*[26] and the *Red Crusader*.[27] The Tribunal concluded that '... only after the appropriate actions fail ... [can] ... the pursuing vessel ... as a last resort, use force. Even then, appropriate warning must be issued to the ship and all efforts should be made to ensure that life is not endangered'.[28]

A consequence of the above information is that firing a weapon to compel a vessel to comply with the legitimate direction of an intercepting vessel may be permissible under international law. However, the LOSC does not directly address the level of force that can be used, instead referring to terms such as 'necessary steps'[29] or 'control necessary'[30] and leaving interpretation regarding what those terms mean to a case-by-case assessment in any given situation.

It is noteworthy that some mention of limitations placed on how a state can exercise law enforcement powers is contained in the LOSC. For example, Part XII of the LOSC contains two articles that address law enforcement activities in the context of measures that can be undertaken for the protection and preservation of the marine environment. However, these provisions only relate to

---

22 *M/V Saiga No. 2* (Saint Vincent and the Grenadines v. Guinea), (1999) ITLOS case no. 2, paragraphs 153–159.
23 Ibid., para 155.
24 LOSC article 293.
25 *M/V Saiga, supra* n 22, para 155.
26 *The I'm Alone* (Canada/United States of America), 3 RIAA 1609.
27 *The Red Crusader* (Commission of Enquiry, Denmark/United Kingdom, 1962), 35 ILR 485.
28 *M/V Saiga, supra* n 22, para 156.
29 LOSC article 25 in relation to action taken in the territorial sea.
30 LOSC article 33 in relation to action taken in the contiguous zone.

who/what can exercise these powers[31] and limitations on the exercise of these powers so that vessels are not unnecessarily endangered.[32] In essence, the powers can only be exercised by duly authorised government officials and '... States shall not endanger safety of navigation or otherwise create a hazard to a vessel or bring it to an unsafe port or anchorage ...'. This clearly indicates that law enforcement powers are to be exercised cautiously against foreign vessels and the *Saiga No. 2* decision reinforces this assessment.[33]

In relation to force that is used against individuals that are onboard a vessel, it is important to recognise there may be a number of distinct categories of persons who are in a vessel when a law enforcement operation is conducted.

The first category are those that are unaware of anything occurring in the vessel other than the routine operations associated with that vessel conducting its activities at sea. Such persons might be quite unaware of any illegal activity taking place in the vessel regardless of the scope of the activity occurring. Accordingly, any use of force against persons in this category would be quite problematic unless there was behaviour from a person that was clearly directed at interfering with legitimate law enforcement actions. The second category are those who are actually involved in the illegal activity, and it is possible that the behaviour of persons in this category might include interference (or even active resistance) to law enforcement activities.

An ancillary question therefore arises as to how it might be possible to identify on any vessel who is actually in each category, and if this can be done, whether there is, or should be, any difference in the level of force that is used in relation to dealing with either group while at sea. The answer will depend on what level of resistance, if any, is provided towards the law enforcement officials, but in either case, only force that is reasonable and necessary in the circumstances would be permitted.[34] This legal test applies regardless of whether action is being taken under international law or domestic legislation.

One aspect of law enforcement that deserves mention is the right of hot pursuit that a coastal State may exercise when a vessel attempts to flee from being apprehended. In broad terms, hot pursuit can be undertaken when '... the competent authorities of the coastal State have good reason to believe that the ship has violated the laws and regulations of that State'.[35] The pursuit must begin

31 LOSC article 224.

32 LOSC article 225.

33 *M/V Saiga, supra* n 22, paras 157–159.

34 The use of excessive force against the persons on board was identified in *M/V Saiga, supra*, n 22, para 158.

35 LOSC article 111 (1).

in a maritime zone (internal waters, territorial sea, contiguous zone, Exclusive Economic Zone or continental shelf) where the coastal State has jurisdiction to deal with the alleged offending.[36] There are other requirements for a valid hot pursuit that are identified in LOSC Article 111, including the provision of a visual or auditory signal to stop at a distance where it can be seen or heard by the foreign ship,[37] and the pursuit must cease when the foreign vessel reaches another State's territorial sea.[38] Further discussion of the practical application of hot pursuit in Australia's law enforcement activities follows below.

In summary, law enforcement measures are regulated under a combination of international law and the domestic law of the State undertaking enforcement action. In conducting law enforcement activities, there is a clear entitlement to use reasonable and necessary force to effect the law enforcement and also in a situation where there is a need to respond to a threat in self-defence. In some circumstances, this could include the use of lethal force, for example if being attacked with a weapon, but the details depend on the precise circumstances that are encountered. There is nothing particularly contentious about force being used against individuals in a law enforcement scenario, although limits must be placed on the amount of force that can be used. Again, the standard of 'reasonable and necessary' is relevant and authority may derive from the principles and standards established under international law, domestic law or a mixture of both.

3 An Example of State Practice – Australia and *MV Tampa*

In late August 2001, the Norwegian flagged container vessel *MV Tampa* rescued 432 persons at sea in the Indian Ocean between Indonesia and Australia. These persons had departed from a port on the southern coast of the Indonesian island of Java by paying large sums of money to people smugglers who crammed them into a small fishing boat, the *Palapa*, which was barely seaworthy. Unsurprisingly, the *Palapa* experienced engine trouble soon after departing the port, and approximately 24 hours after sailing the vessel's engine was dead.[39] The vessel foundered at sea for a number of hours while the question of which maritime rescue authority had responsibility for coordinating the vessel's rescue was passed between Australian and Indonesian rescue centres.

36 LOSC article 111 (1) and (2).
37 LOSC article 111 (4).
38 LOSC article 111 (3).
39 D. Marr and M. Wilkinson, *Dark Victory* (Crows Nest, Allen & Unwin, 2003) p. 7.

Ultimately, the Australian Maritime Safety Authority released a distress call, despite the *Palapa* being in the Indonesian search and rescue zone, that was responded to by the MV *Tampa*.[40]

The people picked up by MV *Tampa* were predominately from Afghanistan, escaping from the Taliban rule in that country, and were seeking to get to Australia in order to claim refugee status. However, the MV *Tampa* was not heading to Australia as its next scheduled port call was Singapore. Therefore, after receiving advice from the Indonesian rescue centre authorities,[41] the *Tampa*'s captain initially proposed to drop off the 'rescuees'[42] at the Indonesian port of Merak which would be the most convenient outcome for MV *Tampa* and allow that vessel to continue on its voyage to Singapore. However, once this decision became known among the 'rescuees' there was a tense stand-off between representatives of those rescued and the *Tampa*'s captain that eventually resulted in the vessel heading towards the Australian territory of Christmas Island.[43]

While events were unfolding onboard the *Tampa*, the Australian government decided that it would prevent the vessel from disembarking the 'rescuees' at Christmas Island. Action taken to achieve this outcome included directing MV *Tampa* to remain outside the territorial sea surrounding Christmas Island and preventing any boats from leaving Christmas Island to visit the ship. Eventually, *Tampa*'s captain decided that the situation onboard his vessel was no longer safe, declared that the vessel was in distress and proceeded into the territorial sea. Once this occurred, the Australian government ordered members of the Australian Defence Force to go onboard MV *Tampa* and seize the vessel. The government also introduced a Bill into the Australian Parliament that would, if passed into law, provide the government with a wide range of powers to deny entry into Australia of people seeking asylum who arrived by sea.[44]

---

40 Ibid., p. 3, p. 9, p. 10 and p. 16.

41 Ibid., p. 20.

42 The term 'rescuees' was used in lieu of other terms such as 'asylum-seekers' or 'refugees' by Justice North of the Australian Federal Court to describe the people who were rescued by MV *Tampa* during a legal challenge to the actions being taken by the Australian government to prevent the people onboard MV *Tampa* entering Australia: Ruddock v Vadarlis (2001) 183 ALR 1.

43 Christmas Island is an Australian offshore territory in the Indian Ocean. It is located approximately 190nm (350km) south of Java, 810nm (1500km) west of the Australian mainland and 1400nm (2600km) northwest of Perth.

44 The *Border Protection Bill* (2001) was defeated in the Australian Senate and never became law.

It is not necessary in this paper to comprehensively address all of the legal issues that arose from the *Tampa* incident, as many of these issues are not directly concerned with the law of the sea.[45] Instead, this paper will concentrate on a few of the key law of the sea issues that arise from the events that took place in and around Christmas Island in August/September 2001, as well as briefly consider some of the subsequent impacts on Australia's maritime border protection operations.

The first issue relates to efforts to keep *MV Tampa* out of the territorial sea around Christmas Island. The Australian government's announcement on this issue occurred during a press conference by the Prime Minster on 27 August 2001 when it was stated that after '... having taken legal advice on this matter and having considered it very carefully ...' *MV Tampa* was not permitted to enter Australia's territorial sea.[46] The precise nature of the legal advice provided to the government has not been disclosed. If the government was relying on LOSC article 25, which permits the temporary suspension of innocent passage in the territorial sea to foreign vessels, there are some important elements of that suspension that must be complied with. First, the suspension must be '... without discrimination in form or in fact among foreign ships ...'[47] Therefore an order that only suspends *Tampa*'s right of innocent passage in the territorial sea, and not the right of other vessels, appears not to conform with the clear requirement of article 25(3) for closure to be without discrimination. Another element of this part of the LOSC is that the temporary suspension of innocent passage can only occur '... if such suspension is essential for the protection of [the coastal State's] security ...' At the time when the closure was announced, the necessity of closing the territorial sea to *Tampa* for essential security reasons was difficult to comprehend. Accordingly, if the real intent of the Prime Minister's announcement that *MV Tampa* '... does not have permission to enter Australian territorial waters ...'[48] was to suspend temporarily the vessel's innocent passage in the territorial sea pursuant to the legal authority

---

45 For example, the status of the 'rescuees' under the 1951 *Convention Relating to the Status of Refugees* 189 UNTS 137 was a critical issue, but not directly relevant to the law of the sea issues that were being addressed.

46 Transcript of the Prime Minister, The Hon John Howard MP, Joint Press Conference with the Minister for Immigration, The Hon Philip Ruddock MP, Parliament House, Canberra (27 August 2001) available at https://pmtranscripts.pmc.gov.au/release/transcript-11989.

47 LOSC article 25(3).

48 Prime Minister's Transcript, *supra* n 46.

provided by LOSC article 25(3), then some legitimate questions can be asked regarding whether this action was validly taken.[49]

The other key law of the sea issue arising from the *Tampa* incident concerns the extent of the obligation to render assistance to vessels in distress at sea under both the LOSC and other parts of international law.[50] The LOSC has codified the customary obligation placed on mariners to provide assistance to persons at sea who are '… in danger of being lost'.[51] The LOSC also requires the master of a vessel to '… proceed with all possible speed to the rescue of persons in distress, if informed of their need of assistance …'[52] and there is no doubt that the master of *MV Tampa* complied with this requirement. The difficulty that arose for the *Tampa* is that neither the LOSC nor the SOLAS and SAR conventions adequately dealt with obligations that arise once persons in danger at sea have been rescued. This shortfall in the international law dealing with the final disposal of persons rescued at sea led to the lengthy standoff between the Australian government, the captain and owners of *MV Tampa* as well as Indonesian and Norwegian authorities. The issue was finally resolved after *Tampa* entered Australia's territorial sea and was subsequently boarded by Australian military personnel, with the 'rescuees' then transferred to an Australian Navy vessel for transport to the small Pacific Island of Nauru.[53]

Subsequently, steps were taken at the International Maritime Organisation (IMO) to prevent a situation like that faced by *MV Tampa* arising again[54] when Norway successfully led the push for an amendment to the SOLAS convention that would allow a vessel to land persons rescued at sea at the nearest available port.[55] The result of this action was the publication, in 2004, of the IMO's Guidelines on the Treatment of Persons Rescued at Sea[56] and an amendment

49 For a detailed analysis of this issue see D.R. Rothwell, 'The Law of the Sea and the MV Tampa Incident: Reconciling Maritime Principles with Coastal State Sovereignty', 13 *Public Law Review* 118 (2002).

50 The other two key instruments are the 1974 *International Convention for the Safety of Life at Sea*, 1184 UNTS 278 ('the SOLAS Convention'), through Regulation V33.1, and the 1979 *International Convention on Maritime Search and Rescue*, 1405 UNTS 97 ('the SAR Convention') through Chapter 2.1.10 and Chapter 1.3.2.

51 LOSC article 98(1)(a).

52 LOSC article 98(1)(b).

53 A synopsis of the 'Tampa incident' can be found at https://www.kaldorcentre.unsw.edu.au/news/tampa-affair-15-years-1.

54 IMO Assembly Resolution A.920(22) adopted on 22 January 2002. A summary of IMO action can be found at https://www.imo.org/en/OurWork/Facilitation/Pages/UnsafeMixedMigration-Default.aspx.

55 Rothwell, D. and Stephens, T., *The International Law of the Sea*, Oxford, Hart Publishing, 2016 (2nd ed) p. 58.

56 IMO Resolution MSC.167(78) (adopted on 20 May 2004).

to the SOLAS Convention that made it clear that an obligation lies with the government of the responsible search and rescue region to coordinate action to disembark survivors as soon as practicable.[57] As a result of these amendments, the procedures used during search and rescue operations in Australia's maritime zones have altered considerably over the past few decades and are now comprehensively addressed in Australia's National SAR Manual.[58]

The arrival of *MV Tampa* in Australian waters in August 2001 signified a changed approach by the Australian government to dealing with unauthorised boat arrivals and the people onboard those vessels who sought to claim asylum in Australia. This changed approach involved more assertive interception of vessels at sea under the military-led Operation Relex I and II, Operation Resolute[59] and the 'whole of government' approach under Operation Sovereign Borders.[60] These activities have not been without controversy, especially between Australia and Indonesia. Unfortunately, a number of vessels that were attempting to reach Australia did not safely complete their journey. Lives have been lost at sea, and questions have been asked about the way in which the Australian government was conducting border protection operations at sea.[61]

Perhaps the most embarrassing moment for Australia since the implementation of the revised border protection policy was when a number of 'inadvertent

57 IMO Resolution MSC.153(78) (adopted on 20 May 2004). For a detailed analysis of the IMO's response to the difficulties encountered by *MV Tampa* see F.J. Kenney Jr. & V. Tasikas, 'The Tampa Incident: IMO Perspectives and Responses on the Treatment of Persons Rescued at Sea', 12 *Pacific Rim Law and Policy Journal*, 2003, 143–177. See also C. Bailliet, 'The Tampa Case and Its Impact on Burden Sharing at Sea', 25 *Human Rights Quarterly* No. 3, 2003, 741–774.

58 The current version of the National Search and Rescue Manual is February 2021 and can be located at https://www.amsa.gov.au/sites/default/files/natsar-manual-february-2021.pdf.

59 Operation Relex I (3 September 2001–13 March 2002); Operation Relex II (14 March 2002–16 July 2006); Operation Resolute commenced on 17 July 2006 and continues: https://www.awm.gov.au/collection/CN500187.

60 Operation Sovereign Borders was established on 18 September 2013 and is a whole of government operation aimed at deterring and preventing people arriving in Australia by boat without authorisation. Statistics relating to Australia's border protection operations, in particular boat 'turnbacks' can be found at https://www.aph.gov.au/About_Parliament/Parliamentary_Departments/Parliamentary_Library/pubs/rp/rp1819/Quick_Guides/BoatTurnbacksSince2001.

61 For example, in 2002 the Australian Senate compiled a report titled 'A Certain Maritime Incident' to inquire into a number of incidents that had occurred at sea since the *Tampa*'s arrival in August 2001, including the loss of 'SIEV X' with approximately 400 persons onboard. The report is available at https://www.aph.gov.au/Parliamentary_Business/Committees/Senate/Former_Committees/maritimeincident/report/index.

incursions' into the Indonesian territorial sea occurred when boat 'turnbacks' were being conducted under Operation Sovereign Borders in late 2013/early 2014.[62] The precise nature of how the turnback operations were conducted has not been disclosed for operational reasons[63] but there are clearly a number of potential law of the sea issues involved in this policy. Key among these issues are the passage rights that exist for foreign flagged vessels in the territorial sea that have been referred to earlier in this paper, as well as the high seas passage freedoms that exist outside the territorial sea. Towing a vessel across the high seas, against the wishes of the master of the vessel, would seem to be inconsistent with the exercise of high seas freedom of navigation.

4 Concluding Remarks

The right to regulate maritime traffic involves a careful balance between the legitimate concerns of a coastal State regarding a range of threats posed by vessels that are in maritime zones under that state's jurisdiction, and the long-standing freedoms of navigation that have existed for many centuries. In asserting their rights, coastal States have, on occasion, pushed the law of the sea's boundaries and Australia has certainly adopted that approach with its approach to maritime border law enforcement operations over the past two decades.

In terms of regulating the movement of people at sea, there is little argument that Australia has a right (and responsibility) to control the entry of people into, and exit from, Australian territory including those maritime zones where Australia has jurisdiction to do so. Further, the potential need for force to be used when dealing with people who are seeking to enter Australia by boat in an unauthorised manner should not be surprising, as there are multiple reasons why law enforcement officials should require their directions be complied with.

---

62 For a critical assessment of these incursions see S. Bateman, 'Incompetence: Australia's incursions into Indonesian waters', Lowy Institute Interpreter, 28 February 2014, available at https://www.lowyinstitute.org/the-interpreter/incompetence-australias-incursions-indonesian-waters.

63 The Australian government has consistently refused to provide details in relation to 'on water matters' regarding Operation Sovereign Borders, although some limited information has been obtained by journalists through Freedom of Information processes: https://www.theguardian.com/australia-news/2017/apr/03/australias-government-muddles-its-way-through-to-hide-details-of-boat-turnbacks.

However, it can be argued that some of the actions taken by Australia in response to people seeking to arrive by boat without authorisation have been inconsistent with international law. Australia has consistently stated that its actions do comply with all relevant international legal obligations, and that its maritime operations uphold the international rules based order. Whether or not this is actually the case in all of the situations that Australia has been involved with over the past two decades since *MV Tampa*'s arrival is still open to question.

CHAPTER 14

Do We Still Need an 'Expansionist/Revisionist' Theory of Self-Defense at Sea?

Kyo Arai

1 Introduction

This paper examines how we should justify the practice of maritime interception operations (MIO) on the high seas against suspected ships sailing under foreign flags, which have been conducted as a part of the War on Terror after 9/11.

Some states and scholars have advocated an expansive interpretation of self-defence for a sweeping legal basis for MIO, in cases where the other rules such as the law of armed conflict including prize law or peacetime law of the sea do not give a legal ground or those are inapplicable.

However, the conclusion here is that such an approach is invalid and unnecessary, at least now. Also, from a policy perspective, it is inadvisable for maintaining the free and open maritime order in the 2020s.

2 Definition

Since 2001, there has been strong advocacy for the expansionist theory of self-defense. In this paper, this "expansionist theory" is defined as a tendency to argue;

1. Self-defense against a non-state armed group in the territory of another state is legally permissible;
2. This is the case, even if the territorial state does not effectively control such group but may have failed to constrain the group's function due to negligence, unwillingness or incapacity; and
3. Necessity and proportionality are measured against the threat by the group, but it is done in a concertina-like quality that is flexibly manipulatable.[1]

1 Nehal Bhuta and Rebecca Mignot-Mahdavi, "Dangerous Proportions: Means and Ends in Non-Finite War," *ASSER research paper 2021-01*, available at: https://ssrn.com/abstract=3790612.

DOI:10.1163/9789004518629_015

At the same time, there is also a "Revisionist theory," a camp that goes one step further regarding the reach of self-defense. This approach was generated by this passage in Harold Hongju KOH's speech in 2010: "a state that is engaged in an armed conflict *or* in legitimate self-defence ..."[2]

Based on this single conjunction "or," it was claimed that the United States could use force for self-defense without being part of an armed conflict. Consequently, under this theory, both the resort to armed force and the execution of specific operations shall be regulated by the *jus ad bellum* only, precluding *jus in bello* assessment and strict regulation for the use of force based on human rights law. In short, this approach produces a legal blackhole where neither human rights law nor the law of armed conflict applies.

3 Expansionist Theory at Sea: Legal Ground for MIO?

This expansive interpretation of the right of self-defense was also asserted in the maritime domain for justifying MIO widely.

As to the maritime interception in the initial phase of the War on Terror, Captain O'Rourke, of the US Navy, advised that "Article 51 of the UN Charter has come to be accepted as the primary basis for such operations."[3] The problem is whether this applied long after the immediate terrorist threat ceased. The revisionist says it is possible.

Indeed, we can find the self-defense justification for MIO in US military doctrines, like the 2007 Commander's Handbook.[4]

> 4.4.4.1.9 Inherent Right of Self-Defense
>
> States can legally conduct MIO Pursuant to customary international law under circumstances that would permit the exercise of the inherent right of individual and collective self-defense.

This paragraph looks straightforward, but reading in conjunction with the other justifications listed here its meaning is unclear. Notably, the relationship between belligerent rights and this self-defense argument is ambiguous.

2 Harold Hongju Koh, "The Role of the Legal Adviser," *Proceedings of American Society International Law*, Vol.104 (2010), p. 207, pp. 219–220.

3 Kenneth O'Rourke, "Commentary: Maritime and Coalition Operations," in *International Law and the War on Terror* (*International Law Series*, Vol.79 (2003)), p. 297, p. 298.

4 US Navy, *The Commander's Handbook on the Law of Naval Operations,* NWP 1–14M, Edition July 2007, para. 4.4.4.1.9.

Suppose one state resorts to self-defense action, and it constitutes an armed conflict. In that case, the maritime operations shall be conducted on the basis of the law of armed conflict, and we do not need a separate justification based on the right of self-defense. So, following the principle of effective interpretation, this paragraph shall be given a distinctive meaning that applies to situations other than armed conflict. This perfectly mirrors what Harold Koh suggested.

Some scholars support this interpretation. In 2010, Professor Heintschel von Heinegg, commenting on the black letter rule 20.09,[5] which is mostly identical to para. 4.4.4.1.9 of the US Navy Commander's Handbook, stated that "this right may very well serve as an operable legal basis for MIO ... taken against foreign vessels and aircraft when encountered in the high seas."[6] Also, Commander Dr Fink of the Netherlands' Navy, commented more directly in 2018,

> States could act against non-state actors on board foreign-flagged vessels under the limited circumstances that a flag State is unable or unwilling to act in order to remedy the situation, for instance in cases of vessels carrying WMD. ..., the doctrine is tempting because ... it allows for the boarding of a foreign-flagged vessel without any form of consent of the flag State ...[7]

He additionally pointed out that it could bypass the controversial legal question of whether the law of naval warfare applies in non-international armed conflict.

Under this revisionist self-defense approach, the MIO started in the context of International Armed Conflict may be legal, regardless of whether the conflict classification changed afterwards, like Operation Enduring Freedom. This point may be the one to which this camp of the debate wanted to push the envelope. Here is the reason. The War on Terror is classified as a non-international armed conflict, where the law of naval warfare has been underdeveloped, or it is executed in a legal grey zone where the applicable rules are shaky. Therefore,

5 Rule 20.09 "States can legally conduct MIO pursuant to customary international law under circumstances that would permit the exercise of the inherent right of individual and collective self-defense." Wolff Heintschel von Heinegg, "Chapter 20: Maritime Interception/Interdiction Operations," Terry D. Gill and Dieter Fleck (eds.), *The Handbook of the International Law of Military Operations* (1st Edition) (Oxford University Press, 2010), p. 375, p. 389.

6 Id., p. 390.

7 Martin Fink, *Maritime Interception and the Law of Naval Operations* (Springer, 2018), pp. 118–119.

advocating the revisionist theory of self-defense at sea is not just claiming that a series of interceptions shall be recognized as necessary and proportionate self-defense to a specific terrorist threat. It aims at, more generally, asserting a sweeping justification blurring the bifurcation of use of force paradigms into the peacetime law-enforcement and wartime belligerent actions.

However, we should pay attention to the same documents recently being updated with more nuance. The 2017 edition of the Commander's Handbook had two additions to the previous edition.[8]

> 4.4.4.1.8 Inherent Right of Self-Defense
>
> States can legally conduct maritime interception operations pursuant to customary international law under circumstances that would permit the exercise of the inherent right of individual, collective, *and national* self-defense *as recognized in Article 51 of the United Nations Charter*. (emphasis added)

The first is the term "national self-defense," and the second is the phrase "as recognized in Article 51 of the United Nations Charter." The text itself does not clarify the intention of this new paragraph. Still, it is safe to say that the emphasis on national self-defense and Article 51 of the UN Charter would not go along with the revisionist camp's direction.

Professor Heintschel von Heinegg also took a more nuanced position in his comment on the 2015 edition of the same Operation Law Handbook, substantially limiting his statement in the previous edition: "States merely agree on the principal applicability of the right of self-defence as a legal basis for MIO. There is no agreement as to the specific measures that may be taken against suspect vessels and persons on board."[9]

4 "Embracing the Uncertainty of Old"?

The next point is that such assertion of a self-defense plea is not novel. Christian Tams pointed out, "Whether States can use force in self-defence

8 US Navy, *The Commander's Handbook on the Law of Naval Operations,* NWP 1–14M, Edition August 2017, para. 4.4.4.1.8.

9 Wolff Heintschel von Heinegg, "Chapter 21: Maritime Interception/Interdiction Operations," Terry D. Gill and Dieter Fleck (eds.), *The Handbook of the International Law of Military Operations* (2nd Edition) (Oxford University Press, 2015) p. 442, pp. 440–441.

against non-state actors abroad is NOT a new issue that suddenly became relevant after 9/11."[10]

The same applies to the maritime sphere. Professors Churchill and Lowe introduced States' attempt to advocate *exceptional measures to* interfere with foreign ships on the high seas on the grounds of self-defense with some examples.

The first and most referenced one is the *Virginius* incident of 1873. There, Spain seized on the high seas an American ship carrying American and British nationals and many weapons for use in the Cuban insurrection. Great Britain accepted that the arrest was justified on the ground of self-defense, while the United States did not. Some scholars refer to this case as supportive evidence for the self-defense argument. However, the reality is that this British reaction was isolated and firmly opposed.[11] Professor Gidel concluded that this was "*prétendument reconnu* (pretended to be recognized)."[12]

The second example is the French practice during the Algerian War. At that time, France asserted a right to visit and search on the ships on the high seas suspected of supporting Algerians, based on the right of self-defense. However, the flag States strongly opposed this. As Professor Michael Byers concluded,

> The evidence of state practice and *opinio juris* generated by opposition to the French policy would still seem to militate against the existence of any extended right of self-defense against weapons shipments on the high seas.[13]

However, in fact, all these debates have been already settled in the past. The International Law Commission, 1956, in a discussion of the High Sea Convention, considered the right to board a vessel committing hostile acts to the intervening State at a time of imminent danger. The Commission did not recognize it, mainly because of the vagueness of terms like "imminent danger" and "hostile acts" that are open to abuse.[14]

---

10 Christian J. Tams, "Embracing the Uncertainty of Old: Armed Attacks by Non-State Actors Prior to 9/11," *Zeitschrift für ausländisches öffentliches Recht und Völkerrecht*, Vol.77 (2017), p. 61, pp. 61–64.

11 Kiara Neri, *L'emploi de la force en mer* (Bruylant, 2013), p. 404.

12 Gilbert Gidel, *Droit international public de la mer* (Mellottée, 1932), t.1, p. 355.

13 Michael Byers, "Policing the High Seas: The Proliferation Security Initiative," *American Journal of International Law*, Vol.98 (2004), p. 526, p. 533.

14 *Yearbook of the International Law Commission*, 1956, Vol.2. p. 284.

Furthermore, Professors O'Connell and Shearer concluded that

> self-defence or national security is an insecure foundation for seeking to qualify the freedom of the seas, for it could lend plausibility to restraints that would not sustain the balance of interests of the international community.[15]

State practice before 2001 shows that there was no overall acceptance of the self-defense exception to the exclusive flag States jurisdiction for the vessels on the high seas.

5 Emerging Self-Defense Justification for MIOs?

Turning to the 21st century, how should we evaluate a twenty-year 'practice'? Dr Fink reported a US DoD organization's opinion in 2005, saying that,

> The MIO has, through accepted practice and custom, developed a new legal regime under which … warships may intercept foreign flag commercial vessels on the high seas, without resorting to any classical belligerent right. This expansion is now well established through over ten years of continuous, unchallenged operations.[16]

Professor Klein contrasts this new practice against the previous one with far less acceptance.[17]

However, careful examination of the case overshadows such claims. From the outset, the participating states to the MIO have different views on the legal basis for the operation. Captain O'Rourke qualified his assertion that the right of self-defense is the primary basis for the MIO by saying that "as time passes, the question will loom larger." He seems to believe in a customary rule permitting the continuance of the MIO. However, his conclusion to this question was, "Only time will tell."[18]

15 Daniel Patrick O'Connell (Ivan Shearer ed.), *The International Law of the Sea*, Vol. II, 1st ed. (Clarendon Press, 1988) p. 797.

16 The Defense Institute of International Legal Studies (DIILS), *Maritime interception operations*, 13 June 2005, cited in Fink, op.cit., p. 120.

17 Natalie Klein, *Maritime Security and the Law of the Sea* (Oxford University Press, 2010), p. 275.

18 O'Rourke, op. cit., p. 298.

Comments by his colleagues in the allied countries, like the United Kingdom and Canada, materialized Captain O'Rourke's concern. According to the UK's statement,

> Although maritime units may use force such as is necessary and proportional, they may be required to do so within the peacetime rules and conventions which apply at sea. ... The UK is simply not prepared to invoke the right of self-defence for such boardings without seeking flag state approval.[19]

This position was also reflected in an operational manoeuvre. In Operation Active Endeavour, which lasted until 2016 in the Mediterranean Sea, the MIO was declared an Article 5, collective self-defense operation, of the NATO Treaty. However, in reality, the boarding took place only when both flag State and the master consented. As Professor Heintschel von Heinegg admitted, "The practice of those States whose navies have taken part in counter-terrorism operations at sea is quite diverse and has not contributed to the emergence of agreed-upon criteria. This explains the importance of other rights of maritime interception."[20]

Additionally, based on research of the national manuals collected by the Stockton Center, it is revealed that recent manuals (Denmark 2020, New Zealand 2019) have maintained the clear bifurcated structure of naval warfare based on the law of armed conflict, including the San Remo Manual on the one hand and maritime law enforcement regulated by the UNCLOS on the other hand. There is no indication of overarching justification of self-defense for MIOs.

The reality is that even the states advocating the self-defense argument obscured their position, trying to secure the alternative ways, such as a bilateral agreement with or *ad hoc* consent of the flag States. On the other hand, opposition states make a clear statement against such an approach. These could not be an indication of the recognition of a new customary rule.

---

19 Neil Brown, "Commentary: Maritime and Coalition Operations," in *International Law and the War on Terror* (*International Law Series*, Vol.79 (2003)), p. 303, p. 305. See also a Canadian military advisor's comment (Jean-Guy Perron, "Commentary: Maritime and Coalition Operations," in *ibid.*, pp. 309–310).

20 Heintschel von Heinegg, op. cit. [2017].

6 Conclusion

Even if this sweeping justification by self-defense is attractive for operational purposes, this paper concludes that it is unnecessary and inadvisable, both from the normative and policy perspective.

Firstly, any claims based on self-defense are, in nature, insecure, provisional, and supplementary. Thus, at best, it could be a second-best basis only. When any alternative cause is available, that will fade from the front stage, remaining an exceptional measure.

Secondly, from a policy perspective, we should recall the conclusion of Professor O'Connell that self-defense would not sustain the balance of interests of the international community.

Admittedly, years just after 9/11, this balance of interests seemingly leaned towards the expansionist direction. However, twenty years after, we should readjust it to the point Professor O'Connell set. In the 2020s, we face other challenges affecting the balance of interests, such as hybrid warfare conducted at sea by sovereign states. Certain states can use hybrid warfare strategies to annoy law-abiding states by intentionally obscuring the legal nature of their actions. Blurring the clear bifurcation of the use of force paradigms would benefit such states the most.

A sweeping national security exception could pave the road to the hazardous attempts by states, ruining the cardinal principles of the Law of the Sea based on vague reasons, such as self-preservation or protection of sovereignty.

CHAPTER 15

In Quest of the Optimal Legal Framework for Maritime Law Enforcement against Foreign State Vessels in the Territorial Sea

Masahiro Kurosaki

1 Introduction

A coastal State may take all necessary measures in accordance with international law to protect its territorial waters—its peace, good order or security—from the conduct of harmful activities by foreign vessels. Yet the matter becomes more complicated when such activities are carried out by foreign state vessels and do not amount to armed attack on the coastal State, which triggers its right of self-defense to use force to repel the attack. Since its law enforcement measures could, depending on circumstances, lead up to the prohibited use of force against the foreign flag State, the coastal State would need to take careful steps to avoid escalating the situation into the use of force and armed conflict, particularly where it forcibly evicts those vessels from its territory.

Against this background, this presentation aims to offer the optimal legal framework for de-escalating a coastal State's maritime law enforcement action against foreign-flagged State vessels—namely warships and other government ships on non-commercial service—navigating in its territorial sea in order to protect its territorial waters as a peaceful maritime engagement without using prohibited armed force. In doing so, I examine three possible options for the legal basis for the coastal State's action: (1) the coastal State's right of protection against non-innocent passage under Article 25.1 of UNCLOS (The UN Convention on the Law of the Sea); (2) a general right of self-protection against a forcible threat to a state's legal rights; (3) the right of an injured state to resort to countermeasures under the law of state responsibility.

1.1 *Option 1: The Coastal State's Exercise of the UNCLOS Right of Protection against Non-innocent Passage in Its Territorial Sea*

The right of self-protection for a coastal State would be the first and foremost legal basis to be considered and relied upon as it is provided in Article 25(1) UNCLOS that is a treaty provision. As such, some would think that it offers the coastal State the solid legal basis, and that it is the best option for the protective action against the foreign state vessels. Yet the problem is that it does not clarify to what extent and what concrete actions the coastal State is authorized to take by this provision.

Article 25(1) does not say anything about the contour of its law enforcement action against harmful activities by foreign state vessels. Thus, some opine that the coastal State is entitled to do anything to protect its territorial waters against foreign state vessels to the extent that it does not amount to the prohibited use of force. On the flip side, others argue that Article 25(1) must be read in conjunction with other UNCLOS provisions that limit maritime law enforcement action taken by the coastal State, highlighting Article 30 and Article 32. Article 30 only permits the coastal State to require foreign warships "to leave the territorial sea immediately," meaning that the coastal State is not allowed to conduct any compulsory measures against foreign flag state vessels because Article 32 does provide "nothing in this Convention affects the immunities of warships and other government ships operated for non-commercial purposes." But, as those diverging views show, the issue remains controversial among international law experts, combined with the scarcity of relevant state practice surrounding Article 25(1) on the coastal State's right of protection.

In this way, the first option is beset by the unresolved issue of whether and to what extent the protective action is inhibited by the immunity and inviolability of foreign state vessels under the UNCLOS regime, which would undermine the legality of the action in question and, as such, runs the risk of escalating the situation into the use of force between the coastal State and the foreign flag State.

1.2 *Option 2: The Coastal State's Exercise of the General Right of Self-Protection against Forcible Threats to Its Maritime Rights*

Alternatively, the coastal State may rely on a general right of self-protection against a forcible threat to its legal rights in emergency situations other than armed attack. As such, this general right does not involve the inherent right of self-defense against armed attack as enshrined in Article 51 of the UN Charter. It has rather been invoked to warrant forcible intervention or minor uses of force that does not amount to the prohibited use of force in the sense of Article 2(4) of the UN Charter. Indeed, the existence of this right was hinted by the ICJ Judgement in the *Corfu Channel* case. In that case, the United Kingdom sent warships into Albanian territorial waters and carried out minesweeping operations therein, and the court found the British violation of Albanian sovereignty. What needs to be noted here is that the ICJ did not find the British violation of the prohibition on the use of force, but instead found its violations of Albanian sovereignty alone. In the same vein, the UK, for its part, relied on the right of self-protection against a forcible threat to its right of innocent passage in Albanian territorial waters. All of these suggest that there exists such a customary right of self-protection distinct from the right of self-defense in international law. Moreover, the right has been advocated predominantly by the British international law scholars like Oxford Professors Humphrey Waldock and Ian Brownlie as well as by the Japanese government in an effort to justify its forcible activities below the threshold of the prohibited use of force carried out outside the sovereign territories of other states, such as in the high seas.

All that said, it is also true that this general right of self-protection has not necessarily attained wide explicit recognition by many states. Besides, there is another thorny issue of how to reconcile this general right of protection with the Caroline doctrine or the Webster Formula on the inherent right of self-defense against imminent threat—which is not limited to armed attack—that the United States has long asserted to warrant its use of force. As such, even if the coastal State seeks to justify its law enforcement actions against foreign state vessels under the general right of protection and argues that those actions are distinct from the prohibited uses of force, the flag State of those foreign state vessels and other states like the United States might still consider them as the prohibited uses of force unless otherwise justified in self-defense or under the authorization by the UN Security Council. If that happens, the second option could end up providing the foreign flag State with the justification for its self-defense against the coastal State's unlawful armed attack on its vessels, inviting the escalation of the use of force between the two. Relying on this second option would thus also likely endanger the situation between the coastal State and the foreign flag State, even granting that the act taken by the costal State vessel is minor or moderate use of force against foreign state vessels.

1.3 *Option 3: The Coastal State's Exercise of the Right to Take Countermeasures against Illegal Entry into Its Territorial Sea*

In contrast, the third option, which concerns countermeasures by the coastal State against the violation of its territorial waters caused by the foreign state vessel's non-innocent passage, is more tenable and instrumental in averting the interstate use of force and armed conflict, compared to other two options. The law of countermeasures is not just a well-established rule of international law on the circumstances precluding wrongfulness, which could justify the coastal State's possible infringement of the immunity and inviolability of foreign state vessels. It also comprehends its own institutional mechanism for de-escalation that is composed of dynamic safeguard procedures to ensure the peaceful settlement of international disputes as provided in Articles 49 to 53 of the UN International Law Commission's Articles on the Responsibility of States for Internationally Wrongful Acts (ARSIWA). Most notably, the notification and negotiation requirements play a crucial and functional role in helping reduce the likelihood of escalating the encounter between the coastal State and the foreign flag State, and therefore should be leveraged in combination with the strengthening and update of the existing maritime confidence-building measures, such as the Code for Unplanned Encounters at Sea among the Pacific nations established in an effort to "facilitate communication when naval ships or naval aircraft encounter each other in an unplanned manner."

As provided in ARSIWA, the countermeasures taken by the coastal State as an injured state shall not involve the use of force in the sense of Article 2(4) of the UN Charter, but, at the moment, there are divergent views on the threshold of the use of force. Some argue that a hostile intent of the state in question is the crucial element for the qualification, and others contend that the intensity of armed violence is everything in the end. Yet whichever of these positions is adopted, de-escalating the situation between the coastal State and the foreign flag State would reduce the hostile intent and the amount of force employed in the situation. Lawful countermeasures, namely proportionate and temporary or reversible countermeasures, aimed at inducing the responsible state to cease the wrongful conduct, and resuming the performance of the obligation breached, would highly likely contribute to the peaceful settlement of the situation between the coastal State and the foreign flag State without the resort to the prohibited use of force. It is therefore not too much to say that among these three options, the option of countermeasures most fits the purpose of peaceful maritime engagement even in such a tense situation.

2 Conclusion

Either of these three options could be relied upon by the coastal State to justify its protective action against the foreign state vessels navigating within its territorial sea. Yet, the foregoing analysis brings us to conclude that the optimal legal framework for the coastal State's protective action in this case is its right to take countermeasures.

It must be admitted that the first two options on the right of protection—namely the UNCLOS right of protection for coastal States and the general right of self-protection for sovereign states—remain highly controversial when applied to a situation where the coastal State forcibly evicts foreign state vessels from its territory. Further, due to their unstable legal bases, these options render the situation more vulnerable to the escalation of the conflict between the coastal State and the foreign flag State into the prohibited use of force and armed conflict. This is all the more so when the conflict erupts in a contested sea area.

The same risk of escalation would also apply to the countermeasures option. However, not only does this option provide the solid legal foundation for the enforcement measures by the coastal State even if it inhibits the immunity and inviolability of foreign state vessels, but its own institutional mechanism for de-escalation also renders it more conducive to the peaceful settlement of conflicts and disputes between those states compared to the other two options that contain no such mechanisms. Apart from the issue of to what extent that mechanism could be workable in actual practice, no one can deny its potential to open a window of opportunity for the peaceful settlement of conflicts and disputes between the states concerned.

PART 3

Arctic Shipping

CHAPTER 16

Governance Considerations on Low Impact Corridors in Canadian Arctic Waters

Aldo Chircop

1 Introduction

There is growing international interest in the use of the Northwest Passage as a navigation route as the Arctic continues to lose sea ice cover and become more accessible for longer periods. Arctic Canada has a coastline of 162,000 km and encompasses circa 4 million km^2 of water. Consisting of seven possible routes, the Passage is navigable largely during the summer months and may be extending into the shoulder seasons. While most current traffic is to resupply Arctic communities and commercial shipping interests discount the likelihood of greater commercial use of the Northwest Passage anytime soon, there continues to be interest from passenger vessel and recreational shipping interests.[1] In addition, there is growing domestic shipping consisting of destinational traffic supporting resource development, government vessel work, and marine scientific research.[2] Since 1990, shipping in Nunavut doubled and the increase included growth of average distances navigated by ships as well as the number and type of vessels.[3] The majority of ships consisted of general cargo vessels and icebreakers, but there was also significant growth of pleasure craft, fishing vessels, tanker, and barge traffic.[4]

---

1 2018 Pilotage Act Review (Transport Canada, 2018) 95–96, online at <https://tc.canada.ca/sites/default/files/migrated/17308_tc_pilotage_act_review_v8_final.pdf>; René Chénier, Loretta Abado, Olivier Sabourin and Laurent Tardif, "Northern Marine Transportation Corridors: Creation and Analysis of Northern Marine Traffic Routes in Canadian Waters", *Transactions in GIS* (2017): 1–13 at 9, DOI: 10.1111/tgis.12295. Frédéric Lasserre and Sébastien Pelletier, "Polar Super Seaways? Maritime Transport in the Arctic: An Analysis of Shipowners' Intentions", (2011) *Journal of Transport Geography* 19(6): 1465–1473.

2 Jackie Dawson, Olivia Mussells, Luke Copland and Natalie Carter, *Shipping Trends in Nunavut 1990–2015: A Report Prepared for the Nunavut General Monitoring Program* (University of Ottawa, 2017). According to Chénier et al., the voyage count tripled between 1990–2014. Chénier et al, *supra* note 1, at 9.

3 Ibid.

4 Dawson et al., *supra* note 2, at 37.

Despite the increase in traffic, the infrastructure needed to support shipping, such as hydrographic data and charting, search and rescue, salvage, and pollution response capacity remain inadequate.[5] Weather, ice and general navigational conditions are frequently hazardous. Multiyear ice is particularly hazardous for all polar class vessels. In 2017, less than 10 percent of Canadian Arctic waters were surveyed and only one percent to modern hydrographic standards.[6] There were passenger vessel groundings in 1996, 2010 and 2018.[7] And yet, even with a decrease of sea ice cover, there is discernible risk-taking in the summer navigation season even by small recreational vessels.[8]

Maritime safety, pollution prevention and protection of indigenous peoples remain primary policy concerns in Canadian Arctic waters. Historically and at this time, Canada has administered Arctic shipping through a system of sixteen Shipping Safety Control Zones (SSCZs), setting out a zone and date system for various classes of ships. Ships navigated the various areas depending on their capabilities. This system is now in transition and paving the way for a different risk assessment system introduced by the Polar Code and implemented by Canada. Separately from the SSCZs, Canada has embarked on a novel initiative to designate corridors for maritime traffic in Arctic waters. In the marine context, 'corridor' has been defined as "an area where there exists a measureable amount of diverse marine transportation with commercial purpose" and "a methodology for planning and prioritization through spatially referencing and comparing specific transportation needs with marine navigational services".[9] Corridor designation provides justification for charting and navigational services.[10]

---

5 *Arctic Marine Shipping Assessment 2009 Report* (Arctic Council, 2009), 186, online: <https://www.pame.is/images/03_Projects/AMSA/AMSA_2009_report/AMSA_2009_Report_2nd_print.pdf> (AMSA).

6 Chénier et al., *supra* note 1, at 10.

7 The groundings concerned the passenger vessels *Hanseatic*, *Clipper Adventurer* and *Akademik Ioffe*. See marine investigation reports M96H0016, M10H0006 and M18C0225 respectively, Transportation Safety Board of Canada, online: <https://www.tsb.gc.ca/eng/rapports-reports/marine/index.html>.

8 For example: "New Zealander sails through Arctic on custom yacht in violation of COVID-19 restrictions", *CBC News* (26 August 2020), online: <https://www.cbc.ca/news/canada/north/new-zealand-yacht-cambridge-bay-nunavut-1.5698347>.

9 Andrew Leyzack, René Chénier and Sean Hinds, "Marine Corridors: a Methodology for Planning and Prioritizing Hydrographic Surveys, Products and Services", presented at the Canadian Hydrographic Conference, 14–17 April 2014, St Johns, Newfoundland and Labrador, at 1, online: <https://hydrography.ca/wp-content/uploads/files/2014conference/8-Leyzack-et-al-Marine-Corridors.pdf>.

10 Ibid. 5.

Consultations are under way with indigenous peoples and other stakeholders on possible routeing of corridors. Five classes of corridors covering approximately 12% of Canadian Arctic waters are proposed, with the primary corridor (class 1) having the highest priority as main traffic highways.[11] The identified corridors coincide with the most heavily trafficked areas and will facilitate focused hydrographic surveys, infrastructure development and provision of services for safe shipping. At this time, it appears shipping will be encouraged to use the corridors rather than other routes, but on a voluntary rather than a mandatory basis.

The development of low impact corridors raises interesting questions in the law of the sea and maritime law. The international legal status of the Northwest Passage remains uncertain and the new measures will affect international shipping. It is unlikely that Canada will seek prior IMO assistance in designating any routeing measures, given Canada's position on the legal status of those waters. However, the non-mandatory nature of the measures may produce a pragmatic compromise between Canada's claim to sovereignty over the interconnecting waters of its Arctic archipelago and international expectations of access and use of the Passage.

This essay discusses the legal consequences of Canada's initiative to designate low impact shipping corridors in its Arctic waters with the participation of indigenous peoples as rights holders and other stakeholders against the backdrop of the international law of the sea, the legal status of Arctic waters and the Northwest Passage, and international maritime regulation. The essay considers Canada's options and processes for the domestic regulation of shipping in the corridors. The essay concludes with reflections on Canada's pragmatic approach on the management of navigation in the Northwest Passage.

11 Ibid. at 3–4, 10. These are described as follows: 1. "Main Corridor (Primary): The main traffic highways in the Arctic, which provide a means to enable secondary access to ports." \ 2. "Approach Corridor (Secondary): Corridors characterized by medium- to low-density traffic levels, which can provide access to navigational ports to fulfill supply links and the movement of passengers. The three types of vessel to use these traffic corridors are cargo, tanker, and passenger vessels." \ 3. "Refuge Corridor (Tertiary): Characterized by medium to low traffic, providing navigational access to places of refuge, including charted anchorage areas located nearest to primary and secondary corridors and furthest away from ports." \ 4. "Private Interest Corridor (Quaternary): Characterized by geographical extents of low buffered density levels. These corridors provide navigational access to resource development and extraction sites, or other private interests (mining sites, research bases)." \ 5. "Projected Corridor (Quinary): Characterized by geographical extents of low buffered density levels, or in the absence of any density analysis or vessel traffic data. These corridors provide navigational access to proposed or potential infrastructure for resource development." \ Ibid. at 4, table 2; Leyzack et al., *supra* note 9, at 6.

2 Context

2.1 *Legal Issues*

Canada's low impact corridors initiative has a backdrop of uncertainty concerning the international legal status of Canadian Arctic waters and international navigation rights therein. That uncertainty has given rise to various diplomatic exchanges on law of the sea and maritime law matters between Canada and other states. A brief consideration of the issues that have emerged is useful as they provide lessons for Canada to consider when introducing new navigation and shipping measures in Arctic waters.

Until the late 1960s, and until challenged by the United States, Canada seems to have assumed that the waters of the Arctic archipelago were an integral part of its sovereign territory. The first passage of the SS *Manhattan* in 1969 served to demonstrate not only that transit was feasible but also that the United States' view was that the Northwest Passage was subject to international navigation rights. The passage occurred barely two years since the catastrophic *Torrey Canyon* casualty on the southwest Atlantic coast of the United Kingdom in 1967, which was fresh on the minds of policy makers and triggering change in the International Maritime Organization (IMO) and adoption of new maritime conventions.

Canada's response to the potential threat of vessel-source pollution in the sensitive Arctic waters was the adoption of the Arctic Waters Pollution Prevention Act (AWPPA) in 1970.[12] It was both revolutionary and controversial. The Act was revolutionary at the time as it unilaterally introduced SSCZs, pollution prevention and construction, design, equipping and manning (CDEM) standards, compulsory insurance and strict liability for shipping in Canadian waters at a time when there were no dedicated international standards for shipping in polar waters. Jurisdiction would be exercised up to a limit of 100 nautical miles (extended to 200 nautical miles in 2009), thus including high sea areas. The enactment was controversial because it extended jurisdiction over international shipping in marine areas adjacent to the coast and beyond the territorial sea, triggering a protest from the United States. The United States discussed with Canada the impending legislation before its adoption, expressing concerns on various law of the sea and national interest grounds.[13] Fearing a precedent once the AWPPA was enacted, the United States criticized

12 RSC 1985, c A-12 (AWPPA).

13 Imminent Canadian Legislation on the Arctic, Information Memorandum for Mr. Kissinger (The White House), Department of State (12 March 1970), online: https://static.history.state.gov/frus/frus1969-76ve01/pdf/d367.pdf.

what it characterized as unilateral infringements of the freedoms of the high seas.[14] Anticipating protests, Canada had previously amended its acceptance of compulsory jurisdiction of the International Court of Justice to except "disputes arising out of or concerning jurisdiction of rights claimed or exercised by Canada in respect of … the prevention or control of pollution or contamination of the marine environment in marine areas adjacent to the coast of Canada".[15]

The AWPPA initiative influenced the agenda of the Third United Nations Conference on the Law of the Sea in 1973–82. In order to address Canadian concerns, Canada, the former Soviet Union and the United States negotiated Article 234 of the ensuing United Nations Convention on the Law of the Sea, 1982.[16] This provision established the unique coastal State jurisdiction for pollution prevention from international shipping in ice-covered areas within the Exclusive Economic Zone (EEZ), and without the requirement of prior consultations through the IMO,[17] even though the IMO was the competent international organization with respect to international shipping. To a great extent, Article 234 had the effect of legitimizing the jurisdiction that Canada claimed and exercised through the AWPPA.

Following the adoption of UNCLOS, the transit of the Northwest Passage by the USCG icebreaker *Polar Sea* in 1985 triggered significant public and political reactions in Canada. In consequence, that year Canada issued a declaration that the Arctic archipelago's waters are subject to its sovereignty on the basis of historic title based on Inuit usage 'since time immemorial' and enacted an Order-in Council delineating straight baselines around the Arctic archipelago and thereby enclosing its interconnecting waters.[18] At that time, the few transits were by icebreakers and consequently in 1988 Canada and the United

14 Dept. of State Press Rel. No. 121 (April 1S, 1970), reprinted in 9 *International Legal Materials* (1970): 605. Bilder commented that Canada appeared to advance a new theory of coastal contiguity in extending jurisdiction over shipping. See Richard Bilder, "The Canadian Arctic Waters Pollution Prevention Act: New Stresses on the Law of the Sea", (1970) *Michigan Law Review* 69(1): 1–54 at 13.

15 Canadian Government's Background Notes on the Arctic Waters Pollution Prevention Bill and the Territorial Sea and Fishing Zones Bill (8 April 1970), 9 *International Legal Materials* (1970): 598.

16 Adopted 10 December 1982 (entered into force 16 November 1994), 1833 UNTS 3 (UNCLOS).

17 Shabtai Rosenne and Alexander Yankov (vol eds), *United Nations Convention on the Law of the Sea 1982: A Commentary* vol IV (Dordrecht: Nijhoff, 1991) (Virginia Commentary), at 396.

18 House of Commons Debates, 33rd Parl, 1st Sess, [Vol 5] (10 September 1985) at 6462–464 (Secretary of State for External Affairs, the Right Honourable Joe Clark).

States adopted an agreement on icebreakers.[19] They agreed to facilitate the transit of icebreakers and to develop cooperative procedures and the United States pledged that "all navigation by U.S. icebreakers within waters claimed by Canada to be internal will be undertaken with the consent of the Government of Canada".[20] However, it was clear that "[N]othing in this agreement of cooperative endeavour between Arctic neighbours and friends nor any practice thereunder affects the respective positions of the Governments of the United States and of Canada on the Law of the Sea in this or other maritime areas or their respective positions regarding third parties".[21] Even so, mutual irritants continued.

When in 1992 Canada acceded to the International Convention on the Prevention of Pollution from Ships, 1973–78 (MARPOL),[22] it issued a declaration that its accession was without prejudice to its Arctic shipping regulation pursuant to Article 234. In re-stating its jurisdictional right under Article 234, Canada considered its accession as being "without prejudice to such Canadian laws and regulations as are now or may in the future be established in respect of arctic waters within or adjacent to Canada".[23] The declaration triggered responses from the United States, and some European states seeking to clarify Canada's international rights and legal obligations.[24] The United States asserted that Canada may enact and enforce laws and regulations on international shipping in the EEZ "that have due regard to navigation and the protection and preservation of the marine environment based on the best available scientific evidence in Arctic waters, and – that are otherwise consistent with international law" including Articles 234 and other UNCLOS provisions.[25] In a

19 Agreement Between the Government of Canada and the Government of the United States of America on Arctic Cooperation, adopted 11 January 1988 (entered into force 11 January 1988), CTS No. 1988/29.

20 Ibid. art 3.

21 Ibid. art 4.

22 Adopted 2 November 1973 and as amended by Protocol of 1978 Relating to the International Convention for the Prevention of Pollution from Ships of 1973, adopted 17 February 1978 (entered into force 2 October 1983), 1340 UNTS 61 (MARPOL).

23 Canada communicated its instrument of accession on 16 November 1992, with effect on 16 February 1993. Status of IMO Treaties: Comprehensive Information on the Status of Multilateral Conventions and Instruments in respect of which the International Maritime Organization or its Secretary-General Performs Depositary or Other Functions (IMO, 15 July 2021), at 133, online: <https://wwwcdn.imo.org/localresources/en/About/Conventions/StatusOfConventions/Status%20-%202021.pdf>.

24 Canada became a party on 16 February 1993. Ibid.

25 Ibid.

similar vein, ten European states held that Canada's declaration "… should be read in conformity with Articles 57, 234 and 236" of UNCLOS and that "the laws and regulations contemplated in Article 234 shall have due regard to navigation and the protection and preservation of the marine environment based on the best available scientific evidence".[26] The exchange serves to clarify that the jurisdiction over Arctic shipping in pursuit of Article 234 must be exercised in conformity with other UNCLOS rules, perhaps most especially concerning due regard to international navigation.

In 2010, Canada communicated to the IMO that its ship reporting system (SRS) in Arctic waters set out in the Northern Canada Vessel Traffic Services Zone Regulations (NORDREG),[27] which previously was voluntary, was now mandatory. The communication triggered an awkward exchange with the United States in the Maritime Safety Committee (MSC). The United States felt that, given the IMO is the organization responsible for the adoption of routeing and reporting measures for international shipping under the International Convention on the Safety of Life at Sea, 1974 (SOLAS),[28] that Canada should first have proposed such measures to IMO.[29] Canada felt it was not obliged to seek prior IMO adoption of the measure, justifying its action under Article 234 of UNCLOS and a provision in Chapter 5 of SOLAS concerning the communication of such measures to the IMO.[30] The MSC could not address the underlying different views on an UNCLOS interpretation matter outside its remit,[31] leaving the matter unresolved.

Differences between the two states appeared to give way to pragmatic mutual predispositions during the Canada-US Joint Arctic Leaders' Statement

26 Ibid. The states concerned were Belgium, Denmark, France, Germany, Greece, Italy, the Netherlands, Portugal, Spain and the United Kingdom.

27 SOR/2010-127 (NORDREG).

28 Adopted 1 November 1974 (entered into force 25 May 1980), 1184 UNTS 2 (SOLAS).

29 Northern Canada Vessel Traffic Services Zone Regulations, Submitted by the United States and INTERTANKO, IMO Doc MSC 88/11/2 (22 September 2010). See the Canadian response in Comments on Document MSC 88/11/2, Submitted by Canada, IMO Doc MSC 88/11/3 (5 October 2010).

30 "Ship reporting systems not submitted to the Organization for adoption do not necessarily need to comply with this regulation. However, Governments implementing such systems are encouraged to follow, wherever possible, the guidelines and criteria developed by the Organization Contracting. Governments may submit such systems to the Organization for recognition". Ibid. chap V reg 11.4.

31 Report of the Maritime Safety Committee on its 88th Session, IMO Doc MSC 88/26 (15 December 2010) at 55.

in 2016, during which President Obama and Prime Minister Trudeau committed to working together to establish consistent policies for ships operating in the region, including sustainable shipping lanes.[32] However, in 2019 former Secretary of State Mike Pompeo issued a statement at the Arctic Ministers meeting in Rovaniemi calling Canada's claim to its Arctic waters as illegitimate, providing a reminder of the differences between the two neighbours.[33]

Cooperation through the Arctic Council is also a significant factor for the establishment of low impact shipping corridors in Canadian Arctic waters. Over the last two decades, Canada embarked on substantial cooperative action to promote safety and pollution prevention in Arctic waters through the IMO and Arctic Council. Canada played important roles in the development and adoption in 2002 of the initial IMO guidelines for safe operations in Arctic waters and their subsequent amendment in 2009.[34] Canada also played a leading role with Finland and the United States in the Arctic Council during the development of the *Arctic Marine Shipping Assessment 2009 Report* that identified pathways for the future governance of Arctic shipping and including support for the future mandatory Polar Code.[35] At the outset of IMO deliberations on the mandatory Polar Code in 2009, Canada submitted a draft of what the future code could look like drawing on its own practical experience in regulating polar shipping and contributed over thirty submissions to facilitate the development of the code.[36] Following the adoption of the Polar Code, Canada worked closely with other Arctic Council states through the Working Group on the Protection of the Marine Environment (PAME) on the implementation of the code. Other cooperation through PAME included the development of a proposal for the adoption of a regional approach to port reception facilities under MARPOL and eventually submitted to the IMO,[37] the launching of an initiative

32 Prime Minister of Canada (20 December 2016) http://pm.gc.ca/eng/news/2016/12/20/united-states-canada-joint-arctic-leaders-statement.

33 "Pompeo calls out Canada, China, Russia over Arctic policy", *CBC News* (6 May 2019), online: <https://www.cbc.ca/news/politics/pompeo-canada-russia-china-arctic-1.5125293>.

34 Guidelines for Ships Operating in Arctic Ice-Covered Waters, IMO Doc MSC/Circ.1056 & MEPC/Circ. 399 (23 December 2002), as amended and revised as Guidelines for Ships Operating in Polar Waters, Resolution A.1024(26) (2 December 2009), IMO Doc A 26/Res.1024 (18 January 2010).

35 AMSA, *supra* note 5, 6–7.

36 Aldo Chircop, Peter Pamel and Miriam Czarski, "Canada's implementation of the Polar Code", (2018) *Journal of International Maritime Law* 24(6): 428–450 at 434.

37 Regional Reception Facilities Plan (RRFP) – Outline and Planning Guide for the Arctic, Submitted by Canada, Denmark, Finland, Iceland, Norway, the Russian Federation, Sweden and the United States, IMO Doc MEPC 72/16 (29 December 2017).

to identify best practices for low impact navigation corridors,[38] and the establishment of the Arctic Shipping Best Practices Forum to support implementation of the Polar Code.[39] Hence, it will be important for Canada to engage its Arctic neighbours for their support and to share experiences on best practices.

2.2 *Indigenous Rights and Arctic Policy*

As noted earlier, Canada claims a historic title to, and consequential sovereignty over the waters of the Arctic archipelago based on longstanding Inuit occupancy and use. Indigenous rights in general international law and constitutional law encumber Canada's sovereignty in the region.[40] Since the adoption of UNCLOS and MARPOL, a body of international indigenous law has arisen in international law and now finds expression in the United Nations Declaration on the Rights of Indigenous Peoples (UNDRIP).[41] Although as a General Assembly resolution UNDRIP *per se* is not legally binding, it evidences general international law in many of its provisions.[42]

In any case, Canada recently enacted the United Nations Declaration on the Rights of Indigenous Peoples Act (UNDRIP Act) to provide a framework for the implementation of the declaration.[43] The Act enables Canada to take "effective measures – including legislative, policy and administrative measures – at the national and international level, in consultation and cooperation with Indigenous peoples, to achieve the objectives of the Declaration".[44] Canadian laws are required to be consistent with UNDRIP[45] and the Minister has a duty to prepare and implement an action plan[46] and report to Parliament.[47]

UNDRIP sets out a comprehensive system of indigenous rights, including rights to ancestral lands, territories, and resources, now crystallized as

38 Overview of Low Impact Shipping Corridors & Other Shipping Management Schemes (Arctic Council/PAME, May 2021), online: <https://www.pame.is/projects-new/arctic-shipping/pame-shipping-highlights/454-low-impact-shipping-corridors-in-the-arctic>.

39 Arctic Shipping Best Practice Information Forum, online: <https://arctic-council.org/projects/arctic-shipping-best-practice-information-forum/>.

40 The Constitution Act, 1982, Schedule B to the Canada Act 1982 (UK), 1982, c 11, s 35.

41 GA Res A/RES/61/295 adopted 13 September 2007.

42 International Law Association, Resolution No. 5/2012: Rights of Indigenous Peoples, adopted at the 75th Conference of the International Law Association, Sofia, Bulgaria, 26–30 August 2012, online: <Committees (ila-hq.org)>.

43 United Nations Declaration on the Rights of Indigenous Peoples Act, SC 2021 c 14 (UNDRIP Act).

44 Ibid.

45 Ibid. s 5.

46 Ibid. s 6.

47 Ibid. s 7.

customary international law.[48] In the Arctic context, those rights include land, marine and ice-covered areas.[49] States have a range of duties towards indigenous peoples, including the duty to protect the environment to enable indigenous rights to be enjoyed. In this respect, the AWPPA anticipated the important role of indigenous rights in Arctic shipping.[50] This is a significant development as consideration of navigational measures in Arctic waters must now be informed not only by UNCLOS and the IMO conventions, but also by international human rights as they concern indigenous peoples. The preamble of the AWPPA reiterated Canada's obligation to ensure that shipping and resource development in the Canadian Arctic take place "in a manner that takes cognizance of Canada's responsibility for the welfare of the Inuit and other inhabitants of the Canadian arctic" as well as environment protection.

Much has transpired in Canada's relations with its indigenous peoples, including Inuit, since the AWPPA and Joe Clark's statement. Recently, the Truth and Reconciliation Commission of Canada issued a report with recommendations that have been accepted by Prime Minister Trudeau on behalf of Canada without reservations.[51] The recommendations call for rebuilding relations with indigenous peoples on nation-to-nation and government-to-government basis. There are several modern treaties negotiated between Canada and its indigenous peoples addressing self-determination, land and resource claims, as well as other rights in the Arctic region. These include the James Bay and Northern Québec Agreement,[52] Inuvialuit Final Agreement,[53] Nunavut Land Claims

---

48 ILA Resolution No. 5/2012, *supra* note 42.

49 Dalee Sambo Dorough, "The Rights, Interests and Role of the Arctic Council Permanent Participants", in Robert C. Beckman, Tore Henriksen, Kristine Dalaker Kraabel, Erik J. Molenaar and J Ashley Roach (eds), *Governance of Arctic Shipping: Balancing Rights and Interests of Arctic States and User States* (Brill, 2017), at 80.

50 AWPPA, *supra* note 12, preamble.

51 "Statement by Prime Minister on release of the Final Report of the Truth and Reconciliation Commission" (15 December 2015), online: <https://pm.gc.ca/en/news/statements/2015/12/15/statement-prime-minister-release-final-report-truth-and-reconciliation>.

52 This agreement reserved hunting, fishing and trapping for the exclusive use of Crees, Inuit and Naskapis. James Bay and Northern Québec Agreement (11 November 1975), online: <https://www.rcaanc-cirnac.gc.ca/eng/1407867973532/1542984538197>. James Bay and Northern Québec Native Claims Settlement Act, SC 1976-77 c 32; Act approving the Agreement concerning James Bay and Northern Québec, SQ 1976 c 46, art 24.7.1. Fishing included the right to conduct commercial fisheries.

53 This agreement covers large areas of the Mackenzie Delta, Beaufort Sea and Amundsen Gulf area, thereby including internal waters, the territorial sea and EEZ, and provides for resource rights. Inuvialuit Final Agreement (as amended) (25 July 1984), Annex A and Annex A-1, online <https://irc.inuvialuit.com/sites/default/files/Inuvialuit%20Final%20Agreement%202005.pdf>.

Agreement,[54] Labrador Inuit Land Claims Agreement,[55] Eeyou Marine Region Land Claims Agreement,[56] and Nunavik Inuit Land Claims Settlement.[57] An integrated management plan for the Beaufort Sea area and marine protected areas in various other Arctic waters have also been established in consultation with Inuit communities.[58] The agreements, integrated management plan and MPAs also concern marine spatial rights and responsibilities and overlap with the navigation routes of the Northwest Passage.

Indigenous rights and concerns are embedded in Canada's Arctic and Northern Policy Framework.[59] Indigenous peoples are recognized as stewards of Northern ecosystems and marine pollution, which has a disproportionate effect on them. Their stewardship is recognized as a pressing concern. Hence, Goal 5 aims, among other, to "[A]pproach the planning, management and

---

54 This agreement includes internal waters and the territorial sea of the east coast of Nunavut, and, among other, protects Inuit resource rights and rights "to participate in decision-making concerning the use, management and conservation of land, water and resources, including the offshore". It also recognizes that "Canada's sovereignty over the waters of the arctic archipelago is supported by Inuit use and occupancy". Agreement between the Inuit of the Nunavut Settlement Area and Her Majesty the Queen in Right of Canada (25 May 1993), online: <http://www.tunngavik.com/documents/publications/1993-00-00-Nunavut-Land-Claims-Agreement-English.pdf>; Nunavut Land Claims Agreement Act, SC 1993, c 29.

55 Among others, this agreement addresses fishing rights and requires the Minister to consult on ocean management and marine protected area initiatives. Land Claims Agreement between the Inuit of Labrador and Her Majesty the Queen in Right of Newfoundland and Labrador and Her Majesty the Queen in Right of Canada (22 January 2005), chaps 6 and 13. online: <https://www.canlii.org/en/ca/laws/stat/schedule-b-to-the-canada-act-1982-uk-1982-c-11/latest/schedule-b-to-the-canada-act-1982-uk-1982-c-11.html>.

56 This agreement addresses the aboriginal title of the Crees of Eeyou Istchee to the use and ownership of lands and resources, including fisheries, in Nunavut and in Hudson Bay and James Bay. Agreement between the Crees of Eeyou Istchee and Her Majesty the Queen in Right of Canada concerning the Eeyou Marine Region (7 July 2010), art 2.23, online: <https://www.rcaanc-cirnac.gc.ca/eng/1320437343375/1542989331999>.

57 This agreement addresses, among other, fishing and wildlife harvesting rights in marine areas in Hudson Bay, Hudson Strait, Ungava Bay and Labrador Sea. Nunavik Inuit Land Claims Settlement (1 December 2006), preamble and art 3, online: <https://www.rcaanc-cirnac.gc.ca/eng/1320425236476/1551119558759#pre>.

58 Beaufort Sea Partnership, "Integrated Ocean Management", online: <https://www.beaufortseapartnership.ca/integrated-ocean-management/integrated-oceans-management-plan/>. Integrated Ocean Management Plan (IOMP) for the Beaufort Sea: 2009 and Beyond (Beaufort Sea Planning Office, 2009), online: <http://www.beaufortseapartnership.ca/wp-content/uploads/2015/04/integrated-ocean-management-plan-for-the-beaufort-sea-2009-and-beyond.pdf>. The plan includes actions on shipping.

59 Canada's Arctic and Northern Policy Framework, online: <https://www.rcaanc-cirnac.gc.ca/eng/1560523306861/1560523330587>.

development of Arctic and northern environments in a holistic and integrated manner" and to "[E]nsure safe and environmentally responsible shipping", and "[S]trengthen pollution prevention and mitigation regionally, nationally and internationally". Goal 6 supports the rules-based international order in the Arctic to effectively respond to new challenges and opportunities. Goal 7 aims at ensuring Northern people are safe, secure and well-defended as the region becomes more accessible. The policy reiterates Canada's sovereignty over its internal waters, which include the Northwest Passage, and notes the unique relationship between the land and waterways in which Inuit have lived on, travelled across, hunted, fished and trapped without distinguishing between frozen land and frozen sea. Hence, Canada will continue to "demonstrate its sovereignty" and "ensure a safe and secure transportation system" involving collaboration by all levels of government with indigenous peoples and allies. Further, Goal 7 objectives include cooperation with international partners and enforcement of marine transportation regulation. Finally, in Goal 8 the policy advances reconciliation through self-determination and other actions, including upholding and implementing indigenous rights.

Accordingly, Canada's corridors initiative in Arctic waters must be informed not only by the permissible jurisdictions in conventional and general international law and generally accepted international rules and standards (GAIRAS), but also by international human rights as they concern indigenous peoples in Arctic waters. Moreover, the designation of corridors cannot be a simple exercise of maritime administration but must involve genuine and respectful consultations in the spirit of reconciliation and indigenous rights as expressed in modern treaties and general international law.

3 Canada's Regulation of Low Impact Corridors

3.1 *Proposed Low Impact Corridors*

The genesis of low impact corridors in Arctic waters was the Northern Marine Transportation Corridors (NMTC) initiative, which emerged in the wake of the federal government's world-class tanker safety system launched in 2013 to address threats posed by oil tanker traffic through a range of legislative and management measures, including the establishment of a Tanker Safety Expert Panel.[60] The NMTC was a joint initiative of Fisheries and Oceans

60 The first addressed spill response capacity and the need for a risk-based approach in Canadian waters, and the second focused on Arctic waters.

Canada – operating through the Canadian Coast Guard (CCG) and Canadian Hydrographic Service (CHS) – and Transport Canada. The current iteration of the NMTC is the Northern Low-Impact Shipping Corridors and includes engagement with indigenous peoples as rights holders, territorial and provincial governments, and stakeholders generally.[61] Public consultations are currently underway.[62] The geographical scope of the corridors will encompass the current area covered by the Northern Canada Vessel Traffic Service Zone (NORDREG Zone) and the Mackenzie River. The corridors consist of the most widely used routes identified on the basis of automatic identification system (AIS) traffic data and CHS information

The purpose of the corridors is to set out a governance framework, enhance maritime safety, minimize the impacts of shipping to designated areas, and enable focused development of infrastructure and essential services. Given the huge geographical extent of Canadian Arctic waters and coastlines, the initiative will enable focused development of nautical charts and products, deployment and maintenance of navigation aids and provision of icebreaking services. As noted earlier, the vast majority of Canadian Arctic waters are uncharted or not charted to modern hydrographic standards. The initiative's focus on corridors will enable prioritization of CHS efforts on 12 percent of those waters, although even these waters are mostly inadequately surveyed at this time.[63] Thus the corridors will not necessarily cover all theoretically possible routes in Canadian Arctic waters, but only the safest and most used routes.

The range of services will include maritime traffic monitoring, navigation aids, hydrographic services, weather and ice forecasts, icebreaking, search and rescue and pollution response,[64] and presumably salvage and places of refuge. Appropriate regulations will accompany the formal designation of corridors.[65] There is a range of routeing and other measures that could be utilized.[66] Unlike the current NORDREG mandatory SRS, the corridors will be voluntary and the

61 Chénier et al., *supra* note 1, at 1.

62 The consultations period is open between 1 April 2021–1 January 2022. Northern Low-Impact Shipping Corridors (Government of Canada, 1 April 2021), online <https://www.dfo-mpo.gc.ca/about-notre-sujet/engagement/2021/shipping-corridors-navigation-eng.html>.

63 Chénier et al., *supra* note 1.

64 Ibid.

65 Ibid.

66 Teresa Clemmer, "Framework and Tools for Developing a Low-Impact Shipping Corridor in the Arctic Ocean", report prepared for WWF-US and WWF-Canada (WWF, 7 September 2018), online: <https://wwf.ca/wp-content/uploads/2020/06/Framework-and-Tools-for-Developing-a-Low-Impact-Shipping-Corridor-in-the-Arctic-2019.pdf>.

fact that they will be serviced should serve as an incentive for shippers to use those routes.

3.2 *Regulations Applicable to the Corridors*

Canada has a well-developed and mature legal regime for Arctic shipping to support low impact corridors, consisting of parent and subsidiary maritime legislation. Some of the legislation is dedicated to polar shipping. Table 16.1 sets out the four principal pillars of the legal regime, consisting of the jurisdictional framework for Arctic shipping, maritime and port law, environmental law, and indigenous and aboriginal law.

Under Canada's constitution, navigation and shipping are a federal legislative power, although in practice there is overlap with provincial powers concerning property and civil rights and local undertakings.[67] When an issue calls for the application of both federal and provincial (and territorial) law, the courts recognize double aspect causes and tend to find a harmonious application of both in the interests of cooperative federalism.[68] It is conceivable that claims concerning aspects of the administration of low impact corridors (for example, where a duty to consult applies because rights are affected) could involve federal maritime law and modern treaties mentioned earlier.

As the principal instrument implementing UNCLOS, the Oceans Act[69] sets out the jurisdictional context for Canada's exercise of its rights as a coastal State and the framework for integrated planning and management of marine areas based on consultations, and CCG services. CCG services are directly relevant to the establishment and maintenance of corridors because its mandate includes "services for the safe, economical and efficient movement of ships in Canadian waters" by providing navigation aids and services, marine communications and traffic management services, icebreaking and ice management services, and channel maintenance.[70] CCG services also include maritime search and rescue, response to wrecks and hazardous or dilapidated vessels, and marine pollution response.[71]

The Federal Courts Act provides for maritime law jurisdiction and suits by and against the federal crown.[72] Hence, any litigation involving claims related to the administration of the corridors will occur in the Federal Court.

---

67 Constitution Act, *supra* note 40, ss 91(10) and 92 (10) and (13).
68 *Canadian Western Bank v Alberta*, 2007 SCC 22, paras 21–24.
69 Oceans Act, SC 1996 c 31.
70 Ibid. s 41(1).
71 Ibid.
72 Federal Courts Act, RSC 1985 c F-7, ss 17 and 22.

TABLE 16.1 Regulatory schemes applicable to Canadian Arctic shipping

Jurisdictional framework	Maritime and port law	Environmental law	Indigenous and aboriginal law
– Constitution Act – Oceans Act – Federal Courts Act	– Arctic Waters Pollution Prevention Act Arctic Shipping Safety and Pollution Prevention Regulations – Canada Shipping Act, 2001 Arctic Shipping Safety and Pollution Prevention Regulations Shipping Safety Zones Control Order Navigation Safety Regulations Northern Canada Vessel Traffic Services Zone Regulations Ship Station (Radio) Regulations, 1999 Vessel Pollution and Dangerous Chemical Regulations, 2012. – Canadian Navigable Waters Act – Wrecked, Abandoned or Hazardous Vessels Act – Pilotage Act – Marine Liability Act – Coasting Trade Act – Canada Marine Act	– Canadian Environment Protection Act Disposal at Sea Permit Application Regulations, SOR/2014–177 Disposal at Sea Regulations, SOR/2001–275 – Fisheries Act – Migratory Birds Convention Act – Canada Wildlife Act – National Marine Conservation Areas Act – Canada National Parks Act – Impact Assessment Act	– Bill C-15 UNDRIP Implementation Act – Nunavut Land Claims Agreement Act – Western Arctic (Inuvialuit) Claims Settlement Act – Labrador Inuit Land Claims Agreement Act

Canada has long regulated Arctic shipping primarily through the AWPPA and subsidiary regulations, and regulations under the Canada Shipping Act, 2001 (CSA 2001).[73] Most importantly, the Arctic Shipping Safety and Pollution Prevention Regulations (ASSPPR) implement the Polar Code.[74] The effect is to replace the previous unilateral CDEM standards for the new GAIRAS of the Polar Code, thus avoiding a potential irritant in the regulation of the corridors. The regulations referentially incorporated Part I of the Polar Code provisions on maritime safety and a new SOLAS Chapter XIV. New regulatory text reproduced the Part II amendments to MARPOL Annexes I (oil), II (hazardous and noxious substances carried in bulk), IV (sewage) and V (garbage). The ASSPPR included consequential amendments to the regulations on navigation safety,[75] radio communications[76] and vessel-source pollution,[77] and repealed the former Arctic shipping regulations containing unilateral CDEM standards.[78]

The ASSPPR contained few and relatively minor departures from the Polar Code. With respect to maritime safety, the previous risk assessment framework consisting of a zone date system, SSCZs and the Arctic Ice Regime Shipping System (AIRSS) will continue to apply to existing ships side-by-side the Polar Operational Limitation Assessment Risk Indexing System (POLARIS) for new ships introduced by the Polar Code.[79] The effect is to phase out the old risk assessment system and phase in POLARIS. The requirement for an ice navigator on board vessels above 300 tons and non-SOLAS vessels continues to apply.[80] Canadian ships are required to have a specific low-air temperature annotation in addition to polar service temperature.[81] The regulations on pollution prevention apply to all ships. The AWPPA absolute 'zero' discharge rule continues even because 'clean ballast', whose discharge is otherwise permissible, may contain up to 5 ppm oil content.[82]

73 SC 2001 c 26 (CSA 2001).
74 Arctic Shipping Safety and Pollution Prevention Regulations, SOR/2017-286.
75 Navigation Safety Regulations, 2020, SOR/2020-216.
76 Ship Station (Radio) Regulations, 1999, SOR/2000-260.
77 Vessel Pollution and Dangerous Chemicals Regulations, SOR/2012-69.
78 Arctic Shipping Pollution Prevention Regulations, CRC c 353 (repealed).
79 Chircop et al., *supra* note 36, 444.
80 Ibid. 445.
81 Ibid.
82 Drummond Fraser, "A Change in the Ice Regime: Polar Code Implementation in Canada", in Aldo Chircop, Floris Goerlandt, Claudio Aporta and Ronald Pelot (eds), *Governance of Arctic Shipping: Rethinking Risk, Human Impacts and Regulation*, (Springer Polar Sciences, 2020), 285–300 at 294.

The definition of Canadian 'Arctic waters' in the AWPPA, which include waters between meridians and maritime boundaries North of 60 degrees, inclusive of internal waters, territorial sea and the EEZ, continues as it largely coincides with the definition in the Polar Code.[83] The ASSPPR do not affect the NORDREG mandatory SRS because the Polar Code does not set out reporting requirements. Finally, the ASSPPR exempt foreign government-owned vessels on non-commercial service from the application of the regulations.[84]

Other regulations under the CSA 2001 will play an important role in regulating low impact corridors, such as those concerning shipping SSCZs in Arctic waters,[85] marine navigation,[86] radio communications,[87] and the NORDREG mandatory SRS in Arctic waters.[88] Other relevant legislation concerns the protection of navigable waters from works,[89] salvage and wreck,[90] rules for pilotage where applicable,[91] civil liability regimes for maritime torts, carriage of goods and passenger vessels,[92] cabotage (such as supplying Northern communities),[93] and ports and harbours.[94]

Several topics addressed by environmental law statutes and subsidiary regulations will apply to the corridors. These include dumping at sea,[95] discharge of harmful substances in fish habitats,[96] discharges in areas frequented by migratory birds,[97] protection of wildlife,[98] and protected areas.[99] It is also conceivable that legislation concerning impact assessments of projects in marine areas will apply to the corridors.[100]

83 AWPPA, *supra* note 12, s 2.
84 ASSPPR, *supra* note 74, s 3.
85 Shipping Safety Control Zones Order, CRC c 356.
86 Navigation Safety Regulations, *supra* note 75.
87 Ship Station (Radio) Regulations, *supra* note 76.
88 NORDREG, *supra* note 27.
89 Canadian Navigable Waters Act, RSC 1985 c N-22.
90 Wrecked, Abandoned or Hazardous Vessels Act, SC 2019 c 1.
91 Pilotage Act, RSC 1985 c P-14.
92 Marine Liability Act, SC 2001 c 6.
93 Coasting Trade Act, SC 1992 c 31.
94 Canada Marine Act, SC 1998 c 10.
95 Canadian Environmental Protection Act, 1999, SC.1999 c 33; Disposal at Sea Permit Application Regulations, SOR/2014-177; Disposal at Sea Regulations, SOR/2001-275.
96 Fisheries Act, RSC 1985 c F-14.
97 Migratory Birds Convention Act, 1994, SC 1994 c 22.
98 Canada Wildlife Act, RSC 1985 c W-9.
99 Oceans Act, *supra* note 69; Canada National Marine Conservation Areas Act, SC 2002 c 18; Canada National Parks Act, SC 2000 c 32.
100 The definition of 'federal lands' includes internal waters, territorial sea, EEZ and continental shelf. Impact Assessment Act, SC 2019 c 28, s 2.

Finally, legislation concerning indigenous and aboriginal law is also relevant. The UNDRIP Act requires that federal law is consistent with UNDRIP.[101] Hence, the regulation of shipping must be undertaken in a manner so as not to infringe on indigenous rights. The modern treaties mentioned earlier are also pertinent because the spatial and resource rights potentially overlap with shipping routes. The Crown has a duty to consult indigenous peoples to ensure that aboriginal and treaty rights are protected.[102] For example, the Labrador Inuit Land Claims Agreement requires the Minister to consult the Nunatsiavut Government before establishing marine navigation services in the zone, issue approvals or exemptions under the Canadian Navigable Waters Act and hydrographic surveys along the shipping routes to Voisey Bay.[103] The Minister is also to consult on ocean management and marine protected area initiatives.[104]

4 Discussion

The designation of corridors in the Northwest Passage is a common sense and pragmatic approach to the facilitation of safe shipping in hazardous, uncharted and unserviced waters with little infrastructure at this time. Focusing shipping in the designated corridors minimizes conflicts and adverse impacts to the particular areas concerned while leveraging potential benefits to the region's inhabitants and international trade. Further, by servicing corridors and building the infrastructure for safe shipping in the region, Canada appears to propose a practical approach to managing disputes concerning the uncertain legal status of its Arctic waters and navigation rights in the Northwest Passage by opening and servicing the Passage.

The corridors initiative should allay past concerns over Canada's unilateral regulation of Arctic shipping. Canada has domesticated the Polar Code as the GAIRAS applicable to Arctic shipping, thus ensuring that the applicable CDEM standards are multilateral rather than unilateral. Moreover, the fact that passage will not be subject to charges, except perhaps for services rendered to particular ships, should allay concerns on the accessibility or hampering of the passage. In this way, Canada will be promoting international navigation in the Northwest Passage while maintaining its position on the legal status of Arctic waters.

101 UNDRIP Act, *supra* note 43, s 5.

102 *Clyde River (Hamlet) v Petroleum Geo-Services Inc*, 2017 SCC 40, para 19.

103 Labrador Inuit Land Claims Agreement, *supra* note 55, ss 6.5.1 and 8.6.6.

104 Ibid. chaps 6 and 13.

If the Polar Code standards turn out to be insufficient to ensure maritime safety and pollution prevention, Canada will have options. First, Canada will likely work closely with Arctic Council member states on a multilateral basis to coordinate a new law reform initiative at the IMO. Past coordinating efforts leading to the AMSA report and ministerial endorsement of its recommendations paving the way to deliberations at the IMO serve as precedent. Second, should Canada feel compelled to act unilaterally, it could act as a coastal State and rely on MARPOL, SOLAS and UNCLOS provisions in scaling up standards. MARPOL provides that "[N]othing in the present Convention shall prejudice ... the present or future claims and legal views of any State concerning the law of the sea and the nature and extent of coastal and flag State jurisdiction".[105] Also, a provision in SOLAS specifies that "[N]othing in this chapter shall prejudice the rights or obligations of States under international law".[106] Canada could argue that under general international law it is entitled to exercise full sovereignty over its internal waters. Doubtlessly, other maritime powers will continue to hold that the Northwest Passage is subject to international navigation rights and the most that Canada could do is to regulate innocent passage and transit passage, subject to the rules of UNCLOS, which include complying with GAIRAS. Canada might consider diplomatic protests as the price for asserting sovereignty from time to time. Third, Canada remains able to adopt unilateral regulations within the EEZ by virtue of Article 234 of UNCLOS, with due regard to international navigation and with scientific justification. Arguing the application of Article 234 to internal waters will be inconsistent with Canada's own position on the legal status of those waters because this provision covers a zone of functional jurisdiction rather than sovereignty. The potential diplomatic costs of the second option and the awkwardness of using Article 234's limited jurisdiction over the EEZ might be sufficient to encourage Canada to proceed with the first option.

It is possible that maritime powers will maintain reservations about Canada's NORDREG mandatory SRS as long as it remains unilateral, rather than as an IMO-designated system. On this point, purely legalistic concerns ought to give way to functional and pragmatic concerns for the safety of human life and shipping generally. Arctic shipping includes a range of vessels that do not necessarily carry AIS and locating them is imperative for the provision of assistance and to mitigate impacts on sensitive areas. In the event of a casualty, the first responders might well be indigenous, and a serious casualty could damage the very sensitive environment and threaten food security of indigenous hunters.

---

105 MARPOL, *supra* note 22, art 16.

106 SOLAS, *supra* note 28, chap XIV reg 2.

Canada is taking a calculated risk in establishing a system to service shipping in this sensitive region. On the other hand, indigenous peoples should benefit from more shipping services to supply communities and help develop local economies, hence the importance of their early engagement in designating the corridors and in building the infrastructure to support them. However, shipping is not neutral and produces a range of environmental impacts, such as atmospheric emissions and waste discharges, radiation of underwater noise, icebreaking disruption of ice routes used by indigenous hunters and animals, community exposure to traumatic events in responding to casualties, and fuel or cargo spills. The costs of mitigating and reinstating environmental damage from an oil spill will be very high.

Canada has not indicated how the corridors will be administered, other than that Transport Canada will lead the development of a collaborative governance model that "will be inclusive of Indigenous people, reflect and respect the modern land claims in place, and oversee the development, implementation, and management of the corridors".[107] Canada does not have an institution exclusively dedicated to the Northwest Passage, such as the St. Lawrence Seaway Authority or the Northern Sea Route Administration in the case of the Northern Sea Route in Russian waters of the Northeast Passage. A related matter is the absence of a legislated definition of the Northwest Passage, unlike the case of the Northern Sea Route in the NSR Regulations.[108] Definition is important to delimit the geographical scope of the corridors and related services, as well as clarifying the mandate of the institution tasked with the administration of the corridors.

The matter of definition is accompanied by overlapping responsibilities and fragmented powers. Under the Oceans Act the CCG is the agency to provide "services for the safe, economical and efficient movement of ships in Canadian waters" and navigation aids.[109] However, the CSA 2001 empowers the Minister of Transport to recommend regulations to the Governor in Council on:

(a) establishing VTS Zones within Canadian waters or in a shipping safety control zone prescribed under the *Arctic Waters Pollution Prevention Act*;

107 Pilotage Act Review, *supra* note 1, at 98.

108 Rules of Navigation in the Water Area of the Northern Sea Route, approved by the Russian Federation Government Decree dated September 18, 2020, No. 1487, appendix 3, online: <http://www.nsra.ru/files/fileslist/137-en5894-2020-11-19_rules.pdf>.

109 Oceans Act, *supra* note 69, s 41(1).

(b) respecting the information to be provided and the procedures and practices to be followed by vessels that are about to enter, leave or proceed within a VTS Zone;
(c) respecting the conditions under which a clearance under section 126 is to be granted;
(d) defining the expression *about to enter* for the purpose of this Part;
(e) respecting aids to navigation in Canadian waters;
(f) regulating or prohibiting the navigation, anchoring, mooring or berthing of vessels for the purposes of promoting the safe and efficient navigation of vessels and protecting the public interest and the environment;

...

(h) specifying classes of persons, or appointing persons, to ensure compliance with regulations made under any of paragraphs (b) and (e) to (g) and specifying their powers and duties; and
(I) prescribing anything that may be prescribed under this Part.[110]

At a minimum, the CCG and Transport Canada have overlapping responsibilities on navigation aids, but vessel traffic services (VTS) are arguably also included in services for the safe movement of ships, a CCG responsibility.

Perhaps the way forward for a 'new collaborative governance model' for the corridors is a new and publicly run institution similar or analogous to the St. Lawrence Seaway Commission, but composed of only Canadian federal, territorial, indigenous people and stakeholder representation with the authority to recommend to the CCG and Transport Canada appropriate measures to service the corridors. Such an institution will need a legal framework, as is the case for the St. Lawrence Seaway.[111] Perhaps the most obvious course of action is to include a new part in the Canada Marine Act dedicated to the corridors and designating or creating a responsible institution, similar to the case of the St. Lawrence Seaway Authority. Using the St. Lawrence Seaway Authority as an example, under the Canada Marine Act:

110 CSA 2001, *supra* note 73, s 136(1).

111 Canada Marine Act, *supra* note 94, part 3. Prior to it the enactment of the Canada Marine Act, the St. Lawrence Seaway Authority had its own dedicated statute, the St. Lawrence Seaway Authority Act. The Canada Marine Act repealed this statute and provided the legal framework in Part 3.

> The Governor in Council may make regulations for the management, control, development and use of the Seaway and property and undertakings in connection with the Seaway, including regulations respecting
> (a) the navigation and use by ships of the navigable waters of the Seaway, including the mooring, berthing and loading and unloading of ships and equipment for the loading and unloading of ships;
> (b) the use and environmental protection of the Seaway or any land used in connection with the Seaway, including the regulation or prohibition of equipment, structures, works and operations;
> (c) the removal, destruction or disposal of any ship, part of a ship, structure, work or other thing that interferes with navigation in the Seaway and the provision for the recovery of the costs incurred;
> (d) the maintenance of order and the safety of persons and property in the Seaway or on any land used in connection with the Seaway;
> (d.1) the information or documents that must be provided by the owner or the person in charge of a ship to the Minister or to any person who has entered into an agreement under subsection 80(5);
> (e) the regulation of persons, vehicles or aircraft in the Seaway or on any land used in connection with the Seaway;
> (f) the regulation or prohibition of the excavation, removal or deposit of material or of any other action that is likely to affect in any way the navigability or operation of the Seaway or to affect any of the lands adjacent to the Seaway; and
> (g) the regulation or prohibition of the transportation, handling or storing in the Seaway, or on any land used in connection with the Seaway, of explosives or other substances that, in the opinion of the Governor in Council, constitute or are likely to constitute a danger or hazard to life or property.[112]

Clearly, the corridors will require additional powers concerning VTS, navigation aids, icebreaking and other services.

The types of routeing and reporting measures needed to service the corridors also raise interesting questions. Chapter 5 of SOLAS provides for the adoption routeing and reporting measures, and the IMO is the responsible organization for their adoption with respect to international shipping. However, as we have seen earlier, Canada did not seek prior IMO adoption

112 Ibid. s 98(1).

before introducing its mandatory SRS in Arctic waters. Canada has an extensive system of domestically designated routeing and other measures in its inland and internal waters and they are not necessarily also IMO adopted.[113] Canada has sought IMO designation of routeing measures in the territorial sea, as was the case with an area to be avoided in Roseway Basin, off Nova Scotia.[114] Given Canada's position on the legal status of its Arctic waters, it is not likely to request the IMO to designate routeing measures for the corridors; rather, and as Canada has acted with respect to the SRS, it will inform the IMO of the measures under the same SOLAS provision it used for the SRS.[115] Canada has indicated the corridors will be voluntary, but it has not indicated whether all routeing measures within the corridors will also be voluntary. There might be good reasons for mandatory traffic separation schemes for collision avoidance in choke points or areas to be avoided near protected areas or where Inuit and animals have ice routes. This is conceivable in Lancaster Sound, a major artery in the Northwest Passage, which has protected areas and Inuit ice routes.

In addition to routeing and reporting measures, it is conceivable pilotage might be needed, most especially because of the lack of charts of Canadian Arctic waters. Perceived as a measure that hampers international navigation, mandatory pilotage has triggered difficult discussions in the IMO in the course of consideration of appropriate protective measures for particularly sensitive sea areas.[116] At this time, there is no pilotage authority or mandatory pilotage in Arctic waters as there is in the Atlantic, Great Lakes and Pacific regions of Canada. However, as seen earlier, there is a requirement for an ice navigator to be on board certain vessels, and this person will have at least some of the knowledge of a pilot. The pilot is a licensed or certified professional person, usually a former mariner, who provides information to the master and officers of the watch on local navigational constraints and requirements for the safe conduct of the vessel. A recent review of Pilotage Act in Canada indicated that

113 Notices to Mariners 1–46: Annual Edition 2021 (Fisheries and Oceans Canada, Canadian Coast Guard, 2021), 130–132, online: <https://www.notmar.gc.ca/publications/annual/annual-notices-to-mariners-eng.pdf>. However, several compulsory routeing systems are also IMO adopted, e.g.: Approaches to Chedabucto Bay, Bay of Fundy and Approaches, Strait of Juan de Fuca and its Approaches, and Haro Straight and Boundary Pass, Strait of Georgia. Ibid. at 130.

114 Establishment of New Recommended Seasonal Area to be Avoided in Roseway Basin, South of Nova Scotia, IMO Doc MSC 83/28/Add.3 (2 November 2007), annex 25.

115 SOLAS, *supra* note 28, reg 11.4.

116 Sam Bateman and Michael White, "Compulsory Pilotage in the Torres Strait: Overcoming Unacceptable Risks to a Sensitive Marine Environment", (2009) *Ocean Development and International Law* 40(2): 184–203.

> Improvements under the Polar Code and formalizing the requirements to become an ice navigator will mitigate the need for Arctic pilotage in the short term. For the longer term, there is potential for pilotage in the north to be developed in conjunction with the Low Impact Shipping Corridors initiatives within the Oceans Protection Plan.[117]

The ideal scenario for ships in Canadian Arctic waters is to have access to pilots who are knowledgeable of those waters, and not simply to ice navigation. The Pilotage Act review considered the possibility of a new pilotage authority for the Arctic and recommended, among others, that

> Transport Canada, the Canadian Coast Guard, and the Canadian Hydrographic Services place a priority on an accelerated timeline to develop and implement the Low Impact Corridors management structure and assess the need for pilotage services as a possible mitigating measure identified by a robust Navigation Risk Assessment Methodology.[118]

Controversial as pilotage might be, it appears it will be a necessity in the low impact corridors.

5 Conclusion

The low impact corridors initiative in Canadian Arctic waters is a grand experiment on a very large scale. While there are many examples of such corridors in other marine regions, and possibly with the exception of the Northern Sea Route, they tend to concern smaller areas and local traffic and do not always concern a marine environment that is so fragile and of global planetary concern. Therefore, it will not be surprising to see international attention turning to what Canada is planning because there is so much at stake. Naturally, at this time it is difficult to fully anticipate how attractive the corridors will be, or for that matter whether the Northwest Passage itself will be attractive to commercial traffic to become a viable international trade route. Like all experiments, it might work, or it might not. What is certain, however, is that this most unique and fragile of regions requires far greater scrutiny of the governance of

117 Pilotage Act Review, *supra* note 1, at viii.

118 Ibid. at 42.

shipping, because shipping will make it even more accessible and subject to cumulative stressors.

That Canada must take action to protect the region in partnership with its indigenous communities is clearly an imperative. To date, Canada appears to be engaging indigenous peoples. It is placing faith in multilateralism more than in unilateralism, whether by working closely with other Arctic Council members on shipping and/or working with the IMO in polar regulatory reform.

CHAPTER 17

Navigational Rights and the Coastal State's Jurisdiction in the Northern Sea Route

Kentaro Wani

1 Introduction

This paper examines Russian Arctic shipping legislation in light of relevant provisions of the United Nations Convention on the Law of the Sea (hereinafter referred to as "LOSC"). The provisions of the LOSC are divided into two categories: *normal* rules and a *special* rule. Article 234 is a *special* rule for ice-covered areas. Provisions other than article 234 are *normal* rules. Section 2 of this paper concerns *normal* rules, and section 3 concerns a *special* rule, article 234.

There are three main routes for Arctic shipping: the Northwest Passage, the Northern Sea Route, and the Trans-Polar Route. Given the present ice conditions, the use of the Trans-Polar route is not a realistic option. It is the Northern Sea Route that has attracted much attention in East Asian countries such as Japan, China, and South Korea.

There are several advantages of the Northern Sea Route for East Asian Countries. First, for example, the distance from the port of Yokohama to the port of Rotterdam is 11,200 nm via the Southern sea route through the Suez Canal. The use of the Northern Sea Route reduces the distance by more than 40 percent. Second, the Northern Sea Route may be used by larger vessels than those admitted for transit through the Suez Canal. (*See* Arctic Council (2009):102, Vylegzhanin, *et al.*(2020):287.)

2 Overview of the Russian Legislation

In 2013, Russia enacted "Rules of Navigation in the Water Area of the Northern Sea Route" (hereinafter referred to as "the Rules of Navigation"). The water area of the Northern Sea Route is defined by the Merchant Shipping Code. The water area of the Northern Sea Route includes the Russian EEZ, the Russian territorial sea, and its internal waters. It does not include the high seas beyond the limits of the Russian EEZ.

 | DOI:10.1163/9789004518629_018

In 1985, Russia drew straight baselines which enclosed several straits in the Northern Sea Route. The validity of these baselines has been the subject of much debate. However, even assuming that the baselines are valid, at the least, the innocent passage regime applies to these straits by virtue of Article 5, paragraph 2 of the 1958 Territorial Sea Convention or Article 8, paragraph 2 of the LOSC. According to these provisions, in internal waters newly enclosed by strait baselines, the regime of innocent passage applies (*see* Brubaker (1999)). Although there has been much debate as to whether these straits are international straits, this paper does not examine this issue.

The purpose of the Rules of Navigation is to ensure the safety of navigation of ships and to prevent pollution from ships. To achieve these purposes, the Rules of Navigation imposes several requirements on ships entering the sea area of the Northern Sea Route. These requirements include a prior authorization requirement, a prior notification requirement and a ship reporting system, ice pilotage, and icebreaker escorting.

The core of the Rules of Navigation is a prior authorization requirement. The entry of a ship to the water area of the Northern Sea Route is permitted or prohibited according to criteria such as the ice class of the ship, ice navigation method, water area, and ice conditions. In the next two sections, I will consider whether these requirements are consistent with relevant provisions of the LOSC

3 Navigational Rights and Coastal State Jurisdiction under *Normal* Rules of the LOSC

Navigational rights under the LOSC are largely divided into three categories: the innocent passage regime, the transit passage regime, and freedom of navigation. The innocent passage regime applies to the territorial sea. It also applies to internal waters newly enclosed by straight baselines. The transit passage regime applies to straits used for international navigation. Freedom of navigation applies to the EEZ and the high seas.

There are three types of standards for the prevention, reduction and control of pollution from ships: discharge standards; construction, design, equipment and manning (CDEM) standards; and navigational standards. For example, a prior notification requirement, pilotage and icebreaker escorting are navigational standards. Ice-strengthening construction standards are CDEM standards. CDEM standards have a special feature as compared with two other types of standards. Ships cannot adjust to divergent CDEM standards during a voyage. Therefore, the LOSC requires coastal States not to apply their laws and regulations to CDEM of foreign ships unless they are giving effect to generally accepted international rules or standards, even within their territorial seas.

Table 17.1 shows the permissibility of three standards of regulations in each sea area.

Three rules are relevant to the subject under discussion. First, in the territorial sea or international straits, a coastal State shall not deny, hamper or impair innocent passage or transit passage (LOSC, art. 24(1), art. 42(2), art. 44). Second, in the territorial sea, a coastal State's laws and regulations shall not apply to CDEM of foreign ships unless they are giving effect to GAIRS (LOSC, art. 21(2)). Third, a coastal State's prescriptive jurisdiction in the EEZ is limited to adopting laws and regulations conforming to and giving effect to GAIRS (LOSC, art. 211(5)).

Now, I will examine coastal States' measures in light of the relevant provisions of the LOSC. A requirement of prior authorization implies the possibility of denying passage, which is clearly in conflict with the duty not to deny innocent passage or transit passage. It is also clearly contrary to the very idea of the "rights" of innocent passage or transit passage. (*See* Hakpää & Molenaar (1999): 138, 144; Churchill (2005): 2753–2761).

Unlike prior authorizations, it could be argued that a requirement of prior notification is compatible with the right of innocent passage and falls within the coastal State's competence under article 21, paragraph (1)(a) relating to the regulation of maritime traffic. In international straits and the EEZ, a coastal

TABLE 17.1 Coastal state jurisdiction under normal rules of the LOSC

		Territorial sea	International straits	EEZ
Discharge	unilateral	+ (art. 21(1)(f))	–	– (art. 211(5))
standards	GAIRS	+	+ (art. 42(2))	+ (art. 211(5))
CDEM	unilateral	– (art. 21(2))	–	– (art. 211(5))
standards	GAIRS	+ (art. 21(2))	?	+ (art. 211(5))
Navigational	unilateral	+ (art. 21(1)(a)(f))	–	– (art. 211(5))
standards	GAIRS	+	+ (art. 41, 42(1))	+ (art. 211(5))

GAIRS: generally accepted international rules and standards
Unilateral: unilateral regulation by a coastal State which exceeds GAIRS
+ permitted
– prohibited

State does not have a unilateral right. A coastal State may adopt ship reporting systems only when they are approved by the IMO. (*See* Hakpää & Molenaar (1999): 134; Churchill (2005): 2755).

The application of CDEM standards exceeding generally accepted international rules and standards is prohibited even within the territorial sea. For stronger reasons, it would be prohibited in international straits and the EEZ.

There has been much debate on the legality of a system of compulsory pilotage. Some authors such as Beckman (2007) have argued that a system of compulsory pilotage would have the practical effect of impairing or hampering the rights of transit passage and innocent passage. This is because the ships must stop to take on a pilot and pay for the pilotage service. Other authors such as Bateman & White (2009) have argued that a system of compulsory pilotage could be operated in such a manner as not to hamper or impair transit passage and innocent passage. For example, if pilots are readily available, they are efficient and competent, and the fee is reasonable, the system does not have the practical effect of hampering or impairing transit passage.

To summarize:

- It is impossible to justify a prior authorization requirement under the normal rules of the LOSC;
- In contrast, it could be argued that a prior notification requirement is permitted in the territorial sea;
- CDEM standards regulation exceeding generally accepted international rules and standards is not permitted even within the territorial sea; and
- The legality of a system of compulsory pilotage is controversial.

In other words, Russian legislation includes requirements that *cannot* be justified by the normal rules of the LOSC. Therefore, the next issue is whether these requirements are justified by a special rule, article 234.

4 Coastal State Jurisdiction under Article 234 of the LOSC

Article 234 provides: “Coastal States have the right to adopt and enforce non-discriminatory laws and regulations for the prevention, reduction and control of marine pollution from vessels in ice–covered areas within the limits of the exclusive economic zone …” The main elements of this article include: “ice-covered areas”; “within the limits of the EEZ”; non-discriminatory; “due regard to navigation”; and “based on available scientific evidence.” What is important is that article 234 refers to neither “generally accepted international rules and standards" nor the approval of "the competent international organization" unlike article 211, paragraphs 5 and 6.

The applicability of Article 234 to the territorial sea is the most controversial issue with respect to this article. There are two opposing interpretations. The first interpretation is that Article 234 applies only to the EEZ (e.g., McRae & Goundrey (1982); Chircop (2009); Franckx & Boone (2017)). The second interpretation is that Article 234 applies to the territorial sea as well as to the EEZ (e.g., Pharand (2007); Yang (2006); Bartenstein (2011a)(2019)).

The logic of the first interpretation is as follows.

1. The limit of the "EEZ" is unequivocally defined by article 55 as "an area beyond and adjacent to the territorial sea";
2. It would be absurd if a coastal State had broader powers in the EEZ than in its territorial sea; and
3. Therefore, powers under article 234 are not broader than those which the coastal State has in the territorial sea.

The logic of the second interpretation is as follows.

1. Powers conferred by article 234 are broader than those conferred by the normal rules applicable to the territorial sea;
2. It would be absurd if a coastal State had broader powers in the EEZ than in the territorial sea; and
3. Therefore, article 234 applies not only to the EEZ but also to the territorial sea.

According to the second interpretation, coastal States' powers under article 234 are broader than the powers which coastal States have in the territorial sea. That is why I call this interpretation "a broad interpretation." In contrast, according to the first interpretation, powers under article 234 are not broader than powers which the coastal State has in the territorial sea. Therefore, I call this interpretation "a restrictive interpretation."

Then, what is the content of coastal State jurisdiction under article 234?

According to the restrictive interpretation, coastal State powers under article 234 are not broader than those under normal rules applicable to the territorial sea. As a result, according to this interpretation, CDEM standards regulation exceeding generally accepted international rules and standards is not permitted under article 234. Also, the coastal State may not require prior authorization for entry into ice–covered areas. (*See* McRae & Goundrey (1982): 221; Franckx & Boone (2017): 1579).

In contrast, many authors who support the broad interpretation consider that CDEM standards regulation exceeding generally accepted international rules and standards is permitted under article 234 (*See* Churchill & Lowe

(1999): 348; Pharand (2007): 47; Bartenstein (2011a): 44–45). However, a total ban on navigation is not permitted. The requirement to have "due regard to navigation" under article 234 presupposes that there exists a certain amount of navigation in ice-covered areas. It is unclear whether a requirement of prior authorization is permitted under article 234. However, Bartenstein (2011b) argues that prior authorization is among the most effective means of preventive action and that the "due regard" obligation is fulfilled by granting an authorization in principle. In other words, by adopting the broad interpretation of article 234, there is room to justify a prior authorization requirement.

The last issue concerning article 234 is its relationship with the Polar Code. The Polar Code was adopted by the IMO and entered into force in 2017. Amendments were made in the Code to SOLAS and MARPOL Annexes to require State parties to these conventions to comply with the mandatory parts of the Polar Code. The Polar Code sets out additional requirements on ships navigating Polar waters. While the Polar Code is the first mandatory standard peculiar to the Polar Sea areas, there still exists a gap between the Polar Code and the requirements imposed by Russian legislation. As Chircop (2016) has pointed out, Russian Arctic shipping legislation includes requirements that do not appear in the Polar Code. For example, ice pilotage and mandatory reporting are not required by the Polar Code.

What is the relationship between the Polar Code and article 234 of the LOSC? The Polar Code is a minimum standard to be implemented by flag States. (*See* Bartenstein (2019): 340). While it constitutes generally accepted international rules and standards, and provides a basis for the coastal State jurisdiction under articles 21, paragraph 2 and article 211, paragraph 5, it does not limit the unilateral competence of coastal States under article 234, which does not refer to generally accepted international rules and standards.

5 Conclusion

Main points of this paper may be summarized as follows.

- The requirements set out by Russian Arctic shipping legislation include those that cannot be justified under the normal rules of the LOSC;
- These requirements may be justified by adopting the broad interpretation of Article 234;
- The Polar Code does not deprive article 234 of its significance. The Polar Code still has shortcomings and gaps. These gaps may be filled by the unilateral coastal State jurisdiction under article 234; and

– Therefore, the interpretation of article 234 is extremely important. Nevertheless, many uncertainties and ambiguities still remain about this article. Further discussion is needed about the interpretation of Article 234.

References

Arctic Council (2009). *Arctic Marine Shipping Assessment 2009 Report.*

Bartenstein, Kristin (2011a). "The 'Arctic Exception' in the Law of the Sea Convention: A Contribution to Safer Navigation in the Northwest Passage?" ODIL 42:22–52.

Bartenstein, Kristin (2011b). "Navigating the Arctic: The Canadian NORDREG, the International Polar Code and Regional Cooperation," *German Yearbook of International Law* 54:77–124.

Bartenstein, Kristin (2019). "Between the Polar Code and Article 234: The Balance in Canada's Arctic Shipping Safety and Pollution Prevention Regulations," ODIL 50:335–362.

Bateman, S., and M. White (2009). "Compulsory pilotage in the Torres Strait: Overcoming unacceptable risks to a sensitive marine environment." *Ocean Development and International Law* [hereinafter cited as ODIL] 40(2): 184–203.

Beckman, R. C. (2007). "PSSAs and Transit Passage: Australia's Pilotage System in the Torres Strait Challenges the IMO and UNCLOS." ODIL 38:325–357.

Bodansky, Daniel (1991). "Protecting the Marine Environment from Vessel–Source Pollution, UNCLOS III and Beyond." *Ecology Law Quarterly* 18:719–777.

Brubaker, R. Douglas (1999). "The Legal Status of the Russian Baselines in the Arctic." ODIL 30: 191–233.

Brubaker, R. Douglas (2005). *The Russian Arctic Straits.* Martinus Nijhoff.

Chircop, Aldo (2009). "The Growth of International Shipping in the Arctic: Is a Regulatory Review Timely?" *International Journal of Marine and Coastal Law* 24:355–380.

Chircop, Aldo (2016). "Jurisdiction over Ice–covered Areas and the Polar Code: An Emerging Symbiotic Relationship?" *Journal of International Maritime Law* 22:275–290.

Chircop, Aldo (2020). "The Polar Code and the Arctic Marine Environment: Assessing the Regulation of the Environmental Risks of Shipping." *International Journal of Marine and Coastal Law* 35:533–569.

Churchill, Robin R. (2005). "The Impact of State Practice on the Jurisdictional Framework Contained in the LOS Convention." in A. Oude Elferink, ed., *Stability and Change in the Law of the Sea: The Role of the LOS Convention* (Nijhoff, 2005), reproduced in Jill Barrett and Jean–Pierre Gauci, eds., *British Contributions to International Law*, 1915–2015: An Anthology Set (Brill, 2021).

Churchill, R.R. and A.V. Lowe (1999). *The Law of the Sea*. 3rd ed. Manchester University Press.

de Mestral, Armand (2015). "Article 234 of the United Nations Convention of the Law of the Sea." In Suzanne Lalonde and Ted L. McDorman, eds., *International Law and Politics of the Arctic Ocean: Essays in Honor of Dornat Pharand*, Brill.

Dremliuga, Roman (2017). "A Note on the Application of Article 234 of the Law of the Sea Convention in Light of Climate Change: Views from Russia," ODIL 48:128–135.

Farré, Albert Buixadé, *et al.* (2014). "Commercial Arctic shipping through the Northeast Passage: routes, resources, governance, technology, and infrastructure." *Polar Geography* 37:298–324.

Franckx, Eric and Laura Boone (2017). "Article 234," in Alexander Proelss, ed., *United Nations Conventions on the Law of the Sea: A Commentary*, C.H. Beck.

Gavrilov, Viatcheslav (2020). "Russian Legislation on the Northern Sea Route Navigation: Scope and Trends." *Polar Journal* 10:273–284.

Hakpää, K. and E.J. Molenaar (1999). "Innocent Passage: Past and Present," *Marine Policy* 23(2): 131–145.

McRae, D.M. and D.J. Goundrey (1982). "Environmental Jurisdiction in Arctic Waters: The Extent of Article 234." *University of British Columbia Law Review* 16:197–228.

Molenaar, Erik Jaap (1998). *Coastal State Jurisdiction over Vessel-Source Pollution*. Kluwer Law International.

Pharand, D. (2007). "The Arctic Waters and the Northwest Passage: A Final Revisit." ODIL 38:3–70.

Solski, Jan J. (2017). "Russia," in Robert C. Beckman, *et al.*, eds., *Governance of Arctic Shipping: Balancing Rights and Interests of Arctic States and User States*. Brill Nijhoff. 173–216.

Vylegzhanin, Alexander, Ivan Bunik, Ekaterina Torkunova and Elena Kienko (2020). "Navigation in the Northern Sea Route: Interaction of Russian and International Applicable Law." *Polar Journal* 10: 285–302.

Yang, Haijiang (2006). *Jurisdiction of the Coastal State over Foreign Merchant Ships in Internal Waters and the Territorial Sea*. Springer.

CHAPTER 18

The Role of East Asian Port States in Addressing Ship-Source Pollution in Arctic Shipping

Zhen Sun

1 Introduction

The continuing reduction of the sea ice coverage has significant implications for shipping through the Arctic Ocean. In particular, it is anticipated that the presence of commercial vessels for international trade between the Asian markets and Europe will continue to grow.[1] The increased presence of various types of vessels will potentially cause significant impacts on the pristine marine environment in the Arctic.[2] The international community has further developed environmental regulations for international shipping in Arctic waters under the umbrella of the United Nations Convention on the Law of the Sea (UNCLOS) and the auspice of the International Maritime Organization.[3] States, particularly flag States, are expected to diligently implement relevant international rules and standards to prevent, reduce and control vessel-source pollution of the Arctic marine environment.[4]

Given the strategic location of ports, it has been acknowledged that the port State could complement the flag State enforcement jurisdiction in ensuring

1 X. Zhou (*et al*), 'Revisiting Trans-Arctic Maritime Navigability in 2011–2016 from the Perspective of Sea Ice Thickness', 13 *Remote Sensing*, 2021, 2766, https://doi.org/10.3390/rs13142766. B. Gunnarsson, 'Recent Ship Traffic and Developing Shipping Trends on the Northern Sea Route – Policy Implications for Future Arctic Shipping', 124 *Marine Policy*, 2021, 104369.

2 J. Svavarsson (*et al*), 'Pollutants from Shipping – New Environmental Challenges in the SubArctic and the Arctic Ocean', 164 *Marine Pollution Bulletin*, 2021, 112004.

3 United Nations Convention on the Law of the Sea (UNCLOS), adopted 10 December 1982, in force 16 November 1994, 1833 *United Nations Treaty Series* 3. International Maritime Organization (IMO), Shipping in Polar Waters: International Code for Ships Operating in Polar Waters (Polar Code), https://www.imo.org/en/MediaCentre/HotTopics/Pages/Polar-default.aspx. This Chapter adopts the definition of 'Arctic waters' as defined in the Polar Code and relevant amendment to MARPOL, *infra* 27.

4 UNCLOS, *supra* 3, Article 94, 211, 217, 218 and 220.

DOI:10.1163/9789004518629_019

ships calling at their ports comply with international regulations.[5] According to customary international law and treaty law, port States may regulate the entry into port, including establishing conditions for granting access, as well as exercise prescriptive and enforcement jurisdiction over recognised activities by a foreign ship.[6] Moreover, in the context of vessel-source pollution and when the conditions are met, the port State may exercise enforcement jurisdiction over discharges that occurred outside its maritime zones in violation of applicable international rules and standards.[7]

Ports located within East Asian States, notably China, Japan, and the Republic of Korea, have the potential to become major departing and destination ports for ships transiting through the Arctic Ocean between Asian and Europe. This chapter argues that these East Asian port States should be more proactive in taking enforcement measures of ship-source pollution which occurred during transit through the Arctic Ocean that is in violation of applicable international regulations. The issue of interest of this chapter is the port State jurisdiction of three East Asian States over visiting foreign vessels that have completed a voyage in the Arctic waters.

2 Port State Power over Foreign Vessels

2.1 *The Legal Basis for Port State Power*

Port serves as an important node between sea-based activities and is the hinterland connection in terms of regulating international shipping. As a matter of geography, a State exercising port State jurisdiction is, with limited exceptions such as a landlocked State connected through rivers, also a coastal State.[8] While there is no official definitions of 'port State' or 'coastal State' in UNCLOS, this chapter will use 'port State' in a narrow sense encompassing prescriptive and enforcement jurisdiction over the port waters only, excluding maritime zones that the State act as a coastal State. Hence, it will not cover jurisdiction

---

5 R. Churchill, 'Port State Jurisdiction Relating to the Safety of Shipping and Pollution from Ships – What Degree of Extra-territoriality?', 31 *The International Journal of Marine and Coastal Law*, 2016, 446 and 463. D. König, 'The Enforcement of the International Law of the Sea by Coastal and Port States', 62 *ZaöRV*, 2002, 14.

6 L. de La Fayette, 'Access to Ports in International Law', 11 *The International Journal of Marine and Coastal Law*, No. 1, 1996, 2–12. UNCLOS, *supra* 3, Articles 25(2) and 211(3).

7 A.N. Honniball, 'The Exclusive Jurisdiction of Flag States: A Limitation on Pro-active Port States?', 31 *The International Journal of Marine and Coastal Law*, 2016, 508–510. UNCLOS, *supra* 3, Article 218.

8 Port of Switzerland, https://www.citizenports.eu/partners/port-of-switzerland/.

exercised by the coastal State at port in relation to vessel-source pollution that occurred within its territorial sea, straits used for international navigation, archipelagic waters and the exclusive economic zone.

Ports, or the permanent harbour works, are regarded as part of the coast that lie within a State's internal waters and therefore fall under its territorial sovereignty.[9] The jurisdictional basis in international law for port State power is the territorial principle that when a foreign ship is voluntarily in port it surrenders itself to the territorial sovereignty of the port State.[10] Customary international law and treaties acknowledge a port State's wide discretion in exercising jurisdiction over its ports, including denying access and establishing conditions for the entry of ports.[11] When regulating access to ports, port State jurisdiction is subject to the general principles such as non-discrimination, good faith and not abuse of right.[12] It is submitted that the port State may exercise both prescriptive and enforcement jurisdiction over the foreign ship voluntarily present within its port waters except matters that are prohibited by international law.[13]

The territorial principle would not cover the exercise of either prescriptive or enforcement jurisdiction in relation to activities by the foreign ship that occurred wholly outside the port State's territory, known as extraterritorial jurisdiction.[14] The port State needs to present a jurisdictional link to justify the exercise of exterritorial jurisdiction over such matters. These links could be based on an international treaty, the person involved in the activity (nationality principle), the interests of the port State affected (protective principle), or the nature of the activity (university principle).[15] The common element

9 UNCLOS, *supra* 3, Article 11.

10 C. Staker, 'Jurisdiction', in M.D. Evans, *International Law* (5th edition, Oxford, 2017), pp. 296–298.

11 UNCLOS, *supra* 3, Articles 25(2), 211(3) and 255. *Case concerning Military and Paramilitary Activities In and Against Nicaragua* (*Nicaragua v. United States of America*), 1986 I.C.J. Rep., at 111, para. 123. A.V. Lowe, 'The Right of Entry into Maritime Ports in International Law', 14 *San Diego Law Review*, 1977, 622. De La Fayette (1996), *supra* 6, 1–4.

12 UNCLOS, *supra* 3, Articles 25(3) and 227. H. Ringbom, *The EU Maritime Safety Policy and International Law* (Martinus Nijhoff, 2008), 253–228. R.R. Churchill and A.V. Lowe, *The Law of the Sea* (Manchester University Press, 1999), 63.

13 Churchill (2016), *supra* 5, 457–458.

14 Report of the International Law Commission (ILC), Fifty-eighth session (1 May-9 June and 3 July-11 August 2006), General Assembly Official Records Sixty-first Session Supplement No.10 (A/61/10), Annex V Extraterritorial Jurisdiction, 515–520.

15 E.J. Molenaar, 'Port State Jurisdiction – Toward Comprehensive, Mandatory and Global Coverage', 38 *Ocean Development and International Law*, 2007, 229. S. Kopela, 'Port-State Jurisdiction, Extraterritoriality, and the Protection of Global Commons', 47) *Ocean Development and International Law*, No. 2, 2016, 92.

among these links is that there is a valid interest of the port State in asserting its jurisdiction to the activity concerned.[16]

2.2 *Port State Jurisdiction under the Law of the Sea*

Jurisdiction derives from the concept of State sovereignty that a State has the competence to regulate the conduct of natural and jurisdiction persons through legislative, executive and juridical measures.[17] Jurisdiction consists of two essential components, prescriptive jurisdiction and enforcement jurisdiction. Prescriptive jurisdiction refers to the legislative action by the State to lay down the regulative framework for activities and persons under its jurisdiction, including transforming applicable international law into domestic law.[18] Enforcement jurisdiction is a State's competence to adopt reasonable measures to compel, induce compliance, or impose sanctions for noncompliance with applicable laws, regulations, or enforceable judgments by means of administrative or executive action or judicial proceedings.[19] The exercise of port State jurisdiction has to comply with the principle of good faith and non-abuse of rights, which also relate to issues of jurisdictional reasonableness, proportionality, and non-encroachment upon the rights of other States.[20]

Port State jurisdiction under UNCLOS can be grouped into four categories: establishing conditions for the entry of ports, exercising jurisdiction over activities occurring within ports, exercising port State control under international instruments, and exercising extraterritorial jurisdiction.[21] The port State needs to adopt domestic legislation, with the exception of auto-implementable international rules and standards, to exercise the enforcement jurisdiction. Enforcement measures could be both executive and juridical depending on the domestic legal system of the port State. For the purpose of this Chapter, it will focus on the jurisdiction over matters which occurred outside of port waters relating to the foreign vessel.

When establishing conditions for the entry of ports by foreign vessels, including requirements for the prevention, reduction and control of pollution of the marine environment, the port State should give due publicity to

---

16 ILC Report (2006), *supra* 14, 521–522.

17 J. Crawford, *Brownlie's Principles of Public International Law* (9th edition, Oxford, 2018), 440.

18 M.N. Shaw, *International Law* (8th edition, Cambridge, 2017), 486–489. Staker (2018), *supra* 10, 294–296.

19 Staker (2018), *supra* 10, 311–313. Crawford (2018), *supra* 17, 462.

20 UNCLOS, *supra* 3, Articles 227 and 300. Crawford (2018), *supra* 17, 468–469.

21 UNCLOS, *supra* 3, Articles 25(2), 38(2), 211(3) and 218.

such requirements and communicate them to the IMO.[22] Such conditions could include more stringent standards than international rules and regulations unless otherwise explicitly prohibited by an international agreement.[23] However, there are concerns over the unilaterality of individual port State measures going beyond the limit of international rules. In cases where such standards have a static nature that relates to the construction, design, equipment and manning of the ship, these standards have extraterritorial effects for they would be required in compliance throughout the ships' voyage beyond the port waters.[24] For example, the United States amended its Oil Pollution Act of 1990 to introduce the double hull requirements and phase-out the schedule for single hull tank vessels operating in its waters before such requirements became generally accepted international standards.[25] The consequence of unilateral port State requirements is that it increases the uncertainly of the scope of port State power and deprives international law of a clear elaboration and development of jurisdictional principles between territorial and extraterritorial jurisdiction.[26]

The port State may carry out what is commonly known as port State control to enforce internationally agreed shipping standards. Port State control was introduced in the International Convention for the Prevention of Pollution from Ships (MARPOL) with the intention to be a back up to flag State implementation and has been adopted in most of the technical conventions developed under the auspice of the IMO.[27] Under the international conventions that

---

22 UNCLOS, *supra* 3, Article 211(3).

23 Churchill (2016), *supra* 5, 457–458. The Agreement on Port State Measures to Prevent, Deter and Eliminate Illegal, Unreported and Unregulated Fishing, adopted 22 November 2009, in force 5 June 2016, Article 4(1)(b).

24 Churchill (2016), *supra* 3, 445–446.

25 National Research Council. 1998. Double-Hull Tanker Legislation: An Assessment of the Oil Pollution Act of 1990. Washington, DC: The National Academies Press. https://doi.org/10.17226/5798. IMO, Tanker safety – preventing accidental pollution, https://www.imo.org/en/OurWork/Safety/Pages/OilTankers.aspx. IMO, Construction Requirements for Oil Tankers – Double Hulls, https://www.imo.org/en/OurWork/Environment/Pages/constructionrequirements.aspx.

26 Kopela (2016), *supra* 15, 92–95 and 105–106.

27 International Convention for the Prevention of Pollution from Ships, 1973, as modified by the Protocol of 1978 relating thereto and by the Protocol of 1997 (MARPOL), entered into force on 2 October 1983. IMO, Resolution A.1138(31), adopted on 4 December 2019, Procedures for Port State Control, 2019, Section 1.4, 'SOLAS 1974 regulations I/19, IX/6.2, XI-1/4 and XI-2/9, as modified by SOLAS PROT 1988; article 21 of LL 1966, as modified by LL PROT 1988; articles 5 and 6, regulation 11 of Annex I, regulation 16.9 of Annex II, regulation 9 of Annex III, regulation 14 of Annex IV, regulation 9 of Annex V and regulation 10 of Annex VI of MARPOL; article X of STCW 1978; article 12 of TONNAGE 1969, article 11

set out detailed regulations of seagoing vessels, most importantly MARPOL for pollution regulations, port States will enforce these treaties to which they are party on all foreign ships regardless of whether or not the visiting vessel's flag State is also a party.[28] Under MARPOL, port State control is limited to verifying that the visiting ship is carrying a valid certificate, and to verifying whether the ship has discharged any harmful substances in violation of the regulations.[29] In cases of a violation, the port State is required to forward the report to the flag State administration, and the requesting State when responding to a request for an investigation of discharge violations, for any appropriate action except to prevent the ship from proceeding to sea if it presents an unreasonable threat of harm to the marine environment.[30] Port State control has proven to be effective in supplementing flag State implementation and eliminating substandard shipping, especially when the procedures and standards are coordinated on both international and regional levels.[31] Furthermore, the limited enforcement measures that a port State can take under these international conventions should not be considered as restricting its power to take measures within its jurisdiction and under other rules of international law.[32]

The truly extraterritorial jurisdiction exercisable by a port State relates to vessel behavior occurring beyond its own maritime zones – on the high seas or in the maritime zones of other States. The port State may undertake investigation and, with sufficient evidence, institute proceedings in respect of any discharge from a vessel outside its maritime zones in violation of applicable international rules and standards established through the IMO or general diplomatic conference.[33] Where such violation occurred within the maritime zone of another State, the port State may only initiate proceedings over the

---

of AFS 2001 and article 9 of BWM 2004 provide for control procedures to be followed by a Party to a relevant convention with regard to foreign ships visiting their ports.'

28 B. Marten, 'Port State Jurisdiction, International Conventions, and Extraterritoriality: An Expansive Interpretation', in H. Ringbom (ed), *Jurisdiction over Ships – Post-UNCLOS Developments in the Law of the Sea* (Brill, 2015), pp. 117–118. MARPOL, *supra* 27, Article 5(4). IMO, Resolution A.1138(31), adopted on 4 December 2019, Procedures for Port State Control, 2019, Section 2.1.

29 MARPOL, *supra* 27, Articles 5(2) and 6(2).

30 MARPOL, *supra* 27, Articles 5(2), 6(2) and (5). Memorandum of Understanding on Port State Control in the Asia-Pacific Region (Tokyo MoU) Section 4.3, http://www.tokyo-mou.org/organization/memorandum_of_understanding.php.

31 IMO, Port State Control, https://www.imo.org/en/OurWork/IIIS/Pages/Port%20State%20Control.aspx. E. Molenaar, *Coastal State Jurisdiction and Vessel-Source Pollution* (Kluwer Law International, The Hague: 1998) 125–131.

32 MARPOL, *supra* 27, Article 9(2). Tokyo MoU, *supra* 30, Section 3.2.2.

33 UNCLOS, *supra* 3, Article 218(1).

foreign ship when requested by the flag State, or the State that is affected by the violation, or when its maritime zones are threated or damaged.[34] When adopted, Article 218 of UNCLOS was considered to be truly innovative given that it goes beyond any existing general basis for justification in international law and was appraised as a progressive development of international law.[35]

It must be acknowledged that the port State enforcement jurisdiction authorised by Article 218 of UNCLOS has not been widely used except as the legal basis for the port State control measures developed by maritime conventions under the auspice of the IMO.[36] Article 218 uses the verb 'may' instead of a more stringent 'shall' to define the port State enforcement jurisdiction, except in the case where the port State is requested to intervene by an affected State or the flag State. Whenever the verb 'may' is used, a port State has discretionary powers to choose whether or not to undertake investigations or institute legal proceedings against a foreign vessel committing a discharge violation.[37] In practice, the port State may lack the political and economic interests to initiative legal proceedings for a violation that derives no immediate benefit but potential prolonged port time of the alleged vessels. In addition, if a port State is too stringent in enforcing extraterritorial jurisdiction, it may become less competitive among neighbouring ports and suffer from a loss of revenue for less port calls from foreign vessels.

With the growing demand to protect the global commons, particularly the marine environment, port State jurisdiction has the potential to further support regulating activities taking place extraterritorially that harm the marine environment.[38] In the context of international shipping in the Arctic waters, the East Asian port States have the legal, political and geographical basis to

34 UNCLOS, *supra* 3, Article 218(2).

35 M.H. Nordquist, N.R. Grandy, S. Rosenne, and A. Yankov (eds), *United Nations Convention on the Law of the Sea 1982: A Commentary, Volume IV*, (Brill, 1990), 260. T.L. McDorman, 'Port State Enforcement: A Comment on Article 218 of the 1982 Law of the Sea Convention', 28 *Journal of Maritime Law and Commerce*, No. 2, 1997, 321. H.S. Bang, 'Port State Jurisdiction and Article 218 of the UN Convention on the Law of the Sea', 40 *Journal of Maritime Law and Commerce*, No. 2, 2009, 298. Molenaar (2007), *supra* 15, 236.

36 IMO, *supra 31*, Port State Control. IMO, LEG/MISC.8, 30 January 2014, Implications of the United Nations Convention on the Law of the Sea for the International Maritime Organization, 58 and 66.

37 T. Keselj, 'Port State Jurisdiction in Respect of Pollution from Ships: the 1982 United Nations Convention on the Law of the Sea and the Memoranda of Understanding', 30 *Ocean Development and International Law*, 1999, 140.

38 C. Ryngaert, *Jurisdiction in International Law* (2nd edition, Oxford, 2015), 186–187. P. Sands and J. Peel, *Principles of International Environmental Law* (3rd edition, Cambridge, 2012), 193.

play an important role in enforcing international rules and standards for ships calling at their ports.

3 Making a Case for the East Asian Port States

3.1 *Regulating Vessel-Source Pollution in the Arctic*

According to the 2019 Special Report on the Ocean and Cryosphere in a Changing Climate published by the Intergovernmental Panel on Climate Change (IPCC), Arctic sea ice has considerably shrunk in the past 30 years, and by the middle of this century, the Arctic Ocean is expected to be almost ice-free during its minimum sea ice season.[39] Simultaneously with a decreasing sea ice cover in the Arctic region, an increase in ship traffic has been experienced in these waters, particularly through the Northern Sea Route (NSR) connecting Asia and Europe.[40] The increased presence of international shipping means a higher probability of accidents and incidents involving various pollutants that might damage the pristine Arctic marine environment.[41]

The regulation of vessel-source pollution in the Arctic follows the jurisdictional framework laid down by UNCLOS. States are expected to establish, through IMO and general diplomatic conference, international rules and standards to prevent, reduce and control pollution of the marine environment from vessels.[42] The flag State has the primary responsibility to ensure that vessels flying its flag comply with, at the minimum, applicable international rules and standards, with supplementary concurrent jurisdiction by coastal and port States under recognised circumstances.[43]

---

39 M. Meredith,, M. Sommerkorn, S. Cassotta, C. Derksen, A. Ekaykin, A. Hollowed, G. Kofinas, A. Mackintosh, J. Melbourne-Thomas, M.M.C. Muelbert, G. Ottersen, H. Pritchard, and E.A.G. Schuur, 2019: Polar Regions. In: *IPCC Special Report on the Ocean and Cryosphere in a Changing Climate* [H.-O. Pörtner, D.C. Roberts, V. Masson-Delmotte, P. Zhai, M. Tignor, E. Poloczanska, K. Mintenbeck, A. Alegría, M. Nicolai, A. Okem, J. Petzold, B. Rama, N.M. Weyer (eds.)], 212–214 and 222–223.

40 J.J. Solski, 'The Northern Sea Route in the 2010s: Development and Implementation of Relevant Law', 11 *Arctic Review on Law and Politics*, 2020, 383–384. Gunnarsson (2021), *supra* 1, 104369. Arctic Council Working Group on the Protection of the Arctic Marine Environment (PAME), 'Arctic Shipping Status Reports: The Increase in Arctic Shipping: 2013–2019', https://www.pame.is/projects-new/arctic-shipping/pame-shipping-highlights/411-arctic-shipping-status-reports.

41 PAME, 'Compendium of Arctic Ship Accidents (CASA)', Final Report (May 2021), https://www.pame.is/projects-new/arctic-shipping/pame-shipping-highlights/457-compendium-of-arctic-ship-accidents.

42 UNCLOS, *supra* 3, Article 211(1).

43 UNCLOS, *supra* 3, Articles 217–220.

The jurisdictional framework of vessel-source pollution has been supplemented by international rules and standards developed under the auspice of the IMO, as the competent international organization for international shipping.[44] States have adopted numerous international conventions to address a wide range of issues relating to the prevention, reduction and control of vessel-source pollution, among which the most comprehensive one is MARPOL and its six Annexes.[45] In 2017, a *lex specialis* set of rules, the International Code for Ships Operating in Polar Waters (Polar Code) developed under the auspice of the IMO, entered into force.[46] The Polar Code covers the whole range of vessels' design, operation, equipment, manning and environmental protection matters relevant to vessels operating in the inhospitable polar regions.[47] It was made mandatory through amendments to the International Convention for the Safety of Life at Sea (SOLAS), MARPOL, and the International Convention on Standards of Training, Certification and Watchkeeping for Seafarers (STCW) and its related STCW Code.[48]

The enforcement of the Polar Code, and relevant amendments to MARPOL relating to discharge regulations, follow the jurisdictional framework established in UNCLOS. The port States, both within the Arctic region and beyond, have the right to verify whether the ship has on board a valid Polar Ship Certificate, and initiate proceedings against discharge violations of the Polar Code. The faithful performance and diligent implementation by relevant port States can become an auxiliary means of effecting compliance with the Polar Code.[49]

---

44 IMO, LEG/MISC.8, 30 January 2014, Implications of the United Nations Convention on the Law of the Sea for the International Maritime Organization, *supra* 36, 7–8.

45 IMO, List of IMO Conventions, https://www.imo.org/en/About/Conventions/Pages/ListOfConventions.aspx.

46 IMO, MEPC 68/21/Add.1, 5 June 2015, Report of the Marine Environment Protection Committee on Its Sixty-Eighth Session, Annex 10, International Code for Ships Operating in Polar Waters (Polar Code).

47 Z. Sun and R. Beckman, 'The Development of the Polar Code and Challenges to Its Implementation', in K. Zou (eds), *Global Commons and the Law of the Sea* (Brill, 2018), 303–325.

48 IMO, Shipping in Polar Waters, https://www.imo.org/en/MediaCentre/HotTopics/Pages/Polar-default.aspx.

49 E. Engtrø, O.T. Gudmestad and O. Njå, 'Implementation of the Polar Code: Functional Requirements Regulating Ship Operations in Polar Waters', 11 *Arctic Review on Law and Politics*, 2020, 63.

3.2 *The Positioning of East Asian Port States*

Ports are the crucial connection of ocean-land-interface for being the departing and destination points of any international voyage. Given this strategic connection, port authorities, as proven, are important actors in ensuring the enforcement and compliance of international regulation of shipping. The three East Asian port States, China, Japan, and the Republic of Korea, have the strategic advantage and legal power to exercise port State jurisdiction over vessels engaged in voyages through the Arctic waters. In addition, as major maritime countries in terms of ship registration and the shipping industries, they all have demonstrated strong political and economic interest in engaging in Arctic affairs and cooperating with the eight Arctic States.

Major ports in the three East Asian States are the windows of the Asian market to both Europe and the North America. To take the NSR for example, there were 378 transit voyages between 2010 and 2020 including both international transit (203 voyages) and transit traffic between Russian ports (175).[50] In 2020, among the 64 transit voyages of NSR, 11 had one of the three East Asian States as departure ports, and 22 as destination ports. Among the 33 vessels which called at those Asian ports before and after the NSR voyages, 20 were foreign flagged vessels other than the port State.[51]

All three East Asian States have shown political commitment to engage in Arctic affairs by becoming Observers to the Arctic Council in 2013 and maintaining their memberships through continuing support to its work.[52] One of the fundamental mandates for the establishment of the Arctic Council is to 'provide a means for promoting cooperation, coordination and interaction among the Arctic States, with the involvement of the Arctic indigenous communities and other Arctic inhabitants on common Arctic issues, in particular issues of sustainable development and environmental protection in the Arctic'.[53] The Republic of Korea, Japan and China all published an Arctic Policy in 2013, 2015 and 2018 respectively.[54] It can be observed that all three States

---

50 CHNL Information Office Information, 'Analysis of Shipping traffic in the NSR waters in 2020', 28 August 2021, https://arctic-lio.com/analysys-of-shipping-traffic-in-the-nsr-waters-in-2020/.

51 Ibid.

52 Arctic Council, Observers, https://arctic-council.org/about/observers/. Arctic Council, 'Compilation of Observer Regular Reports 2019–2020', https://oaarchive.arctic-council.org/.

53 Declaration on the Establishment of the Arctic Council (Ottawa Declaration), Ottawa, Canada, 19 September 1996, Article 1(a).

54 Arctic Policy of the Republic of Korea, http://library.arcticportal.org/1902/1/Arctic_Policy_of_the_Republic_of_Korea.pdf. Japan's Arctic Policy, The Headquarters for Ocean Policy, 16 October 2015, https://www8.cao.go.jp/ocean/english/arctic/pdf/japans_ap_e.pdf.

have committed to promote the protection of the Arctic environment, the sustainable development of the Arctic sea routes and other economic activities, and enhance international cooperation with the Arctic States and other stakeholders.[55]

It has been demonstrated beyond doubt that the pristine Arctic marine environment is very vulnerable to vessel source pollution and requires dedicated protection measures.[56] It could be argued that the three East Asian States could play a more effective role in ensuring compliance of the Polar Code and punish non-compliance occurring during voyages through Arctic waters. In particular, they could exercise enforcement jurisdiction as authorised in Article 218 of UNCLOS to respond to requests from Arctic coastal States to initiate proceedings against discharge violations which occurred within their maritime zones, and initiate proceedings of discharge violations of applicable international rules and standards that occurred on the high seas.

If all three States could take the same position on their port State enforcement jurisdiction, they could establish a safety net at one end of the Arctic shipping routes to prevent substandard ships from entering the Arctic region, and catch the potential perpetrators that have violated the applicable international rules and standards during a transit in Arctic waters. Their collective positions would also ensure that none of their ports would lose a competitive standing because of a stringent enforcement jurisdiction to enforce pollution regulations. The next section will look at the specific matters on how these three States could exercise the extraterritorial enforcement jurisdiction over foreign ships that have committed a violation during a voyage through the Arctic waters.

China's Arctic Policy, The State Council Information Office of the People's Republic of China (中国的北极政策，中华人民共和国国务院新闻办公室), 26 January 2018, http://www.scio.gov.cn/zfbps/32832/Document/1618203/1618203.htm.

55 Ibid. A. Tonami, 'Arctic Policies of Japan, South Korea, and Singapore' and A.M. Brady, 'China's Undeclared Arctic Foreign Policy', in Polar Initiative Policy Brief Series, *Arctic 2014: Who Gets a Voice and Why It Matters* (Wilson Center, 2014), https://www.wilsoncenter.org/publication-series/arctic-2014-who-gets-voice-and-why-it-matters. D. Jin, W.S. Seo and S.K. Lee, 'Arctic Policy of the Republic of Korea', 22 *Ocean & Coastal L.J.*, 2017, 85 -96. A. Moe, 'Asian Countries and Arctic Shipping: Policies, Interests and Footprints on Governance', 10 *Arctic Review on Law and Politics*, 2019, 24–52.

56 Arctic Council, Arctic Marine Shipping Assessment 2009 Report, https://oaarchive.arctic-council.org/handle/11374/54. PAME Work Plan 2021–2023, May 2021, https://pame.is/pame-work-plan.

3.3 *Potential Extraterritorial Enforcement Jurisdiction Matters*

3.3.1 Applicable International Rules and Standards

Under international law, 'the internationally valid exercise of prescriptive jurisdiction in the adoption of a law is a prerequisite for the valid exercise of adjudicative or enforcement jurisdiction with respect to that law'.[57] With respect to the extraterritorial enforcement jurisdiction as envisioned in Article 218, the port State would have adopted, according to its domestic legal system, laws that conform to and give effect to 'applicable international rules and standards' established through the IMO or general diplomatic conference. However, UNCLOS does not give a port State an explicit power to adopt such legislation. Presumably, the prescriptive jurisdiction of the port State must be implicit in Article 218 as otherwise the enforcement jurisdiction would be rendered inoperative.[58] Such implicit prescriptive jurisdiction would clearly be extraterritorial in nature. It is based on the authorization of UNCLOS and includes elements that go beyond any of the traditional customary international law bases of extraterritorial jurisdiction such as links with nationality and effects of the activity.

It must be acknowledged that the phrase 'applicable international rules and standards' as applied in Article 218, as well as Articles 219 and 220, remain to be clarified. There are two distinctions could be made to interpret this phrase. First, it is different from 'particular requirements for the prevention, reduction and control of pollution' in Article 211(3) that refer to domestic legislation for violations which occurred within the port State's port, internal and territorial waters.[59] The port State jurisdiction under Article 211(3) is based on the territorial principle whereby it is not limited to conforming to international rules and standards. Secondly, it is different from the term 'generally accepted international rules and standards' in Article 211(2) and (5) when referring to both flag State (as a minimum requirement) and coastal State prescriptive jurisdiction (as a maximum requirement) over vessel-source pollution. The term 'generally accepted' is not limited to customary international law or binding instruments between the relevant parties, but also those are of non-binding nature but would acquire such status if they were followed in state practice.[60]

The word 'applicable' has a narrower connotation. It intends to limit the exercise of the enforcement jurisdiction to the body of international rules and

57 ILC Report (2006), *supra* 14, 518.
58 Churchill (2016), *supra* 5, 463.
59 McDorman (1997), *supra* 35, 315.
60 International Law Association London Conference (2000), Committee on Coastal State Jurisdiction Relating to Marine Pollution, Final Report, 33–39.

standards that are accepted by the parties involved in the enforcement case.[61] As the delegate of India stated, during the conference that led to the adoption of the 1986 Convention on the Conditions for Registration of Ships, that 'the words applicable international rules and standards, whenever they appear in the text cover only those specific conventions, treaties and protocols to which India is a contracting party. Therefore India would not be able to accept under the proposed convention any other obligation which it had not specifically contracted'.[62] Hence, the port State, under the authorization of Article 218, can only enforce those discharge-related international rules and standards that they have accepted against vessels from States that have also accepted the same international rules and standards.[63]

The source of 'applicable international rules and standards' is the treaties that have been developed by States under the auspice of IMO, as the competent international organization, or general diplomatic conference. Given that the violation defined under Article 218 is limited to 'any discharge' from a vessel, the commonly accepted international rules and standards are those included in MARPOL.[64] Under MARPOL, discharge, 'in relation to harmful substances or effluents containing such substances, means any release howsoever caused from a ship and includes any escape, disposal, spilling, leaking, pumping, emitting or emptying'.[65] It includes both operational and accidental discharges, and discharges into both the water and the atmosphere.

How the port State would adopt these 'applicable international rules and standards' as a legal basis for exercising its enforcement jurisdiction depends on its domestic legal system.[66] China, for example, has adopted a mixed approach to implement the international treaties that it has become a party whereby for most private or civil law matters the treaty provisions can be automatically incorporated into the domestic legal system.[67] For the international

61 Ibid., 41.

62 Report issued during the third session of October 18, 1985, during the Conference for the United Nation's Convention on Conditions for Registration of Ships (UNCCORS), Doc. TD/RS/CONF/19 (1985), 7.

63 McDorman (1997), *supra* 35, 319.

64 DOALOS, Office of Legal Affairs, *The Law of the Sea: Obligations of State Parties under the United Nations Convention on the Law of the Sea and Complementary Instruments* (United Nations, 2004), 54.

65 MARPOL, *supra* 27, Article 2(3)(a).

66 Nordquist, Grandy, Rosenne, and Yankov (1990), *supra* 35, 272.

67 J.T. Xu, 'Several Issues on the Domestic Application of International Treaty', 3 *Chinese Review of International Law*, 2014, 78–79. (徐锦堂，"关于国际条约国内适用的几个问题"，《国际法研究》，2014年第3期，69–79，78–79。).

environmental treaties that China has ratified, the international treaty shall prevail over the domestic law except when in case of a conflict China had expressed reservations.[68] Currently, the Chinese Marine Environment Protection Law only explicitly implements some elements of Article 218 based on the effect principle that applies to violations which occurred beyond its maritime zone but nevertheless polluted its marine environment.[69] It does not deal with discharges that occurred outside of its maritime zones that did not affect the marine environment under the Chinese jurisdiction. In theory, under the authorization of Article 218, a Chinese court would be able to institute judicial proceedings against a foreign vessel for discharge violations of MARPOL outside of its maritime zones regardless of whether its marine environment has been affected.

3.3.2 Instituting Proceedings

The port State may undertake investigations and, where the evidence so warrants, institute proceedings to exercise the extraterritorial enforcement jurisdiction authorized under Article 218. The port State may institute either administrative or judicial proceedings over the foreign vessel, depending on where the violation occurred, upon its own initiative or by request of another State.

The port State may take initiative under two scenarios. The first one is when the discharge violation occurred outside the maritime zone of another State – as on the high seas – regardless of whether such violation affected the port State.[70] The second one is when the discharge violation, occurred either within the maritime zone of another State or on the high seas, has 'caused or is likely to cause pollution in the internal waters, territorial sea or exclusive economic zone' of the port State.[71]

The port State may institute proceedings in response to a request by a coastal State, an affected State, or the flag State over discharge violation by a foreign vessel that has no direct consequence to its marine environment. A coastal State, when aware of a discharge violation that occurred within its internal waters, territorial sea or exclusive economic zone, may request the port State to institute proceedings against the alleged foreign vessel that is voluntarily

68 Marine Environment Protection Law of the People's Republic of China, adopted on 23 August 1982, third amendment adopted on 4 November 2017, Article 96. (中华人民共和国海洋环境保护法（修订），1982年8月23日通过，2017年11月4日第三次修正，第九十六条。).

69 Ibid., Article 2.

70 UNCLOS, *supra* 3, Article 218(1).

71 UNCLOS, *supra* 3, Article 218(2).

within its port.[72] A State that is 'damaged or threatened by the discharge violation' which occurred within the maritime zone of another State, may request the port State which the foreign vessel has entered to take enforcement measures.[73] Finally, the flag State may request the port State to investigate a violation by a vessel that is flying its flag, irrespective of where the violation occurred.[74]

The port State may initiate 'proceedings in a court of law, or in some other type of tribunal, or proceedings of an administrative character' according to its domestic legal system against the foreign vessel should the evidence so warrant.[75] Take Chinese law for example. The Marine Environment Protection Law states that any person, both natural and legal, who violated the discharge regulations is subject to administrative punishment of revoking operational licence and monetary fines among others.[76] Moreover, when the discharge violation has caused major damage to the marine environment and the marine ecosystem, the person is subject to criminal responsibilities.[77] The Chinese Marine Environment Protection Law applies to its internal waters, the contiguous zone, the exclusive economic zone, the continental shelf and other maritime areas subject to the Chinese jurisdiction, but the Criminal Law refers to environment in general without explicitly identifying the marine environment.[78] It is not clear whether the criminal proceedings could be applied for violations which occurred beyond its territorial sea since there has not been any judicial cases brought before a Chinese court.

It could be presumed that, when sending the request, the requesting State would provide the port State with 'evidence' and the legal basis of the discharge violation. It is worth noting that, given the structure of Article 218 whereby paragraph 2 is conditioned on paragraph 1, there are two potential gaps. First, the port State cannot institute proceedings against violations that occurred within the maritime zone of another State unless requested. It is not clear

72 UNCLOS, *supra* 3, Article 218(2).

73 UNCLOS, *supra* 3, Article 218(2).

74 UNCLOS, *supra* 3, Article 218(3).

75 Nordquist, Grandy, Rosenne, and Yankov (1990), *supra* 35, 358.

76 Marine Environment Protection Law of the People's Republic of China, *supra* 68, Articles 73, 76 and 90.

77 Marine Environment Protection Law of the People's Republic of China, *supra* 68, Article 90. Criminal Law of the People's Republic of China, adopted on 1 July 1979, eleventh amendment adopted on 12 December 2020, Article 338. （中华人民共和国刑法，1979年7月1日通过，2020年12月26日修正案(十一)修正，第三百三十八条。).

78 Marine Environment Protection Law of the People's Republic of China, *supra* 68, Article 2.

what measures the port State could take if it uncovered such violation during a routine investigation. The port State could transmit the discovery to the flag State to take action and arguably to the affected State so it could consider issuing a request for action. Secondly, the requesting State could not request the port State to institute proceedings in respect of a discharge violation of their domestic law that exceeded the applicable international rules and standards. There would be a legal gap when the flag State adopted more stringent discharge standards than MARPOL.

The port State is obliged, 'as far as practicable', to comply with all three types of requests for investigation of the alleged discharge violation.[79] This framework could be applied to international shipping in the Arctic. For example, the port authorities in the three East Asian countries could establish a cooperative mechanism with the Arctic coastal States whereby they could adopt a designated procedure to handle requests for investigation of discharge violation of MARPOL occurring within Arctic waters. Moreover, if the port authority uncovered any discharge violation occurred within the maritime zone of an Arctic coastal State, it could communicate more efficiently with the coastal State if the latter would request the port State to undertake further actions. In addition, should the three East Asian countries be so committed to protect the high seas in the Arctic, they could initiate proceedings against any discharge violation by a foreign vessel that is voluntarily in port irrespective of whether its maritime zones have been affected.

3.3.3 Safeguards

The exercise of port State extraterritorial enforcement jurisdiction is subject to a number of safeguards as required by UNCLOS to ensure that the exercise of jurisdiction is reasonable and clearly reflects a legitimate balancing of conflicting interests, which is an integral part of jurisdictional assertions. These safeguards include procedure requirements to facilitate proceedings, a hierarchy of conflicting jurisdiction, duties to exercise jurisdiction in a reasonable and proportional manner, and obligations to assume liability when rights were unduly exercised. They can be grouped into two categories based on the subject of these safeguards, towards the foreign vessel and other relevant States.

The first group of safeguard measures are designed for actions against the foreign vessel. The port State is first required not to discriminate in form or in fact against vessels of any other State, and the exercise of powers of enforcement against foreign vessels should only be undertaken by designated officials

79 UNCLOS, *supra* 3, Article 218(3).

as being authorized to that effect.[80] The port State is further required to avoid adverse consequences to the vessel in the exercise of the powers of enforcement and to avoid undue delay of the vessel when conducting investigations.[81] When an investigation reveals a violation of applicable international rules and standards, the port State should promptly release the vessel subject to reasonable procedures such as the posting of bonding or other appropriate financial security.[82] The port State may impose monetary penalties to discharge violations of applicable international rules and standards committed by foreign vessels beyond the territorial sea.[83] Such penalty may only be imposed within three years from the date on which the violation was committed, and has not been instituted by another State.[84] When the port State, during the exercise of enforcement powers, has taken measures that are 'unlawful or exceed those reasonably required in the light of available information', it should be liable for damage or loss to the foreign vessel.[85]

The second group of safeguard measures are designed to establish a balance of rights and duties among States for their respective role in regulating vessel-source pollution. The port State is obliged to promptly notify the flag State and the requesting State of any measures taken against the foreign vessel and submit to the flag State any official reports concerning such measures.[86] With respect to the requesting State, both the coastal State or the affected State may also request the port State to transmit the records of the investigation.[87] The coastal State is further entitled to request the port State to suspend any proceedings instituted against the foreign vessel that committed a discharge violation within its internal waters, territorial sea or exclusive economic zone.[88] With respect to the flag State, it may institute proceedings against a vessel flying its flag regarding any violation of applicable international rules and standards irrespective of where the violation occurred.[89] If the flag State institutes such proceedings within six months of the date on which proceedings were instituted by the port State in respect of corresponding charges, it

80 UNCLOS, *supra* 3, Articles 224 and 227.
81 UNCLOS, *supra* 3, Articles 225 and 226(1)(a).
82 UNCLOS, *supra* 3, Article 226(1)(b).
83 UNCLOS, *supra* 3, Article 230(1).
84 UNCLOS, *supra* 3, Article 228(2).
85 UNCLOS, *supra* 3, Article 232.
86 UNCLOS, *supra* 3, Article 231.
87 UNCLOS, *supra* 3, Article 218(4).
88 UNCLOS, *supra* 3, Article 218(4).
89 UNCLOS, *supra* 3, Article 217(1).

has the effect to suspend the port State's proceedings.[90] The effect of suspension would not apply when the alleged violation caused 'major damage' to the port State, and when the flag State 'has repeatedly disregarded its obligation to enforce effectively the applicable international rules and standards in respect of violations committed by its vessels'.[91]

International jurisdictional principles are developed on the basis of the ascertainment of jurisdictional links and the balance of conflicting interests. In the context of the port State's extraterritorial enforcement jurisdiction under Article 218, the need of balancing of rights, reasonableness and legitimacy determine the scope of the exercise of enforcement powers and ensure that safeguards exist and are taken into account to prevent undue encroachments upon recognised rights of the accused and States' sovereignty. The encroachment upon the interests of the flag State created by the extraterritorial enforcement jurisdiction of the port State could be justified by the international community's collective interest to protect and preserve the marine environment from vessel-source pollution, particularly in areas of high ecosystem value such as the Arctic. The flag State's interest in this sense has been absorbed rather than been side-lined for the protection of global interests.

4 Conclusion

This chapter presents a case for the three East Asian States to exercise enforcement powers over discharge violations of applicable international rules and standards committed by foreign vessels during a journey in Arctic waters, either within the internal waters, territorial sea, or exclusive economic zone of a coastal State or on the high seas. This extraterritorial enforcement jurisdiction by the port State would supplement the traditional enforcement jurisdiction of the flag State over pollution discharges that can have detrimental effects over the pristine Artic marine environment.

There is a legal basis under UNCLOS for the port State to exercise such extraterritorial enforcement jurisdiction to address discharge violations of applicable international rules and standards. The exercise of such enforcement powers is subject to detailed safeguard measures and requirements to balance rights and obligations between the port State and the accused, as well as between the port State and other concerned States. Moreover, the three East Asian States

90 UNCLOS, *supra* 3, Article 228(1).
91 UNCLOS, *supra* 3, Article 228(1).

have demonstrated political commitment and have economic interests in further engaging in Arctic affairs, including the protection and preservation of the Arctic marine environment and the sustainable development of the Arctic region.

The three East Asian States could take advantage of all the possible jurisdictional options in international law including the exercise of port State extraterritorial enforcement jurisdiction as acknowledged in UNCLOS to ensure compliance with applicable international rules and standards in Arctic shipping. The three States could adopt the same position to assume such extraterritorial enforcement jurisdiction and coordinate their approaches and procedures through the existing platforms including the Tokyo memorandum of understanding on port State control (Tokyo MoU). The effectiveness of such port State enforcement jurisdiction could be further pursued by the collaboration of the Arctic coastal State and the East Asian port States. This could be done through projects undertaken by the working groups of the Arctic Council, or through bilateral arrangement among individual States.

Given the importance of the protection and preservation of the Arctic marine environment, it would be a missed opportunity if States do not utilise all potential channels to implement applicable international rules and standards developed for such purpose. The important element of utilising port State extraterritorial enforcement jurisdiction is to establish a balance that reflects an international consensus with respect to the protection of the Arctic marine environment in line with multilateral instruments and cooperative processes. The aim of the port State jurisdiction should be to enhance the efficiency of the adopted applicable international rules and standards and to create incentives to international cooperation under the same principle of common concern.

PART 4

East China Sea Maritime Boundaries

CHAPTER 19

The Quest for a Win-Win Solution in the Delimitation of Continental Shelf in the East China Sea: An Irreconcilable Conflict between China and Japan?

Hironobu Sakai

1 Introduction

This chapter aims to sort out the issues of maritime boundary delimitation between China and Japan in the East China Sea in accordance with recent international case law on maritime boundary delimitation and to explore the possibilities of a solution which may be acceptable to both states. First, I would like to present a brief outline of the continental shelf delimitation dispute between China and Japan in the East China Sea, including each states' claims on the maritime boundary delimitation. Then, I will deal with some important issues regarding those claims from the viewpoint of international law, in particular, of the case law on maritime boundary delimitation, and finally I would suggest some requirements to normalize the relationship between China and Japan in the East China Sea.

2 Claims to the Continental Shelf by the States Concerned in the East China Sea

2.1 *Geographical and Geomorphological Features of the East China Sea*

The East China Sea is a semi-enclosed sea, with an estimated area of 300,000 square kilometer, bounded by China and Taiwan Island to the west and south, the Korean Peninsula to the north and Japan's Ryukyu islands to the east.[1] The width of this body of water varies from 180 nautical miles at its narrowest

1 The overview of the East China Sea, see, U.S. Energy Information Administration, "East China Sea". Available at https://www.eia.gov/international/analysis/regions-of-interest/East_China_Sea.

points to 360 nautical miles at its widest.[2] The seabed terrain of the East China Sea consists of a broad continental shelf and a steep geological depression, which is known as the Okinawa Trough, alongside the Ryukyu islands chain.[3] The Trough's legal status prevails in the arguments with regard to China's claim to an extended continental shelf in the East China Sea and its delimitation in relation to Japan. It is because there is no agreement on the extent to which this geological characteristic may give some influence on the drawing of the maritime boundary. The area which divides the two states is less than 400 nautical miles.[4]

Thus, the East China Sea dispute on the continental shelf between China and Japan is related to the delimitation situation, in which two states are separated by less than 400 nautical miles of water. Furthermore, the geological and the geomorphological features of the seabed make it possible for one of two states to claim an entitlement to a continental shelf extending more than 200 nautical miles from the baseline of its own coast.

2.2 *Maritime Claims to the Continental Shelf in East China Sea*

2.2.1 China's Claims

China has claimed that its sovereign right covers the shelf extending to the Okinawa Trough, based on the natural prolongation theory.[5] In practice, China operates an offshore platform to exploit an oil and gas field in a full-fledged way at a Chinese-side point 45 kilometers from the median line. That is to say, China sees waters between the median line and the Okinawa Trough as subject to the bilateral dispute, and has demanded that the two states conduct joint development in waters east of the median line.[6] China also seems to stick only

2 Thomas J. Schoenbaum, "Finding Solutions to the Disputes between China and Japan", in *idem* (ed.), *Peace in Northeast Asia. Resolving Japan's Territorial and Maritime Disputes with China, Korea and the Russian Federation* (Edward Elgar, 2008), p. 91.

3 Jianjun Gao, "The Okinawa Trough Issue in the Continental Shelf Delimitation Dispute within the East China Sea", *Chinese Journal of International Law*, Vol.9 (2010), p. 145.

4 Constantinos Yiallourides, *Maritime Disputes and International Law. Disputed Waters and Seabed Resources in Asia and Europe* (Routledge, 2019), p. 94.

5 Haiwen Zhang, "Legal Issues concerning the East China Sea Delimitation – A Chinese Perspective on the Sino-Japanese the East China Sea Dispute – ", *Japanese Yearbook of International Law*, Vol.51 (2008), pp. 125–126. For China's legal position on the continental shelf in general, see, *Working Paper submitted by the Chinese Delegation: Sea Area within the Limits of National Jurisdiction*, UN Doc.A/AC.138/SC.II/L.34, *Report of the Committee on the Peaceful Uses of the Sea-Bed and the Ocean Floor beyond the Limits of National Jurisdiction, Volume III*, GAOR, 28th Session, Supplement No.21 (A/9021), p. 74.

6 It is reported, nevertheless, that in its efforts to develop the offshore oil since 1980, China has limited its exploration and exploitation mainly to its side of the Chinese-Japanese

to the continental shelf delimitation but not the Exclusive Economic Zone (EEZ) delimitation. It is sure that China should avoid a single maritime boundary for a continental shelf and an EEZ,[7] which could be generally based on the equidistant/median line and subjected to coordination to reflect the equitable principle as necessary. This would be a delimitation method to the disadvantage of China's claim.[8]

2.2.2 Japan's Claims

Japan, in contrast, has rejected the applicability of the natural prolongation theory to the maritime delimitation in this area. Japan's position is that under international maritime delimitation law, natural prolongation has no role to play in maritime boundary delimitation where the distance between the coasts of two opposite states is less than 400 nautical miles. Japan, instead, has asserted its claim to a continental shelf extending to a distance of 200 nautical miles from its coastal baseline. Therefore, Japan asserts that the median line between the two states should be the basis for delimiting the boundary, because the distance is less than 400 nautical miles between China and Japan in the East China Sea. Thus, Japan grounds its continental shelf claim on the distance criteria, provided in Article 76 (1) of the United Nations Convention on the Law of the Sea (UNCLOS). To be specific, Japan's position rests on the distance from the relevant coasts irrespective of any geological or geomorphological considerations.[9]

---

equidistance line in consideration of the lack of agreement achieved between the two states. See, Junwu Pan, "Way Out: The Possibility of a Third-Party Settlement for the Sino-Japanese Maritime Boundary Dispute in the East China Sea", *China: An International Journal*, Vol.6 (2008), p. 193.

7 However, the Chinese Government may accept a single maritime boundary if China's claim that its EEZ prolongs naturally to the Okinawa Trough should be upheld. The Ministry of Foreign Affairs of the People's Republic of China, "China's Oil and Gas Development in the East China Sea is Justified and Legitimate", July 27, 2015. Available at <https://www.fmprc.gov.cn/mfa_eng/wjdt_665385/2649_665393/t1284278.shtml>.

8 The delimitation of EEZ in the East China Sea (a principle based on distance) could produce a more disadvantageous result for China than the delimitation of continental shelf (a principle based on natural prolongation). See, H. Schulte Nordholt, "Delimitation of the Continental Shelf in the East China Sea", *Netherlands International Law Review*, Vol.32 (1985), p. 134. For the China's position, see, Ji Guoxing, "Sino-Japanese Jurisdictional Delimitation in East China Sea: Approaches to Dispute Settlement", in Seoung-Yong Hong & Jon M. Van Dyke (eds.), *Maritime Boundary Disputes, Settlement Processes, and the Law of the Sea* (Brill, 2009), pp. 82–84.

9 Ministry of Foreign Affairs of Japan, "Japan's legal position on the development of natural resources in the East China Sea". Available at <https://www.mofa.go.jp/a_o/c_m1/page3e_000358.html>.

2.3 *Conflict between China and Japan in the Maritime Delimitation in the East China Sea*

2.3.1 Disputed Sea Area

The first point is "Where is the disputed sea area between the two states?" China holds that the natural prolongation of the landmass extends to the edge of the Okinawa Trough,[10] where China's continental shelf comes to an end.[11] On the other hand, Japan is of the view that the median line between the baseline of China's coast and the ones of the Ryukyu Islands and other chains of islands that are spread from the mainland of Japan should be the boundary of the continental shelf in the East China Sea.[12] Thus, these claims by the two states have brought the location of the disputed sea area to light. China argues that the disputed sea area stretches into the area west of the median line to Okinawa Trough. Against the Chinese argument, Japan claims that disputed sea area is all waters in the East China Sea wherever both states' claims of 200 nautical miles overlap.[13]

---

10 Goldie compared the Norwegian Trough, which the ICJ took as an example of natural prolongation in the *North Sea Continental Shelf* cases, with the Okinawa Trough, and suggested that the latter divides the seabed of the East China Sea into two major provinces and thus provides a clear boundary in terms of the ICJ's formula of natural prolongation. See, L.F.E. Goldie, "The International Court of Justice's 'Natural Prolongation' and the Continental Shelf Problem of Islands", *Netherlands Yearbook of International Law*, Vol.4 (1973), pp. 252–254.

11 In Chapter "5. Natural Prolongation of Land Territory" in the Executive Summary of the Submission by China to the Commission on the Limits of the Continental Shelf (CLCS) on 14 December 2012, it stated the following: the East China Sea (ECS) "consists of three geomorphologic units: the shelf, the slope and the Okinawa Trough", which is "the natural termination of the continental shelf of ECS". Submission by the People's Republic of China Concerning the Outer Limits of the Continental shelf beyond 200 Nautical Miles in Part of the east China Sea, Executive Summary, pp. 3–5. <https://www.un.org/depts/los/clcs_new/submissions_files/submission_chn_63_2012.htm>.

12 Ministry of Foreign Affairs of Japan, "Japan's Legal Position on the Development of Natural Resources in the East China Sea", August 6, 2015, Available at <https://www.mofa.go.jp/a_o/c_m1/page3e_000358.html>.

13 In this case, the question where the disputed area is situated may be related to the relationship between distance and natural prolongation in the continental shelf delimitation. If distance criterion prevails over natural prolongation, the Japan's 200 nautical miles continental shelf cannot be encroached by the China's beyond 200 nautical miles continental shelf. On this subject, see, Xuexia Liao, "Is There a Hierarchical Relationship between National Prolongation and Distance in the Continental Shelf Delimitation?" *The International Journal of Marine and Coastal Law*, Vol.33 (2018), pp. 79–115. From the Chinese perspective, "if the natural prolongation of one state's land territory exceeds 200 nautical miles from its coast, but the other state's does not, then the "area of overlapping entitlements" will be the area bounded by the limits of the natural prolongation of the former state's land territory on the one hand, which is therefore different from

2.3.2 Single Boundary for Continental Shelf and EEZ

The second point is the possibility of a single maritime boundary. The continental shelf is different from the EEZ by nature, because of the following facts: the continental shelf belongs to coastal states *ipso facto* and *ab initio*, and the legal title to the shelf does not depend on effective or normal occupancy, or explicit declaration; in contrast, explicit acts are required for establishing the EEZ. Therefore, UNCLOS does not necessarily require any single boundary covering both the EEZ and the continental shelf, since the legal title to the EEZ is based on the standard distance of 200 nautical miles while the entitlement to the continental shelf depends upon the continuity or natural prolongation of the onshore geological structure.

But, in State Practice, states have tended to delimitate a common boundary for the EEZ and the continental shelf. Because the continental shelf extending up to 200 nautical miles from the coastline is covered by the EEZ, Japan's position is that only any portion of the continental shelf beyond the EEZ boundary is related to the natural prolongation theory.

In the East China Sea, Japan has the EEZ delimitation as well as the continental shelf delimitation in mind while China adheres largely to the continental shelf delimitation.[14] Drawing a single boundary for a continental shelf and an EEZ between China and Japan might support the Japan's maritime delimitation arguments, because such a single boundary line would be drawn mainly on the basis of the distance criterion.

2.3.3 Applicable Maritime Delimitation Law

The main conflict on the maritime delimitation of the continental shelf between China and Japan is related to the contents of applicable legal principles and rules in delimiting continental shelves. China traditionally relies on the natural prolongation theory for the entitlement of its continental shelf,[15] and claims equitable principle as the applicable law to the continental shelf

---

the "area of overlapping entitlements" in the case of EEZ delimitation. See, Gao Jianjun, "Joint Development in the East China Sea: Not an Easier Challenge than Delimitation", *The International Journal of Marine and Coastal Law*, Vol.23 (2008), pp. 44–45.

14 It does not exclude any possibility that China will agree to median line as the delimitation line of the EEZ with Japan, though China still insists on natural prolongation for delimitation of the continental shelf. In that case, there would be two different delimitation lines in the East China Sea, thus definitely bringing difficulties of law enforcement and exercise of jurisdiction for both states. Zou Keyuan, "China's Exclusive Economic Zone and Continental Shelf: Development, Problems, and Prospects", *Marine Policy*, Vol.25 (2001), pp. 77–78.

15 Zhiguo Gao, "China and the LOS Convention", *Marine Policy*, Vol.15 (1991), p. 205.

delimitation. In contrast, Japan adopts the distance criterion for its continental shelf entitlement, and also claims to draw a median line on the basis of the distance criterion. To resolve this respect of the conflict, it is necessary to confirm the contents of the current legal rules on the maritime delimitation, in particular through the examination of the recent international jurisprudence.

3 Recent Trends of Maritime Delimitation Rules in International Jurisprudence

3.1 *Governing Provision of UNCLOS with Regard to the Delimitation of the Continental Shelf*

China and Japan are parties to UNCLOS, which provides rules and principles for the delimitation of maritime boundaries. UNCLOS has the provision on delimitation of the continental shelf in Article 83 (1), and Article 74 (1) of UNCLOS, which regulates the delimitation of the EEZ, is almost the same as Article 83 (1). While these provisions do not refer to equidistance nor are related directly to the notion of equitable principles, they include the terms only "an equitable solution",[16] the meaning of which is not necessarily clear from their texts.[17] Thus, the texts of these provisions alone cannot provide any definitive solution to the confrontation between the equidistance principle and the equitable principles for the criteria of the maritime delimitation of the continent shelf and EEZ.[18] Therefore, the subsequent international jurisprudence on the maritime delimitation has complemented the contents of "an equitable solution" and contributed to clarify the delimitation method for it.

---

16 Thus, under Article 74 (1) and Article 83 (1) no predominance is given either to equitable principles or to equidistance. See, Satya N. Nandan & Shabtai Rosenne (eds.), *United Nations Convention on the Law of the Sea 1982. A Commentary, Volume II* (Martinus Nijhoff Publishers, 1993), pp. 814, 913. That means a compromise between these two approaches resulted from a common perspective: the need to avoid inequitable solutions. See, Nuno Marqus Antunes, *Towards the Conceptualisation of Maritime Delimitation. Legal and Technical Aspects of a Political Process* (Brill, 2003), pp. 88–89.

17 Article 74 (1) as well as Article 83 (1) "offers scant explanation about the content of 'an equitable solution'. Thus, the equitableness of maritime boundaries must be evaluated on a case-by-case basis". Yoshifumi Tanaka, "Article 83", in Alexander Proeless (ed.), *United Nations Convention on the Law of the Sea. A Commentary* (C.H. Beck, 2017), p. 658.

18 For the confrontation between the equidistance principle and the equitable principles, Malcolm D. Evans, "Maritime Boundary delimitation", in Donald R. Rothwell, Alex G. Oude Elferink, Karen N. Scott & Tim Stephens (eds.), *The Oxford Handbook of the Law of the Sea* (O.U.P., 2015), pp. 256–259.

3.2 *From Theoretical and Practical Confrontation between the Equidistance/Special Circumstances Method and the Equitable Principles/Relevant Circumstances Method to the Adoption of the "Three-Stage Approach" in International Jurisprudence*

3.2.1 Predominance of the Equitable Principles/Relevant Circumstances Method in the International Court of Justice (ICJ) Early Cases on the Maritime Delimitation

In the early cases on the delimitation of the continental shelf, including the *North Sea Continental Shelf* cases,[19] the *Tunisia/Libya* case,[20] and the *Libya/Malta* case,[21] the ICJ rejected the existence of any mandatory equidistance delimitation method of the continental shelf, which is provided by Article 6 of the 1958 Convention on the Continental Shelf, and has followed the equitable principles/relevant circumstances method. Particularly in the *Gulf of Maine* case, the Chamber of the ICJ took a more discretionary approach, referring to the set of fundamental rules.[22] Its formulation is the most result-oriented one, therefore, "it eliminated almost any rule-orientation and turned delimitation into a fully discretionary operation".[23]

---

19 *North Sea Continental Shelf, Judgment, I.C.J. Reports 1969*, pp. 46–47, para. 82. On the other hand, in the *UK/France Continental Shelf* Arbitration, the Court of Arbitration integrated the equidistance-special circumstances rule in the whole body of the rules of law that were to result in delimitation in accordance with equitable principles and observed that a median line would "normally effect a broadly equitable delimitation" in the case of opposite states. *Case concerning the Delimitation of the Continental Shelf between the United Kingdom of Great Britain and Northern Ireland, and the French Republic, Decision of 30 June 1977, R.I.A.A.*, Vol. XVIII, pp. 47–48, para. 75, p. 56, para. 95.

20 *Continental Shelf (Tunisia / Libyan Arab Jamahiriya), Judgment, I.C.J. Reports 1982*, p. 59, para. 70.

21 *Continental Shelf (Libyan Arab Jamahiriya / Malta), Judgment, I.C.J. Reports 1985*, pp. 37–38, para. 43. In this case, however, the Court observed that in the delimitation between states with opposite coasts, "the tracing of a median line between those coasts, by way of a provisional step in a process to be continued by other operations, is the most judicious manner of proceeding with a view to the eventual achievement of an equitable result". Ibid., p. 47, para. 62. See also, Yoshifumi Tanaka, *Predictability and Flexibility in the Law of Maritime Delimitation*, 2nd Edition (Hart Publishing, 2019), pp. 71–72.

22 *Delimitation of the Maritime Boundary in the Gulf of Maine Area, Judgment, I.C.J. Reports 1984*, pp. 299–300, para. 112.

23 Thomas Cottier, *Equitable Principles of Maritime Boundary Delimitation. The Quest for Distributive Justice in International Law* (Cambridge U.P., 2015), p. 407. In the *Guinea/Guinea-Bissau* case, the Arbitral Tribunal also restated the wide-open, discretionary approach, as the Chamber took in the *Gulf of Maine* case. *Affaire de la délimitation de la frontière maritime entre la Guinée et la Guinée-Bissau, sentence du 14 février 1985, R.I.A.A.*, Vol. XIX, pp. 181–182, para. 88.

3.2.2 Searching for an Objective Delimitation Methodology: Restoration of Equidistance Approach and the Appearance of the "Three-Stage Approach"

As the Chamber pointed out properly in the *Gulf of Maine* case, however, "[T]here has been no systematic definition of the equitable criteria that may be taken into consideration for an international maritime delimitation, and this would in any event be difficult *a priori*, because of their highly variable adaptability to different concrete situations".[24] Thus, this concern may induce the international courts and tribunals to look for more objectively determined delimitation methods and criteria, as opposed to subjective equity consideration.

In fact, the ICJ confirmed in the *Jan Mayen* case, that "[P]rima facie, a median line delimitation between opposite coasts results in general in an equitable solution, particularly if the coasts in question are nearly parallel".[25] Most of the subsequent international jurisprudence on maritime delimitation, including the *Qatar v. Bahrain* case,[26] the *Cameroon v. Nigeria* case,[27] the *Eritrea/Yemen* Arbitration,[28] the *Barbados/Trinidad and Tobago* Arbitration,[29] the *Guyana/Surinam* Arbitration,[30] and the *Nicaragua v. Honduras* case,[31] all reaffirmed that a provisional equidistance or median line should be drawn first

24 *I.C.J. Reports 1984*, p. 312, para. 157.

25 *Maritime Delimitation in the Area between Greenland and Jan Mayen, Judgment, I.C.J. Reports 1993*, p. 66, para. 64.

26 *Maritime Delimitation and Territorial Questions between Qatar and Bahrain, Merits, Judgment, I.C.J. Reports 2001*, p. 111, paras. 228–230.

27 *Land and Maritime Boundary between Cameroon and Nigeria (Cameroon v. Nigeria: Equatorial Guinea intervening), Judgment, I.C.J. Reports 2002*, pp. 441–442, paras. 288–290.

28 *Award of the Arbitral Tribunal in the Second Stage of the Proceedings between Eritrea and Yemen (Maritime Delimitation), Decision of 17 December 1999*, R.I.A.A., Vol. XXII, p. 365, paras. 131-132.

29 *Award of the Arbitral Tribunal concerning the Maritime Boundary between Barbados and the Republic of Trinidad and Tobago, Decision of 11 April 2006*, R.I.A.A., Vol. XXVII, pp. 214–215, para. 242.

30 *Award in the Arbitration regarding the Delimitation of the Maritime Boundary between Guyana and Suriname, Award of 17 September 2007*, R.I.A.A., Vol. XXX, p. 95, para. 342.

31 *Territorial and Maritime Dispute between Nicaragua and Honduras in the Caribbean Sea (Nicaragua v. Honduras), Judgment, I.C.J. Reports 2007*, p. 745, para. 281. The Court, however, adopted, instead of the equidistance principle, the bisector method, according to which some form of bisector of the angle created by lines representing the relevant mainland coasts could be a basis for the delimitation, though confirming that equidistance remains the general rule. Ibid., p. 746, para. 287.

as a starting point for the maritime delimitation, and that then modifying it would be necessary for an equitable result.

Finally, in the *Black Sea Maritime Delimitation* case,[32] the Court, following the previous judgments on the object of maritime delimitation,[33] articulated so-called three-stage approach on the delimitation process: first, the decision-maker draws a provisional equidistance line, and second, it considers whether there are factors for adjustment or shifting of that line to achieve an equitable result, and third, it conducts an *ex-post facto* disproportionality test to verify that the adjusted equidistance line does not lead to an inequitable result by reason of any marked disproportion between the ratio of the respective coastal lengths and the ratio between the relevant maritime area of each State.[34] Most of the subsequent maritime delimitation cases, for example, the *Bay of Bengal* cases,[35] the *Nicaragua v. Colombia* case,[36] the *Peru v. Chile* case,[37] the *Ghana/Côte d'Ivoire* case,[38] and the *Costa Rica v. Nicaragua* case[39] follow this three-stage approach in the delimitation of the EEZ and the continental shelf. Therefore, international jurisprudence on maritime delimitation indicates

---

32 *Maritime Delimitation in the Black Sea (Romania v. Ukraine), Judgment, I.C.J. Reports 2009*, pp. 101–103, paras. 115–122.

33 "The purpose of delimitation is not to apportion equal shares of the area, nor indeed proportional shares". "The object of delimitation is to achieve a delimitation that is equitable, not an equal apportionment of maritime area". Ibid., pp. 99–100, paras. 110–111. The court observed that this means that "[E]quity does not necessarily imply equality". *I.C.J. Reports 1969*, p. 50, para. 91. See also, Davor Vidas, "Consolidation or Deviation? On Trends and Challenges in the Settlement of Maritime Delimitation Disputes by International Courts and Tribunals", in Nerina Boschiero, Tullio Scovazzi, Cesare Pitea & Chiara Ragni (eds.), *International Courts and the Development of International Law. Essays in Honour of Tullio Treves* (Springer, 2013), p. 328.

34 See also, Mathias Forteau et Jean-Marc Thouvenin (dir.), *Traite de Droit International de la Mer* (Pedone, 2017), pp. 600–607 [Alain Pellet].

35 *Delimitation of the Maritime Boundary in the Bay of Bengal (Bangladesh / Myanmar), Judgment, ITLOS Reports 2012*, pp. 67–68, paras. 238–240; *The Bay of Bengal Maritime Boundary Arbitration between the People's Republic of Bangladesh and the Republic of India, Award of 7 July 2014, R.I.A.A.*, Vol. XXXII, pp. 104–106, paras. 337–346.

36 *Territorial and Maritime Dispute (Nicaragua v. Colombia), Judgment, I.C.J. Reports 2012*, pp. 695–698, paras. 190–199.

37 In this case, the Court said that "[I]n the first, it constructs a provisional equidistance line unless there are compelling reasons preventing that". *Maritime Dispute (Peru v. Chile), Judgment, I.C.J. Reports 2014*, p. 66, para. 180.

38 *Delimitation of the Maritime Boundary in the Atlantic Ocean (Ghana / Côte d'Ivoire), Judgment, ITLOS Reports 2017*, p. 103, para. 360.

39 *Maritime Delimitation in the Caribbean Sea and the Pacific Ocean (Costa Rica v. Nicaragua)* and *Land Boundary in the Northern Part of Isla Portillos (Costa Rica v. Nicaragua), Judgment, I.C.J. Reports 2018*, p. 190, para. 135.

that equidistance is now a well-established standard for drawing an initial boundary line to be adjusted for equity, if necessary.

3.3 *Rejecting Natural Prolongation as a Relevant Factor in Delimitation of Continental Shelf within 200 Nautical Miles*

On the other hand, the natural prolongation theory, which China adopts for maritime delimitation, as a criterion of delimitation of continental shelf within 200 nautical miles has been rejected by the recent international jurisprudence.

It is in the *North Sea Continental Shelf* cases[40] that the ICJ first referred to the natural prolongation as a criterion of boundary delimitation of the continental shelf. In the *Tunisia/Libya* case,[41] the Court rejected geological and geomorphological circumstances for considering the delimitation of the boundary, but in fact, it reserved the possibility of their consideration in future cases.[42] Thus, later, in the *Gulf of Maine* case,[43] the Chamber of the Court observed the applicability of geological circumstances in delimiting a single boundary of the continental shelf and the EEZ within 200 nautical miles in the Gulf of Maine area. It is on these judgments that China's legal contention is based in the maritime delimitation in the East China Sea where according to China, the Okinawa Trough presents the natural break between the Chinese and the Japanese continental shelves.

In the *Libya/Malta* case,[44] however, the Court refused the parties' arguments based on geology and geomorphology, and rejected natural prolongation as a relevant factor in so far as the continental shelf within 200 nautical miles was concerned.[45] Moreover, in the *Nicaragua v. Colombia* case, the Court also rejected Nicaragua's contention based upon natural prolongation, and

40 *I.C.J. Reports 1969*, p. 32, para. 43, p. 54, para. 101 (C) (1).

41 *I.C.J. Reports 1982*, p. 57, para. 66.

42 Yiallourides, *supra* note 4, p. 113.

43 *I.C.J. Reports 1984*, p. 327, paras. 194–195.

44 *I.C.J. Reports 1985*, pp. 35–36, paras. 39–40.

45 To the contrary, some authors argue that the Court left open the possibility that the geological features on the seabed might be relevant to delimitation of the continental shelf beyond 200 nautical miles from the baselines. David A. Colson, "The Delimitation of the Outer Continental Shelf between Neighbouring States", *American Journal of International Law*, Vol.97 (2003), pp. 102–103; Øystein Jensen, "Maritime Boundary Delimitation beyond 200 Nautical Miles: The International Judiciary and the Commission on the Limits of the Continental Shelf", *Nordic Journal of International Law*, Vol.80 (2015), pp. 599–600; Bjarni Már Magnússon, *The Continental Shelf Beyond 200 Nautical Miles* (Brill, 2015), p. 17.

repeated its own observation in the *Libya/Malta* case that "geological and geomorphological considerations are not relevant to the delimitation of overlapping entitlements within 200 nautical miles of the coasts of States".[46] In addition to the ICJ, the recent jurisprudence of the International Tribunal for the Law of the Sea (ITLOS) and the Arbitral Tribunal constituted under Annex VII to UNCLOS, for example, in the *Bay of Bengal* cases,[47] verifies that the geological and geomorphological features of the seabed are not likely to give any influence upon maritime boundary delimitation,[48] even if the continental shelf extends beyond 200 nautical miles.[49] Thus, while natural prolongation is relevant only for ascertaining whether an overlap of outer continental shelf entitlement exists,[50] it would not have further influence once the overlap is confirmed.[51] This explains that natural prorogation theory, according to international jurisprudence, is not relevant at least for the criteria of maritime

46 *I.C.J. Reports 2012*, p. 703, para. 214.

47 "In the view of the Tribunal, the delimitation method to be employed in the present case for the continental shelf beyond 200 nautical miles should not differ from that within 200 nm". *ITLOS Reports 2012*, p. 117, para. 455. See also, *R.I.A.A.*, Vol.XXXII, p. 138, paras. 457–458.

48 Tanaka, *supra* note 21, p. 295.

49 All of the tribunals in the *Bay of Bengal* cases and the *Ghana/Côte d'Ivoire* case decided to use the "equidistance/relevant circumstances method in the delimitation of the outer continental shelf. Jianjun Gao, "The Delimitation Method for the Continental Shelf Beyond 200 Nautical Miles: A Reflection on the Judicial and Arbitral Decisions", *Ocean Development & International Law*, Vol.51 (2020), p. 124. Davenport acknowledges that "[A]fter the *Bangladesh/Myanmar* Case, it may be difficult for China to continue to argue that natural prolongation is still a valid basis of entitlement under international law", though not denying the possibility that China is entitled to an extended continental shelf in area less than 400 nautical miles. Tara Davenport, "The China-Japan Dispute over Entitlement in the East China Sea: Legal Issues and Prospects for Resolution", in Clive Schofield, Seokwoo Lee & Moon-Sang Kwon (eds.), *The Limits of Maritime Jurisdiction* (Brill, 2014), p. 308.

50 Paik said that "the concept of natural prolongation was destined to be involved with the question of the outer limits and its consequent impact on delimitation" (Jin-Hyun Paik, "The Origin of the Principle of Natural Prolongation: North Sea Continental Shelf Cases Revisited", in Lilian del Castillo (ed.), *Law of the Sea, From Grotius to the International Tribunal for the Law of the Sea. Liber Amicorum Judge Hugo Caminos* (Brill, 2015), p. 589.), but the questions of entitlement of continental shelf and of its delimitation, even if they are complementary, should be clearly distinct. *I.C.J. Reports 1985*, p. 30, para. 27.

51 Nuno Marques Antunes & Vasco Becker-Weinberg, "Entitlement to Maritime Zones and Their Delimitation. In the Doldrums of Uncertainty and Unpredictability", in Alex G. Oude Elferink, Tore Henriksen & Signe Veierud Busch (eds.), *Maritime Boundary Delimitation: The Case Law* (Cambridge U.P., 2018), p. 67.

delimitation of the continental shelf in the area less than 400 nautical miles,[52] like between China and Japan in the East China Sea.[53]

4 Diving or Digging into the Search for a Tolerable Panacea in the East China Sea?

4.1 *Possible Results of the Application of the Current Legal Rules to the Delimitation of the Continental Shelf between China and Japan in the East China Sea*

4.1.1 Application of the Three-Stage Approach to the Continental Shelf Delimitation between China and Japan

International case law supports the thesis that the three-stage approach dominates in recent international jurisprudence. According to this method, first, the provisional equidistance/median line should be drawn between the relevant coastlines of China and the ones of Japan. This way seems to favor Japan's position on the continental shelf delimitation, because Japan has consistently argued the median line as the continental shelf boundary between China and Japan in the East China Sea. Thus, apparently the case law on the maritime delimitation may provide some advantages with the Japanese side. But this median line is still provisional, and it could be adjusted if there are any relevant factors for the equitable results. Usually, the equidistance/median line may give both coastal States the equitable results, but there is no principle without exception.

4.1.2 Existence of the Relevant Factors Which Could Adjust the Provisional Median Line for the Equitable Result

As for the relevant circumstances, most noteworthy here is coastal length disparity, which could by itself determine the adjustment of an equidistant/median line. The case law on the maritime delimitation acknowledges that "a substantial difference in the lengths of the parties' respective coastlines may be a factor to be taken into consideration in order to adjust or shift the

52 Hyun Jung Kim, "Natural Prolongation: A Living Myth in the Regime of the Continental Shelf?" *Ocean Development & International Law*, Vol.45 (2014), p. 382.

53 It is asserted that by the mid-1990s international jurisprudence on maritime delimitation has indicated the contemporary trend to disregard geological features, which means that the Okinawa Trough is unlikely to affect the maritime boundary delimitation. See, Jonathan I. Charney, "Central East Asian Maritime Boundaries and the Law of the Sea", *American Journal of International Law*, Vol.89 (1995), p. 740.

provisional delimitation line".[54] The point is whether or not there is any coastal length disparity between the parties' respective coastlines in the East China Sea, and to what extent, if any, this disparity requires the provision of median line to be adjusted.[55]

In the *Nicaragua v. Colombia* case, the ICJ observed that "it is normally only where the disparities in the lengths of the relevant coasts are substantial that an adjustment or shifting of the provisional line is called for".[56] The Court then found that the result achieved by the application of the provisional line in a ratio of 8.2:1 coastal length in Nicaragua's favour "does not entail such a disproportionality as to create an inequitable result".[57] In the case of the East China Sea, even if the geographical features seem to show approximately a ratio of 2:1 coastal length in China's favor,[58] which is dependent upon how to specify where is the respective relevant coasts of the two states, in my view, it is not very convincing that this ratio should be decisive for the provision of the median line to be adjusted in China's favor, compared with other similar cases.[59]

The existence of islands can be also one of the relevant circumstances for the equitable results. Islands may give some impact on the maritime delimitation under the condition that it belongs decisively to one of the parties to the dispute. In the East China Sea, China argues that the Senkaku/Diaoyu Islands

54 *I.C.J. Reports 2002*, p. 446, para. 301.

55 It is to be noted that coastal length disparity, which is related to a relevant circumstance at the second stage, and disproportionality, which leads the Court to assess the ratio between the marine areas allocated to each state at the third stage, have distinct functions in the three-stage approach. Massimo Lando, *Maritime Delimitation as a Judicial Process* (Cambridge U.P., 2019), p. 281.

56 *I.C.J. Reports 2012*, p. 702, para. 210. The Court also observed in the *Black Sea Maritime Delimitation* case that "[W]here disparities in the lengths of coasts are particularly marked, the Court may choose to treat that fact of geography as a relevant circumstance that would require some adjustments to the provisional equidistance line to be made". *I.C.J. Reports 2009*, p. 116, para. 164.

57 *I.C.J. Reports 2012*, p. 717, para. 247.

58 "[T]he proportionality between the lengths of the coastal states' respective coastlines in the South Region would result in a delimitation of the continental shelf in a ratio of approximately 64 to 36 in favor of China", when the East China Sea would be divided into North and South regions along 30°N. See, Wei-chin Lee, "Troubles under the Water: Sino-Japanese Conflict of Sovereignty on the Continental Shelf in the East China Sea", *Ocean Development & International Law*, Vol.18 (1987), p. 599.

59 In the *Jan Mayen* case, the Court observed that the ratio of relevant coasts was approximately 1:9 in Denmark's favour (*I.C.J. Reports 1993*, p. 65, para. 61.), but even in this case, it did not consider a ratio of approximately 1:2.7 relevant area in Denmark's favour to be significantly disproportionate. See, *I.C.J. Reports 2012*, p. 717, para. 246.

are "an inseparable part of the Chinese territory" over which China enjoys indisputable sovereignty. Against China's argument, Japan, which occupies these islands effectively, maintains that there is no doubt that the Senkaku Islands are clearly an inherent part of the territory of Japan in light of historical facts and based on international law, and that there exists no issue of territorial sovereignty to be resolved concerning the Senkaku Islands.

As for the Senkaku/Diaoyu Islands, apart from the questions of the existence or non-existence of dispute and the holder of territorial sovereignty over it, whether or not they should satisfy the objective pre-conditions set forth in Article 121 (3) of UNCLOS, especially in light of the requirements which the *South China Sea* Arbitration Award clarified,[60] remains to be seen. However, it can be safely said that, whether or not they qualify as fully entitled islands, their potential effects on the future maritime boundary delimitation in the East China Sea is likely to be very limited.[61] In fact, the Senkaku/Diaoyu Islands need not to be considered as relevant circumstances for the adjustment of the provisional median line.[62]

4.1.3 Possibility of Separate (but Partially Overlapping) Maritime Boundaries?

Many cases concerning single maritime boundaries can be seen in international jurisprudence,[63] but in State Practice, there are only a few cases in which the parties concerned agreed to create two separate maritime boundaries.[64]

60 *The South China Sea Arbitration between the Republic of the Philippines and the People's Republic of China, Award of 12 July 2016, R.I.A.A.*, XXXIII, pp. 387–390, paras. 539–551.

61 Yiallourides, *supra* note 4, pp. 137–138.

62 The legal status of the Senkaku/Diaoyu Islands would give little influence upon the maritime boundary delimitation, because it is possible to separate the issue of maritime boundary delimitation from that of ownership of the Senkaku/Diaoyu Islands, given the recent development of international jurisprudence ignoring small islets in seabed boundary delimitations between opposite states. Suk-Kyoon Kim, "Perspectives on East China Sea Maritime Disputes: Issues and Context", in Schofield, Lee & Kwon (eds.), *supra* note 49, p. 291.

63 "The Court observes that the concept of a single maritime boundary does not stem from multilateral treaty law but from State practice". *I.C.J. Reports 2001*, p. 93, para. 173. For the state practice and international jurisprudence of a single maritime boundary line, see, Laurent Lucchini, "Plaidoyer pour une ligne unique de délimitation", in Rafael Casado Raigón et Giuseppe Cataldi (dir.), *L'évolution et l'état actuel du droit international de la mer. Mélanges de droit de la mer offerts à Daniel Vignes* (Bruylant, 2009), pp. 564–570.

64 The regimes of the EEZ and the continental shelf "are separate, but to avoid the difficult practical problems that could arise were one Party to have rights over the water column and the other rights over the seabed and subsoil below that water column, a single maritime boundary can be drawn". *R.I.A.A.*, Vol. XXX, pp. 92–93, para. 334.

The 1997 maritime delimitation treaty between Australia and Indonesia provides a good example of separate continental shelf and EEZ boundaries. This was the situation in which there was a conflict between an entitlement to a continental shelf extending beyond 200 nautical miles based on the criterion of natural prolongation on the one hand, and a combined claim to an EEZ and continental shelf based on the 200 nautical miles distance criterion on the other hand, in an area less than 400 nautical miles.[65]

At first glance, this example might be used to support China's legal reasoning in relation to Japan's position. Nevertheless, the 1997 Australia / Indonesia Treaty can be argued to be inconsistent with UNCLOS, because the EEZ not only contains rights in the water column but it also covers continental shelf rights in the seabed and subsoil. Under the relevant provisions of UNCLOS, the EEZ is difficult to be considered exclusively to concern activities on the water column, in separation from the seabed.[66] It is natural, from the practical viewpoint as well as the legal one, that the states concerned should seek a single boundary line in the maritime delimitation.

Finally, the 1997 Treaty, though signed, has not entered into force. The main reason is that Indonesia withdrew from East Timor in October 1999. Later on, in 2018, Timor-Leste sought to negotiate a permanent EEZ and continental shelf boundary with Australia, on the basis of equidistance line. Both states concluded a comprehensive treaty setting maritime boundaries between the two states in the Timor Sea, with the assistance of a Conciliation Commission. As this example shows, the possibility that separate and partially overlapping continental shelf and EEZ boundaries may overcome debate over the role of geographical factors in maritime boundary delimitation should not be denied. However, considering that the 1997 Treaty was never ratified, the value as a precedent of the Treaty is very limited for the East China Sea dispute.[67]

4.2 *Towards Strengthening a Joint Development Framework between China and Japan*

4.2.1 "Rediscovery" of the 2008 Agreement

China and Japan have already shared a common position as a restarting point for win-win solution. Since 2004, China and Japan negotiated to proceed for

65 For the text of the 1997 Treaty establishing an EEZ Boundary and Certain Seabed Boundaries and the commentary on it, see, Jonathan I. Charney & Robert W. Smith (eds.), *International Maritime Boundaries*, Vol. IV (Brill, 2002), pp. 2697–2727.

66 Max Herriman & Marti Tsamenyi, "The 1997 Australia – Indonesia Maritime Boundary Treaty: A Secure Legal Regime for Offshore Resource Development?" *Ocean Development & International Law*, Vol.29 (1998), pp. 364–365.

67 Yiallourides, *supra* note 4, pp. 120–124.

the successful maritime delimitation of the EEZ and to deal with China's advances in extracting hydrocarbon resources to the west of the median line which China does not officially recognize.[68] On June 18, 2008, the Foreign Ministries of China and Japan announced at separate press conferences that the "two sides will conduct cooperation in the transitional period prior to delimitation without prejudicing their respective legal positions".[69] Under this Joint Press Statement, China and Japan would jointly explore and develop natural resources in a 2,700 squares kilometer area of the East China Sea that extends across Japan's proposed median line.[70] Concluding of this Agreement ("Principled Consensus" by the Chinese Government) had the following advantages at that time. First, China and Japan confirmed that the joint development would not harm their respective legal positions on the EEZ or continental shelf delimitation. Second, the stable framework of joint development would attract a Japanese private sector that has been hesitant to develop resources in the East China Sea owing to the absence of a delimited boundary. Third, joint development is significant for economically efficient drilling of each oil and gas deposit, and the parties could jointly drill a point for the most efficient production and share output.[71]

From the view of managing any conflict between China and Japan in the East China Sea, in particular on the resources under that sea area, the 2008 Agreement should and could be an important starting point, because the

68 Reinhard Drifte, "The East China Sea. Sea of Regional and Global Confrontation", in Gordon Houlden & Nong Hong (eds.), *Maritime Order and the Law in East Asia* (Routledge, 2018), p. 41; Chung-min Tsai, "Sino-Japanese Relations Over the East China Sea: The Case of Oil and Gas Fields", *Journal of Territorial and Maritime Studies*, Vol.3 (2016), pp. 74–76.

69 Ministry of Foreign Affairs of Japan, "The Current Status of China's Unilateral Development of Natural Resources in the East China Sea". Available at <https://www.mofa.go.jp/a_o/c_m1/page3e_000356.html> For the full text of the Agreement, see, Jianjun Gao, "A Note on the 2008 Cooperation Consensus Between China and Japan in the East China Sea", *Ocean Development & International Law*, Vol.40 (2009), pp. 302–303. See also, Clive H. Schofield & Ian Townsend-Gault, "Choppy Waters Ahead in "a Sea of Peace Cooperation and Friendship"?: Slow Progress towards the Application of Maritime Joint Development to the East China Sea", *Marine Policy*, Vol.35 (2011), pp. 29–30.

70 The conclusion of this Agreement is in line with the spirit and provisions of UNCLOS which encourages States concerned to work out provisional arrangements including joint development agreement pending the settlement of their maritime boundary disputes. Keyuan Zou, "Maritime Conflict and Cooperation in East Asia. Recent Developments and Future Prospects", in Barthélémy Courmont, Frédéric Lasserre & Éric Mottet (eds.), *Assessing Maritime Disputes in East Asia. Political and Legal Perspectives* (Routledge, 2017), p. 41.

71 Shigeki Sakamoto, "Japan-China Dispute over Maritime Boundary Delimitation – From a Japanese Perspective – ", *Japanese Yearbook of International Law*, Vol.51 (2008), p. 118.

cooperation of the two states is at the heart of the Agreement and should be still essential for a win-win solution between them.

4.2.2 Conditions for the Revival of the June 2008 Agreement

Regrettably, the cooperative atmosphere created by this Agreement between two states has been wrecked,[72] in particular after the recurrence of the Senkaku/Diaoyu Islands sovereignty problem in 2012. Nevertheless, China and Japan have the obligation to make every effort not to jeopardize or hamper the reaching of the final agreement under Article 83 (3) of UNCLOS, which requires them to refrain from engaging in unilateral action that may aggravate a dispute.[73] In reality, there is no choice but to shelve this problem for a while, whether the perception that there is a territorial dispute between two states should be recognized or not. The 2008 agreement should be re-estimated as a starting point for next stage, so that China and Japan may rebuild trust in each other in the East China Sea.

The restart of the joint development between two states requires cooperation which implies that there should be prevailing feelings of goodwill and friendliness between them. It is true that the joint development agreement should facilitate coordinated and systematic operations in the disputed sea area, but ultimately, it is very important for the parties to demonstrate the required level of political goodwill in support of this cooperative solution.

In December 2018, when China deployed a jack-up drilling rig near the provisional median line between China and Japan in the East China Sea, Japan protested against China, considering that drilling operations so close to the provisional median line entailed the risk of tapping the petroleum reserve straddling the maritime areas of the two states. Unfortunately, an unsettled atmosphere still prevails between China and Japan in developing their indigenous seabed energy resources in the East China Sea. Access to such valuable

72 Taisaku Ikeshima, "Recent Developments in Maritime Delimitation: Any Implication for Territorial and Maritime Boundary Disputes in East Asia?" *Graduate School of International Culture and Communication Studies*, Vol.4 (2017), p. 83. The two states failed to conclude a provisional arrangement of a practical nature on some kind of cooperation on hydrocarbon exploitation. Zhang Xinjun, "Why the 2008 Sino-Japanese Consensus on the East China Sea Has Stalled: Good Faith and Reciprocity Considerations in Interim Measures Pending a Maritime Boundary Delimitation", *Ocean Development & International Law*, Vol.42 (2010), p. 61.

73 Sean D. Murphy, "Obligations of States in Disputed Areas of the Continental Shelf", in Tomas Heidar (ed.), *New Knowledge and Changing Circumstances in the Law of the Sea* (Brill, 2020), pp. 198–200.

resources is at the heart of all the main controversies that characterize the maritime disputes between the two states.

That is why China and Japan tried to rebuild confidence with the respective political will to implement the 2008 agreement effectively. To increase the friendly relationship between the two states, at first, Japan should cooperate with China in implementing the petroleum operations in the area near the median line, while China should respect the significance of the median line in this maritime sea area, even if it does not officially recognize the median line.

5 Conclusions

First, the continental shelf between China and Japan in the East China Sea should be delimited in accordance with the case law on maritime delimitation, that is, the "three-stage approach", just in case both states would agree to the conclusion of a maritime boundary treaty. Second, in reality, however, the current situation is becoming so intense that it is now difficult to negotiate any work of maritime delimitation between them. Third, China and Japan should do their best to gain the confidence from its counterpart in order to reactivate joint development operations in the East China Sea. The 2008 Agreement might be a starting point for their cooperation.

To build confidence each in other, China and Japan should take into consideration the following: First, they should refrain from conducting any measure which might deteriorate their relationship, including any such activities with regards to the Senkaku/Diaoyu problem. Second, while China should avoid drilling unilaterally in the area across the median line between the two states, Japan should consider the possibility of increasing the joint development operation within its 200 nautical miles area from its coast.

I hope and deeply believe that only such strong efforts to build mutual confidence by the two states must turn the East China Sea into a "Sea of Peace, Cooperation and Friendship" in the near future.

CHAPTER 20

State Practice as a Factor Impacting Potential East China Sea Boundaries

Stuart Kaye

1 Introduction

The delimitation of maritime boundaries can be a difficult process for States, particularly where there are unusual geographical features in the relevant area, or where the presence of significant resources add complexity to negotiations. Maritime boundaries can also be complicated where there are a number of States with potential jurisdiction in a relatively small area of ocean space, or where there are sovereignty disputes. The East China Sea is bounded by three littoral States, namely China; Japan; and the Republic of Korea. It is also largely free of islands save those close to the coasts of the littoral States, and, save for the Senkaku/Diaoyu Islands disputed between China and Japan in the south of the East China Sea, there are no sovereignty disputes. Yet for all of this, there are almost no maritime boundaries agreed between any of the East China Sea's littoral States. This chapter considers whether State practice in the region has impacted upon the possible conclusion of a maritime boundary, and what impact, if any, it might have on the conclusion of a possible boundary.

The chapter will commence with consideration of applicable State practice, namely the use of territorial sea baselines, and the making of submissions to the Commission on the Limits of the Continental Shelf. This will begin with a brief introduction of the applicable law in the United Nations Convention on the Law of the Sea,[1] before a discussion of the applicable practice of each of the littoral States in turn. It will then be followed by an analysis of principles of maritime boundary delimitation, with emphasis on the relevance of territorial sea baselines and areas of continental shelf beyond 200 nautical miles. The chapter will then conclude with the possible impact on State practice upon potential maritime boundaries, noting the application of the relevant law.

---

1 *United Nations Convention on the Law of the Sea*, 1833 UNTS 397.

2 Regional Geography

Before considering regional State practice, it is first necessary to consider the geography of the East China Sea which is illustrated in Map 1. The International Hydrographic Organization published a definition of the East China Sea in 1953.[2] This provided for a western limit along the coast of mainland China, and eastern limit based the Ryukyu Islands, the northern tip of the island of Taiwan to the south and a line from the Chinese mainland to Jeju Island to Kyushu. The only littoral States bordering this area of sea are China, Japan and the Republic of Korea.

Consideration of the maritime boundaries in the East China Sea therefore can only include the maritime boundaries between China, Japan and the Republic of Korea. The Japan-Korea maritime boundary[3] also extends through the Tsushima Strait and up into the Sea of Japan or East Sea, which is clearly beyond the scope of this chapter, but the parts of a potential Japan-Korea boundary south of the Tsushima Strait, and the northern extremities of the potential China-Republic of Korea maritime boundary are only just outside the geographical limits of the East China Sea. Therefore, in the context of this chapter those parts of the Yellow Sea south of the Shandong Peninsula will also be considered, as they are likely to be relevant in any diplomatic exchange between the littoral States over East China Sea boundaries.

3 Territorial Sea Baselines

3.1 *Applicable International Law*

Part II of the Law of the Sea Convention deals, *inter alia*, with territorial sea baselines. Its antecedents come from, in part the 1958 Convention on the Territorial Sea and Contiguous Zone,[4] which itself can be traced back to the *Anglo-Norwegian Fisheries Case*.[5] The Case permits straight baselines to be drawn in a range of circumstances, but in the absence of such circumstances makes use of the "low water line" along the coast to be the "normal baseline".[6]

2 International Hydrographic Organization, *Limits of Oceans and Seas*, (Monaco, 3rd Edition, 1953) IHO Special Publication 23.

3 *Agreement between Japan and the Republic of Korea Concerning the Establishment of Boundary in the Northern Part of the Continental Shelf Adjacent to the Two Countries*, 1225 UNTS 1981.

4 *Convention on the Territorial Sea and Contiguous Zone*, 516 UNTS 205.

5 *Fisheries (Norway v United Kingdom)* ICJ Reports 1951 p. 116.

6 *United Nations Convention on the Law of the Sea*, Article 5.

MAP 1 East China Sea

In the practice applicable to the East China Sea, the provision for straight baselines under the Law of the Sea Convention that is most relevant is Article 7. None of the littoral States appear to have applied baselines based upon reefs around islands or atolls, nor directly across the mouth of a river, although some do draw baselines between islands that are located beyond the estuaries of some quite substantial rivers. While there are also many juridical bays, the vast majority of the baselines used do not appear to be based upon the rules for such bays contained in Article 10 of the Law of the Sea Convention.

Article 7 of the Law of the Sea Convention provides, in part:

1. In localities where the coastline is deeply indented and cut into, or if there is a fringe of islands along the coast in its immediate vicinity, the method of straight baselines joining appropriate points may be employed in drawing the baseline from which the breadth of the territorial sea is measured.
2. Where because of the presence of a delta and other natural conditions the coastline is highly unstable, the appropriate points may be selected along the furthest seaward extent of the low-water line and, notwithstanding subsequent regression of the low-water line, the straight baselines shall remain effective until changed by the coastal State in accordance with this Convention.
3. The drawing of straight baselines must not depart to any appreciable extent from the general direction of the coast, and the sea areas lying within the lines must be sufficiently closely linked to the land domain to be subject to the regime of internal waters.
4. Straight baselines shall not be drawn to and from low-tide elevations, unless lighthouses or similar installations which are permanently above sea level have been built on them or except in instances where the drawing of baselines to and from such elevations has received general international recognition.

Some of the phrases used in Article 7 above, including "deeply indented and cut into", "fringe of islands" and "general direction of the coast" were derived directly from Article 4 of the Convention on the Territorial Sea and Contiguous Zone, which in turn can be traced back to the *Anglo-Norwegian Fisheries Case*.[7] The contention that has flowed from the interpretation of Article 7 is largely because these phrases are essentially subjective, and lacking a precise definition are capable of multiple interpretations.[8] As a result, there are huge variations in the approaches of States in the construction of straight baseline systems. One certainty is that the United States protests whenever another State produces territorial sea baselines which do not meet the criteria which it

7 *Fisheries (Norway v United Kingdom)* ICJ Reports 1951 p116 at 128–129.

8 J.R.V. Prescott & C.H. Schofield, *The Maritime Political Boundaries of the World*, (Leiden, Martinus Nijhoff, 2nd Edition, 2005) 139–156.

believes reflect the correct interpretation of Article 7,[9] and over time in addition to lodging protests, the United States has also published its views on the legality of territorial baselines adopted by other States.[10] Each of the baseline systems adopted by the littoral States in the East China Sea, which are illustrated in Map 2, have been the subject of such consideration.

3.2 *China*

The coastal geography of China from the Shandong Peninsula to the 25th parallel runs in a generally north-south direction, with Hangzhou Bay being a natural divide. North of Hangzhou Bay, the coastline is largely free of offshore islands, although there are some significant embayments, notably Jiaozhou Wan near Qingdao, and Haizhou Bay. There are some small islands off the coast, including Darshan Island, some 28 nautical miles off Lianyungang, Chaolian Island, around 30 nautical miles east-southeast of Qingdao, and Sheshan Island, around 19 nautical miles east off the estuary of the Yangtze River. Off Hangzhou Bay is the Zhoushan Archipelago, which consists of over 1300 islands, 103 of which are permanently inhabited. The archipelago covers over 20,000 square kilometres in area with a land area of over 1,000 square kilometres. Southward from there, the coastline is flanked by numerous small islands and embayments, particularly in the vicinity of Fuzhou.

China declared a system of territorial sea baselines along its coast, from the Shandong Peninsula to Hainan Island in 1996,[11] pursuant to Article 3 of the 1992 *Law of the Territorial Sea and Contiguous Zone*.[12] Neither the legislation nor the declaration provide for any methodology for the baselines, with the former requiring only coordinates for basepoints, and the latter providing the coordinates themselves. This is not unusual, with most States in their national legislation rarely providing any explanation for any individual baselines.

China ratified the Law of the Sea Convention on 7 June 1996, less than three weeks after it proclaimed its territorial sea baselines. Given the baselines have not been altered in the quarter of a century since their promulgation, it can be

9 US State Department, "Developing Standard Guidelines for Straight Baselines" (1987) 106 *Limits in the Seas* 1 at 6–7.

10 The full collection of *Limits in the Seas* is at <https://www.state.gov/limits-in-the-seas/>.

11 See Declaration of the Government of the People's Republic of China on the baselines of the territorial sea, 15 May 1996: <https://www.un.org/Depts/los/LEGISLATIONANDTREATIES/PDFFILES/CHN_1996_Declaration.pdf>.

12 See <https://www.un.org/Depts/los/LEGISLATIONANDTREATIES/PDFFILES/CHN_1992_Law.pdf>.

assumed that the baselines were intended to be consistent with China's interpretation of the Law of the Sea Convention, and therefore many, if not all of the baselines are based upon the application of Article 7 of the Law of the Sea Convention.

The northern portion of the territorial sea baselines are characterised by a tendency to over-reach what would be legitimate. The baselines from the south-eastern extremity of the Shandong peninsula south to the mouth of the Yangtze River do not touch the Chinese mainland at any point. The coastline concerned is not deeply indented, and China has made use of a number of widely spaced relatively small features, including Darshan Island and Chaolian Island. South of Darshan Island to the Yangtze Estuary, the basepoints appear to be either undeveloped low tide elevations or open sea, each many miles apart, and not consistent with international law. Further south, the presence of numerous small islands off the coast sees the length of the baselines substantially reduce, and the case for the islands fringing the coast grows stronger. Nevertheless, the baselines have still attracted a protest from the United States.[13]

On 13 September 2012, China deposited with the United Nations a document entitled *The Chart of Baselines of Territorial Sea of Diaoyu Dao and its Affiliated Islands of the People's Republic of China* showing the baselines and the outer limits of the territorial sea of China,[14] as well as a list of geographical coordinates of points defining the baselines of China, as contained in the *Statement of the Government of the People's Republic of China on the Baselines of the Territorial Sea of Diaoyu Dao and its Affiliated Islands* of 10 September 2012. This resulted in a *note verbale* from Japan dated 24 September 2012 in which Japan claimed sovereignty over the Senkaku Islands.[15]

3.3 *Korea*

The western coast of the Korean Peninsula is relatively complex, with numerous bays and offshore islands. Some of the islands are well out to sea from the Korean mainland. Most of the larger features are inhabited, or at least were historically inhabited prior to the creation of national parks upon some

13 US State Department, 'Developing Standard Guidelines for Straight Baselines' 106 *Limits in the Seas*, 1987, 1–35.

14 See <https://www.fmprc.gov.cn/mfa_eng/topics_665678/diaodao_665718/t968769.shtml>.

15 *Note verbale* dated 24 September 2012: reprinted at <https://www.un.org/Depts/los/LEGISLATIONANDTREATIES/PDFFILES/DEPOSIT/communicationsredeposit/mzn89_2012_jpn.pdf>.

of the islands. South Korea proclaimed territorial sea baselines in 1978.[16] The baselines, which were updated in 2013,[17] enclose deeply indented coastlines around the southern half of the Korean Peninsula, commencing off the coast near Pusan, and extending to Soryeong-do to the southwest of Seoul. The coordinates were proclaimed again in 2002, without any significant modification.

Although the baselines enclose what is clearly a deeply indented coastline, around which baselines could certainly be applied, they are not without difficulties. Firstly, there is a lack of clarity as to where the internal waters begin and end in both the west and the east. In the west, the baselines end on a small island well off the mainland coast of South Korea, leaving a substantial area of water on the maritime approaches to Inchon that may or may not be claimed as internal waters of South Korea.[18] This uncertainly is in part motivated by the proximity to the DMZ boundary with North Korea, and presumably a desire not to unduly provoke North Korea.

The baselines also are quite generous in their formulation, to an extent that may be contrary to international law from the point of view of some States, although not inconsistent with regional State practice. While there is no length limitation on baselines made under Article 7 of the Law of the Sea Convention for fringing islands and deeply indented coastlines, some of the baselines are long with seven of the 19 baselines drawn pursuant to Article 7 being longer than 24 nautical miles, and two of these exceed 48 nautical miles.[19] The baselines have been the subject of protest by the United States, and were the subject of a Freedom of Navigation Program protest by US navy ships in 1999.[20] Japan does not appear to have protested the baselines as part of the acceptance that they would not be extended to incorporate Jeju Island.

3.4 *Japan*

Japan initially moved to proclaim baselines to enclose the Seto Naikai or Seto Inland Sea, between Shikoku and Honshu Islands in 1977.[21] In addition to these waters, Japan also has an extensive system of straight baselines around

---

16 Enforcement Decree of[the] Territorial Sea and Contiguous Zone Act promulgated on 20 September 1978.

17 <https://www.un.org/Depts/los/LEGISLATIONANDTREATIES/PDFFILES/DEPOSIT/mzn130-coordinates.pdf>.

18 Prescott & Schofield, *supra* note 8, p. 150.

19 US State Department, 'Straight Baselines and Territorial Sea Claims: South Korea' 121 *Limits in the Seas*, 1998, 5–6.

20 See J.A. Roach, *Excessive Maritime Claims* (Leiden, Brill Nijhoff, 4th Edition, 2020) 108.

21 *Law on the Territorial Sea* (Law No. 30 of 2 May 1977) and Cabinet Order No.210 of 1977.

its Home Islands, as well as Tsushima, Okinawa and some of the Kurile Islands, which were proclaimed in the 1990s.[22] The baselines enclose relatively large areas of sea and land, including the whole of the waters around Kyushu and Shikoku islands. The baselines were the subject of analysis by the Office for Ocean Affairs within the US State Department in 1998.[23] Their analysis considered the length of various baselines and their compliance with the requirements of Articles 7 and 10 of the Law of the Sea Convention. As a result of this analysis, the United States protested the validity of some of these baselines, largely on the basis of length. Among those baselines that are the subject of a negative analysis, territorial sea baselines to the west of Okinawa and northwest of Amami Oshima were criticised as being too generous, as well as baselines linking a series of islands to the southwest of Kyushu, which extend a total of 80 nautical miles and well off the coast of Kyushu.[24]

4 Continental Shelf

4.1 *Applicable International Law*

The definition of the continental shelf in the United Nations Convention on the Law of the Sea is found in Article 76 of the Convention. Article 76 provides a coastal State's land territory will generate a continental shelf based upon the application of one of three techniques. The first, and most simple, is to extend the continental shelf in the same fashion as the EEZ, that is to a distance of 200 nautical miles, regardless of water depth or the configuration or composition of the seabed. The second and third techniques are applicable when the coastal State asserts a continental shelf beyond 200 nautical miles. The second is to identify the foot of the continental shelf and extend the continental shelf seaward of this point by 60 nautical miles. This is generally referred to as the "Hedberg Line", in honour of the American geographer who proposed the concept. The third technique, known generally as the "sediment thickness formula" again uses the foot of the continental slope, but continues beyond it to

---

22 Enforcement Order of the Law on the Territorial Sea and the Contiguous Zone (Cabinet Order No. 210 of 1977 amended by Orders No. 383 of 1993, No. 206 of 1996 and No. 434 of 2001): reprinted at <https://www.un.org/Depts/los/LEGISLATIONANDTREATIES/PDFFILES/DEPOSIT/jpn_mzn61_2008.pdf>.

23 US State Department, 'Straight Baselines and Territorial Sea Claims: Japan' 120 *Limits in the Seas*, 1998.

24 *Ibid.*, 6–13; Roach, *supra* note 20, 107–108.

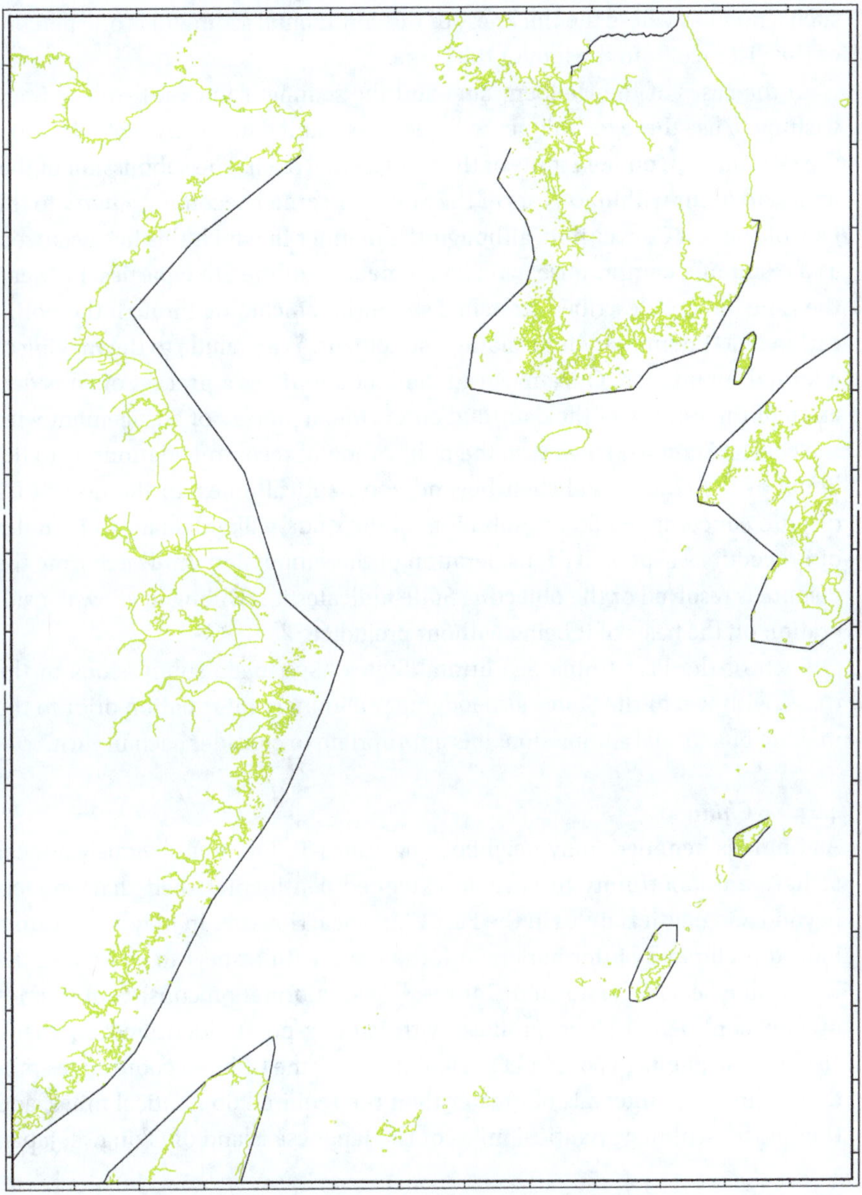

MAP 2 Territorial Sea baselines in the east China Sea

such a point as where the thickness of the continental sediment is one percent of the distance from the foot of the slope.[25]

In the cases of the Hedberg Line and the sediment thickness rule, a State wishing to use these techniques will need to submit data justifying their use to the Commission on the Limits of the Continental Shelf. The submission of this data is to occur within 10 years of the State concerned becoming a party to the Law of the Sea Convention, although the manner in which this has occurred, as a result of a compromise agreed at a meeting of the State parties, has seen the time limit as described stretched somewhat, including through the notification of a "Preliminary Information" statement, as a prelude to the making of a formal submission. Once received, the CLCS initiates a process of consideration of the validity of the data, and enters into a process of engagement with the coastal State with a view to the publication of recommendations as to the limits of the continental shelf beyond 200 nautical miles. In the event of a dispute concerning a State's submission, the CLCS will, pursuant to its Rules of Procedure, suspend its consideration of the submission until such time the dispute is resolved or the objecting State indicates it is willing to allow consideration on the basis of it being without prejudice.[26]

Each of the East China Sea littoral States have made submissions to the CLCS, with two of the States also lodging preliminary information prior to the making of a formal submission. It is appropriate to consider each in turn.

4.2 *China*

As China is hemmed in by neighbouring States, it does not obviously appear to have an opportunity to have an extended continental shelf that projects beyond 200 nautical miles in the East China Sea. However in May 2009, China lodged preliminary information with the CLCS with respect to an area in the East China Sea, to the north of Taiwan.[27] The information consists of a series of four continental slope profiles, with various points identified on them. Using those points to construct a "Hedburg line", the Chinese coordinates produce a line with intervals of greater than the required 60 nautical miles, and that passes within 35 nautical miles of the Japanese island of Okinawa. Japan

---

25 M.H. Nordquist (ed.), *United Nations Convention on the Law of the Sea 1982: A Commentary* (The Hague: Martinus Nijhoff, 1993) Vol.2, 873 et seq.

26 *Rules of Procedure of the Commission on the Continental Shelf*, UN Doc. CLCS/40/Rev.1, 17 April 2008 Rule 46, and Annex I, clause 5(a).

27 See *Preliminary Information Indicative of the Outer Limits of the Continental Shelf Beyond 200 Nautical Miles of the People's Republic of China*, 11 May 2009: reprinted at <https://www.un.org/depts/los/clcs_new/submissions_files/preliminary/chn2009preliminaryinformation_english.pdf>.

protested the preliminary information, pointing out its territory is within 400 nautical miles of China.[28]

On 14 December 2012, China lodged a partial submission with CLCS concerning the East China Sea essentially in conformity with its Preliminary Information. It also used the baselines contained in the charts deposited with the United Nations on 13 September 2012 in the claim for extended continental shelf.[29] On 28 December 2012, Japan protested the Submission for the same reason as it protested the Preliminary Information as well as the use of the baselines for the Senkaku Islands/Daiyou Dao.[30] On 13 August 2013, Japan reiterated its view that because of the concerns expressed in its *note verbale* of 28 December 2102 that the Commission should not consider the Chinese submission.[31]

4.3 *Korea*

South Korea also appears to have no potential for a continental shelf beyond 200 nautical miles because of its proximity to neighbouring States. However it also lodged preliminary information with the CLCS[32] and a Submission in December 2012.[33] The preliminary information essentially relates to the portions of the Japan – Korea petroleum joint development zone (JDZ)[34] more than 200 nautical miles from the nearest Korean territory, while the

28 *Note verbale* dated 23 July 2009: reprinted at <https://www.un.org/depts/los/clcs_new/submissions_files/preliminary/jpn_re_chn2009e.pdf>.

29 *Submission of the People's Republic of China Concerning the Outer Limits of the Continental Shelf beyond 200 Nautical Miles in Part of the East China Sea: Executive Summary*, 14 December 2021: reprinted at <https://www.un.org/depts/los/clcs_new/submissions_files/chn63_12/executive%20summary_EN.pdf>.

30 *Note verbale* dated 28 December 2012: reprinted at <https://www.un.org/depts/los/clcs_new/submissions_files/chn63_12/jpn_re_chn_28_12_2012.pdf>. China responded on 5 August 2013: reprinted at <https://www.un.org/depts/los/clcs_new/submissions_files/chn63_12/chn_re_clcs63_08_2013_e.pdf>.

31 *Note verbale* dated 13 August 2013: reprinted at <https://www.un.org/depts/los/clcs_new/submissions_files/chn63_12/jpn_re_chn_13_08_2013.pdf>.

32 See *Preliminary Information regarding the Outer Limits of the Continental Shelf*, 11 May 2009: reprinted at <https://www.un.org/depts/los/clcs_new/submissions_files/preliminary/kor_2009preliminaryinformation.pdf>.

33 *Partial Submission to the Commission on the Limits of the Continental Shelf Pursuant to Article 76 Paragraph 8 of the United Nations Convention on the Law of the Sea: Executive Summary*, 26 December 2012: reprinted at <https://www.un.org/depts/los/clcs_new/submissions_files/kor65_12/executive_summary.pdf>.

34 *Agreement between Japan and the Republic of Korea Concerning Joint Development of the Continental Shelf Adjacent to the Two Countries*, reprinted at in J.I. Charney & L.M. Alexander (eds), *International Maritime Boundaries* (Dordrecht: Martinus Nijhoff, 1996) Vol. 1, 1065–1068.

submission moves further south and east towards Japanese territory. This area is well within 200 nautical miles of Japanese territory, so Japan responded as might be expected. A Japanese *note verbale* protesting to that effect was made in May 2009[35] to the Preliminary Information and similar protests were made by Japan to the Submission in 2012.[36]

4.4 *Japan*

While Japan has made a submission to the CLCS, none of the submissions pertain to areas within the East China Sea.[37] One area of Japan's submission, to the south of Okinotorishima has been the subject of *notes verbale* from China[38] and the Republic of Korea,[39] but it is well to the east and south of the East China Sea. Both *notes verbale* were lodged on the basis that Okinotorishima was in fact a rock for the purposes of Article 121(3) of the Law of the Sea Convention, and therefore Japan was not entitled to generate a continental shelf from the feature.[40]

---

35 *Note verbale* dated 23 July 2009: reprinted at <https://www.un.org/depts/los/clcs_new/submissions_files/preliminary/jpn_re_kor2009e.pdf>.

36 *Note verbale* dated 11 January 2012: reprinted at <https://www.un.org/depts/los/clcs_new/submissions_files/kor65_12/jpn_re_kor_11_01_2013.pdf>. See also subsequent notes verbal from Japan dated 30 April 2013 and 28 August 2013 reprinted at <https://www.un.org/depts/los/clcs_new/submissions_files/kor65_12/jpn_re_kor_30_04_2013.pdf> and <https://www.un.org/depts/los/clcs_new/submissions_files/kor65_12/jpn_re_kor_28_08_2013.pdf>; and the Republic of Korea's responses on 23 January 2013 and 26 August 2013 reprinted at <https://www.un.org/depts/los/clcs_new/submissions_files/kor65_12/kor_re_jpn_23_01_2013.pdf> and <https://www.un.org/depts/los/clcs_new/submissions_files/kor65_12/kor_re_jpn_26_08_2013.pdf>.

37 *Japan's Submission to the Commission on the Limits of the Continental Shelf pursuant to Article 76, paragraph 8 of the United Nations Convention on the Law of the Sea: Executive Summary*, 12 November 2008: reprinted at <https://www.un.org/depts/los/clcs_new/submissions_files/jpn08/jpn_execsummary.pdf>.

38 *Note verbale* dated 6 February 2009: reprinted at <https://www.un.org/depts/los/clcs_new/submissions_files/jpn08/chn_6feb09_e.pdf>. See also n*ote verbale* dated 3 August 2011: reprinted at <https://www.un.org/depts/los/clcs_new/submissions_files/jpn08/chn_3aug11_e.pdf>.

39 *Note verbale* dated 27 February 2009: reprinted at <https://www.un.org/depts/los/clcs_new/submissions_files/jpn08/kor_27feb09.pdf>. See also *Note verbale* dated 11 August 2011: reprinted at <https://www.un.org/depts/los/clcs_new/submissions_files/jpn08/kor11aug11.pdf>.

40 For Japan's responses on 25 March 2009: reprinted at <https://www.un.org/depts/los/clcs_new/submissions_files/jpn08/jpn_25mar09.pdf>; 26 August 2009: reprinted at <https://www.un.org/depts/los/clcs_new/submissions_files/jpn08/jpn_26aug09.pdf>; 9 August 2011: reprinted at <https://www.un.org/depts/los/clcs_new/submissions_files/jpn08/jpn_09aug11.pdf>; 15 August 2011: reprinted at <https://www.un.org/depts/los/clcs_new/submissions_files/jpn08/jpn_15aug11.pdf>; 9 April 2012: reprinted at <https://www.un.org/depts/los/clcs_new/submissions_files/jpn08/jpn_09apr12.pdf>.

5 Existing Boundary Arrangements

It would be wrong to suggest that the East China Sea had been entirely devoid of maritime boundary activity, which is evident in Map 3, and is discussed below. Japan and the Republic of Korea concluded only a partial maritime continental shelf boundary, as well as a petroleum joint development zone. The boundary is a continental shelf boundary concluded in the 1970s and is essentially an equidistance line.[41] South of the Korean Straits, the two States came into dispute over the course of the boundary, once Jeju Island became a factor in the calculation, and so the boundary ceased. With South Korea insisting on a boundary owing much to the configuration of the seabed, and Japan favouring a line of equidistance, the two States agreed to share the disputed area in a joint development zone where they would have shared jurisdiction over petroleum-related activity.[42] The JDZ terminates in the south at an approximate equidistance tripoint with China's EEZ.[43] It was a temporary arrangement, with a lifespan of 50 years from its entry into force.[44]

China has also negotiated a series of provisional fisheries agreements with Korea,[45] and Japan.[46] In both cases these agreements straddle either side of a possible median line and provide for cooperation in fisheries management.[47] In 2008, Japan and China also agreed to a small petroleum joint exploration zone, although whether the "principled consensus" will amount to treaty status is questionable. It provides for cooperation on petroleum in an area adjacent to the larger Japan-Korea petroleum JDZ.[48]

---

41 *Agreement between Japan and the Republic of Korea Concerning the Establishment of Boundary in the Northern Part of the Continental Shelf Adjacent to the Two Countries, supra* note 3.

42 *Agreement between Japan and the Republic of Korea Concerning Joint Development of the Continental Shelf Adjacent to the Two Countries, supra* note 34.

43 Prescott & Schofield, *supra* note 8, p. 436.

44 *Agreement between Japan and the Republic of Korea Concerning Joint Development of the Continental Shelf Adjacent to the Two Countries, supra* note 34, Article XXXI.

45 *Agreement of Fisheries between the Republic of Korea and the People's Republic of China*, 3 August 2000, reprinted in Sun Pyo Kim, *Maritime Delimitation and Interim Arrangements in North East Asia* (The Hague: Martinus Nijhoff, 2004), 347–356.

46 *Agreement on Fisheries between the People's Republic of China and Japan*, 11 November 1997, reprinted in Sun Pyo Kim, *Maritime Delimitation and Interim Arrangements in North East Asia* (The Hague: Martinus Nijhoff, 2004), 338–347.

47 For a discussion of these arrangements see G. Xue, 'Bilateral Fisheries Agreements for the Cooperative Management of the Shared Resources of the China Seas: A Note' 36 *Ocean Development & International Law*, 2005, 363–374.

48 *China and Japan Reach Principled Consensus on the East China Sea Issue*, 2008: reprinted at <https://www.fmprc.gov.cn/ce/ceun/eng/fyrth/t448632.htm>.

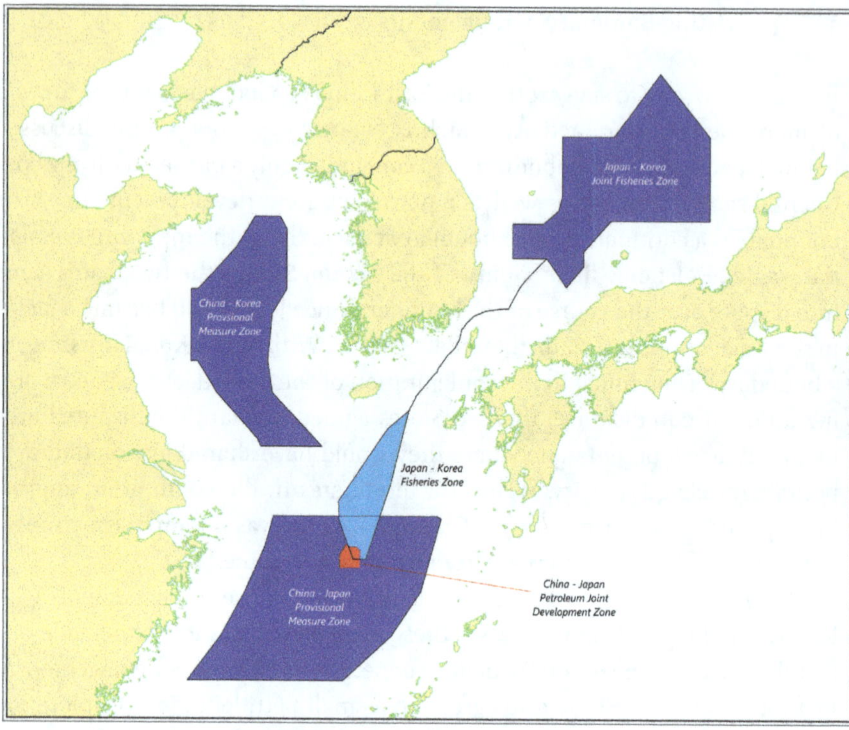

MAP 3 Maritime boundaries and joint development areas

Korea has also negotiated a provisional fisheries agreement with Japan.[49] The joint fisheries zone is in two parts: a northern portion in the vicinity of Liancourt Rocks in the Sea of Japan/East Sea, and a southern portion, south of the delimited continental shelf boundary. There is overlap between this southern zone and the China-Japan fisheries zone, although the application towards the southern limit of the Japan-Korea zone is left vague to ensure the text does not provoke a dispute with China.[50]

Except for the small portion of continental shelf boundary between Japan and the Republic of Korea in the extreme northeast of the area under consideration in this chapter, all of these arrangements are designed to be temporary and without prejudice to a permanent boundary. While it might be expected

49 *Agreement on Fisheries between the Republic of Korea and Japan of 1999*, 1999: reprinted in Sun Pyo Kim, *Maritime Delimitation and Interim Arrangements in North East Asia* (The Hague: Martinus Nijhoff, 2004), 327–338.

50 See *Ibid.*, Annex I and Agreed Minutes, para. 2.

that permanent boundaries, if agreed, would fall within these joint development zones, as a matter of law there is no basis for this to occur.

6 Maritime Boundary Delimitation

6.1 *Law of the Sea Convention Provisions*

While the Law of the Sea Convention has three articles that address maritime boundary delimitation, only two are relevant to the littoral States of the East China Sea. The geography in question means that, with the exception of the delimited maritime boundary in the Tsushima Strait between Japan and Korea, there is no location where the territories of any of the littorals is within 24 nautical miles of each other, obviating the need for a territorial sea boundary.[51] As such, the only provisions of the Convention that are applicable in the relevant region are Articles 74 and 83 of the Convention, dealing with the delimitation of EEZ and continental shelf boundaries respectively. Both articles are identical save for the reference to the applicable zone:

1. The delimitation of the exclusive economic zone/*continental shelf* between States with opposite or adjacent coasts shall be effected by agreement on the basis of international law, as referred to in Article 38 of the Statute of the International Court of Justice, in order to achieve an equitable solution.

The Law of the Sea Convention therefore provides no methodology for States to move forward in delimiting their boundaries beyond doing so by agreement. Articles 74(3) and 83(3) do provide for "provisional arrangements of a practical nature", in order to foster cooperation during the period prior to the conclusion of a boundary, however such arrangements are to be "without prejudice to the final delimitation". As such, the framing of a methodology has been left to international courts and tribunals, or observed through State practice, which in the latter case is of limited utility in providing an assessment of future boundaries. That is to say what States may agree in one part of the world will not be binding upon them, or other States, in a different part of the globe. It is therefore useful to briefly consider the approach of the courts.

51 Even in that case, Japan and the Republic of Korea both decided to keep the territorial seas of their possessions on either side of the Tsushima Straits to 3 nautical miles in width, avoiding a territorial sea boundary: see Suk Kyoon Kim, *Maritime Disputes in Northeast Asia*, (Leiden, Brill Nijhoff, 2017) 39.

6.2 *Approach to Maritime Boundary Delimitation by International Courts and Tribunals*

Various international courts have considered a range of factors when undertaking the delimitation of maritime boundaries. Since 2005, the International Court of Justice has fixed upon a procedural approach that has been applied with consistency by that Court, as well as *ad hoc* arbitrations and the International Tribunal for the Law of the Sea. The process was applied in detail in the first instance in the *Black Sea Case* (*Romania v Ukraine*),[52] although the Court ascribed the elements of the process to earlier jurisprudence. The process is a three step process:

1. The Court will draw a provisional equidistance line, using all the features identified in the relevant area;
2. The Court will then test and if necessary adjust the provisional equidistance line to reflect an equitable result; and
3. The Court will assess whether the result produces a manifestly disproportional result.

The process has been applied in a number of cases subsequent including:

- Nicaragua/Colombia[53]
- Peru/Chile[54]
- Bay of Bengal (Bangladesh/Myanmar)[55]
- Bay of Bengal (Bangladesh/India)[56]
- Ghana/Côte d'Ivoire Case[57]
- Nicaragua/Honduras Case[58]
- Somalia/Kenya Case[59]

Based on this practice, the method is the most appropriate in assessing the possible approach of an international court should there be future litigation concerning the maritime boundary between any of the littoral States or informing the negotiating positions. There are three factors which are potentially relevant

52 *Black Sea Case* (*Romania v Ukraine*) I.C.J. Reports, 2009, p. 101 at para 115–122.

53 *Territorial and Maritime Dispute* (*Nicaragua v Colombia*) I.C.J. Reports 2012, p. 624.

54 *Maritime Dispute* (*Peru v Chile*) I.C.J. Reports, 2014, p. 3 at para 180.

55 *Bay of Bengal* (*Bangladesh v Myanmar*) I.T.L.O.S. Reports 2012, p. 4 at para 233.

56 *Bay of Bengal* (*Bangladesh v India*), 7 July 2014: reprinted at <http://www.pcacases.com/web/sendAttach/383>, at para 336 et seq.

57 *Dispute concerning delimitation of the maritime boundary between Ghana and Côte d'Ivoire in the Atlantic Ocean* (*Ghana v Côte d'Ivoire*), I.T.L.O.S. Reports 2017, p. 4 at para 360.

58 *Territorial and Maritime Dispute between Nicaragua and Honduras in the Caribbean Sea* (*Nicaragua v. Honduras*), I.C.J. Reports 2007, p. 659.

59 *Maritime Delimitation in the Indian Ocean* (*Somalia v Kenya*) I.C.J. Reports 2021 at para 122.

in the East China Sea – the use of straight baselines; the treatment of islands; and the assertion of continental shelf claims. Each will be considered in turn.

6.2.1 Use of Territorial Sea Baselines in Delimitation

The use of territorial sea baselines in maritime boundary delimitation appears to be limited. In the context of decisions of international courts and tribunals, the reasons for this are eloquently expressed by the International Court of Justice in the *Black Sea Case*:

> The Court observes that the issue of determining the baseline for the purpose of measuring the breadth of the continental shelf and the exclusive economic zone and the issue of identifying base points for drawing an equidistance/median line for the purpose of delimiting the continental shelf and the exclusive economic zone between adjacent/ opposite States are two different issues. In the first case, the coastal State, in conformity with the provisions of UNCLOS (Articles 7, 9, 10, 12 and 15), may determine the relevant base points. It is nevertheless an exercise which has always an international aspect (see *Fisheries* (*United Kingdom v. Norway*), Judgment, I.C.J. Reports 1951, p. 132). In the second case, the delimitation of the maritime areas involving two or more States, the Court should not base itself solely on the choice of base points made by one of those Parties. The Court must, when delimiting the continental shelf and exclusive economic zones, select base points by reference to the physical geography of the relevant coasts.[60]

Ultimately, the Court preferred to decide the location of basepoints relevant to the delimitation, rather than utilise lines identified by the coastal State. Certainly, the proclaimed territorial sea baselines used by Bangladesh and Myanmar did not figure in their litigation before the International Tribunal for the Law of the Sea,[61] and the formulation used by the ICJ in the Black Sea quoted above was explicitly adopted in the case of *Bay of Bengal* (*Bangladesh/ India*).[62]

Given the Law of the Sea Convention does permit coastal States to use any method they can agree upon to apply, State practice does appear to have seen the application of straight baselines in the calculation of the course of

60 *Black Sea Case* (*Romania v Ukraine*) I.C.J. Reports, 2009, p. 101 at para 137.

61 *Bay of Bengal* (*Bangladesh v Myanmar*) I.T.L.O.S. Reports 2012, p. 4 at para 264.

62 *Bay of Bengal* (*Bangladesh v India*), 7 July 2014: reprinted at <http://www.pcacases.com/web/sendAttach/383>, at paras 221–222.

a maritime boundary. Identification of such practice can be problematic, as States rarely proscribe a methodology for the calculation of the maritime boundary, which is usually just defined with a series of coordinates. Louis Sohn in 1996 undertook consideration of the employment of straight baselines in boundary delimitation practice, generously stretched to include archipelagic States. In his study, he noted there were 20 instances of straight baselines being taken into account, but 50 instances where they were disregarded.[63]

Sohn also makes the point that often the basepoints that will be used to anchor the territorial sea baselines will be the same basepoints used in the calculation of a boundary, effectively meaning the straight baselines make no material difference in the creation of the boundary.[64] This observation is correct, at least where the baselines employed by a State are relatively conservative. Examples of the straight baseline itself providing additional basepoints are harder to identify and significantly rarer. Ultimately, since there is no compulsion to use territorial sea baselines, either in the Convention or in the decided cases, it will be entirely a matter for the negotiating States, who will be motivated only by whether the use of baselines would be in their interest.

6.2.2 Treatment of Islands

The treatment of islands by international courts has varied considerably, but some common factors can be deduced. Even the smallest features considered in the above cases generated a full territorial sea, save St Martin's Island, whose proximity to the Myanmar coast prevented this from taking place, although the island was given full effect in the creation of an equidistance line within 12 nautical miles.[65] Features such as Quitasueño in Nicaragua/Colombia are very small,[66] consisting in that case of some isolated rocks on a reef structure, and yet Quitasueño received a full territorial sea.[67]

The treatment of islands beyond the generation of a territorial sea has seen variation, although much of this has to the specific geography of each case.

63 L.B. Sohn, 'Baseline Considerations' in J.I. Charney & L.M. Alexander (eds), *International Maritime Boundaries* (Dordrecht: Martinus Nijhoff, 1996) Vol. 1, 153 at 157.

64 *Ibid.*, 156–158.

65 *Bay of Bengal* (*Bangladesh v Myanmar*) I.T.L.O.S. Reports 2012, p. 4 at paras 298–319.

66 See <http://www.shipspotting.com/gallery/photo.php?lid=2635873>.

67 *Territorial and Maritime Dispute* (*Nicaragua v Colombia*) I.C.J. Reports 2012, p. 624 at paras 181–183.

The typical approach over a long period of time has been to ignore or reduce the impact of the island where that feature was perceived to exert a disproportionate effect upon the course of the median line, relative to its size.[68] In the cases since 2005, the same approach was applied with the treatment of Serpents Island in the *Black Sea Case*,[69] the numerous small islands in *Nicaragua v Colombia*[70] and *Nicaragua v Honduras*,[71] and St Martin's Island in the *Bay of Bengal* (*Myanmar/Bangladesh*).[72] The most extreme situation can be seen in the treatment of Quitasueño and Serrana in *Nicaragua v Colombia*. These features were enclaved within the Nicaraguan EEZ, explained by the Court as because they were remote from the remainder of the Colombian

68 See *Newfoundland/Nova Scotia Arbitration*, 26 March 2002: reprinted at <https://www.cnsopb.ns.ca/sites/default/files/pdfs/phaseii_award_english.pdf>: Sable Island (which was part of Nova Scotia) was not used in the calculation of the boundary as it would cause a disproportionately negative impact on the boundary for Newfoundland. The island's territorial sea was unaffected, given its significant distance from the boundary; *Anglo-French Channel Arbitration* 18 ILM 397 (1979): the Channel Islands, which were within a few miles of the French coast, were enclaved within the French continental shelf, while the more remote Scilly Isles and Ushant were given a reduced effect on the calculation of a boundary; *Dubai/Shajah Arbitration* 91 ILR 543 (1981): Abu Musa was restricted to a 12 nautical mile territorial sea because of the disproportionate impact upon Shajah of a median line; *Tunisia/Libya Continental Shelf Case* I.C.J. Reports 1982, p. 18: the Kerkennah Islands were given a reduced effect in the calculation of the maritime boundary; *St Pierre et Miquelon Arbitration* 31 ILM 1148 (1992): islands belonging to France (St Pierre and Miquelon) were given reduced effect, but still received an entitlement beyond the territorial sea; *Qatar/Bahrain Case* [2001] ICJ Reports 40: the International Court of Justice effectively discounted small isolated features from both States that each would have exerted a profound effect on the course of a median line; *Eritrea/Yemen Boundary Arbitration* http://www.pcacases.com/web/sendAttach/518, 3 October 1996: a number of Yemeni islands in the vicinity of the median lime were given reduced effect; *Jan Mayen Case* I.C.J. Reports 1993, p. 38: the small island of Jan Mayen was given a reduced effect in the calculation of a boundary between it and Greenland; *Gulf of Maine Case* (*Canada v United States*) I.C.J. Reports 1984, p. 246: the effect of Seal Island was reduced due to the disproportionate effect it would have on a median line; *Libya/Malta Case* I.C.J. Reports 1985, p. 15: the International Court of Justice reduced the effect of Malta itself in the calculation of the continental shelf boundary, due to its small size relative to Libya; *Guinea/Guinea-Bissau Arbitration* 25 ILM 251 (1986): the impact of Alcatraz Island was reduced to its vicinity, and so as to not impact on a continuing basis out to sea.

69 *Black Sea Case* (*Romania v Ukraine*) I.C.J. Reports, p. 101.

70 *Territorial and Maritime Dispute* (*Nicaragua v Colombia*) I.C.J. Reports 2012, p. 624 at para 167 et seq.

71 *Territorial and Maritime Dispute between Nicaragua and Honduras in the Caribbean Sea* (*Nicaragua v. Honduras*), I.C.J. Reports 2007, p. 659 at para 304 et seq.

72 *Bay of Bengal* (*Bangladesh v Myanmar*) I.T.L.O.S. Reports 2012, p. 4.

EEZ, and their linking to it would have been unfair to Nicaragua.[73] In the most recent *Somalia/Kenya Case,* the ICJ declined to use the small and arid Diua Damasciaca islets as basepoints in the construction of the maritime boundary as they "would have a disproportionate impact on the course of the median line in comparison to the size of these features".[74]

From the cases, a number of factors can be identified:

1. Relatively small islands are not treated equally as compared to large mainland territories;
2. Even very small islands receive a full territorial sea unless within 24 nautical miles of the opposing State's coast;
3. Small islands usually receive a reduced effect in the calculation of a median line, or may be discounted depending on whether their likely impact on a boundary would be very great; and
4. The enclaving of islands in another State's jurisdiction is unusual, and always stems from a grossly disproportionate impact were they to receive treatment to link with their remaining territory's EEZ.

Another factor relevant in the treatment of islands in delimitation is whether the island generates any maritime jurisdiction beyond a territorial sea, assuming it is a natural feature clear of the water at high tide. Article 121(3) of the Law of the Sea Convention provides that a rock that is not capable of human habitation or an economic life of its own, will be limited to a territorial sea, and not generate an EEZ or continental shelf. The Annex VII Tribunal in the *South China Arbitration*[75] took an approach to the interpretation of this provision that set a very high standard for demonstrating what constitutes human habitation or an economic life of its own. By discounting actual habitation as a basis, and focusing on the creation of a largely self-sustaining community,[76] it found that none of the features in the South China Sea qualified as capable of human habitation or an economic life of their own. The Tribunal made this finding in spite of the many hundreds of military personnel from China, Malaysia, the Philippines, Taiwan and Vietnam living on these islands on a permanent basis as government personnel sent to crew a military outpost would not qualify as a settled community.[77] This included the largest island in the Spratlys, Itu Aba, which the Tribunal noted was over forty hectares in area,

73 *Territorial and Maritime Dispute* (*Nicaragua v Colombia*) I.C.J. Reports 2012, p. 624 at para 167 et seq.

74 *Maritime Delimitation in the Indian Ocean* (*Somalia v Kenya*) I.C.J. Reports 2021 at para 114.

75 *South China Sea Arbitration* (*Philippines v China*), 12 July 2016: reprinted at <http://www.pcacases.com/web/sendAttach/2086>.

76 *Ibid.,* at para 520.

77 *Ibid.,* at para 620.

possessed numerous fruit trees and some potable water, as well as a population of several hundred Taiwanese armed forces personnel.[78]

6.2.3 Delimitation of the Continental Shelf beyond 200 Nautical Miles

Another issue that is potentially relevant to the region centres on maritime boundary delimitation of areas of continental shelf beyond 200 nautical miles. In 1969, the ICJ in the *North Sea Continental Shelf Cases*[79] held that the appropriate principle to use in the delimitation of the continental shelf was "natural prolongation". That is to say, where there is a significant submarine feature in the continental shelf, such as a trench or trough that constitutes a break in the seabed, that break should be used as the location of a continental shelf boundary. The concept fell out of favour in subsequent cases, with the ICJ noting in the *Libya/Malta Case* that with the advent of a continental shelf based entirely on distance within 200 nautical miles, the configuration of the seabed was irrelevant to delimitation. The ICJ stated:

> ... the law applicable to the present dispute, that is, to claims relating to continental shelves located less than 200 miles from the coasts of the States in question, is based not on geological or geomorphological criteria, but on a criterion of distance from the Coast or, to use the traditional term, on the principle of adjacency as measured by distance. [80]

However, this approach still left open the use of natural prolongation beyond 200 nautical miles, as the ICJ acknowledged in the same judgment:

> This is not to suggest that the idea of natural prolongation is now superseded by that of distance. What it does mean is that where the continental margin does not extend as far as 200 [M] from the shore, natural prolongation, ... , is in part defined by distance from the shore, irrespective of the physical nature of the intervening sea-bed and subsoil. The concept of natural prolongation and distance are therefore not opposed but complementary; and both remain essential elements in the juridical concept of the continental shelf. [81]

78 *Ibid.*, at paras 580–614.
79 *North Sea Continental Shelf Cases* I.C.J. Reports 1969, p. 3 at para 19.
80 *Libya/Malta Case* I.C.J. Reports 1985, p. 15 at para 61.
81 *Ibid.*

In more recent cases, this window to continue using natural prolongation in delimitation beyond 200 nautical miles has seemingly closed, with judgments stressing a single approach to delimitation that does not distinguish between parts of the continental shelf.[82] In the *Bay of Bengal* (*Bangladesh/Myanmar*) ITLOS was explicitly clear on this issue:

> In the view of the Tribunal, the delimitation method to be employed in the present case for the continental shelf beyond 200 nautical miles should not differ from that within 200 nm. Accordingly, the equidistance/relevant circumstances method continues to apply for the delimitation of the continental shelf beyond 200 nm. This method is rooted in the recognition that sovereignty over the land territory is the basis for the sovereign rights and jurisdiction of the coastal State with respect to both the exclusive economic zone and the continental shelf ...[83]

The same approach was used by the Annex VII Tribunal in the *Bay of Bengal* (*Bangladesh/India*).[84] In the *Somalia/Kenya Case*, the ICJ merely continued the geodetic used to set the boundary within the EEZ, indicating no change in methodology.[85]

7 Possible Boundaries

7.1 *China/Republic of Korea*

In applying the approach to boundary delimitation used in the Black Sea Case, a possible maritime boundary between China and the Republic of Korea would be initially marked out through the drawing of a median line and making adjustments to account for any features that might have a disproportionate impact upon the course of the boundary. Since both States are relatively far apart, with no inconveniently located islands or peninsulas, in theory this should be straight-forward. However, drawing the median line will require consideration of which basepoints are to be used in its construction, as both States have extensive straight baseline systems facing each other across the

82 *Barbados/Trinidad & Tobago Arbitration*, XXVII R.I.A.A. 147 (2006), para 213.
83 *Bay of Bengal* (*Bangladesh v Myanmar*) I.T.L.O.S. Reports 2012, p. 4 at para 455.
84 *Bay of Bengal* (*Bangladesh v India*), 7 July 2014: reprinted at <http://www.pcacases.com/web/sendAttach/383>, at para 457.
85 *Maritime Delimitation in the Indian Ocean* (*Somalia v Kenya*) I.C.J. Reports 2021 at para 196.

East China and Yellow Seas, with neither having a relevant basepoint on their mainland territory, save for the terminal point of the Chinese baselines.

The relevance of the baselines and their possible use can be seen in the accompanying map. It shows the control lines used in the construction of the median line, identifying the basepoints used in the construction of the line. What is interesting from this map is that it demonstrates the Chinese baselines are far more significant in the construction of the median line than their Korean counterparts. Since the Chinese baselines mask large sections of the coast, including those connecting the small islands south of the Shandong Peninsula, the baselines themselves become relevant to the construction of the median line. This is even more stark in the baselines employed between Darshan Island and Sheshan Island. These baselines are very long, and according to the analysis in *Limits in the Seas* are anchored on undeveloped low tide elevations, which is inconsistent with Article 7 of the Law of the Sea Convention.[86] These baselines provide a large number of control points in the construction of the median line in Map 4. While the Korean baselines are also relevant in this fashion in places, a much larger portion of the Korean control points are based on islands.

On this basis, the Republic of Korea would be much better served through the use of a median line constructed from actual land features, while China does much better from using its baseline system. In the unlikely event that an international tribunal were ever to consider a possible boundary, the treatment of territorial sea baselines in international case law in the construction of a boundary would greatly favour the Korean position.

On the Korean side, the islands used in the baseline systems do appear, from the information available, to be entitled to generate the full range of maritime zones (Mara Island; Soheugson-so and Hong-do), with the exception of North Clifford Island to the west of Taean, which has only a lighthouse. If this island could not be used to generate an EEZ, there are four inhabited islands closer to the coast within the limits of the Taeanhaean National Park just to the east, so the impact upon Korean jurisdiction would be limited. On the Chinese side, the critical features are the Zhoushan Islands, which extend the Chinese baselines to the east of Shanghai. Although the islands are small, many have been inhabited for many centuries.

86 US State Department, 'Straight Baselines: China' (1996) 117 *Limits in the Seas* 1 at 3–8.

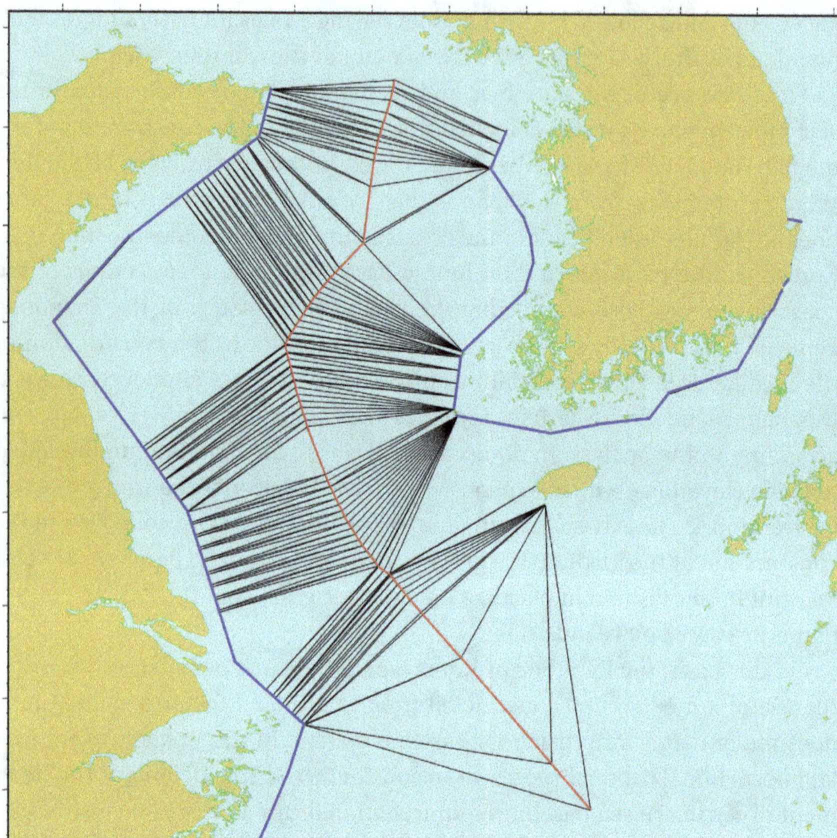

MAP 4 Theoretical equidistance line and control points

7.2 *China/Japan*

For the maritime boundary between China and Japan, there are a number of complicating factors. First is the disputed status of the Diaoyu/Senkaku Islands. Since maritime jurisdiction is based upon sovereignty over land territory, where there is a dispute over sovereignty it is effectively impossible to resolve the course of a maritime boundary involving maritime zones generated from such territory. Since neither Japan nor China has shown any sign of a compromise involving the islands, the dispute makes the conclusion of a maritime boundary impossible in the southern quadrant of the East China Sea.

Even if a solution to the sovereignty dispute could be found, it is unclear whether the Islands would generate the full range of maritime zones. They have not been inhabited since before World War II, and from 1945 until 1972 they were under the control of the United States, which mainly used them as a site for military training. The first recorded permanent settlement of the Islands was in 1900 when a fish processing facility was built by a Japanese businessman. His venture failed in 1940 and the Islands have remained uninhabited since that time. On that basis, applying the definition of "capable of human habitation", as used in the *South China Sea Arbitration*, might be problematic, as there would seem to be a lack of a settled community, and the only economic activity was essentially extractive in nature.

The presence of the island of Taiwan in the south also adds to the complexity. Japan does not recognize the government in Taipei, but is unlikely to treat with China to determine a maritime boundary between its territory and Taiwan as the island is not under the control of Beijing. The government in Taipei has proclaimed territorial sea baselines, enclosing the two small islands (P'eng-chia Yu and Mien-hua Yu) to the north of the main island,[87] but there has been no adoption of those baselines nor a separate proclamation by Beijing.

Further north, the maritime boundary between the Ryukyu Islands of Japan and China is also problematic. In this instance, there are a full set of territorial sea baselines on only one side of the delimitation. China's baselines shield its entire mainland coast while the Japanese baselines around Okinawa and Amami Oshima are irrelevant in the calculation of a median line as other Japanese islands are closer to the Chinese coast. The baselines enclosing a number of offshore features to the southwest of Kyushu are relevant in the construction of a median line.

In the vicinity of Okinawa, a median line would rely upon only three Japanese islands in its construction: Kume Island, Torishima and Iōtorishima. The first of these is inhabited and certainly would generate the full range of maritime zones under Article 121(3) of the Law of the Sea Convention, even with the most conservative interpretation. The remaining two islands are problematic. Torishima is a small isolated feature 38 kilometres north of Kume, and is uninhabited. It has been used as a bombing range for the American and Japanese militaries, and in physical area, it is less than one tenth the size of Itu Aba Island in the South China Sea, which was found to be a rock in the *South China Sea Arbitration*. North of Okinawa, Iōtorishima, which is 2.5 square kilometres in area, is an active volcano that remained inhabited for hundreds of years until 1958 when the residents were evacuated for their own safety. Whether this historic occupation would be sufficient, given there was formerly a settled community as required from the formulation used in the *South China Sea*

87 *Law on the Territorial Sea and the Contiguous Zone*, 21 January 1998, Annex 2.

Arbitration, or whether the abandonment of the island for over 50 years is too long and is recognition that the island is not inhabited is a moot point.

Moving northward, Yokoatejima and Takarajima represent potential basepoints for Japan, however only Takarajima is inhabited, as Yokoatejima is a steep sided volcano which was last active in the 19th Century. Even if it were unable to be used, the availability of Takarajima would see little change in the course of the median line. Enclosed with the baselines surrounding Kyushu, the basepoints generated by and Suzume Island (part of the Uji Islands) and Kusagaki-gunto would also be relevant. Neither of these features are inhabited.

On the Chinese side, while there are a large number of fringing islands scattered along the southern coast from Shanghai southwards, the baselines employed are very long, with five of the six used being in excess of 34 nautical miles in length, and half more than 69 nautical miles long. As is evident from Map 4, these baselines are used as control points for a median line, which is disadvantageous to Japan, although given the numbers of other features inboard of the baselines, the impact upon the course of the median line would not be great. The Chinese islands anchoring the basepoints appear to be either inhabited islands, or smaller features with navigational aids upon them.

A distinct factor in the possible China/Japan boundary in the East China Sea is the existence of the Okinawa Trough, and the extended continental shelf claimed by China in its submission to the Commission on the Limits of the Continental Shelf. The Chinese submission runs to the edge of the Trough and approaches to between 20 and 25 nautical miles from Japanese territory. This appears to indicate that China views the trough as the logical boundary between its jurisdiction and Japan's jurisdiction. However since the Trough is more than 200 nautical miles from the nearest Chinese territory this presumably mean that there would have to be a water column boundary much further to the west.

The existence of the Okinawa Trough would be unlikely to sway an international court or tribunal that it should be used as the maritime boundary between China and Japan. As noted above, cases have not used submarine features in this fashion nor referred positively to such an approach since the *North Sea Continental Cases* in 1969, and more recently have indicated that there should be no distinction in the approach used to delimit the continental shelf whether within 200 nautical miles or beyond it. As such, China's position with respect to the Trough is not strong.

On the other hand, the positions of China and Japan are analogous to that of Nicaragua and Colombia in their maritime boundary delimitation case. Colombia's small and remote offshore islands were faced with the mainland coast of Nicaragua, masked with its own small offshore islands, and a similar description could be made of the geography of Chinese and Japanese territories across the East China Sea, albeit much further apart. In that case, the ICJ held that the smaller Colombian islands should be given less weight, and the median line drawn was adjusted to Nicaragua's favour. A tribunal might therefore be of the view some adjustment in China's favour is appropriate, although unlike that case, most of the Japanese islands are inhabited, so should not be discounted altogether. While the amount of such an adjustment is entirely speculative, given the Japanese islands are much further from the coast of China than the Colombian islands, the scale of the adjustment might be less than in that case.

7.3 *Japan/Republic of Korea*

A median line between the republic of Korea and Japan is dominated by Jeju Island on the Korean side, and a number of small features on the Japanese side. For Japan, the Danjo Islands are located to the west of Kyushu and fall outside of the joint development zone agreed between the two States in 1974. The Danjo Islands are uninhabited, although there has been a manned lighthouse on Me Island, in the southwest of the group, for many years. To the north of the group is a small feature on the charts marked as Torinoshima, consisting of two outcrops with elevations of 17 and 9 metres. All of these features would generate a territorial sea, but it is likely that Korea would dispute their ability to generate an EEZ, and as much seems to be reflected in the course of the joint development zone around them.

If the Danjo Islands are ignored, the Japanese features that exert impact on a median line are Fukue Island and its smaller near neighbour, Saganoshima, both of which are inhabited. Using these islands and Jeju Island produces a median line as marked on Map 5. The theoretical line is not affected by Japan's straight baselines and is much closer to the western side of the joint development zone.

The Republic of Korea, like China, has also made a claim to an area of shelf beyond 200 nautical miles which is influenced by the presence of the Okinawa Trough. The claimed area of shelf is even closer to the Japanese islands than the Chinese claim, and for the reasons discussed above in that context, is unlikely to influence the course of a possible maritime boundary.

8 Conclusions

There is little likelihood of an international court or tribunal having a role in determining any of the maritime boundaries in the East China Sea. While

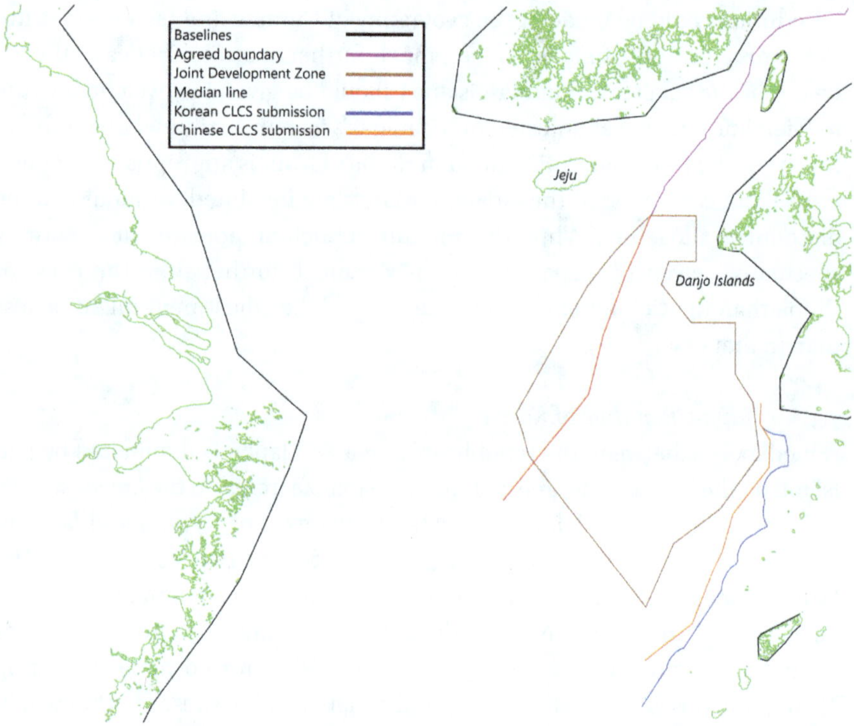

MAP 5 East China Sea continental shelf claims

Japan has not made a choice of procedure for disputes under the Law of the Sea Convention, nor sought any exemption from jurisdiction for boundary disputes, both China and the Republic of Korea have sought to use the optional exception for maritime boundary disputes under Article 298. As such, Japan could avoid a referral of a boundary dispute with its Chinese or Korean neighbours on the basis of reciprocity.

A negotiated boundary would not be assisted by reliance upon the State practice on the parties. Chinese territorial sea baselines impact upon the course of median lines if they are used in their calculation, and the continental shelf submissions to the CLCS made by China and Korea would make negotiation of a maritime boundary based on those submissions virtually impossible. When combined with the disputed status of the Senkaku/Diaoyu Islands and the presence of the island of Taiwan, there seems little prospect at present of concluding maritime boundaries. That said, the littoral States have been able to agree to joint arrangements with respect to fisheries, which is suggestive that some accommodation between each may be possible, if unlikely.

CHAPTER 21

ASEAN and Peaceful Management of Maritime Disputes in the South China Sea

Robert Beckman and Vu Hai Dang

1 Introduction

This chapter examines the role of ASEAN (the Association of Southeast Asian Nations) in the peaceful management of disputes in the South China Sea. It begins with a brief history of ASEAN, the "ASEAN way" and the concept of "ASEAN Centrality". It then summarizes the sovereignty and maritime disputes among States bordering the South China Sea and the early attempts of ASEAN to assist in managing these disputes, including the 1992 ASEAN Declaration on the South China Sea. The chapter also analyses the ASEAN position relating to the South China Sea disputes. Next, it focuses on efforts of ASEAN to manage the South China Sea disputes between China and the ASEAN Member States through the 2002 ASEAN-China Declaration on the Conduct of Parties in the South China Sea and the ongoing negotiations between China and ASEAN on a Code of Conduct for the South China Sea. Finally, it explains the role that ASEAN can play in the peaceful management of the maritime disputes in the South China Sea.

2 ASEAN: A Brief Historical Background

2.1 *Foundation*

ASEAN came into being at the height of the Cold War between the United States and the Soviet Union. In 1967 in Bangkok, Thailand, the Ministers of Foreign Affairs of Indonesia, Malaysia, the Philippines, Singapore and Thailand signed the ASEAN Declaration,[1] which formally established "an Association for Regional Cooperation among the countries of South-East Asia to be known as the Association of South-East Asian Nations (ASEAN)".[2] The aims and purposes of ASEAN were, among other things, to accelerate economic growth, social

1 The ASEAN Declaration, 8 August 1967, Bangkok, Thailand.

2 Ibid., Art. 1.

 | DOI:10.1163/9789004518629_022

progress and cultural development in the region, promote regional peace and stability, promote active collaboration and mutual assistance on matters of common interest, collaborate more effectively for the greater utilization of their agriculture and industries, the expansion of their trade, the improvement of their transportation and communications facilities and the raising of the living standards of their peoples.[3]

2.2 *ASEAN Community*

ASEAN has since doubled its membership, from its five founding Member States in 1967 to ten. Brunei became ASEAN's sixth member in 1984, Viet Nam joined as its seventh member in 1995, Laos and Myanmar joined in 1997, and Cambodia joined as its tenth member in 1999.

At the 9th ASEAN Summit in 2003, ASEAN Leaders adopted the Declaration of ASEAN Concord II which provided for the establishment of an ASEAN Community.[4] According to the Concord, the future ASEAN Community would comprise of three pillars: political and security, economic and socio-cultural. The ASEAN Security Community was established to bring ASEAN's political and security cooperation to a higher plane to ensure that countries in the region live at peace with one another and with the world at large in a just, democratic and harmonious environment. The ASEAN Economic Community is the realization of the end-goal of economic integration to create a stable, prosperous and highly competitive ASEAN economic region. The ASEAN Socio-Cultural Community envisaged a Southeast Asia bonded together in partnership as a community of caring societies.[5]

2.3 *ASEAN Centrality*

ASEAN has established a network of regional mechanisms involving major players in the Indo-Pacific through its ASEAN Plus meetings. Many of these mechanisms deal with security and maritime issues. They include the East Asia Summit,[6] the ASEAN Regional Forum,[7] the ASEAN Defense Ministerial

---

3 Ibid., Art. 2.

4 Declaration of ASEAN Concord II (Bali Concord II) adopted at the 9th ASEAN Summit, 7–8 October 2003, Bali, Indonesia.

5 Ibid.

6 The EAS is a forum between Leaders of 18 countries of the Asia-Pacific region formed to further the objectives of regional peace, security and prosperity. EAS Membership includes 10 ASEAN Member States, Australia, China, India, Japan, New Zealand, Republic of Korea, Russia and the United States. See India at the East Asia Summit (August 2018) online: Ministry of External Affairs of India <http://mea.gov.in/aseanindia/about-eas.htm>.

7 ASEAN Regional Forum serves to foster constructive dialogue and consultation on political and security issues of common interest and concern and to contribute to

Meeting Plus[8] and the Expanded ASEAN Maritime Forum.[9] These initiatives have not only been a tool for ASEAN to engage with major regional powers (China, the United States, India, Japan, South Korea and Australia) but also serve as fora where the participating States can discuss and exchange views on important regional matters. For this reason, ASEAN has actively promoted and upheld the principle of "ASEAN centrality" in order to maintain its central role in discussing and solving issues which are relevant to its Member States and the region.

2.4 *The ASEAN Way*

ASEAN is well-known for its "ASEAN Way". This refers to its tradition of dealing with regional and international issues, especially the resolution of inter-State conflicts, in a manner strongly influenced by Asian traditions and values. It prefers consensus, consultation, informality, and non-confrontation, rather than the legally binding, high institutionalization and compliance-oriented approaches followed in regional groups such as the European Union.[10] The influence of the ASEAN Way may be observed in the ASEAN decision-making process, enshrined in the article 20 of the ASEAN Charter, which states that "[a]s a basic principle, decision-making in ASEAN shall be based on consultation and consensus".[11]

3 ASEAN and the South China Sea Dispute

The South China Sea dispute refers to the sovereignty and maritime disputes between China and the ASEAN Member States bordering the South China

---

confidence-building and preventive diplomacy in the Asia-Pacific region. It is held annually between ASEAN Member States, observers and ASEAN partners. For details see online: ASEAN Regional Forum <http://aseanregionalforum.asean.org/about-arf/>.

8 ADMM-Plus involves Ministers of Defence from 10 ASEAN Member States and 8 ASEAN Dialogue Partners, namely Australia, China, India, Japan, New Zealand, Republic of Korea, Russian Federation, and the United States. It meets yearly to discuss how to strengthen security and defence cooperation for peace, stability and development in the region. For more details, see online: ASEAN Defence Ministers' Meeting <https://admm.asean.org/>.

9 The EAMF was initiated in 2011 to encourage dialogue between East Asia Summit participating countries to utilise opportunities and address common challenges on maritime issues. It is held annually back-to-back with the ASEAN Maritime Forum. For details, see 1st EAMF Chairman's Statement, 5 October 2012, Manila, Philippines.

10 A. Acharya, 'Ideas, Identity and Institution-building: From 'ASEAN Way' to the 'Asia-Pacific Way'?', *The Pacific Review* 10, Issue 3 (1997), 319.

11 Charter of the Association of Southeast Asian Nations, 20 November 2007, Singapore, Art. 20.

Sea – Brunei, Indonesia, Malaysia, Philippines and Viet Nam. Viet Nam claims sovereignty over all the features in the Paracel Islands and Spratly Islands; Philippines claims sovereignty over most of the Spratly Islands in what it refers to as the Kalayaan Islands; and Malaysia and Brunei claim some features in the southern part of the Spratly Islands.[12] China claims sovereignty over four groups of features in the South China Sea (Paracel Islands, Spratly Islands, Pratas Island and Macclesfield Bank) and rights and jurisdiction over the surrounding waters.[13] Although the legal basis of China's claim to rights and jurisdiction in the South China Sea is shrouded in ambiguity, it is usually depicted by the 'nine-dash line map' that China attached to the diplomatic note it sent to the UN Secretary-General in May 2009.[14] The nine-dash lines on the map cover about 80% of the South China Sea and extend as far as the waters near the Natuna islands of Indonesia. Although Indonesia does not claim sovereignty over any of the disputed islands in the South China Sea, and its sovereignty over the Natuna Islands is not in dispute, China's claim to rights and jurisdiction in the South China Sea overlaps with the EEZ claim of Indonesia from the Natuna Islands. Consequently, there is a dispute between Indonesia and China with respect to China's maritime claims in the South China Sea.

3.1 *ASEAN and the South China Sea Disputes: A History*

ASEAN began addressing the South China Sea issues in the late 1980s when tensions rose after China occupied six features in the Spratly Islands. In 1988, China used force to drive Viet Nam off Johnson Reef.[15] Tensions between China and Viet Nam increased in the early 1990s over oil concessions in Vanguard Bank, off the southern coast of Viet Nam.[16]

In January 1990, Indonesia convened the first Workshop on Managing Potential Conflicts in the South China Sea. This workshop process was headed by Ambassador Hasjim Djalal of Indonesia and Professor Ian Townsend-Gault

---

12 R. (Pete) Pedrozo, *China versus Vietnam: An Analysis of the Competing Claims in the South China Sea* (August 2014) CNA Occasional Paper and J. A. Roach, *Malaysia and Brunei: An Analysis of their Claims in the South China Sea* (August 2014) CAN Occasional Paper.

13 *Statement of the Government of the People's Republic of China on China's Territorial Sovereignty and Maritime Rights and Interests in the South China Sea,* (12 July 2016) online: Ministry of Foreign Affairs of the People's Republic of China <https://www.fmprc.gov.cn/nanhai/eng/snhwtlcwj_1/>.

14 Note No. CML/17/2009 dated 7 May 2009 from the Permanent Mission of the People's Republic of China to the United Nations to the Secretary-General of the United Nations.

15 B. Hayton, *The South China Sea: The Struggle for Power in Asia* (London: Yale University Press, 2014), 81–84.

16 Ibid., 125.

of Canada, with funding from Canada, and became an important informal policy-oriented Track 1.5 forum for discussions on the South China Sea. The Workshops were attended by ASEAN member States, China and Chinese Taipei.[17]

The first official ASEAN joint declaration on the South China Sea was issued in 1992.[18] This could have been a response to the adoption by China of the Law on the Territorial Sea and Contiguous Zone in February 1992,[19] which had prompted negative reactions from Indonesia, Malaysia and Philippines.[20]

Tensions between China and the Philippines increased in 1995 after China occupied Mischief Reef, a low-tide elevation in the exclusive economic zone of the Philippines.[21] From the mid-1990s onward, there were regular incidents between China and Viet Nam, and between China and the Philippines.[22] Malaysia had also occupied several of the Spratly Islands in the early 1980s, but there were no reported incidents between Malaysia and China in the 1990s.

In May 2009, Malaysia and Viet Nam jointly submitted to the Committee on the Limits of the Continental Shelf (CLCS) their claim for an extended continental shelf in the Southern area of the South China Sea. At the same time, Viet Nam also made a separate submission to an extended continental shelf in the South China Sea. These submissions to the CLCS prompted China to send an official protest note to the UN Secretary-General and to attach its nine-dashed line map to its diplomatic note. Malaysia, Vietnam, Philippines and Indonesia then responded to challenge the claims in China's diplomatic note.[23]

---

17 H. Djalal & I. Townsend-Gault, 'Preventive Diplomacy: Managing Potential Conflicts in the South China Sea' in: Chester Crocker, Fen Osler Hampson, and Pamela Aall (eds), *Herding Cats: Multiparty Mediation in a Complex World*, Washington, DC: United States Institute of Peace Press, 1999, 107.

18 ASEAN Declaration on the South China Sea, 22 July 1992, Manila, Philippines. For a reproduction of the text, see: H. T. Nguyen, 'Vietnam and the Code of Conduct for the South China Sea', *Ocean Development and International Law* 32, No.2, 2001, 105 at 124–125.

19 The Law claims sovereignty over China's mainland and offshore islands, including the Spratlys. See Law on the Territorial Sea and the Contiguous Zone of the People's Republic of China, 25 February 2020, online: UN DOALOS <https://www.un.org/depts/los/LEGISLATIONANDTREATIES/PDFFILES/CHN_1992_Law.pdf>, Art. 2.

20 L. Buszynski, 'ASEAN, the Declaration on Conduct, and the South China Sea', *Contemporary Southeast Asia* 25, No.3, 2003, 343 at 348.

21 B. Hayton, *supra* note 15, at 84–89.

22 I. Storey, 'Creeping Assertiveness: China, the Philippines and the South China Sea Dispute', *Contemporary Southeast Asia* 21, No.1 1999, 95 at 98 and R. Amer, 'The Sino-Vietnamese Approach to Managing Boundary Disputes', *IBRU Maritime Briefing* 3 (2002), 23.

23 The Joint Submission of Malaysia & Vietnam, China's protest, and the Notes Verbale of Vietnam, Malaysia, Philippines and Indonesia are available at https://www.un.org/depts/los/clcs_new/submissions_files/submission_mysvnm_33_2009.htm.

One of the most significant developments on the South China Sea was the decision by the Philippines in 2013 to institute arbitral proceedings against China under Annex VII of the 1982 United Nations Convention on the Law of the Sea (1982 UNCLOS).[24] China refused to participate in the case and adopted a policy of non-participation and non-compliance. Nevertheless, the case proceeded, and the Arbitral Tribunal made its decision on the merits of the case in July 2016.[25] The award of the arbitral tribunal was consistent with the practice of the ASEAN States on maritime claims and contrary to the claims of China to rights and jurisdiction in the waters inside its nine dashed line in the South China Sea. The arbitral tribunal ruled that none of the features in the disputed Spratly Islands was an island entitled to an Exclusive Economic Zone or continental shelf of its own. In addition, it ruled that whatever "historic rights" China may have had to the resources in the South China Sea in areas that are now within the EEZ of other States, it gave up such historic rights when it became a party to UNCLOS. Although China decided not to participate in the arbitration, the Award of the Tribunal is nevertheless final and binding on the two parties to the case, the Philippines and China. However, China has declared that in its view the award of the tribunal is null and void.

In December 2019, Malaysia made a separate submission to the CLCS for an extended continental shelf in the South China Sea. China immediately objected by submitting an official protest. China's diplomatic note provoked a "notes verbales war" between China and the ASEAN member States surrounding the South China Sea in which the ASEAN member States challenged the legality of China's maritime claims in the South China Sea. In addition, States from outside the region also submitted notes or statements to the UN Secretary-General questioning the legal basis of China's claims. This included the United States, Australia, the United Kingdom, Germany, France, Japan and New Zealand.[26] Several of the diplomatic notes cited the 2016 Award of the Arbitral Tribunal as a basis for challenging China's maritime claims in the South China Sea.

24 United Nations Convention on the Law of the Sea, Montego Bay, Jamaica on 10 December 1982, UNTS 1833, at 397 (entered into force 16 November 1994), Annex VII.

25 PCA Case No 2013–19, in the Matter of the South China Sea Arbitration, The Republic of the Philippines v. The People's Republic of China, Award of 12 July 2016, online: PCA <https://docs.pca-cpa.org/2016/07/PH-CN-20160712-Award.pdf>.

26 For details about Malaysia and Viet Nam's submissions, see: Commission on the Limits of the Continental Shelf https://www.un.org/depts/los/clcs_new/submissions_files/submission_mys_12_12_2019.html.

3.2 *Implications of ASEAN's Policy of Making Decisions by Consensus*

The South China Sea is one of those issues on which ASEAN Members have divergent interests. Five of the ten ASEAN member States have a direct interest in the maritime and sovereignty disputes in the South China Sea. Brunei, Malaysia, the Philippines and Viet Nam border the South China Sea and are "claimant States" in the sense that they claim sovereignty over some or all of the disputed features in the Spratlys or/and Paracels. Indonesia is not a claimant State, but it borders the South China Sea and China's claim to sovereign rights and jurisdiction inside its nine dash-line map overlaps with Indonesia's claim to an Exclusive Economic Zone from the Natuna Islands. In addition, the maritime claims of the Philippines may also overlap with the maritime claims of Malaysia and Viet Nam.

On the other extreme, two of the ASEAN Member States have almost no interest in the South China Sea. Laos PDR is a land-locked State and Myanmar borders the Andaman Sea. While Cambodia and Thailand border the Gulf of Thailand rather than the South China Sea, they have an interest in the commercial shipping routes connecting the Gulf of Thailand and the South China Sea. Singapore also has an interest in the South China Sea because the major shipping route between the Indian Ocean and East Asia passes through the Straits of Malacca and Singapore before entering the South China Sea.

Not only do the ASEAN Member States have divergent national interests in the maritime and sovereignty disputes in the South China Sea, but they also have different relationships with the major powers which have interests in the South China Sea, especially China. As a result, it is sometimes extremely difficult for the Member States to reach a consensus on statements concerning the South China Sea.

An example of the difficulties inherent in the ASEAN policy of decision-making by consensus is the failure of the ASEAN Foreign Ministers' Meeting to reach a consensus on the South China Sea paragraphs in the AMM Joint Communiqué, at the 45th AMM in July 2012 in Phnom Penh. Because of a deadlock on the wording relating to the South China Sea issue, the annual meeting of the ASEAN Foreign Ministers did not conclude with the customary Joint Communiqué for the first time.

Another example is ASEAN's silence after the Award of the Arbitral Tribunal in the South China Sea Case. Although this case was obviously of great interest to the ASEAN claimant States in the South China Sea, the ASEAN Foreign Ministers were unable to reach a consensus on any language about the arbitration case in their annual statements on the South China Sea.

3.3 ASEAN *Common Position on the South China Sea Dispute*

The common position of ASEAN relating to the South China Sea dispute has been set out in the official statements issued at the close of meetings of the ASEAN Foreign Ministers.[27] At its latest 54th meeting in August 2021, the Foreign Ministers affirmed the need to enhance mutual trust and confidence, exercise self-restraint in the conduct of activities, avoid actions that may further complicate the situation, and pursue peaceful resolution of disputes in accordance with the universally recognised principles of international law, including the UNCLOS. They emphasised the importance of non-militarisation and self-restraint in the conduct of all activities by claimants and all other states. They reaffirmed the importance of maintaining and promoting peace, security, stability, safety, and freedom of navigation in and overflight above the South China Sea and recognised the benefits of having the South China Sea as a sea of peace, stability, and prosperity. They underscored the importance of the full and effective implementation of the DOC in its entirety and looked forward to further progress towards the early conclusion of an effective and substantive COC that is in accordance with international law, including UNCLOS. They emphasised the need to maintain and promote an environment conducive to the COC negotiations and welcomed practical measures that could reduce tensions and the risk of accidents, misunderstandings and miscalculation. They stressed the importance of undertaking confidence building and preventive measures to enhance, among others, trust and confidence amongst parties, and reaffirmed the importance of upholding international law, including the 1982 UNCLOS.[28]

4 China-ASEAN Negotiations on a Code of Conduct

4.1 *2002 Declaration on Conduct of Parties in the South China Sea*

The establishment of a Code of Conduct (COC) for all relevant parties in the South China Sea was first suggested in the 1992 Declaration on the South China Sea by ASEAN Ministers of Foreign Affairs at the 25th AMM.[29] The first codes of conduct on the South China Sea were adopted bilaterally between the Philippines and China, and the Philippines and Viet Nam in 1995.[30] The

27 Overview, online: ASEAN Foreign Ministers' Meeting <https://asean.org/asean-political-security-community/asean-foreign-ministers-meeting-amm/#12e7a8305876ob4da>.

28 Joint Communiqué of the 54th ASEAN Foreign Ministers Meeting, 2 August 2021, ss 89–90.

29 1992 ASEAN Declaration on the South China Sea, *supra* note 18.

30 Joint Statement of the RP-PRC on the South China Sea and on Other Areas of Cooperation, 9–10 August 1995, and Joint Statement of the 4th Annual Bilateral Consultations between

proposal for a regional Code of Conduct was then endorsed at the 29th AMM in Jakarta, Indonesia in 1995. The ASEAN Draft Code of Conduct was presented to China during the 6th ARF Meeting in 1999.[31] China was reluctant about the idea at first, but later it seemed to be interested and suggested its own version of the draft code.[32] The 1st ASEAN-China Consultation on the Code of Conduct on the South China Sea was held in Hua Hin, Thailand in 2000.

During the negotiations between the ASEAN and China on the COC important disagreements appeared. For example, China rejected the mention of Paracels in the disputed areas and in the commitment to refrain from occupying new islands, reefs, or shoals. ASEAN objected to China's proposal to ban multilateral military exercises and military patrols in the Spratly Islands. To resolve the deadlock in negotiations, Malaysia suggested at the 35th AMM in July 2002 in Brunei to have a "declaration" on the conduct of parties which would be less binding than a "code" of conduct.[33] This suggestion was endorsed by the AMM.[34] China also accepted the idea of a declaration of conduct. The result was the adoption of the 2002 Declaration on the Conduct of Parties in the South China Sea by Ministers of Foreign Affairs of China and ASEAN in November 2002 in Phnom Penh, Cambodia (DOC).[35]

The DOC has no provisions on the controversial issues that had been raised by the parties in the negotiations. It only refers to the South China Sea and does not state exactly where it applies. It does not ban military exercises or military patrols. Its provisions include respect for international law, peaceful resolution of disputes, respect for freedom of navigation and overflight, the exercise of self-restraint, confidence-building measures, and cooperative activities. However, the DOC also reaffirmed that the adoption of a code of conduct in the South China Sea would further promote peace and stability in

---

the Republic of Philippines and the Socialist Republic of Viet Nam, Hanoi, 7 November 1995. For a reproduction of the text of these two codes of conduct see Nguyen, *supra* note 18, at Appendixes 2 & 3.

31 R. Amer, "Ongoing Efforts in Conflict Management" in: Timo Kivimäki (ed.), *War or Peace in the South China Sea,* Copenhagen: NIAS Press, 2002, 117 at note 27. See also 6th ARF Chairman's Statement, 26 July 1999, Singapore, para. 11.

32 H. T. Nguyen, 'The Declaration of Conduct of Parties in the South China Sea: a Vietnamese Perspective 2002–2007', in: Bateman, Sam, and Emmers, Ralf (eds), *Security and International Politics in the South China Sea: Towards a Co-operative Management Regime,* London: Taylor and Francis, 2009, 207 at 209; and L. Buszynski, *supra* note 20, 355.

33 Buszynski, *supra* note 20, 356.

34 Joint Communiqué of the 35th AMM, 29–30 July 2002, Brunei, paras. 40–41.

35 Declaration on the Conduct of Parties in the South China Sea, Phnom Penh, 4 November 2002, online: ASEAN <https://asean.org/declaration-on-the-conduct-of-parties-in-the-south-china-sea-2/>.

the region, and reiterated the Parties' commitment to working, on the basis of consensus, towards the eventual attainment of this objective.[36] The one paragraph in the DOC that arguably reduced tensions is paragraph 5 in which the parties agreed to exercise self-restraint in the conduct of activities that would complicate or escalate the disputes, including refraining from inhabiting any presently uninhabited features.

4.2 *2011 Guidelines for Implementation of the 2002 Declaration of Conduct*

In 2004, the 1st ASEAN-China Senior Officials Meeting for the implementation of the DOC (SOM-DOC) was convened in Kuala Lumpur, Malaysia to set up a Joint Working Group to implement the DOC (JWG-DOC).[37] Its Terms of Reference stated that the JWG would formulate recommendations in guidelines and action plans for the implementation of the DOC, specific cooperative activities in the South China Sea, a register of experts and eminent persons who may provide technical inputs, non-binding and professional views or policy recommendations to the JWC-DOC, and the convening of workshops, as the needs arose.[38]

Due to the disagreements between the two sides on the specific content of the guidelines for the implementation of the DOC, it took seven years for China and ASEAN to reach an agreement on the guidelines.[39] At the 44th ASEAN PMC+1 Session with China in July 2011, a set of Guidelines for Implementation of the DOC was adopted.[40] It contained principles to guide the implementation of possible joint cooperative activities, measures and projects as provided

36 Ibid.

37 Press Release of the 1st SOM-DOC, 7 December 2004, Kuala Lumpur, Malaysia.

38 Terms of Reference of the ASEAN-China Joint Working Group on the Implementation of the Declaration on the Conduct of Parties in the South China Sea, adopted by the ASEAN-China Senior Officials' Meeting on the implementation of the DOC, 07 December 2004, Kuala Lumpur, Malaysia. See also C. Thayer, 'China-ASEAN and the South China Sea: Chinese Assertiveness and Southeast Asian Responses' in Yann-Huei Song and Keyuan Zou (eds), *Major Law and Policy Issues in the South China Sea: European and American Perspectives*, London: Routledge, 2016, 25 at 44.

39 China objected to a clause which specified "ASEAN will continue its current practice of consulting among themselves before meeting with China". China insisted that outstanding disputes should be resolved by bilateral consultations "among relevant parties" and not with ASEAN. See C. Thayer, 'Chinese Assertiveness in the South China Sea and Southeast Asian Response', *Journal of Current Southeast Asian Affairs* 30, No.2 (2011), 77 at 91.

40 Chairman's Statement on the ASEAN PMC+1 Sessions, 21–22 July 2011, Bali, Indonesia.

for in the DOC such as step-by-step approach, voluntary participation and respect for consensus.[41]

4.3 ASEAN-*China Confidence-Building Measures from 2014 to 2018*

From 2014 to 2018 a series of confidence building-measures were adopted by China and ASEAN to build trust and confidence between the parties. In 2014, at the 17th ASEAN-China Summit in Nay Pyi Taw, Myanmar, Leaders of ASEAN and China agreed to support "the adoption of the first list of commonalities on COC [Code of Conduct] consultation, the establishment of a hotline platform among search and rescue agencies, a hotline among foreign ministries on maritime emergencies, and a table-top exercise on search and rescue to promote and enhance trust and confidence in the region".[42] These measures were considered "early harvest measures" to build trust and confidence among relevant parties and to avoid miscalculations and incidents on the ground in the South China Sea.[43]

At the 19th ASEAN-China Summit in 2016, Leaders of both sides adopted the Joint Statement on the Application of the Code for Unplanned Encounters at Sea (CUES)[44] in the South China Sea, and the Guidelines for Hotline Communications among Senior Officials of the Ministries of Foreign Affairs of ASEAN Member States and China in Response to Maritime Emergencies in the Implementation of the DOC.[45] The Joint Statement on the Application of the CUES reaffirms the commitments of China and ASEAN to the CUES, in order to improve the operational safety of naval ships and naval aircraft in air and at sea. The statement contains the parties' agreement to use the safety and communication procedures for the safety of all their naval ships and naval aircraft, as set out in the CUES, when they encounter each other in the

41 Guidelines for the Implementation of the DOC, adopted at the ASEAN-China Senior Officials' Meeting at the 44th ASEAN PMC+1 Session with China, 21–22 July 2011, Bali, Indonesia.

42 17th ASEAN-China Summit Chairman's Statement, 13 November 2014, Nay Pyi Taw, Myanmar, paras. 9–11.

43 Joint Press Briefing on the 14th SOM-DOC, 18 May 2017, Guiyang, Guizhou Province, China.

44 The CUES was adopted at the 2014 Western Pacific Naval Symposium in Qingdao, China by navies of 35 Pacific countries to provide communication and manoeuvring procedures among naval vessels and aircraft when they operate in close proximity, see Code for Unplanned Encounter at Sea, version 1, adopted at 24th Western Pacific Naval Symposium, 22 April 2014, Qingdao, China.

45 19th ASEAN-China Summit Chairman's Statement, 7 September 2016, Vientiane, Laos, paras. 20–21.

South China Sea.[46] The Guidelines for Hotline Communications provide for the designation of a contact point for the Ministries of Foreign Affairs' hotline communications, and procedures for undertaking actions.[47] ASEAN Member States and China successfully conducted a hotline test exercise from 18 to 24 April 2017.[48]

In addition, a maritime exercise between ASEAN and China was organized in 2018 as another confidence-building measure. The maritime exercise took place in two phases. The first phase was a table-top exercise from 2 – 3 August 2018 hosted in Changi Naval Base, Singapore, in which navies from ASEAN Member States and China developed plans to deal with maritime incidents such as search and rescue operations, and medical evacuations.[49] The second phase was a field training exercise taking place from 22 – 27 October 2018 in Ma Xie Naval Base, Zhejiang, China, in which 1000 personnel and eight ships from both sides undertook joint search and rescue operations, and medical evacuation drills with the use of helicopters.[50]

The Declaration for a "Decade of Coastal and Marine Environmental Protection in the South China Sea" was adopted on 13 November 2017 at the 20th ASEAN-China Summit in Manila, Philippines, on the occasion of the 15th anniversary of the signing of the DOC.[51] The Declaration declared that 2017 – 2027 would be the "Decade for the Protection of Coastal and Marine Environment in the South China Sea". Governments of ASEAN Member States and China committed to taking action for the protection, preservation, and

---

46 Joint Statement on the Application of the Code for Unplanned Encounters at Sea in the South China Sea, adopted at the 19th ASEAN-China Summit Chairman's Statement, 7 September 2016, Vientiane, Laos.

47 Guidelines for Hotline Communications among Senior Officials of the Ministries of Foreign Affairs of ASEAN Member States and China in Response to Maritime Emergencies in the Implementation of the DOC, adopted at the 19th ASEAN-China Summit Chairman's Statement, 7 September 2016, Vientiane, Laos.

48 Joint Press Briefing on the 14th SOM-DOC, 18 May 2017, Guiyang, Guizhou Province, China.

49 "Singapore Navy Hosts Table-Top Exercise as part of Inaugural ASEAN-China Maritime Exercise" (3 August 2018) online: Ministry of Defence of Singapore <https://www.mindef.gov.sg/web/portal/mindef/news-and-events/latest-releases/article-detail/2018/august/03aug18_nr2/!ut/p/z0/fY0xE8FAFIR_iyLlzbuEiDY0MEgT5lyTOTxxJC-SO8G_d6FR6XZ3vt0FCQIkqVbnyuqKVOH8Tg6zKJlOZnwQrJMw9Xm8TdNlOF7PN9EQFiD_A25BX-paxiAPFVl8WhClpiOe2MeT9fi5KtHjhA_DFB0Zti41Hi-URWNZgwUqgy4IuD_yuLrnd-NavO-UP8q0CbqXoFlNVjnIm7JnpulUgeh4EF8exC9_u8r96xH33p0VbGg!/>.

50 Koh S. L. C., "Inaugural ASEAN-China Maritime Exercise: What to Expect" (3 August 2018) RSIS Commentary No.131.

51 20th ASEAN-China Summit Chairman's Statement, 13 November 2017, Manila, Philippines, paras. 12–14.

sustainable management of the coastal and marine environment of the South China Sea.[52]

4.4 *Renewed Negotiations on the Code of Conduct Leading to Single Draft Negotiating Text*

China expressed interest in renewing the negotiations for a COC with ASEAN in 2013.[53] At the 19th ASEAN-China Senior Officials' Consultation in April 2013, Chinese officials announced their willingness to commence discussions with ASEAN on a COC later in the year.[54] On August 2013, at a press conference in Hanoi, Viet Nam, Chinese Minister of Foreign Affairs, Mr. Wang Yi, stated that China and ASEAN had "agreed to hold consultations [as distinct from negotiations] on moving forward the process on the Code of Conduct in the South China Sea under the framework of implementing the Declaration on the Conduct of Parties in the South China Sea (DOC)".[55] ASEAN and China held their first formal consultation on the COC at the 6th ASEAN-China SOM-DOC and the 9th ASEAN-China JWC-DOC in Suzhou, China, 14–15 September 2013. At the consultation, it was agreed that parties would adopt a step by step approach to reach a consensus on the COC process through consultation, starting from identifying the consensus before gradually expanding it and narrowing differences.[56] At the 16th ASEAN-China Summit in October 2013, leaders of both sides welcomed the positive outcomes achieved at the first official consultation on the COC and agreed to maintain the momentum of regular official consultations, and work towards the adoption of the COC.[57]

52 Declaration for a Decade of Coastal and Marine Environmental Protection in the South China Sea (2017–2027), adopted at the 20th ASEAN-China Summit, 13 November 2017, Manila, Philippines, paras. 12–14.

53 C. Thayer, 'New Commitment to a Code of Conduct in the South China Sea?' (9 October 2013) The National Bureau of Asian Research. For details about the South China Sea arbitration, see 2.2. Implications of ASEAN's Policy of Making Decisions by Consensus.

54 Ibid. See also '19th ASEAN-China Senior Officials' Consultation' (4 April 2013) online: ASEAN <https://asean.org/19th-asean-china-senior-officials-consultation/>.

55 'Foreign Minister Wang Yi on Process of "Code of Conduct in the South China Sea' (05 August 2013) online: Ministry of Foreign Affairs of the People's Republic of China <https://www.fmprc.gov.cn/mfa_eng/wjb_663304/wjbz_663308/activities_663312/t1064869.shtml>.

56 'The Sixth Senior Officials Meeting and the Ninth Joint Working Group Meeting on the Implementation of the "Declaration on Conduct of Parties in the South China Sea" Are Held in Suzhou' (15 September 2013) online: Ministry of Foreign Affairs of the People's Republic of China <https://www.fmprc.gov.cn/mfa_eng/zxxx_662805/t1079289.shtml>.

57 16th ASEAN-China Summit Chairman's Statement, 9 October 2013, Brunei, paras. 15–16.

After two rounds of consultations, both sides agreed on a first list of commonalities on COC consultation at the 8th SOM-DOC in August 2014.[58] At the 17th ASEAN-China Summit in 2014, China and ASEAN considered the adoption of the first list of commonalities on COC consultation as an "early harvest measure" to promote and enhance trust and confidence in the region.[59] At the 9th SOM-DOC in July 2015, they concluded that by adopting the second list of commonalities, and the COC consultation had entered a new stage.[60] At the 10th SOM-DOC in October 2015, two preliminary documents were formulated, namely the list of crucial and complex issues and the list of elements for the outline of a COC.[61] At the ASEAN PMC 10 + 1 Session with China in August 2015, the Meeting welcomed the recent agreement between ASEAN Member States and China to proceed to the next stage of consultations towards the establishment of the COC, and looked forward to expeditious negotiations on the framework, structure and elements of the COC.[62] At the same time, the Ministers of Foreign Affairs of ASEAN and China issued a joint statement on the full and effective implementation of the DOC, in which the Parties reaffirmed that the adoption of a code of conduct in the South China Sea would further promote peace and stability in the region, and agreed to work towards the eventual attainment of this objective on the basis of consensus.[63]

At the 14th SOM-DOC in May 2017, a draft framework was submitted to the ASEAN PMC 10+1 session with China in August 2017 in Manila, Philippines.[64] The Ministers of Foreign Affairs of China and ASEAN adopted the Framework and tasked their Senior Officials to start substantive consultations and negotiations on the COC. The Framework contains three parts: Preambular Provisions,

58 'ASEAN-China cooperation moves forward at the 8th ASEAN-China SOM' (24 October 2014) online: Ministry of Foreign Affairs of the Kingdom of Thailand <http://www.mfa.go.th/main/en/media-center/28/50886-ASEAN-China-cooperation-moves-forward-at-the-8th-A.html>.

59 17th ASEAN-China Summit Chairman's Statement, 13 November 2014, Nay Pyi Taw, Myanmar, paras. 9–11.

60 L. Li, *China's Policy towards the South China Sea: When Geopolitics Meet the Law of the Sea*, New York: Routledge, 2018, 192.

61 'Tenth Senior Officials Meeting on the Implementation of the Declaration On the Conduct of the Parties In the South China Sea Held in Chengdu' (20 October 2015) online: Ministry of Foreign Affairs of the People's Republic of China <https://www.fmprc.gov.cn/mfa_eng/wjbxw/t1307573.shtml>.

62 Chairman's Statement of the ASEAN PMC 10+1 Sessions with Dialogue Partners, 5 August 2015, Kuala Lumpur, Malaysia.

63 Joint Statement of Ministers of the Foreign Affairs of ASEAN and China on The Full and Effective Implementation of the Declaration on the Conduct of Parties in the South China Sea, 25 July 2016, Vientiane, Laos.

64 Joint Press Briefing on the 14th SOM-DOC, 18 May 2017, Guiyang, Guizhou Province, China.

General Provisions and Final Clauses. Most of the provisions and principles are similar to the DOC, but there are some notable differences. For example, the Framework states that the COC is not an instrument to settle disputes and that it is necessary to have a monitoring mechanism.[65]

At the 15th SOM-DOC in June 2018, a Single Draft COC Negotiating Text (SDNT) was adopted by officials from ASEAN and China. The officials agreed that this would be a living document; it would serve as the basis for the negotiations and its content would be kept strictly confidential throughout the entire process. They further agreed that there would be at least three readings of the SDNT.[66] At the ASEAN PMC 10 + 1 Session with China in August 2018 in Singapore, Ministers of Foreign Affairs of ASEAN and China "noted that ASEAN Member States and China had agreed on a Single Draft Code of Conduct in the SCS (COC) Negotiating Text at the 15th ASEAN-China Senior Officials' Meeting on the Implementation of the Declaration on the Conduct of Parties in the SCS in Changsha, China on 27 June 2018, and encouraged further progress towards an effective COC".[67]

During 2019, ASEAN and China completed the first reading of the SDNT and exchanged views on the second reading at the SOM-DOC level.[68] At the ASEAN PMC 10+1 Session with China and 22nd ASEAN-China Summit, both sides welcomed the completion of the first reading of the SDNT and the commencement of the second reading of the SDNT. They also welcomed the aspiration to conclude the COC within a three-year timeline as proposed by China.[69]

---

65 Framework of a COC, adopted by at the ASEAN PMC 10+1 Session with China, 6 August 2017, Manila, Philippines. For a comprehensive assessment of the Framework of the COC, see Ian Storey, 'Assessing the ASEAN-China Framework for the Code of Conduct for the South China Sea' (8 August 2017) ISEAS Perspective No.62/2017.

66 C. Thayer, 'ASEAN and China Set on Agree on Single Draft South China Sea Code of Conduct' (27 June 2018) online: The Diplomat <https://thediplomat.com/2018/07/asean-and-china-set-to-agree-on-single-draft-south-china-sea-code-of-conduct/>.

67 Chairman's Statement of the ASEAN PMC 10+1 Sessions with Dialogue Partners, 2–3 August 2018, Singapore.

68 'The 17th Senior Officials' Meeting on the Implementation of the Declaration on the Conduct of Parties in the South China Sea (DOC) Held Successfully in China' (19 May 2019) online: Ministry of Foreign Affairs of the People's Republic of China <https://www.fmprc.gov.cn/nanhai/eng/wjbxw_1/t1665134.htm> and 'The 18th ASEAN-China Senior Officials' Meeting on the Implementation of the Declaration on the Conduct of Parties (DOC) in the South China Sea Successfully Held' (16 October 2019) online: Ministry of Foreign Affairs of the People's Republic of China <https://www.fmprc.gov.cn/mfa_eng/wjbxw/t1708862.shtml>.

69 Chairman' Statement of the ASEAN PMC 10+1 Sessions with Dialogue Partners, 31st July – 1 August 2019, Bangkok, Thailand, and 22nd ASEAN-China Summit Chairman's Statement, 3 November 2019, Bangkok/Nonthaburi, Thailand, para. 18.

Despite COVID-19, both sides have been discussing the issue via videoconference and recently were able to agree provisionally on the Preamble section of the SDNT during 2021.[70]

5 Conclusion: What Role ASEAN Can Play in the Peaceful Management of Maritime Disputes in the South China Sea?

It is clear that ASEAN does not take a position on the sovereignty or maritime disputes in the South China Sea and it does not take sides on how the disputes should be resolved. The major objective of ASEAN is to preserve peace and stability in the South China Sea and to see that South China Sea disputes are managed in a peaceful manner. That explains the silence of ASEAN with respect to the Award of the Arbitral Tribunal in *South China Sea case* and with respect to the "notes verbales war" following the submissions of Malaysia and Vietnam to the CLCS.

On the other hand, based on the centrality principle, ASEAN wants to maintain its central role in dealing with regional issues and remain neutral in the competition between the major powers. That is the reason why some ASEAN Member States, while willing to see more balance to China's domination in the region, have been reluctant to welcome initiatives such as Quad and AUKUS. They are concerned that increased tensions between the United States and China will force Southeast Asian countries to take sides and undermine the central role of ASEAN in maintaining peace in the region.

At the 34th ASEAN Summit in June 2019, ASEAN Leaders adopted the ASEAN Outlook on the Indo-Pacific to help guide ASEAN's engagement and cooperation in the wider Indo-Pacific region.[71] The Outlook envisages ASEAN centrality as the underlying principle for promoting cooperation in the Indo-Pacific region, with ASEAN-led mechanisms such as East Asian Summit serving as platforms for dialogue and cooperation. It also defines four broad range of areas in which ASEAN will undertake cooperation: maritime cooperation, connectivity, UN sustainable development goals 2030 and economic and other areas.[72] The content of the ASEAN Outlook relating to maritime cooperation can shed some light on the future ASEAN policy on the South China Sea. Pursuant to

70 84th AMM Joint Communiqué, 2 August 2021, s90.

71 Chairman's Statement of the 34th ASEAN Summit, 23 June 2019, Bangkok, Thailand, para. 56.

72 ASEAN Outlook on the Indo-Pacific, adopted at the 34th ASEAN Summit, 23 June 2019, Bangkok, Thailand.

the Outlook, ASEAN will "prevent, manage and eventually resolve" maritime issues such as unresolved maritime disputes, unsustainable exploitation of maritime resources, and marine pollution in a more focused, peaceful and comprehensive way. This language suggests that ASEAN will continue to place greater emphasis on the prevention of conflict and on peaceful management of the sovereignty and maritime disputes in the South China Sea, rather than on the resolution of such disputes. At the same time, ASEAN will also continue its efforts to play the primary role as a facilitator by providing forums for the relevant parties to meet to discuss how to manage the disputes, prevent conflict and enhance cooperation.

PART 5

Preservation of the Marine Environment, Including the Hazard of Plastic Debris

CHAPTER 22

Designing an International Instrument for Combating Marine Plastic Pollution

Tomofumi Kitamura

1 Introduction

1.1 *Problem of Marine Plastic Pollution*

It is estimated that more than eight million tons of plastics leak into the ocean each year, and if no action is taken, this is expected to quadruple by 2050. An alarming result of this is that the ocean might, by weight, contain more plastic than fish by the same year.[1] Marine plastic pollution has serious impacts on the marine environment. Industries such as fisheries and tourism are affected. It may cause serious risks to human health, especially in the case of microplastics. As to the source of pollution, most of the marine plastic pollution is from land sources. Asia is by far the biggest source of pollution, with just five developing countries in the region accounting for around 60% of global pollution.[2] As to the types of measures to cope with the problem, there is a growing consensus that downstream measures such as improvement of waste management infrastructures and implementation of clean-up programs are important but not sufficient. Therefore, an immediate response involving not only developed countries but also developing countries is required. The response needs to include not only downstream measures but also upstream measures focusing on reduction, reuse, and recycling of plastics.

1.2 *Existing International Institutions*

The response to date of the international community to the problem is best described by the concept of "fragmentation" as used in the literature of global governance theory: a policy domain marked by "a patchwork of international institutions that are different in their character (organizations, regimes, and implicit norms), their constituencies (public and private), their spatial scope

1 Ellen MacArthur Foundation, *The New Plastics Economy: Rethinking the Future of Plastics* (2016), p. 12.

2 Peter Dauvergne, "Why is the Global Governance of Plastic Failing the Oceans?" *Global Environmental Change* 51 (2018), p. 25.

 | DOI:10.1163/9789004518629_023

(from bilateral to global), and their subject matter (from specific policy fields to universal concerns)."[3] There already exist in the policy domain of marine plastic pollution a number of binding/non-binding regional/global instruments, with different levels of involvement of private actors, addressing different sources and aspects of pollution, with different levels of specificity.[4] This patchwork of existing international institutions, however, has fallen short of effectively responding to the problem.

1.3 *Proposed Options for the Way Forward*

In the Assessment Report circulated in 2017, the United Nations Environment Programme (UNEP) provided three options with which to combat marine plastic pollution: maintaining the status quo (Option 1), strengthening existing international framework (Option 2), and creating a new international legally binding instrument (Option 3).[5] Whereas Option 1 is not a true option and can be eliminated immediately, the line between Option 2 and Option 3 is not necessarily clear. If the choice between these options is non-binding or binding instruments, what is at issue may be understood as a question of tradeoffs between feasibility and effectiveness; that is, binding instruments may be more effective in inducing compliance, whereas it may not be politically feasible for countries to accept them. Alternatively, if the choice is whether we want multiple institutions operating somewhat independently or a single institution playing a central role, the issue may be a question of whether a fragmented approach or an integrated approach is more effective for the purpose of environmental governance. This is a question which has been widely discussed in the literature of global governance theory, but the debate is not conclusive.[6] On the one hand, a fragmented approach may induce forum-shopping behaviors with each country choosing environmental standards and actions it can achieve without much effort. On the other hand, a fragmented approach may

---

3 Frank Biermann *et al.*, "The Fragmentation of Global Governance Architectures: A Framework for Analysis," 9 *Global Environmental Politics* 4 (2009), p. 16.

4 See, for detailed analysis of these instruments, UNEP, "Combating Marine Plastic Litter and Microplastics: An Assessment of the Effectiveness of Relevant International, Regional and Subregional Governance Strategies and Approaches," UN Doc UNEP/AHEG/2018/1/INF/3 (8 May 2018), pp. 22–55.

5 *Ibid.*, pp. 74–99. See, also, Karen Raubenheimer *et al.*, "Towards an Improved International Framework to Govern the Life Cycle of Plastics," 27 *RECIEL* 3 (2018), pp. 215–219.

6 See, Frank Biermann and Rakhyun E. Kim, "Architectures of Earth System Governance: Setting the Stage," in Frank Biermann and Rakhyun E. Kim, eds., *Architectures of Earth System Governance: Institutional Complexity and Structural Transformation* (2020), pp. 11–13; Frank Biermann *et al.*, "Governance Fragmentation," in *ibid.*, pp. 168–172.

facilitate quicker, more innovative and more far-reaching decision-making among like-minded countries. In either case, the choice between Option 2 and Option 3 seems to depend on what kind of binding instrument is being created. Even if we create a new plastic treaty, the outcome may not be much different from a non-binding instrument or multiple instruments operating independently, if the treaty leaves almost everything to the discretion of each country and each country can just choose whatever standards or actions with which they are comfortable.

2 Design of New Plastic Treaty

2.1 *Models of New Plastic Treaty*

Regarding the question of what kind of binding instrument should be created to address marine plastic pollution, there are two streams of ideas: one is that the new plastic treaty should be modelled after the Montreal Protocol on Substances that Deplete the Ozone Layer, and the other is that the Paris Agreement on climate change is the more appropriate model.[7] The characteristic of the Montreal Protocol is its top-down approach. The Protocol lists certain substances in its Annexes and obliges the parties to phase out the use of those substances. This obligation applies not only to developed countries but also to developing countries being subject to different timeframes. In contrast with this is the approach of the Paris Agreement. The Agreement sets the global target at "well below 2 degrees Celsius above pre-industrial levels." However, instead of providing mandatory reduction targets and actions for each party, the Agreement allows each party to set its own level of ambition and develop its own action plans. The Montreal Protocol model is attractive, because the Protocol is considered one of the most successful environmental treaties ever created. However, in certain contexts, it is simply not feasible because it is too ambitious. The Kyoto Protocol is a good example. On the other hand, the bottom-up approach of the Paris Agreement seems to be feasible in most contexts, but it may not be sufficient to solve the problem. It is too early to say anything about the performance of the Agreement, but the experience

7 See, for example, Elizabeth A. Kirk, "The Montreal Protocol or the Paris Agreement as a Model for a Plastic Treaty," 114 *AJIL Unbound* (2020). See, also, Nils Simon and Maro Luisa Schulte, *Stopping Global Plastic Pollution: The Case of an International Convention* (2017); Karen Raubenheimer and Alistair Mcllgorm, "Is the Montreal Protocol a Model that Can Help Solve the Global Marine Plastic Debris Problem?" *Marine Policy* 81 (2017); Nordic Council of Ministers, *Possible Elements of a New Global Agreement to Prevent Plastic Pollution* (2020).

of the Convention on Biological Diversity (CBD) which is also characterized by its bottom-up approach seems suggestive. Therefore, an obvious but important lesson is that there is no panacea which will solve all environmental problems. What we need in designing an environmental treaty is rather a diagnostic approach which takes into account different features and contexts of each problem and provides case-specific prescriptions.[8]

2.2 *Factors to Be Examined*

There are a variety of factors that may be examined in diagnosing environmental problems, five examples of which are herein considered. First, one of the most basic questions to be asked is "where does the damage occur?" If it occurs within a territory of a specific country, as in the case of transboundary movements of hazardous waste, the best response may be to let that country itself to decide what to do by introducing procedural obligations such as prior informed consent. In a case where the damage occurs in territories of unspecified number of countries or in public domain, substantive obligations setting standards and actions would be necessary.

Second, another important question that may be asked is "whether a polluter and a victim can be identified?" If both can be identified, liability and compensation mechanisms may be a good way to incentivize parties to prevent damages. In a case where a victim can be identified, but not a polluter, creation of an international fund for compensation may be worth considering. If it is only a polluter that can be identified, creation of an entity which receives compensation on behalf of the international community may be an option.

The third question is "whether alternative technologies are technically and economically available?" When this is the case, the ambitious top-down approach such as the one of the Montreal Protocol may be feasible. In fact, studies suggest that an important reason for the success of the Protocol was that solutions were already available that were profitable for the industries.[9]

The fourth question is "is a problem visible to the public?" A good counterexample is the CBD. Many factors have contributed to the underperformance of the Convention, but one of the most important is arguably a low visibility of the problem. It is hard for the public to understand what exactly is lost when biodiversity is lost. As a result, countries have been struggling to mobilize

---

8 Oran R. Young, "Research Strategies to Assess the Effectiveness of International Environmental Regimes," 1 *Nature Sustainability* 9 (2018), pp. 461–463.

9 See, for example, Ina Tessnow-von Wysocki and Philippe Le Billon, "Plastics at Sea: Treaty Design for a Global Solution to Marine Plastic Pollution," *Environmental Science and Policy* 100 (2019), p. 95.

political support from the public. Conversely, if the problem is highly visible to the public, an ambitious approach may be feasible. Consumer information schemes such as eco-labeling may work well, and awareness raising programs may be effective.

Finally, one of the key factors which has a strong impact on the structure and content of environmental treaties is "who pays the cost and who receives the benefit of environmental protection?" Again, the experience of the CBD seems relevant. The reason is that every country has to pay to preserve biodiversity, but those who have to pay the most are developing countries, because biodiversity is especially abundant in those countries. It is also the case that every country benefits from preservation of biodiversity, but those who will benefit the most are probably the bioindustries in developed countries. In such a situation, strong corporations are unlikely to emerge.

2.3 *Some Preliminary Observations*

The results of examinations according to the factors just described of some environmental problems including marine plastic pollution are shown in Table 22.1 below. While there are a lot of oversimplifications in the table, it nevertheless may provide a broad idea of what a new plastic treaty might look like. Let us make three observations. First, as to the above second question, "whether a polluter and a victim can be identified," various scenarios may be considered in the case of marine plastic pollution. For example, in an enclosed or semi-enclosed sea, it may be possible to identify where plastics come from and where they end up. Additionally, if it is possible to track the movement of plastic debris using satellite technologies, polluters and victims may be identified in broader circumstances. Even then, various questions have to be addressed including whether it is a government or an industry or a company which should assume liability.[10] Still, some type of compensation mechanism may be worth considering as a technique to incentivize prevention.

Second, as to the fourth question, "is a problem visible to the public," the problem of marine plastic pollution seems highly visible. This suggests consumer information schemes such as eco-labelling and awareness raising programs work particularly effectively.

Third, regarding the fifth question, one of the most important characteristics of the problem of marine plastic pollution is that there is a large overlap between "who pays the cost and who receives the benefit of environmental

10 Sandrine Maljean-Dubois and Benoît Mayer, "Liability and Compensation for Marine Plastic Pollution: Conceptual Issues and Possible Ways Forward," 114 *AJIL Unbound* (2020), pp. 207–208.

TABLE 22.1 Examinations of selected environmental problems

Problems Factors	Biodiversity loss	Depletion of ozone layer	Climate change	Marine plastic pollution
1. Does the damage occur within the territory of specific country?	No	No	No	No
2. Can a polluter and a victim be identified?	Both hard to identify	Both hard to identify	Both hard to identify	Various scenarios
3. Are alternative technologies reasonably available?	No	Yes	No	No
4. Is the problem visible to the public?	Low visibility	Medium	Medium	High visibility
5. Who pays the cost and who receives the benefit?	Large divide	All parties pay and receive	Some divide	Large overlap

protection." The countries which contribute to pollution the most are the countries which suffer from the pollution the most. This is quite a contrast to the case of the CBD, and this may suggest that there is no strong reason to adopt the bottom-up approach as if it is the only feasible choice.

3 Design of New Plastic Treaty Continued: Factor of International Trade

3.1 *International Trade and Unilateral Regulations on Plastics*

Lastly, let us examine another factor which may greatly impact the design of a new plastic treaty, namely, the factor of international trade. The bottom line here is that when markets are highly integrated throughout the supply chain of a product, as in the case of plastic products,[11] unilateral regulations by one country can be *de facto* international regulations, especially when that country or region is a large economy. For example, one important measure to tackle the issue of marine plastic pollution is to introduce product design requirements restricting certain additives and polymers so that plastics can be reused and recycled efficiently. Now, if country A imposes such product design requirements on products sold within its market, all products which end up in this market in one way or another have to comply with those requirements. Furthermore, producers may be incentivized to follow these requirements even for the products which do not end up in the market of Country A, as using different additives and polymers for different markets might not make sense economically. The logic here is best described by a passage from the EU circular economy action plan 2020: "the single market provides a critical mass enabling the EU to set global standards in product sustainability and to influence product design and value chain management worldwide."[12]

3.2 *Unilateral Regulations on Plastics and the WTO Agreement*

Crucially, however, certain unilateral regulations are prohibited by the WTO Agreement, and therefore legally not available. The question of what types of regulations are consistent or inconsistent with the WTO Agreement requires extensive analysis which goes far beyond the scope of this paper. What is of particular importance in this context is the distinction of whether the regulations are directed towards the risks involved in the product itself or the risks involved in the production process of the product. An example of the first type of regulations is a ban on products which contain asbestos. An example of the second is a ban on shrimp which were caught without using technologies to prevent the bycatch of sea turtles. According to the jurisprudence of the WTO Dispute Settlement Body, the first type of regulations is likely to be consistent with the WTO Agreement as long as the regulations are reasonably designed. Conversely, the second is highly controversial, and more likely to be inconsistent with the WTO Agreement, as illustrated by the following well-known passage from the Appellate Body's decision in the Shrimp-Turtle case:

> ... it is not acceptable, in international trade relations, for one WTO Member to use an economic embargo to require other Members to adopt

---

11 Carolyn Deere Birkbeck, "Strengthening International Cooperation to Tackle Plastic Pollution: Options for the WTO," *Global Governance Brief 2020/1* (2020), pp. 4–6.

12 European Commission, *Circular Economy Action Plan: For a Cleaner and More Competitive Europe* (2020), p. 6.

> essentially the same comprehensive regulatory program, to achieve a certain policy goal, as that in force within that Member's territory, without taking into consideration different conditions which may occur in the territories of those other Members.[13]

Between these two types of regulations, product design requirements on plastics fall into the first type, because it is the design, additives, and components of the product itself that are addressed by the regulation.

3.3 *Case for Negotiated International Regulations*

The examinations in the above two paragraphs indicate that in the case of plastic design requirements, countries are likely to be able to impose these requirements unilaterally, and especially when it is a large economy such as the European Union or the United States, those unilateral regulations may be *de facto* international regulations. This is a positive thing for the purpose of combatting marine plastic pollution, but the problem of this approach is that strict regulations unilaterally or collaboratively set by some large economies become *de facto* international regulations, without taking into consideration different conditions and different development needs of other countries, especially developing ones. This is arguably one of the most important points to be considered when designing a new plastic treaty, particularly because in the existing literature, it is sometimes argued that the purpose of international regulations on plastic design is to create a level playing field for industry and governments,[14] or that these regulations are not appropriate or feasible since this kind of top-down regulations touch upon sensitive aspects of national sovereignty.[15] The reality, however, may be the other way around. Large economies can set *de facto* international regulations unilaterally or collaboratively anyway. If this is the case, it may be more appropriate to set the international regulations through multilateral negotiation, so that some flexibilities and some schemes for technical and financial assistance can be agreed upon together with those regulations.

---

13 Appellate Body Report, United States – Import Prohibition of Certain Shrimp and Shrimp Products, WT/DS58/AB/R, 12 October 1998, para. 164.

14 See, for example, Nordic Council of Ministers, *supra* note 7, p. 75.

15 See, for example, Simon *et al.*, *supra* note 7, pp. 34–36.

4 Conclusion

In conclusion, if we can agree upon some top-down rules in a multilateral instrument, it may make more sense to make that instrument legally-binding and let that binding instrument play a central role in the combat against marine plastic pollution. Political and social contexts for such an ambitious instrument may not be as favorable as the issue of ozone layer depletion, but may be more favorable than the issue of biodiversity loss or climate change. Therefore, what we may want is a hybrid of top-down and bottom-up approaches, and if this is the case, an important question is what kind of standards and actions should be imposed from top-down, and what kind of standards and actions should be left to the discretion of each country. This, of course, requires a thorough examination, but product design requirements may be a good candidate for a top-down approach.

CHAPTER 23

Common but Differentiated Responsibilities as a Guiding Principle towards a Potential International Treaty on Plastic

Aleke Stöfen-O'Brien

1 Introduction

Plastics are an enduring representation of our time. They provide convenience in packaging food, cosmetics and any number of other consumables. Most recently and importantly during the Covid-19 pandemic, they have proven to be an effective means of facilitating hygiene standards, thereby ensuring a certain degree of human health protection against the spread and effects of the virus. However, increased plastic consumption has resulted in a significant increase in marine environmental pollution by plastic in the form of marine litter. This type of pollution challenges the architecture of international public law and ocean governance. Whereas developed countries engineer the plastics and export the waste, they are generally not the major source polluting countries. Their contribution to the marine litter pollution load tends to be relatively limited due to the existence of an adequate infrastructure for waste management and recycling.[1] Mismanaged waste mostly makes its way into the ocean from a range of States in Asia and Africa, all of which have in common that they are considered developing countries.[2] Considered in light of pollution from other sources, such as those emitting CO_2 emissions, a dichotomy between high and low emitters is being pursued.[3]

This chapter argues that there may be a need to move away from these approaches in the context of plastic pollution and adopt a more nuanced

1 The Economist Plastics Management Index, October 2021 at https://backtoblueinitiative.com/?utm_source=Referral&utm_medium=SustainabilityProject&utm_campaign=BackToBlue2021.

2 J.R. Jambeck, R. Geyer et al., 'Plastic waste inputs from land into the ocean', 347 *Science*, 768–771, 2015, p. 771.

3 J. Depledge and F. Yamin 'The global climate change regime: a defence', in: Helm and Hepburn (eds.), *The economics and politics of climate change* (Oxford: Oxford University Press, 2009), pp. 533–453, p. 443.

 | DOI:10.1163/9789004518629_024

architecture of burden-sharing. In addition, the legal framework must serve to better distribute responsibility for plastic pollution, taking into account the complex interactions and supply chain of plastics on a global scale. In this regard, the application of the principle of common but differentiated responsibilities (CBDR) may be suitable to guide such (preliminary) discussions, which are currently getting underway regarding a potential new international legally binding instrument on plasticbeing discussed within the framework of the UN Environment Programme.

Admittedly, the complexity of any such regime is complex and cannot be reduced to or solved by the application of a principle. Nonetheless, giving further thought to the operationalisation of CBDR in an effort to foster greater equity in the overall governance approach is of upmost importance. It has the potential to go some way towards addressing the asymmetry in the global governance system pertaining to marine litter, a system characterised by a dearth of effective regulatory instruments on national and regional levels and compounded by partial data availability (particularly in certain parts of the world)[4] as well as aspects of parachuting science, whereby only research is conducted by some few countries (also in third countries) without the involvement of local governments, researchers and/or organisations.[5] CBDR may also serve to guide towards the resolution of conflicts of interests along the prevailing North-South divide in international politics.[6]

2 Marine Litter as a Long-Term and Persistent Environmental and Societal Challenge

Marine litter includes all durable, manufactured or processed persistent materials that enter the marine environment through accidental or intentional introduction. Besides materials such as rubber, metals, fabrics/textiles, glass, wood or paper, plastic is the most frequently found material with a share of > 75%. Plastics have become an expression of our throwaway society – they can

4 United Nations (UN), 'Chapter: 12', *The Second World Ocean Assessment* (*WOA II*), Volume II, ISBN: 978-92-1-1-130422-0 (2021), W. Lau et al., 'Evaluating scenarios toward zero plastic pollution', 369 *Science*, 2020, pp. 1455–1461.

5 A. Stöfen-O`Brien, K.K. Ambrose et al.,'Parachuting science through a regional lens: marine litter research in the Caribbean Small Island Developing States and the challenge of extra-regional research', 174 *Marine Pollution Bulletin*, 2022.

6 P.G. Harris, and J. Symons, 'Norm conflict in climate governance: greenhouse gas accounting and the problem of consumption', 13 *Global Environmental Politics*, No.1, 2013, p. 10.

be easily and quickly industrially produced and processed and are often given away cheaply or even for free (plastic straws, bags etc.). Recent studies estimate that globally between 1.8 % and 4.6 % of the plastic waste produced in 192 States ends up in the oceans, which amounted to somewhere between 4.8 to 12.7 million tons in 2010.[7] The reasons for this are many and variable: poor or inadequate waste management, especially in Southeast Asia and emerging and developing countries; low recycling rates; societal factors contributing to intensive plastic consumption; and, lack of awareness of the consequences of careless disposal of waste in the environment (littering).

In addition to large-particle waste such as plastic bottles or plastic bags, microplastics (plastic particles < 5 mm) are increasingly a matter for concern.[8] So called secondary microplastics are formed by the fragmentation of larger plastic parts and during the use of products (e.g., in the form of synthetic fibers through the washing of textile products, as abrasion from shoe soles and car tires, and the weathering of facade or marine paints). Primary microplastics are deliberately added to products in micronized form (e.g. cosmetic and hygiene products and abrasives) or enter the environment through leakage/accidents.[9] Due to the longevity and very slow decomposition rate of plastics, it may take centuries for the material to be broken down by physical, chemical and biological processes in the oceans.[10] Physical conditions such as wind, waves, and currents can transport and disperse trash in the ocean over long distances from the point of entry. Consequently, plastic is now present in all aquatic habitats, and is distributed throughout the marine food web, even far from populated areas such as uninhabited islands in the polar regions and Arctic ice.

Globally, marine litter comes largely from land-based sources and the remainder from sea-based sources. However, sources vary by geographic location, and the amount and composition of litter are influenced by, for example, urban and industrial areas, ports, shipping lanes, or fishing areas. The remaining inputs consist of municipal waste, which enters the oceans primarily from

---

7 Jambeck, 2015, p. 768.

8 UN, WOA II, Chapter 12, 2021.

9 N.B. Hartmann et al., 'Are We Speaking the Same Language? Recommendations for a Definition and Categorization Framework for Plastic Debris', 53 *Environmental Science & Technology*, 2019, pp. 1039–1040, p. 1039.

10 D.K.A. Barnes et al., 'Accumulation and Fragmentation of Plastic Debris in Global Environments', 364. *Philosophical Transactions of the Royal Society B: Biological Sciences*, 2012; F. Thevenon et al., 'Plastic Debris in the Ocean: The Characterization of Marine Plastics and their Environmental Impacts' (IUCN 2014) Situation Analysis Report, p. 14.

careless discarding of waste in public spaces through rivers or canals, as well as via industrial or wastewater treatment plants or stormwater discharges along the coasts. Source identification is relevant to derive efficient prevention and reduction measures. Approximately ten percent of the litter entering the seas can be attributed to fishing gear lost or left in the sea. These so-called ghost nets pose a lethal threat for decades to marine mammals, seabirds, and fish. Although most nets sink to the bottom of the sea, they can remain upright and continue to "fish" there for sometimes long periods of time. Other risks include the ingestion and accumulation of chemical substances. Plastics often contain chemical additives and, in addition, small particles are said to have a vector property whereby they adsorb chemical substances (e.g., Persistent Organic Pollutants (POPs)) from the water. By ingesting plastic parts (especially microplastics), it cannot be excluded that these substances accumulate in the food chain. Furthermore, trash can act as a vector for non-native species.

Overall, marine litter is a complex topic characterised by knowledge gaps relating to sources and impacts and an uneven distribution of environmental pressures and externalities of plastic pollution among different countries. It is closely associated with the challenge of wealth distribution and relates, first, to the issue of access to resources, and, second, to burden-sharing and the allocation of responsibilities. Access to resources may include food and a healthy environment, but equally also an inclusive participation of marginalized people and minorities, countries as well as sectors in political decision-making and economic processes.[11] Given the complex sources and impacts, a broad range of stakeholders needs to be included and addressed in any effective regulatory regime. Moreover, establishing an equitable system for the allocation of risks, burdens and responsibilities among States and other actors is of key importance.[12] The long-term nature and persistence of plastic pollution in the marine environment places it at the nexus between distributive justice and equity of social, economic and environmental costs as well as benefits between different countries and generations.[13]

11 M.G.B Lima and J. Gupta, 'The policy context of biofuels: a case of non-governance at the global level?', 13 *Global Environmental Politics* 2, 2013, p. 47.

12 F. Biermann et al., *Earth System Governance: People, Places and the Planet. Science and Implementation Plan of the Earth System Governance Project,* ESG Report (Bonn, IHDP: The Earth System Governance Project, 2009), p. 60.

13 Sarah Burch et al., 'New directions in earth system governance research', 1 *Earth System Governance*, 2019, p. 9.

3 Challenges of the Current Regulatory Framework of Marine Litter

Addressing marine litter is a complex and multifaceted problem and as has been the subject to numerous analyses.[14] From a legal perspective, the current regulatory landscape is flawed in that it permits a fragmentation between different regulatory regimes.[15] This finds its root-cause in the structure of the United Nations Convention on the Law of the Sea (UNCLOS),[16] in particular in the relevant section thereof, namely Part XII UNCLOS.[17] A clear obligation on States Parties to protect and preserve the marine environment is mandated in Article 192 UNCLOS. This duty has been met by partial responses that are sectoral in nature and rely largely on a source-based approach divided among land-based and sea-based pollution. A further factor compounding the inadequacy of many prevailing regimes, is that the introduction of marine plastic pollution is typically a matter of chronic, persistent oftentimes even systemic pollution and is generally not caused by singular events.[18] A number of international instruments, many developed against the backdrop of broader mandates and objectives than plastic pollution, establish rules in respect of this subject matter. Even though marine litter is known to have impacts on the marine environment and biodiversity, its management has for a long time been approached through limited sectoral instruments. The first indication of its potential adverse consequences was acknowledged in the 1960s and the fact that the International Convention for the Prevention of Pollution from Ships (MARPOL)[19] as well as the Convention on the Prevention of Marine Pollution

14 A. Stöfen-O'Brien, *The International and European Legal Regime Regulating Marine Litter in the EU* (Boston/Hamburg: Nomos, 2015); L. Raubenheimer, *Towards an Improved Framework to Prevent Marine Plastic Debris* (Doctor of Philosophy Thesis, Australian National Center for Ocean Resources and Security (ANCORS), University of Wollongong 2016); UN Environment, *Combating Marine Plastic Litter and Microplastics: An Assessment if the Effectiveness of Relevant International Regional and Subregional Governance Strategies and Approaches* (Nairobi, 2017), UNEP/EA.3/INF/5.24–25.

15 UN Environment, *Combating Marine Plastic Litter and Microplastics: An Assessment of the Effectiveness of Relevant International, Regional and Subregional Governance Strategies and Approaches* ((15 February 2018), UNEP/EA.3/INF/5, p. 15).

16 United Nations Convention on the Law of the Sea (UNCLOS) (Montego Bay) of 10 December 1982, in force 14 November 1994; 1833 UNTS 3.

17 Stöfen-O'Brien, 2015, p. 399.

18 Ibid, p. 68.

19 International Convention for the Prevention of Pollution from Ships (Adopted 2 November 1973) 1340 UNTS 184, as amended by the Protocol Relating to the 1973 International Convention for the Prevention of Pollution from Ships (Adopted 17 February 1978, entered into force 2 October 1983) 1340 UNTS 61 ('MARPOL Convention').

by Dumping of Waste and Other Matter (London Dumping Convention),[20] adopted in 1978 and 1975 respectively, demonstrate that the world community must have had an understanding of its detrimental impacts. Both agreements adopted measures to prevent plastic entering the marine environment from shipping and dumping through specific Annexes and guidelines.[21] Yet the diverse regimes created only do so within the strict remit of their respective geographical, in the case of regional seas agreements, and material scopes. Considering the material scope, this applies on the one hand to sea-based sources of marine litter, such as MARPOL, addressing waste from shipping, and the London Convention and London Protocol,[22] both of which address dumping. On the other hand, the Global Programme of Action for the Protection of the Marine Environment from Land-based Activities (GPA)[23] on Land-Based solutions also explicitly addresses marine litter as a source of pollution, but is hindered by its mandate as a non-binding soft law instrument.

Since 2011, another regulatory layer of marine litter management was added through the adoption of Regional Action Plans under Regional Seas Conventions. Adopting regional responses, in line with Article 122 of UNCLOS, may prove to be successful in seeking integrated approaches to the issue of marine litter.[24] To date, over 14 regional action plans have been developed, with differing legal natures, scopes and objectives.[25] However, they have been largely modelled on four main pillars: (1) Addressing land-based sources; (2) Addressing sea-based sources; (3) Monitoring and Assessment; and, (4) Awareness and Education. These Regional Actions Plans have proven to be

20 Convention on the Prevention of Marine Pollution by Dumping of Wastes and Other Matter (Adopted 13 November, entered into force 30 August 1975) 1046 UNTS 120 ('London Convention').

21 See for an in-depth analysis: Stöfen-O'Brien, 2015, p. 125 *et seq.*

22 Protocol to the Convention on the Prevention of Marine Pollution by Dumping of Wastes and Other Matter (Adopted 7 November 1996, entered into force 24 March 2006) 36 ILM 1 ('London Protocol').

23 Global Programme of Action for the Protection of the Marine Environment from Land-based Activities (GPA), Intergovernmental Conference to adopt a Global Programme of Action for the Protection of the Marine Environment from Land-Based Activities, 05.12.1995, UNEP (OCA)/LBA/IG.2/7.

24 Admittedly, during the negotiations towards adopting UNCLOS, the issue of semi-enclosed seas was not without controversy. One of the key aspects of that time related to the determination of what constitutes regions which was coined by the political status quo, which was coloured by ideological regionalism, see Alexander, *Ocean Development & International Law* 2 (1974) 151.

25 UN Environment Programme, Global Partnership on Marine Litter, Action Plans, last accessed 19.10.2021.

successful in raising awareness of the issue. In addition, the regional approach has enabled specific regional challenges related to the marine litter issue to be addressed at an effective local level with immediate results visible in some instances.[26] Due to the smaller circle of States Parties, Regional Action Plans may be revised in a more efficient manner than any global instruments and may target specific regional pressures and sources. This is also the case for riverine inputs of marine plastics for which river basin organisations could provide a suitable regulatory framework.[27]

Increasingly, other, non-law of the sea, intergovernmental agreements take up the issue of marine litter and plastic pollution. One of the most prominent examples is undertaken in the framework of the Basel Convention on the Control of Transboundary Movements of Hazardous Wastes and Their Disposal[28] (Basel Convention) in which framework an amendment to include plastic has been adopted in 2019 and which came into force in January 2021.[29] Beyond the global and regional regulatory approaches, there are also numerous national initiatives and regulations in place. Increasingly, industry establishes (voluntary) initiatives on marine litter and marine litter management addressing plastic along the entire life cycle. Yet, despite the different global and regional instruments in place, a preliminary assessment by the United Nations Environment Programme (UNEP) has outlined that "[n]o global agreement exists to specifically prevent marine plastic litter and microplastics or provide a comprehensive approach to management".[30] It is clear that gaps in the global

26 Stöfen-O'Brien, 2015, p. 382.

27 L. Finska and J. Gjørtz Howden, 'Troubled Waters-Where is the Bridge? Confronting Marine Plastic Pollution from International Watercourses', 27 *Review of European, Comparative and International Environmental Law*, No. 3, 2018; N. Lebreton et al., 'River Plastic Emissions to the World's Oceans', 8 *Nature Communications*, 2017; C. Schmidt et al., 'Export of Plastic Litter by Rivers into the Sea', 51 *Environ. Sci. Technol.* 21, 2017, 12246–12253. Certain rivers have River Basin Organization in place, such as the Rhine or Danube River, which may develop measures to address the pollution of the marine environment through their watershed. However, some of the most affected rivers by plastic pollution in the world are not governed by a river basin organisation. Examples of this are the Amur River, a shared watercourse between China and Russia or the Ganges-Brahmaputra-Meghna a shared watercourse between China, India, Bangladesh and Nepal.

28 Basel Convention on the Control of Transboundary Movements of Hazardous Wastes and their Disposal (Adopted 22 March 1989, entered into force 5 May 1992) 1673 UNTS 57 (Basel Convention).

29 Basel Convention Plastic Waste Amendments, Conference of the Parties 14, 29 April 10 May 2019 available at: http://www.basel.int/Implementation/Plasticwaste/Amendments/Overview/tabid/8426/Default.aspx.

30 UN Environment, 2018, p. 15.

regulatory landscape exist and that these gaps necessitate a paradigm shift in the way this single pollution may be addressed by the global community.

4 The United Nations Environment Assembly as a Catalyst for Change: Yet Another Treaty of Public International Law?

The increasing concern of an uncomprehensive regulatory regime further weakened by fragmentation and inadequate regulatory enforcement mechanisms[31] (a not uncommon problem in international environmental law) to effectively address marine litter has meant that this subject has begun to be discussed in a number of different fora. The United Nations Environment Assembly (UNEA) under the auspices of UN Environment can be described as a catalyst for change in this regard. UNEA has paved the way for a formal and worldwide intergovernmental movement to attempt to negotiate a new international treaty on plastic. During different sessions of UNEA, key turning points include the establishment of an ad-hoc open-ended expert group (AHEG) on marine litter and plastics in 2018. The AHEG has met four times between 2018 and 2020.[32] During AHEG 1, delegates exchanged views on barriers to combat marine litter and microplastics and considered the work of existing mechanisms addressing this issue. The option of establishing a new global governance structure was also raised. During its fourth meeting in November 2020, AHEG concluded work on a Chair's Summary,[33] which included a non-exhaustive list of recommendations for future action on marine litter and microplastics. The Group reflected on a growing consensus to address plastic pollution in a broader manner, developed a set of recommendations to address the identified gaps, including voluntary measures, and raised the necessity to establish an Intergovernmental Negotiation Committee towards a new global agreement.

UNEA has also passed a number of resolutions to discuss the best ways to address the issue.[34] Whereas in previous years, the idea to pitch an international

31 Stöfen-O'Brien, 2015, p. 320.

32 UNEA Resolution 3/7 established an *Ad Hoc* Expert Group (AHEG) on marine litter and microplastics to identify, *inter alia*: the range of national, regional, and international response options, including actions and innovative approaches and voluntary and legally binding governance strategies and approaches; and environmental, social, and economic costs and benefits of different response options (2018).

33 UNEA, *Report of the Fourth Meeting of the Ad-Hoc Open-Ended Expert Group on Marine Litter and Microplastics Annex 1 Chair's Summary*, 13 November 2020.

34 See for an overview: UNEA 2/11 'Marine Plastic Litter and Microplastics' (23–27 May 2016) UN Doc UNEP/EA.2/Res.11; UNEA Res 3/7 'Marine Litter and Microplastics'

plastic treaty was unsuccessful during the UNEA session, UNEA-5.1., held virtually in February 2021, proved to be of key importance in moving this agenda item forward. It was agreed that a Ministerial Conference on Marine Litter and Plastic should be convened and one took place from 01 to 02 September 2021 in Geneva. The outcomes of this meeting are then to be used to understand the scope and approach for formal discussions on this topic during UNEA-5.2., which is scheduled to take place in spring 2022.

4.1 *Preparatory Workshops and Meetings*

In preparation for the Ministerial Conference on Marine Litter and Plastic Pollution, two preparatory meetings were organized by the co-convenors Ecuador, Germany, Ghana and Vietnam in May and June 2021. The two preparatory meetings were co-chaired respectively by two of the four co-convenors and separated into different workstreams. These were 1) common goal/vision and objectives of a potential global instrument; 2) data, monitoring and reporting; 3) national and regional cooperation, coordination, and implementation; and, 4) financial and technical support. The discussion on a common goal and vision set the scene for what governments (and some other stakeholders) envisioned, broadly framed in terms of an ambitious goal/vision with a broad scope to address the root causes of marine litter and plastic pollution.[35] After the two preparatory meetings, there was a certain agreement among the participants that a message be sent to the Ministerial Conference on Marine Litter and Plastic Pollution requesting the establishment of an Intergovernmental Negotiating Committee on Marine Litter and Plastic Pollution at UNEA-5.2. In framing this recommendation, certain key aspects seemed to stand central in moving this item forward.[36] These relate on the one hand to acknowledging that there are still many knowledge gaps on the sources and (socio-economic) impacts that would need to be identified and quantified. Also, that measures and incentives including economic instruments which likewise extend to different actors, including the business and industry sector, should aim, among others, to internalize environmental costs of plastic pollution. The participants highlighted that there must not be a duplication of already on-going efforts on a global and regional level and within different sectors. Several participants

(4–6 December 2017) UN Doc UNEP/EA.3/Res.7; UNEA Res 4/6 'Marine Plastic Litter and Microplastics' (11–15 March 2019) UN Doc UNEP/EA.4/Res.6; UNEA Res 4/9 'Addressing Single-use Plastic Products Production' (11–15 March 2019) UN Doc UNEP/EA.4/Res.9.

35 Co-Convenors, Preparatory Workshop Outcomes, May and June 2021, document is with the author.

36 Ibid.

highlighted that measures along the entire life cycle of plastic products and alternatives should be considered and that the waste hierarchy should be implemented and reflected in the new legal regime. Some countries strongly emphasised that capacity building and technical and financial assistance must stand central in assisting countries to develop measures to meet the objectives of a new treaty. Although some stakeholders argued differently, there seemed to be a majority in favour of stating as an agreed objective that all plastic pollution and marine litter should be addressed in its totality. This included adopting a risk-based approached for those types of plastic that are considered to present particular risks to the environment and health due to chemical additives, and for products regarded as impossible to collect and manage safely.

4.2 *Ministerial Conference on Marine Litter and Plastic Pollution*

On the 1 and 2 September 2021, the Ministerial Conference on Marine Litter and Plastic Pollution took place.[37] The Ministerial Declaration of this Conference stated that the participating countries affirm to propose at UNEA-5.2 the establishment of an Intergovernmental Negotiating Committee on Marine Litter and Plastic Pollution at UNEA-5.2., with the aim of achieving a new Global Agreement with ambitious goals, wide participation and means of implementation.[38] The Ministerial Declaration highlighted the need to adopt a Global Agreement based on a clear and common vision with ambitious objectives to, among others, eliminate or minimize all negative impacts of plastic throughout its life cycle. This would include the significant reduction and progressive elimination of direct and indirect discharges of plastic into the environment. The primacy of the preventive approach was highlighted by participants throughout the Conference. Delegates also touched on the human health dimension, including particular reference to the disproportionate impacts of pollution on women and children. A draft resolution on an internationally legally binding instrument on plastic pollution intended for adoption at UNEA-5.2 was presented by Peru and Rwanda and co-sponsored by a significant coalition consisting of Costa Rica, Ecuador, the European Union and its Member States, Guinea, Norway, Philippines, Senegal and Switzerland. The resolution requests the Executive Director of UNEP to convene a negotiation committee (NC) under the auspices of UNEA to prepare for an international legally binding instruments commencing in 2022 with the goal of completing it by the sixth session of UNEA in (most likely) 2023. The call in this resolution for the

---

37 Ministerial Conference on Marine Litter and Plastic Pollution, see at: https://ministerialconferenceonmarinelitter.com/, last accessed 19.10.2021.

38 Ibid., Ministerial Statement, paras. 1, 4 and 5.

completion of the work of the NC within one year is certainly commendable, yet experience from other more recent treaty negotiations, such as the negotiations towards an International Legally Binding Treaty on biodiversity in areas beyond national jurisdiction[39] would seem to indicate that reality may prove otherwise and that intractable negotiations should not be precluded. In particular, the sheer breadth and complexity of questions to be addressed reasonably allow the conclusion that this timeframe is very ambitious in its scope. At the same time, the ambition of certain States Parties is commendable.

The instructions provided by States Parties in the resolution adopted at UNEA-5.2. are particularly instructive and for that reason it is worth reproducing these in their entirety. In the resolution, the NC is invited to consider:

> (a) To specify the objectives of the instrument and establish as necessary targets, definitions, methodologies, formats, and obligations;
> (b) To achieve sustainable production and consumption of plastics, including the uptake of secondary and alternative raw materials;
> (c) To address product design and use, including compounds, additives and harmful substances as well as intentionally added microplastics;
> (d) To promote national action plans to prevent, reduce and remediate plastic pollution, tailored to local and national circumstances and the characteristics of specific sectors, and to support regional and international cooperation and coordination;
> [...]
> (g) To provide scientific and socio-economic assessments and to monitor and report on plastic pollution in the environment;
> [...]
> (i) To specify financial and technical arrangements, as well as technology transfer assistance, to support implementation of the convention;
> (j) To address implementation and compliance issues;
> (k) To promote research and development into innovative solutions, among others.

As may be concluded from this list, the objectives are manifold and indeed transcend across the boundaries of the current regulatory framework. In

39 G. Wright et al., *The long and winding road: negotiating a treaty for the conservation and sustainable use of marine biodiversity in areas beyond national jurisdiction* (Paris: IDDRI, Studies N°08/18, 82, 2018).

particular, the ambition to address plastic consumption and production, including design and raw material is in particularly important in achieving a comprehensive approach to effectively address plastic pollution. Furthermore, the mandate specifically includes to fill knowledge gaps and to emphasise that financial and technical arrangements need to be specified. However, significant uncertainties still prevail. Some open questions are as to whether what type of marine litter and/or plastic will be included in a new treaty draft and how this may be done in practice. Judging from the current state of readiness and preparedness in many developing countries, some of the intended objectives could rightly be categorised as overly ambitious, particularly when understood against the backdrop of limited countries with regular and harmonized monitoring programmes in place to monitor litter, e.g., beach litter. The lack of socio-economic assessments and knowledge available for developing countries as well as infrastructure relating to recycling, for example, is a further hindrance for which solutions will have to be found. In the following, some considerations how to meaningful incorporate the needs and corresponding obligations for Developing States, Small Island Developing States (SIDS) and Least Developed Countries (LDCS) in such a regime will be analysed while drawing on the burden-sharing principle of common but differentiated responsibilities (CBDR).

5 Dichotomy of Marine Plastic Pollution Management: Polluting Countries vs. Receiving Countries

As outlined by Picard and Barsalou,[40] the development and structure of international law around sovereignty and the right to exploit one's resources has led to structural disadvantages faced by the global South with regard to plastics. It is argued that the export of a disproportionate amount of waste to certain countries of the global South leads to ecological debts.[41] Picard and Barsalou coined the term as being indicative of an asymmetry of affluence (distribution of wealth) and effluence (pollution and waste).[42] This also applies to legacy pollution which impacts the marine environment and economic sectors in

40 M.H. Picard and O. Barsalou 'Exploring the planetary boundaries' wasteland: international law and the advent of the Molysmocene', in: Duncan, and Kotzé (eds.), *Research Handbook on Law, Governance and Planetary Boundaries*, Cheltenham: Edward Elgar Publishing Ltd, 2019.

41 A. Hornborg and J. Martinez-Alier, 'Ecologically Unequal Exchange and Ecological Debt, 23 *Journal of Political Ecology*, No. 328, 2016.

42 Picard and Barsalou, 2019, p. 207.

many countries of the global South.[43] The transboundary nature of the plastic pollution and the collective responsibility to reduce and prevent the overall pollution load in the marine environment necessitate a meaningful and effective integration of the countries of the global South. Regarding the prevailing dichotomy between polluters and plastic producing countries, it is important to reflect on the principle of CBDR and its role on equity and fairness regarding a new legal regime on plastic pollution. In essence, the objective of the CBDR principle is twofold: first, States are required to take environmental measures (the element of commonality), yet the form and nature of these measures will, in the second element, depend on the States′ capacity. Hence, different commitments and obligations apply (the element of differentiation).[44] Two legal consequences primarily follow: A dual standard in favour of developing States exists and developed States are responsible in assisting developing States. It may be seen as an expression of the general principle of equity common to many domestic legal regimes in international law.[45]

This commentary has been strongly emphasised in the deliberations during the preparatory meetings and the Ministerial Conference 2021. In particular, the financial and technical support of developing countries to meet the objectives of the reduction and elimination of direct and indirect discharges of plastic into the marine environment was often stressed and highlighted as a *conditio sine qua non* for a progression of the current plans. Indeed, paragraph 1 of the Ministerial Conference states that the objectives of a Global Agreement must also consider and account for the local and national circumstances as well as specific needs of developing countries, especially SIDS and LDCs.[46] The topic of solidarity among all actors involved was raised several times during the meeting and found its way into the Ministerial Declaration.[47] During the deliberations, the means of implementation was strongly emphasised by a majority of representatives from SIDS and Developing Countries which asked

43 K. K. Ambrose, 'Coordination and harmonization of a marine plastic debris monitoring program for beaches in the Wider Caribbean Region: Identifying strategic pathways forward', *Mar Pollut Bull.* 14, 2021.

44 T. Honkonen, *The common but differentiated responsibility principle in multilateral environmental agreements: regulatory and policy aspects* (New York: Kluwer Law International, 2009).

45 P. Sands et al., *Principles of international environmental law*, 3rd ed. (Cambridge: Cambridge University Press, 2012), p. 233.

46 Ministerial Statement, Ministerial Conference on Marine Litter and Plastic Pollution, 1 and 2 September 2021, https://ministerialconferenceonmarinelitter.com/ENDORSEMENTS/.

47 Ibid.

for concrete and already determined means of implementation. However, some delegations felt that this was too prescriptive at this point of the deliberations and stated strongly that certain means of implementation may not be considered as this point, mainly relating to waste management in countries. The importance of the means of implementation evokes the relevance of the principle of CBDR, which was however not referred to in the Ministerial Declaration. The discussion on means of implementation not only relates to what kind of means are envisioned within a given regime, but also how different countries are differentiated according to their needs and responsibilities. This in particular relates to the engagement and differentiation of responsibilities of developing countries and some even argue that, relating to the climate regime, "[w]ithout a firm, effective and mutually acceptable bedrock definition defining the scope and depth of developing country involvement, any truly global negotiation will almost inevitably fall apart."[48] This certainly also holds true for plastic pollution and marine litter. This is however challenged by the engagement of emerging economies and their role within a system of CBDR. Overall, one needs to address the question what is common and what is different between states and how may it look like? In order to structure the debate, three central conceptual pillars are proposed:

1. *Approach:* How to target which countries and responsible actors?
2. *Differentiation:* How does one achieve to differentiate pollution reduction and prevention responsibilities?
3. *Participation Mechanisms:* How to achieve a universal participation and is that something which is feasible and necessary?

Determining which countries or stakeholders ought to be included in the common responsibilities can be done in manifold ways. Lessons may be learnt from legal scholarship and approaches from other regimes. The CBDR principle has been implemented in different international agreement and has been guiding implementation. Most notably, the United Nations Framework Convention on Climate Change (UNFCCC)[49] applies this in the general principles based on respective capabilities. However, the convention's section on commitments (among others Art. 4) does not refer to CBDR, but to "specific national and regional development priorities, objectives and circumstances," which may seem subject to interpretation.

48 S. Walsh, et al., 'China and India's participation in global climate negotiations', 11 *International Environmental Agreements: Politics, Law and Economics*, No.3, 2011, p. 264.

49 United Nations Framework Convention on Climate Change, New York, 09 May 1992, 1771 UNTS 107 (entered into force 21 March 1994).

The approach to determine responsible actors and sectors has been analysed in-depth in the context of the development of a climate change regime. One of the most accessible ways may be the sectoral-based approach[50] within a given plastic regulatory regime which focuses on specific sectors within the plastic pollution management. These include, *inter alia*, plastic production, shipping, construction, personal care, medical sector, car industry, waste management and so forth. What is more, and this may admittedly be too ambitious in terms of the overall achievable scope of what ostensibly purports to be an international environmental treaty, is also the role of finance and development institutions through which support could be provided by financial means targeted at the sustainable development in these sectors under a given regulatory and integrated regime. Any such determination of responsible actors will almost invariably require a reliance and indeed, in the first instance, the availability of scientifically viable data.[51] This is not currently the case for several aspects of the plastic life cycle and supply chain as well as countries and regions. Before any sectoral policies could be implemented or arguably before an international treaty could be concluded, additional steps must be taken to address the scarcity of reliable information in the form of monitoring and verification processes.[52]

Differentiation has been undertaken in diverse fora, most significantly within the context of the UNFCCC in which a distinction is drawn between Annex I (developed) and Annex II (developing) countries.[53] Such a differentiation regarding plastic pollution may be done by determination of the historical responsibility[54] based, by way of example, on plastic production and consumption, the kind of plastic being produced and exported, vulnerability to the impacts of plastic, a hot spot approach and/or transboundary movement of plastic. Admittedly, these are only very rudimentary considerations and scientific, economic and other factors would need further consideration. These would have to be understood as being dynamic as opposed to static differentiation between Annex I and Annex II countries within the UNFCCC regime

50 A. Sawa, *A sectoral approach as an option for a post-Kyoto framework* (Cambridge, Mass.: Harvard Project on International Climate Agreements Discussion Paper 2008–23, 2008), p. 25.

51 Honkonen, 2009, p. 145.

52 UN, WOA II, Chapter 12, 2021; Lau et al., 2020, p. 1461.

53 Sawa, 2008, p.26.

54 T. Deleuil, 'The common but differentiated responsibilities principle: changes in continuity after the Durban Conference of the Parties', 3 *Review of European Community & International Environmental Law*, No. 21, 2012, p. 272.

with no mechanism to change and adjust as may be required.[55] Differentiation of applicable responsibilities may be achieved through same obligations but different commitments, for example recycling targets. One may draw from the experience of regional differentiation found in the United Nations Convention to Combat Desertification (UNCCD) (Art. 7).[56] An additional layer of differentiation may be achieved by grouping certain countries with differentiated responsibilities. Again, identifying scientific criteria would seem paramount and a benchmarking process ought to be considered. This could draw on production and consumption and/or recycling targets, among others. Comparable examples may be found in Article 4 (3) UNCCD, which stipulates the eligibility for assistance based on affected or non-affected countries. Applied to the plastic pollution, this could also be done by developing sustainability criteria and criteria relating to vulnerability to the impacts of plastic pollution. The means of participation may include financial compensation which may be targeted for a specific objective or action as defined in the material scope of a Convention, technology transfer and the exchange of information through a Clearing-House Mechanism and capacity building.

Overall, the implementation of the CBDR in this regime, be it within a new treaty or new responses, must represent the notion of equity in international law, but should also reflect that the widest possible cooperation among countries and indeed also, indirectly, private actors, is needed to combat the problem of plastic pollution. The dichotomy which exists with regard to a two-tiered grouping of countries may not be feasible for this regime. Indeed, further research and work has to be undertaken along the dissection of responsibilities and fault lines of those actors engineering and owning the property rights of plastic and those who are obliged to clean-up and mitigate the waste either washed ashore or importing the plastic waste.[57]

---

55 Depledge/Yamin, 2009, p. 441.

56 United Nations Convention to Combat Desertification in Countries Experiencing Serious Drought and/or Desertification, especially in Africa of 14 October 1994 (*1954 U.N.T.S. 3, UNCCD*). The convention explicitly singles out Africa as a priority region (UNCCD Art. 7) and furthermore entails five regional annexes that specify the "particular conditions" for the regions of I. Africa; II. Asia; III. Latin America and the Caribbean; IV. Northern Mediterranean; and V. Central and Eastern Europe, and spells out regional needs and guidelines for the respective affected country parties.

57 Picard and Barsalou, 2019, p. 209.

6 Conclusion

The principle of CBDR recognizes each States' individual circumstances. Depending on the outcome of negotiations on an international treaty on plastic, there are many options available on the application and operationalisation of the CBDR in this regime. The principle of CBDR may provide an opportunity to reflect on difficult questions relating to the dichotomy and asymmetry between plastic engineering and trading countries and those which are impacted by imported waste and washed ashore from transboundary movement. The interconnectedness and transboundary scale of the problem necessitates that global efforts to address the structural root causes of this type of pollution must also include those countries which do not have the capacity yet to implement effective marine litter reduction and prevention measures. It is argued that within these confines, the focus may not be on end-of-pipe technologies, such as for waste management. Rather, the means of implementation should emphasise measures which support the application of the waste hierarchy, with a preference for prevention and reduction of plastic, followed by recycling and as a last resort, disposal. This could include recyclability improvement, redesign of materials as well as, if necessary, sustainable low-carbon waste/ material management schemes. A new plastic treaty needs to therefore outline concrete and measurable targets and indicators which provide certainty and predictability for developing countries in achieving these by successful mobilization of resources, technology transfer and capacity-building.

Author Addendum

This contribution considers relevant events until October 2021. It does not include any subsequent developments, such as the United Nations Environment Assembly Resolution 5.14 to End Plastic Pollution: towards an internationally legally binding instrument which was adopted in March 2022.

CHAPTER 24

Implications of a New Treaty for Marine Biodiversity for the Asia-Pacific Region

Joanna Mossop

1 Introduction

At the time of writing, negotiations are underway for a treaty for the conservation and sustainable use of marine biodiversity in areas beyond national jurisdiction (BBNJ Treaty or Treaty). The Treaty negotiations were authorised by the United Nations General Assembly in Resolution 72/249. However, discussions around the topic of the Treaty have been ongoing since 2006.[1]

Although it is obviously impossible for the author to predict the outcome of the final negotiations, this chapter will explore some of the implications of the draft Treaty for the Asia-Pacific region. It will explore the positions of key states from the region in the negotiations. It is not possible to identify a common interest of states in the region because the Asia-Pacific is a very diverse region with a combination of developed and less developed states, who have different concerns about the new treaty. However, identifying the positions of states in the negotiations can reveal the opportunities and potential challenges that the BBNJ Treaty presents for the Asia-Pacific.

This focus on the Asia-Pacific region reflects two important factors. First, a regional approach to cooperation for the conservation and sustainable use of marine biodiversity is both permitted and encouraged by the draft text of the Treaty. Considering how the Treaty may interact with existing regional governance mechanisms can provide a useful indication where the regional architecture might be improved. Second, the variety of interests in the region mirror the wider range of interests in the negotiations. Comparing the positions across the Asia-Pacific provides some perspective on the challenges of finalising the Treaty.

1 See, e.g. Kristina Gjerde et al, 'Building a platform for the future: The relationship of the expected new agreement for marine biological diversity in areas beyond national jurisdiction and the UN Convention on the Law of the Sea' (2019) 33 *Ocean Yearbook* 3–44; J Ashley Roach, 'The BBNJ Process: Gaps and Prospects for Success' (2021) 35 *Ocean Yearbook*, 52–84.

DOI:10.1163/9789004518629_025

First, what is the Asia-Pacific region? There is currently a movement in strategic circles to use Indo-Pacific rather than Asia-Pacific as a regional descriptor.[2] However, this concept is subject to some controversy, and I intend to use Asia-Pacific in a descriptive capacity. Thus, this chapter will consider littoral countries in Asia as well as the Pacific region. The small island States of the Pacific are often overlooked in discussions using an Asia-Pacific lens. This chapter will discuss both. I will not be considering countries such as Australia, New Zealand, or those in North or South America.

This chapter first provides a brief overview of the negotiations to date. Next, it covers the key characteristics and positions of states from the Asia-Pacific region and highlights some selected implications for the region.

2 Overview of the Negotiations to Date

The international community began to discuss issues associated with the conservation and sustainable use of marine biodiversity in an *ad hoc*, informal working group, established by the General Assembly in 2006.[3] At the time, a range of concerns prompted the discussions. These included concerns about the sectoral and divided governance of areas beyond national jurisdiction (ABNJ), the absence of a regulatory mechanism for new uses of the oceans, and the need for a mechanism to establish marine protected areas for ABNJ. A key issue from the beginning was the call by many developing states to include marine genetic resources, especially those on the deep seabed, as common heritage of mankind. This caused very deep divisions in the discussions because many developed states considered that the freedom of the high seas applied to the exploitation of marine genetic resources in ABNJ.

A series of working group meetings were held in subsequent years. In 2011, states agreed on elements of a 'package' that would focus the discussions and potentially move towards a new instrument.[4] In 2015 the General Assembly

2 See, e.g. Felix Heiduk and Gudrun Wacker, 'From Asia-Pacific to Indo-Pacific: significance, implementation and challenges', (SWP Research Paper, Berlin, September 2020) https://doi.org/10.18449/2020RP09; Rory Medcalf, 'Reimagining Asia: From Asia-Pacific to Indo-Pacific' in Gilbert Rozman and Joseph Chinyong Liow (eds) *International Relations and Asia's Southern Tier* (Springer, 2018) 9–28.

3 General Assembly Resolution 59/24, para 73.

4 General Assembly Resolution 66/231, para 167.

authorised four sessions of a Preparatory Committee,[5] and then in December 2017, the General Assembly authorised four sessions of an Intergovernmental Conference (IGC) to be held in 2018 and 2019.[6] The first three sessions of the IGC were held as planned, but the fourth IGC was postponed due to the COVID-19 pandemic.[7] At the time of writing, the fourth session is yet to be held.

General Assembly Resolution 72/249 directed states to discuss the issues identified in the 2011 package,

> namely, the conservation and sustainable use of marine biological diversity of areas beyond national jurisdiction, in particular, together and as a whole, marine genetic resources, including questions on the sharing of benefits, measures such as area-based management tools, including marine protected areas, environmental impact assessments and capacity-building and the transfer of marine technology.

A further important aspect of the Resolution was the instruction that 'this process and its results should not undermine existing relevant legal instruments and frameworks and relevant global, regional, and sectoral bodies' (GRSBs).[8] This instruction was intended to ensure that the new Treaty would not override or upset existing arrangements. However, it has proven to be one of the hardest issues to resolve during the negotiations. While there is general agreement that a Conference of the Parties (COP) will be established, along with a secretariat and a scientific and technical committee, it is not yet agreed whether (and how) the COP will be able to make decisions on subject matters that intersect with other bodies. There has been much discussion about whether the institutional arrangements will be based on a global, hybrid or

5 General Assembly Resolution 69/292, 19 June 2015. Paragraph 1(a) tasked the Preparatory with making substantive recommendations to the General Assembly on the elements of a draft text of an internationally legally binding instrument under UNCLOS.

6 General Assembly Resolution 72/249.

7 A number of authors have written summaries of the BBNJ negotiations. See for example, Rachel Tiller et al, 'The once and future treaty: Towards a new regime for biodiversity in areas beyond national jurisdiction' (2019) 99 *Marine Policy* 239–242; E Mendenhall et al, 'A soft treaty, hard to reach: the second intergovernmental conference for biodiversity beyond national jurisdiction' (2019) 108 *Marine Policy* 103664; Elizabeth De Santo et al, 'Stuck in the middle with you (and not much time left): The third intergovernmental conference on biodiversity beyond national jurisdiction' (2020) 117 *Marine Policy* 103957; E Papastavridis, 'The Negotiations for a new implementing agreement under the UN Convention on the Law of the Sea Concerning Marine Biodiversity' (2020) 69 (3) *International and Comparative Law Quarterly* 585–610.

8 General Assembly Resolution 72/249, para 7.

regional approach.[9] For example, will the COP be able to establish a Marine Protected Area (MPA) itself, or will it be limited to identifying potential areas for an MPA, relying on sectoral or regional institutions to implement it? What if there is no competent body authorised to establish MPAs? These questions remain unanswered following IGC 3.

The President of the Conference, Ambassador Rena Lee, has released two versions of a draft text. The first was discussed at IGC 3,[10] and the revised draft text will be discussed at IGC 4.[11] A key characteristic of both draft texts is that much of the language is bracketed (i.e. not yet agreed). This reflects ongoing disagreements among states about key aspects of the treaty. The following analysis is, in part, based on the author's observations of the three IGCs.[12]

3 Key Issues in the Negotiations

As mentioned above, four key elements are being negotiated in the IGC, plus a number of cross-cutting issues.

3.1 *Marine Genetic Resources* (MGRs)

The first issue is the legal regime for access to and benefit sharing of MGRs in ABNJ. MGRs have the potential to be the source of new biotechnology such as pharmaceuticals, and developing countries initially argued that species found on the seabed should be governed by the principle of common heritage of mankind, in the same way as mineral resources. This would allow all states to benefit from the exploitation of resources found in commons areas.

Many industrialised states have argued that high seas freedoms should apply, and unfortunately there doesn't seem to be much agreement about the applicable principles. Although the general approach in the current negotiations is that the regime will apply to MGRs in all ABNJ, high seas and seabed, the question is what principles will apply to the regime.[13] The first draft of the

9 Andrew Friedman 'Beyond "not undermining": possibilities for global cooperation to improve marine environmental protection in areas beyond national jurisdiction' (2019) 76 *Journal of Marine Science* 452–456; Nicola Clark, 'Institutional arrangements for the new BBNJ agreement: moving beyond global, regional and hybrid' (2020) 122 *Marine Policy* 104143.

10 <https://www.un.org/bbnj/content/third-substantive-session>.

11 <https://www.un.org/bbnj/content/fourth-substantive-session>.

12 Although the author is an observer with the New Zealand delegation, all views expressed here are her own and do not represent the views of the New Zealand government.

13 Vito de Lucia, 'The question of the common heritage of mankind and the negotiations towards a global treaty on marine biodiversity in areas beyond national jurisdiction: No

text excluded common heritage of mankind from the text which was vigorously opposed by the G77. Other issues include what types of research will be covered in the treaty, what access provisions might apply, and whether monetary or non-monetary benefits might result.

Some of the larger economies in Asia potentially could develop marine genetic resources in ABNJ. Japan is one country that has a clear commercial interest in MGRs, including in ABNJ.[14] The other large states are also in a position to participate in high-cost activities such as research into MGRs in ABNJ, in comparison to smaller economies.[15] It is therefore not surprising that those countries have emphasised the importance of not infringing the freedom of scientific research.

Other states in the region, such as the Pacific Small Island States (PSIDs) grouping and the Philippines, made it very clear (both individually and as part of the G77) of the importance of using the common heritage of mankind principle to structure the MGRs section of the Treaty. In light of the reluctance of developed states to directly refer to common heritage of mankind, it is difficult to see how the issue will be resolved.

3.2 *Area-Based Management Including Marine Protected Areas*

The second element focuses on area-based management tools (ABMT) including marine protected areas (MPAs). Currently, a number of GRSBs can, and do, impose area-based measures. For example, regional fisheries management organisations (RFMOs) will sometimes impose seasonal or permanent closures of certain areas.[16] Other organisations have created more permanent area-based restrictions for environmental protection.[17] But these are hard to

---

end in sight?' (2020) 16 *McGill International Journal of Sustainable Development Law and Policy* 138–157; Alice Vadrot et al, 'Who owns marine biodiversity? Contesting the world order through the 'common heritage of mankind' principle' (2021) *Environmental Politics*, DOI: 10.1080/09644016.2021.1911442.

14 David Leary, 'Marine genetic resources in areas beyond national jurisdiction: do we need to regulate them in a new agreement? (2018) 5 *Maritime Safety and Security Law Journal* 22–47.

15 Alex D Rogers et al (2021) 'Marine genetic resources in areas beyond national jurisdiction: Promoting marine scientific research and enabling equitable benefit sharing' (2021) 8 *Frontiers in Marine Science*, 600.

16 Carole Durussel et al, 'Strengthening the Legal and Institutional Framework of the Southeast Pacific: Focus on the BBNJ Package Elements' (2017) *International Journal of Marine and Coastal Law* 635–671.

17 E.g. Cassandra Brooks et al, 'Reaching consensus for conserving the global commons: The case of the Ross Sea, Antarctica' (2020) 12(1) *Conservation Letters* DOI: 10.1111/conl.12676; Elisa Morgera, 'Whale sanctuaries: An evolving concept within the International Whaling Commission' (2004) 35 *Ocean Development and International Law* 319–338.

get agreement on, and they are almost never cross-sectoral in nature. While states seem to agree that a process is needed for the identification of suitable areas, there is still significant debate about how the Conference of the Parties (COP) will interact with existing bodies and frameworks. For example, if the COP agrees that there is a vulnerable area in a place in which an RFMO exists, what is the appropriate division of responsibilities between the COP and the RFMO? What happens when there is no RFMO? Can the COP establish an MPA, or will an RFMO be formed?[18]

At IGC3, the larger economies such as China and Japan were resistant to the possibility that non-state parties might propose areas for ABMTs. They were also concerned about the possibility that the COP might impose compulsory measures which touch on the mandate of other organisations. China mentioned both the Ross Sea MPA and the Arctic Fisheries Agreement as good examples of what can be done in a regional setting. It is interesting to note that both these initiatives for protection expire after a specified period of time. In contrast, PSIDS were much more open to the idea that non-state actors might make proposals for ABMTs.

3.3 *Environmental Impact Assessments*

The third element is environmental impact assessments (EIAs). Article 206 of UNCLOS requires states to undertake environmental assessments of activities likely to cause significant and harmful changes to the marine environment. According to article 205, those assessments are meant to be reported to the competent international organisations which should make them available to all states. However, this obligation has been poorly complied with.[19] Perhaps due to a growing international familiarity with EIAs, this element of the package has achieved more consensus than other elements. The draft texts have included quite extensive provisions about how environmental impact assessments are to be conducted. However, questions remain about the types of activity that will require an EIA, and the threshold at which an EIA would be required.[20]

---

18 Amy Hammond and Peter JS Jones, 'Protecting the "blue heart of the planet": Strengthening the governance framework for marine protected areas beyond national jurisdiction' (2021) 127 *Marine Policy* 104260.

19 Deqiang Ma et al, 'Current legal regime for environmental impact assessment in areas beyond national jurisdiction and its future approaches' (2016) 56 *Environmental Impact Assessment Review* 23–30.

20 Robin Warner, 'Environmental impact assessment in the world's oceans beyond national jurisdiction: Crafting a comprehensive regime' in World Maritime University, *Workshop and side events report: biodiversity beyond national jurisdiction: Towards the development*

Japan, South Korea and China have taken the position that EIAs should be undertaken and assessed by states parties only. They prefer that the COP or committees under the COP play a minimal role. In contrast, PSIDS prefer that the institutional arrangements provide both an additional evaluation of the EIAs, and assistance for states with lesser capacity. The Philippines was very keen to ensure that adjacent coastal States will be included and consulted.

3.4 *Capacity Building and the Transfer of Marine Technology*

The fourth element is capacity building and the transfer of marine technology.[21] There is a general acknowledgement that Part XIV of UNCLOS has been poorly implemented. While there is no opposition to the idea that capacity building and transfer of marine technology are necessary, there is something of a divide between developed and developing countries about whether it will be compulsory for developed states to provide financial assistance under the Treaty.

3.5 *Cross-Cutting Issues*

Among the cross-cutting issues, there is a fundamental question about the institutional relationship between existing institutions and the COP. The requirement in the GA Resolution that the new treaty 'not undermine' existing frameworks and GRSBs has created some tensions within the negotiations. It is often stated that there are three possible approaches to the institutional framework: global, regional or hybrid. A global approach would allow the COP to play a lead in developing new regulations and processes. Prior to the agreement to 'not undermine' existing bodies, some proponents of the global approach argued that the COP should be able to override other bodies. Now, proponents of the global approach are keen for the institutions under the Treaty to perform as much of the decision making as possible. A regional approach, in contrast, would limit the role of the COP when there are existing bodies with a mandate to regulate activities in the high seas. A strong version of a regional approach would result in COP having no mandate to address

---

of a balanced, effective and universal international agreement (2020) 64 Report 33–40, <https://commons.wmu.se/lib_reports/65>.

21 Marjo K Vierros and Harriet Harden-Davies, 'Capacity building and technology transfer for improving governance of marine areas both beyond and within national jurisdiction' (2020) 122 *Marine Policy* 104158; Harriet Harden-Davies and Paul Snelgrove, 'Science collaboration for capacity building: Advancing technology transfer through a treaty for biodiversity beyond national jurisdiction' (2020) 7 *Frontiers in Marine Science* <https://doi.org/10.3389/fmars.2020.00040>.

these issues. Closely connected to this is the possibility that fisheries might be excluded from the scope of the agreement.[22] A hybrid approach implies a mixture of these approaches, but there is a variety of views on how a hybrid regime might work.

4 The Asia-Pacific Region and Oceans Governance

4.1 *Characteristics of the Asia-Pacific Region*

The Asia-Pacific contains essentially two distinct areas within the region. On the one hand we have North and South Asia. In this part of the world there are fewer areas of the high seas, as well as considerable debate about territorial sovereignty and the appropriateness of claims to maritime zones. The finding of the South China Sea arbitral tribunal, if implemented, would have resulted in an area of the high seas in the middle of the South China Sea.[23] However, the outcome is not accepted by China. Most of the remaining ocean area is dominated by EEZs. It is really the edge of the Pacific where significant high sea areas begin.[24]

In the Pacific, coastal State EEZs dominate the southwest Pacific, but there are still plenty of large areas of high seas. Pacific states often express concern about the management of 'high seas pockets' created by gaps between the EEZs. They are particularly concerned about the impact of fishing in these areas. Beyond the Southwest Pacific, there are large stretches of oceans that are ABNJ.

Although the two areas have a different mix of EEZs to ABNJ, one important thing to note is that ocean ecosystems are interconnected. Ecosystems can be connected to distant parts of the ocean either passively (through ocean currents) or actively through the migratory patterns of sea birds, sea turtles, sharks and marine fish.[25] Ecosystem connectivity means that the interests of

---

22 See draft article 8, which includes options for excluding fishing from the part on MGRs, or from the Treaty as a whole. See also Richard Barnes, 'The proposed LOSC implementation agreement on areas beyond national jurisdiction and its impact on international fisheries law' (2016) *International Journal of Marine and Coastal Law* 583–619.

23 George K Ndi, 'Philippines v China: Assessing the implications of the South China Sea arbitration' (2016) 8(4) Australian Journal of Maritime and Ocean Affairs 269–285.

24 For the purposes of this chapter, I include the ABNJ west of the Philippines and Japan in my analysis of Asia. Some of that area is covered by the North Pacific Fisheries Commission, but not all.

25 Ekaterina Popova et al, 'Ecological connectivity between the areas beyond national jurisdiction and coastal waters: safeguarding interests of coastal communities in developing

distant coastal States may be affected by activities in ABNJ. So even for parts of the world that are dominated by EEZs, what happens in the high seas can have an impact in areas of national jurisdiction.[26]

When thinking about the interests of states in the region, it is clear that there is a diversity of interest based on national circumstances. States range from industrialised counties with significant economies, to middle income countries with large EEZs, to small island developing States. The larger states in the region also are distant water fishing nations. For these countries, protection of their access to fisheries is a priority. Although they are engaged in the negotiations, they are perhaps more conservative than others in acknowledging a potential role for the COP created by the Agreement. They tend to prefer an institutional structure that gives considerable deference to existing institutions, which would include RFMOs.

Smaller economies may be highly dependent on their EEZ for providing income – this is especially true of Pacific small island developing States (often referred to as PSIDS). They are often conscious of the impact that high seas activities have on their own EEZs. They are more likely to be hopeful that the MGR regime will provide financial benefits, and to support a more active COP.

There is also the matter of diversity between parts of the region.

The Asian region is, of course, dominated by disputes in relation to maritime zones. This includes disputes over the sovereignty of islands and other features, as well as disputes about the entitlement to maritime zones from those features. This means it can sometimes be difficult to identify where ABNJ are and to cooperate in their regulation. Although there are examples of regional and bilateral cooperation, such as with fisheries, these tend to be limited, and modest in nature.

In the Pacific, almost the opposite is true. While there are a few disputes about maritime zones, these are fairly limited in comparison to Asia. The defining characteristic of this region is the high level of cooperation between states on maritime matters such as fishing and pollution.[27] Organisations in

---

countries' (2019) 104 Marine Policy 90–102; Popova et al, 'So far, yet so close: ecological connectivity between ABNJ and territorial waters', International Institute for Environment and Development (IIED), Briefing, February 2019, https://pubs.iied.org/pdfs/17500I IED.pdf (accessed 18 September 2019); Daniel P. Costa et al, 'New Insights into Pelagic Migrations: Implications for Ecology and Conservation' (2012) 43 *Annual Review of Ecology, Evolution and Systematics* 73–96.

26 A-L. Harrison et al, 'The political biogeography of migratory marine predators' (2018) 2 *Nature Ecology and Evolution* 1571–1578.

27 See, e.g., Joanna Vince et al, 'Ocean governance in the South Pacific region: Progress and plans for action' (2017) 79 *Marine Policy* 40–45; Andrew Wright et al, 'The cooperative

the Pacific are doing a fairly good job of ensuring that the use of ABNJ are sustainably managed. For PSIDS, there is a considerable amount of concern about the regulation of fishing and other activities in the high seas pockets in the Western Pacific. States have long been worried that activities on the high seas might undermine efforts in the region to conserve biodiversity.

RFMO coverage is good in the South and North Pacific, but less so in the ABNJ bordering Asia. Although the tuna RFMOs tend to achieve good coverage, there are overlapping areas of jurisdiction where coordination can be a problem.[28] For non-tuna RFMOs, it is striking to see the number of gaps in regional coverage. There are parts of the Asian region where no RFMO exists – this may in part due to the fact that non-tuna RFMOs tend to focus on high seas areas, and there are fewer of those in Asia. But it is also likely the lack of RFMO reflects the problems in engaging in cooperation when significant disputes exist about sovereignty and maritime zones.

A final type of regional body are regional seas agreements (RSAs). They tend to focus on the prevention of pollution and tend not to have much jurisdiction over ABNJ. Although there is a RSA that exists in the Asian region, it is not extremely active and not particularly focused on regulation of activities. In the Pacific, the Secretariat of the Pacific Environment Programme (SPREP) is the secretariat charged with supporting the work of PSIDS to address environmental management challenges, including oceans.

4.2 *The Different Positions of Asia-Pacific States and Implications*

While larger Asian states, including Japan, China and South Korea, are happy to negotiate the Treaty, they are interested in ensuring that the scope of the treaty is limited, particularly when it comes to fisheries. They tend to favour decision making in the COP to be based on consensus, which means that states retain the ability to essentially veto proposals that they consider to be not in their best interests. While some larger states are part of the G77 and China grouping, it seems that there is some divergence between the interests of the larger states and smaller states on the role of the common heritage of mankind principle.

---

framework for ocean and coastal management in the Pacific Islands: Effectiveness, constraints and future direction' (2006) 49(9) *Ocean & Coastal Management* 739–763. Genevieve Quirk and Harriet Harden-Davies, 'Cooperation, Competence and Coherence: The Role of Regional Ocean Governance in the South West Pacific for the Conservation and Sustainable Use of Biodiversity beyond National Jurisdiction' (2017) 32(4) *International Journal of Marine and Coastal Law* 672–708; Carole Durussel et al, above n 16.

28 E.g. The overlap between IATTC and WCPFC.

A key issue for the distant water fishing states in the region is to ensure that the COP does not gain a mandate to impose measures, or even suggest them, in relation to sectoral areas where there are existing organisations. RFMOs are much smaller entities, in which key players can exert much more influence than in a COP open to all states. However, other states are keen to see the COP take measures that are complementary to the mandate of existing organisations.[29] The outcome of this would be a role for the international community to examine the performance and mandate of regional organisations, which might make some members of RFMOs uncomfortable.

Of course, one can anticipate problems if it is proposed that, say, measures to regulate fishing in an area that is not covered by an RFMO, be established under the COP. In parts of the Asian maritime region, there are disputes about the ability of small features to generate EEZs. There are also unresolved disputes over sovereignty and maritime zones which means it is harder to agree on which areas are under national state jurisdiction and which are areas beyond national jurisdiction. This has proven to be a challenge to cooperation among states in relation to fishing, for example.[30] It might be worthwhile including some provisions about what to do in situations when states are in dispute.

Draft article 6 requires states to cooperate for the purposes of conservation and sustainable use. The third paragraph reflects the tension between the global and regional approaches. On the one hand, many states believe that if there is no existing body, then the COP should have the ability to impose measures to protect biodiversity. On the other hand, proponents of a more regional approach argue that if no such body exists, one should be created. Paragraph 3 is still in brackets, which indicates it is not accepted yet.

If the Treaty does require the establishment of regional organisations where there are currently none, this means that the Asian region may need to be considered. One option is for existing organisations to be extended to cover the area. Another is to create a bespoke organisation. This may prove to be a challenge given the disagreements around maritime zones and territorial sovereignty.

The problem of the relationship between the COP and GSRBs is also found in draft article 15 about how ABMTs should be established. Under the current draft, there are a number of possibilities about how an ABMT could be established. First, through existing bodies. Second, by the COP to complement measures in other bodies. This latter is controversial and opposed by those who

29 See e.g., draft article 15(b).

30 Hongzhou Zhang, 'Fisheries cooperation in the South China Sea: Evaluating the options' (2018) 89 *Marine Policy* 67–76.

would argue that the existence of a body with a mandate over an activity means that it is up to that body to regulate all aspects of the activity. In their view, if an RFMO exists, the COP would not be able to issue measures for fishing activities. Third, there are alternative approaches to the situation where no relevant body exists. The first option is that the COP could implement ABMT measures itself. The second option is that the COP cannot create ABMTs, a body must be created to take those decision. This debate is still far from settled at present.

Smaller economies particularly in Southeast Asia may benefit from capacity building and any benefit sharing that is created by the MGR regime.

In the Pacific, smaller states are more likely to favour an institutional framework for the BBNJ that is more centralised and supportive of states with low capacity to implement the Treaty. The Pacific already has a well-developed institutional architecture in place to manage oceans, especially fisheries, and would not want to lose their autonomy. For PSIDS, the new Treaty is an opportunity to incentivise states to improve their focus on marine biodiversity in ABNJ, which strongly affects biodiversity in their own maritime zones. They are keen to see compulsory monetary contributions to build capacity and hope that their obligations under the treaty can be supported by a stronger, well-resourced set of BBNJ institutions.

The Pacific has much to gain from the BBNJ agreement. Requirements on parties to cooperate to ensure sustainable use of biodiversity may empower small states to raise the issues in existing bodies and may help to tip the balance in favour of expanding mandates of GRSBs to include biodiversity protection where necessary.

The cooperative approach in the Pacific is very visible in the BBNJ negotiations, where the group representing PSIDS is extremely active and engaged. It does a great job of ensuring that the voice of the region is heard loud and clear.

A key issue for PSIDS has been the inclusion of traditional knowledge on a similar footing to science as a source of knowledge.[31] Despite some initial reluctance on the part of some states, the use of 'scientific information and relevant traditional knowledge of indigenous peoples and local communities' is now found in several places in the revised draft text.[32]

On the other hand, PSIDS will not get everything they would like. The efforts to raise the role of coastal States in adjacent areas of the high seas, such as in high seas pockets have so far been resisted by many states. Any ability to benefit from capacity building and MGRs may be inhibited by the reluctance

31 Clement Yow Mulalap et al, 'Traditional knowledge and the BBNJ instrument' (2020) 122 *Marine Policy* 104103.

32 E.g. draft articles 5(i), 16(1), 21(4), 31(2).

of larger states to agree to monetary benefit sharing or compulsory financial contributions to support benefit sharing.

And finally, the shape of the relationship between the relatively effective regional architecture in the Pacific and the COP is not yet clear. This will depend on the shape of the final text.

5 Conclusion

The requirement that the Treaty negotiations 'not undermine' global, regional and sectoral bodies makes some sense. Regional arrangements can be an effective approach to managing activities. As Durussel et al have acknowledged, 'working at the regional level has been shown to drive better legal commitment and policy convergence between regional States, thus leading to large-scale changes being more efficiently tackled in the longer term.[33] Despite this argument, it has also been shown that regional organisations can be ineffective, especially in relation to RFMOs.

The draft text still reflects considerable disagreement about key aspects of the treaty. Many have their doubts that the fourth session of the negotiations will result in an outcome given the wide gaps in positions that have no obvious solution. Those wide gaps are also present in the region.

Although Asia and the Pacific are very different in terms of the interests of the coastal States and the institutional framework, the agreement does have promise that it might lead to a renewed focus on cooperation for the purposes of conserving marine biodiversity. And smaller states in particular may benefit from the provisions on MGRs and capacity building.

33 Durussel et al, above n 16.

PART 6

Issues Arising Out of Climate Change

CHAPTER 25

The BBNJ Agreement: Strengthening the Oceans-Climate Nexus?

Karen N. Scott

1 Introduction

This paper explores the ocean-climate nexus in the context of the proposed internationally legally binding instrument (ILBI) under the United Nations Convention on the Law of the Sea on the conservation and sustainable use of marine biological diversity of areas beyond national jurisdiction. The ILBI – often referred to as the Biodiversity Beyond National Jurisdiction (BBNJ) Agreement – is arguably the most significant global oceans instrument to be negotiated in almost 30 years. The ILBI proposes to "ensure the [long-term] conservation and sustainable use of marine biological diversity of areas beyond national jurisdiction through effective implementation of the relevant provisions" of the 1982 United Nations Convention on the Law of the Sea (UNCLOS).[1] Work exploring options for managing activities in areas beyond national jurisdiction (ABNJ) began as early as 2004,[2] but it was a decade before the BBNJ working group recommended to the United Nations General Assembly (UNGA) that an internationally legally binding instrument (ILBI) be adopted.[3] A Preparatory Committee (PrepCom) was established by the UNGA in 2015[4] and, in 2017, the UNGA decided to convene an intergovernmental

1 Revised draft text of an agreement under the United Nations Convention on the Law of the Sea on the conservation and sustainable use of marine biological diversity of areas beyond national jurisdiction, A.CONF.232/202/3 (18 November 2019), Art 2 [hereinafter, ILBI Draft Text] available at: https://documents-dds-ny.un.org/doc/UNDOC/GEN/N19/372/88/PDF/N1937288.pdf?OpenElement.

2 UNGA, *Report on the Work of the United Nations Open-ended Informal Consultative Process on Oceans and the Law of the Sea,* 5th Meeting, UN Doc. A/59/122 (2004); UNGA Res. 59/24 *Oceans and the Law of the Sea* (17 November 2004) [73].

3 *Letter dated 13 February 2015 from the Co-Chairs of the Ad Hoc Open-ended Informal Working Group to the President of the General Assembly* A/69/780 (2015).

4 UNGA Res. 69/292, *Development of an international legally binding instrument under the United Nations Convention on the Law of the Sea on the conservation and sustainable use of marine biological diversity of areas beyond national jurisdiction,* (19 June 2015).

conference, under the auspices of the UN, to consider the recommendations of the PrepCom.[5] The Intergovernmental Conference was slated to run for four sessions. The third session took place in August 2019, but the fourth session has been postponed at the time of writing owing to the COVID-19 pandemic. Nevertheless, a comprehensive revised draft text of the ILBI was circulated by the President of the Intergovernmental Conference in November 2019.[6]

Over the twenty years or so that the work relating to the BBNJ Agreement has been undertaken, understanding of the impacts of climate change and ocean acidification on the oceans has increased. Impacts include, but are not limited to, sea level rise, coral bleaching, toxic algae events, latitudinal abundance shifts in marine species including fisheries, reduced biodiversity and decline in fish populations owing to falling oxygen levels, and an increase in the number of extreme weather events.[7] Although more is known about the potential impacts of climate change on coastal water ecosystems, it is generally acknowledged that climate change and ocean acidification are significant threats to the deep ocean, in particular, to deep seafloor ecosystems and cold water corals and sponges.[8] The Second World Ocean Assessment, released in 2021,[9] highlighted the increase in marine heat waves over the last two decades that can penetrate multiple hundreds of metres into the deep ocean and which have affected all ocean basins.[10] The authors estimate that marine heat waves have doubled in frequency between 1982 and 2016.[11] It is predicted that rising ocean temperatures may lead to enhanced stratification, nutrient limitation and shifts towards small phytoplankton, and this will impact pelagic species.[12]

---

5 UNGA Res. 72/249, *International legally binding instrument under the United Nations Convention on the Law of the Sea on the conservation and sustainable use of marine biological diversity of areas beyond national jurisdiction Statement of financial implications*, (24 December 2017). See the *Report of the Preparatory Committee established by General Assembly resolution 69/292: Development of an international legally binding instrument under the United Nations Convention on the Law of the Sea on the conservation and sustainable use of marine biological diversity of areas beyond national jurisdiction* A/AC.287/2017/PC.4/2 (2017).

6 ILBI Draft Text, note 1.

7 See generally, *IPCC Special Report on the Ocean and Cryosphere in a Changing Climate* [H-O Pörtner, DC Roberts, V Masson-Delmotte et al.] (1999) available at: https://www.ipcc.ch/srocc/ especially chapters 4, and 5.

8 NL Bindoff, WWL Cheung, JG Kairo et al., "Changing Ocean, Marine Ecosystems, and Dependent Communities" in *IPCC Special Report on the Ocean and Cryosphere in a Changing Climate*, ibid, 448, 486–492.

9 United Nations, *The Second World Ocean Assessment, Volumes I and II* (2021) available at: https://www.un.org/regularprocess/woa2launch.

10 Ibid, Volume II, 58.

11 Ibid.

12 Ibid, 62.

The Assessment also highlights the potential impact of ocean acidification, including changes in gene expression, physiology, reproduction and behaviour with particular risk to deep-water corals.[13]

The climate-oceans nexus, while increasingly understood from a scientific and ecological perspective, has yet to fully underpin legal-policy approaches to climate change and oceans governance.[14] This paper will explore the climate-oceans nexus in the context of the BBNJ Agreement and examine the extent to which this instrument is likely to address mitigation of and adaptation to the impacts of climate change on the oceans. It will highlight the specific references to climate change and ocean acidification in the current draft of the Agreement and focus on the two areas where these two issues are most relevant: area-based protection and environmental impact assessment. This paper will conclude, however, with the observation that while there is potential in the BBNJ Agreement to integrate climate issues more effectively into the conservation of biodiversity and ecosystems beyond national jurisdiction, it is unlikely to do so owing to a lack of ambition and to resistance by some negotiating states.

2 The Climate-Oceans Nexus

There is no comprehensive, overarching global strategy or regime that addresses the impacts of climate change and ocean acidification on the oceans. Rather, this issue is the subject of what is commonly described as a regime complex: functionally overlapping parallel regimes and institutions that are non-hierarchical but which nevertheless affect one another's sphere of operations.[15] Obligations to mitigate climate change, including emissions reductions, are largely confined to the climate change regime, comprising the 1992

13 Ibid, 63–64.

14 See for example, Karen N. Scott, "Climate Change and the Oceans: Navigating Legal Orders" in Myron H. Nordquist, John Norton Moore, and Ronán Long (eds), *Legal Order and the World's Oceans: UN Convention on the Law of the Sea* (Koninklijke Brill, Leiden) (2017) 124. For a comprehensive discussion of the ocean-climate nexus see: Jan McDonald, Jeffrey McGee and Richard Barnes (eds), *Research Handbook on Climate Change, Oceans and Coasts* (Edward Elgar, 2020); Elise Johansen, Signe Veireud Busch and Ingvild Ulrikke Jakobsen (eds), *The Law of the Sea and Climate Change. Solutions and Constraints* (CUP, 2021).

15 See further K. J. Atler and S. Meunier, "The Politics of International Regime Complexity" (2009) 7 *Perspectives on Politics* 13; T. Gehring and B. Faude, "The Dynamics of Regime Complexes: Microfoundations and Systemic Effects" (2013) 19 *Global Governance* 119.

United Nations Framework Convention on Climate Change (UNFCCC),[16] 1997 Kyoto Protocol[17] and 2015 Paris Agreement.[18] However, the climate change regime is primarily focused on the atmosphere and has historically marginalised the oceans. While the climate system is defined under the 1992 UNFCCC as "the totality of the atmosphere, *hydrosphere*, biosphere and geosphere and their interactions",[19] climate change is defined as "a change of climate which is attributed directly or indirectly to human activity that alters the composition of the global *atmosphere* …".[20] Although the oceans constitute the largest sink for carbon dioxide (CO_2),[21] the focus of the climate regime has been on forests and other land-based sinks in the context of climate change mitigation.[22] The emission reduction targets under the 1997 Kyoto Protocol allowed parties to choose from a 'basket' of six (increased to seven)[23] greenhouse gases in order to meet the global commitment of a reduction in greenhouse gas emissions of 5 percent below 1990 levels,[24] but no specific targets were set in respect of CO_2, the principal cause of ocean acidification. Under the 2015 Paris Agreement, parties determine their own commitments at the national level in order to meet the Agreement's overarching objective to limit global temperature rise to 2° C with the aim of limiting the rise to 1.5° C.[25] The legally binding temperature target of 2° is generally agreed to be too high in the context of ocean temperature rise,[26] and there is no equivalent target relating to ocean pH.

---

16 United Nations Framework Convention on Climate Change (UNFCCC), adopted on 9 May 1992, entered into force 21 March 1994, 1771 UNTS 107.

17 Kyoto Protocol to the United Nations Framework Convention on Climate Change, adopted on 11 December 1997, entered into force 16 February 2005, 2303 UNTS 214.

18 Paris Agreement on Climate Change, adopted on 12 December 2015, in force 4 November 2016, (2016) 55 *ILM* 743.

19 1992 UNFCCC, Art 1(3) [emphasis added].

20 1992 UNFCCC, Art 1(2) [emphasis added].

21 M Rhein et al, 'Observations: Ocean' in T F Stocker et al (eds), *Climate Change 2013: The Physical Science Basis. Contribution of Working Group I to the Fifth Assessment Report of the Intergovernmental Panel on Climate Change* (Cambridge, Cambridge University Press 2013) 255, 260.

22 1992 UNFCCC, Art 4(2)(a) and 1997 Kyoto Protocol, Art 4(2)(a).

23 The list of greenhouse gases under the 1997 Kyoto Protocol was amended in Doha in 2012. See Decision 1/CMP.8 (2012) *Amendment to the Kyoto Protocol pursuant to its Article 3, paragraph 9 (the Doha Amendment)*.

24 1997 Kyoto Protocol, Article 3(1).

25 2015 Paris Agreement, Article 2.

26 See OD Hoegh-Guldberg, M Jacob, M Taylor, et al., "Impacts of 1.5°C Global Warming on Natural and Human Systems" in *Global Warming of 1.5°C. An IPCC Special Report on the impacts of global warming of 1.5°C above pre-industrial levels and related global greenhouse gas emission pathways, in the context of strengthening the global response to the threat of climate change, sustainable development, and efforts to eradicate poverty* [VP

States party to the 1982 United Nations Convention on the Law of the Sea (UNCLOS)[27] are under a general obligation to protect and preserve the marine environment,[28] to prevent pollution from any source,[29] and to specifically adopt laws and regulations to prevent, reduce and control pollution from land-based sources[30] and from or through the atmosphere.[31] These obligations provide a clear mandate for states to address climate change and ocean acidification, and, arguably states have a due diligence obligation to take such action.[32] However, outside of the specific context of vessel-source air emissions,[33] parties to UNCLOS have largely left such action to the climate change regime. Thus, climate change and ocean acidification and, in particular, their mitigation, have largely fallen between the climate and the ocean regimes.

This legal-policy disconnect in the ocean-climate nexus is, however, changing. Increasingly, regional fisheries management organisations and regional seas organisations are considering the implications of climate change in the context of fisheries or ocean management.[34] The UNGA, in its 2020 resolution on oceans and the law of the sea, commended the efforts of the 25th conference of the parties (COP) to the UNFCCC to "the mainstreaming of issues relating to the ocean and climate nexus into the relevant multilateral ocean and climate change processes".[35] This momentum was carried forward by COP 26 in Glasgow in 2021. The Glasgow Climate Pact notably invites the Chair of the Subsidiary Body for Scientific and Technical Advice to hold an annual dialogue, beginning in 2022, in order "to strengthen ocean-based action".[36] More

---

Masson-Delmotte, HO Zhai, D Pörtner, et al. (eds)] (2018) available at: https://www.ipcc.ch/sr15/ 221–235.

27 United Nations Convention on the Law of the Sea (UNCLOS), adopted 10 December 1982, entered into force 16 November 1994, 1833 UNTS 397.

28 1982 UNCLOS, Art 192.

29 1982 UNCLOS, Art 194(1).

30 1982 UNCLOS, Art 207.

31 1982 UNCLOS, Art 212.

32 See Karen N. Scott, "Ocean Acidification: A Due Diligence Obligation under the LOSC?" 35 (2020) *International Journal of Marine and Coastal Law* 382. On the relationship more generally between Part XII of UNCLOS and climate change see Alan Boyle, "Protecting the Marine Environment from Climate Change. The LOSC Part XII Regime" in Elise Johansen, Signe Veireud Busch and Ingvild Ulrikke Jakobsen (eds), note 14, 81.

33 See International Convention for the Prevention of Pollution from Ships as modified by the Protocol of 1978 Relating Thereto (MARPOL 73/78), adopted on 2 November 1973, entered into force 2 October 1983, 1340 UNTS 62, Annex VI.

34 See Erik J. Molenaar, "Integrating Climate Change in International Fisheries Law" in Elise Johansen, Signe Veireud Busch and Ingvild Ulrikke Jakobsen (eds), note 14, 263.

35 UNGA Res. 75/340 (2020) *Oceans and the Law of the Sea* [56].

36 Decision -/CP.26 *Glasgow Climate Pact* (2021) [61].

generally, the Pact calls on relevant work programmes and constituted bodies under the UNFCCC to "consider how to integrate and strengthen ocean-based action in their existing mandates".[37] Importantly, from an oceans perspective, the Glasgow Pact strengthened the commitment to limit temperature increases to 1.5° compared with 2°[38] and, for the first time, introduced a specific target to reduce CO_2 by 45 percent by 2030 relative to 2010 levels and to net zero around mid-century.[39] This is specifically relevant to ocean acidification, which is largely caused by excess emissions of CO_2. Equally relevant is the first explicit reference to fossil fuels (a significant source of CO_2), although the call to "phase out unabated coal power" was weakened to "phasedown"[40] during the final stages of the negotiation.[41]

As, arguably, the most important global instrument of application to biodiversity beyond national jurisdiction, the negotiation of the BBNJ Agreement provides an opportunity to deepen and strengthen the ocean-climate legal-policy nexus. The indications thus far, however, indicate that this may be an opportunity missed.

3 The BBNJ Agreement, Climate Change and Ocean Acidification

In advance of the postponed fourth negotiating session for the ILBI, in November 2019, the Chair of the BBNJ negotiations released a revised draft text of the proposed Agreement.[42] It is anticipated that the Agreement will cover four broad areas relating to the conservation and sustainable use of biodiversity in ABNJ: marine genetic resources including questions relating to the sharing of their benefits; area-based management tools including marine protected areas; environmental impact assessment (EIA); and capacity building and transfer of technology.[43] The Agreement explicitly operates within

37 Ibid, [58].
38 Ibid, [16].
39 Ibid, [17].
40 Ibid, [20].
41 Valerie Volcovici, "How a dispute over coal nearly sank the Glasgow Climate Pact" *Reuters*, 15 November 2021 available at: https://www.reuters.com/business/cop/how-dispute-over-coal-nearly-sank-glasgow-climate-pact-2021-11-14/.
42 ILBI Draft Text, note 1.
43 Ibid. For an overview of issues and progress relating to the BBNJ negotiations see: Robin Warner, "Conserving Marine Biodiversity in Areas Beyond National Jurisdiction: Co-Evolution and Interaction with the Law of the Sea" in Donald R. Rothwell, Alex G Oude Elferink, Karen N. Scott et al., (eds), *The Oxford Handbook of the Law of the Sea* (OUP, Oxford, 2015) 752; Rachel Tiller, Elizabeth De Santo and Elizabeth Mendenhall et al., "The

the framework of UNCLOS and is intended to implement the relevant provisions of UNCLOS in order to ensure the conservation and sustainable use of biodiversity.[44]

It is clear from the draft text that neither climate change nor ocean acidification are priority issues for the Agreement. Although identified early on by the working group as "an area of concern for oceans and biodiversity",[45] the focus has been on their relevance to ecosystem resilience and area-based measures rather than as stand-alone issues.[46] Thus, the Agreement will not provide for express obligations to mitigate climate change and ocean acidification, notwithstanding their status as significant threats to biodiversity and ecosystems beyond national jurisdiction. This is unsurprising. The BBNJ Agreement is designed to support and work in conjunction with existing sectoral and regional agreements,[47] which would include the climate regime. Although it might be argued that the climate regime does *not* in fact adequately address the impacts of climate change and ocean acidification on the oceans, and is therefore not sufficient to comply with the due diligence obligations under UNCLOS to prevent marine pollution,[48] there has never been any serious discussion about developing specific mitigation obligations under the Agreement. Similarly, there is no indication that the BBNJ Agreement will expressly regulate activities that seek to exploit the oceans in order to mitigate climate change, such as marine geoengineering. There is in fact no overarching regime applicable to marine geoengineering, although the 1996 Protocol to

Once and Future Treaty: Towards a New Regime for Biodiversity in Areas Beyond National Jurisdiction" (2019) 99 *Marine Policy* 239; Elizabeth M De Santo, Elizabeth Mendenhall, Elizabeth Nyma, et al., 'Stuck in the middle with you (and not much time left): the third intergovernmental conference on by adversity beyond national jurisdiction'(2020) 117 *Marine Policy* 103957.

44 ILBI Draft Text, note 1, Art 2.

45 Nilufer Oral, 'Ocean acidification: falling between the legal cracks of UNCLOS and the UNFCCC?' (2018) 45 *Ecology Law Quarterly* 9, 27.

46 Ibid. See also Joanna Mossop, "Ocean acidification and a new treaty on marine biodiversity in areas beyond national jurisdiction" in David L VanderZwaag, Nilüfer Oral and Tim Stephens, *Research Handbook on Ocean Acidification Law and Policy* (Edward Elgar, 2021) 61, 67; Christian Pip, "Integrating Climate Change in the Goverance of Areas beyond National Jurisdiction" in Elise Johansen, Signe Veireud Busch and Ingvild Ulrikke Jakobsen (eds), note 14, 336, 342–345; Siddharth Shekhar, Kristina Maria Gjerde, "The ocean, climate change and resilience: making ocean areas beyond national jurisdiction more resilient to climate change and other anthropogenic activities" (2020) 122 *Marine Policy* 104184.

47 ILBI Draft Text, note 1, Art 4.

48 I have argued this elsewhere in Karen N. Scott, note 32.

the 1972 London Convention[49] regulates ocean fertilization for scientific purposes[50] and does provide a potential platform from which to regulate other forms of marine geoengineering.[51] Marine geoengineering for climate – or indeed any other purpose – however, will not be directly addressed by the BBNJ Agreement, although the Agreement's provisions relating to environmental impact assessment and area-based protection are likely to be indirectly relevant to future marine geoengineering activities.

Nevertheless, the draft text of the Agreement does currently explicitly refer to both climate change and ocean acidification in a number of different places. The first reference is in the definition section of the draft Agreement (draft Article 1) in the context of the definition of "cumulative impacts" as "[impacts on the same ecosystems resulting from different activities, including past, present or reasonably foreseeable activities, or from the repetition of similar activities over time, including *climate change, ocean acidification* and related impacts.]"[52] It is notable that the entire definition is in square brackets, indicating a current lack of consensus among negotiating states on this draft article. Draft Article 5 sets out General [principles] [and] [approaches] and includes a strong endorsement of ecosystem resilience, defined as "[a]n approach that builds ecosystem resilience to the adverse effects of *climate change* and *ocean acidification* and restores ecosystem integrity".[53] Both threats are also explicitly identified in draft Article 14, which sets out the objectives of area-based management measures, including marine protected areas (MPA) under the Agreement. Draft sub-paragraph E, which in its entirety is currently in square brackets, exhorts states to "[[r]ehabilitate and restore biodiversity and ecosystems, including with a view to enhancing their productivity and health and building resilience to stressors, including those related to *climate change, ocean acidification* and marine pollution;]".[54] The indicative criteria for the

49 Protocol to the London Convention on the Prevention of Maine Pollution by Dumping of Wastes and Other Matter, adopted on 8 November 1996, entered into force 24 March 2006, (1997) 36 ILM 1.

50 The Protocol was amended in 2013 in order to prohibit ocean fertilization activities for any purpose other than scientific research. See the 1996 London Protocol, Art 6*bis* and Annexes 4 and 5. The amendments have yet to enter into force.

51 1996 London Protocol, Art 1(5*bis*) and Art 6*bis* (1) as amended in 2013 (amendments not yet in force).

52 ILBI Draft Text, note 1, Art 1(6) [emphasis added].

53 ILBI Draft Text, note 1, Art 5(h) [emphasis added]. See generally, Catherine Blanchard, Carole Durussel, Ben Boteler, "Socio ecological resilience and the law: exploring the adaptive capacity of the BBNJ agreement" (2019) 108 *Marine Policy* 103612.

54 ILBI Draft Text, note 1, Art 14(E) [emphasis added].

identification of areas appropriate for protection includes, in draft paragraph F, vulnerability, including to *climate change* and *ocean acidification*.[55] Indirectly, a number of the principles and/ or approaches endorsed or proposed for inclusion in the Agreement under draft Article 5 are strongly supportive of directly considering climate change and ocean acidification in decision-making. These include, in addition to ecosystem resilience, an ecosystem approach, the precautionary [principle] [approach] and [an integrated approach].[56]

What emerges from these express references to climate change and ocean acidification, as well as from the PrepCom negotiations,[57] is that these threats are most relevant to decision-makers in the context of area-based protection and environmental impact assessment.

3.1 *The BBNJ Agreement, Climate Change and Area-Based Management*

Thus far, the part of the BBNJ Agreement that most actively responds to the risks posed by climate change and ocean acidification is Part III, which sets out the provisions relating to area-based management tools, including marine protected areas. While less politically fraught than the issue of access to and benefit sharing of deep-sea marine genetic resources, the question of area-based protection on the high seas is arguably more legally complex.[58] Issues yet to be resolved through negotiation include the impact of area-based protection on traditional high seas freedoms such as navigation and fishing, and the relationship between area-based protection under the BBNJ Agreement and comparable measures under other global and regional instruments.

The 2019 draft text defines an "area-based management tool" as "a tool, including a marine protected area, for a geographically defined area through which one or several sectors or activities are managed with the aim of achieving particular conservation and sustainable use objectives [and affording higher protection than that provided in the surrounding areas]".[59] At the time of writing all the objectives of area-based protection are listed in square brackets, but will potentially include: the promotion of a "holistic and cross-sectoral approach" to ocean management/conservation; the establishment of

55 ILBI Draft Text, note 1, Annex I(f) [emphasis added]. At the time of writing, Annex I in its entirely is in square brackets, indicating a current lack of consensus on the text of the draft.

56 ILBI Draft Text, note 1, Art 5 (f), (e) and (g).

57 Nilufer Oral, note 45, 28.

58 See Karen N. Scott, "Area-based Protection Beyond National Jurisdiction: Opportunities and Obstacles" 4 (2019) *Asia-Pacific Journal of Ocean Law and Policy* 158, 173–180.

59 ILBI Draft Text, note 1, Art 1(3).

a system of ecologically representative marine protected areas; the designation of areas that support food security, safeguard aesthetic, natural or wilderness values and that create scientific reference areas for baseline research.[60] As noted above, draft Article 14(e) refers to the designation of protected areas for the rehabilitation and restoration of biodiversity and ecosystems in order to build resilience to stressors, including those related to climate change and ocean acidification. Areas requiring protection "shall be identified on the basis of the best available [science] [scientific information and relevant traditional knowledge of indigenous peoples and local communities], the precautionary [approach] [principle] and an ecosystem approach".[61] Specifically, vulnerability, "including to climate change and ocean acidification" comprises one of 21 indicative criteria that can be used in order to identify areas to be protected.[62] Thus, if adopted as per the current draft, the BBNJ Agreement will be the first global instrument to provide an undisputed legal mandate for the establishment of area-based conservation measures beyond national jurisdiction with the objective of enhancing ecosystem resilience in the context of climate change and ocean acidification.[63]

At the time of writing, the process of establishing protected areas has yet to be decided. Currently there is disagreement on whether a BBNJ institution (such as a conference of parties) will have a mandate to designate protected areas generally or, more likely, in areas that are not covered by any existing organization or regime, or whether the BBNJ agreement will rely on existing institutions to designate protected areas, with its role confined to a coordinating or advisory body.[64] Therefore, while a mandate to designate marine protected areas or other area-based measures in order to respond to the threats of climate change and ocean acidification and to increase ecosystem resilience is likely to be created under the Agreement, the extent to which that mandate will be implemented depends, to a large extent, on how active BBNJ institutions are permitted to be in designating or coordinating the designation

60 ILBI Draft Text, note 1, Art 14.

61 ILBI Draft Text, note 1, Art 16(1).

62 ILBI Draft Text, note 1, Annex I. It should be noted that the text of Annex I is currently in square brackets.

63 On the contribution that MPAs may make to enhancing ecosystem resilience in the context of climate change see: Ingvild Ulrikke Jakobsen, "Marine Protected Areas and Climate Change" in Elise Johnasen, Signe Veierud Busch and Ingvild Ulrikke Jakobsen (eds), note 14, 234; Danielle Smith, "A global network of MPAs: an important tool in addressing climate change" in Jan McDonald, Jeffrey McGee and Richard Barnes (eds), note 14, 425.

64 ILBI Draft Text, note 1, Art 19 at the time of writing provides for the three alternative models in its draft text.

of such protection. Positively, the draft Agreement provides for a process of monitoring and periodic review by the Scientific and Technical Body and a process whereby the Conference of the Parties may decide to extend, amend or revoke area-based management tools on the basis of an adaptive management approach, taking into account best available science, traditional knowledge, the precautionary [principle] [approach] and an ecosystem approach.[65] The inclusion of regular review and adaptive management is crucial in the context of area-based protection in dynamic ecosystems and in the context of climate change where the nature of the impact of warming and acidifying oceans will inevitably lead to changes in ecosystem nature and function.

Nevertheless, taken as whole, Part III of the BBNJ Agreement, as currently drafted, is arguably wholly inadequate in supporting area-based protection for climate change and ocean acidification purposes.

First, notwithstanding the endorsement of an ecosystem approach, it is unclear, at the time of writing, whether fisheries will be excluded from the general mandate of the BBNJ Agreement.[66] In terms of ecosystem impact, fishing is undoubtedly the most important activity taking place on the high seas. Implementing area-based protection in order to enhance ecosystem resilience against climate change and ocean acidification would arguably be undermined if such measures are not also able to address fisheries.

Second, the BBNJ Agreement makes no reference to climate refugia in the area-based measures objectives in Part III of the 2019 draft or in the criteria for selecting areas for protection in draft Annex I. Climate refugia refer to areas or ecosystems that are not currently impacted by or are believed to be resilient to climate change and ocean acidification, and therefore should be protected in order to manage other activities in order to create climate refuges.[67] Although it could be argued that draft Article 14(e), which refers to "building resilience to stressors, including those related to climate change [and] ocean acidification", is broad enough to permit the designation of climate refugia, its emphasis on "rehabilitat[ing] and restor[ing] biodiversity and ecosystems" may preclude its application to ecosystems that are currently healthy and resilient. A more

65 ILBI Draft Text, note 1, Art 21.

66 See B Haas, M Haward, J McGee et al., "Regional fisheries management organizations and the new biodiversity agreement: Challenge or opportunity?" 22 (2021) *Fish and Fisheries* 226.

67 See Kendall R. Jones, Carissa J. Klein, Benjamin S. Halpern et al., 'The Location and Protection, Status of Earth's Diminishing Marine Wilderness' (2018) 28 *Current Biology* 2506, 2506.

robust approach to climate resilience would explicitly provide for a right if not an obligation to create climate refugia.

Finally, the 2019 draft BBNJ Agreement does not adequately address the inherent tension between the static nature of an area-based measure and the highly dynamic nature of the ocean environment, exacerbated by the impacts of climate change and ocean acidification. Although, as noted above, the draft Agreement does provide for a process of review, and also refers briefly to the concept of adaptive management, it is unlikely that these provisions will prove adequate in face of the level of change likely to occur as a consequence of climate change and ocean acidification.

In this context it is useful to refer to a recent assessment of area-based management tools in the north Atlantic, which was highly critical of the relatively well-developed network of area-based protection in the region, finding that the majority of measures adopted are likely to become redundant or less fit for purpose within the next 15 to 20 years owing to climate change.[68] This was primarily because, notwithstanding references to climate change in the relevant regimes, the area-based management measures are "still being applied on the basis of contemporary environmental conditions and habitat distributions".[69] The authors recommended the application of adaptive management, a focus on ecosystem function[70] and the identification of refugia so that "areas that are not currently seen as high biomass or density areas for a species of conservation interest ... [are] included in the implementation of ABMTs to safeguard against climate change".[71]

More generally, there is increasing recognition that area-based management must be temporally and biologically as well as spatially adaptive.[72] In addition to an explicit mandate for such an approach, this form of adaptive management also requires responsive and expert-based institutional infrastructure that can review and adapt area-based measures as appropriate. The current draft of the BBNJ Agreement not only adopts a narrow, spatially focused definition of area-based protection, but is also unlikely to establish decision-making

68 David Johnson, Maria Adelaide Ferreira and Ellen Kenchington, "Climate change is likely to severely limit the effectiveness of deep-sea ABMTs in the north Atlantic'" (2018) 87 *Marine Policy* 112, 119.

69 Ibid, 113.

70 Ibid, 120.

71 Ibid.

72 See Guillermo Ortuño Crespo, Joanna Mossop, Daniel Dunn et al., 'Beyond static spatial management: scientific and legal considerations for dynamic management in the high seas' (2020) 122 *Marine Policy* 104102.

bodies with the appropriate mandate and expertise to respond to the challenges posed by climate change and ocean acidification.

3.2 *The BBNJ Agreement, Climate Change and Environmental Impact Assessment*

The second area in which the BBNJ agreement can potentially contribute towards measures related to climate change and ocean acidification is environmental impact assessment and strategic environmental assessment as set out in draft Part IV of the Agreement.[73] As is the case for area-based protection, much of Part IV of the draft Agreement remains in square brackets and there are significant differences between the alternative proposed obligations relating to the nature and extent of an EIA, the threshold at which an EIA is required and the relationship between the BBNJ agreement and other international and regional instruments as they relate to EIA. Depending on the decisions made between these alternative texts, the impacts of climate change and acidification on the oceans could be important factors to consider in the assessment of activities within or affecting ABNJ, or entirely peripheral to such processes.

In contrast to Part III of the draft BBNJ Agreement, there is no explicit reference in draft Part IV to climate change and ocean acidification. However, Article 21bis, which sets out the objectives of the Part, expressly refers to the consideration of cumulative impacts when carrying out an EIA.[74] As noted above, cumulative impacts, as defined in draft Article 1(6), includes "climate change, ocean acidification and related impacts". Moreover, draft Article 25 is devoted to the issue of cumulative impacts, which "shall [, as far as possible,] be [taken into account] [considered] in the conduct of environmental impact assessments".[75] This would create, for the first time, an express obligation to consider climate change and ocean acidification as part of the EIA for all activities carried out in ABNJ.

Unsurprisingly, the question of which activities in ABNJ are subject to EIA processes under the Agreement is contested. The first option would require an EIA when states have reasonable grounds to believe that activities under their jurisdiction or control may cause substantial pollution of or significant harmful changes to the marine environment, or, more boldly, more than a minor or transitory impact on the environment.[76] The second option, draws inspiration

73 See generally, Robin Warner, "Oceans in transition: incorporating climate change impacts into environmental impact assessment for marine areas beyond national jurisdiction" (2018) 45 *Ecology Law Quarterly* 31.

74 ILBI Draft Text, note 1, Art 21bis [(b)]. This text is at the time of writing in square brackets.

75 ILBI Draft Text, note 1, Art 25(1).

76 ILBI Draft Text, note 1, Art 24(1) [Alt 1].

from the 1991 Environmental Protocol to the 1959 Antarctic Treaty,[77] and provides for a two stage assessment process depending on whether the activity is likely to have more than a minor or transitory effect or cause substantial pollution or significant harmful changes to the marine environment.[78] In the latter case, the results of the EIA must be submitted for a technical review in accordance with Part IV of the Draft Agreement.[79] There is provision in the current draft of the Agreement for the EIA threshold and criteria to be set out in the Agreement or developed, at a later date, by the Scientific and Technical Body.[80] From the perspective of climate change and ocean acidification, it is clear that the lower threshold for carrying out an EIA is more appropriate. The nature of an EIA is that it is the individual activity that is subject to assessment, and while the Agreement requires cumulative effects to be considered, it is unlikely, outside the context of geoengineering, that any individual activity in ABNJ will lead to "significant and harmful" climate change and ocean acidification effects.

One option under consideration is for a list of activities that require, or which do not require an EIA to be specified in an annex to the BBNJ Agreement or set out in voluntary guidelines prepared by the Conference of the Parties on the basis of recommendations from the Scientific and Technical Body.[81] This option provides an opportunity for the BBNJ Agreement to regulate activities in ABNJ that directly contribute to or are closely connected with climate change or ocean acidification. The obvious example of such an activity is marine geoengineering. As noted above, while the 1996 Protocol to the London Convention will regulate ocean fertilisation once the 2013 amendments to the Protocol enter into force, and has a mandate to regulate other forms of geoengineering, its scope is arguably limited to geoengineering that involves the placement of matter into the oceans.[82] There is currently no global organisation with a mandate to regulate marine geoengineering more generally.[83] This

77 Protocol on Environmental Protection to the 1959 Antarctic Treaty, adopted on 4 October 1991, entered into force 14 January 1998, 30 ILM 1461, Art 8 and Annex I.

78 ILBI Draft Text, note 1, Art 24(1) [Alt 2].

79 Ibid.

80 ILBI Draft Text, note 1, Art 24[(2)]. The entire provision is in square brackets in addition to the two alternative options set out within the paragraph.

81 ILBI Draft Text, note 1, Art 29(1). This option is currently in square brackets.

82 1996 London Protocol, Art 6*bis* (1). Article 6*bis* (1) was adopted as an amendment to the Protocol in 2013 and has not yet entered into force.

83 See generally, Karen N. Scott, "Geoengineering and the Law of the Sea" in Rosemary Rayfuse (ed), *Research Handbook on International Marine Environmental Law* (Edward Elgar Publishing, 2015) 451.

lacunae could be partially filled by a BBNJ Agreement that specifies that geoengineering activities in ABNJ must comply with an EIA subject to the terms of the Agreement. A similar argument could be made in relation to other activities that have climate implications such as renewable energy technologies.

Arguably the most significant factor that will influence how relevant the BBNJ Agreement EIA provisions are to activities with climate change or acidification implications for the oceans is whether the EIA process will apply only to activities carried out in ABNJ or whether it will apply to activities that have an *effect* "on areas within or beyond national jurisdiction".[84] The latter option is potentially very broad and, in theory, might encompass activities under the jurisdiction of states (within their territory) but which affect the oceans – in terms of temperature rise, deoxygenation or pH change – beyond national jurisdiction. In fact, it is largely land-based activities, rather than activities within ABNJ, that are contributing to climate change and ocean acidification. At the time of writing, one option in the draft BBNJ Agreement defines an EIA (draft Article 1(7) [Alt.1]) as "a process to evaluate the environmental impact of an activity [to be carried out in areas beyond national jurisdiction [*, with an effect on areas within or beyond national jurisdiction*]] [, taking into account [, interrelated [socioeconomic] [social and economic], cultural and human health impacts, both beneficial and adverse].][85] The alternative definition confines the process to activities taking placed beyond national jurisdiction.[86] From the perspective of addressing the climate-related impacts on the oceans, it is clear that the broader definition that would require an EIA in respect of activities under the control of states wherever they are located if they affect ABNJ, is preferred. Politically, however, it is unlikely that states will agree to such a far-reaching obligation.

Finally, connected to the issue of EIA breadth, draft Article 28 provides for a process of strategic environmental assessment (SEA) of plans and programmes. Currently poorly defined under the draft BBNJ Agreement,[87] SEA builds on and is broader than the process of EIA in that it focuses on an assessment of the environmental and other impacts (such as health) of government

84 ILBI Draft Text, note 1, Art 7 [Alt. 1].

85 Emphasis added.

86 ILBI Draft Text, note 1, Art 7 [Alt. 2]: ["Environmental impact assessment" means a process for assessing the potential effects of planned activities, carried out in areas beyond national jurisdiction, under the jurisdiction and control of State Parties that may cause substantial pollution of or significant and harmful changes to the marine environment.].

87 See ILBI Draft Text, note 1, Art 1[13].

programmes and plans.[88] It therefore has the potential to be highly relevant to programmes, plans and policies that have implications for climate change and ocean acidification such as shipping and offshore oil and gas production. Again, a key question is whether the BBNJ SEA obligation will be confined to activities conducted in ABNJ or whether it will apply to activities under the control of parties that affect ABNJ. Both options are currently provided for in square brackets in draft Article 28. The broader option is potentially very far reaching with the SEA obligation, in principle, of application to industrial and energy plans and programmes under a state's jurisdiction, including on its territory, where those plans and programs contribute to the cumulative effects of climate change and ocean acidification in ABNJ. While extremely positive from the perspective of climate change, it is again unlikely that states will agree to such a far-reaching SEA obligation.

3.3 *The BBNJ Agreement, Institutional Infrastructure and Climate Change*

The final area worthy of consideration is the institutional infrastructure associated with the BBNJ agreement. A challenge in developing the global law of the sea is that UNCLOS has few institutions that have the capacity to develop and implement the Convention.[89] In contrast to the UNFCCC and indeed most other multilateral environmental treaties, the UNCLOS conference of the parties deals only with technical matters and does not provide a forum for the discussion of substantive issues.[90] By contrast, it is proposed a number of institutions be established to support the implementation of the BBNJ Agreement. The creation of dynamic institutional infrastructure is important in the context of responding to an equally dynamic ocean environment.

Draft Article 48 of the BBNJ Agreement establishes a conference of the parties with a potentially broad mandate to adopt decisions on all aspects of the agreement. It is likely that the standard model of consensus decision-making will be adopted[91] and in practical terms this may inhibit progressive action in the context of climate change and ocean acidification. Positively, draft

88 See generally, Robin Warner, "Strategic Environmental Assessment and Its Application to Marine Areas beyond National Jurisdiction" in Richard Barnes and Ronán Long (eds), *Frontiers in International Environmental Law: Oceans and Climate Challenges* (Brill, 2021) 430.

89 See generally, James Harrison, "The Law of the Sea Convention Institutions" in Donald R. Rothwell, Alex G Oude Elferink, Karen N. Scott et al., note 43, 373.

90 1982 UNCLOS, Art 319(2)(e). See also ibid, 376–378.

91 ILBI Draft Agreement, note 1, Art 48 [3bis]. The article provides for the procedures adopted by the conference of the parties to apply if consensus cannot be achieved.

Article 49 is slated to establish a Scientific and Technical Body to provide scientific and technical advice to the conference of the parties. The Body may have the power to make recommendations associated with the assessment of area-based protection measures and EIA proposals, although all of these functions are currently in square brackets and there is no consensus yet on the extent of the mandate of the Scientific and Technical Body. Other bodies likely to be established by the Agreement include a secretariat,[92] a clearing house mechanism for information exchange and dissemination[93] and a financial mechanism.[94] Although not directly connected to climate change and ocean acidification, the establishment of responsive and scientifically-based institutions are fundamental in supporting the adoption of adaptive measures appropriate to the dynamic ocean environment in the context of climate change and ocean acidification.

4 Concluding Remarks

The ocean-climate nexus is now largely acknowledged by policy-makers, although progress towards implementing integrated oceans-climate measures is slow. The BBNJ Agreement provides a meaningful opportunity to more effectively integrate climate change and ocean acidification impacts into the management and conservation of high seas biodiversity and ecosystems. Climate change and ocean acidification are both expressly identified as factors relevant to oceans resilience, and as such, need to be considered as part of EIA and SEA processes, assuming the bracketed definition of cumulative effects remains as it is currently drafted. It has yet to be agreed as to whether the BBNJ EIA/ SEA processes will apply to activities taking place outside ABNJ under a state's jurisdiction, but which may impact on biodiversity beyond national jurisdiction. This is currently an option in the draft Agreement, and from the perspective of integrating climate change and ocean acidification into broader decision-making, would undoubtedly be preferable to the narrower approach which restricts EIA/ SEA processes to activities actually taking place beyond national jurisdiction. The inclusion of an SEA process in the draft BBNJ Agreement is particularly notable in the context of climate change and ocean acidification as the SEA obligation applies to programs and plans more generally that take place within or potentially impact on ABNJ. A broad interpretation of

92 ILBI Draft Agreement, note 1, Art 50.

93 ILBI Draft Agreement, note 1, Art 51.

94 ILBI Draft Agreement, note 1, Part VII.

this obligation could require states to consider activities such as shipping or offshore oil and gas exploitation from the perspective of climate change and ocean acidification.

More particularly, climate change and ocean acidification are expressly identified as factors that undermine ecosystem resilience, justifying area-based management mechanisms under the Agreement. However, Part III of the Agreement on area-based protection is arguably inadequate as currently drafted as a response to the dynamic challenges posed by climate change and ocean acidification. The definition of area-based management is spatially focused and lacks a meaningful temporal and biological adaptive dimension. Moreover, while acknowledging that the process of designating protected areas has yet to be determined under the BBNJ Agreement, the provisions in the draft that relate to review and adaptation are arguably insufficient to respond to the very dynamic nature of ocean ecosystems. This constitutes something of a lost opportunity to develop processes and principles for area-based management on the basis of modern scientific and ecological research. Finally, the conception of area-based protection is quite narrow under the 2019 draft of the BBNJ Agreement in that the focus is on areas that are currently vulnerable to climate change and ocean acidification, and there is no express provision for protecting so-called climate refugia. That is, areas that are currently resilient and should be protected in order to maximise ecosystem resilience, or areas that are likely to become vulnerable in the future.

More generally, the apparent exclusion of fisheries from the draft BBNJ Agreement inevitably limits the application of an integrated and ecosystem approach and, in practice, undermines the potential effectiveness of measures adopted under the Agreement seeking to build resilience in the face of climate change and ocean acidification.

While climate change and ocean acidification are expressly identified as cumulative impacts, and as factors that contribute towards ecosystem vulnerability, neither threat is front and centre of the draft Agreement. The BBNJ Agreement will not contribute to obligations to mitigate carbon dioxide emissions and other causes of climate change and ocean acidification, and it will not address the regulatory in lacuna which exists in relation to ocean acidification. It is unlikely to provide a forum within which marine geoengineering can be generally regulated outside of the broad provisions relating to environmental impact assessment and area-based protection.

Significantly however, climate change and ocean acidification are at risk of being entirely marginalised within the BBNJ Agreement. In the textual proposals submitted by state and other delegations in February 2020,[95] in response to the 2019 draft, a number of states indicated a desire to water down or omit altogether the references to climate change and ocean acidification. For example, the EU and its member states have proposed the deletion of "climate change, ocean acidification and related impacts" from the definition of cumulative impacts in Article 1(6).[96] The Republic of Korea has suggested that the entire definition of cumulative impacts be removed altogether.[97] Indonesia has suggested the omission of Article 14(e), which includes building resilience stressors, including those related to climate change and ocean acidification, among the objectives of area-based protection.[98] This proposal is endorsed by the Republic of Korea, which has suggested paragraph (e) of Article 14 be moved to the Preamble of the Agreement.[99] In relation to EIA, the EU, Indonesia and the Republic of Korea have all endorsed confining the process to activities taking place in ABNJ.[100] Korea is in favour of removing Article 25 (on cumulative impacts) entirely from the draft and dealing with cumulative and transboundary impacts in draft Article 35(2)(d), which sets out a description of the potential effects of a planned activity as part of the preparation and content of EIA reports.[101] The EU, Indonesia and the Philippines favour limiting the obligation to carry an SEA under draft Article 28 of the Agreement to activities taking place within ABNJ[102] and Korea has suggested that Article 28 and SEA be omitted altogether.[103] This compilation of proposals is far from complete and notably does not include the views of China and Russia.

---

95 Textual proposals submitted by delegations by 20 February 2020, for consideration at the fourth session of the Intergovernmental conference on an international legally binding instrument under the United Nations Convention on the Law of the Sea on the conservation and sustainable use of marine biological diversity of areas beyond national jurisdiction (the Conference), in response to the invitation by the President of the Conference in her Note of 18 November 2019 (A/CONF.232/2020/3) at: https://www.un.org/bbnj/sites/www.un.org.bbnj/files/textual_proposals_compilation_article-by-article_-_15_april_2020.pdf.

96 Ibid, 9.

97 Ibid, 15. By contrast, South Africa, has indicated its very strong support for including a definition of cumulative effects, including the reference to climate change and ocean acidification. See ibid, 17.

98 Ibid, 122.

99 Ibid, 125.

100 Ibid, 219–221.

101 Ibid, 242.

102 Ibid, 249.

103 Ibid, 250.

At the time of writing therefore, the BBNJ Agreement has the potential to strengthen the ocean-climate nexus and to better integrate climate and ocean acidification into the conservation and management of biodiversity and ecosystems beyond national jurisdiction. However, it is very unlikely that this potential will be realised in a way that is meaningful and effective. Not only is the BBNJ Agreement unambitious in relation to climate change and ocean acidification, but the few references and innovations the current draft provides for are at distinct risk of being diluted by the negotiating states, including, rather surprisingly, the EU. Bridging the climate and law of the sea regimes and integrating climate concerns into oceans governance is a global priority and this is slowly being recognised by institutions such as the UNFCCC. But the BBNJ Agreement is unlikely to be the instrument that constitutes such a bridge.

CHAPTER 26

Regime Interaction between the Law of the Sea and Climate Change Law

Naoki Iwatsuki

1 Introduction

Climate change impacts, such as sea-level rise, water-warming, acidification, have various implications for ocean spaces and the utilization of marine natural resources.[1] Considering these impacts, the law of the sea, embodied principally in the United Nations Convention on the Law of the Sea (UNCLOS), must be implemented to protect the marine environment and adapt to changing ocean conditions. In this respect, the law of the sea may work in *collaboration* with climate change law to achieve the prime objective: the protection of the climate system for present and future generations.[2]

On the other hand, issues are arising from the endeavor to alleviate the effect of climate change and to reduce the emissions of carbon dioxide (CO_2) or other greenhouse gases (GHGs). Researchers have discussed the availability and feasibility of using ocean spaces as a CO_2 reservoir by applying innovative forms of geo-engineering, such as ocean fertilization and sub-seabed carbon storage.[3] Undoubtedly, the development of new methods contributing to the reduction of GHGs is highly desirable from the perspective of the climate change law, embodied in the United Nations Framework Convention on Climate Change and its protocols. However, such ocean space utilization must

1 See generally, R.S. Abate and S.E. Krejci, 'Climate Change Impacts on Ocean and Coastal Law: Scientific Realities and Legal Responses', in: R.S. Abate (ed.), *Climate Change Impacts on Ocean and Coastal Law: U.S. and International Perspectives* (New York, Oxford University Press, 2015), pp. 2–24.

2 For different types and forms of regime interaction, see H. van Asselt, *The Fragmentation of Global Climate Governance: Consequences and Management of Regime Interactions* (Cheltenham, Edward Elgar, 2014), pp. 44–59.

3 See generally, D.P. Keller, 'Marine Climate Engineering', in: T. Markus and M. Salomon (eds.), *Handbook of Marine Environment Protection: Science, Impacts and Sustainable Management* (Cham, Springer, 2018), pp. 261–278. Also see, H. Ginzky, 'Marine Geo-Engineering', in: *ibid.*, pp. 997–1012; K.N. Scott, 'International Law in the Anthropocene: Responding to the Geoengineering Challenge', 34 *Michigan Journal of International Law*, 2013, No. 2, 309–358.

DOI:10.1163/9789004518629_027

be performed in consonance with the obligations under the law of the sea.[4] In this respect, there may be some conflict between the law of the sea and climate change law. Thus, appropriate *coordination* between these two legal regimes should be sought.

2 Collaboration between the Law of the Sea and Climate Change Law

2.1 *Key Points of Collaboration*

I will first present the possibilities and limits of collaboration between the two regimes. The key to collaboration between the law of the sea and climate change law is Chapter XII of UNCLOS. The first article of that Chapter, Article 192, obliges states to protect and preserve the marine environment. Under this general obligation, Article 194, paragraph 1, specifies that states shall take all measures necessary to prevent, reduce, and control pollution of the marine environment *from any source*.

Additionally, paragraph 3 of that article specifies that measures to be taken by states pursuant to Chapter XII shall deal with *all sources* of marine environment pollution. This includes, *inter alia*, measures designed to minimize toxic, *harmful*, or noxious substance-release from land-based sources.

Based on these provisions, some authors maintain that states are obliged to take measures to control and regulate the activities contributing to climate change. For example, one author contends that, under Articles 192 and 194 of UNCLOS, states are obliged to control and reduce CO_2 emissions from any source likely to pollute the marine environment and cause harm to other states.[5]

As argued by some authors, Articles 192 and 194 may represent the legal basis for the encouragement of states to conduct further efforts toward more efficient reduction of GHGs. However, one may question the precise substance of the obligation at issue. The arbitral tribunal in the *South China Sea* arbitration noted that the obligation under Articles 192 and 194 is an obligation

4 On this issue, an excellent series of works by K.N. Scott must be referred to. Among others, K.N. Scott, 'The Day After Tomorrow: Ocean CO_2 Sequestration and the Future of Climate Change', 18 *Georgetown International Environmental Law Review*, 2005, No. 1, 57–108; *idem*, 'Regulating Ocean Fertilization under International Law: The Risks', 2013 *Carbon & Climate Law Review*, No. 2, 2013, 108–116; *idem*, 'Ocean Acidification: A Due Diligence Obligation under the LOSC', 35 *International Journal of Marine and Coastal Law*, 2020, 382–408.

5 E.g., Alan Boyle, 'Law of the Sea Perspective on Climate Change', 27 *International Journal of Marine and Coastal Law*, 2012, 834.

of conduct, requiring the 'due diligence' by a state not only to adopt appropriate rules and measures but also to ensure a 'certain level of vigilance in their enforcement and the exercise of administrative control'.[6] So far, so good. However, what actually matters is the level of vigilance regarding the reduction of CO_2 emissions required to mitigate impacts of climate change on the marine environment. On this point, it is suggested that the law on climate change is relevant, and that the Paris Agreement sets a standard for giving effect to the obligation *under* UNCLOS. According to this argument, the Paris Agreement indicates the necessary measures related to GHG emissions, and, as such, it constitutes the generally accepted international rules or standards for that purpose.[7]

2.2 *Limits for Collaboration*

Assuming that the impacts of climate change, such as water-warming and acidification, constitute 'pollution' as defined by UNCLOS,[8] one may agree with that line of thought. However, in my opinion, it is necessary to note one caveat. I question whether Articles 192 and 194 may be interpreted as a clause of *automatic* incorporation of the standards laid down *outside* the law of the sea regime. UNCLOS has such incorporation provisions, for example, in relation to the laws and regulations on shipping and marine transportation.[9] Admittedly, Article 212 under Chapter XII appears to be similar in that it requires states to take into account internationally agreed rules, standards and recommended practices and procedures in adopting laws and regulations with respect to pollution from or through the atmosphere. However, the phrase 'taking into

6 *The South China Sea Arbitration* (*the Republic of Philippines v. the People's Republic of China*), *Award of 12 July 2016*, para. 944.

7 Alan Boyle, 'Litigating Climate Change under Part XII of the LOSC', 34 *International Journal of Marine and Coastal Law*, 2019, 466–467.

8 Article 1, Paragraph 1 of UNCLOS defines 'pollution of the marine environment' as '*the introduction by man, directly or indirectly, of substances or energy into the marine environment*, including estuaries, *which results or is likely to result in such deleterious effects as harm* to living resources and marine life, hazards to human health, hindrance to marine activities, including fishing and other legitimate uses of the sea, impairment of quality for use of sea water and reduction of amenities' (emphasis added).

9 See, Articles 21, 39, 94, 211. For example, Article 94 (Duties of the flag State), Paragraph 5 provides: 'In taking the measures called for in paragraphs 3 and 4 [measures for ships flying its flag as are necessary to ensure safety at sea] *each State is required to conform to generally accepted international regulations, procedures and practices and to take any steps which may be necessary to secure their observance*'. (emphasis added).

account' in Article 212 is the 'weakest of the qualifications used' in relation to the obligations of the states regarding internationally agreed measures.[10]

Furthermore, the level of vigilance for the prevention and mitigation of the impacts of climate change on the marine environment is not necessarily the same as that set out by climate change law.[11] More precisely, even if the law of the sea and climate change law commonly oblige states to seek to alleviate the impacts of climate change to protect the environment, the required level of vigilance for that purpose may be determined differently within the respective regimes. Concerning climate change law, the stabilization of GHG concentrations in the atmosphere at a level needed to prevent dangerous anthropogenic interference with the climate system is essential.[12] However, what is at stake for the law of the sea is to promote the protection and preservation of the marine environment *together with* the equitable and efficient *utilization* of the ocean spaces and their natural resources.[13] Thus, the different objectives of each regime would lead to divergent standards to be applied.

Having said that, I do not intend to emphasize the problem of fragmentation resulting from the distinctiveness of each regime. Rather, my point is that the incorporation of the standards of one regime into another *should be carried out* with due respect for the differences in the objectives and structure of each regime. The aim of collaboration for effective climate change mitigation is not to integrate the two regimes. Rather, collaboration should be sought through continuous adjustments of relevant regime operations, while keeping in mind the distinctiveness of the respective regimes. Such adjustments may be better attained through dialog among relevant international organizations and

10 Myron H. Nordquist (ed.), *United Nations Convention on the Law of the Sea 1982: A Commentary*, Vol. IV (Dordrecht/Boston, M. Nijhoff, 1991), p. 132; Alexander Proelss (ed.), *United Nations Convention on the Law of the Sea* (München, Hart, 2017), p. 1385.

11 Scott, *supra* note 4 (Due Diligence Obligation), 402–403.

12 Article 2 of the United Nations Framework Convention on Climate Change (1992) provides: 'The ultimate objective of this Convention and any related legal instruments that the Conference of the Parties may adopt is to achieve, in accordance with the relevant provisions of the Convention, stabilization of greenhouse gas concentrations in the atmosphere at a level that would prevent dangerous anthropogenic interference with the climate system'.

13 Preamble, fourth paragraph, of the United Nations Convention on the Law of the Sea (1982) stipulates: 'Recognizing the desirability of establishing through this Convention [...] a legal order for the seas and oceans which [...] will promote the peaceful uses of the seas and oceans, the equitable and efficient utilisation of their resources, the conservation of their living resources, and the study, protection and preservation of the marine environment'.

forums *than* through automatic incorporation of the standards of one regime into another.

3 Coordination between the Law of the Sea and Climate Change Law

3.1 *Conflict between the Regimes*

Now, let us turn to the second issue, coordination between the law of the sea and climate change law. Here, I aim to discuss coordination as a matter of conflict between legal regimes.

As I have just mentioned, the law of the sea and climate change law represent two distinct legal regimes. Nevertheless, implementation measures of one regime may conflict with the regulations of the other. Such regime conflict has increasingly arisen in relation to so-called ocean-based mitigation options. Among these, I will discuss here two options: ocean fertilization and sub-seabed carbon storage.

Ocean fertilization is a geo-engineering project for transferring carbon from the atmosphere to the ocean. Its fundamental idea is to add inorganic nutrients, such as iron, nitrate, phosphate, and urea, to the near-surface ocean to stimulate the biological production of organic matter.[14] Introducing such nutrients to seawater stimulates phytoplankton blooms and increases the seawater's atmospheric CO_2 uptake.

Several studies show positive estimates for ocean fertilization as a means of mitigating GHG s. However, there are numerous uncertainties regarding the process. Indeed, the Intergovernmental Panel on Climate Change perceives ocean fertilization negatively, indicating the risks of unintended side effects and low acceptability.[15] Nevertheless, experimental research on the feasibility and effectiveness of ocean fertilization is underway, although such experimental research has provoked considerable concern regarding compatibility with the obligations imposed by the law of the sea, particularly Articles 195 and 210 of UNCLOS.[16]

---

14 High Level Panel for a Sustainable Ocean Economy, *The Ocean as a Solution to Climate Change: Five Opportunities for Action* (2019), p. 75 (available at <https://oceanpanel.org/sites/default/files/2019-10/HLP_Report_Ocean_Solution_Climate_Change_final.pdf>).

15 *IPCC Special Report on the Ocean and Cryosphere in a Changing Climate* (2019), p. 454 (available at <https://www.ipcc.ch/srocc/>).

16 Robin Warner, 'Marine Snow Storms: Assessing the Environmental Risks of Ocean Fertilization', 2009 *Carbon & Climate Law Review*, 2009, No. 4, 429–431; A.C. Lin, 'International Legal Regimes and Principles Relevant to Geoengineering', in: W.C.G. Burns and A.L. Strauss (eds.), *Climate Change Geoengineering: Philosophical Perspectives,*

Article 195 establishes an obligation 'not to transfer [...] damage or *hazards* from one area to another or transform one type of pollution into another' (emphasis added). Article 210 specifically requires states to take measures, as necessary, to prevent, reduce, and control pollution of the marine environment *by dumping*. Dumping is defined under Article 1, paragraph 5, as '*any deliberate disposal of wastes or other matter* [...] at sea' (emphasis added). This definition is sufficiently broad to cover the activities of ocean fertilization.[17]

This also applies to sub-seabed carbon storage. The idea is relatively simple: injecting concentrated and compressed CO_2 into sub-seabed geological formations.[18] Sub-seabed carbon storage is promising, and its practical utilization has been actively explored by states. In Japan, for example, feasibility studies have been successfully completed, and it is reported that progress is now underway toward commercialization by 2030.[19]

Sub-seabed storage can be implemented within territorial seas. However, the point is that injecting CO_2 into the seabed might be qualified as deliberate disposal at sea wherever it is performed; as such, sub-seabed storage might be qualified as dumping to be regulated by the law of the sea.[20]

3.2 *Coordination between the Regimes*

If these ocean-based mitigation options for disposing of CO_2 are indispensable for attaining the objective of the law on climate change, the law of the sea should be interpreted, or, if necessary, revised, to accommodate those novel methods as long as they are proved to be acceptable in light of the precautionary approach as adopted in the law of the sea.[21]

Legal Issues, and Governance Frameworks (New York, Cambridge University Press, 2013), pp. 191–193.

17 However, it must be noted that, in line with the London Convention and Protocol, UNCLOS attaches a reservation clause to this broad definition, which excludes 'placement of matter for a purpose other than the mere disposal thereof, provided that such placement is not contrary to the aims of this Convention'. Whether fertilisation should be admitted as sort of placement is a question in point. Warner, *supra* note 16, 433–434; Scott, *supra* note 4 (Regulating Ocean Fertilization), 111–114.

18 P. Verlaan, 'Geo-engineering, the Law of the Sea, and Climate Change', *Carbon & Climate Law Review*, Issue 2009, No. 4, 448; *Ocean as a Solution, supra* note 14, 70.

19 Agency for Natural Resources and Energy (Japan), <https://www.enecho.meti.go.jp/about/special/johoteikyo/ccs_tomakomai_2.html> (in Japanese).

20 Scott, *supra* note 4 (The Day after Tomorrow), 73–79; Mark A. de Figueiredo, *The International Law of Sub-Seabed Carbon Dioxide Storage: A Special Report to the MIT Carbon Sequestration Initiative*, August 2015, 13–14 (available at <https://sequestration.mit.edu/pdf/international_law_subsea_co2_storage.pdf>).

21 *Responsibilities and Obligations of States Sponsoring Persons and Entities with Respect to Activities in the Area, Advisory Opinion of 2011*, paragraph 135; Joanna Mossop, 'Can We

Indeed, such coordination has been sought, particularly in relation to the London Protocol to the Convention on the Prevention of Marine Pollution by Dumping. Under the London Protocol, any deliberate disposal into the sea of wastes or other matter is prohibited as dumping, except those listed in Annex 1 to the Protocol. In response to the growing interest in sub-seabed storage, the amendment of Annex 1 with a new item 'Carbon dioxide streams from carbon dioxide capture processes for sequestration' was proposed and adopted in 2006 at the first Meeting of the Contracting Parties. This amendment opened a legal avenue for sub-seabed carbon storage, subject to the permit procedure under Annex 2. Importantly, permissible carbon storage under this amendment is limited to the disposition into sub-seabed geological formation *only* (Annex 1, paragraph 4.1), not into other ocean spaces, such as the water column above the seabed.[22]

Regarding ocean fertilization, a more cautious attitude has been observed. At the third Meeting of the Contracting Parties in 2008, a resolution regarding the regulation of ocean fertilization was adopted by consensus. This resolution accepts ocean fertilization *only if* it is legitimate scientific research. Proposed projects are to be scrutinized following the assessment framework established by the 2010 Resolution adopted at the fifth Meeting of the Contracting Parties. If approved as legitimate scientific research, implementation of the project is regarded as a 'placement of matter' under Article 1.4.2.2 of the London Protocol.[23] It is noteworthy that the 2008 Resolution also specifies that 'given the present state of knowledge, ocean fertilization other than legitimate scientific research should be considered contrary to the aims of the Protocol and not currently qualify for any exemption from the definition of dumping of the Protocol'. This implies that states consider that the admissibility of ocean-based mitigation options should be examined carefully in light of the precautionary approach as embedded in the law of the sea.[24]

The 2006 amendment of the London Protocol and the adoption of relevant resolutions are exactly what is envisioned by Article 210, paragraph 4 of UNCLOS. This article requires states to endeavor to establish rules and standards

Make the Oceans Greener? The Successes and Failure of UNCLOS as an Environmental Treaty', 49 *Victoria University of Wellington Law Review*, No. 4, 2018, pp. 588–589.

22 See David Langlet, 'Exporting CO_2 for Sub-Seabed Storage: The Non-Effective Amendment to the London Dumping Protocol and Its Implications', 30 *International Journal of Marine & Coastal Law*, 2015, 405–410.

23 See Harald Ginzky & Robyn Frost, 'Marine Geo-Engineering: Legally Binding Regulation under the London Protocol', 2014 *Carbon & Climate Law Review*, 2014, No. 2, 83–85.

24 *Ibid.*, 83. See Scott, *supra* note 4 (Due Diligence Obligation), 400.

relating to marine environment pollution caused by dumping, acting through competent international organizations or diplomatic conferences. It is hoped that further coordination between the law of the sea and climate change law regarding ocean-based geo-engineering options are pursued through such endeavors. Consultation and cooperation among relevant international institutions and organs are indispensable for that purpose.

4 Concluding Remarks

Instead of concluding remarks, I will make reference to the dispute settlement system under UNCLOS. Some argue that this system offers a mechanism for ensuring effective implementation of the rules and standards concerning climate change, as it provides compulsory judicial procedures not available within the law on climate change.[25] Indeed, it may be possible and desirable that the rules and standards to be followed by states are ascertained and established by the International Tribunal for the Law of the Sea or the International Court of Justice, considering the adverse impact of climate change on the ocean. However, given the complexity of climate change and its impacts on the marine environment, it would be challenging for the Court and Tribunals to identify the level of vigilance required to establish the illegality of alleged acts and appropriateness of risk assessment by states concerned.[26]

Therefore, if the compulsory judicial procedures under UNCLOS effectively contribute to the mitigation of climate change, it will be through the interpretation and application of specified international rules and standards that are established through competent international organizations or diplomatic conferences for the protection and preservation of the marine environment.[27] Importantly, those international rules and standards established through international organizations or international conferences are specifically placed under the jurisdictional scope of the Court and Tribunals by Article 297, paragraph 1 (*c*).[28] The judicial settlement mechanism under UNCLOS may

---

25 Boyle, *supra* note 7, p. 474.

26 Mossop, *supra* note 21, 590.

27 See Scott, *supra* note 4 (Due Diligence Obligation), 406–408.

28 *Chagos Marine Protection Area Arbitration* (*Mauritius v. United Kingdom*), *Award of 2015*, paras. 316 ('The Tribunal also notes that, in certain respects, Article 297(1) expands the jurisdiction of a Tribunal over the enumerated cases beyond that which would follow from the application of Article 288(1) alone. In addition to describing disputes relating to the interpretation and application of the Convention itself, *each of the three specified cases in Article 297(1) includes a renvoi to sources of law beyond the Convention itself* [...].

be expected to work effectively if collaboration and coordination between the law of the sea and climate change law are pursued through the standard-setting efforts within the relevant international institutions along with inter-institutional dialog for that purpose.

Article 297(1) thus expressly expands the Tribunal's jurisdiction to certain disputes involving the contravention of legal instruments beyond the four corners of the Convention itself and ensures that such disputes will not be dismissed as being insufficiently related to the interpretation and application of the Convention' (emphasis added)). See also *ibid.*, paras. 319–322.

Index

www.ingramcontent.com/pod-product-compliance
Lightning Source LLC
LaVergne TN
LVHW012053011026
849162LV00018B/193